THE INTER-AMERICAN HISTORICAL SERIES

Edited by JAMES A. ROBERTSON

A HISTORY OF ARGENTINA

The Capitol, Buenos Aires; photograph by the Translator.

A HISTORY OF
ARGENTINA

By RICARDO LEVENE

PROFESSOR OF ARGENTINE HISTORY IN
THE NATIONAL UNIVERSITY OF LA PLATA

Translated and Edited by

WILLIAM SPENCE ROBERTSON

PROFESSOR OF HISTORY IN THE
UNIVERSITY OF ILLINOIS

NEW YORK

RUSSELL & RUSSELL · INC

1963

PREFACE BY THE GENERAL EDITOR

THE "INTER-AMERICAN HISTORICAL SERIES," of which this is the first volume, had its inception during the Pan American Congress which was held at Panama in 1926 on the one hundredth anniversary of the famous Bolivarian congress of 1826. Before that commemorative congress, Dr. Charles W. Hackett, one of the three commissioners for the United States on that occasion, proposed the publication in the United States of a series of volumes under the title of "Bolivarian Historical Series." Elaborating his proposal, Dr. Hackett gave a brief outline of the series he had in mind. It was to consist of the translation into English of that volume for each country of Hispanic America, written in each case preferably by a national of the respective country, which would best set forth the history of the country, and which would have the approval of the higher institutions of learning and of reputable scholars. Volumes selected for translation and publication in the United States were to fulfil certain requirements. They were to be sound and were to reflect the best canons of historical writing. The series, as a whole, was intended to reveal to Anglo Americans how writers of history of Hispanic America regard the history of their own countries. The value of this as a factor in the intellectual coöperation between Anglo and Hispanic America needs no brief.

The Bolivarian Congress unanimously approved Dr. Hackett's proposal. Accordingly, the latter reported his proposal and its reception by the Congress to the Hispanic American History Group at the annual meeting of the American Historical Association in December, 1926; and at the same time he recommended its consideration by the Group. That body voted unanimously that a series of the nature purposed was highly desirable and appointed a committee under the chairmanship of Dr. Hackett to give further study to the matter and report at the next annual meeting of the American Historical Association in 1927.

In 1927, the name of the series was changed from "Bolivarian Historical Series" to "Inter-American Historical Series," since it was considered that this title better expressed the purpose of such a series. Attention was given also to the choice of books for translation, to translators and editors, and to actual publication.

The University of North Carolina Press had expressed an interest in the plan from the very beginning and on circularizing libraries and individuals found enough interest in the series to warrant making plans for publication. When attempts to obtain financial aid from foundations interested in Hispanic America failed, it was determined to undertake the series without such aid. To the University of North Carolina Press, therefore, are due the thanks of those who use the series, for it is owing to its management that the series is published.

The plan visualizes the publication of translations covering each country of Hispanic America. It is probable that the Central American countries will form one single volume inasmuch as a considerable part of their history has been in common; and the Dominican Republic and Haiti will probably appear in one volume. Each of the other republics will have a volume devoted to it, and a compendium touching the history of the whole of Hispanic America will form a fitting volume of the series. An historical atlas has also been planned and was, in fact, to be undertaken by the late Professor William R. Shepherd, but new arrangements must now be made for this.

Volumes already chosen for translation, and the translators and editors of them, are as follows: for Argentina, Ricardo Levene, *Lecciones de Historia Argentina*, 2 vols. — translator and editor, Dr. William Spence Robertson; for Brazil, João Pandiá Calogeras, *A Formação historica do Brasil* — translator and editor, Dr. Percy Alvin Martin; for Chile, Luis Galdames, *Estudio de Historia de Chile* — translator and editor, Dr. Isaac Joslin Cox; for Colombia, J. M. Henao and G. Arrubla, *Historia de Colombia* — translator and editor, Dr. J. Fred Rippy; for Mexico, Luis Pérez Verdía, *Compendio de la Historia de Mexico* — translator and editor, Dr. Charles W. Hackett; for Peru, Carlos Wiesse, *Historia del Perú*, 4 vols. — translator and editor, Dr. William Whatley Pierson; for Bolivia, Alcides Arguedas, *Historia General de Bolivia*—translator and editor, Dr. J. Lloyd Mecham. Other volumes for the other republics have not yet been definitely chosen as the choice involves much careful study. Those scholars who will participate in the series for whom volumes have not yet been chosen are the following: for Uruguay, Dr. Alfred Hasbrouck; for Central America, Dr. N. Andrew N. Cleven; for Cuba, Dr. Charles E.

Chapman; for the Dominican Republic and Haiti, Dr. Arthur S. Aiton; for Ecuador, Dr. W. H. Calcott. No statement can yet be made with regard to Paraguay and Venezuela. The compendium of Hispanic American History will be translated and edited by Dr. Herbert E. Bolton. He has wisely chosen as the book to be translated by him, Carlos Navarro y Lamarca's *Compendio de Historia general de America,* in two volumes. The historical atlas mentioned above will be published only in case special funds are secured for its preparation and publication.

It is fitting that the series should commence with the history of Argentina as a colony and as a republic. And it is eminently fitting that this volume should be translated and edited by Dr. William Spence Robertson who for so long has been an acknowledged authority on this and on all the countries of Hispanic America. The author of this work has written other works on the history of his country and most of them if not all have gone through various editions. Dr. Levene occupies a secure position in the field of history. He has an understanding of the history of Argentina not surpassed by any of his countrymen and he writes in an easily understood manner. His volumes can be judged by the best canons of historical writing and his method of treatment is sound throughout.

It is the hope of those connected with the series that this volume, as well as those which will follow it, will draw closer the intellectual and cultural bonds between Anglo and Hispanic America.

July, 1937   JAMES A. ROBERTSON.

PREFACE BY THE TRANSLATOR AND EDITOR

PRESIDENT ROOSEVELT'S peace mission to Buenos Aires has directed attention to the most progressive nation that sprang from the ruins of the Spanish colonial Empire. To those persons who are interested in the politics and the history of the Argentine Nation this volume offers an instructive narrative. After the translator was chosen by the Hispanic American group of the American Historical Association as the chairman of a committee to select a history of Argentina for translation into English, he examined the histories of that country of approximately the right length and scope. He not only solicited the views of scholars well versed in South American history but also asked for the verdict of the Argentine Ministry of Education. The consensus of opinion was that the work in two volumes of Señor Ricardo Levene entitled *Lecciones de Historia Argentina* would be the best suited for the English reader.

Señor Ricardo Levene is an influential figure in what has appropriately been styled the new school of history at Buenos Aires—a group of scholars who by virtue of their important and learned publications have won for their native land the leading position in Latin-American historical scholarship. This eminent Argentine historian has for several years held a chair in both the University of Buenos Aires and the National University of La Plata. He has been further honored by election to an honorary professorship in the University of Chile and in the University at Rio de Janeiro. He is the President of the *Junta de Historia y Numismática Americana* of Buenos Aires and is general director of the monumental coöperative *Historia de la Nación Argentina* which has just begun to issue from the press of Buenos Aires.

The distinguished author kindly gave the translator permission to render his narrative into English. The translator then undertook to prepare an English version of the eleventh edition of Levene's *Lecciones de Historia Argentina* which was published at Buenos Aires in 1928. That work had long been widely used as a text in the *colegios* or secondary schools of the Argentine Republic. Synopses and tables of contents have been left out of the translation. Three chapters of the work, which were concerned with historical sources, with sciences auxiliary to history, and with the discovery of America were also omitted but replaced by a brief "Introduction" by the translator which dealt with the discovery and the physiography of the extensive region included within the present limits of Argentina. As, in the meantime, Señor Levene had in the fifteenth edition of his *History* brought the story of his country up to the year 1933, the translator replaced the last three chapters of the eleventh edition with the last four chapters of the fifteenth edition, thus including the author's fresh narrative of the last decades of Argentine history.

Throughout the text, wherever possible, the translator has made certain of the accuracy of the quotations and of the footnotes. In many cases the footnotes have been abbreviated. Whenever quotations had been taken from an English work, the original language has been supplied. Omissions which the author had made from treatises that he quoted have been indicated by the editorial three dots. His parentheses in the body of the text have been retained. Brackets have been used to indicate words interpolated in the narrative. Such references to authorities as have been added by the translator to the author's footnotes have been followed by the initials W. S. R. Whenever Levene's footnotes have been in juxtaposition with those of the translator, the latter's notes have been enclosed in brackets. An endeavor has been made to standardize the footnotes. Titles of works cited there are printed in the original languages. Printer's errors and minor slips in the Spanish text have been corrected by the translator without cluttering up the English narrative by footnote references or the insertion of brackets. In the translation parentheses have been inserted by the translator only to enclose words or the titles of books equivalent to or explanatory of terms used in the text. He has furnished bibliographical notes at the end of the book in the hope that they may be useful to some readers.

The translator and editor has appreciated the uniform helpfulness of the staff of the University of Illinois Library where a large collection of Argentiniana has been most useful in the preparation of the manuscript. He is also grateful to the staff of the Library of Congress for courtesies extended during his labors in that center of historical study. Dr. Leo S. Rowe, Director of the Pan American Union, has given valuable assistance and counsel to the translator during the preparation of this book. To his one-time pupil, Dr. Pelham H. Box, of King's College, London, the translator is indebted for aid in securing from the British Museum data which were not available in Urbana. The translator was given helpful suggestions concerning his draft translation of a part of the first volume of Levene's *Historia* by Dr. James A. Robertson, the general editor of the Inter-American Historical Series. On difficult passages in the last part of the work the translator has profited by the wise advice of Dr. M. E. Butterfield of the Oklahoma College for Women. Professor John Van Horne of the University of Illinois opened to the translator the fountains of his Romance knowledge.

Here and there to promote clarity the translator has completely recast the structure of a sentence employed in the original text. For his purpose was not to produce a line for line translation but to present a version of the *Historia* which would adequately convey the author's views to an American audience. In preparing the index the translator has aimed to place the enormous fund of information in this volume at the ready disposal of English readers. The staff of the University of North Carolina Press has given the translator and editor many helpful editorial suggestions concerning the form of this *History*. Lastly, he must acknowledge the aid which he received in reading the proof of this book from his son and his daughter.

WILLIAM SPENCE ROBERTSON.

University of Illinois.

CONTENTS

ILLUSTRATIONS

A HISTORY OF ARGENTINA

INTRODUCTION

As THE DAWN of modern times drew near, a new spirit heralded
the era of discovery. Among others a Franciscan, called Friar
John, who was sent on a missionary trip to Asia, brought back
intriguing reports about the Great Khan, the Mongolian monarch
whose career had fascinated the world. Friar John startled Europe
by describing Cathay, or China, as bordered by an eastern sea.
After his return from China about 1295 an enterprising Venetian
merchant named Marco Polo dictated the story of his experiences
in a book concerning "the Kingdoms and Marvels of the East."
Marco Polo pictured broader travels than had ever before been
described to Europeans. He told of China, Tibet, Burma, Siam,
Cochin-China, Japan, the Indian Archipelago, Sumatra, and India,
either from direct experience or hearsay. From Arab sailors he
learned of Zanzibar, Madagascar, and Abyssinia; he even gathered
information about Siberia. Though sober statements in Marco
Polo's book were received with incredulity, yet it was widely circulated, translated into German, and printed in the early days
of the press. In diverse ways the geographical horizon of men was
vastly widened.

The advance of geographical knowledge was efficiently promoted by science. An Englishman named John Holywood, adapting
ideas of the ancient geographer Ptolemy, prepared a useful treatise
concerning the stars and the planets. The art of preparing sea-
charts was much improved. Utilizing the knowledge of Arabian
geographers, various attempts were made to institute a systematic
notation of longitude. The astrolabe, which had long been used
to find the altitude of heavenly bodies, had been improved so that by
the aid of tables of declination it could be employed at sea to
determine approximately a ship's latitude. Tables had been prepared that showed the sun's declination for each day in the year.
The magnetic needle, which had been used by Norsemen in their
adventurous voyages, gradually became a serviceable instrument.
Mariners might now launch forth on the Sea of Darkness with more
assurance as to their course.

High on the roll of those leaders who undertook to utilize the
knowledge amassed by science and travel is inscribed the name of

Prince Henry, the son of King John the Good of Portugal. Though invited by various European monarchs to take a military post in their armies, yet he refused; for he had set his heart on the exploration and conquest of Africa. Under the quickening influence of that prince, hardy Portuguese mariners gradually pushed their way down the African coast. The Azores, Cape Bojador, Cape Verde, and the Gulf of Guinea were discovered or re-discovered before the death of Prince Henry in 1460.[1] In 1486, Bartholomeu Dias rounded the southern end of Africa which the Portuguese king named the Cape of Good Hope. Sailing beyond that point on Christmas Day, 1497, Vasco da Gama got a glimpse of a land that he named Natal, and on May 6, 1498, he caught sight of the highlands of India. After rounding Cape Verde a Portuguese noble named Pedro Alvares Cabral, who was sent with a formidable expedition to establish commercial relations with India, changed his route, and on April 22, 1500, came in sight of a mountain in South America. On May 1, Cabral took formal possession of Brazil for Portugal.[2]

It was in Portugal, said a son of the Great Discoverer, that Columbus began to surmise that if the Portuguese sailed so far south one might also sail westward and find land in that direction. According to the most critical scholarship, Christopher Columbus was born at Genoa in the autumn of 1451.[3] He attended a school established by the wool weavers of his native city. In his youth he went on voyages to the island of Chios in the Aegean. While he was on a voyage to England in Genoese ships in 1476 the flotilla was attacked by a French corsair. The ship that bore Columbus took fire; he leaped into the sea, was fortunately picked up, and landed on the Portuguese coast near Lisbon. Thence he continued his voyage to England. On his return he took up his residence in the Portuguese capital where about 1480 he married a daughter of Bartholomeu Perestrello, who had planted a colony in Madeira.[4]

[1] Oliveira Martins, *The Golden Age of Prince Henry the Navigator* (translated by J. J. Abraham and W. E. Reynolds, London, 1914), pp. 211-27.

[2] *Diccionario historico, geographico e ethnographico do Brasil* (2 vols. Rio de Janeiro, 1922), I, 766.

[3] Henry Vignaud, *A Critical Study of the Various Dates assigned to the Birth of Christopher Columbus* (London, 1903).

[4] *Idem., Histoire critique de la grande entreprise de Christophe Colomb* (2 vols. Paris, 1911), I, 31-39.

His mother-in-law gave Columbus some papers of Perestrello which perhaps first directed his attention toward discoveries in the west. Meantime, he accompanied Portuguese expeditions down the African coast. In 1483 or 1484, he presented to King John II of Portugal, his design for a western voyage. He asked for three caravels equipped and provisioned for one year, the title and prerogatives of grand admiral, the viceregal authority and perpetual government over all islands and mainlands that might be discovered, and, among other advantages, one-tenth of the produce from such lands. This proposal was submitted to a council of experts. They rejected it, however, probably because of the excessive demands of the petitioner or because of errors in his calculations.[5]

Shortly afterward, Columbus left Portugal for Spain. For five years he lived a precarious existence near the Spanish court, occasionally encouraged by small donations of money. Late in 1490, a council to which his design had been submitted reported adversely. Encouraged, however, by his acquaintance with leading navigators of southern Spain, Columbus laid his proposal before another commission which also rejected it. Upon the point of leaving the Peninsula, his cause was espoused by a court functionary named Luis de Santangel, and on April 17, 1492, an understanding was reached between the visionary adventurer and the Spanish crown. This agreement was formulated in the capitulation of Santa Fe. It stipulated that Columbus and his heirs were to have the office of admiral in all islands and lands that he might discover. The admiral was to become viceroy over such lands. He was to get one-tenth of the pearls, precious stones, and spices that might be found, bought, or bartered within his admiralty. Columbus or his deputy was to have the sole power to judge all disputes arising out of traffic between the new countries and Spain. The admiral was to be allowed to contribute one-eighth of the expense of other expeditions to these countries and was to have the same share of the profits. Significant is the fact that although presumably the Indies were in the mind of the great admiral, yet the capitulation mentioned simply the discovery of islands or lands.[6] This agreement was the

---

[5] *Ibid.*, pp. 41, 368-91.

[6] E. G. Bourne, ed., *The Northmen, Columbus, and Cabot, 985-1503* ("Original Narratives of Early American History," vol. I, New York, 1906), pp. 77-80.

first of a series of contracts between Catholic monarchs and daring adventurers who undertook to explore and conquer new realms for Spain.

On August 3, 1492, a small flotilla in charge of Columbus set sail from Palos. It comprised three caravels, the *Nina*, the *Pinta*, and the *Santa María*. The expedition was composed of some ninety seamen, thirty Spanish officials and servants, besides pilots, a physician, and an interpreter. Leaving the Canary Islands on September 6, the ships were steadily wafted westward. According to his *Journal*, the admiral kept two reckonings of the voyage; one of distances really traveled for his own guidance; and another of lesser distances for his crew. A landfall was made on October 12, 1492, at an isle called by the natives Guanahani, an island that is now generally identified as Watling's Island. Whatever may have been the original intention of Columbus, upon discovering Guanahani, Cuba, and Santo Domingo, he felt that he had reached Cathay or the gorgeous Indies.[7]

On March 9, 1493, Columbus recorded in his *Journal* that in an interview with King John of Portugal that monarch had asserted that by a Spanish-Portuguese treaty of 1479 the newly-discovered lands would belong to him. The admiral replied that he had purposely refrained from sailing in the direction of Guinea, which was recognized as a Portuguese possession. The prospect of a contention between Spain and Portugal concerning the title to the new lands provoked an appeal to the Pope who at that time was supposed by Catholic peoples to exercise a species of hegemony over non-Christian dominions. Hence on May 3, 1493, Pope Alexander VI issued a bull granting the Spanish sovereigns exclusive rights over newly-discovered lands not in the possession of any Christian prince. According to Spanish jurists, this bull conferred upon the kings of Spain complete sovereignty over the Indies. A bull issued on the following day sketched an imaginary line from the North Pole to the South Pole one hundred leagues west of the Azores or Cape Verde Islands. Unknown lands discovered west of this line were to belong to Spain. However, this did not settle the dispute between Spain and Portugal which was

---

[7] *Ibid.*, pp. 93-128.

not adjusted until 1494 when a treaty of demarcation between those nations was signed at Tordesillas.[8]

In a letter from Columbus to Ferdinand and Isabella concerning the colonization and trade of Santo Domingo, the admiral proposed measures that entitle him to be styled a colonial administrator. He proposed that emigration to that island should be permitted to the number of two thousand families, that gold hunting should be carried on only by inhabitants of towns and cities by special permission and during particular seasons, that three or four towns should be established at convenient places with governments like those in Castile, that churches should be founded with priests or friars to administer the sacraments and to instruct the Indians, that all vessels trading with Santo Domingo should unload their cargoes exclusively at one or two ports, and that all ships returning from that island should unload at Cadiz.[9]

Some of these suggestions were incorporated in the letter of instructions which the monarchs gave Columbus for his second voyage. On that voyage he explored Cuba and discovered Jamaica. On his third voyage he struck the northeastern coast of South America near the Orinoco River. On his fourth voyage he skirted the eastern coast of Central America.

We must now notice the exploration of the eastern coast of South America. Here the chief names are those of Juan Díaz de Solís, Ferdinand Magellan, and Sebastian Cabot. In 1508, Díaz de Solís accompanied Yáñez Pinzón on a voyage to northern South America for the purpose of discovering a strait or an open sea. In 1512, Solís was appointed chief pilot of Spain to succeed Amerigo Vespucci. On November 24, 1514, a capitulation was signed between Solís and King Charles I. This agreement provided that Solís should explore the eastern coast of the new continent in search of a strait that was supposed to connect the Atlantic Ocean with the western sea which had been discovered in 1513 by Vasco Núñez de Balboa.[10] Solís sailed from Sanlúcar on October 8, 1515. From the

---

[8] *Ibid.*, p. 254; F. G. Davenport, *European Treaties bearing on the History of the United States and its Dependencies* (3 vols. Washington, 1917, 1929, 1934), I, 58-93.   [9] Bourne, *op. cit.,* pp. 273-77.

[10] J. T. Medina, *Juan Díaz de Solís* (2 vols. Santiago de Chile, 1897), I, ccxxvii-ccxxx.

Canary Islands he proceeded to South America. He skirted the
coast of Brazil southward from the Bay of Rio de Janeiro to
about 35° south latitude where, in 1516, the sweetness of the
water convinced him that he had reached the mouth of a great
river. Solís named this estuary the "Mar Dulce," and took formal
possession of the adjacent lands for the king of Spain. Landing
with a few companions on the island of Martín García, he fell
into an ambuscade and was killed by the Indians.[11]

The object of the unfortunate Solís was attained by a brave
and honorable Portuguese navigator named Ferdinand Magellan,
who seems to have entertained the idea that he could actually reach
the famed Spice Islands by sailing west. On March 22, 1518,
Magellan signed a contract with the king of Spain by which he
bound himself to discover within the Spanish demarcation islands
and mainlands and rich spice lands. One-fifth of the profits of the
expedition was to go to the king. Provided with five old ships, and
some two hundred and fifty men, on September 20, 1519, Magellan
sailed from Sanlúcar for South America. In December, he reached
the Brazilian shores near Rio de Janeiro, and coasted south. He
reached the "Sweet Sea," disembarked at various places along the
coast, and encountered the aborigines. On October 21, Magellan
discerned the straits that bear his name. Passing through the
dangerous channel he reached the sea which he christened the Pacific
Ocean. Then he proceeded by way of the Ladrone Islands and
Guam to the Philippines which he sighted in the middle of March
1521.[12] Soon afterward, Magellan was killed in a skirmish with
the savages. Only one ship of the expedition, the *Victoria*, reached
Spain and thus completed the first circumnavigation of the globe.

The task of the discovery and exploration of southern South
America was next taken up by Sebastian Cabot, a son of the dis-
coverer of eastern North America. Sebastian Cabot had become
chief pilot to the king of Spain. In 1526, he accepted the command
of a fleet of four vessels that had been equipped by merchants of
Seville for a voyage to the Moluccas by way of Magellan's Straits.
Relinquishing this design, he decided to follow the route of Solís.
Leaving two of his vessels near the mouth of the great estuary

[11] *Ibid.*, pp. ccxlix-cclxiii.
[12] Antonio di Pigafetta, *Magellan's Voyage around the World* (translated by
James A. Robertson, 2 vols. and index, Cleveland, 1906), I, 31-99.

discovered by that mariner, Cabot sailed up the Paraná River to its junction with the Carcarañá, where he founded Fort Sancti Spiritus. Thence he proceeded up the Paraná to its junction with the Paraguay and then ascended that river beyond the site of Asunción.[13]

Meantime, a follower of Solís named Diego García had sailed from Coruña with another expedition destined for the Moluccas. But he also changed his plans and followed the wake of Cabot up the Paraná River. The two adventurers met near Fort Sancti Spiritus. After an acrimonious discussion they reached an agreement and undertook to explore the Pilcomayo River. Hearing that the Indians had made an attack on Sancti Spiritus, they returned to that fort but found that it had been destroyed. Then they sadly withdrew to the coast where for more than a year they awaited reënforcements. As these did not arrive, they returned to Spain.[14]

Although the companions of Magellan had applied to the "Mar Dulce" the name Río de Solís after its discoverer, yet early in the sixteenth century that estuary came to be called the Río de la Plata, apparently because of the notion that somewhere upon its banks there were quantities of silver. Seated in this river basin, within a favored region which in colonial days was often styled "La Plata," separated from outlying territories that once pertained to the viceroyalty of La Plata, is the modern nation of Argentina. It is scarcely an exaggeration to say that few modern peoples have had their lines of development so definitely plotted by physiographic conditions as the Argentine Nation.

Argentina stretches from the tropics almost to the Antarctic Circle. By the discovery of the "Sweet Sea" Solís and his followers had reached one of the great gateways to the American continent. The Plata River System, composed of the estuary known as the Río de la Plata with its affluents, drains an area which is more than two and one-half times as large as the entire South Pacific slope of the Andes. This drainage basin not only includes a large portion of present Argentina, southeastern Bolivia, and Uruguay, but also considerable portions of Brazil. The geographic fact that the Paraná River, "the Mother of the Sea," with tributaries in the

---

[13] Medina, *op. cit.*, II, 185-92.

[14] J. Guevara, "Historia del Paraguay, Río de la Plata y Tucumán," *Anales de la Biblioteca* (Buenos Aires, 1908), V, 165-73.

heart of the continent, and the Uruguay River, both empty into the
Plata River, has had a profound influence upon the history of the
Platean countries. Indeed, the yearnings of people locked within
this vast basin for an unobstructed outlet to the sea have at times
incited international rivalries. Just off the southeastern coast
of South America lie the Falkland Islands, a group of rocky isles
located in the center of a whale-fishing region. Strategically, these
islands command the entrance to the Straits of Magellan.[15]

The coast line of Argentina on the east, including the funnel-
shaped estuary of the Río de la Plata, has an extent of about
sixteen hundred miles. This extensive littoral on the most frequented ocean on the globe would naturally attract its inhabitants
to the sea. To the south of the Plata River this coast is dotted
with harbors. The estuary of Bahía Blanca furnishes a minor gate-
way to the continental interior. Farther south, the rocky Tierra
del Fuego is separated from the continent by a "mighty rent in
the Andes"—the Straits of Magellan. In the southern part of
Argentina, the climate is cold; the central portion has a temperate
climate; while the northern part gradually merges into the sub-
tropics. This land stretches over thirty-three degrees of latitude.
Because of the influence of prevailing winds, because of a great
diversity of altitude, and because of proximity to large bodies of
water, it has great climatic variations. The climate of central
Argentina resembles that of the southern part of the United
States. The city of Buenos Aires lies as far south of the equator
as Memphis, Tennessee, lies north of that line.[16]

The four main physiographic provinces of Argentina are the
pampas, the semitropical northern plain, the Andean mountain
region, and Patagonia. A considerable portion of the drainage
basin of the Plata River may be included within what are styled
the pampas. These extensive, undulating, treeless plains covered
with grass, which extend from the Río Colorado, in Patagonia,
north to the river Saladillo, include about a quarter of the area
of Argentina. The soil of the pampas is fine, porous, deep, and very

---

[15] The Argentine viewpoint as to the strategic position of the Falkland Islands
is indicated in S. R. Storni, *Intereses argentinos en el mar* (Buenos Aires, 1916),
pp. 26-28.

[16] B. Willis and others, *Northern Patagonia, Character and Resources* (New
York, 1914), I, 2.

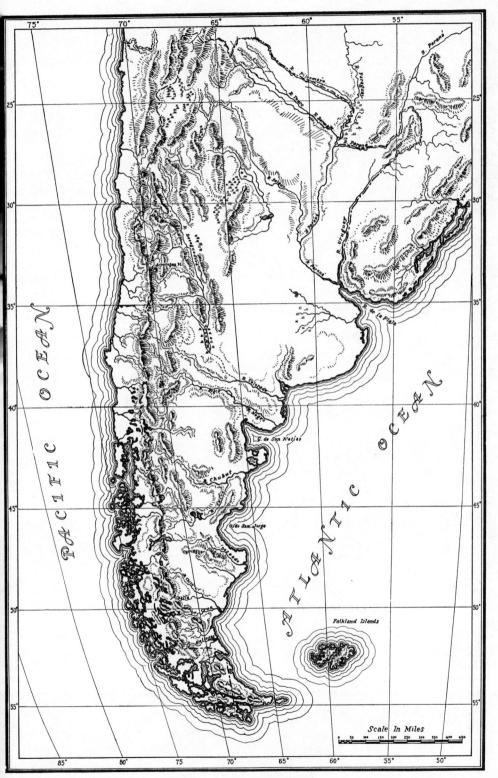

PHYSICAL MAP OF ARGENTINA

fertile. The region has an advantage over the prairie lands of the Mississippi Valley, which it resembles, because it lies close to the seaboard. Supplied in many parts with a reservoir of underground water, the pampas are admirably adapted for agriculture and the pastoral industry. A considerable portion of the pampean plain is today included within the bounds of the important province of Buenos Aires.

The semitropical northern plain includes about one-fifth of the territory of Argentina. This region is largely composed of moist lowlands. Much of it is covered with hardwood forests which are occasionally broken by savannas. Here snow never falls, while frost rarely occurs. The most distinctive portion of this plain is the region designated the Chaco which is drained by the meandering rivers Bermejo and Pilcomayo that are constantly seeking for new channels and at flood times overflow large stretches of territory. In this northern region there flourish yerba mate or Paraguayan tea as well as quebracho trees which are a great source of tannin.[17] To the southeast, lying between the rivers Paraná and Uruguay, is an intermediate physiographic province with rich alluvial soil, traversed by low hills, where the plain merges into the pampas. In part this tract is composed of the delta formed by the silt of the Paraná. It is well watered, has gigantic waterfalls at Iguassú, and forests that abound in valuable woods. This rich and diversified section, which includes the provinces of Corrientes and Entre Ríos, was appropriately styled by the French traveler, Martin de Moussy, the Argentine Mesopotamia.[18]

On the west the Andean mountain region walls in the Platean basin from the Pacific Ocean. The cordillera expands as it enters Argentina and proceeds southward in a series of parallel branches that gradually decline in altitude and finally bury themselves in antarctic isles. These mountain chains inclose a number of small, elevated plateaus which in the north are sometimes covered by salt marshes. In the southern spurs of the cordillera are some beautiful lakes among which is Lake Nahuel Huapí. Glorious scenery has won for this section the name of the "Argentine Switzerland." Ripe

---

[17] G. E. Church, *South America, an Outline of Its Physical Geography* (London, 1901), pp. 61-63.

[18] J. A. V. Martin de Moussy, *Description géographique et statistique de la Confédération Argentine* (3 vols. Paris, 1860-69), I, 266.

forests of cedar and Andean beech thinly cover many of the steep, eastern slopes of the mountains. Various minerals are scattered through the subsoil of this region, especially in the barren plateau known as the Puna of Atacama.

The region designated Patagonia extends on Atlantic shores from the Río Negro to the Straits of Magellan. This section has some physical features of both the pampas and the cordillera. Patagonia rises from the east by a series of immense gradations until it merges into the foothills of the Andes. In general, it is a land of semiarid grassy plateaus which are finally lost in the forest-clad slopes of the cordillera. The varied, mountainous region of Argentine Patagonia has a heavier rainfall than the so-called desert to the east.[19]

The nucleal region of Argentina is thus composed of lands that border the navigable Paraguay, Uruguay, and Paraná rivers. These pampean and delta lands, which are dowered with a temperate climate, productive soil, and easy communication with the outside world, furnish the natural home of a great agricultural and pastoral people.

[19] Willis, *op. cit.*, especially pp. 14-26.

Stress on grazing & agriculture

CHAPTER I

THE ABORIGINES

NUMEROUS AND VARIED were the people who occupied the territory of present Argentina when the Spaniards conquered and colonized it in the sixteenth century. It is not easy to classify them according to linguisitic or anthropological characteristics. Modern authors have made the following classification according to geographic distribution:[1] (1) the historic peoples of the mountains of the northwest, (2) of the Chaco forests, (3) of the great rivers, (4) of the plains, (5) of Patagonia, (6) of the Magellan Archipelago.[2]   *andean*

In the time of the Spanish conquest the region of the present government of the Andes, the present provinces of Jujuy, Catamarca, Tucumán, La Rioja, San Juan, the western part of Salta, the eastern and southern parts of Santiago del Estero, the northern part of Córdoba, Mendoza, and San Luis were inhabited by aborigines known as Diaguitas, also called Calchaquians, who are now extinct.[3]

The territory occupied by the Diaguitas was distinguished by its aridity, and by a vegetation composed of mesquite, talas, canes, and teasels. The Diaguitas lived on maize, which they ate either roasted or ground, peas, gourds, the fruit of the chañar tree,[4] and prickly pears. They prepared drinks, and, to judge by some clay pipes that have been found, it would seem that they smoked.

There are many ruins in this region which show the kind of habitations built by the Diaguitas. These were made of stones which were piled on top of each other without mortar. The villages

[1] L. M. Torres and others, eds., *Manual de historia de la civilización argentina* (Buenos Aires, 1917), I, 69-70. See further, C. O. Bunge, *Historia del derecho argentino* ("Estudios editados por la facultad de derecho y ciencias sociales de la Universidad de Buenos Aires," vols. I and III; 2 vols. Buenos Aires, 1912-13), I, 31.

[2] F. F. Outes and C. Bruch, *Los áborigines de la República Argentina* (Buenos Aires, 1910), pp. 49-141.

[3] F. Heger, "XVII Congreso internacional de Americanistas; sesión de Buenos Aires," *Revista de Derecho, Historia y Letras* (Buenos Aires, 1912), VI, 476-98.

[4] The chañar tree was a kind of mimosa. Some varieties of it produced wood useful for building purposes and bore pleasant fruit.—W. S. R.

Diaguitas

agriculture

irrigation

war

were densely populated and were located either upon hills or in valleys.

Their chief industries were agriculture and the manufacture of pottery. They made such articles as plates, pitchers, and urns in which to bury the dead, all of which they ornamented with designs and pictures. They tilled extensive strips of land; and, when water was lacking, they constructed canals in order to conduct it to the cultivated fields.

With regard to organization, each tribe had its chief. To judge by the ruins of fortresses which were constructed out of fragments of rock, the Diaguitas must have waged frequent and bloody wars. Their arms were the bow and arrow, the sling, and the hatchet. The fortresses which they built, and which they used strategically for protection, were called Pucará.

The historic peoples of the Chaco forests inhabited the region of the Chaco and Formosa and part of the present provinces of Santa Fe, Santiago del Estero, and Salta. These people were nomadic, pugnacious, and warlike, and were composed of four great tribes: Matacos-Mataguayos, Chorotes, Guaycurúes, and Chiriguanos. The Matacos constructed habitations composed of branches set in the ground and joined overhead in the form of an arch. The making of textiles was their most important industry. These Indians also made a large quantity of nets; and they knew how to make canoes from the trunks of large trees. The Chorotes lived upon the products of hunting and fishing, and, like the Matacos, produced fire by twirling in their hands a cylindrical bit of wood placed horizontically upon another piece until the resulting sawdust flared up. Among the Guaycurúes, the Tobas Indians were the most important and the most characteristic because of their imposing stature and general physical development.

The historic peoples of the littoral of the great rivers inhabited the provinces of Entre Ríos and Corrientes, the coast of the province of Santa Fe, and Misiones territory. The tribes that occupied this region, designated among others as the Timbúes, Caingúas, Mocoretas, Charrúas, and Agaces, have now entirely disappeared. The Charrúas were a nomadic tribe which came from the present territory of Uruguay and which also occupied Entre Ríos and Corrientes. Out of stone and bone they fashioned such utensils as knives and mortars. They lived by hunting and did

Study of Zapicán, a Charruan chief, by the Uruguayan sculptor, Nicanor Blanes. This work is in the Museum of Fine Arts, Montevideo; photograph by the Translator.

not engage in agriculture. The Caingúas inhabited the district later known as the Argentine and Paraguayan mission region. They were sedentary aborigines who built two kinds of habitations: one a slight edifice composed of branches and trunks of trees; and the other a more permanent building covered with clay. The textile industry was the most important. The Caingúas used the cane of tacuarembó and the leaves and fibres of the palm to make hats and baskets of various sizes.[5]

The historic people of the plains inhabited a part of the present provinces of Mendoza, San Luis, and Córdoba, as well as the entire province of Buenos Aires, and the present territory of La Pampa. This region was inhabited by three great indigenous tribes: the Querandíes, the Puelcheans, and the Araucanians. The Querandíes were a tribe of considerable culture and were very warlike. They resisted the colonizing work of the first Spanish conquerors. The Puelcheans possessed customs and a civilization very similar to that of the Patagonians.

The Araucanians at first occupied the present territory of Neuquén and a part of the province of Mendoza. When the Querandíes and Puelcheans were destroyed, the Araucanians advanced up to the eastern plains. After the Diaguitas, the Araucanians were the most civilized aborigines who existed within the limits of present Argentina. In war, they used the lance and bolas, the latter being composed of stones fastened to thongs. They carried on trade with neighboring peoples; in exchange for whose products, they gave cloth, hides, and ostrich plumes.

The historic peoples of Patagonia occupied the Argentine territory bearing this name. Their industries consisted in the preparation of pelts and the manufacture out of stone of such weapons as knives, drills, and balls. As they were nomadic tribes, they lived chiefly by hunting. The chase of the guanaco was carried on by imprisoning a small animal of that species in a certain place, while the hunters awaited the approach of the large herds. Ostriches were hunted in an original fashion. An Indian covered himself with ostrich plumes, and in this guise deceived the flocks of ostriches and led them to the place where the hunters were concealed. When

[5] The word "tacuarembó" comes from the Guaraní language and was used to designate a tall, slender, flexible cane employed in weaving baskets and mats. —W. S. R.

horses were introduced in the days of Spanish conquest, the Indians mounted those animals and carried on the chase by means of bolas.

The historic peoples of the Magellan Archipelago inhabited the western part of the present territory of Tierra del Fuego. They were composed of two indigenous groups: the Onas and the Yamanas. Some of the Onas, who were a nomadic tribe, still exist. They did not construct habitations and their families slept in the open. The Yamanas were canoemen who skirted along the coast of Tierra del Fuego.

Within the present dominions of the republics of Peru, Ecuador, Bolivia, and northern Chile there existed during the period of the Spanish conquest a vast and powerful empire, that of the Incas, whose capital was the city of Cuzco. In an age much earlier than the sixteenth century, there lived in this extensive territory divers peoples who made war on one another, until Manco Capac, son of the sun, united them all and became their civilizer. According to tradition, from that time dates the organization of the empire of the Incas, which succeeded in developing one of the most brilliant civilizations of the American aborigines. The Inca, as absolute monarch, had unlimited power, and was lord of all the land, which, in accordance with his wishes, had been divided into four portions that pertained respectively to the sun, the Inca, the nobles, and the community. The Peruvians had constructed extensive roads, and one of the most original features of this civilization was the organization of a postal service. The Inca Empire extended its civilization into the territory of some of the present Argentine provinces, as is shown by the ruins of stone buildings of an architectural style similar to that used by the Incas.[6]

---

[6] Bunge, op. cit., I, 37-38.

1. Stress on Argentine agriculture
2. Acceptance of Indian destruction
3. Admiration of Spain
4. Admiration of private enterprise

CHAPTER II

THE FIRST ADELANTADO

SPAIN SUDDENLY and unexpectedly became mistress of the immense continent discovered by Columbus. That country had to undertake the difficult task of conquering it, of subjugating the aboriginal tribes that inhabited it, and later of colonizing it in order to establish there centers of Spanish and European civilization. The enterprise was prodigious and in itself constitutes one of the purest glories of Spain.

Two historic facts made Spain's task of colonizing America even more difficult: (1) Spain was not in a condition to become a colonizing nation. (2) The immense territorial expanse of the continent, its imposing geographic features, and the savage and warlike instincts of many tribes that inhabited it made the distribution therein of the gifts of civilization a very hazardous enterprise.

In fact, a country is in a condition to colonize only when it is impelled by economic or political motives. Such is the case, for example, when there is an excess of population, as is true of the peoples of present Europe, who emigrate to new continents where the struggle for life is easier; or when people emigrate for political reasons—for example, to the colonies of North America, which were settled during the seventeenth century by emigrants who fled in large numbers from England from the political and religious tyranny of the Stuart kings.

Spain of the sixteenth century was not in this condition; for that country had no such excess population; nor did political motives impel the migration of the Spanish people. And yet, Spain launched into the work of colonizing America because she was its mistress, and because she was inspired to do so by virtue of the audacious, generous, and daring instincts of the race. It should be added that because of the institutional organization adopted during the war with the Moslems, Spain was prepared to found a democracy in the New World.

The second fact that made the colonization of America difficult was the vast territorial extent of the continent that stretched from pole to pole and its physiographic features—mighty and impassable rivers, inaccessible mountains, forests that had never been trodden by human foot, and extensive pampas. The rivers of Europe—the Seine, the Thames, and the Tiber—were rivulets in comparison with the immense volume and extent of the American rivers—the Orinoco, the Magdalena, the Paraná, and the Plata. And the Spanish adventurers, animated by the desire to gain glory and booty, surmounted the physiographic obstacles, only to face, not the tranquil possession of the lands which they explored but war with the aboriginal tribes.[1]

The subjugation of La Plata differed from the conquest of other parts of the aboriginal empire, for, in contrast with Mexico and Peru, it lacked mineral wealth. Further on in this narrative, it will be shown how this economic fact influenced the early structure of the society of La Plata. On the other hand, the aborigines who inhabited this region, with the exception of those in northwestern Argentina, had neither the organization nor the culture of the Incas or the Aztecs. Hence it can be affirmed that the real character of the conquest of La Plata was such as to make it from the very beginning an actual colonization.[2]

Spain began the colonization of America with the well-known system of adelantados—a system employed during the conquest of the Moslem who had occupied the Peninsula for centuries. According to this system noblemen undertook at their own expense the task of gradually expelling the invader, in return for the title conferred upon them by the king of governor and master of the lands conquered by them. This system was soon extended to America. Those persons who led expeditions and took charge of the government and administration of the lands taken from the Indians were called adelantados.

The advantage of this system consisted in the fact that it intrusted to private enterprise a task of such large dimensions as was that of colonization by stimulating private interest through the hope of the control of the land and the riches that it possessed. But this advantage was outweighed by the disadvantages of the

---

[1] A suggestive description of episodes of the Spanish conquest is found in L. Lugones, *El imperio jesuítico, ensayo histórico* (Buenos Aires, 1907) pp. 131-34.

[2] P. Groussac, "La expedición de Mendoza," *Anales de la Biblioteca* (Buenos Aires, 1912), VIII, xii-xiii.

system. Evidently the adelantado system constituted a definitive contract made by the king with individuals who were commercially interested in the work of colonization. The adelantados accordingly engaged in colonization for the purpose of reimbursing themselves for the expense of the enterprise and with the design of exploiting these lands in order to obtain various benefits and advantages. Besides, the kings of Spain delegated absolute powers to them; and thus the adelantados had complete political, military, and judicial authority.

Not for long and never completely

Throughout all of Spanish America the history of the adelantados was a melancholy one. The first adelantado was Bartholomew Columbus. From the Gulf of Mexico to Buenos Aires all the inhabitants suffered from the consequences of the powers exercised by these officials. King Philip II decided to end this system, and substituted for it the system of governors who received a salary and were appointed and removed directly by the king. The last adelantado of Río de la Plata was Juan Torres de Vera y Aragón who advised the Spanish king to suppress the system because of the disadvantages caused by it.

Under this system the king signed contracts on the same day for both the conquest of Chile and that of La Plata. The first was with Almagro and Alcazaba and the second with Pedro de Mendoza. The conquest of La Plata was very important, not only because of the legend of the fabulous mineral riches of that region but also because of the necessity of erecting a bulwark against the extension of the Portuguese conquest.

The contract between the Spanish king and Mendoza, which was signed in 1534, provided as follows: "We promise to make you our governor and captain general of the said lands, provinces, and peoples of said Río de la Plata, and of the said two hundred leagues of coast of the South Sea, which commence at the limits that we have set to the government of said Marshal Diego Almagro. You are to hold these lands during all the years of your life with a salary of two thousand ducats of gold each year and two thousand ducats annually in aid of the expenses, which are in all four thousand ducats, which you shall enjoy from the day upon which you set sail from our kingdom in order to undertake this conquest and colonization. These four thousand ducats for salary and for aid in the expenses of settlement shall be paid from the incomes and profits pertaining to us in that land which we may have, during the period of your government, and in no other manner." [3]

Pedro de Mendoza was an illustrious man of his time. Of him the Argentine critic, Pablo Groussac, said: "We are absolutely ignorant what motives could have impelled him, with his courtly position and customs, to engage in an adventure so expensive and perilous, above all an adventure so remote in nature from the enterprises that had hitherto enlisted his cupidity or ambition. In order to limit and perhaps to settle these conjectures, we shall say only that Mendoza was able to interest so much personal and pecuniary aid in the success of his venture that it would appear to be very likely that this decidedly lightened the expense of his preparations." [4]

Because of his illness, Mendoza postponed the expedition one year. It finally sailed from the port of Sanlúcar on August 24, 1535, in eleven vessels carrying about twelve hundred men. The admiral was Diego Mendoza, a brother of the adelantado. The chief posts in the expedition were filled by notable men, including Juan de Ayolas, Juan de Osorio, Domingo Martínez de Irala, Juan de Salazar, Gonzalo de Mendoza, and Francisco Ruíz Galán. They took with them as instruments of colonization, horses and mares, and tools and implements of all sorts. The expedition sailed to the Canary Islands and from thence to the Cape Verde Islands, where it was supplied with provisions. By the end of November, 1535, the party had reached Rio de Janeiro.

As the adelantado became ill in Rio de Janeiro, he gave the direction of the expedition to his chief commander, Juan Osorio. Enemies of this worthy chief made Mendoza believe that he was conspiring against his authority. The adelantado, acting quickly, gave credit to this slander and ordered his captains to put Osorio to death. Ayolas cast him into prison, and notified the adelantado, who repeated his order. Ayolas then struck Osorio with a dagger

---

[3] J. F. Pacheco and F. de Cárdenas, *Colección de documentos inéditos relativos al descubrimiento, conquista y colonización de las posesiones españolas en América y Oceanía* (42 vols. Madrid, 1864-84), XXII, 352. Groussac, "La expedición de Mendoza," *Anales de la Biblioteca*, VIII, 1v, note, comments on the ignorance of the terrain displayed by the council of the Indies in early capitulations.

[4] *Ibid.*, p. liv.

until "his soul left his body." Groussac states: "Even if the entire guilt of the accused were admitted, the mere idea of condemning and executing him without hearing his defense, and simply because of the assertions of his enemies, is—and was at that time—an abominable proceeding which even in inquisitorial Spain of the sixteenth century would have scandalized honorable souls." [5]

The expedition spent fourteen days in Rio de Janeiro. Then it proceeded to La Plata, and ascended the river. The small vessels reached the Riachuelo in February, 1536, and at its entrance in the low lands along the banks of the "little river of the ships" the adelantado founded the city of Puerto de Santa María del Buen Aire. At that place, Mendoza built a church, a house for the adelantado, and a large number of huts composed of straw and clay. Out of one hundred horses and mares that had been embarked in Spain, seventy-two were landed—a fact that we should notice, for some time later the plains were covered by their wild progeny, which became the basis of the great Argentine wealth in livestock.

A colonial historian states that the first person who landed was Sancho del Campo, who noticing the purity of the air, its good quality, and freshness, said: "What good airs [Buenos Aires] are those of this land!" This was the origin of the name given to the settlement. Other historians have raised doubts about the veracity of this exclamation, and have observed that the origin of the name "Buenos Aires" was due to another cause. In fact, it is known that there existed in Seville, in the section known as Triana, a hospital and brotherhood of merchants who had a chapel under the protection of Our Lady of Buen Aire. Evidently, its constitution dated from 1561, which is subsequent to the date of the first foundation of our city. But, in any case, there already existed "Our Lady of Buen Aire" on the island of Sardinia, a possession of the crown of Castile. [6] The image of Buenos Aires which was cherished by the sailors explains the origin of the name of the port of Santa María de Buenos Aires.

In a concise, but correct, page of his annals, the German chronicler, Ulrich Schmidel (who arrived in the expedition of the first adelantado) mentions that they found in the new land a people

---

[5] *Ibid.*, p. cx.   [6] *Ibid.*, p. cxxi.

composed of almost two thousand Indians called Carendíes (Querandí). Schmidel said: "These Carendíes brought to our camp
and shared with us their miserable victuals of fish and game for
fourteen days, and there was not more than one day when they
did not come. Then our general, Don Pedro de Mendoza, sent
an alcalde named Juan Pavón with two other Spaniards on horseback to visit those Carendíes who were four miles [leagues] from
our camp, and when they reached the place where the Indians
were, the three men were severely treated and had to return to
our camp. As soon as Pedro de Mendoza, our captain, knew of
this event by the mouth of our alcalde (who for this purpose
had created a disturbance in our camp), he sent to the Indian
village his own brother, Diego de Mendoza, with three hundred
lancers and thirty well-armed horsemen; I went with them. The
orders were indeed severe: to capture or to kill all the Carendíe
Indians and to take possession of their village. But when we
approached them they numbered some four thousand men, for they
had summoned their friends." [7]

As a result of the ensuing battle Diego Mendoza and about
thirty other Spaniards were killed. Soon afterward, the settlement was fortified in expectation of a fresh attack. The misery
was so great that the colonists began to suffer from hunger. "Thus
it happened that necessity and misery reached such a point," continued Schmidel, "that by reason of the famine there were not
left any rats or mice, or snakes, or even any reptiles that might
nourish us in our great necessity and unprecedented misery. We
even ate all the shoes and the hides." [8] A little later the Indians
to the number of twenty-three thousand attacked the fort and
burned it. [9]

Before these events took place, Ayolas had sailed up the Paraná
River and had founded near Coronda the town of Corpus Christi.
In view of the success of this first exploration and of others that
followed it, Pedro de Mendoza decided to proceed up the Paraná
River in small vessels with seven hundred men, leaving one hundred
and sixty in the port of Riachuelo. They went up the Paraná

---

[7] U. Schmidel, *Viaje al Río de la Plata* (edited by B. Mitre and S. A. Lafone
Quevedo, Buenos Aires, 1903), pp. 148-49.

[8] *Ibid.*, pp. 151-52.

[9] *Ibid.*, pp. 154-55.

River as far as the mouth of the Carcarañá, where the adelantado founded, a few leagues below Corpus Christi, the port of Nuestra Señora de Buena Esperanza, whence Ayolas sallied forth in search of the land of gold. Soon afterward, Mendoza left some men at Buena Esperanza, and, falling ill, he returned to Buenos Aires.

The men who accompanied the adelantado on this expedition suffered all sorts of privations. On the feast day of St. John the Evangelist, in 1536, the Indians burned four boats containing Spaniards. An ensign and thirty soldiers lost their lives.

Having heard nothing from Ayolas, early in 1537, Pedro de Mendoza sent Juan de Salazar and Gonzalo de Mendoza in search of him. Three months passed after the departure of the latter without the receipt of any news. In view of the privations which they were suffering, the hostility of the Indians, and his own illness, the adelantado decided to return to Spain. He arranged that Juan de Ayolas should remain as lieutenant governor and captain general; and that, pending the latter's return, Captain Francisco Ruíz Galán should act as head of the colony. In the last days of April, 1537, the adelantado sailed from America for Spain. He left two hundred and fifty men in Buenos Aires. Soon after leaving these coasts, Mendoza's illness became worse; and he died on June 23, 1537. His body was buried at sea.

Meantime, Ayolas proceeded up the Paraná and Paraguay rivers to a port which he named Candelaria, where he left Domingo Martínez de Irala as his lieutenant, with orders to await his return. Ayolas continued on his venturesome expedition. After enduring many hardships, he reached Upper Peru—now called Bolivia—and came back laden with gold and silver. He returned to Candelaria three months after his departure from that port, and not finding there Martínez de Irala—who had descended the Paraguay River to Asunción to repair his ships—after a painful voyage of more than four hundred leagues, his party stopped to rest among the Payaguae Indians, who seemed to be friendly; but these Indians treacherously killed them while they were crossing a swamp.

Upon his departure for Spain, Pedro de Mendoza had, as we have said, intrusted the command to Ruíz Galán. It will be remembered that Juan de Salazar and Gonzalo de Mendoza had left Buenos Aires in search of Ayolas. They reached Candelaria where they learned from Martínez de Irala that Ayolas was on the way to Upper Peru. The emissaries returned, but while descending the Paraguay River, in August, 1537, they paused to construct a fort on the site where the city of Asunción was soon to be founded by Martínez de Irala. Gonzalo de Mendoza remained there with thirty men, while Juan de Salazar returned to Buenos Aires. Ruíz Galán decided to proceed to Asunción, and reached that place when Martínez de Irala returned from Candelaria in order to repair his vessels. At this meeting the first clash of authorities in the colony took place; for Ruíz Galán declared that he was the representative of Pedro de Mendoza, while Martínez de Irala alleged that he was the representative of Ayolas. Martínez de Irala proceeded with his ships to Candelaria, while Ruíz Galán, after taking steps to promote the growth of the city of Asunción, went to Corpus Christi and then to Buenos Aires. A little later, fresh complications arose, for the inspector Alonzo Cabrera arrived at Colonia with a royal cédula prepared in Spain when the death of Adelantado Pedro de Mendoza became known. In this cédula, dated September 12, 1537, it was arranged that, in case the adelantado had not left a representative, the colonists should be assembled in order to elect "the person who according to God and their consciences seemed to them best fitted to take command." When Cabrera learned that the lieutenant left by Mendoza, pending the return of Ayolas from his expedition, was Ruíz Galán, accompanied by the latter, he went in search of Ayolas to the city of Asunción. There they met Domingo Martínez de Irala, who upon returning again from Candelaria, had framed a document in which, mentioning the death of Mendoza, the disappearance of Ayolas, and his appointment by the latter, he instituted himself as the legitimate successor of Ayolas in the government. Martínez de Irala assumed command on July 31, 1539, being supported in this step by Ruíz Galán and Cabrera.

As the population of Asunción was decreasing from day to day, Martínez de Irala decided to collect the colonists of Buenos Aires and to concentrate them in the new settlement, which was destined to be for almost half a century the center of colonization and conquest of the colony of La Plata. For this purpose, he and the inspector, Alonzo de Cabrera, left Asunción in March, 1541. When they reached Buenos Aires, they found that the colonists were refusing to obey the order of Martínez de Irala. Nevertheless, he proceeded to distribute the movable goods. He also removed the church, a ship that served as a fortress, and the houses that had been built out of wood. As Madero observes: "By the middle of the year 1541 there remained at Buenos Aires no other trace of Spain than the horses and mares which had been brought by Pedro de Mendoza, and of which the Querandí Indians began to make use." [10]

[10] E. Madero, *Historia del puerto de Buenos Aires* (Buenos Aires, 1902), p. 176.

CHAPTER III

ALVAR NÚÑEZ CABEZA DE VACA, MARTÍNEZ DE IRALA, JUAN DE GARAY

EMPEROR CHARLES V had meantime granted permission to Alvar Núñez Cabeza de Vaca to prepare an expedition for the Río de la Plata with the prerogatives of adelantado, in case Ayolas had died.[1] On December 2, 1540, Cabeza de Vaca left Cadiz; and, after a voyage of almost four months, he reached Santa Catalina. At this place two Franciscans gave him information concerning the distance between Santa Catalina and Asunción. After making certain explorations that had been ordered by the adelantado, the expedition proceeded overland with two hundred and fifty soldiers, leaving one hundred and fifty at Santa Catalina. The journey they undertook was a perilous enterprise; for the route traversed inaccessible forests, ascended mountains, and crossed great rivers. The men reached Iguassú, where they must have marveled at the spectacle afforded by the great falls.[2] After appeasing the hostilities of certain indigenous tribes, Adelantado Cabeza de Vaca entered the city of Asunción on March 11, 1542, after a journey that had lasted about one hundred and twenty days.

The journey of Cabeza de Vaca across Brazil was of special importance. According to the terms of the agreement that had been signed, Santa Catalina was an integral part of this district. By means of its adelantados, Spain asserted its right to the ownership of these territories.

Upon his arrival at Asunción, Cabeza de Vaca assumed control. He named Domingo Martínez de Irala second in command. The adelantado was there informed that Martínez de Irala had undertaken to depopulate Buenos Aires in order to concentrate the colonists in one place. Cabeza de Vaca then expressed a wish

[1] Pacheco and Cárdenas, *op. cit.,* XXIII, 8-33. [Cabeza de Vaca had previously accompanied Pánfilo de Narváez on a daring expedition into Florida, had been a castaway in Texas, and had made thence an heroic trip overland to the city of Mexico.—W. S. R.]

[2] A. Núñez Cabeza de Vaca, *Relación de los naufragios y comentarios de Alvar Núñez Cabeza de Vaca* ("Colección de libros y documentos referentes a la historia de América," vols. V and VI, Madrid, 1906), p. 185.

to repopulate that city; but the colonists, who vividly remembered the miseries and hardships they had suffered during their sojourn in Buenos Aires, showed great displeasure at this decision. The adelantado therefore relinquished his design.

According to the provisions of his contract with Charles V, Cabeza de Vaca was to seek a route of communication with Peru. In fulfillment of this obligation, he dispatched Martínez de Irala who again ascended the river Paraguay up to sixteen degrees of latitude, where he found a port which he named Los Reyes. Martínez de Irala returned to Asunción with excellent reports, and Cabeza de Vaca prepared an expedition under his own leadership to journey to the famous lands of Peru. He left Asunción in the beginning of September, 1543, with 400 Spaniards, 1,200 friendly Indians, 10 ships, and 120 canoes. He traversed the course of the Paraguay River throughout almost its entire extent and then proceeded overland in a northwesterly direction. But he was unable to advance farther because of the numerous obstacles encountered—either obstructions of nature or the hostility of Indian tribes. With his followers ill and worn by fatigue, he returned to Asunción without having accomplished his purpose, but more fortunate than Ayolas, who had met death on the way.

After the adelantado's return to Asunción, a revolutionary uprising took place which was led by royal officials (functionaries who had charge of the administration of the royal treasury). Cabeza de Vaca was deposed and cast into prison,[3] where he remained ten months. During this time the Spaniards divided into two factions: the loyal colonists who were partisans of the adelantado; and the seditious colonists, who were partisans of Martínez de Irala. After ten months of imprisonment, Cabeza de Vaca was sent to Spain, where the Council of the Indies instituted a suit against him and condemned him; but a little later, the indictment was reconsidered and he was absolved. In his account of this uprising the Argentine writer, Enrique Peña, says:

"On April 26, the day after the adelantado was imprisoned, there assembled the inspector, Alonso Cabrera, the accountant, Felipe de Cáceres, the fiscal, Pedro Dorantes, and the treasurer,

[3] *Correspondencia de los oficiales reales de hacienda del Río de la Plata con los Reyes de España* (edited by R. Levillier, Madrid, 1915), I. 58-69, 73-79, 83-94.

García Vanegas, as well as the clerks Orue, González, and Balderas. After having brought against the adelantado a series of charges as proof of his bad administration, such as having failed to carry out the royal wishes, and having committed all sorts of abuses, they stated that they had resolved to incarcerate him, and that he would be sent to Spain and judged there. The royal officials also decided that while they were framing formal charges and preparing the caravel for his transportation, they would designate Martínez de Irala as lieutenant governor—and, indeed, did so in this instrument. On the afternoon of the same day the clerks who had attended the meeting went to the house of Martínez de Irala in order to inform him of his nomination as lieutenant governor and captain general—a position in which he had served before the arrival of Cabeza de Vaca. When they had finished reading the statement of what had been done by the royal officials, a large number of conquistadors who were present, declared that they also nominated Martínez de Irala as lieutenant governor.[4]

Once installed in the government, Martínez de Irala was able to reëstablish order among the inhabitants of Asunción who were divided into factions by contentions that had precipitated the formation of the two parties which we have mentioned, composed of the loyal colonists and the contumacious colonists.

Martínez de Irala then undertook to carry out his plan of establishing communication between La Plata and Peru. Just as he was ready to start with the expedition, a general uprising of the Guaraní Indians obliged him to postpone his attempt. By the end of November, 1547, however, Martínez de Irala was ready to leave Asunción with 250 Spaniards and 3,000 friendly Indians. He again ascended the Paraguay River, and then marched in a northwesterly direction until he reached the frontiers of Peru. Upon hearing of the civil war led by Gonzalo Pizarro, the king of Spain had sent the commissioner La Gasca to Peru in the rôle of peacemaker. Martínez de Irala profited by this circumstance to inform the royal commissioner of the changes that had taken place in Asunción. For this purpose, he dispatched Nuflo de Chaves, who reached Lima and then returned to the port of San

[4] E. Peña, introduction to "Relación de Alvar Núñez Cabeza de Vaca," *Revista de Derecho, Historia y Letras* (Buenos Aires, 1906), XXV, 354-55.

Fernando. Martínez de Irala awaited the return of Chaves for some time, but as his soldiers clamored for a speedy return to Asunción, he had to relinquish his post, and the mutineers started back under the command of Gonzalo de Mendoza.

During the absence of Martinez de Irala the government of Asunción had been intrusted to Captain Francisco de Mendoza. As the absence of the governor was prolonged for almost a year, the inhabitants voted that Diego de Abreu should act as substitute for Martínez de Irala. Mendoza felt himself slighted by this choice, and attempted to lead an uprising with his followers, but Abreu made him a prisoner and had him beheaded at Asunción.

When the followers of Martínez de Irala returned they asked him to withdraw his resignation and to take charge of the government as a necessary means of restoring order and reëstablishing peace. Martínez de Irala agreed to assume the government and the people were appeased. In a short time Nuflo de Chaves and his companions returned; they brought with them the first sheep and goats that came to the land of La Plata. Martínez de Irala soon proceeded to make new grants of lands and Indians, in order to exploit the first and to secure the subjugation of the second. He assigned to the colonists about 26,000 Indians.

In 1552, by a royal cédula, Martínez de Irala was confirmed in his post as governor. He died in 1556 at about sixty years of age. Because of his active disposition and organizing ability, Martínez de Irala was one of the great figures of the colonial epoch.

Some historians of the colonial period have judged him harshly because of his personal dissensions with Adelantado Cabeza de Vaca, and because of his ambition and lust for command. The political activity of Martínez de Irala was so intense that it was natural he should have had bitter enemies and loyal adherents. But viewed down the vista of the centuries his figure becomes great; for to him the nascent colony of La Plata owed wise and just laws for securing the submission of the Indians; and the encomienda system employed in La Plata, which although it degenerated in practice, was in principle an advanced system of colonization. Martínez de Irala was the first governor in whose election the colonists had taken part. This is a fact worth noting, for it will aid us to explain later the slow and gradual formation of a democratic spirit in the colony of La Plata.[5]

Almost two years after Cabeza de Vaca had reached Spain, and because of repeated complaints against Martínez de Irala, Emperor Charles V signed at Monzón on July 22, 1547, a contract with Juan de Sanabria "for the conquest and settlement of Río de la Plata." This agreement also obliged Sanabria to make a settlement at the port of San Francisco (between Paranaguá and Santa Catalina). It conferred upon him the title of adelantado. But just as he was about to sail, he died at Seville. His son Diego asked for the post, which the emperor conceded to him by a contract signed at Valladolid on March 12, 1549. As Diego Sanabria could not at once come to America, his mother, Doña Mencia Calderón, who had supplied him with the money to prepare the fleet, sailed with three of the ships.

Doña Mencia reached the Brazilian coast where the ships were lost. Accompanied by her two daughters, María and Mencia, and fifty men, she crossed the continent from the river San Francisco to Paraguay. Diego Sanabria left Spain later with two ships. At the mouth of La Plata River he encountered a storm in which he lost one of the vessels. Some soldiers who escaped in boats went to the coast of Brazil and proceeded by land to Paraguay. The other ship—which carried Diego de Sanabria—sailed along the coast to Brazil, and was wrecked and "completely destroyed" at the island of Margarita.[6] In the expedition of Doña Mencia came Hernando de Trejo who at San Francisco married María de Sanabria, the daughter of the adelantado. From this marriage there sprang Fernando de Trejo y Sanabria, who became bishop of Tucumán.

Martínez de Irala had provided in his will that upon his death his son-in-law, Captain Gonzalo de Mendoza, should take charge of the government. Mendoza directed Nuflo de Chaves to found a village "in the province of the Xarayes and their districts." For

[5] R. Levene, *Lecturas históricas argentinas* (2 vols. Buenos Aires, 1913), I, 24-30. A eulogy of Martínez de Irala will be found in F. Azara, *Descripción é historia del Paraguay y del Río de la Plata* (2 vols. Madrid, 1847), II, 157-59.

[6] Madero, *op. cit.*, p. 183. The capitulation with Sanabria is published in Pacheco and Cárdenas, *op. cit.*, XXIII, 118-31.

this purpose, Chaves left with one hundred and fifty Spaniards. However, he did not execute his commission, but on February 26, 1561, he founded the city of Santa Cruz de la Sierra (which is located in the present province of Chiquitos). Soon afterward, he distributed the Indians in encomiendas. Among the encomenderos was Juan de Garay.

Mendoza died in the course of that year and by vote of the colonists in accordance with the royal cédula of 1537 another son-in-law of Martínez de Irala named Ortiz de Vergara was chosen as head of the government. In order to legalize this choice it was necessary for the king to confirm him in his post. As he could not send an agent to Spain for that purpose, Ortiz de Vergara decided to prepare an expedition for Peru in order to request the viceroy to confirm him in office. Contrary to Ortiz de Vergara's expectations, upon his arrival at Chuquisaca, the viceroy deprived him of his command and appointed Juan Ortiz de Zárate as third adelantado of La Plata.

When he designated Ortiz de Zárate as adelantado, the viceroy of Peru imposed as a condition that the king should confirm him in the office. The viceroy also made an agreement with the adelantado that had important consequences upon the destinies of the colony. According to this agreement, the new adelantado was to bring from Spain families of agriculturists and laborers, as well as cattle, horses, and sheep.

After appointing Felipe de Cáceres as his representative in Asunción, Ortiz de Zárate departed for Spain via Panama. Dissensions and struggles now took place in Asunción because some colonists were in favor of recognizing the government of Cáceres, while others were partisans of Ortiz de Vergara and of Bishop Latorre. The people were thus divided into factions as in the days of Cabeza de Vaca and Martínez de Irala. Upon a certain occasion when Cáceres organized an expedition to the Río de la Plata, with the expectation of meeting the adelantado there, his enemies received him when he returned with signs of hostility, and one day when Cáceres was in church, the friends of Ortiz de Vergara confined him in the monastery of the Order of Mercy in a small cell where he was bound with two pairs of fetters and a heavy chain. After a year in prison, Cáceres was shipped to Spain.

After Cáceres, Martín Suárez de Toledo assumed the command; he was later confirmed in his post by the vote of the chief inhabitants.

With the expedition of Pedro de Mendoza, seventy-two horses and mares had been introduced into Buenos Aires. When the fort was given up, the horses and mares were left on the pampas. In 1580, when Buenos Aires was recolonized, the stock of horses had multiplied amazingly. The first goats and sheep were introduced by Nuflo de Chaves into Paraguay. To that region, Portuguese from São Vicente brought the first cows. Such was the original nursery of livestock; for, from Asunción, livestock were taken for the founding of Corrientes, Santa Fe, and for the resettlement of Buenos Aires. Upon the arrival of the expedition of Ortiz de Zárate, which brought a large contingent of laborers and horses, our wealth of livestock was insured and a great development took place.

While these events were taking place in Asunción, the figure of Juan de Garay, the founder of Santa Fe, became prominent in the history of La Plata. It was he who brought about the real founding of the city of Buenos Aires. Garay was fourteen years of age when he came to South America with his uncle, the lawyer Pedro Ortiz de Zárate, as part of the retinue of Viceroy Blasco Núñez Vela. Garay remained in Peru from 1544 to 1548. When Juan Núñez Prado left Peru in 1549 to colonize the provinces of Tucumán, Garay accompanied him. He began to reside at Asunción in December, 1568, and had reached the age of thirty-nine when he was given his first post in the provinces of La Plata.

Garay himself states that when the passions of the bishop and of Felipe de Cáceres were stilled, the new governor, Martín Suárez de Toledo, gave him a commission to come and plant a settlement in the Platean provinces. Suárez de Toledo made this appointment "because of the warmth with which I declared," wrote Garay, "that we should open gates into that region and that we should not be inclosed." He ascended the river La Plata, then went up the Paraná, and entered the Río Salado. Garay was accompanied by "nine Spaniards and seventy-five young men who were natives of the land." "With these followers," says Madero, "who were almost entirely creoles, Juan de Garay founded the city of Santa Fe on Sunday, November 15, 1573. As alcaldes, he appointed Juan de Espinosa and Ortuño de Albido, and as regidors, Benito de Morales, Hernando de Salas, Mateo Gil, Diego de Ramírez, Lázaro de Banialbo, and Juan de Santa Cruz. The extent of jurisdiction of the new colony was thus marked out: 'by way of the road to Paraguay as far as the end of the over-flowed Chicos; and down the river on the road to Buenos Aires twenty-five leagues below Sancti Spiritus' (that is, twenty-five leagues to the south of Carcarañá); and 'toward the province of Tucumán, fifty leagues, and into the interior from the banks of this river to the Paraná River and on the other side of the Paraná another fifty leagues.' " [7]

The founding of the city of Santa Fe was of great importance. We have noticed that the Spanish colonizing movement had be-gun at Buenos Aires and, after the destruction of that city, had been centered around Asunción. It was, however, necessary to seek an outlet to the sea, and the founding of Santa Fe prepared the way for the second founding of Buenos Aires. This city was destined to become the center of the Platean colony—a center which had direct communications with Spain.

The adelantado, Ortiz de Zárate, had signed the agreement above mentioned by which he undertook to bring five hundred men, eight thousand cows and sheep, and eight hundred goats, mares, and horses.[8] He sailed from Spain in 1572, and entered the Río de la Plata in the following year. At the island of Martín García he met Juan de Garay and they at once set out for Asun-ción. There the discouragements of Ortiz de Zárate had even in-creased, for he had met with difficulties of every sort.[9] He had been able to found only a temporary settlement on the banks of the Río de la Plata and the people of Asunción did not yield him proper obedience. Two years after his arrival, he died; in his will he provided that whoever married his daughter, then residing in Peru, should be his successor. In the meantime, he designated as his lieutenant Diego de Mendieta, a restless youth whose admin-istration was short and reckless. Ortiz de Zárate's daughter mar-

---

[7] Madero, op. cit., p. 231.

[8] On the preparations made for this expedition, see P. Groussac, "Juan de Garay," Anales de la Biblioteca (Buenos Aires, 1915), X, cli-clii.

[9] On the personnel of Zárate's expedition, see B. Mitre, Historia de Belgrano y de la independencia argentina (4 vols. Buenos Aires, 1902), I, 11.

ried Juan Torres de Vera y Aragón, who consequently became
the new adelantado of the Río de la Plata.[10]

Torres de Vera y Aragón named Garay lieutenant governor,
an appointment which was very well received. During the government of Garay occurred the expedition against the cacique Oberá,
which was due to an uprising of the Guaraní Indians. This cacique
revolted with all his tribe; he announced that he was the son of
God and had been directed to redeem his race. Garay fought a
sanguinary combat with the Indians and was able to subjugate
them.

Upon returning from his campaigns, Garay gathered the men
and supplies that were needed for the resettlement of the city of
Buenos Aires. We noticed that Buenos Aires had been founded in
1536 by the first adelantado of La Plata, Pedro de Mendoza,
that, after its destruction by the Indians, Martínez de Irala had
ordered that it should be abandoned, and that all the colonists
had been concentrated in the city of Asunción. In 1544, the second
adelantado, Alvar Núñez Cabeza de Vaca, had tried to reëstablish
Buenos Aires, but his followers displayed their displeasure at the
project, and he desisted. Lastly, in 1570 and 1572, Felipe Cáceres
had also attempted the enterprise in vain.[11]

To Juan de Garay belongs the honor of being the second founder of the city of Buenos Aires. He gathered more than sixty
men, with the necessary farm implements and munitions, one
thousand horses, and five hundred cows. He left Asunción on
March 9, 1580. At the end of May or the beginning of June, the
party disembarked and Garay, with the chief men who accompanied him, selected the site on which the city was to be built. On
Saturday, June 11, 1580, the day of St. Barnabas, the founding
of the city of Buenos Aires took place.

Garay's account runs as follows: "On this day, Saturday, the
day of the feast of St. Barnabas, the eleventh day of the month of
June in the year of the birth of our redeemer, Jesus Christ, one
thousand five hundred and eighty, being in this port of Santa
María de Buenos Aires in the provinces of the Río de la Plata,
recently styled Nueva Vizcaya, I establish and found at the above-

---

[10] Groussac, "Juan de Garay," *Anales de la Biblioteca*, X, cxcvi-cxcix.

[11] On the rôle of Matienzo in this movement, see R. Levillier, *El licenciado
Matienzo, inspirador de la segunda fundación de Buenos Aires* (Madrid, 1910).

mentioned site and port a city, which I am settling with the soldiers and civilians whom I have brought with me for that purpose. . . .

"One of the facts not mentioned by history, but which is most worthy of notice, and which has undoubtedly contributed to the character of the people of Buenos Aires, is that of the sixty-three companions with whom Juan de Garay planted the city anew, only 'ten were Spaniards, while the others had been born in this land.' We have seen that the founders of Santa Fe were composed in about the same proportion of creoles and Spaniards. . . . Thereafter, as will soon be seen, the creoles began proudly to claim their communal fueros or privileges and to display marked tendencies to govern themselves." [12]

On October 17, 1580, Garay issued an ordinance for the distribution to the settlers of "sites for houses," "strips of land outside of the city for the Indians who served them, stones for their farm lands and haciendas, and even ranches for their oxen and beef cattle." All this is demonstrated by cédulas or memoirs signed by Juan de Garay. Regarding the new Buenos Aires, Madero makes this comment: "I do not know whether in tracing the plan of the city, which according to his notion, would be the 'port of the land,' Juan de Garay followed principles or rules of aesthetic and architectonic foresight. It is believed that he did not do so; and yet, the plan was in harmony with the tradition of the ancient Greek cities which faced the sea, for the principal square of Buenos Aires was placed almost upon the banks of the river." [13]

The new city had a frontage on the river of 2,416 yards and a depth toward the west of 1,370 yards. Garay selected the site for the church and appointed the alcaldes and regidors for the first cabildo. With the resettlement of Buenos Aires, the movement for the colonization of La Plata, which for half a century had been centered in Asunción, returned to its original point of departure.[14]

Torres de Vera y Aragón entered the city of Asunción in

[12] Levene, *op. cit.*, I, 45-50.

[13] Madero, *op. cit.*, p. 264.

[14] The colonial historians Lozano, Guevara, and Azara assert that the founder of Buenos Aires died in the beginning of 1584. But M. P. Leguizamón in his books *La iconografía de Juan de Garay* (La Plata, 1910), *El supuesto retrato de Garay* (La Plata, 1910), and *Páginas argentinas* (Buenos Aires, 1911), proves that the conquistador died in 1583.

August, 1587. At the beginning of the following year he proceeded with the aid of Hernando Arias de Saavedra and eighty men, to found a new city. On April 5, 1588, he built a fort on the eastern bank of the Paraná which bore the name of San Juan de Vera de las Siete Corrientes. Some months afterward, the adelantado departed for Charcas, leaving his nephew, Alonso Vera, as lieutenant governor at Asunción.

CHAPTER IV

THE CONQUEST OF THE INTERIOR

IN ORDER to check the grievous dissensions that had arisen among the conquerors of Peru, the king had sent Vaca de Castro to act as peacemaker. When this agent had succeeded in establishing order, he rewarded the services of his soldiers by sending them to conquer unexplored lands. This is the historic explanation of the expedition of Diego de Rojas, who left Peru at the head of two hundred men about May, 1543—an expedition that did not end until September, 1546. The party passed the gorge of Humahuaca and entered an imposing region. The members of the expedition had to fight many times with the indigenous tribes, and in one of these combats Rojas was killed. Francisco de Mendoza, one of the officers of the expedition, took charge, penetrated to the river Carcarañá, and skirted its banks until he reached its outlet in the Paraná River, where stood the ruins of Fort Sancti Spiritus, which had been founded by Cabot. The explorers then decided to retrace their steps, but on the journey Mendoza was murdered by one of his companions.[1]

Meantime the dissensions in Peru had not ceased. Gonzalo de Pizarro rebelled against the viceroy, Blasco Núñez de Vela, and the latter had him executed. President La Gasca established order in Peru and, in his turn, rewarded the services of his followers. Among others, he rewarded Juan Núñez de Prado, whom he charged to plant a colony in the territory that had been traversed by Rojas.[2] Núñez de Prado left in 1549 with an expedition composed of about eighty soldiers. After subjugating the Calchaquian Indians, he founded the city of Barco.

The colonizing stream that proceeded from Peru came into violent contact with another stream which, coming from the same

---

[1] P. Gutiérrez de Santa Clara, *Historia de las guerras civiles del Perú* ("Colección de obras y documentos referentes á la historia de America," vols. II, III, IV, X, XX, XXI; Madrid, 1904-29), III, 147 ff. See further, R. Levillier, *El descubrimiento del Norte Argentino* (Lima, 1925).

[2] With regard to the extent of the territory designated as "Tucumán," see R. Jaime Freyre, *El Tucumán colonial* ("Documentos y mapas del archivo de Indias," vol. I, Buenos Aires, 1915), pp. 8-9.

place, had proceeded to Chile and penetrated into Tucumán. The great conqueror of Chile, Pedro de Valdivia, had, indeed, sent Francisco Villagra to Barco because he considered that those regions pertained to the jurisdiction of Chile. Francisco de Aguirre, a new emissary from the government beyond the Andes, deprived Núñez de Prado of the command, and sent him a prisoner to Chile. Aguirre distributed more than 40,000 Indians among the encomenderos and transferred the city to the banks of the river Dulce. In a spot that was not subject to floods he founded the settlement of Santiago del Estero, "a land of promise."

In 1558, the governor of Chile sent Juan Pérez de Zurita to take charge of the province of Tucumán. Pérez de Zurita founded the cities of Londres, Cañete, and Córdoba del Calchaquí which were very short-lived, for they were destroyed by the Indians. As the authorities in Chile undertook to appoint a successor to Pérez de Zurita, the colonists protested to the government of Peru and declared that the towns of the region of Tucumán were not within the jurisdiction of Chile. This important matter was settled by a royal cédula of August, 1563, which provided that Tucumán was dependent upon the audiencia of Charcas. This decision was made, not only because of the conflicts that had taken place, but also because it was preferable that the inhabitants, for reasons of convenience and distance, should be dependent in their affairs upon Charcas and not upon Lima, even in case an audiencia were established in Chile. The viceroy of Peru then appointed as governor Francisco de Aguirre, the leader who had transferred the colonists from Barco to Santiago del Estero. After Tucumán was made dependent upon the government of Peru, there began an organic period of the founding of important cities. Sent out by Aguirre, Diego Villarroel founded San Miguel de Tucumán on May 31, 1565, on the very spot where Pérez de Zurita had earlier planted the city of Cañete which had been destroyed by the Indians.

Aguirre made a daring expedition to the region of Córdoba; but because of various motives his soldiers mutinied against him and sent him back to Charcas as a prisoner. The figure of Francisco de Aguirre is of exceptional importance, because he conceived a vast plan for the planting of settlements. Among these was to be one located on the shore of the Atlantic Ocean in order to furnish direct communication with Spain. Thus he anticipated the projects of the oidor of Charcas, Juan de Matienzo, as well as the work of Juan de Garay.[3]

In 1571, the government of Peru appointed Jerónimo Luis de Cabrera to the vacant post at Tucumán. He immediately placed himself at the head of an expedition for the purpose of exploring certain territories to the south of Santiago del Estero. On July 6, 1573, Cabrera founded on the central plain the city of Córdoba, which he considered an intermediate step necessary in seeking an exit by water and communication with Spain. In fact, with forty horsemen and some officials, Cabrera set out toward the east and reached Cabot's fort. Notice that it was in this very year that Garay founded the city of Santa Fe. We shall later consider the clash that took place between Cabrera and Garay.

When Cabrera's term ended, he was succeeded by Gonzalo de Abreu, who founded with little success a town in the valley of Salta. He also undertook an unsuccessful expedition to the legendary city of the Caesars, which was supposed to be located in the Patagonian region, and which was famed as unique because of its wealth of gold and precious stones. Hernando de Lerma, the new governor who was appointed in 1577, founded in 1582 the city of San Felipe de Lerma (Salta), a place of communication and defense between Santiago del Estero and Peru.

In 1586, Ramírez de Velazco arrived in the province of Tucumán to take over the post of Hernando de Lerma. In 1591, the new governor founded the cities of La Rioja and Jujuy. His successor, Fernando de Zárate, came to occupy temporarily the government of Tucumán and La Plata at an opportune time, for it was necessary to strengthen the defenses of the city of Buenos Aires against the constant attacks of corsairs and pirates. During the rule of the governors who succeeded one another in Tucumán, it was necessary to carry on sanguinary struggles with the Indians. War was the ordinary mode of subjugating them.

The bishopric of Tucumán was established in 1570. We shall consider this event in its proper place. During the episcopate of Fray Fernando de Trejo, the work of evangelization which had been intrusted to Christian missionaries became important.

[3] R. Levillier, *Francisco de Aguirre y los orígenes del Tucumán* (Madrid, 1920); and A. A. Figueroa, *Santiago del Estero, tierra de promisión* (Buenos Aires, 1924).

Outstanding is the apostolic figure of Father Francisco Solano
of the Franciscan order, who has been canonized by the church.
By his kind treatment and his habits of labor and order, Francisco
Solano subdued the Indians. It is related that he won his way into
their hearts by means of music and chanting.[4]

The two chief colonizing streams which penetrated Argentine
territory laid the foundations of cities at almost the same time.
This simultaneousness made it inevitable that the two streams
advancing into this territory should come into violent contact.

When, in 1516, Juan Díaz de Solís touched at an island in La
Plata River, the explorers in the north following the footsteps of
Vasco Núñez de Balboa, who had discovered the South Sea in
1513, took possession of the Pearl Islands in the Pacific Ocean.
In the same year, 1527, Francisco Pizarro planted himself on the
island of Gallo, and Sebastian Cabot founded the fort of Sancti
Spiritus—the first European colony in La Plata—at the junction
of the Paraná and the Carcarañá. In 1535, the city of Lima was
founded, which became the center of the conquest in Peru, and
Buenos Aires was founded in 1536. In the same year, 1573, the
conquistadors of Peru founded the city of Córdoba, and the colonists of La Plata established Santa Fe. Some time afterward, the
colonizing movement which was descending from Peru, and the
one which was advancing from the east came into conflict at Fort
Sancti Spiritus. The leaders of the expeditions from Peru and
from La Plata, Jerónimo Luis de Cabrera, and Juan de Garay,
both claimed to have exclusive jurisdiction over the coastal territory.[5] The superior tribunals decided the conflict by taking the
view that this jurisdiction pertained to the colonizers who came
from the east.

There were two causes for the conflict between the northern and
the eastern colonizing movements: (1) The simultaneousness of
the settlements made by these movements, which were destined to
clash because the exploration of Argentine territory was being
carried on gradually; and (2) the fact that the colonizing stream

---

[4] J. M. Estrada, *Lecciones sobre la historia de la República Argentina* (vols.
II and III of his *Obras*, 2 vols. Buenos Aires, 1896-98), I, 120-21. [The title
"Fray" was used before the names of priests belonging to certain religious
orders.—W. S. R.]

[5] Groussac, "Juan de Garay," *Anales de la Biblioteca,* X, cxxxix.

from the north, after founding the city of Córdoba, doubled toward the east, impelled by the necessity of finding a port of exit that would afford direct communication with Spain.

Because of the territorial limits assigned in 1548 to Pedro de Valdivia, the district of Cuyo depended upon the jurisdiction of Chile. The provinces included in this region remained under the control of Chile until the creation of the viceroyalty of La Plata in 1776. At that date, those provinces became an integral part of the new political division. Sent out by the governor of Chile, García Hurtado de Mendoza, in 1561, Pedro del Castillo founded the city of Mendoza. In 1562, Captain Juan Jufré, who had been appointed lieutenant governor of Cuyo, founded the city of San Juan de la Frontera. About the year 1596, the city of San Luis was founded.

The colonization of a country does not signify merely the importation of men, animals, and implements of labor. There is also inherent in colonization a spiritual element which includes the habits, beliefs, and customs that the colonizing people bring with them. Thus the spirit of Spanish colonization is very characteristic. With the settlers there came the spirit of the race, that is, the habits and beliefs of the Spanish people.

The spirit of Spanish colonization in La Plata was distinguished by three characteristics: (1) The warlike spirit: the Spanish race, in fact, became active during the era of colonization because of the fighting instinct that had been formed during the protracted war which the Spaniards had to carry on in the Peninsula in order to expel the Moslem. Later, among the creoles of Spanish America this bellicose spirit became a spirit of rebellion and of love for independence. (2) The spirit of municipal organization: in the Spanish cities there existed municipal councils, to which the people elected representatives who interpreted their needs and defended their rights. It was Martínez de Irala who founded among us the first municipal organization or cabildo, in the city of Asunción, by summoning the colonists and giving them the privilege of participating in the discussion of public affairs. But above all else the cabildos promoted the formation of towns and cities, for they paternally supervised the needs of the inhabitants. (3) The spirit of labor: this characteristic was the result of adaptation to the environment. As for silver, the colony of La Plata had

This may be true. Due to environment the settlers of Argentine may have developed this characteristic uniquely.

only the name; and its riches were destined to result from the cultivation of the soil and not from the exploitation of mines as in Mexico and Peru. The fruits had to be torn from the soil; and to do this labor was necessary. In the words of the distinguished Argentine historian and statesman, Bartolomé Mitre: "All these elements combined, and in a sense modified, constituted a rudimentary democracy, turbulent by nature, and industrious from necessity, with instincts of individual independence and communal liberty, and at the same time with a tendency to arbitrariness. . . . " [6]

---

[6] Mitre, *op. cit.*, I, 12.

CHAPTER V

DEMOCRATIC ORIGINS

FROM ITS very beginnings there existed in the colony of La Plata the first germs of a turbulent democracy. We have said that Spanish colonization was marked by a warlike and rebellious spirit, because of the municipal organization which was transplanted from Spain, and because of the imperious necessity of tilling the soil in order to make a living. These causes were influential in the formation of democracies based on equality; for as Mitre observed: "In reality there existed neither rich nor poor, for all were more or less poor; from this there resulted a kind of equality or social equilibrium which very early held the germs of a free society, springing from human spontaneity." [1]

In the colony of La Plata, in contrast with Mexico and Peru, it was necessary to till the soil that held the productive wealth within its breast; and from this necessity of labor there resulted a relationship of solidarity, the union of the Spanish conqueror and the vanquished aborigine. Thus among us the two races became fused, while in the other Spanish colonies in America, where the only occupation was the extraction of metals, this miscegenation did not take place. From the second half of the sixteenth century, when the races had begun to fuse in La Plata, those persons born in the colony were already characteristic types because of their rebelliousness and love of liberty.

Thus it happened, for example, in Santa Fe, where in 1577 and 1580, four years and seven years respectively after the founding of the city, two uprisings occurred which reveal the spirit and the desire of the creoles. We remember that Juan de Garay founded Santa Fe in 1573, with "nine Spaniards and seventy-five young men who were natives of this land."

Adelantado Ortiz de Zárate provided in his will that his nephew Diego Ortiz de Zárate Mendieta should temporarily carry on the government. This youth had not yet reached the age of twenty years and had led so licentious a life that the people of Asunción

---

[1] Mitre, *op. cit.*, I, 8-9.

had displayed hostility toward him. In 1577, he came to Santa Fe where he prepared to continue his dissolute career. The inhabitants rose to seize him, but, warned in time, Mendieta informed the lieutenant governor, who found asylum for him in a church. The people repaired thither, and seized Mendieta, who relinquished the baton of command to the ayuntamiento and was sent a prisoner to Spain.

In 1580, a communal movement broke out in the city of Santa Fe which denounced the schism that existed between Spaniards and creoles. The facts were as follows: the creoles of Santa Fe desired to take part in the government, and in the absence of Garay, the inhabitants assembled in the house of Lázaro de Venialvo, decided to revolt, and deposed the lieutenant governor, the alcalde, and the Spaniards who held offices. These inhabitants had previously invited all the people freely to elect their governmental officials, and had delegated all civil authority to Cristóbal Arévalo and all military authority to Venialvo. Both these men were creoles, but disputes which arose over the delimitation of authority weakened the strength of the movement, and the Spaniards took advantage of this to suppress it in bloody fashion.

In 1583, there occurred in Buenos Aires an important act which served as an expression of the common will. As already noticed, according to a cédula of 1537, in case of the death of the titular governor, the inhabitants were to elect the person who "according to God and their consciences should seem to them best fitted to take the command." In Buenos Aires, upon the death of Garay, those persons born in the country presented Juan Fernández de Enciso as their candidate, while the Spaniards put forth Alonso de Vera y Aragón. The creoles were in the majority, for we know that of the seventy-three companions with whom Garay resettled Buenos Aires in 1580, "ten were Spaniards and the others were natives of the country." The resistance which they made on this occasion was such that despite the arrival of sixty soldiers from Asunción to restore order in Buenos Aires, an agreement was reached between them and the Spaniards and by common accord they elected Rodrigo Ortiz de Zárate as governor.

In 1589, the cabildo of Buenos Aires passed an important resolution. Fray Pablo Velazco had presented a request on behalf of the order of Our Lady of Mercy, asking to be conceded the wild horses. The cabildo refused to make such a grant and stated that it "pertains to the children of the first conquerors to enjoy these wild horses as persons who inherited them from their fathers and as persons who sustain the said land at their own cost without being aided by his Majesty or any other person." [2] This important declaration asserted the superior right of the children of the conquerors to the possession of the land and the animals.

In 1588, the cabildo of Córdoba furnished another manifestation of this rebellious spirit. The governor of Córdoba, Juan Ramírez de Velazco, addressed a note to the cabildo asking it to nominate candidates for certain alcaldes and regidors who belonged to that body of officials and whose appointment was made by its active members. The cabildo met and protested against the interference of the governor, freely elected the regidors, and its members declared that in case this election should not be respected "they would at once relinquish the wands of office of alcaldes and the positions of regidors." [3] Governor Ramírez de Velazco was obliged to approve the elections.

During the sixteenth century there also occurred in the province of Tucumán the first conflicts between ecclesiastical dignitaries and the civil power. These conflicts provoked a civil war which divided the people into factions.

The struggle took place between Governor Hernando de Lerma and Dean Salcedo. The latter had been authorized by a royal cédula to designate four persons who were to hold benefices of the cathedral church, without indicating whether they referred to greater or smaller beneficiaries. The dean claimed that they were greater beneficiaries while the governor refused to recognize this right. Salcedo was exiled to Talavera, where he harbored in a monastery the fugitives who had escaped from prison, young men, old men, and children; he proposed to leave the city with them and to present a complaint to the audiencia. But Lerma was advised in time, and sent some soldiers who thwarted Salcedo's plan, and fought against him in the street. A suit was brought against the dean and he was exiled to Peru.

Yet the inhabitants of Tucumán were not appeased. Because

---

[2] *Acuerdos del extinguido cabildo de Buenos Aires* (Buenos Aires, 1886), I, 51; Levene, *op. cit.,* I, 145.

[3] *Archivo municipal de Córdoba,* as quoted in Levene, *op. cit.,* I, 186.

of fresh disorders Lerma was deposed. Complaints were laid before the audiencia in the form of accusations and extensive memorials that asked for the expulsion of the governor. In a detailed study R. J. Cárcano interprets the conflict as follows: "The struggle against Lerma was not, however, fruitless. A general movement of opinion took place, which being well directed, revealed a collective, vigorous, and indomitable force asserting its own rights. The deposition of licentiate Lerma served to teach the people of Tucumán that, if under a system of absolute rule, they could not give themselves the government which they desired, they could destroy a government which they disliked by using their own energy in a concerted and decided fashion." [4]

The cabildo was an institution whose members, namely, alcaldes and regidors, according to the laws, should be freely chosen. Every year the outgoing regidors selected from among the inhabitants of the city the persons who were to succeed them. The governors oppressed the spirit of the inhabitants by intervening arbitrarily in the elections. Just as the cabildo of Córdoba had in 1588 protested against this interference, so also a protest was made in Corrientes in 1589, which furnishes another proof of the strength of the creoles. Among the founders of the city of Córdoba, which was settled in 1588, was the creole Hernando Arias de Saavedra, who led in this expedition "many soldiers at his own expense, supplied them with everything that was necessary, and brought overland many munitions, horses, mares, and cows." In the act of protest it was stated that the lieutenant governor "at the time when the election takes place sends out of the city certain members of the chapter whom he suspects will not cast their votes for the persons desired by the said governor, and thus manages the elections just as he desires—a method which has caused the death of republics and good government." [5] The protest asked for the intervention of superior tribunals in order to assure the free election of regidors.

We have already explained that the population of the city of Asunción was divided into two factions: the loyal persons who

[4] R. J. Cárcano, "Gobernación del Tucumán; primeras luchas entre la iglesia y el estado," *La Biblioteca* (Buenos Aires, 1898), VII, 405.

[5] *Revista del archivo de la provincia de Corrientes,* as quoted in Levene, *op. cit.,* I, 186.

supported the adelantado, Cabeza de Vaca, and those who supported Martínez de Irala, who were called instigators of rebellion.
During the first forty years of its foundation, that is, from 1536
to 1576, there occurred in Paraguay such events as the following:
the imprisonment of the adelantado, Cabeza de Vaca, the popular
elections in favor of Martínez de Irala; the execution of Francisco
de Mendoza on a public scaffold because he had desired to seize
control of the province, and the death of Diego de Abreu for the
same reason; the transportation of Felipe de Cáceres to Spain in
chains; and the usurpation of authority by Martín Suárez de
Toledo. With regard to the government of Paraguay, the historian
Lozano declared: "It is clear that from the time the Spaniards
set foot here an unbridled ambition was manifested by some persons (the governors) by others (the subjects) an excessive inso-
lence, and in general such restlessness of spirit as provoked perni-
cious novelties from the very beginning." [6]

As we have seen, there took place in the colony of La Plata
during the sixteenth century democratic movements that burst
forth in a stormy fashion. The rebellious spirit was destined to
increase steadily during the seventeenth and eighteenth centuries,
each time becoming more general and important. These democratic
movements soon revealed that the destiny of the colony was independence. Democracy loves liberty and aspires to self-government,
good or bad.

These revolts and subversive movements became stronger and
stronger, and during the three centuries of the colonial era the
spirit of the creoles was being trained for the great Revolution of
1810. The Revolution of 1810 was a result of our democracy.

---

[6] P. Lozano, *Historia de las revoluciones de la provincia del Paraguay* (2 vols.
Buenos Aires, 1905), I, 1-2.

And the Revolution of 1810 in Mexico, Venezuela?

CHAPTER VI

ARIAS DE SAAVEDRA

In 1591, Juan Torres de Vera y Aragón, the last adelantado of
La Plata, was in Spain; he had left a number of relatives as lieutenant governors.[1] In 1587, the audiencia of Charcas had issued an
order prohibiting the adelantado from filling governmental posts,
such as lieutenants, alcaldes, and alguacils, with relatives even to
the fourth degree of consanguinity. Two years later the audiencia
repeated this order. Nevertheless, Alonso de Vera, who was nicknamed Cara de Perro (Dog-Face) because of his ugly face, was
still exercising the functions of lieutenant governor of Asunción
in the beginning of 1592. It was in the middle of that year that
his Majesty appointed the creole, Hernando Arias de Saavedra,
as lieutenant governor of that city.

With good reason, Hernando Arias de Saavedra has been styled
the first patriot of La Plata.[2] A legitimate son of Martín Suárez
de Toledo and Doña María de Sanabria, he was born in Asunción
in 1561.[3] In the city of Santa Fe, at the age of twenty-one, he
married Jerónima de Contreras, the daughter of Juan de Garay.
At fifteen years of age he served under the orders of the governor
of Tucumán, Gonzalo de Abreu, and soon entered the service of
Licenciate Hernando de Lerma.

When Alonso de Vera y Aragón passed through Santa Fe to
found the city of Concepción, he asked Hernando Arias de Saavedra to join him with his soldiers and friends. Arias de Saàvedra
soon placed himself under the orders of Juan Torres de Vera y
Aragón. He inspired the adelantado with so much confidence that
the latter asked for his company in founding the city of Las Siete
Corrientes. As we have seen, Arias de Saavedra brought to Co-

---

[1] With regard to the relatives of this adelantado, see A. Larrouy, "Cronología
de los gobernadores del Paraguay y Río de la Plata," *Revista de la Universidad
de Buenos Aires* (Buenos Aires, 1907), VII, 247-48.

[2] According to Eduardo Madero, this name was given to Arias de Saavedra
by Doctor V. F. López.

[3] Both paternal and maternal family names were not always borne by the
children of Spaniards in the Indies before great houses were founded and the
custom of entail introduced.

rrientes "many soldiers at his own expense, he supplied them with everything necessary, and he brought overland many munitions, horses, mares, and cattle."

The administration of Arias de Saavedra as lieutenant governor of Asunción, which lasted three years, was worthy of praise. In the words of Madero, "he exercised his functions quietly and to the satisfaction of the inhabitants; he cleared the city of vagabonds and vicious persons, compelled the idle to work, punished thieves and persons of evil life, dispensed justice with an even hand, rebuilt the cathedral church and constructed temples, seeing that divine service was offered in them decorously; and not only did he improve the other public works of his native city, but in order better to protect it he sent expeditions against the Guaycuru Indians who were hostile to it and also against the Pasancos." [4]

Fernando de Zárate, governor of Buenos Aires (1593-1595), as a reward for the services of Arias de Saavedra, made him lieutenant governor of Santa Fe. The new governor, Juan Ramírez de Velazco (1595-1597), at once named him lieutenant governor of Asunción. This compelled Arias de Saavedra to leave Santa Fe for his native city, where he continued to perform important services which, as a document of this era states, "he always did at his own cost, without being given any favor in remuneration for it" and that "his many needs and his poverty did not permit him to live according to his quality."

Up to this time, Arias de Saavedra had exercised only the functions of lieutenant governor in Corrientes, Asunción, and Santa Fe. But upon the death of the governor, Juan Ramírez de Velazco, and according to the royal cédula of 1537 which has been cited more than once, "the inhabitants assembled and elected the person who according to God and their consciences seemed to them best fitted for command." Arias de Saavedra was elected by the town as the first magistrate of Buenos Aires. Soon afterward, in December, 1597, the viceroy of Lima appointed him governor. Madero says further of him:

"It is a great satisfaction for us to be able to assert that to Arias de Saavedra pertains the glory of having at this time made the first attempts to furnish public education. 'He drew up a plan

---

[4] Madero, *op. cit.*, p. 334.

so that the sons of this country might have an opportunity to study, and provided those who should teach and instruct them. For this purpose he collected all the people of the district who lived in the mountains and other sections where there was much need of such ministrations' (Memorial of 1612). This single fact would be enough to honor his memory—adorned with other virtues—and it is an eloquent proof that God had endowed him with the instinct of a statesman, for he duly appreciated the first social need. He, who was acquainted with only a part of the woods and fields of the New World, was, nevertheless, the precursor of public education. Three centuries ago, 'anxious to preserve miserable children from vice,' he succeeded in reversing the practices that then abandoned to negligence and barbarism the descendants of Spaniards in America. Public spirit and political liberty, the fruits of education, owe him a tribute. . . . The city fortified, the Indians pacified, the lawsuits and dissensions among the inhabitants ended, and the first school founded, the governor, whom in youth Garay had imbued with his theory of 'opening the gates to the land,' decided to make a visit to the cities of Concepción, Corrientes, and Santa Fe, and to live for a time at Buenos Aires, the portal of the future greatness of the republic." [5]

In the beginning of 1599 the new governor, Diego Rodríguez de Valdés y de la Banda, arrived in Buenos Aires with troops for the defense of the port against the constant attacks of pirates who preyed upon this region. This governor died in Santa Fe in 1600, leaving as lieutenant governor Francés de Beaumont y Navarra, who served until January, 1602, when Arias de Saavedra was designated governor.

The second term of the governorship of Arias de Saavedra lasted until December 22, 1609. During this period he visited the cities, "had the coast north of La Plata River surveyed; issued ordinances, examined the accounts of the public revenues, organizing their bookkeeping and the archives of the cabildos and customhouses; founded asylums for orphan girls; increased to one hundred and fifty the number of students in the schools that he founded; subdued the Indians by persuasion and without bloodshed; stimulated the people, organizing excursions to cut timber

_____
[5] *Ibid.*, p. 341.

and groups of workmen to manufacture tile in order to rebuild economically the cathedrals of Asunción and Buenos Aires; promoted agriculture and coöperated in the construction of windmills; promoted commerce with the coast of Brazil; and—what was at this time extraordinary and ever the chief aspiration of people and rulers—preserved peace, and displayed all this foresight, activity, and energy in order that—as he himself wrote in Buenos Aires in words which happily for his glory and our affection have been kept indelible—'this country may develop which we should love as a fatherland.' " [6]

On December 22, 1609, Diego Marín de Negrón was received as governor of Buenos Aires. During his term there were framed the ordinances of Francisco de Alfaro, oidor of the audiencia of Charcas, who visited these provinces and inspected the organization and labors to which the Indians were subjected. Upon the death of Marín de Negrón, the king appointed as governor of Buenos Aires, Francés Beaumont y Navarra, who had been lieutenant governor. He remained only a short time in his new post; for on September 7, 1614, Hernando Arias de Saavedra was appointed governor for the third time.

During his third term two important steps were taken: religious colonization by the system of Jesuit missions, and the division of the land of La Plata into two jurisdictional areas. Soon after his third appointment, Arias de Saavedra retired to Santa Fe where, as a colonial historian wrote, "he lived as a great example, free from other cares, revered as the father of his country, although he paid so little heed to these attentions that after he left office he did not wish the people to address him as 'your lordship,' as is customary here, nor to accord him any other of the honorary titles he had well merited; and became angry when they addressed him by any other title than his name; and he was right, for he knew how to make it so glorious that until the present day it is mentioned only with praise in these provinces. He finally died, in 1634 in the city of Santa Fe, full of glory and merit." [7] And,

[6] *Ibid.*, p. 363.

[7] P. Lozano, *Historia de la conquista del Paraguay, Río de la Plata y Tucumán* (5 vols. Buenos Aires, 1873-75), vol. III, chap. 3. On Hernando de Arias, see further, V. F. López, *Historia de la República Argentina* (10 vols. Buenos Aires, 1913), I, 238.

Wise leadership of arias de Saavedra helped establish area

added the historian who has been quoted: "As a personage who was conspicuous in the arts of peace and war, the officials of the house of trade at Seville had his portrait hung in an honorable place among pictures of the notable men of the New World that adorned one of its halls."

Because of causes that we shall mention further on, in 1617, the king divided the land of La Plata into two jurisdictional areas: the district of La Guayra which included the present republic of Paraguay, with the city of Asunción as its capital; and the district of Buenos Aires or Río de la Plata, which was composed of the regions of Buenos Aires, Banda Oriental, Entre Ríos, Corrientes, Santa Fe, Patagonia, and the Great Chaco.

The division of the territory of La Plata into two governmental districts marked an important point in colonial history. Various reasons induced Arias de Saavedra to propose this division. One of these was the extensive territory included in La Plata, which having only one main residential center, made the work of colonization and government difficult. Another more important reason was the increasing prosperity of Buenos Aires and the decadence of Asunción. In fact, when Garay resettled Buenos Aires in 1580, he gave that city a great stimulus by placing it in direct communication with Spain, so that trade routes were directed toward the new city. In the thirty-seven years between 1580 and 1617, Buenos Aires became the center of population of La Plata, as well as its capital and its market. Said Mitre:

"Meantime Paraguay, isolated, reduced to its own resources, deprived of the vivifying currents of immigration and the interchange of products, became stagnant and ceased to be the center of a fruitful and expanding civilization. In contact with Portuguese civilization in the southern part of Brazil, the Paraguayans collided with it on the frontiers of the Upper Paraná, and had to withdraw vanquished; the province of La Guayra was raided by the Brazilian-Portuguese frontiersmen of São Paulo and three towns disappeared forever. Simultaneously with this decadence another decomposing element was operative, which, although consigned to eternal sterility, yet affected Paraguayan society. We refer to the famous Jesuit missions, which at this time (1617) already constituted a theocratic empire exclusively composed of indigenous elements, subjected to a communistic régime and to a monastic discipline. Although these reductions exercised a favorable influence in so far as they served as a dyke against the Brazilian-Portuguese invasions, yet in the main their effect was fatal to Paraguay. They restrained the movement of a colonization dominated by the European element, the only element that carried within itself the gift of reproduction. They interposed an obstacle to the miscegenation which was working for pacific conquest, and also withdrew the aborigines from contact with European immigration. Thus efficient social forces in Paraguay were paralyzed, a new antagonism was created, and the constitution of the nascent society was enervated." [8]

Lastly, another condition which made it necessary to divide the territory of La Plata into two districts was the contraband trade carried on by the Portuguese through Buenos Aires. Through the medium of Brazil, Portugal mocked the commercial restrictions imposed by Spain, and carried on a contraband trade at the same time that it kept alive its claim to the possession of the Banda Oriental del Uruguay. The new government seated at Buenos Aires could watch the activities of Portugal more closely than had hitherto been feasible.

Important also is the arrangement of 1620 by which the bishopric of Buenos Aires was created, with jurisdiction over a region which had hitherto been dependent upon the bishopric of Paraguay. We shall consider this matter when we deal with the ecclesiastical organization of La Plata; meantime, we mention its special significance, namely, the fact that the creation of the bishopric of Buenos Aires followed closely the royal cédula of 1617 by which the district of Buenos Aires was organized into a distinct governmental area.

---

[8] Mitre, *op. cit.*, I, 15-16.

CHAPTER VII

THE MANAGEMENT OF THE ABORIGINES

TURNING ASIDE, for the moment, from the narrative of colonial history, in this chapter we shall consider the relations between the Spaniards and the aborigines. We shall begin by considering the apostleship of Las Casas. The vehement spirit of Bartolomé de Las Casas so far transcends his writings and so agitates his fitful life that—as a noted author has said—it is impossible to write his biography without considering the events and the passions that animated him. His love for the Indians was not based merely upon tenderness and tolerance. He was a pugnacious apostle who hurled terrible words, like projectiles, which wounded selfish and sensitive spirits. The fact that he did not yield a single point to the threats of the powerful, intensifies the imperturbability of his character.

Passionate and upright, he was capable of telling the whole truth even in the presence of the emperor and of placing the blame where it belonged. He showed this when he disclosed in his *Historia* the hidden ulcer of the venality and sordid self-interest of many defenders of the encomiendas, whether he was criticizing the Franciscans or Archdeacon Fonseca and other councillors who had distributed Indians among themselves, or stigmatizing the encomenderos by their true name, "hungry wolves."

The heat of the struggle, the conflict of the passions involved and the hazards of a long fight during which, although he held aloft the standard of his principles, he lost ground in each encounter as the power of the interests was the stronger—all these necessarily stirred the heart of this extraordinary man and induced him to cite extreme or exaggerated figures concerning the mortality of the Indians, perhaps because he hoped that by making fantastic statements he might obtain some action which would promote justice. Historical criticism has pointed out these errors of Las Casas—the fruits of his zeal and disillusionment—and this is inevitably the stain which, instead of veiling, has thrown into sharper contrast the white light of his apostolic spirit.

Las Casas proceeded to the island of Cuba in 1512 and at once began his defense of the Indians. In 1515, he went to Castile and was promised an interview with King Ferdinand that did not materialize because of the latter's death. In Madrid, he informed Cardinal Cisneros of the excesses committed by Spaniards in the Indies. He condemned the laws of Burgos to which he attributed the miseries of the aborigines. He assembled a junta of theologians, who framed new ordinances and intrusted their application to the Jeronymite fathers; for the Dominicans were partisans of Las Casas, while the Franciscans were his opponents. Although the intervention of the Jeronymites was significant, yet it did not produce results.

In 1517, Las Casas returned to Spain where he was appointed universal protector of the Indians. The new king and his ministers listened to his protests. In order to alleviate the condition of the Indians, he proposed that peasants should be sent to America from Castile and that the importation of Negroes should be freely permitted for use on sugar plantations and in the exploitation of mines. At the proper time, this last proposal will be explained; for it implies a contradiction in the philosophic doctrines of Las Casas. He asked for a grant of one thousand leagues of land on the coast of Tierra Firme, where he might subdue the aborigines without the aid of either soldiers or sailors. This project was referred to the king's councillors; but Las Casas objected to some of them and especially to the bishop of Burgos. A new junta was formed which approved the proposed contract.

When the bishop of Darien, Fray Juan Cabedo, a man of high reputation, arrived in Spain instructed to discuss affairs of the Indies, a solemn conclave was held in the presence of the emperor. This was a memorable conference. It was also a preliminary polemic. The chancellor told the bishop to speak. The latter showed pleasure at finding himself in the presence of his sovereign but as he had secret information to impart, he asked that all persons who did not belong to the council should be required to leave the hall. He referred to Las Casas. He persisted in his refusal to speak; but finally, under compulsion, he said in essence with respect to the Indians that they were serfs "by nature."

Las Casas then took up the theme. Doffing his hat, and making a profound obeisance, he delivered a speech that lasted for three-quarters of an hour. The exposition which he made on this occasion—and which is described in detail in his *Historia*—is admirable in form and content. He proved in the light of law and of philosophy that the Indians were not serfs "by nature," that the Roman Catholic faith was adapted to all the nations of the world, and that it received all people on equal terms without depriving any individual of his liberty.

The grant made to Las Casas in 1520 conceded him only two hundred and seventy leagues of land. But the enterprise failed in his hands. Much discouraged, he took the religious vows in a monastery of the Dominican Order. In 1527, he began to write his *Historia de las Indias* which he was destined to complete a few years before his death. In Guatemala, he composed *De unico vocationis modo* in which he proved that the only method instituted for the instruction of men in religion and culture was by reasonable and pacific measures.

In Spain, after the end of 1539, he intervened in all the questions which were considered in juntas concerned with the better government of the Indies. In 1541-1542 he wrote the famous plea *Brevíssima relación de la destrucción de las Indias* (Very Short Narrative of the Destruction of the Indies), which was printed in Seville in 1552, and which was translated into various languages in the sixteenth and seventeenth centuries. His self-deceptions and the painful experiences which he had suffered caused him to assert that the rapacity of the conquistadors had caused the destruction of fifteen million Indians—an incredible number. It has now been demonstrated that the extinction of entire races—a phenomenon that has been repeated among modern peoples—can be explained by ethnological reasons, by the introduction of epidemic diseases, and by the aggravation of endemic diseases or of diseases peculiar to the race. In fine, although he had written in his *Historia* that he had seen with his own eyes what he related and "had not read it in histories which might contain lies," he had failed to see with the eyes of a serene spirit that told the truth.[1]

In 1542, the New Laws of which we have already spoken were issued. Besides the measures adopted by the emperor to insure their execution, Las Casas was appointed bishop of Cuzco in 1543 but did not accept the post. Later he was made bishop of Chiapas. He

---

[1] A facsimile reproduction of the *Brevíssima Relación* is found in B. de Las Casas, *Colección de Tratados* (Biblioteca argentina de libros raros americanos, vol. II, Buenos Aires, 1924).—W. S. R.

had to reconcile himself to this mandate against his will; for he was compelled to lend his aid to execute the laws which he had inspired. Having finally accepted the post, when he reached the New World he was able to estimate the hatred entertained for him by the men who pointed him out as the chief author of those governmental acts by virtue of which their encomiendas were to be torn from them. With the feeling that he had been defeated in the land of reality, he returned to Spain in 1547 and then entered into a dispute with Sepúlveda, putting into this new polemic—as he did into the first—the same passion and unchangeable faith.

As has been shown by historians, Las Casas was not the first person to advise the enslavement of Negroes in the Indies; for, in 1505, the peninsular government itself gave orders to Obando to admit some Negroes for the purpose of relieving the Indians. In 1517, when the Jeronymite fathers came to the Indies, they praised this policy. About the same time, Las Casas proposed in a memorial that each colonist should be permitted to bring with him two Negroes and two Negresses. In the contract which he made with the government for the colonization of Cumaná, Las Casas and his associates were each authorized to bring with them three Negro slaves, and even as many as seven apiece. It is, therefore, indisputable that the apostle of the liberty of the Indians, inspired by a love for those humble beings who composed the great majority, had favored the enslavement of the Negroes who were in a minority. His policy of spreading Negro slavery culminated in the royal cédula of 1526 in which it was ordered that the children of Negroes were not to be free, even though their fathers had contracted legitimate marriages.

What should be emphasized in this place is the fact that in view of the enormous development of the slave trade in the Indies, Las Casas, who had criticized the Aristotelian doctrine and had set against it the doctrine of natural law, changed his views concerning the traffic in Negroes and inscribed in his *Historia de las Indias that* "the enslavement of Negroes was as unjust as Indian slavery."

In a consideration of the legal and economic system to which the Indians were subjected, it is necessary to notice the following organizations that were adopted: reductions, personal services, encomiendas, and missions.

The Indians had to be induced to live in villages called reductions. If they composed a group of eighty houses, two alcaldes and regidors were to be appointed who should have charge of the government of the reduction. The Indian alcaldes could punish by scourging or imprisonment those persons who became drunk or who failed to attend mass. A poll tax was levied upon them, the proceeds being destined for the benefit of the particular community. Indians between the ages of eighteen and fifty years were to pay the tax designated as "tribute." This tax was to be paid in kind: such as wheat, maize, chickens, or fish. The error of the reduction system probably lay in prohibiting every kind of communication with the Spaniards.

In June, 1500, the Catholic monarchs had declared the Indians to be free, a juridical and humane principle that did honor to the motherland. The Indian was forced to work in order to prevent idleness and vice; while his labor was to be remunerated by suitable wages. He could be assigned to the building of houses in cities or towns which were being settled, as well as to labor on ports and bridges; or to the cultivation of fields where wheat, maize, and barley were sown, but not to the culture of grapes and olives; for such culture was prohibited in America, because these products were similar to those of Spain.

A jurist of the seventeenth century thus defined the encomienda: "It is a right conceded by royal grant to those persons in the Indies who have merited such favor, in order that they may collect for themselves the tributes of the Indians who are intrusted to them for the term of their lives and the life of one heir, according to the law of succession, with the charge of caring for the spiritual and temporal welfare of the Indians, and of inhabiting and defending the provinces that are conquered." In the course of the conquest of America, the Spaniards needed the aid of the Indians for labor in the mines and in the cultivation of the fields. Thus the "repartimientos of Indians" came into existence. The encomenderos tried to promote their own interests exclusively; hence the brutal treatment to which they subjected the Indians.

The grants of encomiendas were originally made only for a term of two lives and could not be acquired by purchase or exchange. The encomiendas were composed of Yanacona Indians who in general were engaged in agricultural labors, and of Mitayo[2] Indians who were engaged in mining. In the very virtue of the system was rooted its chief vice. By this concession the encomendero was limited to the collection of tribute from Indians belonging to his own encomienda. "If we assume" (said a writer named Hernández), "that an encomendero had one hundred Indians (with a tax of four pesos in silver) his annual income would amount to four hundred pesos. From this was to be deducted the *sinodo* or the fifth part, in order to provide a curate for the Indians and whatever was necessary to furnish arms and horses for war."

In place of tribute the encomenderos preferred personal service, that is, making the Indians labor for their profit, either in domestic or agricultural employment. In order to restrain the greed of the encomenderos, Licenciate Francisco de Alfaro was sent to La Plata. In 1611, ordinances were issued bearing the name of the visitor Alfaro, and including eighty-four provisions which, in fine, extinguished personal service and replaced it by the tribute. This tribute was set at five pesos of current money, but as the Indian was allowed to choose between personal service amounting to thirty days and the payment of a tax, the abuses continued. In 1679, an order was issued to transform the encomiendas of Yanaconas into Mitayas, and to reduce these to Indian villages. The voices of protest raised against this measure compelled the government to refrain from carrying it into execution.[3]

In the opening of the nineteenth century the policy was begun of assigning to the crown the titles to the encomiendas that fell vacant. The Revolution of May, 1810, was especially concerned with the condition of the Indians, for it viewed them as free men.

The special type of encomienda styled the *mita* is derived from a Quechua word that signifies "turn"; for in practice the Indians of a reduction were renewed in turns in order to perform the service. The most famous mitas existed in Potosí. They included one hundred and thirty-nine Indian villages whose inhabitants were

---

[2] For an explanation of the terms "yanacona" and "mita" (from which "mitayo" is derived—meaning those affected by the mita); see W. S. Robertson, *History of the Latin-American Nations* (New York, 1932), p. 93.—W. S. R.

[3] A. de León Pinelo, *Tratado de confirmaciones reales de encomiendas, oficios y casos, en que se requiren, para las Indias Occidentales* (Buenos Aires, 1922). —W. S. R.

employed in the mines. The Indians were to work one week and to rest two weeks, in such a manner that during a year the Indian labored four months in all. In the mita all the abuses culminated. In Upper Peru a magistrate of great talent and probity, Victorián de Villalva, fiscal of the audiencia of Charcas at the end of the eighteenth century, who filled the office of protector of the Indians, wrote a learned work entitled *Discurso sobre la Mita* in which he lovingly defended the apostle of Indian liberty. Villalva developed the following points in his study: (1) That the labor in the mine of Potosí was not of a public nature; (2) That although it were of a public nature, it conferred no right to compel the Indians to work; (3) That the Indian was not as indolent as ordinarily supposed; (4) That even though the Indian were lazy to the highest degree, he must not be compelled to perform this labor by force. The intendant of Potosí, Paula Sanz, responded to Villalva's brief to the effect that he considered the natural condition of the Indians to be one of slavery.

The Society of Jesus, which was founded by Ignatius Loyola came to have as one of its chief purposes the conversion of pagans. By the discovery of the New World, this society had disclosed to it a vast field for the spread of the Roman Catholic faith. Having obtained the authorization of the Spanish sovereigns, the Jesuits spread throughout the Spanish dominions. By 1549, they had reached Brazil; a few years later (1553) a priest of this order, named José Anchieta, founded São Paulo. At the end of the sixteenth century the bishop of Tucumán introduced into his diocese the first Jesuit missionaries in Spanish America.

The principal academy of the Jesuits was founded in the city of Córdoba. Another academy was established at Asunción, where Fathers José Cataldino and Antonio Ruíz de Montoya performed a distinguished service. The latter is the author of important works concerning aboriginal linguistics and ethnology.

In accordance with a royal cédula of Philip III, Hernando Arias de Saavedra directed the Jesuit missionaries to carry out in Paraguay the new ordinances issued as a result of the visit of the oidor Francisco de Alfaro. The Jesuits first organized four villages or reductions which soon increased to ten and later to seventeen. The missionaries succeeded in gathering 110,000 Indians into reductions, but they had to struggle constantly against the invasions of the mamelucos of Brazil who sought gold and slaves.[4] Besides, there were disguised emissaries, like the famous João Preto, sent out by the Portuguese of Brazil in order to provoke discord among the missions. There were also tribes of Indians who were constantly attacking the reductions.

The highest political authority in the missions was the corregidor, then followed the lieutenant corregidor, alcaldes, and so on. In reality the true authority was that of the priests. The superiors of the society explained this intermeddling by declaring that the Indians gladly yielded to the authority of the fathers.

Conditions compelled the missionaries to adopt a military organization. As the colonial officials could not aid the missions with military force, the Jesuits were authorized to obtain firearms and to teach the Indians how to use them. In order to judge of the importance of this military organization, it should be remembered that after the signing of the Treaty of 1750 (by which Spain transferred to Portugal the provinces of Santa Catalina and Río Grande and seven Jesuit reductions in exchange for the colony of Sacramento), the Indians of these missions revolted and waged the Guaraní War that lasted for three years, simply in order to resist the execution of the treaty.

In respect to economic organizations, it should be said that the Indians enjoyed the private ownership of movable property (such as utensils and clothing), but that real property was held in common. The *Tupambaé* (from "Tupa," meaning God and "embaé," meaning property) was the common field with its crops and livestock. All the inhabitants of a reduction took part in tilling it at least two days per week. The missionaries claimed that the proceeds of this labor in rich and abundant fruits of the soil were devoted to the relief of the sick, the widow, and the orphan, and to the construction of temples.

An attempt has been made to justify the communism of Tupambaé by certain antecedents, such as the custom in Aragon where the forests were held in common for the gathering of firewood and acorns, where the grassland was also held in common so that each inhabitant might, if he wished, drive his livestock there

[4] "Mamelucos" were the hybrids that resulted from the miscegenation of whites and Indians in Brazil. See R. Southey, *History of Brazil* (3 vols., London, 1817-22), II, 622; III, 787.—W. S. R.

to pasture. The analogy is not exact: in the case of the forests and pastures of Aragon, one is concerned with the use of a "gift of nature" that has not been cultivated; while in the case of the missions, the productive labor of the Indian was destined for certain purposes of debatable importance.[5]

It would be necessary to shut one's eyes to the evidence if one failed to recognize the actual mildness by which the Jesuits accomplished the spiritual conquest of the Indians. From this viewpoint, that of sentimental well-being, the missions were more fortunate than the lay and civil settlements where, as we have seen, the encomiendas were the practical means of the exploitation and severe treatment of the aborigines. Let us notice again that lay colonization of the Indians failed, not because it lacked virtue in principle, but because the encomenderos undertook to deaden and corrupt the system.

Of course

Nevertheless, an institution of government is not to be judged by sentiment, but according to its works, by the results produced in view of the economic and social condition of the people and of the age. If the Paraguayan reductions placed in high relief the virtue and beneficence of the priests, they demonstrated the incapacity of the Jesuits to undertake the great work of government and administration which was required by the colonization of a continent.

There are two fundamental objections that can be brought against the Jesuit mission system: one of an economic character, and the other of a moral character which relates to their administration. (1) The Jesuits established in the missions the economic régime of communism by prohibiting the transfer of property either by contract or by inheritance and by ordaining that the fruits and products of labor should be the property of the community. In defense of this system, it has been said that "the best proof that it suited the Indians is the fact that the successors of the Jesuits were forced to continue the system almost up to the present time, and that its destruction, which was not wrought by skilful and paternal measures, has had no other result than to plunge the aborigines into misery. At the present hour their

---

[5] A discussion of the economics of the Jesuit missions is found in Lugones, *op. cit.*, pp. 164-66.

remnants bitterly lament the absence of that régime, which was doubtless imperfect but the best adapted to their instincts and customs.[6] This argument is more apparent than true. The affirmation is correct that the system of communism was most suitable and adaptable to the instincts and customs of the Indians. Primitive peoples, nomadic and restless, do not, in fact, recognize individual ownership. They live by hunting and fishing, and the land belongs to all and not to any particular individual. When a more civilized people arrive, who are sedentary in their habits, they cultivate the soil, they settle on it, and become its owners.

To say that communism with respect to the land was the system most suitable to the instincts and customs of the aborigines is to assert that the Jesuits, who undertook such a type of colonization, proposed to maintain the Indians in their original condition as a nomadic race, without any firm attachment to the soil. The communistic régime destroys a great incentive and a great motive of progress, that is, individual ownership as a result of one's own efforts and labor.[7]

and slavery?

(2) The Jesuits treated the Indians, as has indeed been said, "like big children," and kept them in isolation, avoiding all contact with the world. The great benefit of the encomienda system, according to Martínez de Irala, lay in the fact that the Indian was to be educated and prepared for free and civilized life. Instead, the Jesuit missions kept the Indians under a government, gentle, it is true, but immutable. This was a serious error, for the fatal destiny of subjugated races is to live indefinitely under the rule of others.

But he wasnt.

Spiritual colonization demonstrated only the Christian virtue and resignation on the part of many priests; but secular colonization not only revealed in profile such great colonizing figures as Martínez de Irala and Garay but also stimulated the progress of the colony through the founding of important cities.

---

[6] Martin de Moussy, *op. cit.*, III, 717-18.

[7] V. G. Quesada, *La vida intelectual en la América Española durante los siglos XVI, XVII y XVIII* (Buenos Aires, 1910), pp. 164-65, comments upon the remarkable results secured by the Jesuits in teaching the Indians certain arts and crafts.

CHAPTER VIII

THE GOVERNORS OF BUENOS AIRES, 1617-1658

ALONSO PÉREZ DE SALAZAR was governor of the province of Buenos Aires, when, on February 7, 1622, an interior custom-house was established at Córdoba. As will be explained in an opportune place, this custom-house was established in response to the efforts of the merchants of Lima. The custom-house formed a legal wall of non-communication between the coast and the interior; for only after the payment of fifty per cent of the regular duties were goods introduced by way of Buenos Aires allowed to pass into the provinces of the hinterland.

During the rule of Salazar's successor, Francisco de Céspedes, the Dutch, who had recently been freed from Spanish rule planted themselves at Bahia. During the administration of Céspedes, the Franciscan fathers founded a reduction in the territory of the Banda Oriental, which roughly corresponds to present Uruguay. This was the town of Santo Domingo Soriano which was established on the banks of the Río Negro. In 1646, Jacinto de Lariz became governor of Buenos Aires. His rule was marked in colonial history by innumerable incidents and internal dissensions which he precipitated with the cabildo and the bishop. Lariz may be characterized as the audacious and unscrupulous type of governor.[1]

Ascarate du Biscay came to Buenos Aires in a Dutch ship with a commercial license in 1658. He left a description of Buenos Aires which contains interesting data. At that time, the city was composed of four hundred houses built of clay, with roofs of reeds and straw. Life was simple and cheap. The inhabitants of the city were the owners of extensive farms, and livestock was considered common property.[2] Ascarate du Biscay did not confine himself solely to a consideration of the material welfare of the growing settlement; for he also exalted the virtue of its inhabitants,

---

[1] E. Peña, *Don Jacinto de Lariz; turbulencias de su gobierno en el Río de la Plata* (Madrid, 1911).

[2] "Un libro curioso y raro 'Relación de los viajes de Monsieur Ascarate du Biscay al Río de la Plata, y desde aqui por tierra hasta el Perú, con observaciones sobre estos paises'" (translated by D. Maxwell), *La Revista de Buenos Aires* (Buenos Aires, 1867), XIII, 3 ff.

and in particular of the women whom he praised because of their beauty and chastity. According to the census taken some years later (1664), the city of Buenos Aires contained 211 families making 854 inhabitants, exclusive of priests, soldiers, and slaves.[3]

Governor José Martínez Salazar came to Buenos Aires to found the tribunal of the audiencia which was established in 1661. The principal reasons that induced King Philip IV to introduce this institution were of an economic nature. He calculated that by this measure contraband trade would be checked, as well as graft in the royal exchequer. The new tribunal was composed of a president, three oidors, and a fiscal.[4] This first foundation was made during the period of the greatest economic decay of Buenos Aires. As the audiencia opposed the admission of any vessels into that port, one can say that this tribunal was established in order to strengthen and defend the monopolistic policy of Peru. It was suppressed in the year 1671.

In a separate chapter, we shall discuss the origin and complications of the civil dispute that arose between Spain and Portugal. Here, we should notice that in 1705 Colonel Baltazar García Ros, at the head of an army composed of Spaniards, creoles, and Indians, besieged and captured the colony of Sacramento which was held by the Portuguese. This colony had passed into the power of the Portuguese in 1713; but the king signally rewarded the city of Buenos Aires for its important part in the war against the Portuguese by conferring upon it the title "very noble and very loyal."

After the opening of the eighteenth century, scientific journeys and new explorations in South America became important. Worthy of mention is the exploration made by Father Quiroga in 1745 along the coasts of Patagonia; and that of Fathers Cardiel and Falkner who during the following year founded a reduction near Cape Corrientes.

[3] With respect to the rights of the colonists at Buenos Aires, see P. Groussac, "Introducción al 'Viaje de un buque holandés al Río de la Plata.' " *Anales de la Biblioteca* (Buenos Aires, 1905), IV, 359. See further, J. de Solórzano Pereira, *Política indiana* (Antwerp, 1703); and the *Recopilación de leyes de los reinos de las Indias* (4 vols. in 2, Madrid, 1841), libro IV, titulo X, ley VI.

[4] E. Ruíz Guiñazú, *La magistratura indiana* ("Estudios editados por la facultad de derecho y ciencias sociales de la Universidad de Buenos Aires," vol. VII, Buenos Aires, 1916), pp. 161-69.

Juan and Ulloa traveled in mid-eighteenth century

It was also at this time that two distinguished Spanish scientists, namely, Jorge Juan and Antonio de Ulloa, made a voyage of circumnavigation that had great scientific significance. The studies of these two scientists were also of political and social value, for in a secret report which they made to King Ferdinand VI, they detailed the vices and errors of government in the colonies, of the Indian villages, and of the management of the royal treasury. This report was long kept secret. It was published in 1826 under the title of *Noticias Secretas de América.*[5]

In 1764, the French made a settlement in the Falkland Islands in order to promote the whale-fishing industry. When a claim to their ownership was made by Spain, the French colony was given up in return for a compensation. The Spaniards then founded the port of Soledad in the Falklands. In 1766, the English founded a colony under the name of Port Egmont, but they were dislodged by an expedition sent out by Bucarelli, the governor of Buenos Aires. The English government denounced this act of violence, and was upon the point of opening hostilities against Spain. The court of Madrid then made amends: it returned Port Egmont to the English, but under the express condition that this act should not affect the question of anterior right concerning the sovereignty of the Falkland Islands. In consequence, the English took possession of Port Egmont for the second time in 1771; but in 1774 they voluntarily evacuated it because they had been accorded the satisfaction that they demanded. In the light of these antecedents the policy of England, which took possession of the Falkland Islands again in 1833, appears incomprehensible.

[5] See Arthur P. Whitaker, "Antonio de Ulloa," *Hispanic American Historical Review,* XV (May, 1935), 155-94; and Lewis Hanke, "Dos Palabras on Antonio de Ulloa and the *Noticias Secretas,*" *Hispanic American Historical Review,* XVI (November, 1936), 479-514.—W. S. R.

Anti-English sentiments here on issue of Falklands.

CHAPTER IX

THE GOVERNMENTS OF TUCUMÁN AND PARAGUAY

AT THE OPENING of the seventeenth century Alonso de Ribera was governor of Tucumán. He founded the cities of San Juan de la Ribera and Talavera de Madrid (the latter formed by the union of the town of Estero with the town of Madrid de las Juntas which was founded by Juan Ramírez de Velazco). In 1612, the bishop of Tucumán, Fray Fernando Trejo, by founding the chief college of the Jesuits, laid the foundations of the famous University of Córdoba which was inaugurated in 1613.

Because of an insult offered to the person of a cacique, a bloody uprising of the Calchaquians occurred in Tucumán during the governorship of Felipe de Albornoz. Some Calchaquian chiefs undertook to extend him a welcome. In order to punish certain misconduct, the governor had the caciques unjustly scourged and ordered that their hair should be cut. The Indians swore to avenge the offense. In token of a conspiracy they secretly passed an arrow from tribe to tribe. An uprising soon took place, in which the rebellious Indians laid siege to the chief cities of the province, destroyed the wheat fields, sacked the church, burned crops and houses, and cut the throats of all Spaniards that fell into their hands, including women, children, and priests. This war lasted ten years, and only after great efforts were the Spaniards able to drown this uprising in blood.[1]

In 1655, Alonzo Mercado y Villacorta was governor of Tucumán. He had an arrogant disposition, and was little fitted to maintain pleasant relations with the Calchaquians. At this time, there fled from Peru and Chile to Tucumán one Pedro Chamijo, known by the name of Pedro Bohorquez, who was said to be a descendant of the Incas of Peru. He called himself Hualpa Inca, and the Indians began to believe that he was a descendant of their race who came to recover the throne which the Spaniards had usurped.

---

[1] See the letter of Albornoz, March 1, 1633, published by E. Boman, "Tres cartas de gobernadores del Tucumán sobre todos los Santos de la Nueva Rioja y sobre el gran alzamiento," *Revista de la Universidad de Córdoba* (Córdoba, 1918), año V, núm. 1, pp. 164-91.

The chiefs did homage to him and thus made him supreme lord of the Calchaquians. Bohorquez then informed Governor Mercado y Villacorta that he possessed the secret of valuable treasures which had been hidden by the Indians. The covetousness of the governor induced him to receive Bohorquez with great pomp and even to name him lieutenant governor and captain general of the valley of Calchaquí. However, discord soon arose between them, for Bohorquez then had more power than the governor himself. The latter now conferred again with the false Inca but could accomplish nothing, for Bohorquez exhorted the Indians to wage war. The governor made a strong resistance with the troops of Tucumán, Jujuy, and Salta, and the Calchaquians were vanquished. But with the purpose of pacifying them the Peruvian viceroy pardoned Bohorquez. However, the latter was so persistent an imposter that on his departure from Tucumán he undertook to incite the Calchaquians anew, for which he was sentenced to death and executed in the early part of 1667. The valley of Calchaquí was constantly agitated by numerous uprisings of the aborigines. Governor Mercado y Villacorta was only able to suppress them completely by distributing the Indians among different cities.

In 1681, Fernando de Mendoza Mate de Luna was governor of Tucumán. Two years later he founded the city of Catamarca. Some of his predecessors had attempted without success to explore the territory of the Chaco in order to reduce the Indians, and thus to relieve the Spanish settlements from the constant threats to which they were subject. The governor of Tucumán penetrated the Chaco with Jesuit missionaries in order to reduce its inhabitants. Governors Gaspar de Baraona and Félix de Arache also made important military expeditions into the Chaco. Later, in 1774, Governor Jerónimo Matorras penetrated the Chaco from the right bank of the Bermejo River as far as Cangayé; but the most important explorations were made during the rule of Viceroy Vértiz y Salcedo.

Paraguay continued to be the turbulent municipal republic of origins. Singular democratic movements took place in La Plata as reactions against the prevailing misrule. One of these notable events was the revolt of the "*comuneros* of Paraguay," which has significance as being a movement that had the definite object of emancipation.

In 1721, Diego Reyes governed Paraguay. José de Avalos, the oldest and most influential regidor in the cabildo of Asunción, opposed the governor. The audiencia of La Plata ordered that Reyes should be impeached and sent José Antequera, a Spanish-American by birth, to judge him. He seized the governor of Paraguay and the people named him to act as substitute. Reyes escaped from prison, proceeded to Buenos Aires, and found there a new order of the viceroy directing him to continue to act as governor of Paraguay. Antequera then decided to relinquish the government in obedience to the viceroy's orders. For that purpose he assembled the members of the cabildo in the hall of the ayuntamiento, "into which each member entered showing by gestures the novelty of that junta. . . . Antequera stood forth with serene countenance, for the fear of sustaining a loss did not destroy his poise. He had the clerk read a copy of the viceroy's order; then he offered to lay down the baton of command and to transfer it to Reyes, unless they considered this measure inadvisable. He besought each one of them freely to express his opinion, without being restrained by private reasons, but considering solely the public weal, as fathers of the country."[2] The cabildo asked him to remain in office until the viceroy should appoint another governor than Reyes. Antequera then commanded that Reyes should be seized, and demanded that the governor of Buenos Aires should refuse to set the prisoner at liberty. Thereupon, the viceroy of Peru dispatched a new governor and captain general. Antequera summoned a new open council meeting and exhorted the people to deliberate with respect to the advantage of his Majesty and the public welfare. The chief alcalde asked Antequera to withdraw from the junta, "leaving the members alone in order that each one might vote with greater freedom, and without misgiving in regard to him." When Antequera retired "they discussed the matter at length, with more license than liberty for the former is more pleasing in assemblies in which disobedience to the prince is decided upon," says the historian Lozano, and they decided that it would not be wise to allow the new governor to come. They wrote to the latter to declare that the mere news of his approach had agitated the entire province and besought him to not enter Asunción. After other mishaps and conflicts, Ante-

---

[2] Lozano, *Historia de las revoluciones de la provincia del Paraguay*, I, 48.

quera was cast into prison and condemned to be beheaded. On the day set for his execution the crier announced: "This is the justice commanded by the king our lord, and in his royal name by his Excellency the viceroy of this kingdom, with the approval of this audiencia in regard to the person of José Antequera, because of his having on various occasions invited all the men of the province of Paraguay to take up arms in sedition and rebellion."

The rebellions initiated by Antequera were continued in the insurrection of the comuneros, an important uprising that throws much light upon the movement for the independence of Spanish America. The person who started this new rebellion was Fernando Mompó who came to Asunción near the end of 1730, after having been imprisoned in Lima, "where he had formed an intimate friendship with José Antequera, learning his maxims and acquiring his spirit." As he was recommended to the principal men of Asunción, the adherents of Antequera welcomed him, and in the house of the chief alcalde he "spent much time in secret conferences. From that house, as though he were a professor, he gave lessons to those who wished to profit thereby. To this rebellion the name of '*común*' has been given, and to its adherents the name '*comuneros*.' It hatched the egg that Antequera had laid . . . and put into practice what was originally only a theory. Mompó spoke of the power of the community of whatsoever republic, city, town, or village. He taught that it was more powerful than the king himself, and that it was in the hands of the community to accept a law or a governor as it saw fit, for although the prince might give these, yet if the community did not desire them, it might justly object and renounce obedience."[3] From the powerful influence of this preaching upon the spirit of the colonists of La Plata arose an idea described in the words of the historian Lozano who in his character of Spanish subject and priest criticizes these events: "It was a pleasing thing to see and to hear a peasant, who came casually to the city and happened to hear Mompó, when he left full of amazement upon meeting another peasant in the country say to him, arching his eyebrows, and displaying in his countenance all the amazement that possessed

[3] *Ibid.*, II, 4. Interesting data are furnished in a letter by Herrán to the viceroy of Peru printed in M. Lobo, *Historia general de las antiguas colonias hispano-americanas desde su descubrimiento hasta el año mil ochocientos ocho* (31 vols. Madrid, 1875), II, 257-64.

[Margin note: Revolutionary ideas of Fernando Mompó. Rights of community opposed to power of king]

his soul: 'Ah, brother, what great things I have heard from a learned man in the city concerning what the community can do; he says that we can do more than the king and at times even more than the Pope. Behold, brother, what we had, without being aware of it. In truth how well they concealed this blessing from us, and would not teach it to us, so that we might not know how easily the community may cease to obey the viceroy.' The listener would make the sign of the cross; and, indeed, this was necessary lest the devil enter into one's soul with this doctrine." Thus the new ideas gained ground and revolutionary principles were disseminated.

Upon the approach of another governor named by the Peruvian viceroy, the community rose in rebellion. Mompó stimulated this movement by instilling a spirit of resistance to the entrance of the new governor to whom a letter was sent declaring that he had better not come to receive the baton of command. Further, a memorial was sent to the viceroy in which the rebels declared that it was disadvantageous to nominate a person who was a friend of the Jesuits and of kings, and proceeded to say that his Excellency was exceeding the bounds of his authority. The historian Lozano exclaims: "Lord Almighty! Is it possible that ignoramuses secluded in a corner of the world have had the audacity to attempt to advise a viceroy of Peru, surrounded by the most capable ministers of all this empire, and that they have dared to speak to him with such scandalous and licentious irreverence? But what will a person not do who has lost respect for God and the world?" The new governor soon arrived; whereupon the comuneros seized him and compelled him to return to Lima.

Because of another political incident the majority of those persons who belonged to the king's party deserted his cause and declared for the comuneros. Partisans of the latter undertook to march to the city with the intention of besieging it, and, despite the opposition of the cabildo, they halted within one league of it. The members of the cabildo, under pretext of celebrating the memory of St. Augustine, decided to proceed to the cathedral church bearing the royal standard in order to pray fervently to the divine Majesty to intercede to secure the peace of the republic. The comuneros prevented the departure of the cabildo and intimated that none of its members should dare to leave their hall. They tore down the staircase which ascended to the hall of the cabildo in order to detain its members. Then the militia of the comuneros entered the city, with the cry, "Death to the bad government!" The chief magistrate, disdaining the risk of life which he ran, went out to speak from the balcony so as to bring them to order. From the crowd a voice rang out: "Honorable sir! What does 'vox populi, vox Dei' mean? Answer what you like, but understand that it means the voice of the commune."

Thirty years later, in 1762, a movement took place in Corrientes known as "the comuneros of Corrientes." This occasioned a suit because of the disturbance that took place in the city of Corrientes when Lieutenant General Pedro Cevallos was governor of the province of La Plata. The people of Corrientes lived in a constant struggle with the Indians who were always besieging them. Thus, abandoning their homes and their interests, they were obliged to make frequent expeditions of exploration and conquest and to furnish military service.

In accordance with an order of Governor Cevallos a great expedition was organized composed of the militia of Paraguay, Corrientes, and Tucumán, under the direction of commander Bernardo López, in company with a chaplain of the Society of Jesus. The object of this expedition was to open a road of communication between the cities of Corrientes and Tucumán. By order of the leaders of the expedition, the route was altered and directed toward the confluence of the Bermejo and Paraguay rivers. The expedition was thus compelled to march during the winter by hazardous routes and amid rains.

When Governor Cevallos undertook to besiege the colony of Sacramento, he ordered that two hundred militiamen of Corrientes who had just been placed under the command of Bernardo López should cross the frontier at the Río Pardo, and place themselves at the disposal of the Jesuits. So great were the privations suffered by the militiamen that they deserted.

On various occasions the cabildo of Corrientes had presented complaints on behalf of the inhabitants, and at another time it sided with a new resistance which the people of Corrientes made when Governor Cevallos ordered that an additional 200 men be sent to take the places of deserters, who had left the command of Barrenechea. The chief men of the city were convoked in cabildo abierto,[4] which resolved that it "was convenient and necessary for the common welfare" to suspend Barrenechea and to inform his Excellency, Governor Cevallos, that they had revolted and to send with this message a memorial from the cabildo and, so to speak, from the republic. Cevallos received the memorial of Corrientes and, according to the historian, Dean Funes, gave the city "in reply a silence that was more severe than the most bitter reproof." Later, Cevallos ordered that some persons should be imprisoned, and that others should be sentenced to death in the name of justice and public security. And, in order to impose his absolute authority, he appointed as his lieutenant governor Manuel de Rivera y Miranda, who was a partisan of the Jesuits. On the night of October 29, 1764, the people of Corrientes revolted, attacked the house of the lieutenant governor, cast him into prison, and replaced his authority with that of the cabildo. The legal advisor, Dr. Rocha y Rodríguez, who prepared the charges against the disturbers of the peace at Corrientes, said: "It is not easy to explain the community idea or concept of these people upon seeing that by their own confessions many of them wished to show that not only is an uprising of this sort not an offense, but that the commune of these revolted people merits the name of government." Some of the imprisoned conspirators undertook to give apparent reasons for having considered that tumult lawful; and the same historian further added: "If on beholding this fate doled out to him who was ruling that city in the name of his Majesty, if on seeing the offenders themselves seize their judge, take control of his suits and processes, cause masses to be read in thanksgiving for the unhappy victory that they had gained, and verses to be sung in praise of those who had distinguished themselves in this barbarous action, one should refrain from making that miserable city an example of punishment, what might this give rise to in the future? What scandal might not

---

[4] A cabildo abierto, an open meeting of a cabildo or town council, was the Spanish-American assemblage which most closely resembled a town meeting. Ordinarily it might be convoked only with the consent of the chief executive residing in the respective city. In troublous times open meetings of town councils often served as the organs through which colonists might express their views. An excellent record of the functioning of a revolutionary cabildo abierto is found in *Días del Mayo; actas del cabildo de Buenos Aires, 1810* (La Plata, 1910).—W. S. R.

occur in neighboring cities which were known to be inclined to similar disturbances? What judge would have enough courage constantly to act with integrity in order to correct and castigate the disobedience of unruly, wayward, and insolent persons?"

As may be deduced from the foregoing narrative, the revolutionary spirit in La Plata was increasing. In the preceding chapter mention was made of the democratic movements during the sixteenth century; we have just seen that in the seventeenth century two significant revolts (not to mention other movements) took place in Paraguay and in Corrientes which were the forerunners of the emancipation of Spanish America.

CHAPTER X

PROBLEMS CONCERNING THE SPANISH-PORTUGUESE BOUNDARY

DURING TWO centuries of the colonial era Spain had an irritating controversy with Portugal concerning their respective boundaries in America. In the period when navigators were seeking a maritime route that would connect them with eastern Asia, Pope Alexander VI conceded to Portugal the land which its navigators might discover. But as Spain had also undertaken maritime enterprises in search of this route, King Ferdinand asked the Pope to concede him an equal right of ownership over lands that he might discover in Asia. In order to eliminate conflicts between the two powers, the Pope proposed to them that the lands which lay east of a line drawn one hundred leagues west of the Azore and Cape Verde Islands and parallel to the axis of the land should belong to the Portuguese, while the lands which lay west of the same line should belong to the Spaniards. Portugal accepted the proposal, but on condition that this imaginary line should pass not one hundred leagues west of the Azores but three hundred and seventy leagues west of those islands. Spain also accepted this modification and the Treaty of Tordesillas was signed by the two parties on June 7, 1494. We should notice that this line of demarcation was concerned with lands of the Old World; for in the year when the treaty was signed it was not yet known that the lands discovered by Columbus belonged to a new continent.

A Portuguese navigator named Pedro Alvares Cabral led an expedition in the year 1500 along the route taken by Vasco da Gama, who had reached Asia by skirting the western coast of Africa and doubling the Cape of Good Hope. Instead of following the route of Vasco da Gama to Asia, however, Alvares Cabral turned west and reached the coast of Brazil at a place which he named Porto Seguro.

Portugal, thereupon, declared itself mistress of Brazil for two reasons: (1) because that region was east of the line traced by Pope Alexander VI, according to the Treaty of Tordesillas; and

(2) because it was a Portuguese mariner, Pedro Alvares Cabral, who had first discovered Brazil.

Spain did not make a fundamental issue of this dispute, although the rich and extensive lands of Brazil belonged to that country by virtue of two reasons: (1) the Treaty of Tordesillas had been framed in the belief that the dividing line would cross the lands of Asia and not those of America, the existence of which was then unknown; and (2) Spain had the prior right in the discovery because three months before the voyage of Cabral, the Spanish navigator Yáñez Pinzón had touched the Brazilian coast. Nevertheless, the Spaniards continued to occupy parts of the coast of Brazil; thus the expedition of Cabot sojourned a year in the lagoon of Los Patos, and the expedition of Adelantado Cabeza de Vaca landed at Santa Catalina and on its way to Asunción, traversed territory claimed by Portugal. We should also keep in mind the landing and sojourn of the expedition of Sanabria on the Brazilian coast.

The Portuguese colonized Brazil by dividing it into ten captaincies. The most southerly of these was that of São Vicente in the Bay of Santos. But later they tried in every way to extend their authority to the eastern bank of the Río de la Plata. Portuguese diplomats let slip no opportunity to display this intention, and, as we have seen, they were determined that the Río de la Plata should not bear the name of its discoverer, Solís, which indicated its dependence upon Spain, but the name Río Dulce.

During the reign of Prince Pedro of Portugal, in accordance with a royal order, the governor of Rio de Janeiro, Manuel Lobo, undertook to found a colony on the north bank of the Río de la Plata. On January 1, 1680, Lobo carried out this order at the island of San Gabriel. José Garro, the governor of Buenos Aires, hastened to transmit news of this step to the viceroy of Peru and to the king of Spain and to suggest that governmental measures should be limited to a claim by diplomatic negotiations. Meantime, the Portuguese extended their settlement on the island of San Gabriel. Without orders from his superior, Governor Garro attacked the colony with a force of Spaniards, creoles, and Indians, and defeated the Portuguese. Worthy of notice is the decisive rôle played in this first military success by the soldiers of Buenos Aires, Santa Fe, and Corrientes under the command of a native of Santa Fe, Colonel Antonio Vera Mujica.

The king of Spain had meantime initiated the proper diplomatic proceedings; but upon receiving news of the capture of Sacramento by force of arms, in view of threats from Portugal, he disapproved of the conduct of Garro, and the two nations agreed to appoint boundary commissions in order to carry out the terms of the Treaty of Tordesillas. The difficulties that arose were very great. In the first place, the Spanish commissioners wished to make use of geographical charts that had been drawn by the Dutch, who were acquainted with the region but did not desire to possess it; while the Portuguese commissioners used their own charts which had been prepared with the obvious purpose of falsifying the truth, for according to them the eastern coasts of America extended many degrees into the ocean.[1]

Another fundamental difference arose because of the vagueness of the terms of the Treaty of Tordesillas, which merely mentioned three hundred and seventy leagues west of the Azore and Cape Verde Islands without indicating from which one of those islands the reckoning should begin. The Spaniards rightly maintained that it should be the most central island (San Nicolás), while the Portuguese argued that it should be the most westerly island (San Antonio). While the commissioners debated this very complicated scientific and political question, Spain directed that Sacramento should be returned to Portugal.

When Philip V ascended the Spanish throne, Portugal took up arms against him, because of its opposition to the coronation of a grandson of Louis XIV as king of Spain. Because of this attitude, the governor of Buenos Aires was ordered to reconquer Sacramento. Colonel Baltazar García Ros, in command of a body of soldiers composed largely of creoles and Indians, beseiged and captured that colony. This feat of arms, as we have already explained, secured for Buenos Aires the title of "very noble and very loyal" city.

By the Treaty of Utrecht (1713), which put an end to the War of the Spanish Succession, Philip V was recognized as king of Spain. By Article VI of that treaty, the colony of Sacramento was

---

[1] According to geographers of Portugal, the demarcation line laid down by the Treaty of Tordesillas would have included the city of Buenos Aires in the Portuguese dominions. See L. L. Domínguez, *Historia argentina* (Buenos Aires, 1870), p. 181.

returned to Portugal.[2] A temporary solution, disastrous to Spanish interests, was thus reached in the boundary dispute with Portugal. Thenceforth, the pretensions of the Portuguese increased. This tendency influenced the court of Madrid to instruct the new governor of Buenos Aires, Bruno Mauricio de Zabala (1717), to oppose an obstacle to Portuguese advance.

The forecast came true. The Portuguese landed on the beach of Montevideo,[3] and declared that they did so because Portugal held the title to that territory. Governor Bruno Mauricio de Zabala then prepared an expedition to attack the Portuguese by both land and sea. The Portuguese commander abandoned the shore of Montevideo, but while on the march Zabala decided to proceed to that place in order to fortify it. With one thousand Indians from the Jesuit missions he began to construct the fortifications, and numerous families of Buenos Aires went to Montevideo on the promise that they would be given exemptions and privileges. In addition, the king sent fifty families to promote the growth of the new city, which was started in 1726 and officially founded on December 20, 1729. Until 1751, Montevideo depended upon the government of Buenos Aires. On that important date, there was created the political and military jurisdiction of Montevideo proper. Colonel Joaquín Viana was appointed its first governor.

In 1750, the "treaty of exchange" was signed by Spain and Portugal. According to its terms, Spain ceded to Portugal the provinces of Santa Catalina and Río Grande and seven of the Jesuit reductions of Paraguay in exchange for the colony of Sacramento. In the words of Mitre, "The Treaty of 1750, the product of an agreement between the reigning families of Spain and Portugal, seemed to bring peace to the contending parties without settling their disputes. By its terms, Spain implicitly recognized the Portuguese right of sovereignty over the colony of Sacramento by the act of accepting the cession of that colony in exchange for seven Jesuit reductions located on the left bank of the Uruguay. With

---

[2] On the attempts made by the king of Spain, in accordance with Article VII of the Treaty of Utrecht, to secure the restitution of Sacramento, see A. Bermejo de la Rica, *La colonia del Sacramento* (Toledo, 1920), pp. 131 ff.

[3] On the origin of the name "Montevideo," see R. Montero Bustamante, "La etimología del nombre Montevideo," *La Prensa,* Buenos Aires, January 3, 1926.

more foresight than the monarch, the Jesuit fathers resisted the transfer of those reductions." [4]

This treaty provoked the so-called Guaraní War, which was waged by the Guaraní Indians who, incited by the Jesuits, rose against the united forces of Spain and Portugal. The agents selected to carry out the treaty of exchange, who represented Spain and Portugal, were received in the missions as enemies. Then an appeal was made to force, and a sanguinary war began that lasted for three years. Finally the Indians were vanquished. Nevertheless, the missions were not transferred to Portugal; for the treaty of exchange was annulled shortly after Charles III ascended the throne of Spain. Soon afterward, because of the complicated European situation, Spain and Portugal were in opposite camps (in consequence of the Treaty of the Family Compact signed in 1761 by Spain and France, which Portugal refused to sign). Gomes Freire, viceroy of Brazil, accordingly ordered fresh forces to the colony of Sacramento in anticipation of any attack that might be made by Pedro Cevallos, the governor of Buenos Aires. In fact, after war was declared, the latter attacked the colony in October, 1762, with an army of six thousand men. It was easy for Cevallos to conquer Sacramento, in spite of the resistance of the Portuguese. He soon advanced as far as the Portuguese province of Rio Grande, where he received news that a new treaty had been signed in Europe between Spain and Portugal which suspended hostilities. This was the peace of Paris (1763) which increased the colonial empire of England at the expense of France. With respect to the dispute between Spain and Portugal, this treaty provided for the return of Sacramento to Portugal, but Spain was left mistress of the banks of the Rio Grande and the southern bank of the Yacuy.

Some years later, the honor devolved upon Cevallos of terminating the question that had been raised a century earlier concerning the title to the colony of Sacramento. In 1776, the king appointed Cevallos viceroy of La Plata and furnished him with the largest expedition that had come to South America during the colonial period. It was composed of one hundred and sixteen vessels and

---

[4] Mitre, *op. cit.*, I, 41. On the Portuguese claims to territory in South America, see further, Domínguez, *op. cit.*, pp. 199-200.

some ten thousand men. On February 20, 1777, Cevallos disembarked at the island of Santa Catalina, where the Portuguese surrendered without a struggle. On June 4, the Portuguese garrison of Sacramento capitulated. Immediately afterward, Cevallos prepared to continue his operations against the province of Rio Grande, when he was informed by the king that peace had been made. The Treaty of San Ildefonso signed by Spain and Portugal on October 1, 1777, provided that the colony of Sacramento and the missions east of the Uruguay River should be transferred to Spain. In exchange, the Portuguese secured large concessions; for they retained Santa Catalina, both banks of the rivers Yacuy and Rio Grande, and the regions explored in La Guayrá and Matto Grosso by frontiersmen from São Paulo.[5]

On March 27, 1767, King Charles III of Spain signed a notable decree ordering the expulsion of the Jesuits from Spain and the Indies. Minister Aranda transmitted the royal decree to all the governors, including Francisco de Paula Bucarelli, who was governor of Buenos Aires. In May, 1768, the latter expelled the Jesuits from their missions, and deported the missionaries to Spain.

This expulsion was one of the most important measures of King Charles III, who was the most liberal and progressive of the Spanish monarchs. During the second half of the eighteenth century, the political atmosphere of Europe began to be charged with new and liberal principles concerning political and religious affairs. Everything announced approaching changes on the stage of the Old World. These may be likened, indeed, to a pacific revolution in matters of belief and principle. Monarchs themselves reflected the new signs, and from the elevation of their thrones they themselves began to carry out the new reforms. Minister Pombal in Portugal; Ministers Turgot and Malesherbes in France; Minister Tanucci in Naples; Joseph II of Austria; Frederick II of Prussia; Catherine II of Russia; and the great ministers of King Charles III of Spain, Campomanes and Floridablanca—these statesmen are the highest expressions of this new revolutionary era.

There was in Spain a powerful institution which exercised a

---

[5] With regard to the difficulties involved in surveying the line laid down by the treaty of 1777, see V. G. Quesada, *Historia diplomática latino-americana* (3 vols. Buenos Aires, 1918-20), II, 13-28.—W. S. R.

decisive influence on the management of political affairs. This was
the Society of Jesus, which since the age of its founder, Ignacio
de Loyola, had expanded throughout Spain and its colonies, and
had become rich and powerful. It had monopolized immense do-
mains and in reality constituted a state within a state. King
Charles III realized that in order fully to develop his liberal policy,
the power of the Jesuits had first to be humbled. This fundamental
reason impelled the government to issue the decree for the expulsion of the Jesuits. The authors of this decree were influenced by
various motives. For Spain, the expulsion of the Jesuits was a
matter of life and death. In the Indies, the Jesuits had not gained
such political power that they caused fear. And, as we have said
in mentioning the spiritual conquest, they performed a task of virtue and beneficence in the colony of La Plata though not an organic task of colonization.[6]

One of the articles of the pragmatic sanction that followed the
royal decree of expulsion provided "that the sequestration of the
temporalities of the Society of Jesus included the properties and
effects, both real and personal, as well as the ecclesiastical revenues that they possessed within the kingdom." By virtue of this,
the rich possessions of the Jesuits became the property of the
royal treasury. In order to manage this property, administrative
boards were established in each province and city.

Furnishing a conclusive proof of the purely political object that
had incited him to expel the Jesuits, the king provided that the
incomes arising from the administration of the confiscated temporalities should be assigned to the development of general culture
and public welfare. With respect to the missions founded by the
Jesuits in Paraguay, their management was intrusted to a lieutenant governor, subject to the supervision of the governor of
Buenos Aires.[7]

---

[6] J. Ingenieros, *La evolución de las ideas argentinas* (2 vols. Buenos Aires,
1918-20), I, 93.

[7] L. M. Torres, *La administración de temporalidades en el Río de la Plata*
(Buenos Aires, 1917), discusses the legal antecedents of this affair.

CHAPTER XI

THE ADMINISTRATION OF THE SPANISH INDIES

IN ORDER to judge properly the colonial institutions established by Spain in America, one must understand the age, that is, the dominant ideas of the period. The seventeenth century is, so to speak, the century of absolutism in history. In France, it was the absolutism of a divine character represented in its king, Louis XIV. Despite its great democratic tradition, England beheld the temporary absolutism of the ruling house of the Stuarts. Spain also had its absolute government. This was the period in which governments emanated from God or from the king but not from the people. In Spanish America, the governments had this dominant vice: the authorities did not represent the people but the will of the king.

The authorities created by Spain in its American colonies had a definite sphere of action and developed separately. In the colonial government, there did not exist an absorbing centralization, but on the contrary the different authorities which were created balanced each other. Thus, for example, the viceroy, who was the highest authority, was secretly watched by the audiencia, which was a tribunal of justice, and when he ended his term of office he was subjected to the judgment of residencia in order that his conduct and honesty while in office might be examined. Naturally, the equilibrium that existed among the colonial authorities was not perfect, for one should remember that not until 1748 did the French philosopher Montesquieu enunciate the principle of the separation of departments as the condition of existence for a free government. Besides, the Laws of the Indies provided that the officials should remain only temporarily in their posts, thus establishing the principle of changes in the personnel of office-holders.[1]

After May, 1493, Juan de Fonseca, a member of the council of Castile, was intrusted with affairs relating to the Indies. In conjunction with Columbus he had made preparations for that ad-

---

[1] Comment upon the political organization provided by the Laws of the Indies is found in Estrada, *op. cit.,* I, 210-11.

miral's second voyage. During the first decade of the discovery, Archdeacon Fonseca exercised the functions of minister of the Indies.

On January 2, 1503, were framed "the instructions to establish a house of trade (*casa de contratación*) in Seville for the business of the Indies." In the warehouse of this new institution were to be deposited the goods that were to be sent to the Indies; in it were to be received the products that came from them. In its beginnings the purpose of the house of trade was to furnish the elements necessary to carry on the official colonization of America. At a later time important judicial functions were added (it became the superior court of commerce), as well as scientific and geographic functions (the preparation of maritime charts and maps of the Indies).

Within the Council of Castile "another board was formed to deal with matters of the Indies," until in 1524, the Council of the Indies was formally established. In October of that year, "the king fell ill of an ague" and he authorized the last-mentioned council to decide judicial matters (as a court of appeal) without consulting him.[2] The jurist, Juan de Solórzano, has rightly said that the Council of the Indies is a part of that of Castile, for it came from the breast of the older council.

The jurisdiction of the Council of the Indies included all political, judicial, and military affairs concerning either the house of trade of Seville or the eleven audiencias existing in the Indies. The council consulted with the king in civil matters pertaining to such offices as viceroys, oidors, presidents, royal officials, governors, and corregidors, and in spiritual matters pertaining to such offices as a patriarch, six archbishops, and thirty-two bishops. As an immediate result of this ascendancy of the Council of the Indies—and of a combination of causes relating to the fact that the era of the great geographic explorations had passed—a decline naturally took place in the functions and importance of the house of trade.[3]

---

[2] A. de Herrera y Tordesillas, *Historia general de los hechos de los Castellanos en las Islas y Tierra Firme del Mar Océano* (5 vols. Madrid, 1726-28), libro VI, cap. XIV, p. 203.

[3] Solórzano Pereira, *op. cit.,* p. 535. See further R. Levene, *Notas para el estudio del derecho indiano* (Buenos Aires, 1918), chap. I. [The oidors were judges.—W. S. R.]

The viceroy was the representative of the king in the colony. In order to insure his independence, he was prohibited from engaging in business or owning land; for in this manner, declared the legal code known as the "Laws of the Indies," "the authority of the viceroys was stronger." In La Plata there did not exist the pompous court of the viceroys of Peru, nor did the social and economic condition lend itself to such corruption as that which existed in Lima.[4] In this respect, eloquent, indeed, is the fact that the household goods of Baltasar Hidalgo de Cisneros, the last viceroy of Buenos Aires, did not amount to four thousand pesos.

In the second half of the eighteenth century, four viceroyalties existed in Spanish America: New Spain or Mexico; Peru, from which New Granada was carved in 1718; and Río de la Plata. There also existed in the colonies the captaincies general of Guatemala and Chile. The captain general directly represented the authority of the king: he commanded the armies, and administered the public treasury. Within the viceroyalties there existed governors with powers of their own, but dependent in the last resort upon the superior authority of the viceroy. At the end of their terms of office, the viceroys, captains general, governors, and oidors of the audiencias were subjected to the judgment of residencia. By this procedure an inquest was made of the administration of the functionary, particularly in what concerned his management of financial affairs. This judgment was made at the end of an official's term.[5]

The creation of the viceroyalty of La Plata was a part of the general plan of reform adopted by the Bourbon kings, and especially by Charles III. With regard to this, it suffices to remember that in 1739 the viceroyalty of New Granada had been definitely reëstablished. In general terms, it can be said that these organizations of a political character resulted from a more exact knowledge of the geography of the New World and from the evident economic progress that took place in the Indies as a result of the commercial privileges granted after 1720.

In the creation of the viceroyalty of La Plata other special

---

[4] J. A. García, *La ciudad indiana* (Buenos Aires, 1909).

[5] These political institutions were of Castilian origin. On the origin of the viceroys of the Spanish Indies, see Solórzano Pereira, *op. cit.*, p. 446.

causes were influential. Among these the three following should be mentioned: (1) In 1771, the fiscal of the audiencia of Charcas, Tomás Álvarez de Acevedo, prepared an interesting report in which he proposed the creation of a new viceroyalty to be composed of the province of Cuyo (to be separated from the captaincy general of Chile), and the districts of Paraguay, Buenos Aires, and Tucumán. This fiscal mentioned as the chief reason for the founding of this new political organism, the vast territorial extent of these colonies. In the official papers relating to this matter Manuel Amat y Junient, the viceroy of Peru, expressed himself in terms similar to those employed by Acevedo.

(2) The proposal of the fiscal of the audiencia of Charcas was made at a time when it was complicated with the question of the boundaries between Spain and Portugal, a fact that decided King Charles III to prepare a powerful expedition commanded by Pedro Cevallos, to whom was given the title of viceroy. In this manner, the problem of the colony of Sacramento became the decisive cause for the creation of the viceroyalty, for the purpose of settling the dispute with Portugal.

The permanence of this jurisdiction, which had been provisionally created because of the expedition of Cevallos, was decided on October 27, 1777, by the appointment of Juan José Vértiz y Salcedo as viceroy of La Plata. The governments of Chile and Peru opposed the decision to make that viceroyalty permanent. Manuel Guirior, the new viceroy of Peru, wrote to the Council of the Indies (May 20, 1779), and declared that it was inadvisable to create the viceroyalty of La Plata: "This news (of its permanent establishment) astounded merchants and common people and they became apprehensive concerning the fate of the property which they possessed in the provinces of the new viceroyalty and began to presage the most fatal effects because of the separation of the jurisdiction of a territory (Upper Peru) in which were found their greatest interests in ships or corregidors and in commissions of private individuals." In addition, they believed that this division of Peru into two jurisdictions would cause rivalry or controversy in the discovery of mines and would weaken the military strength of both viceroyalties, which would consequently not be able to resist a hostile invasion. In order to explain this opposition of Peru, it is sufficient to remember the commercial policy that had been consistently developed by Lima, which tended to keep the port of Buenos Aires closed to foreign commerce.

(3) Another principal cause was the fear entertained at the court of Madrid concerning the threats of English or Portuguese expeditions that planned to occupy the Patagonian coast. Remember that the French had gained control of the Falkland Islands. After those islands were returned to Spain the English occupied them. These proceedings were affected by the importance of fishing for whales and other sea mammals.

In this respect, it would be enough to add that a great maritime company founded near the end of the eighteenth century with privileges conceded by the king, undertook to promote whale fishing and other maritime industries. It should also be remembered that in June, 1778, the court of Madrid directed Viceroy Vértiz y Salcedo to establish forts and settlements which would tend to insure the control of Patagonia. For this purpose, the explorations of Francisco and Andrés Biedma, of Juan de la Piedra, and of the pilot Villarino were made.[6]

The age of the viceroys represented the constitutional era of La Plata, that is, the era of organization. During this last stage of Spanish domination, the bases were laid for the economic relations that were reëstablished after the battle of Caseros; the administration was organized in which the viceroy figured as a moderate but not absorbing entity; and the limits of the future state were defined. It became evident, even during the age of the viceroys, that Upper Peru, Chile, and the Banda Oriental were opposed to being considered subordinate to Buenos Aires, just as Buenos Aires had for two centuries resisted its absurd economic and political subordination with respect to Peru.

We have said that on October 27, 1777, the viceroyalty was permanently established by the appointment of Juan José Vértiz y Salcedo. On March 21, 1778, the intendancy of the army and the royal treasury was provided for La Plata; soon afterward, a customs service was organized. In 1782, a royal ordinance was issued concerning the intendancy of the army and the provinces; in 1794, a consulado or tribunal of commerce was founded. Thus,

[6] E. Ravignani, "Creación y permanencia del virreynato del Río de la Plata," *Anales de la facultad de derecho y ciencias sociales* (Buenos Aires, 1915), XV, 413-39.

all of these institutions were being slowly formed by a process of increase and development.

During the age of the viceroys, a phenomenon of decomposition and political and financial bankruptcy occurred at the very time when revolutionary ideas were spreading. We can mention the following as being among the events that were affecting the viceregal political organism: (1) the cabildo abierto of August 14, 1806, and the war junta of February 10, 1807, which deposed Viceroy Sobremonte and thus initiated the great crisis of political right in the Indies; (2) the separation of Montevideo which established a local junta (September, 1808), the first junta or self-governing assembly formed in America in imitation of the type of those existing in the Peninsula because of the Napoleonic usurpations; (3) the riot of January 1, 1809, in Buenos Aires, for the purpose of deposing Viceroy Liniers, just as in 1807 Viceroy Sobremonte had been deposed; (4) the revolutions at Chuquisaca and La Paz (May 25 and July 16, 1809).

With respect to the profound financial crisis which destroyed the colonial fiscal régime, it should be said that, after 1806 the annual budgets showed a deficit of no less than one-third of the total revenue needed to cover the cost of the entire administration. This trying condition caused the introduction of extraordinary imposts, loans, and patriotic contributions that did not improve the economic and financial depression until November 6, 1809, when the port of Buenos Aires was opened to English trade.

Lastly, emancipatory or revolutionary proposals became more and more organic in the shadow of the political decomposition that affected the viceroyalty and the bankruptcy that afflicted the treasury. The projects of emancipation should indeed be mentioned: (1) under an English protectorate (1807); (2) under the pretext of crowning Princess Carlota (1808-1809); (3) invoking the right to form local juntas of government similar to those which had been formed in Spain, a formula which, accepted by the patriots after the middle of 1809, scored a triumph in the cabildo abierto of May 22, 1810.

At the proper time, the vast plan of economic reforms carried out by the Bourbon kings in Spain and America will be explained. Among the most important reforms of a political character instituted in the motherland and soon transplanted to the colonies should be mentioned the intendancies of army and province, which King Philip V created for Spain in 1718. Though suppressed in 1721, they were reëstablished in 1749 by King Ferdinand VI.

After 1776, intendancies of the army and royal treasury were transplanted to the continent of America. On March 21, 1778, this institution was established at Buenos Aires. Manuel Fernández was made intendant general. He was to take "special cognizance of all the revenues or taxes that in any form or manner belong to my royal treasury with everything incidental or annexed to them, as also the finances of the military organization." This reform was extended to the four departments of the treasury, justice, police, and war. These were the intendancies "of war and province" which were created in 1782 for the viceroyalty of Buenos Aires, and at later dates for other parts of the Spanish continental dominions. They were, in reality, "two organizations that supplemented each other; for they were the outcome of the same centralistic policy that was applied in certain cases to the department of the treasury and war, and in other cases also to the departments of police and justice." [7] We shall explain the functions of the intendant when we consider colonial economic institutions.

During the period when cities were being established in the territory of La Plata, the institution designated as the cabildo was being organized. This was a municipal organization with social and political functions. Its members were called regidors. Judges of the first and second degree, who were charged with the administration of justice in minor cases, formed an integral part of it. In order to become a member of a cabildo, one had to be an inhabitant of the respective city. Descendants of the conquistadors were preferred for such posts. The offices were not salaried, and their acceptance, under a guarantee of faithful performance, was obligatory. Connected with the cabildo, there was also the royal ensign, who bore the standard in public ceremonies as a representative of the royal authority; the procurer general, who proposed re-

---

[7] L. M. Torres, introduction to vol. IX of *Documentos para la historia argentina* (13 vols. Buenos Aires, 1913-21), p. lvi. [A special type of intendant had, however, been earlier introduced into the island of Cuba. Instructions for that intendant were signed on October 31, 1764, by Julián de Arriaga, minister of the navy and the Indies. See W. W. Pierson, "The Establishment and Early Functioning of the *Intendencia* of Cuba," *The James Sprunt Historical Studies* (Chapel Hill, 1927), vol. XIX, no. 2, pp. 113-33.—W. S. R.]

forms, took care of the cabildo's needs, and always defended the institution; the majordomo, who managed religious ceremonies and feast-days; the public clerk, who subscribed the acts of the cabildo; the official of justice, the jailor, the chief military officer of the city, the judge of minors, the defender of the aborigines, and the chief constable: all of these interests had their places or their legal representatives in the cabildo.[8]

According to law, the cabildos were organized in the same manner and form as the ayuntamientos or cabildos which existed in the motherland. Upon their introduction into a different milieu, various factors partly modified the constitutional significance of these municipal councils.

The political régime of the cabildos was as follows: the first regidors were selected when the city was founded by the adelantado or the conquistador. Soon afterward, the regidors themselves undertook to designate annually the persons who were to succeed them, for it was assumed that they could best select the persons to fill the vacant offices. Accordingly, the inhabitants of the city did not participate directly in the selection of the regidors. After the election took place the result was made known to the people, and it might be contested in the cabildo. Further, the election had to be sanctioned by the governor or the viceroy, who sometimes declined to approve it.

It has been said that the cabildos were the cradle of Argentine liberty or a school of democracy. As has been seen, the people only voted indirectly, for the regidors selected their successors. That practice was justified in the minutes of the early cabildo of Buenos Aires: "In view of the principle that, because of the scanty population or small size of the district those who had just ceased to administer its interests were the judges most competent to choose in any given district the persons best fitted to carry on their functions with the same spirit and the same attention to the general welfare." [9] Certain authors, like Sarmiento, have exalted the political importance of the cabildos. "The cabildo of Córdoba," said the author of *Conflictos y armonías de razas (The Conflicts and Harmonies of Races)*, "for many years occupied as elevated a

---

[8] On the transplantation of the cabildo from Spain to America, see Solórzano Pereira, *op cit.*, libro V.

[9] *Acuerdos del extinguido cabildo de Buenos Aires*, II, 40.

place as the English parliament. . . ." Alberdi said of the cabildos: "Before the republic was proclaimed, the sovereignty of the people existed in South America in fact and in principle in the municipal system that was given to us by Spain. Policy and administration were separated: policy was determined by the government, while administration belonged to the people directly." [10]

The cabildos exercised administrative, judicial, and police functions. They intervened in lawsuits and quarrels as a good father of a family would do. Any inhabitant might present complaints or requests to the respective cabildo. These municipal organizations distributed lots, granted permission for hunting cattle and for the extraction of grease and tallow, attended public entertainments, and regulated processions; they presented a bulwark against the advances of the ecclesiastical authority, granted permission for the construction of buildings, inspected stores in order to learn the prices and qualities of the merchandise on sale, fixed the price of meat, yerba mate, tobacco, and other products, protected the poor from the oppression of the rich, and compelled the latter in case of need to give up the surplus of their harvests and products for the common welfare. Thus, for example, the cabildo of Córdoba resolved as follows with respect to the quantity of grain that should be collected for the use of the people who needed it: "In the city of Córdoba . . . there met in the cabildo hall, the illustrious members of the cabildo of this city . . . they said that they had by common consent attended this council in order to consider matters concerning the service of God, our Lord, and of his Majesty the king, and concerning the welfare of this city and its republic. They considered that it was proper to gather one hundred fanegas of wheat for the maintenance of the inhabitants of this city who have neither gathered food nor have any, and to pay a moderate price for this wheat. These gentlemen decided that one peso should be paid for each fanega of food thus taken and distributed, and that this peso was to be paid in clothing, linen, sheep, and wool; the sheep should be reckoned at the rate of a peso

---

[10] In contrast with the views of Sarmiento and Alberdi, some writers maintain that the cabildos had no significance as political institutions. However, the correct view is that the cabildos exercised much political authority during the early colonial period because of their functions which were intimately concerned with colonial society.

apiece, and the wool at two pesos per each twenty-five pounds, and the said sheep must be good to use in exchange." [11]

The influence of the cabildo must accordingly have been powerful in the social order; for its decisions sought inspiration from the most general interests and common needs, always assuming the function of the defense and the protection of society. Possibly the most important and general acts or political events of Spanish America scarcely found an echo in the decisions of the cabildo. Matters of high policy and administration appertained to authorities and functionaries of a superior class residing either in Spain or America. But small interests, elementary and urgent needs, arising from the people themselves and, therefore, important and significant to them, were considered by the cabildos. Not a single military, economic, or political act was decided upon without their participation. Their character and their highest political significance, accordingly, depended upon the fact that they aided and promoted the formation of towns, cities, and communities. But if one should judge of the value and importance of institutions, not according to a superior and perfect ideal, but according to an ideal that is adaptable and efficient, one must consider the social function of the cabildos in the protection and defense of the common interests, and in paternal administration and vigilance, as of high significance for the destinies of the developing communities.[12]

[11] *Archivo municipal de Córdoba,* as quoted in Levene, *Lecturas históricas argentinas,* I, 172-73. A "fanega" was a Spanish grain measure, which was equivalent to about 1.6 bushels.—W. S. R.

[12] R. Levene, *Los origenes de la democracia argentina* (Buenos Aires, 1911), p. 105.

CHAPTER XII

THE VICEROYS

PEDRO DE CEVALLOS carried out at once a series of fundamental reforms for the nascent viceregal organization of La Plata. In June, 1777, he issued a proclamation directed against the exportation of metals to Lima: "Because I understand that from those provinces of this viceroyalty which produce gold and silver, a large quantity of these metals is taken to La Ciudad de los Reyes under the pretext that they will be smelted in the mint of that capital, to the prejudice of the mint established in the imperial town of Potosí." By this manifesto Cevallos began the policy of reaction against the absorbing pretensions of Peru. Another act inspired by the same motive was concerned with the problem of transporting quicksilver by way of the port of Buenos Aires. Viceroy Cevallos thought that quicksilver from Almadén could be imported directly into Buenos Aires, instead of extracting it from the mines of Guancavélica, which was much more expensive.

Anticipating the idea of Manuel Belgrano, secretary of the tribunal of commerce, regarding the necessity of promoting the cultivation of hemp and flax, Viceroy Cevallos asked "that the Indians and the mixed classes of these dominions should apply themselves to the sowing, the cultivation, and the harvesting of hemp and flax in order that these products might be taken to Spain, as raw materials for the manufacture of canvas and cordage, free of all duties."

Under date of November 17, 1777, Cevallos issued a proclamation concerning the regulation of peon labor which should be mentioned separately because of the progressive spirit that it revealed: "As the production of cereals and legumes . . ." so ran the proclamation—"is one of the activities most conducive to the public welfare and particularly to the present expedition which deeply concerns the royal service, and since I have become aware of the disorders and wastes due to the peons who labor in the harvest fields, which have caused the loss of much wheat because of floods, fires, and the grain that is left on the stubble, I have judged it politic to prevent this and hence order as follows: . . . The better peons who labor in these harvests shall not be paid more than four reals per day, and the boys two reals or at most three reals. . . . They shall take a siesta, as is customary, but on the days when they have no siesta, as on threshing-days and on other days when it is necessary to use the wind for winnowing purposes, the wages shall be increased one real per day. . . . The peons shall rise at four o'clock in the morning in order to drink mate; then they shall immediately go to work, and at the end of one hour and a half they shall be given another mate; a half hour later they shall be given breakfast; an hour later they shall be given another mate; and they then shall be given all the cold water that they wish until they stop work. . . . At half-past eleven o'clock they shall retire to the house where they shall rest half an hour, and at twelve they shall be given something to eat in order that they may sleep during the siesta. At two o'clock they shall be awakened, given mate, and then they shall at once return to the harvest field. There, at equal intervals, they shall be served two other mates, and after that as much cold water as they wish until they all stop work which will be one hour after sunset." [1]

Indeed, one of the most serious tasks of the government was to regulate the work of laborers. The proclamation of Viceroy Cevallos shows that this need was anticipated by the framing of a protective regulation.

But the fundamental measure of Cevallos was the ordinance concerning importation and free commerce dated November 6, 1777. In its explanatory clauses, he said that the viceroyalty having been founded, it was necessary to have "freedom and liberty of the active and passive commerce of each province and city with other provinces and cities, both with respect to the products which they raise and with respect to those that enter the port of Buenos Aires from ports of Spain in licensed ships. Without the aid of this measure, which is a stimulus to colonization, they can never make the least progress." He designated this freedom of commerce as a "natural right" and declared that as the colony had recovered its strength, the plight which justified "the closing of the port of Buenos Aires had ceased to exist"; he added that this liberty "is

---

[1] *Documentos para la historia del virreynato del Río de la Plata* (3 vols. Buenos Aires, 1912-13), I, 222-23.

for all those subjects who until the present have been deprived of it because of distance and the lack of communications."

Upon the basis of this ordinance, the king issued the decree of February 2, 1778. The economic and financial results accruing to La Plata by the regulation concerning free commerce of October 12, 1778 (which concerned all the ports of America, in contrast with the decree of February 2, which only related to Buenos Aires) were very important. The poor colony of yesterday became a respectable community, because of the increase of the revenues, the development of its business, and the active interprovincial commerce that began. In 1776, the difference between the receipts and expenditures of La Plata was 286,000 pesos; in 1777, it rose to 1,200,000; in 1779, it fell to 195,000 pesos. This condition was due to the war between England and Spain with the resulting commercial limitations and restrictions.

After 1780, the tendency was toward a return to normal conditions. The economic progress that subsequently took place in La Plata must have been due especially to the beneficial results of royal provisions concerning free traffic in Negroes (1791), concerning commerce with the colonies of other nations (1795), and commerce with neutral powers (1797).[2]

Pedro de Cevallos did not remain two years at the head of the government. On June 12, 1778, Juan José de Vértiz y Salcedo became viceroy. Vértiz y Salcedo was a native of Mexico, who showed a decided love for the colonists. The policy of Viceroy Vértiz y Salcedo was varied and intense. He took the initiative in all matters of administration, and left everywhere the impression of a beneficent and enduring work. During his rule, an era of intellectual renovation and of liberalism was inaugurated. In Mitre's words: "We began to enter upon a new epoch. Great events, which changed the face of the country, were soon to take place. The stage of public life began to expand; new actors in the drama of history appeared. A new law and a new force began to appear, each supporting the other. The old skeleton of the colonial system began to moulder and even its own custodians unconsciously promoted this tendency."[3]

[2] See further, R. Levene, *Investigaciones acerca de la historia económica del virreynato del Plata* (2 vols. La Plata, 1927).

[3] Mitre, *op. cit.*, I, 84.

At this moment, the figure of Vértiz y Salcedo stands out, like a governor of the modern type. Thus, the viceroy learned that indigenous tribes roamed between the rivers Paraná and Uruguay but "he did not order troops there to force them to observe the rights of the others." Instead he sent pioneers who planted in the heart of the desert the towns of Gualeguay, Concepción del Uruguay, and Nogoyá. Of the theater, Vértiz y Salcedo said "that it was the best school of customs, of speech, and of general urbanity"; of the printing press he said "that, besides furnishing some revenue to the foundling hospital, it also provided the public with the useful effects of the printing press"; of the school he said "that not only was it convenient for many public purposes which are assured by the good education of individuals, but it was also necessary in this capital in order to check the disorders of childhood and to shield the youth who are generally endowed with clear understandings." Vértiz y Salcedo even undertook to sketch a plan for a university which was to be founded in Buenos Aires, in order to furnish instruction "free from the bias of schools."[4]

As we have said, at this time Vértiz y Salcedo directed an intellectual reform so pronounced and characteristic that when King Charles III of Spain issued an invitation to Spanish universities to improve their instruction, the University of Salamanca replied that "there were no innovations to make, for the systems of Newton and Descartes very illy accorded with revealed truth," while the secular cabildo of Buenos Aires, through the intervention of Viceroy Vértiz y Salcedo, recommended "the policy of not imposing any precise system upon professors of philosophy." In this manner, he advocated liberty of teaching and the toleration of all ideas.

One of the most important establishments founded by Vértiz y Salcedo was the Academy of San Carlos. During its first year the academy had more than one hundred students enrolled. Included in the administrative and teaching corps of this institution were Baltazar Maciel, Juanzaras, Dr. Luis José Chorroarín, and a priest named Fernández.

A certain author affirms that "ignorant theologians" were trained in the Academy of San Carlos—alluding to the fact that

---

[4] J. M. Gutiérrez, *Noticias históricas sobre el origen y desarrollo de la enseñanza pública superior en Buenos Aires* (Buenos Aires, 1868), *passim*.

its teaching was much influenced by religion and scholasticism.[5] Perhaps this was not true, for in the cloisters of the Academy of San Carlos were trained such students as Saavedra, Belgrano, Rivadavia, French, and Berutti. As Gutiérrez has aptly said, the Academy of San Carlos educated the men who launched the May Revolution and honored the country by their talents.

With regard to the printing press and trade in books in the Indies, the legislation of Spain was prohibitive. In the Laws of the Indies it was provided "that in the western Indies, islands, and mainlands of the Ocean Sea, judges should not consent or permit any book to be printed or sold which dealt with the affairs of the Indies, without the special and previous authorization of the Council of the Indies; and they were ordered to have collected as speedily as possible all the books that might be found and all booksellers were to be forbidden to sell or to print them." It was even necessary—as V. G. Quesada said—for manuscripts to be sent to the Council of the Indies for examination and censure; and these would probably be condemned if their author was not sufficiently rich to present them personally and to influence the proceeding.

The Jesuits were the first to introduce the printing press. It has been proven that in the Paraguay missions they published books concerning Christian doctrine and dictionaries in Spanish and Guaraní during the years from 1703 to 1725. The Jesuit father, José Serrano, translated into the Guaraní language the book entitled *Diferencia entre lo temporal y lo eterno*, which had been written by Father Eugene of Nuremberg. In 1724, there was printed an edition of the book entitled *Arte de la lengua Guaraní* by Father Antonio Ruíz de Montoya.[6]

The Jesuits established a center in the city of Córdoba, where they founded a university. They had a printing press there also on which they published educational books. When the Jesuits were expelled, the management of the university devolved upon the

---

[5] Manuel Moreno, *Vida y memorias del Dr. Mariano Moreno* ("Memorias y autobiografías, museo histórico nacional," vol. II, Buenos Aires, 1910), p. 18. *Cf.* E. Ravignani, "Constituciones del Real Colegio de San Carlos," *Revista de la Universidad de Buenos Aires* (Buenos Aires, 1917), XXXV, 530-45. See further, A. de Souza Arguello, *Colegio real de San Carlos* (Buenos Aires, 1918).

[6] See Lawrence C. Wroth's "The Origins of Typefounding in North and South America," in *Ars Typographica,* April, 1927, for interesting data on early typefounding in the New World.—W. S. R.

Franciscans. They did not use the printing press which remained there until Viceroy Vértiz y Salcedo ordered it transferred to Buenos Aires, where it was used to establish the printing office of the Foundling Hospital. Upon reporting this event the viceroy said: "Later there was purchased and put into use a press that had been idle for many years in the Royal Academy of Monserrat. In addition to the purchase price, its reëstablishment was very costly. Besides bringing some revenue to this hospital, that measure also furnished the public with the useful influence of a printing press." [7] Without fear of exaggeration, it may be said that this act of Viceroy Vértiz y Salcedo involved a principle of spiritual regeneration, for the press became an instrument for the diffusion of a developing culture.

Viceroy Vértiz y Salcedo founded a theater upon the site that had been occupied by the central market. Covered with a straw roof, it was a modest structure but one which was destined to furnish hours of recreation to society. A certain author relates that a priest exhorted the women from the pulpit to the effect that, if they were devout Roman Catholics, they would not attend theatrical performances. Vértiz y Salcedo removed this priest from his post for making such recommendations, and society attended the performances of the playhouse, the income from which had the noble end of aiding in the support of the Foundling Hospital.

During the administration of Vértiz y Salcedo, there was also established the Foundling Hospital that was supported by the income accruing from the press which was brought from Córdoba and by the profits of the theater. Besides, he also founded a hospice for beggars, an orphan asylum, and a hospital for women. He also organized the tribunal of royal physicians. Among the most notable material reforms, we should mention the construction of sidewalks and the paving of the two principal streets of Buenos Aires. During a heavy rainstorm, the city was apt to be cut off from the adjacent country for many days. The reforms mentioned improved those public services which were necessary for the well being of the inhabitants. Vértiz y Salcedo also installed a public lighting system by means of tallow candles. During his term a census was taken

---

[7] On the circulation of prohibited books in the viceroyalty of la Plata, see R. Rojas, *La literatura argentina* (4 vols. Buenos Aires, 1917-23), II, 20-24.

which gave the city 24,754 inhabitants, and the adjacent country, 12,925.

The Indians were constantly menacing the colonists by making raids on the city. Vértiz y Salcedo directed that forts should be constructed to protect the frontiers. A contingent of soldiers designated as "Blandengues" was assigned the task of checking the Indian advance but proved unable to fulfil that duty. Vértiz y Salcedo pushed the frontier line forward; he established forts at Chascomús, Monte, and Rojas, and intermediate posts at Ranchos, Lobos, Navarro, and Areco. Although he expended considerable sums on these defenses, yet they were also ineffective, for shortly afterward the Indians repeated their raids. The rectification of the frontier line was again undertaken during the viceregal term of Melo de Portugal.

At this time a great uprising of the Quechua Indians, to the number of sixty thousand, took place in Upper Peru. The disaffection soon spread into the province of Salta. A cacique of the province of Tinta named José Gabriel Tupac Amaru, a descendant of the Incas, who had been educated in the universities of Cuzco and Lima, put himself at the head of the rebellion. The Indians complained of the ill treatment that the Spaniards accorded them in the working of the mines. In order to suppress this movement, Viceroy Vértiz y Salcedo sent forces which arrived triumphantly at the city of Chuquisaca. The Peruvian viceroy also sent an army which numbered seventeen thousand men upon its arrival at Cuzco. Finally, the uprising was put down in sanguinary fashion, and Tupac Amaru was executed. Of this insurrection, Pedro de Angelis, a scholar of Italian birth, who edited a collection of documents on South American colonial history, said: "The only useful result of this great rebellion was the new organization that the court of Spain gave to the administration of its transatlantic provinces, and the abolition of *repartimientos*. In this fashion, the principle that Tupac Amaru had invoked for the improvement of the lot of the Indians was legitimized; for, in their delegates, they later found administrators who were more responsible and hence more upright than the corregidors." [8] The orgy of cruelty displayed in suppressing the insurrection also serves to demonstrate that the Spanish

---

[8] P. Angelis, ed., *Colección de obras y documentos relativos á la historia antigua y moderna de las provincias del Río de la Plata* (5 vols. Buenos Aires, 1910), IV, 272.

authorities had no slight fear of the contagion that might be spread by this insurrection, which we cannot consider as having been entirely without effect upon the spirits of the Americans.[9]

When the revolt of Tupac Amaru was put down, the problem of the status of the Indian was upon the tapis. At the beginning of the nineteenth century the abuses of the *mita* system continued in all their rigor, especially in Potosí, where the figure of Francisco de Paula Sanz became prominent. He was the advocate of the miners, maintaining that the Indian was irrational, and supporting the mita system with all its brutal practices which originated with the first conquerors of America, just as if centuries had not elapsed since then. Opposed to him was Victorián de Villalva, fiscal of the audiencia of Charcas, who championed the principle of the liberty of the Indian. Recollect what has already been said earlier in this respect regarding the influence of Villava on the education of Mariano Moreno who, to fulfil the requirements for the degree of licenciate in law, composed a thesis entitled *Disertación jurídica sobre el servicio personal de los Indios en general* (*Juridical Dissertation regarding the Personal Service of the Indians in General*). We repeat that the problem of the Indian is fundamental in the study of the Spanish-American Revolution. After 1810, the officials of the patriot government became concerned about the immediate amelioration of the condition of the aborigines.[10]

We have already mentioned the importance of the Patagonian expeditions made by the Jesuit fathers José Quiroga and Thomas Falkner. Concerning the latter it should be added that in 1774 he published in England the work entitled *A Description of Patagonia and the Adjoining Parts of South America*, undoubtedly for the purpose of attracting the attention of his country to the riches and strategic value of those territories, as may be deduced from a paragraph of his book.

In consequence Viceroy Vértiz y Salcedo received an order from

---

[9] Estrada, *op. cit.*, I, 243-44. On the punishments imposed on the rebels, see G. Funes, *Ensayo de la historia civil de Buenos Aires, Tucumán y Paraguay* (2 vols. Buenos Aires, 1856), II, 264.

[10] The political importance of these movements of the aborigines is shown by a document in the Archivo del Gobierno de Buenos Aires, 1810, Archivo general de la Nación, entitled "Instrucción que doy a mi Sucesor en el Gorno, de esta Proa. de Salta arreglada a las qe. he recibido de la Excma. Junta Gubernativa y a los conocimtos, practicos que he adquirido," which was prepared by Chiclana for his successor.

the court of Madrid—in anticipation of constant threats by England and Portugal—to establish forts on the Patagonian coast. In response to this order, new and important explorations and settlements were made in this territory by Francisco, Antonio, and Andrés Viedma, by Juan de la Piedra, and by the pilot Villarino. "The pilot, Manuel Bruñel, and Pedro García, an infantry lieutenant, in accordance with the orders of Juan de Piedra (commissary-superintendent of the 'bottomless bay') with the smack *San Antonio de Oliveira*, made a reconnaissance of a part of these extensive coasts and reached the mouth of the Río Negro. The appearance of the bar vividly impressed him, and he did not dare to attempt its passage, but returned to San José, where the people assured him that entrance was impossible. Speaking of the Río Negro, Falkner said in his account: 'This river, the greatest of all Patagonia, empties itself into the western ocean, and is known by various names; as the Second Desaguadero or Second Drain; the Desaguadero of Nahuel Huapí, or Drain of Nahuel Huapí; by the Spaniards called the Great River of Sauces or Willows; by some of the Indians, Choele Choel; by the Puelches, Seubucomó or the River by Antonomasia; and Curú Leuvú, that is, Río Negro, or Black River by the Huiliches and Pehuenches.' The pilot, Villarino, who for many reasons is entitled to our respectful consideration, undertook to demonstrate the risk of the assertions concerning the navigability of the Río Negro and proved it, being the first white man to navigate the waters of that large river." [11]

On February 22, Villarino reconnoitered the entrance of the Río Negro. He sent out a boat which made soundings for the pilot and the brig was able to advance. On the next day, he continued the exploration of the river and received on board some natives of the region. On February 28, the explorers returned to the Atlantic Ocean.

In 1779, Colonel Fernández Cornejo undertook to navigate the Río Bermejo, which traverses the Chaco from Peru. When Fernández Cornejo was about to abandon the enterprise, a priest of the Franciscan order, Father Morillo, went on and met Commandant

---

[11] T. Falkner, *A Description of Patagonia and the Adjoining Parts of South America* (Hereford, 1774), p. 79 is quoted by J. J. Biedma, *Crónica Histórica del Río Negro de Patagones* (Buenos Aires, 1905).

Arias who had established some Indian reductions in the center of the Chaco. Because of his meeting with Morillo, Arias relinquished the exploration of Río Bermejo and proceeded to the city of Corrientes.

In order to colonize Patagonia numerous families had been brought from Spain, chiefly from the Asturias and Galicia, but as this enterprise was about to be abandoned, Viceroy Vértiz y Salcedo founded with them the towns of Gualeguay, Gualeguaychú, and Concepción del Uruguay in Entre Ríos; and in the Banda Oriental, San Juan Bautista, San José, and San Francisco de Minas.

In March, 1784, Nicolás del Campo, marquis of Loreto, succeeded Vértiz y Salcedo as viceroy of La Plata. During his term, Loreto chiefly promoted cattle-raising and its related industries (especially the salting of meat), as well as agriculture. He also ordered the improvement of the port of Buenos Aires by means of a mole planned by the engineer, Domingo Pallares. The most important event of his administration was the installation of the audiencia on August 8, 1785. In the survey of his administration which Vértiz y Salcedo left to the Marquis of Loreto, the former particularly recommended, to one who was a man of letters, the project which he had cherished of founding a university in Buenos Aires. But the Marquis of Loreto did not promote this plan which would have brought him considerable glory and would have greatly benefited the colony.

In December, 1789, Nicolás de Arredondo succeeded the Marquis of Loreto. During his term of office, Arredondo promoted the colonization of the Patagonian coast, and stimulated the whale fishing industry by means of a great company to which the king granted liberal privileges. During this administration, the tribunal of commerce was founded, the importance and significance of which we have already noticed where we observed that economic questions began to be discussed among its members, thus revealing revolutionary sentiment.

The following viceroys followed Arredondo in chronological order: Pedro Melo de Portugal y Villena (1795-1797), Antonio Olaguer Feliú (1797-1799), Gabriel Avilés de Fierro (1799-1801), Joaquín del Pino (1801-1804), during whose administration the first periodicals were published in La Plata, namely the

Telégrafo Mercantil, edited by Francisco Cabello, and the *Semanario de Agricultura y Comercio*, edited by Hipólito Vieytes. We shall devote a separate chapter to this important event in another part of this book. The Marquis of Sobremonte (1804-1807) succeeded Viceroy del Pino. During Sobremonte's administration, the English invasions of La Plata took place.

CHAPTER XIII

COLONIAL COMMERCE

IF POLITICAL events occurring before 1810 are considered, the colonial history of Argentina falls into the corresponding periods of the adelantados, the governors, and the viceroys. In view of economic facts that are marked by struggles for adaptation to the environment which is destined to support life, colonial history is divided into distinct epochs. These epochs are as follows: (1) from the beginnings of the Spanish conquest up to the establishment of the interior custom house at Córdoba in 1622; (2) to 1713, when the Treaty of Utrecht was signed; (3) to 1796, when a war with England broke out which had grave economic and political consequences; (4) to 1810.

The first epoch of the economic history of La Plata was one of relative commercial liberty. In 1595, a royal cédula was issued authorizing Pedro Gómez Reynel to introduce six hundred Negroes per annum into these provinces for a term of nine years.[1] In 1602, a royal ordinance permitted the exportation of colonial products to Brazil and Guinea for a term of six years in exchange for clothing, footwear, iron, and other necessary articles.[2] During the rule of Arias de Saavedra twenty vessels visited Buenos Aires; fourteen entered that port during the rule of Diego de Góndora. At this time, Negroes sold at prices varying between sixty and seventy pesos.

In 1608, for the first time, and again in 1614, the privilege conceded in 1602 was extended. For a term of five years there could be exported from La Plata two thousand fanegas of flour, five hundredweight of resin, and twenty hundredweight of tallow. When these grants expired the fiscal of the city of Buenos Aires made fresh representations to the king; but the latter on September 8, 1618, limited the grant to a period of three years, and upon the express condition that the colonists could only export their products in vessels not exceeding one hundred tons apiece plying to Brazil to sell flour, resin, and tallow in exchange for sugar and

---

[1] Reales cédulas y provisiones, Archivo general de la nación, folio 45.

[2] Pacheco and Cárdenas, op. cit., XVIII, 324-25.

timber, and then sailing to Seville where they were to get clothing and other articles necessary for the colonists.[3] The cabildo discussed the grant of 1618, and stated that this would not satisfy the pressing needs of the inhabitants, for the voyage to Seville would consume a year, while the previous concession of 1622, twice extended to permit trade with Brazil, made possible two voyages in that time. Although the cabildo rejected the grant of his Majesty, yet the governor respected it and proceeded to carry it out. But upon returning from Seville, on the pretext that they were forced into harbor by distress, the ships touched at Brazil so that they might take on more merchandise for immediate introduction into Buenos Aires.

In fact, the commercial activity that developed during this epoch was not solely that which was included within the terms of the legal grant. Illicit foreign commerce was continually carried on. Dutch and Portuguese vessels approached to within a short distance of Buenos Aires and transferred much foreign merchandise to Spanish barks.

These facts provoked protests from the merchants of Peru, whose viceroy had the political superintendence over all the provinces of La Plata. These protests originated from the fact that the introduction of goods through the port of Buenos Aires produced competition with the exorbitant prices of articles introduced by way of Peru. People in the interior and the northern part of La Plata were the object of an insatiable exploitation on the part of the merchants of Lima. In Potosí, prices were four times as high as in Lima; while in Tucumán, prices were twice as high as in Potosí, so that, as compared with Lima, prices in Tucumán were eight times as high.[4]

The loss of the Argentine markets induced the merchants of Lima to make the necessary representations to the king. These were successful; for on February 7, 1622, the interior custom-house of Córdoba was established, which was, so to speak, a wall interposed between the coast and the interior; for only upon the payment of fifty per cent of the regular duties were goods that had been freely introduced into Buenos Aires permitted to penetrate into the remote provinces. After the establishment of the custom-house

---

[3] *Acuerdos del extinguido cabildo de Buenos Aires*, V, 18-24.

[4] R. Levene, *La moneda colonial del Plata* (Buenos Aires, 1916), pp. 20-21.

at Córdoba, every commercial concession in favor of La Plata caused protests from Peru. Governor Francisco de Céspedes exerted all his influence to change this state of affairs, but without avail.

The stringency of the system was increased by other provisions, by virtue of which no more specie could be brought to the coast than was actually necessary; neither could there be taken from the port of Buenos Aires gold or silver either in the form of money or as gold ware, silver ware, ingots, or ore. Spain absurdly persisted in adopting measures so stringent that they could not be applied—measures which definitely stimulated the contraband trader. Buenos Aires was a natural port, and its lands contained rich resources which made exportation necessary. It was impossible to watch the exit of products. The first foundation of the audiencia of Buenos Aires (1661) made for this purpose, was a noisy failure, and, as a document states, people began to despair of the outcome of similar measures "in view of the fact that the obstacles in the way of the enforcement of restrictive regulations were superior to their forces which were not sufficient for success in such open regions." This document adds that "the port of Buenos Aires has been a beautiful mistress for foreigners who have not refrained from wooing her by the most expensive measures." [5]

This second period in the economic history of La Plata coincides with the era in which Spain became a commercial monopolist. It adopted what may be designated as the policy of a single port of clearance from Spain and a single port of entry into the Indies. From the viewpoint of Spanish-American history, this policy was pursued from 1561 to 1713.

On the former date the régime of fleets and galleons was organized which is mentioned in title XXX of book IX of the *Recopilación de Indias (Laws of the Indies)*. Each year, two merchant fleets left Seville, Cadiz, and Sanlúcar, accompanied by a royal squadron. One of these fleets was destined for New Spain, while the other went to Tierra Firme. The royal squadron was to convoy and protect the fleets as well as to transport the treasure belonging to the king and to private persons. All these vessels were to proceed equipped, armed, supplied, and manned with the

---

[5] *Documentos para la historia argentina*, V, 322.

forces necessary to punish enemies. The cargoes were destined for
Cartagena and Porto Bello where fairs were held that lasted for
a month.

The motherland was compelled to adopt this régime, however
absurd it may appear, because of the following reasons: (1) The
war waged by corsairs and filibusters which made union necessary
for defense. (2) The system of commercial monopoly which was
general during this epoch. France, Portugal, Holland, and England also followed it toward their colonies. (3) From the middle
of the sixteenth century there occurred in Spain the phenomenon
of a rise in prices of articles necessary for subsistence owing to
the receipt of large quantities of precious metals from America
which were at once coined into money. But in the belief that the
prevailing high cost of living was due to the demand in the Indies
for European products, the proctors who represented the Spanish cities at court demanded that the king prohibit the exportation
of products and goods to the Indies. In large part, these petitions
were in accordance with the policy of placing restrictions upon
commerce, of opening only one port to trade, and of restricting
exportations to the infrequent voyages of fleets and galleons.

One of the provisions which most helped to aggravate the Spanish monopolistic régime was that stipulating that the colonies
could not carry on commercial intercourse with each other, but
that each of them should either trade separately with Spain or
should bring its products to the markets provided by the fairs.

In 1713, the Treaty of Utrecht was signed which ended the War
of the Spanish Succession. That date marked the beginning of a
new colonial policy initiated by Europe. The importance of the
Treaty of Utrecht is particularly American, with the cession of
Newfoundland and Acadia in North America (which gave to
England the entrance to the river St. Lawrence and the control
of part of present Canada); the grant to the English of the
privilege of carrying on the slave traffic for thirty years in the
ports of Spanish America; and the recognition that the colony of
Sacramento belonged to Portugal. Following this treaty, England
put agents in all the ports of Spanish America upon the pretext
of introducing Negroes, but at the same time it developed a trade
in various articles, because it did not hesitate to secure Spanish-
American markets. Faced by the peril of being commercially elim-

inated by England, and with the desire of promoting a revival of its industries, Spain initiated a liberal policy and developed better relations with the Indies.

The commercial concessions that Spain began to grant to its colonies after the opening of the eighteenth century were the work of the Bourbon kings, Philip V, Ferdinand VI, Charles III, and Charles IV, and their ministers. Misery had struck deep roots in Spain and had undermined its national fountains of wealth. Many economists pointed out the evil and proposed remedies. The monarchs hearkened to them, and formulated a complex plan of reform, particularly of an economic character, according to notions suggested by various economists. Among these economists should be mentioned Jerónimo Uztariz, author of the work entitled *Teórica y práctica del comercio y de marina (The Theory and Practice of Commerce and Navigation)*, in which he criticized vigorously the imposing régime that prevailed in Spain, especially the tax designated the alcabala which affected every transaction in the nature of a purchase or a sale. Uztariz viewed the alcabala as the cause of the death of Spain's domestic and foreign commerce. King Ferdinand VI commissioned an Irishman named Bernard Ward to make a trip of investigation through Europe in order to compare the colonial policy of other nations and to propose a plan of reform. Ward soon published his famous treatise entitled *Proyecto Económico* in which he advocated the adoption of liberal measures in the commercial and industrial order. During the reigns of Charles III and Charles IV, two great economists stood out conspicuously: Campomanes and Jovellanos. The former is the author of the notable studies on *Educación popular de los artisanos (Popular Education of Artisans)*, *Fomento de la industria popular (The Promotion of Popular Industry)*, *Fuentes de la industria (Sources of Industry)*, and *Abusos de la Mesta (Abuses of the Mesta)*, in which he disputed the principle that it was sufficient to stimulate agriculture in order to insure the happiness of the kingdom. Campomanes reasoned that it was also necessary to stimulate other industries, and that it would be politic to spread a knowledge of technical and professional education. Jovellanos wrote the famous *Informe en el expediente de la ley agraria (Report concerning the Agrarian Law)* in which he developed a vast plan of agrarian development based upon the principle of removing the obstacles furnished by prejudice, by laws, and by the nature of the soil.

In April, 1720, King Philip V framed a "project for the fleets and galleons of Peru and New Spain and for registered and mail ships that should sail to both viceroyalties." By these means he proposed to improve commercial relations with the colonies. In order to insure success, he sent a circular order to the intendants of the provinces of Spain to the effect that they should favor manufacturers and merchants by encouraging them to send their goods to the Indies and instructing them that the duties had been considerably decreased. Soon afterward, the necessary steps were taken for the departure of fleets and galleons to Mexico and South America. In 1735, the despatch of galleons to Tierra Firme was suspended because it had not produced the beneficial results that had been expected. In 1740, the system of fleets and galleons was suppressed; and in 1754, it was reëstablished solely for New Spain.

In place of the old system, the plan of single registered vessels destined for a port in the Spanish Indies was made general. Many permits were issued for this trade with Spanish America. The authorization necessary for the clearance of registered vessels came directly from the king. This was a most important innovation which produced a real economic revolution by "opening the natural routes of commerce which up to that time had been obstructed by monopoly, as it permitted registered ships to go direct to commercial ports of their own selection and to proceed by way of Cape Horn to the South Sea, an ocean hitherto closed like a lake and condemned to be supplied solely by Porto Bello and Panama." [6]

For no other colony did the new policy of registered vessels have such significance as for La Plata. By virtue of this policy, the emancipation of La Plata from the economic domination of Peru was begun. In December, 1721, a license was signed permitting Salvador García Posse to transmit through Buenos Aires merchandise worth seven hundred thousand pesos as far as Charcas and Chile. In spite of the protests of Lima which became more and more furious, new registered vessels came to Buenos Aires, among them those of Urquiju and Alzaibar (1727) with authorization to

---

[6] B. Mitre, *Comprobaciones históricas* (2 vols. Buenos Aires, 1916), I, 38.

bring in exchange as much as two million pesos worth of goods.[7] La Plata thus entered upon a period unprecedented in its activity of commerce and trade. European goods entered in sufficient quantities to satisfy needs and at prices that appeared improbable. The wealth of the colony was stimulated by the demand for colonial produce.

In 1774, provoked by the concessions made to Lorenzo del Arco for sending a ship of three hundred tons to Buenos Aires the commercial tribunal of Lima sent to the viceroy of Peru a notable document entitled "Consulta y Representación" ("Opinion and Representation") in which they requested the suspension of the clause permitting goods to be allowed to enter the provinces of Peru and Chile, and demanded that merchandise should not be allowed to pass beyond the provinces of Salta and Jujuy, under penalty of confiscation. Evidently, the king did not take the pretensions of Peru seriously, for a little later he granted to Pedro de Arriaga, Roque San Martín and Company permission to despatch a ship of two hundred tons under the same terms as those conceded to Lorenzo del Arco.

Up to the opening of the eighteenth century the official communications of the motherland with its colonies were narrowly restricted. In 1764, Charles III established a maritime mail service; he ordered that one mail packet per month should leave the port of Coruña for North America and that another mail packet should leave every two months for South America. In 1767, the benefits of this reform were extended to Buenos Aires.

By a decree of October 16, 1765, an end was put to the policy of having only one port of clearance from Spain and one port of entry in the Indies. This decree opened the ports of Cadiz, Seville, Alicante, Cartagena, Málaga, Barcelona, Santander, Coruña, and Gijón for trade with Cuba, Santo Domingo, Puerto Rico, Margarita, and Trinidad. This permission completely swept away the absurd restrictions of the monopolistic policy; it left merchants free to choose the port of clearance and the port of entry from the list of authorized ports, and relieved commerce from onerous imposts. In 1768, this permission was extended to include the province of Louisiana as well as Yucatan and Campeche.

Freedom of ports 1765

---

[7] Archivo general de la nación, Hacienda, legajo 1, expediente 12.

At the very time when Charles III conceded these privileges concerning the commercial relations of Spain with the Indies, he also began to frame liberal regulations concerning intercolonial trade. Among these may be mentioned: (1) The royal cédula of 1768 concerning freedom of commerce between the viceroyalties of New Granada and Peru; (2) the authorization of 1774 by which Peru, New Spain, New Granada, and Guatemala could exchange their own products; and (3) the extension to La Plata (1776) of the privileges of reciprocal commerce embodied in the royal cédula of 1774.[8] The permission to trade freely with Buenos Aires was extended on February 2, 1778, because of a report of Viceroy Cevallos who based his views upon the effects of an ordinance dated November 6, 1777, concerning the opening of the port of Buenos Aires to free importation. This ordinance of Cevallos tended to promote interprovincial commerce.

On October 12, 1778, the permission to carry on commerce was made general by the issue of the royal "regulations and tariff for the free commerce of Spain and the Indies" which were embodied in fifty-five articles. By Article IV, thirteen ports in Spain, the Balearic Isles, and the Canary Islands were opened to Spanish-American commerce. By Article V, twenty-four additional ports were opened in America. Articles XVI and XVII grouped Spanish-American ports into major and minor classes. The minor ports were to collect duties ranging from one and one-half per cent upon the value of Spanish products to four per cent upon the value of products of foreign countries; while the major ports were to collect duties ranging from three per cent upon the value of Spanish products to seven per cent upon the value of foreign products. Article XXII stipulated that all goods manufactured in Spain from wool, cotton, hemp, and flax were to be exempt from duties for ten years. In order to stimulate the development of the national merchant marine, article XXXIII provided that the owners of Spanish ships carrying national products exclusively should enjoy a reduction of one third of all the duties, while ships carrying cargoes two-thirds of which consisted of national products were to enjoy a reduction of one-fifth of the imposts.

The results of these regulations were extraordinary and imme-

---

[8] See R. Levene's introduction to vols. V and VI of *Documentos para la historia argentina*.

[margin handwritten note: lower tariffs in minor ports would tend to build their commerce]

diate. With respect to Buenos Aires, in each year of the period from 1792 to 1796—years of the greatest economic prosperity— foreign commerce amounted to 7,212,000 pesos, of which 2,545,000 pesos were imports, and 4,667,000 pesos, exports. Thus there was a favorable balance of trade amounting to about 2,000,000 pesos per annum.[9] Between 1772 and 1776, scarcely thirty-five ships had entered Buenos Aires, while after 1792 the figures were as follows:

Years	Vessels	Exports in Pesos
1792	62	4,511,594
1793	59	3,744,112
1794	62	5,715,009
1795	51	5,134,071
1796	77	5,470,675[10]

The slave trade was carried on from the age of discovery by means of commercial licenses. With respect to Buenos Aires, as early as 1591, permits were granted for the introduction of Negro slaves for a term of ten years. The system known as the asiento, that is, a contract between an individual or a company and the government, was also used. The first asiento was signed in 1595 with Gómez Reynel for a term of nine years. This provided that he should bring 4,250 slaves annually into Spanish-American ports, six hundred of whom were to be brought to La Plata.

On November 24, 1791, permission was granted to carry on the slave traffic with numerous ports. Negro slaves were to be admitted free of duty. In return, vessels could take cargoes of specie and produce upon which they were to pay a duty of six per cent. As the concession to this traffic was made to promote agriculture, in addition to Negroes, vessels were permitted to introduce farm implements. This commerce might be carried on by foreigners, and in such cases the Laws of the Indies prohibiting the entrance of foreigners into Spanish-American ports were annulled.

On March 4, 1795, a royal order was issued regarding commerce with colonies of foreign nations. The French islands, which had been conquered by the English (for England was then allied with Spain), needed meat and flour that could be supplied by Buenos

---

[9] Azara, *op. cit.*, vol. I, table opposite p. 290.

[10] Núm. 5,554, Colección de manuscritos de la Biblioteca Nacional.

Aires. Considering that the exportation of these products would benefit La Plata, the royal order permitted such trade (which was soon extended to all foreign colonies) under the following conditions: (1) colonial products not designed for Spain could be taken from Buenos Aires; (2) while goods and products that were similar to the products of Spain might not be introduced into this port, yet Negroes, money, and certain products (sugar, coffee, and cotton) could be introduced; (3) their importation was to be free of duties.

The third period in the economic history of La Plata ended in 1796, when an event of capital importance for all the colonies took place, namely, the rupture of relations between Spain and England. This was equivalent, so to speak, to a rupture with all nations; for Great Britain exercised undisputed control over the ocean. The resulting interruption of intercourse between Spain and its colonies lasted until 1802, and was destined to create in America unalterable conditions of fact arising from the free commercial and political relations maintained by the colonies with other powers because they could not be taken care of by the motherland.

The royal order concerning trade with neutral powers bears the date 1797. After the declaration of war with England, in order to avoid so far as possible the interruption of commerce with America, numerous merchants had solicited permission to carry on trade "in neutral vessels" from a national or foreign port. The king permitted such expeditions under the following prescribed conditions: (1) these ships could not transport prohibited goods (consequently only Negroes, specie, and produce were allowed); (2) this commerce could be carried on both in national ships and foreign ships from foreign ports but only "on condition that they should return to the ports of Spain"; and (3) they were to pay the same duties as though they sailed from national ports, that is, duties upon importation into Spain, and both import and export duties in America.

This permission failed to produce the results expected; for the condition of returning to Spain was absurd during a time when the Peninsula was almost blockaded, and soon (as commerce was permitted only in a few products) the colonies needed many more imports. From this developed a situation of imperious actuality:

namely, that of allowing the entrance of goods classed as contraband without requiring a return voyage to Spain. Even Spanish
officials proclaimed the necessity of permitting this free trade in
order to alleviate the misery of the colonists.[11]

When peace was signed between Spain and England in 1802,
commercial relations between Spain and its colonies were reëstablished; but in 1805 a new war with England broke out which in
its turn furnished a pretext for the English invasions of La
Plata (1806-1807).

Abnormal years continued. In 1808, the armies of Napoleon
invaded Spain. In 1809, the situation became grave: after 1806,
the budget had large deficits. It was difficult to burden the people
with new imposts or loans. In this state of affairs the culminating
phase of the economic conflict was traced and interpreted in the
Representación de los Hacendados (*Memorial of the Landowners*)
composed by Mariano Moreno.

In August, 1809, two English merchants, J. Dillon and J.
Thwaites, asked Viceroy Cisneros to permit them to sell the goods
carried in their vessels. The viceroy sent a communication to the
cabildo and the tribunal of commerce recommending a study of this
petition. He told them that "the petition and the offer with which
the merchants tried to support it would under other circumstances
justify an emphatic refusal and even the vigorous measures which
the laws of these dominions had provided to prevent them; but
that, at the present time, existing political circumstances impelled
him to suspend such measures." Because of the fact that sufficient
force was lacking to repel the foreign vessels anchored near the
capital, and because opposition to the petition "would mean opening the port to contraband traffic," Viceroy Cisneros was inclined
to admit the goods from English vessels under certain principles
that would make this concession less prejudicial to the commerce
of the motherland. He concluded by proposing the convocation
of a general junta of commerce in which the whole matter might
be discussed and the government notified concerning "what the
majority thought the proper course to follow." [12]

---

[11] R. Levene, *Un precursor del comercio libre en el Plata* (Buenos Aires, 1915),
pp. 19 ff.

[12] *Documentos referentes á la guerra de la independencia y emancipación
política de la República Argentina* (2 vols. Buenos Aires, 1914-17), I, 213.

The syndic of the tribunal of commerce, Gregorio Yáñez, presented a report unfavorable to the petition of the English merchants; but the tribunal favored it on condition that this commerce should conform to certain regulations embodied in fourteen articles. Among other stipulations, these provided that the English should name as their Spanish attorneys persons who had registered in the tribunal of commerce; that there should be prepared tariffs of values at the current wholesale prices and that articles of luxury should be heavily taxed while necessities should be taxed lightly; that, in return, the merchants should load their vessels with cargoes composed in two-thirds of raw hides and the rest in other products of the country. In its decision the cabildo declared "that if it is not an advantage to allow the English any kind of commerce with us, yet at least under the existing circumstances it is a necessary and indispensable evil."

Next, Fernández de Agüero, the attorney of the commercial tribunal of Cadiz, asked that he be allowed to see the report of the proceedings. He then composed his representation. This is a plea in favor of the Spanish commercial monopoly. The argument adduces the decisive prohibition of the Laws of the Indies, and the menace of ruin to the merchant marine and industry of Spain. It contains very judicious, though evidently interested, words, in defense of national industries. "What would become of the unhappy artisan who always merits the protection of an enlightened government? Is it not true that the shoemaker, the blacksmith, the carpenter, and a multitude of other artisans who honorably support many large families by the sweat of their brow would be compelled to shut their stores and to abandon their shops forever? It is a report only too common that a single one of the ships which we can see carries in its cargo nineteen thousand pair of shoes. . . . What a calamity is this, your Excellency, to the guild of shoemakers and to the tanners of every kind of hide or pelt!"

In place of removing the prohibition of commerce with the English, the Cadiz agent proposed that the viceroy should resort to other measures to relieve the pressing needs of the treasury: such as the floating of a loan; the levying of moderate taxes upon the ownership of farm land, and the income from real estate; the reduction of the salaries of civil, ecclesiastical, and military officials, and the establishment of a great lottery.

In order to reply to the arguments formulated by the agent of the commerce of Cadiz—the strength of which was more apparent than real—the landowners and laborers of the eastern and western banks of the Río de la Plata selected Dr. Mariano Moreno as their representative. That moment when Moreno intervened was decisive for the important question under discussion. From his pen there flowed spontaneously his "Memorial" which is a formidable essay directed against the prevailing economic régime.

Below are given a few paragraphs which embody the thought of this plea:

"For more than two years it has been the first concern of this government to formulate measures that will make up the deficit in the treasury; but all the attempts have produced only fatal disillusions. The agent of the commercial tribunal of Cadiz adduces all the projects which have been so often discredited, and adds others that provoke laughter because of their absurdity. . . . These straits will be remedied with dignity when freedom of commerce opens the inexhaustible sources of rapid circulation which importations and their respective returns will then have; when your Excellency is freed from the needs which now afflict and bind you, you can develop to their full extent the beneficent ideas that will make your administration memorable, the motherland will receive large resources, and the country will be happy because it has effective resources that assure its internal and external tranquility. What can restrain your Excellency from making so magnanimous a decision? The need is notorious; it is urgent and will brook no delay. This step is the only measure which can furnish a remedy; two years of continual attempts at a solution should convince your Excellency of the inadequacy of other measures. It is imperative, therefore, that most respectable considerations should be sacrificed for the salvation of the country. . . . There are truths so manifest that it is an offense to reason to try to demonstrate them. Such is the proposition that it is politic for the country to allow the free importation of products which it does not produce, and the exportation of those products which are so plentiful that they are wasted because they have no exit. In vain does private interest, which is often opposed to the public welfare, denounce a system from which it fears loss; in vain will it disguise the motives of its opposition, borrowing words contrary to the intentions that animate it; the force of conviction will prevail despite all its sophisms. . . . Those who believe that an abundance of foreign products is an evil for the country are certainly ignorant of the first principles of the economy of states. Nothing is more beneficial for a province than a great abundance of those goods which it does not produce, for by such goods becoming common the price falls, which results in a cheapness useful to the consumer. To the advantage gained by the introduction of foreign goods there is added a similar advantage to the country through the exportation of its own products. How rapid would be the development of our agriculture, if by the opening of our ports to all exportable fruits, the farmer could count with security upon a lucrative sale. Those persons who now engage timidly in agriculture because of the uncertainty of sales would then labor with the steadfastness inspired by the certainty of profit."

With the conviction and the energy illustrated by the passages cited above, Mariano Moreno pleaded for the freedom of commerce. With the same passion he pleaded for democracy and championed the cause of social equality. He said: "The audacity with which the syndic of the tribunal of commerce in one of his memorials to that tribunal asserts that it is the common people who are anxious that the plan suggested be carried out is not to be tolerated. This is an insult. . . . The most useful, the most distinguished, the most noble part of society directs its protests to your Excellency, and pleads for a cause upon which the stability of the government and the welfare of the country depend. This noble object is intimately linked to national prosperity, and it can prove fatal only to four merchants who fear lest they will lose the profit which they were expecting from clandestine transactions."

The succeeding pages were devoted to a criticism of the various measures which were proposed by Fernández de Agüero in place of free trade, and concluded with these words: "These are the wishes of twenty thousand proprietors whom I represent, and this plan constitutes the only means of establishing with the dignity suitable to the character of your Excellency the principles conducive to our felicity and to the solvency of the treasury."

The value of this brief does not depend solely upon its liberal ideas but upon the fact that its author opposes all the clogs and restrictions proposed by the tribunal of commerce upon a grant of permission to engage in trade.

The *Representación de los Hacendados* (*Memorial of the Landowners*) of Moreno was translated into Portuguese by the great Brazilian economist and jurist, José da Silva Lisboa, and was published in Rio de Janeiro in 1810. Not satisfied merely by a translation of the essay of Moreno, Silva Lisboa supplemented it by other related studies, such as those regarding the commerce of Spain with its colonies in time of war, and reflections concerning freedom of trade in Brazil. Besides, the translation was accompanied by a laudatory comment in the preface by Silva Lisboa, who characterized the author of the *Memorial of the Landowners* as "the wise advocate of the farmers and proprietors of La Plata who was endowed with a vigorous mentality and was well versed in political economy." The important fact that ought to stand out is as follows: Silva Lisboa published the treatise of Moreno in Rio de Janeiro in order to controvert the Portuguese monopolists who were trying to convince the prince regent, whose capital was at Rio de Janeiro, that it was necessary to revoke the commercial privileges which had been conceded.[13]

After other pleas and briefs had been annexed to the proceedings which we are studying, on November 6, 1809, a general junta presided over by Viceroy Cisneros decided to admit to trade "any friendly, neutral or national ship proceeding from foreign ports with a cargo of goods and produce." A regulation composed of fifteen articles fixed the duties which were to be paid and the formalities to be observed.[14] That is to say, permission to trade with

---

[13] R. Levene, "La traducción y publicación portuguesa de 1810 de la 'Representación de los hacendados de Moreno,' " *Nosotros* (Buenos Aires, 1918), XXIX, 498-525.

[14] D. L. Molinari, *La "representación de los hacendados" de Mariano Moreno; su ninguna influencia en la vida económica del pais y en los sucesos de Mayo de 1810* (Buenos Aires, 1914), pp. 147-48, and notes; R. Levene, *Ensayo histórico sobre la revolución de Mayo y Mariano Moreno* ("Estudios editados por la facultad de derecho y ciencias sociales de la Universidad de Buenos Aires," vols. VIII and IX, 2 vols. Buenos Aires, 1920-31), I, 247-50.

the English was granted, but it was hampered because of the clogs and restrictions adopted in accordance with the proposals of the tribunal of commerce. The great merit of Mariano Moreno consists in the fact that in 1810 he swept away all restraints upon freedom of commerce.

CHAPTER XIV

THE ECONOMIC LIFE OF LA PLATA

UNDER THIS general title we include a study and explanation of the economic facts concerning La Plata, in particular during the eighteenth century. We shall present a brief summary of the condition of agriculture, mining, the cattle-raising industry, and other industries and conclude with some observations in respect to the money of this era.

The first animals left by Spanish explorers in La Plata multiplied prodigiously. They spread by thousands throughout the land. From the beginning until past the middle of the eighteenth century, the pampas of La Plata, as far as the Río Negro, were so covered by wild cattle that not being restrained they extended to Chile, Mendoza, Córdoba, and Santa Fe. Of the livestock products only the hides were utilized. Contemporaneously with the policy of commerce in registered vessels, which was begun in the eighteenth century, a very large exportation of hides took place so that at the time the viceroyalty of La Plata was created the cattle-raising industry was in danger of dying out. Between 1770 and 1775, the cabildo of Buenos Aires had urged the governor to guard against the abuse that had been introduced of killing cows, heifers, and young bulls, an abuse which in large part was a result of rounding up the cattle and the constant slaughtering of wild animals. "Each rancher reported to the authorities the number of head of cattle that he had lost and obtained a license to breed according to this number in unappropriated lands or in those that were adjacent to his establishment." [1]

Up to the date (1778) when the regulation concerning free commerce was issued, the annual exportation of hides may be calculated at 150,000; after that date, it increased rapidly until it reached 800,000 and after the peace of Paris in 1783 (which terminated the war with England), the number of hides annually exported aggregated 1,400,000. [2]

---

[1] R. Pillado, *El comercio de carnes en la República Argentina* (Buenos Aires, 1909); J. A. Pillado, *Origenes del ganado argentino* (Buenos Aires, 1909), p. 11.

[2] On the pastoral industry, see further, P. Ezcurra, "Ganadería y Agricultura," *La Nación, 1810—25 de Mayo—1910* (Buenos Aires, 1910), pp. 265-66.—W.S.R.

Proposals to promote the salting of meat in the provinces of La Plata date from 1776. In that year Minister José Gálvez wrote Governor Vértiz y Salcedo of Buenos Aires, and submitted to his judgment a project for the development of this industry. The governor assembled a cabildo abierto, and informed it that these provinces could supply annually five thousand tons of salt meat, but this required that barrels with iron hoops be imported from Spain and that warehouses be erected in the city. The first attempts produced excellent results. The salting was performed in the following manner: when the animal was slaughtered it was hung up in the ordinary way and then cut up into convenient pieces for salting and packing in barrels. The pieces of meat were placed in brine, in cases composed of wood or other material where they were left for at least a month. The meat was then packed in barrels holding from two hundred to two hundred and fifty pounds each, and covered with salt, the precaution being taken to leave some openings stopped with corks that could easily be removed in order to refill the barrel whenever any leakage was observed.[3] Viceroy Loreto promoted this industry with special care. In the first place its importance depended upon the price of salt. During the seventeenth century that price had fluctuated between ten and fifteen pesos per fanega. Loreto stimulated regular expeditions to Salinas Grandes, to the southwest of Buenos Aires, thus causing a fall in the price of salt amounting to five pesos per fanega. Then numerous factories for salting meat began to be established by private persons. The meat was exported to Spain and to Havana. However, there was need of new master coopers and meat salters. This condition and the commercial interruptions and isolations from which the colony suffered, because of the wars in which Spain became involved, checked the initial impulse that had been given to this industry.

In 1794, the landowners of Buenos Aires and Montevideo presented a memorial to Minister Gardoqui concerning the means of promoting the industry of salting meat. The ranchers stated that on the average 600,000 head of cattle were annually slaughtered in La Plata. Buenos Aires, Montevideo, Santa Fe, Corrientes; and the mission reductions consumed the meat of 150,000 beeves.

---

[3] Archivo general de la nación, Reales ordenes, 1778.

Thus there were left for salting, 450,000 head. In the belief that each beeve produces 150 pounds of jerked beef or two barrels and a half of salt meat, and considering that each barrel would hold from 175 to 200 pounds, it is seen that some 390 vessels of from 250 to 300 tons could be annually laden with the meat, tallow, hair, and horns from 450,000 head of cattle. This estimate does not include the hides that would amount in value to about 8,000,000 pesos. The ranchers proposed that the salt meat could be sent to Africa and also to Asia. Further, they proposed that all the other products of La Plata, including horse hair, hog's bristles, butter, cheese, tongues, mutton, tallow, beef suet, and the hides of such animals as dogs, cattle, sheep, viscachas, and nutrias,[4] should also be exported. In this memorial some economic ideas of importance were explained and the optimistic and flattering declaration was made "that this is the richest country in the world." [5]

Colonial agriculture did not attain the importance of the pastoral industry; still it was not so backward as has been ordinarily supposed. In 1788, were issued the first royal orders by which the right to export wheat to Spain was granted. But this trade was immediately interrupted because of the failure of Francisco Ximenez de Mesa, the superintendent of the customhouse of Buenos Aires, who dragged down with him one of the concessionaries. Other royal cédulas, like that of 1791, concerning the slave trade by admitting agricultural implements and Negroes for farm labor, promoted the development of agriculture; but there was lacking the permission for free exportation which by stabilizing the prices of products would promote their cultivation.

This commerce was hampered by the action of the cabildo, an institution which believed it was promoting the interests of the city by preventing the exportation of grain in order to supply it with cheap bread. The cabildo was animated by sane intentions. It did not systematically oppose the free exportation of grain, but did so only when the farmers combined with the bakers to fix prices arbitrarily.

---

[4] The "viscachas" (vizcachas) and the "nutrias" are small animals resembling rabbits.—W. S. R.

[5] Gutiérrez, "Memorial al ministro D. Diego Gardoqui para los hacendados de Buenos Aires y Montevideo en el año 1794," *Le Revista de Buenos Aires* (Buenos Aires, 1866), X, 17.

In 1793, the farmers of Buenos Aires asked the king not to prevent the exportation of their products. "Who doubts, sir," they said, "that farming land is the source of wealth? The conditions prevailing in this country tend to cause this: its location in a temperate climate, the good quality of its lands which raise good crops without the use of fertilizers; the boundless territory which it has for cultivation; the disposition of the country people to cultivate wheat and legumes, even without other hope than the market afforded by the consumption of this city; and as this is not a manufacturing country its people are prevented from following any other occupation, nor do they have any other property than the products of the soil. Although they are in the midst of such opportunities as we have indicated, the farmers of these extensive plains are in a state of the greatest poverty and depression because they have no market for their products on account of the lack of commerce and exportation." [6]

The farmers stated that such was the depression in agriculture that when the expedition of Cevallos arrived in 1777, because of the fear that the normal sowings would not yield enough harvest, one thousand tons of flour were brought from the neighboring colony. The same thing happened in 1781 on the occasion of the war with England in anticipation of an attack by the English squadron. Following the example of England, the farmers proposed free trade, whenever the price of a fanega of wheat in the public market reached a certain figure which they set at thirty-two reals. By this policy, which considered the needs of foreign markets, they sought to prevent a fall in the price of a fanega of wheat when there was an excess of production.

In 1798, the farmers sent another representation to the cabildo, based upon the same principles as that of 1793. These were very trying times for the colony. After the middle of 1796, because of the war with England, misery spread throughout the entire viceroyalty. The leading alcalde of the capital supported the petition of the farmers and proposed that free trade should be declared, but that the price of a fanega of wheat should never exceed four pesos (thirty-two reals). The dean of the municipal magistrates, Gregorio Ramos Mejía, opposed this and expressed his opinion

---

[6] V. G. Quesada, "Representación al Rey de los labradores de Buenos Aires (1793)," *La Revista de Buenos Aires* (Buenos Aires, 1868), XVII, 174.

in an extensive plea. He maintained that liberty in setting the price would benefit only the sellers who would speculate in order to secure a high price from the consumers. He estimated that there was only an excess of about 24,000 fanegas of wheat, and lost sight of the fact that freedom of commerce would induce a larger production. With only the vote of Ramos Mejía in opposition, the cabildo forwarded the petition to the viceroy, at a juncture when the superintendent of the custom house and the commercial tribunal were meditating upon the need of rescuing the colony from the miserable situation in which it was placed by opening the port of Buenos Aires to a free trade not only in grain but also in all kinds of goods.

At the instance of the king, Viceroy Cevallos had promoted the cultivation of hemp and flax, in order that the product could be transported to Spain as raw material free of duty where it was needed for the manufacture of linen, canvas, and cordage. In his position as secretary of the commercial tribunal of Buenos Aires, Manuel Belgrano had furnished all the necessary facilities to promote the cultivation of these crops, not only in order to supply the necessities of the motherland, but particularly to furnish occupation to many people who were without work. Belgrano developed this topic in his memoir of the year 1797. He said that hemp and flax necessitated several operations of the farmer, such as sowing, reaping, and retting, and also of women, such as combing and spinning. In this connection, he devoted some interesting pages to the need of incorporating women into the economic life of society. In fact the feminine sex, especially in the capital city, did not engage in any industry and was exposed to misery and illness.

Despite its name, the colony of La Plata did not possess the mineral wealth of other Spanish-American colonies. This was an economic fact of prime importance which was not without influence on its social life. As the historian Mitre pertinently observes: "The colonization of La Plata was peculiar in that it was the only society in South America that did not owe its establishment, its formation, and its gradual development to the lure of the precious metals, even though this was the incentive that attracted colonists. . . . Thus, Argentine colonization was born and developed in the midst of hunger and misery; it asked subsistence from mother earth; it fortified itself in the midst of painful sufferings, and afforded the only example in South America of a society that was the offspring of reproductive labor." [7]

Gold mines existed in Maldonado, Punta de San Luis, and Jachal; silver mines in Mendoza; copper mines in Córdoba, and quicksilver in the Guaraní mission district. But none of these districts mentioned yielded minerals of importance. The richest mine was the one at Potosí. It was discovered in January, 1546; and a numerous population soon clustered around it. This population was divided into "factions of Andalusians and Basques" whose struggle might pass for civil wars similar to those of Marius and Sulla, in a smaller but not less bloody theater.[8] During the second half of the eighteenth century the riches of the hill of Potosí began to diminish because of the low grade of the ores extracted. It produced from 250,000 to 300,000 marks of silver of eight ounces each which were sold in the bank of exchange at seven and seven and one-half pesos apiece. Each mark of silver yielded to the royal treasury about a peso because of the king's tenth and other taxes.

Throughout Spanish America, industrial activity was slight, but it increased somewhat during the seventeenth century, as a consequence, in the first instance, of the decline of Spanish industry and poor communications. The manufacturing activities of Mexico and Peru were especially noteworthy. Solórzano says of the textiles made in many places "that they could almost be compared with the best that were brought from Spain at so great an expense." The first industries of La Plata also developed during the seventeenth century—the period of provincial isolation.

The cultivation of the vine had gained such importance that the wine sufficed for home consumption. There were vineyards in Mendoza, San Juan, La Rioja, and Catamarca. The king had prohibited viticulture in America in order to prevent competition with wines produced in the Peninsula; but, despite this prohibition, freedom of cultivation existed in fact. The people of San Juan sold wine in Buenos Aires at thirty-six pesos per barrel; one must deduct from this, however, about fourteen to sixteen pesos for freight. In 1802 there were sent from San Juan to Buenos Aires 9,263 barrels of ordinary spirits; 430 barrels were taken to Salta in the same year, and to Córdoba 518 barrels.

---

[7] Mitre, *Historia de Belgrano*, I, 6-7.

[8] Archivo general de la nación, Legajo Potosí, 1784-1788.

The ruin of this wine industry in San Juan and in the rest of La Plata began with the active commercial intercourse occasioned by the regulations of 1778. The people of San Juan made known this fact in 1803 by reporting the ruined condition of viticulture which could not compete with the foreign liquors because of the excessive cost of freight.

In Córdoba, Catamarca, and Corrientes, manufactures of various kinds were carried on, such as linens, woolen cloth, ponchos, and blankets. The deputy of the tribunal of commerce of Catamarca lauded the skill of the women who were engaged in the manufacture of linens, and said "there is neither a house nor a ranch in this entire district that does not have one or two looms with one spindle for carding and another for spinning cotton." [9] "Corrientes was noted for another trait: it was the manufacturing center, par excellence, for the tackle and spars that supplied the entire viceroyalty. After the English invasions this local industry, as well as another of the more important ones, disappeared forever." [10]

In Tucumán, rice was cultivated but at the opening of the nineteenth century, when an active commerce with Brazil began, the rice of Tucumán could not compete with that imported from Rio de Janeiro. The abundance of excellent wood in Tucumán encouraged its inhabitants to construct good carts, which were not so large as those made by the people of Mendoza. In Upper Peru, the city of Cochabamba consumed every year in its looms from 750,000 to 1,000,000 pounds of cotton. This industry furnished employment to many people.

Because of their geographic position, Paraguay and Corrientes used their timber in the construction of vessels. Their futtock timbers were of carob wood, covered with *lapacho* wood; and faced with red *timbó*. They were equipped with rigging, sails, and iron fittings. In 1801, five frigates, eight brigantines, and four smacks were built in the shipyards of Paraguay, without including sloops and other smaller craft.

In describing the pastoral industry we have said that the only trade originally resulting from that resource was the exportation of hides. In order to prevent the stagnation of so precious a source

---

[9] *Ibid.*, Consulado, Catamarca, Santiago del Estero, núm. 13.

[10] C. L. Fregeiro, "Resumen histórico," *Segundo censo do la República Argentina*, p. 624.

of wealth, near the close of the eighteenth century the industry of salting meat was started, which we have elsewhere considered.

The tanning industry also began to prosper. Alexander Durand asked permission from the tribunal of commerce to bring as many as six master tanners from the United States with the tools necessary for the establishment of a tannery in Buenos Aires for the purpose of manufacturing sole-leather, calfskin, and tanned leather of every sort. The tribunal granted the petition. A year later, its secretary, Manuel Belgrano, devoted his annual report to praise of the tanning industry. He urged that foreign master tanners should be secured, or, better still, that six or eight young men should be given financial allowances by the tribunal of commerce in order that they might visit those European countries where hides were most expertly tanned for the purpose of learning the theory and practice of the industry.

The trades were socially despised by the Spaniards who landed in America. Thus it was that they were for the most part carried on by mestizos or by foreigners. Eventually, silversmiths constituted in Buenos Aires a corporation with many members. In other parts of Spanish America, the guild of silversmiths amassed considerable wealth, because of the large number of mines. The industrial growth of the art of the silversmith was also a result of the religious sentiment of the age.

In Buenos Aires, the establishment of the guild of silversmiths dates from the year 1788, at which time Intendant General Paula Sanz issued an ordinance of organization providing that no person might open a shop and set up a show-case "unless he could show that he had served five years as an apprentice and two more years as an artisan under a skilled master who at the right time gave him proper certification." Any person violating this ordinance was to be punished by the confiscation of all his materials and tools. As a result of this action, the cabildo made a list of the silversmiths who had opened shops—forty-seven in all, a total showing the importance attained by this industry. Even more suggestive is the distribution by nationalities: twenty-five were creoles, fifteen, Portuguese, and seven, Spaniards. These figures show that the foreigners and creoles engaged in this industry far outnumbered the Spaniards.

The shoemaker's guild had more than fifteen years of history.

In 1788, the master shoemakers complained of the condition of their trade; they reasoned that their apprentices needed exact information concerning the use of their tools, their materials, the manner of preparing them, and "the proper way to do their stitching," all these being indispensable to the comfort of those persons who wear shoes, because "many persons, without being more than botchers open shops, seek for workmen, engage apprentices, and sell their shoes to the public." In view of these circumstances they proposed to organize a guild, after the fashion of the silversmiths, which should provide for an apprenticeship of four years, two years' service as a workman, and an examination.[11]

The proceedings during the formation of this guild were very noisy. Foreigners, who constituted a considerable number, protested because they had been excluded from the management of the guild. Negroes and mulattoes, who were master shoemakers, were also excluded. Cornelio Saavedra, who was then acting as syndic of the cabildo of Buenos Aires, wrote a notable opinion in which he advised the superior authorities not to permit the formation of such a guild. In his report, Saavedra said of the guilds "that far from being useful and necessary, they should be considered prejudicial to the general welfare, because they weakened the rights of men, increased the misery of the poor, encumbered industry, were repugnant to the inhabitants, and caused many other disadvantages. He opposed the guild, in the name of the freedom of labor, and affirmed that "the right to work is the most sacred and indestructible privilege known to humankind." As has been shown, attempts at guild organization in La Plata before the outbreak of the revolution against Spain had been frustrated.

Up to the end of the sixteenth century, metallic money was almost completely lacking in La Plata. The price of goods was reckoned in money, but it was translated into local values. A yard of linen was commonly worth two reals, that is, sixty-eight maravedís. In 1574, the cabildo of Córdoba decided upon a kind of currency and its value by resolving that goats and horseshoes should be used as media of exchange. A goat was to be worth one peso, while a horseshoe was to be worth a peso and a half. Later, it was agreed that wool, tallow, rams, and ewes should also serve as cur-

[11] R. Levene, "Los gremios durante la época colonial," *Anales de la facultad de derecho y ciencias sociales* (Buenos Aires, 1916), XVI, 137-51.

rency. As is seen, the usual currency consisted of products of the soil, which served instead of metallic money, because they were media of exchange and measures of all values. The wedge of iron, which was also used, was soon discarded because of the fluctuations in its value.

In Paraguay, the media of exchange were yerba mate and tobacco. Twenty-five pounds of mate were worth sixteen ounces of silver, or two *"pesos huecos,"* or twelve reals (on the basis that every peso hueco was worth six reals). Tobacco used as money was leaf tobacco tied in bundles which were fastened with Paraguayan broom, and not that which had been stripped or powdered. The value of the tobacco was double that of yerba mate; twenty-five pounds of it were worth four pesos.[12]

The scarcity of regular currency lasted for a long time. In October, 1618, because of the scarcity of money, King Philip II declared that, with respect to the payment of imposts and tributes, the money of the country would be considered as specie, "and that anything valued at one peso in that medium should by a just and common estimate be worth six reals in silver." According to this declaration, the medium of exchange of La Plata suffered a devalorization with respect to its equivalent in metallic money. The king ordained in fact that the peso which represented eight reals in silver throughout Spanish America, should be reduced by one fourth in value in La Plata, making it worth six reals.[13] Thus there came into existence the peso hueco, which was worth two reals less than the "peso fuerte," the current unit of value.

The metallic coins circulating in Spanish America were the same as those of Spain. The gold coins consisted of the doubloon of eight, worth sixteen pesos fuertes; the doubloon of four, worth eight pesos; the gold doubloon, worth four pesos, and the escudo, worth two pesos.

The silver coins consisted of the peso worth eight reals, and the half-peso worth four reals. The real was valued at thirty-four maravedís. The ducat—merely a nominal coin—was worth eleven reals plus one maravedí. In addition, there were minor coins made of copper and silver alloy. It was during the reign of Alfonso XI

---

[12] Levene, *La moneda colonial del Plata,* p. 17.

[13] *Recopilación de leyes de los reinos de las Indias,* libro IV, título XXIV, ley VII.

(1312-1350) that the real was minted—a silver coin which was destined to figure permanently in the monetary régime of Spain and the Indies. After the real came into circulation, no other coin of Castile was more used. It may even be asserted that the value of all the other coins was estimated in relation to the value of the real.

The first pesos fuertes coined in Spanish America seem to have been struck off during the reign of Philip II in the mints of Mexico and Potosí.[14] Because of the extensive counterfeiting of this coin in America in the middle of the seventeenth century, orders were given that a new peso should be minted with a device that bore on one side the arms of León and Castile, and on the other side the columns of Hercules with the legend "plus ultra" in the middle. In order to demonstrate their genuineness, these coins were also to be inscribed with the year, the name of the mint, and that of the assayer. These pesos constituted the so-called columnar money.

A mint existed at Potosí, which became dependent upon Buenos Aires after the creation of the viceroyalty of La Plata. The mint of Potosí became notorious because of the bad workmanship of its coins, not only on account of their imperfect technique but also on account of rascality practiced in their manufacture. Much money was made out of silver alloy *(plata sencilla)*, that is, in minting the coins, a much less quantity of the noble metal was used than was necessary. With the quantity of silver that was required to coin a peso of eight reals, more than ten pesos were minted and even as many as fourteen. Almost all the coins that circulated in the city of Buenos Aires in the middle of the eighteenth century were composed of silver alloy.

There were also in circulation other silver coins of irregular weight styled macuquino money,[15] which were accepted at their nominal value in domestic transactions. The king had ordered that these cut macuquino coins should be withdrawn from circulation and brought to the mints where they should be re-coined. But such was the scarcity of money in La Plata, that the macuquino money

---

[14] A Peruvian writer states that rude mints were established at Cuzco in 1534, at Lima in 1572, and at Potosí in 1572 where tokens and coins were minted. Upon the establishment of the mint at Potosí, pesos fuertes were coined there. See Alejandro Garland, *Estudio económico sobre los medios circulantes usados en el Perú* (Lima, 1908), pp. 18-20.—W. S. R.

[15] Coins with the milled edges cut away.—W. S. R.

continued to circulate until the middle of the nineteenth century, notwithstanding divers royal provisions ordering its withdrawal.

We have said that the money in circulation was almost all "*sencillo*" or macuquino money. The money made of "*plata doble*"— or that which conformed to the weight established by law—was sent to Spain. Accordingly, the scarcity of this standard silver (plata doble) caused it to appreciate greatly so that, after the issuance of an ordinance by Vértiz y Salcedo, the money thus minted enjoyed a premium of three per cent. This premium had as its further object the establishment of a fund from the excess value for the payment of soldiers. A thousand pesos of salary in La Plata were thus worth only 970 pesos.

A similar phenomenon occurred with respect to the gold money. The king arranged that the salaries of government employees should be paid in silver money, and that the surplus of the total revenues should be sent to Spain in gold specie. This circumstance stimulated an excessive appreciation in this kind of money. By the above-cited decree of Vértiz y Salcedo the premium was fixed at eight per cent.

From the viewpoint both of the quantity and of the quality of money, the colonial period in the history of La Plata was marked by an undoubted monetary poverty. This is an essential factor in our financial history; it is an antecedent which explains the precarious character of the circulating medium during that entire period of our national life which extends up to the time of our economic organization.

CHAPTER XV

THE ROYAL TREASURY

THE OFFICIALS who were intrusted with the collection of the revenues and the despatch of the treasures of the Indies to Spain were royal functionaries. The Laws of the Indies (law LXVI, of book VIII, title IV) defined their duties. They were to keep a general account of incomes and expenditures, which should contain a statement of the revenues received by the monarch with an explanation of the reasons therefor. The royal officials were also administrative judges who could compel debtors to pay their tribute by judicial decisions. From the beginning of the eighteenth century, tribunals of the exchequer were established (in Lima, Mexico, and Bogotá), which were also called auditorships, that heard appeals in all cases concerning royal officials.

In 1767, the general instructions of the auditing office of the Indies were issued providing for the establishment of the tribunal of the superior office of audit of accounts for the provinces of La Plata, Paraguay, and Tucumán by virtue of which the treasuries of those provinces were to cease making reports to the tribunal at Lima, and were thenceforth to render account to the superior auditing office established in Buenos Aires.[1]

Imposts were grouped in three classes. The first class was that of the royal treasury, the taxes of which had a fixed purpose, namely, to meet the salaries of officials of the political, military, and ecclesiastical administration. The second class, or that of particular revenues, included those imposts which had diverse and special uses. The third class, or that of distinct branches, included those imposts in the expenditure of which the king had no share. Belonging to the first class were such imposts as tenths of silver, taxes on sales of lands and on retail stores for the sale of liquors, cigars, and so on, tributes, import and export duties, and taxes on sales and exchanges. To the second category belonged ecclesiastical allowances (*mesadas*), such revenues as those arising from

---

[1] Archivo general de la nación, instrucciones y reglamentos, libro 1, núms. 2, 3, and 4.

vacant benefices of a major and minor character, and fines imposed by courts of justice that were due to the royal treasury. The third class included ecclesiastical half-annats, excise duties, the military pension fund, and so on.

The tenths of the products of the silver mines constituted one of the oldest taxes collected at the mines. At the beginning, a fifth was paid free of all costs, but in the first half of the eighteenth century, this was reduced to a tenth.

Tributes were collected only from the Indians, who paid them in kind. Their quota varied, according to the condition of the particular province. A large part of this revenue was destined for such purposes as the construction of churches and the salaries of teachers, while the balance went to the royal treasury. In La Plata the tributes amounted to eight, nine, or ten pesos per capita.

The *almojarifazgo* was a customs duty which was laid upon the export of goods and products of Spain and upon their importation into the colonies. Up to the end of the seventeenth century it amounted to 10 per cent. In the regulation of free commerce (1778) the almojarifazgo was put at 7 per cent for foreign goods and 3 per cent for national products in the major ports. In the minor ports the rate was respectively 4 per cent and 4½ per cent. Buenos Aires was one of the major ports.

The *alcabala* was the tax levied upon every business transaction, purchase, sale, or donation. At the end of the sixteenth century 2 per cent was collected in this manner. Later the rate was increased by 2 per cent and by 1776 it was increased to 6 per cent.

The ecclesiastical allowance was the tax that ecclesiastics paid to his Majesty. It consisted in the contribution of a month's income out of the annual income of the holder of a benefice. The incomes arising from the greater vacancies were the revenues of the bishoprics and archbishoprics that fell vacant because of promotions or deaths, and pending the appointment of a successor. The incomes arising from minor, vacant benefices referred to the unallotted revenues of the dignities and prebends of the church. Fines were imposed by the tribunals of justice as penalties for infractions of laws in force.

The ecclesiastical half-annats were the duties that the king could levy every six months upon all ecclesiastics holding benefices. They were established because of the large sums which the royal treasury had to spend in the propagation of the Roman Catholic faith. These clerics who paid the half-annats did not have to pay the ecclesiastical allowance. Parish priests could pay the allowance in order to be relieved from the half annats.

The impost of the *sisa,* or tax for fortifications, was established in Buenos Aires and Santa Fe upon certain articles (wine, spirits, Paraguayan yerba mate, and leaf tobacco), to furnish revenues for the maintenance of fortifications. This tax was levied in most of the cities.

The *propios* and *arbitrios* were resources employed by the cities to meet their ordinary expenses. They were ordinarily employed in paying the salaries of alguacils, macebearers, and clerks, in meeting the expenses of the religious feasts of Corpus Christi and San Martín which were celebrated with great solemnity, and the expenses due to the ceremonies of taking the oath of allegiance to a new sovereign.

In the seventeenth century, the resources of the city of Buenos Aires were reduced to the income from licenses of four retail stores for the sale of liquors, cigars, and so on, each paying twenty pesos apiece, the income from a tax of a real upon each bottle of wine that entered the city and the anchorage dues of the vessels arriving in that port. The total amount of propios and arbitrios for a year did not exceed four hundred pesos. These resources were so meager that the city made known to the king that merely in the purchase of wax for religious festivals it annually spent about five hundred pesos.[2] As indicated, these municipal revenues were very modest in their origins; but they increased so markedly with the development of the population and the cities that they became the economic basis of the political autonomy of the municipalities.

An approximate estimate of the annual revenues from all the imposts in the Indies might reach nine million pesos—a sum much less than the fabulous amount indicated by some authors. The viceroyalty of New Spain had an income of from five to six million

---

[2] V. G. Quesada, ed., "Documentos para servir á la historia, rentas municipales, 1708-1768," *La Revista de Buenos Aires* (Buenos Aires, 1870), XXI, 7-8. [Propios and arbitrios furnished revenues for the support of Spanish-American towns and cities in colonial times. Propios were composed of real properties owned by a local community. Arbitrios were excise duties levied by a municipality on goods or products brought within its limits.—W. S. R.]

pesos; Peru, one million; Buenos Aires, from six to seven hundred thousand pesos; New Granada, from four to five hundred thousand; and the remaining colonies scarcely produced what was needed to cover the expenses of administration.

The period of the greatest financial and commercial prosperity in La Plata was the five years from 1790 to 1794. The total of all revenues accruing to the royal treasury, special and distinct, amounted to 20,227,258 pesos; and the total expenses of the royal treasury, for war, and for political and ecclesiastical administration, came to 19,446,524 pesos.[3] If one should add to the difference between these amounts the income from the tobacco monopoly, the annual surplus during the five-year period under consideration would not exceed three hundred thousand pesos.

[3] V. G. Quesada, "Noticias sobre el gobierno del virrey Arredondo," *La Revista de Buenos Aires* (Buenos Aires, 1869), XVIII, 170 ff.

CHAPTER XVI

ECONOMIC INSTITUTIONS

THE COLONIAL institutions of La Plata may be classified as economic, political, judicial, ecclesiastical, and administrative, according to their dominant functions. Each of the colonial institutions performed at the same time functions of a diverse character; but each one had in its charge certain specific objects which may be classed as economic, political, judicial, or otherwise. Among the chief economic institutions located in America may be mentioned the custom-house, the mint, the intendancies, and the tribunal of commerce.

After the viceroyalty of La Plata was created and the port of Buenos Aires was opened to direct and free commerce with numerous ports of the peninsula, it became imperatively necessary to organize an administrative institution that would take care of the collection of the revenue. In fact, on July 25, 1778, the king established the custom house of Buenos Aires. By the same royal cédula he appointed Francisco Ximenez Mesa as its first superintendent.

From its very beginnings, the custom-house had consultative functions of importance. It was not simply a fiscal collecting office. It was an institution of the treasury and had a decisive influence upon the thought and action of the intendants general and the viceroys. Not a single matter of a commercial or financial nature was decided without hearing the views of the administrator of the custom-house. This important rôle is explained when one realizes that the customs revenues served to cover a large part of the expenses of colonial administration.

In the year 1796, Ángel Izquierdo took charge of the administration of the custom house. He assumed his duties at a moment pregnant for the future of the Spanish-American colonies. That year was only half over when the economic situation began to get worse. Spain was at war with England, a condition that lasted until 1802. During that period, the Spanish-American colonies suffered a great scarcity of European goods, while they were not able to export their own products. A severe crisis occurred. The prices of foreign products tripled in value. The exports, which had amounted to 5,470,675 pesos in 1796, declined to 334,708 pesos in 1797.

In such a delicate situation the cabildo presented a memorial to the viceroy soliciting permission to export produce and to import merchandise in neutral vessels. Viceroy Olaguer Feliú showed the memorial to the administrator of the customs. His report is a notable document. Izquierdo asserted that "it is advisable to open and extend the commerce of America in order that it may be possible to carry it on by means of neutral vessels by transporting the products of these colonies to other Spanish colonies or to those foreign ports whither the merchant may send them."[1] He accordingly urged the need of opening the port of Buenos Aires to free commerce.

In another of his valuable reports, Izquierdo said: "When great numbers of ships are tied up at the wharves, accumulating as much expense as they are worth, and entirely unable to procure supplies necessary for their preservation; when bumper crops that farmers produce go to waste and do not bring in enough to meet their needs; when merchants have no business and when mercantile transactions bring no profit; then commerce will commit the crime of placing itself outside the law, for our lawgivers have had nothing to say about unforeseen cases, when international justice and nature itself cry out and cannot support the law." As a result of this intervention of Ángel Izquierdo the disembarkation of foreign goods, transported in foreign vessels, was allowed in the ports of Montevideo and Buenos Aires.

Until 1777, the customs revenues of Buenos Aires had not exceeded twenty thousand pesos per annum. In 1778, on the occasion of the opening of the port of Buenos Aires, the customs revenues amounted to 53,974 pesos. During the years from 1791 to 1795, this increasing prosperity continued and produced an average revenue of 400,000 pesos. At the end of 1796 began the critical period mentioned above. In 1798, the custom-house did not collect over 100,000 pesos. After 1802, the revenue increased no-

---

[1] Colección de manuscritos de la Biblioteca Nacional, manuscript no. 5954. The attitude of the administrator of the customs is further shown in Levene, *Un precursor del comercio libre en el Plata.*

tably; it reached 1,000,000 pesos in 1804 and 1805. The English invasions (1806-1807), and that of Napoleon into Spain (1808), interrupted commerce with the colonies and suspended all the customs revenues. It was necessary to create new taxes and extraordinary imposts in order to meet the expenses of the budget. This was the situation admirably described by Mariano Moreno in the *Representación de los Hacendados* (*Memorial of the Landowners*). Thus the solution of the problem was found by opening the port of Buenos Aires to free trade with the English.

The first mint founded in America was at the city of Mexico. Later, others were established at Potosí, Lima, and elsewhere. The mints acquired the metal necessary for their operations. At the end of the sixteenth century the viceroy of Peru arranged to receive offers for the disposal of silver by public contract. This system continued up to the middle of the eighteenth century, when a company was organized among the producers of quicksilver who worked mines and reduction plants. Later a bank for purchase by barter was organized which operated until it was incorporated in the crown in 1779.

After 1777, the mint of Potosí acquired annually about 2,000 ingots of silver of various weights and sizes. The new ordinances provided that the highest price which could be paid for ingots of legal standard (286 grains) was 7 pesos and 4 reals. Wrought silver or silver plate was received, but purchased at a lower rate, namely, 6 pesos and 4 reals per ingot, because of the alloy that they contained. In these operations the bank for purchase by barter was using 70,000 pesos every week. For the management of this bank, and the performance of its functions there were a superintendent, a director, two smelters, an accountant, a treasurer, and other officers. The superintendent of the mint was also superintendent of the bank. He had special jurisdiction over all the governmental, economic, and judicial interests of the bank, to the exclusion of the authority of the audiencias and other tribunals and with the right of appeal to the superior board of the royal treasury of Buenos Aires. This jurisdiction was concerned with matters pertaining directly or indirectly to the business of the bank or of the mint, but in all other matters the employees of the mint and of the bank were subject to the ordinary judges.

The office of director was of great importance: his principal duty was the purchase or exchange of silver. He was responsible with his property for all the damages that he might cause to the bank or to other parties in the regulation of prices and also for the profit resulting from the transaction. The treasury could make neither payment nor collection in transactions in which the accountant had not participated and inspected the accounts. The ordinance provided that "the porter must be of suitable age and have the necessary qualifications for the care of the mint, the door of which he has to tend."

The creation of the viceroyalty of La Plata made necessary a new internal organization, both political and economic. By that step four important provinces had been segregated from the viceroyalty of Peru, namely, Charcas (in which was located the famous University of Chuquisaca), the archbishopric of La Plata (with an influential clergy), Potosí (a commercial and mining center), and La Paz. From the captaincy general of Chile had been separated the province of Cuyo with a highly developed wine industry. The governments of Buenos Aires, Tucumán, and Paraguay, with the provinces segregated from Chile and from the viceroyalty of Peru, composed the extensive viceroyalty of the Río de la Plata. Its organization was regulated in 1782 by the "royal ordinance for the instruction and establishment of the intendant of the army and of the provinces."

Two conditions were mainly responsible for the establishment of intendancies in La Plata: (1) the vast territorial extent of the viceroyalty which demanded the creation of autonomous organs, in order that all the administrative and economic functions might not be vested in the viceroy; and (2) the necessity of substituting officials of higher rank and responsibility for the corregidors, who had made of the provinces under their charge veritable markets of exploitation.

The royal ordinance for the establishment of intendants, with the reforms introduced by a royal cédula in the following year (1783), created eight intendancies and various subordinate districts distributed as follows: (1) The superintendency general, upon which all the intendancies depended, was located in the city of Buenos Aires, which was also the seat of an intendancy; (2) The intendancy of Paraguay; (3) The intendancy of Salta del Tucumán including Tucumán, Santiago del Estero, Cata-

marca, and Jujuy; (4) The intendancy of Córdoba del Tucumán
including Córdoba, San Juan, Mendoza, and La Rioja; (5) The
intendancy of Cochabamba; (6) The intendancy of La Paz;
(7) The intendancy of Charcas; and (8) The intendancy of
Potosí. The subordinate districts were Montevideo, the Guaraní
mission region, and the provinces inhabited by the Moxo and the
Chiquito Indians. The general superintendency was suppressed in
1788, as the officials who managed it by virtue of authority conferred by royal instructions had conflicted with the viceroys. The
only superintendents that Charcas had were Manuel Ignacio Fernández and Francisco de Paula Sanz.

The royal instructions classified the functions of intendants as
judicial, police, financial, and military. Each of the intendants
had a legal assistant appointed by the king, who exercised civil
and criminal jurisdiction. From the judgments or sentences pronounced by the legal assistants in their character as ordinary
judges an appeal might be taken to the audiencia. They were especially urged to study the Laws of the Indies and the laws of Spain,
the latter of which were to be applied in matters that the former
code did not include. In the section treating of powers the royal
instructions made all the provisions necessary for a new plan for
the management of the propios and arbitrios by establishing a general auditing office in Buenos Aires under the direction of the superior board of the treasury. The intendants were to require from
cities and towns a punctual report upon the propios and arbitrios
and upon the property of the community.

Among the police functions, it was provided that the intendants
were to have engineers prepare topographical maps of their respective provinces showing mountains, woods, rivers, lakes, and
other features. These maps were to give information of the quality
of the land of each province, of its natural products belonging to
the three kingdoms, of its industry and commerce, of its navigable
rivers, of the new canals that might be opened for the irrigation
of agricultural lands, and of the condition and means of improvement of roads and bridges. On their own part and by means of
their deputies who represented them in the different cities of the
intendancies, they were to study the inclinations, life, and customs
of the people in order to reform the idle. They were likewise
charged to teach the aborigines how to sow and cultivate hemp

and flax, and if it became necessary to distribute royal lands among them in order to promote this important end, they could do so. They were also recommended to promote the gathering of wax, apiculture (both wild and domestic), the cultivation of cotton, agriculture in general, and the raising of grain. The intendants were in charge of the policing of the roads and the sanitation and adornment of the streets. Every four months they were to report to the viceroy concerning the abundance or scarcity of products and their current prices.

With respect to the financial functions, it was provided that the management of the royal revenues was in future to be under the special supervision of the intendants. Jurisdiction concerning disputes which had been conferred by the Laws of the Indies on royal officials in order to make possible the collection of duties was transferred to the intendants in their respective provinces. Accordingly, in matters relating to the revenues, the intendants acted beyond the authority of all tribunals and audiencias, with the exception of the superior board of the treasury. This board, which sat in Buenos Aires, was composed of the two oldest ministers of the tribunal of accounts, the counsellor, the auditor general, and the fiscal of the royal treasury. It had to meet once weekly without including extraordinary sessions. Its chief duty was "so far as possible, to establish on the same basis the government and the administration of justice in matters concerning the royal treasury and the financing of military affairs." [2]

The intendants were to carry with them the "general account book of my royal treasury," in order that the funds might be managed in orderly fashion. They were to take note of the source, apportionment, and final disposal of all the royal incomes and duties. This chapter of the royal ordinance is the most extensive, for it contains a complete list and a minute regulation of all the taxes, from monopolies to propios and arbitrios. The ordinance also devotes some articles to determining the duties corresponding to the department of war in so far as these were related to the royal treasury. Thus the intendants had to look after the subsistence of the soldiers stationed in their respective territories, but

---

[2] *Documentos referentes á la guerra de la independencia y emancipación política de la República Argentina,* I, 32.

in whatever concerned the army itself, the entire supervision pertained to the military inspectors.

Argentine writers have raised the query as to whether the royal
ordinance for intendants was intended to promote the autonomy
of the provinces, or, on the contrary, to promote fiscal and political centralization. This problem is closely related to the study
of the origins of Argentine federalism, a topic which it is not convenient to develop in connection with this theme. Doubtless, the
intendancies restricted not a few of the functions of the cabildos,
and from this viewpoint would seem to point toward a centralizing
organization. But attention should be called to the fact that the
cabildos were not organs of the provinces proper but rather of
the cities, and that perhaps it would be an exaggeration to ascribe
important effects upon the internal political régime to institutions
like the intendancies which were introduced near the end of the
period of Spanish domination. The intendancies rather promoted
the autonomy of distinct regions which had been in formation since
the founding of the colonies.

The establishment of the intendancies signified in the dominions
of the viceroyalty of La Plata the highest degree of administrative
and financial organization. It can be said that this was the organic
period, the period of the most rapid evolution of the provinces of
the viceroyalty.

Commercial tribunals had existed in Spain since the middle ages.
Such a tribunal was more commonly designated as "the university
of merchants." This was an association of merchants, shipowners,
and bankers of Castile who organized themselves into a guild, and
aided their associates in everything relating to insurance, maritime freight, and the payment of sea tithes. At the end of the
fifteenth century, the Catholic monarchs conceded mercantile jurisdiction to the University of Burgos so that it might decide
disputes between merchants concerning matters of a commercial
nature.

Up to the second half of the eighteenth century only two commercial tribunals had been founded in Spanish America, those of
Mexico and Lima. This fact is explained if one remembers that up
to this time the commercial life of the Spanish-American people
was confined to Porto Bello and Callao. After 1778, the date of

the opening of all the peninsular ports, new commercial tribunals began to be founded in America.

On January 30, 1794, the royal cédula for the founding of the commercial tribunal of Buenos Aires was issued. In many of its provisions this followed the royal cédula issued by Charles III in 1784 establishing the commercial tribunal of Seville. The commercial tribunal of Buenos Aires was composed of a prior, two consuls, nine counsellors, a syndic, a secretary, an accountant, and a treasurer. It had the double character of a judicial tribunal intrusted with the most expeditious administration of justice in mercantile cases, and a board for the protection and development of commerce in all its branches.

As a board of promotion, the commercial tribunal was required to assemble twice a month to promote the progress of agriculture, the cultivation of crops, the introduction of machines and implements, and the ease of internal traffic. It was required to select deputies with jurisdiction over mercantile affairs who should represent the tribunal in ports and places of considerable commercial importance. A special fund was created for this institution consisting of the income from the duty on merchants or merchandise that was styled *avería* and the sums accruing from the fines that the commercial tribunal imposed. The legal organization of the commercial tribunal was completed by regulations which were framed later. In 1797, a most important provision was made—namely, a stipulation that its members should be composed in equal numbers of merchants and landowners.

Manuel Belgrano, who had just returned from Europe with a thorough grounding in economic matters, was appointed secretary of the commercial tribunal. But when this institution was founded, the majority of its members were monopolistic merchants who, in the first instance, defended their own personal interests which were also the interests of their compatriots residing in Cadiz whom many of them represented.

Within the tribunal a bitter struggle took place between the tendency of the monopolists and those members who represented the interests of the crown. One of the first matters, the consideration of which had to be appealed to a higher court, was that relating to the importation of Negroes and the exportation of products of the country. Tomás Antonio Romero had been granted permission to bring a thousand Negroes to La Plata from Brazil. Viceroy Loreto prohibited this traffic, because the transportation was to be undertaken in a foreign ship. An appeal was taken from this decision to the king, and as it was sustained by him, Romero later secured permission to export to foreign ports domestic products valued at 500,000 pesos. This concession provoked a very animated debate in which the general sentiment was opposed to the exportation of domestic products, or rather hides, to foreign ports. The group of monopolists who sat in the commercial tribunal tried to prove that hides were not domestic products, and in order to prevent their exportation, they presented arguments of a juridical and economic nature.

Another question which was raised in the commercial tribunal was that relating to the concession to engage in trade with colonies of other nations. The tribunal protested against that concession and alleged that it resulted in abuses and difficulties. Upon that occasion certain arguments were presented which showed the great difference between the viewpoints of such divergent interests. Francisco Antonio Escalada said that the special interests should be silent in the face of the general interest and that the monopolists themselves ought to prefer "the country which shelters them and which has perhaps produced their entire fortune," and "if they do not do so we must ourselves enter the fight for the general welfare of the state and of our children." Another member of the commercial tribunal, Tomás Fernández, said that the question could not be settled except in the light of the principles of political economy, "a science as much studied at the present time in Europe as it is neglected in these countries." The syndic, Ventura Miguel Marcó del Pont, addressed the king and argued for free trade with the colonies of other nations. He asked this for the benefit of the landowners and farmers, "the two classes most worthy of consideration in this republic. . . . Although since free commerce between Spain and the Indies was inaugurated a large number of hides have been taken to the Peninsula, there still remains in this province an equal or even greater amount that cannot be exported, so that even should the number of vessels arriving at these ports be tripled, they would all soon find cargoes. With respect to wheat, a benign heaven, regular seasons, virgin lands which reward a rude and superficial culture with prodigious usury, so that there can be gathered not only all the wheat necessary for the maintenance of the capital and its jurisdiction that consume annually 80,000 to 90,000 fanegas—twice as much as does Spain—but also for the trade with Europe, for the supply of Havana and other Spanish colonies, and for export to the foreign lands which need this cereal. . . . In view of this, what argument of equity and justice can be adduced to prohibit its exportation to foreign colonies in America? The syndic regidor can neither present nor can he discover such arguments." [3]

Some years later, the commercial tribunal had evolved in a liberal manner. A not inconsiderable number of landowners, who represented the interests of the country, belonged to it. Thus it was that, as in the sessions of October, 1798, the commercial tribunal decided in favor of the cabildo and of the administrator of the customs, who asked that the port of Buenos Aires should be opened to foreign commerce in order to save the colony from the painful situation into which it had fallen.

In his character as secretary, Belgrano had to read annually a report on economic affairs. In 1796, he wrote one on "the general methods of promoting agriculture, stimulating industry, and protecting the commerce of an agricultural country." In this memorial he criticized the empirical methods of exploiting the soil; he asserted that it was necessary to found a school of agriculture in which young men should be taught the general principles of the exploitation and improvement of farm lands.

He was a champion of the free exportation of the products of the country. He asserted that "the farmer must not be compelled to sell his products at a fixed price in order that the cities may buy them at a suitable figure. . . . Neither should he be prevented from selling them where he can get the most for them; for the farmer should enjoy entire freedom in his sales and exports which, if they yield him the profit on which he has taken a chance, will encourage him to continue his labors."

In his report of the following year Belgrano developed a theme on the "advantages which will result to these provinces and to the peninsula from the cultivation of hemp and flax; the mode of their cultivation; the land most suitable for it, the manner of harvesting

---

[3] Colección de manuscritos del Museo Mitre, Arm. B, cajón 27, núm. 15.

these two crops; and lastly the way to teach farmers to devote themselves constantly to this kind of agriculture." In 1798, Belgrano considered the advantages accruing to the country from coöperation between merchants and landowners.

CHAPTER XVII

JUDICIAL INSTITUTIONS

AFTER THE conquest of Spanish America began, Spain undertook to dictate laws for the New World. This legislation had among its primary objects the establishment of authorities, the distribution of functions, and the organization of relations between civil and ecclesiastical officials. This legislative policy began after the signing of the capitulations with Columbus and continued until the colonies had won their independence. A half century after the discovery of America, the bulk of the laws issued had become enormous, and the need arose of codifying them, that is, of arranging the laws according to a chronological or systematic order, so as to facilitate their study and application. In 1556, Antonio Maldonado, the fiscal of the audiencia of Mexico, had faced this task. Seven years later an oidor of the same audiencia named Vasco de Puga, by royal authorization and under charge of the viceroy, had printed in one volume a collection of cédulas that was called the *Cedulario de Puga*. In 1599, Diego de Encinas of the secretariat of the Council of the Indies collected in four volumes the royal cédulas issued up to that time. Similar labors were carried on by Aguiar y Acuña, Antonio de León Pinelo, and that distinguished student of affairs of the Indies, Juan Solórzano y Pereyra, author of the works entitled *De Jure Indiano* and *Política Indiana*. At the end of the seventeenth century, a board of councillors was formed to complete the compilation. Finally, in 1680, King Charles II promulgated the *Recopilación de leyes de los reinos de las Indias* commonly known as the Laws of the Indies.

This code is divided into nine books. The first book concerns the church, taxes of an ecclesiastical character (tithes, ecclesiastical allowances, holy crusade, etc.), universities, and learning. The second book concerns the Council of the Indies, the audiencia, and general and special visitors. The third concerns viceroys, war, the army, arms, fortifications, captains, soldiers, corsairs and pirates, order of precedence, ceremonies, courtesies, and the mails. The fourth is devoted to discoveries, settlements, cities, and cabildos, the sale, arrangement, and distribution of land, public works, and the miners of quicksilver and other metals. The fifth is devoted to governors, corregidors, and alcaldes, the cognizance and jurisdiction of suits and judgments, appeals, and the residencia.[1] The sixth book includes laws concerning the life of the Indians, reductions and towns, tributes, caciques, and encomenderos, and the postal service. The seventh book deals with divers matters, as games and gamblers, crimes and punishments, Negroes and mulattoes. The eighth and ninth books deal with the auditing department, the royal treasury, and colonial commerce.

As has been stated, the code was published in 1680, and hence does not include the legislation of the eighteenth century, the work of the Bourbon kings, which was a frank reaction against the policy of the preceding century. A new code was prepared during the reign of Charles III which, however, was not published. Nevertheless, it is known that the compilation of the first book was completed in the reign of Charles IV, and that it was applied in the Indies to some isolated cases.[2]

The audiencia of Buenos Aires was founded for the second time in 1783. The reasons for this reëstablishment were of a different nature than those that prevailed in 1661. Even by the end of the eighteenth century, La Plata was a vast political and administrative organism with a developed population, wealth, and commerce. In 1776, the viceroyalty was founded; in 1779, the custom-house; and in 1782, the intendancies. The need was felt of a local audiencia that would function as a superior tribunal of justice, just as at a later time the need was felt of creating a commercial tribunal.

The functions of the audiencias were political and judicial. Even upon the establishment of the first audiencia at Buenos Aires, the royal cédula creating it declared that in matters of government the governor should have the final decision, "except that, for his better judgment, we command that, in matters and cases of importance relating to government, the said governor must consult

[1] The "residencia" was an official inquiry made into the conduct of important Spanish colonial authorities at the end of their term of office.—W.S.R.

[2] A detailed consideration of the Laws of the Indies is found in Levene, *Notas para el estudio del derecho indiano*.

5. Governors, corregidores, etc
6. Indians
7. diverse matters including Negroes
8 & 9 auditing, treasury, commerce

with the oidors of that audiencia in order to get their advisory opinions." [3] Its essential function was civil, criminal, and commercial justice. Appeal might be taken from its judgments to the council of the Indies, provided the sum in dispute amounted to 6,000 pesos.

It has been stated that besides being a junta for public improvement, the commercial tribunal was a court of commercial justice. Beginning with 1794, therefore, these tribunals were made special tribunals of commerce. The administration of justice was in charge of this tribunal which was composed of a prior and two consuls; it had cognizance of lawsuits arising between merchants and traders regarding purchases, sales, exchanges, insurance, accounts of partnerships, the freighting of vessels, and similar matters. In passing judgment "a simple style, recognized truth, and good faith" were to be observed. The decision was oral and settled the matter. When the suit involved over 1,000 pesos, an appeal might be taken to the appellate tribunal which was composed of the dean of the audiencia and two colleagues named by the dean himself, who was to select one colleague from a list of two nominees made by each party to the dispute.

There were two municipal alcaldes, of the first and second class; they formed a part of the cabildo. They acted as judges of the first instance in civil and criminal affairs. The Laws of the Indies prescribed that the alcaldes in ordinary should be honorable, capable, and qualified persons who could read and write. No debtor to the royal treasury could be made an alcalde. The term of office of alcaldes was one year and they could not be reëlected until two years had elapsed. In case of the death of the governors and the lack of a lieutenant governor, the alcaldes in ordinary were to act as governors. The presidents of the audiencias and the oidors could not infringe upon the jurisdiction of ordinary judges. Appeals from the judgments of the alcaldes might be taken to the audiencias.

Besides the above-mentioned officials, other functionaries in

[3] *Recopilación de leyes de los reinos de las Indias,* libro II, título XV, ley XIII. [The ordinances of the commercial tribunal of Bilbao, which were sometimes used as the basis for the organization of such tribunals in Spanish America, are found in the *Novísima recopilación de las leyes de España* (5 vols. Paris, 1854), V, apéndice.—W.S.R.]

America exercised judicial powers. The corregidors, for example, who were assigned to the chief towns of the Indies, were intrusted with the administration and supervision of judicial affairs. They became notorious because of the spirit of avarice and arbitrariness which was their salient trait. These offices were filled directly by the king.

The royal ordinance of intendants created a new judicial functionary, namely, the legal assistant *(teniente letrado)*, who had civil and criminal jurisdiction. The tribunal of accounts was an administrative body, for it had power to constrain debtors of the royal treasury. In this matter, other tribunals had no jurisdiction. Another special tribunal, composed of the superintendent and high officials of the mint, exercised jurisdiction in all questions concerning the infraction of the ordinances promulgated for the regulation of the mints.

CHAPTER XVIII

THE CHURCH

AMERICA WAS discovered during an age of profound religiousness in Spain. The Spanish sovereigns were the champions of Roman Catholicism in Europe. After the age of Ferdinand and Isabella, while the New World was being conquered, the dominant sentiment was the propagation of the Catholic religion. The Catholic monarchs exerted all their efforts for the conversion of the American aborigines to Christianity; and their devotion to this religious ideal led them in July, 1500, to make a declaration of a juridical nature that honors the motherland, namely, the assertion that the Indians were free and equal to the Spaniards. Remember that Europe had just emerged from the feudal age and was reviving the Roman law which had proclaimed slavery. According to the prevailing notion of the era, the status of being a free man arose from the condition of being a Christian.

In order to carry on the huge task of conversion, the monarchy needed prodigious sums. Hence, King Ferdinand obtained from Pope Alexander VI the bull of 1501 which conceded to the Spanish sovereigns the revenues accruing from the tithes, for it was considered that this income would found and maintain churches in the New World. Fabié y Escudero made this appropriate comment: "This pontifical disposition gave a special character to the patronage of the Spanish kings in the church of the Indies; for, in contrast with what occurred in the motherland, religion and its ministers were not supported by the patrimony and the special incomes of the church, but by the assignments which the monarchs as representatives of the state set apart for these objects." [1] Later Pope Julius II conceded to the Spanish kings the right of making appointments to all ecclesiastical benefices in America. [2]

---

[1] A. M. Fabié y Escudero, *Documentos legislativos* ("Colección de documentos inéditos relativos al descubrimiento, conquista y organización de las antiguas posesiones españoles de ultramar," second series, vols. V, IX, and X, Madrid, 1890-97), I, xl.

[2] The bull of Pope Julius II, issued July 28, 1508, which declared that he conceded to the Catholic monarchs "the right of patronage and the right to present suitable persons to cathedrals, churches, and benefices in the Indies,"

Consequently, the true pontiffs of the Spanish-American church were the kings; for they were the masters of the revenues of ecclesiastical origin, and they filled all the vacancies. In all the cities founded by the Spaniards, conflicts arose between ecclesiastical and civil authorities, but these struggles never assumed the character of a clash between the temporal and the spiritual power. They were rather differences between two authorities of the same state.

In the first rank of the ecclesiastical hierarchy were the high dignitaries, namely, archbishops, bishops, and deans. In the second rank were the clergy composed of curates or parish priests, doctrinal curates or teachers of Catholic doctrine, and missionaries. The curates officiated in the parishes, the doctrinal curates served in the villages occupied by Indians who had been subjected to the civil authority, while the missionaries were dedicated to the pacification, conversion, and management of the unconquered Indians.

The secular clergy lived in America in complete independence and not infrequently in magnificence. The immense majority of them were Spaniards who had left the motherland, like the civil conquerors, animated by a spirit of adventure.

The religious orders that were most active in America were the Franciscans, Dominicans, Augustinians, and Jesuits. Their members were more distinguished than the secular clergy. The most elevated posts of the ecclesiastical hierarchy in Mexico and Peru were filled by members of the regular clergy. The learned historian, William Robertson, says of them: "They are almost the only Spanish ecclesiastics, from whom we have received any accounts, either of the civil or natural history of the various provinces in America. Some of them, though deeply tinged with the indelible superstition of their profession, have published works which give a favorable idea of their abilities. The natural and moral history of the New World, by the Jesuit Acosta, contains more accurate observations, perhaps, and more sound science than are to be found in any description of remote countries published in the sixteenth century." [3]

---

is found in L. Ayarragaray, *La iglesia en América y la dominación española* (Buenos Aires, 1920), pp. 161-64.—W. S. R.

[3] William Robertson, *The History of America* (4 vols. London, 1812), IV, 51-52.—W. S. R.

The religious orders mentioned above devoted themselves especially to teaching. The Franciscans and the Dominicans had charge of primary instruction; they were the instructors who taught the rudiments of knowledge until the eighteenth century was far advanced, when the majority of the cabildos supported with their own revenues the teachers in primary schools.

The Jesuit order has displayed a manifold activity in America. The majority of the "missions" were founded by them. From the viewpoint of the spirit of sacrifice and labor for the organization and civilization of the Indians they were unsurpassed. They promoted higher education in the New World. They were the founders of many universities. In the cities they had a notable influence upon the governing class.

The religious orders had constant dissensions. In Córdoba a serious conflict took place between the Dominicans and the Jesuits, because of the fact that the latter had founded a university there, while the former, as they were furnishing the necessary instruction in their monastery, claimed the right to confer the degrees of master and doctor. The Jesuits cited the royal cédulas which authorized their order to grant diplomas to the graduates. The royal audiencia of Charcas, which was located at Chuquisaca, intervened in the dispute and directed that the Dominicans could not grant the degree of doctor.[4]

In 1570, the bishopric of Tucumán was created with its seat at Santiago del Estero. Four years before it was established, Fray de Villa Carillo was designated to administer the new diocese until he obtained his confirmation. In 1577, the Reverend Fray Francisco de Victoria, of the Dominican order, occupied the bishopric. He was confirmed by Pope Gregory XIII. Engaged in the work of converting the Indians, he invited to Tucumán the Theatin fathers, some members of the Dominican order, and the first Jesuits. During the period when he was at the head of the bishopric numerous disputes arose with the governors.

In 1592 the Reverend Father Fernando Trejo y Sanabria, one of the finest figures of the Spanish-American church, was made bishop of Tucumán. In order to unify activities in the development

---

[4] J. Ingenieros, "Notas sobre la mentalidad colonial," *Revista de Filosofía* (Buenos Aires, 1917), año III, núm. 2, pp. 249-96.

of the work of evangelizing the aborigines, he convoked the first synod or general assembly of the towns and cities of the diocese which was composed of civil and ecclesiastical delegates. In his biography of the worthy bishop, Fray José María Liqueno thus described the proceedings of the assembly: "Having decided that it was faced by three classes of problems—faith, worship, and morality—the synod organized its labors into three divisions. 'The first division considered religious doctrine, the method by which it should be taught, and all other matters relating thereto. The second considered the sacraments, their proper administration, and all other related matters. The third considered various matters such as the observance of church feasts and the reforming of customs.' " [5]

Furthermore, Trejo y Sanabria was a great defender of the liberty of the Indians. He devoted himself to this cause with great religious fervor in order to contend against the personal service and exploitation of the Indian. In 1678, Fray Manuel Mercadillo took possession of this bishopric. During his episcopate the cathedral seat was transferred from Santiago del Estero to Córdoba.

The last bishop of the colonial era was Rodrigo Antonio de Orellana who took possession of his diocese near the end of 1809. In the next year the revolt against Spanish rule began. In Córdoba a counter-revolutionary movement was organized in which Orellana took part. His companions, who had acted as leaders of this movement, were shot; Orellana escaped death only by virtue of his ecclesiastical dignity.

In 1620, the bishopric of Buenos Aires was created in the region which up to that time had been dependent upon the Paraguayan episcopate. Two years later the erection was confirmed by Bishop Carranza. In the words of Rómulo D. Carbia: "On May 12, 1622, the bishop finally decided to issue the ordinance erecting the cathedral church which was soon solemnly proclaimed, on Sunday, June 26. The document to which I have just alluded organized all the functions of the church, which was the head of the bishopric, in the form that was demanded by its needs, so far as the means

---

[5] J. M. Liqueno, *Fray Fernando de Trejo y Sanabria* (2 vols. Córdoba, 1916), I, 77-78.

at disposal allowed." [6] By one of the clauses of this ordinance, the vestments of the priests were specified, namely, "a cassock, open or closed and reaching down to the feet," black in color, "or of any other color that is decorous, with the hair worn short and having a tonsure of the size of a silver real." The communicants were ordered to pay first fruits and tithes. The latter might be paid in wild cattle, hides, or other products.

This prelate had a stormy dispute with Governor Céspedes. The notary of the Holy Office, Juan de Vergara, a disturbing instigator, had been cast into prison by order of the governor. The bishop asked the governor whether Vergara depended directly upon his command and demanded that the latter be set free. Céspedes declined to set him free; the bishop then assembled the clergy, and placing himself at their head, proceeded to the prison and liberated Vergara. Supported by his soldiers, and two pieces of artillery, the governor pursued the clerics. Nothing tragic occurred, however, and Vergara remained at large.[7] The second bishop was Fray Cristóbal de Aresti. During his episcopate a new conflict with the civil authority occurred, but it was not of the magnitude of the one just mentioned. In 1660, Antonio Azcona Imberto was elected bishop of Buenos Aires.

Peña says of the church edifice: "It is known that, upon the founding of this city, Juan de Garay selected a site for the mother church, which is the same as that now occupied by the cathedral. The first church was built of earthen walls, probably adobe, which were repaired by Bishop Carranza, who built the choir and the sacristy. This building fell into a ruined state. Bishop Azcona Imberto reconstructed it and covered it with a roof of Paraguayan cedar. He spent over eighty thousand pesos in cash in rebuilding this church." [8]

In the middle of the eighteenth century the illustrious Masellano y Agramont became bishop of Buenos Aires. He raised a question about the solemnities that should be observed in the ceremony of his reception. The bishop claimed that the members of the ayunta-

---

[6] R. D. Carbia, *Historia eclesiástica del Río de la Plata* (2 vols. Buenos Aires, 1914), I, 130-31.

[7] V. G. Quesada, "Noticias sobre los ilustrísimos obispos del Río de la Plata," *La Revista de Buenos Aires* (Buenos Aires, 1896), XVIII, 330-31.

[8] E. Peña, "Don Francisco de Céspedes," *Anales de la Academia de Filosofía y Letras* (Buenos Aires, 1916) vol. V., pt. 1.

Coat of Arms granted to the City of Buenos Aires in 1744; now preserved in
the Museo Histórico Nacional, Buenos Aires. From *Días de Mayo;
actas del cabildo de Buenos Aires, 1810.*

miento should carry the rods of the pallium on entering the cathedral. The king deliberated about this matter, but, in view of the fact that the bishop had desired to be received with the pallium upon his entrance into the city, reminded him that this was a ceremony reserved for the royal person alone, and not even allowed to viceroys. Nevertheless, he sanctioned the custom by which bishops were received under the pallium in cathedral churches and not at the gates of the cities. At this time the cathedral church collapsed, which made necessary its speedy reconstruction.

One of the most important bishops was Manuel Antonio de la Torre (1757-1765). He was distinguished by the numerous reforms which he introduced into church ceremonies, and by his serious quarrel with the governor, which originated, mainly because of the supposed participation of the regular and secular clergy in the revolutionary movement in the city of Corrientes in 1764.

During that bishopric and during the interregnum under Maciel, a new dispute took place with Governor Vértiz. The latter had authorized the dance called the fandango. A priest condemned this custom as immoral. The king directed that such dances should be suppressed.

"Parallel with the relaxation of public customs went the relaxation of monastic life. In the province of Buenos Aires and its jurisdiction, there were at this time 366 friars and 79 nuns concerning whom the civil cabildo entertained opinions that were scarcely favorable." [9] The objections were raised that minors entered monasteries, that prisoners were not instructed, that the sick were not ministered unto, that the friars did not preach, and that they did not have a fixed tariff for such ceremonies as funerals and services for the dead.

The last bishop of Buenos Aires during the colonial era was Benito de Lue y Riega, who was appointed in 1802. This bishop proposed to elevate the diocese to an archepiscopate and founded a seminary. He took part in the cabildo abierto of May 22, 1810, where he championed the rights of Spain and of all Spaniards to govern the colonies.

[9] Carbia, *op. cit.*, II, 170-71.

After the beginning of the eighteenth century many churches were built in Buenos Aires. Two Jesuit priests, who were architects, namely, Blanqui and Primoli, had arrived to direct the construction of the church of San Ignacio. Their services were also required to build the churches of San Francisco, San Telmo, and La Merced. A rivalry among the Jesuits, the Franciscans, the Order of Mercy, and other orders induced them to stimulate the interest of their communicants by asking them to make gifts for the construction of churches. The religious sentiment of the population was so profound that most of the churches constructed were the result of the contributions of persons with property and reputation. The Argentine diplomat and scholar, Vicente G. Quesada aptly states:

"The church of Monserrat was in the beginning a chapel constructed by Pedro Sierra. The promoters of the construction of the church of La Merced are the married couple whose pictures are seen at the entrance to the church and whose names we do not know. The church of San Miguel was due to the zeal of the priest, José González Islas. Manuel Gómez began the construction of the church of Nuestra Señora de la Piedad. . . . The church of Nuestra Señora de la Concepción was in the beginning a chapel constructed by Matías Flores. The Socorro was another chapel erected by Alejandro de Valle. The old church of Balvanera was started by the Franciscan father, Fray Juan Rodríguez. . . . The chapel of San Juan was erected by a military commander named Juan de San Martín, and the church of San Nicolás by Don Francisco Araujo. . . . Many wealthy citizens contributed to the funds for building the fine churches of San Ignacio, Santo Domingo, and even the cathedral church." [10]

In the Dominican and Franciscan monasteries and those of the Order of Mercy and the Bethlehemites there were professorships of theology, philosophy, grammar, elementary instruction, and other subjects which attracted many students. The convent of Cataline nuns was authorized in 1717 but was not inaugurated until 1745. It was provided that the maximum number of these nuns should be forty, and that those women who so desired might enter the convent in order to receive an education or an asylum

[10] "Noticias sobre la edificación del templo de Santo Domingo en Buenos Aires," *La Revista de Buenos Aires* (Buenos Aires, 1869), XXI, 163.

provided they had previously secured permission from the bishop
of the diocese. The inauguration of this convent was a solemn act in
which all the civil and ecclesiastical authorities and the people
took part. Twenty-five years after its foundation, the convent had
grievous tribulations. It scarcely possessed 1,910 pesos for the
support and vestments of the nuns who numbered forty-five
instead of forty as stipulated by the royal cédula that provided
for its foundation.[11]

In 1745, the king granted a license for the founding of a convent of Capuchin nuns in the block where the church of San
Nicolás de Bary was located, but as the site in question was
unhealthful, it was installed in the church of San Juan Bautista.

One of the conditions that proved fatal for the prestige of the
Church was the corruption of the clergy. Many of its members
came to America with the intention of satisfying their desires and
their avarice. In order to check this overflow many measures were
taken, but these were ridiculed. Ferdinand VI prohibited members
of religious orders from taking charge of parishes by directing
that when posts fell vacant they should be filled by secular priests
who were subject to the jurisdiction of their bishop.

One result of the condition that we have mentioned was the
slow progress made in the conversion of the Indians to Christianity; for although as early as 1537 Pope Paul III had declared
the Indians to be rational creatures capable of being converted to
Christianity, the propagation of the Catholic faith had not gone
on rapidly. It is indeed true that the primitive condition of the
aboriginal civilizations helps to explain this phenomenon.

It has already been stated that the religious orders devoted
themselves to the promotion of education. They were the teachers
in the schools and the universities. But in both organization and
teaching plan these institutions were a faithful reflection of
Spanish schools and universities, that is, they were vitiated by
verbosity and theology.

After the middle of the eighteenth century, the liberal doctrines
of economists, philosophers, and encyclopedists began to spread
in the Spanish Indies. Members of the clergy were slowly impreg-

---

[11] V. G. Quesada, "Noticias históricas sobre la fundación y edificación del
convento de monjas catalinas en Buenos Aires," *La Revista de Buenos Aires*
(Buenos Aires, 1864), III, 43-60.

nated by this new spirit. This tendency is made much more evident by considering the fact that when the Revolution of 1810 took place, the great majority of the clergy embraced the revolutionary cause. Rómulo D. Carbia states: "With regard to the clergy, the gifts of books made in 1810 to the public library which the junta ordered to be established in Buenos Aires reveals that the books read privately by the clergy were not only those of a religious character. If it can be said that this intellectual background to which I have alluded was anywhere frankly manifested, it was in the Franciscan cloister of Buenos Aires where a spirit of scientific amplitude dominated everything. . . . The commissary of the Franciscan order in the Indies, Fray Manuel Manso Truxillo, a man . . . influenced by the desire for improvement prevailing at this time, had scarcely entered upon his duties when he addressed to all his American subordinates a 'pastoral exhortation' inciting them to the cultivation of letters and intellectual development. . . ." [12] Father Truxillo ordered that two hundred pesos should be assigned to them every three years for the purchase of works on education for members of his order. This antecedent explains the intellectual life of the Franciscan cloister, "the library of which was rich in profane works, whose friars entertained such liberal ideas, and in whose halls a course of study was given in natural philosophy."

In the cabildo abierto of May 22, 1810, of two hundred and forty-six persons present, twenty-six were priests. Monsignor Agustín Fiaggio thus describes the rôle of the clergy: "The clergy represented by members of religious orders who occupied respectable positions in their respective communities, and by priests who were all doctors, and by various others who were curates or canons, responded in respectable numbers to the invitation to attend the meeting. It appears that the clergy had awaited this moment with anxiety, as may be deduced from their presence in the cabildo and even more by the views expressed when they cast their votes." [13]

[12] R. D. Carbia, "La revolución de Mayo y la Iglesia," *Anales de la facultad de derecho y ciencias sociales* (Buenos Aires, 1915), XIV, 199-201. [In other parts of Spanish America than La Plata, the clergy often supported the royalist cause.—W. S. R.]

[13] A. Fiaggio, *Influencia del clero en la independencia argentina* (Barcelona, 1912), p. 7.

CHAPTER XIX

INTELLECTUAL LIFE

Aside from the cultural labor carried on by the religious orders in America, the monarchy had charge of the founding of educational institutions. In the middle of the sixteenth century the universities of Mexico and Lima were founded. Numerous American writers appeared, especially in Mexico and Peru. There should be mentioned here, the *Historia de los Indios de Nueva España* by Toribio de Motolivia; the *Historia de las Indias de Nueva España* by Fray Diego Durán; *Vida y Religión Mejicanas* by Fray Bernardino de Sahagún; the *Historia natural y civil de las Indias* by Father José Acosta which has been already mentioned. Garcilaso de la Vega wrote a work concerning the empire of the Incas; Alonso de Sandoval, S. J., is the author of a treatise concerning Africa and the Negroes; Antonio León Pinelo is perhaps the greatest American scholar and bibliophile; his thought and action contributed in the highest degree to bring to a head codification of the Laws of the Indies. Among his productions should be mentioned the following works: *Discurso acerca de la importancia, forma y disposición de la recopilación de las leyes de Indias* (*Treatise on the Importance, Form, and Arrangement of the Compilation of the Laws of the Indies*); *Política de las Indias* (*Politics of the Indies*); *Bulario Índico* (*Papal Bulls concerning the Indies*); *Tratado de las confirmaciones reales* (*A Treatise of Royal Confirmations*); *Historia del Supremo Consejo de Indias* (*History of the Supreme Council of the Indies*); and the *Historia eclesiástica y política de las iglesias de América* (*Political and Ecclesiastical History of the Churches of America*).

We have not mentioned, except to serve as illustrations, the works written by certain Americans which might serve as an index of the intellectual level of the New World; but it should be noticed that Spain transmitted European culture by sending to America not only conquerors and men of the sword but also students and men of learning. The late Dr. Edward G. Bourne made the following estimate of Spanish achievements in education:

"That the Spanish authorities in church and state did much to promote education is abundantly evident, and the modern sciences of anthropology, linguistics, geography, and history are profoundly indebted to the labors of the early Spanish-American scholars and missionaries. It is in these fields that their achievements shine, for in these fields they could work unhampered by the censorship of the press and the Inquisition. In philosophy and in politics the mind was less free. The part which the Inquisition played in confining intellectual work to the well-beaten track of traditional orthodoxy makes appropriate a brief consideration of its activities in America, about which great misconceptions have prevailed."[1]

It is essential to suggest some notions about the condition of primary education in the colony, which will permit us to estimate the condition of general culture in the year when the revolution against Spain began. Primary education was in the hands of the religious orders, of "the schools of the king," and especially of the municipal schools that had either been created or had developed without special act. According to a report of the year 1773, seven hundred and seventy-five boys were attending the schools of Buenos Aires to receive primary instruction (the census taken by order of Vértiz y Salcedo in 1778 gave the city a total of 24,205 inhabitants, of whom only 15,719 were whites) ; four hundred and three were being educated in the monasteries of the Dominicans, the Franciscans, the Order of Mercy, and the Bethlehemites; one hundred and forty were in charge of municipal teachers in the parishes of Piedad, San Nicolás, Concepción, Monserrat, and San Miguel; and the remainder, two hundred and thirty-two, were in the Academy of San Carlos.[2] After the establishment of the viceroyalty, the income of the cabildo of Buenos Aires from propios and arbitrios notably increased;[3] and, because of this, the

---

[1] E. G. Bourne, *Spain in America, 1450-1580* ("American Nation Series," vol. III, New York, 1904), pp. 311-12.—W. S. R.

[2] Gutiérrez, *Noticias históricas sobre el origen y desarrolla de la enseñanza pública superior en Buenos Aires,* p. 407.

[3] Archivo general de la nación, Gobierno colonial, cabildo de Buenos Aires, propios, 1772-1782, legajo 4. [A table listing the revenues derived by the cabildo of Buenos Aires from propios and arbitrios in 1809 is given by R.

municipal action exerted for the development of primary instruction was important. In 1808 the cabildo directed that municipal teachers should be paid four hundred pesos a year, besides fees and gratuities.

During the last period of Spanish domination in La Plata, no one espoused the cause of public education with greater zeal than did Manuel Belgrano, as can be shown by facts that we shall mention later. In the numbers of the *Correo de Comercio* for March 17 and 24, 1810, Belgrano spoke of education with the love of a teacher: "How can it be expected that men can love labor, that customs can be regulated, that there will be plenty of honorable citizens, that virtue will overcome vice, and that the government will receive the fruits of its cities, if there is no public instruction and if ignorance is handed down from generation to generation with greater and greater increments?"

The measures for opening schools were adopted as Belgrano advised. He desired that elementary schools should be supported by the propios and arbitrios of cities and towns and that the benefits of such establishments should be extended to the country. He further proposed that in order to meet these expenses the prosperous parents should pay a moderate salary to the teachers.[4]

With respect to the content of primary education a contemporary has written the following judgment: "In the schools there was no system of education; the teachers of elementary subjects were for the most part ignorant and vicious; their entire teaching was what might be expected of them. Each child read the books that he could bring from home: profane histories, the narratives of which neither they nor their teachers understood; books of chivalry or similar productions; the most pious fathers gave their sons ascetic works to read which were products of an ill-digested piety or lives of the saints which had been written by authors with-

Levene, *Ensayo histórico sobre la revolución de Mayo y Mariano Moreno*, I, 124, footnote.—W. S. R.]

[4] Regarding an interesting decree of Viceroy Cisneros concerning compulsory elementary education, see Archivo del gobierno de Buenos Aires, título 10, caps. LV-LXXVII, Archivo general de la nación. See further, R. Levene, "Un decreto del virrey Cisneros sobre instrucción primaria obligatoria," *Revista de Filosofía* (Buenos Aires, 1918), año IV, núm. 4, pp. 70-75.

out judgment and were consequently laden with apocryphal passages and pretended miracles." [5]

In Buenos Aires, secondary education developed—general culture, philosophy, and theology—in the Academy of San Carlos, which we considered in the chapter describing the administration of Viceroy Vértiz y Salcedo. The Academy of Monserrat of Córdoba was founded by the priest, Ignacio Duarte, who transferred it to the Society of Jesus in 1695. It was not exactly an institution of education, but rather a boarding-school. In that academy students received a moral education and also attended classes at the University of Córdoba. The Academy of Monserrat was inaugurated with six scholarships, but it soon acquired great importance, for parents adopted the custom of placing their sons as pupils in the academy by virtue of the payment of a certain sum. After the expulsion of the Jesuits in 1767, the Academy of Monserrat passed into the hands of the Franciscans.

In the city of Chile the Society of Jesus had founded the Academy of Máximo which was transferred to Córdoba in 1614 and called the Academy of Loreto or the King's Academy. This academy served as a basis for the foundation of the University of Córdoba; the honor of doing this pertains to Fray Fernando de Trejo y Sanabria, an American who was a son of Hernando de Trejo and María de Sanabria. For a long period the University of Córdoba was the only center of higher education in the colony of La Plata; all the young men who were anxious to study flocked to its halls.

That university was composed of two colleges: the college of theology, and the college of arts. The college of arts included the study of logic, philosophy, ethics, metaphysics, and natural philosophy extending over a period of three years. The college of theology developed a more extensive plan of studies that extended over four years. The colonial life of the University of Córdoba included two periods: the Jesuit period (1613-1767); and the Franciscan period (1767-1808).

In 1791, a professorship of jurisprudence was created at the University of Córdoba, but it was the only university in southern

[5] J. I. de Gorriti, *Reflecciones sobre las causas morales de las convulsiones interiores en los nuevos estados Americanos y examen de los medios eficaces para reprimirlas* (Buenos Aires, 1916), pp. 120-21.

Spanish America that did not teach civil law. Hence, in order to take the doctorate in law, young men of La Plata went to the University of Chile or to the University of Chuquisaca. The last-mentioned institution was founded a century after the University of Córdoba. In the year 1808, a professorship of mathematics was created at Córdoba at the instance of Dean Gregorio Funes. Although famous because it was the oldest university, yet the University of Córdoba did not fulfill the aspirations of youth because of the quality and direction of its teaching.

After the University of San Marcos, which was located at Lima, the most famous university of South America was the university at Chuquisaca. Attracted by the fame of its college of law, young men of La Plata went to the University of Chuquisaca, for there juridical and literary teaching was given. From that university there went out such patriots as Moreno, Castelli, Monteagudo, and Vicente López y Planes. In order to understand the liberal spirit that animated the students of the University of Chuquisaca, it is enough to cite the example of Mariano Moreno who later republished, with a prologue, a Castilian edition of Rousseau's *Social Contract*.

The Carolinian Academy, which was created at Chuquisaca in 1780 like others in the Indies in imitation of academies founded in Spain in the eighteenth century, was composed of a group of practicing lawyers, who provided an advanced course of the University of Chuquisaca. It functioned under the direction of a member of the royal audiencia, but chose its own officers and had special archives and a library as well as its own hall. A student attending this academy was styled an academician, while the licentiate or doctor who had left its hall was called an alumnus. In accordance with a custom of the age, a candidate was only admitted to this academy after complying with certain formalities, such as declarations concerning legitimacy and purity of descent. For two years he was expected to attend its courses that dealt with law in general and with the Law of the Indies.[6] The study of national codes moulded a generation of men who were well versed in the legislation and administration of Spain and its colonies.

---

[6] L. Paz, *La Universidad Mayor Real y Pontificia de San Francisco Javier de la capital de los Charcas* (Sucre, 1914), pp. 235-37.

By the aid of new sources of information we can suggest more ample viewpoints concerning the teaching of philosophy during the colonial epoch. Such factors were the following treatises: *Lecciones de lógica* (*Lessons in Logic*), by Professor L. J. Chorroarín of the Royal Academy of San Carlos of Buenos Aires (1783); *Física (Natural Philosophy)* by Professor Fray Elías del Carmen of the Royal Academy of Córdoba (1784); *Apuntes de filosofía moral (Principles of Moral Philosophy)*, a work that has remained anonymous up to the present day but which probably was composed by some noted professor of the University of Córdoba; *Conclusiones sobre toda la filosofía (Conclusions relative to all Philosophy)*, by Francisco Xavier Martínez de Aldunate (1790).

In Chorroarín's *Lógica* it was affirmed, on the one hand, that the authority of all the holy fathers is an irrefutable rule in moral matters, but that, on the other hand, in the natural sciences one must adhere to it only in case the fathers were versed in the scientific discipline that it considers. Father Elías del Carmen in his *Física* admits experimental proof in natural phenomena and, on the other hand, maintains that the body of Christ passed through the stone of the sepulchre and the doors of the room in which the Last Supper was eaten, "for impenetrability might actually be lacking from a body without it ceasing to exist for that reason." Similar viewpoints are found in the anonymous work on the *Apuntes de filosofía moral* and in the *Conclusiones* of Aldunate.[7]

From the middle of the eighteenth century the study of Spanish law was stimulated as a reaction against the tendency in teaching in vogue up to that time which ascribed greater importance to Roman and canon law than to the laws and ordinances of Spain and the Indies. On the occasion of the discussion concerning the founding of the University of Buenos Aires, the ecclesiastical cabildo declared with reference to the plan of juridical studies, that it did not censure the establishment of chairs for the study of the code, the institutes, and other features of Roman law, but that it was absurd to omit instruction in that other legitimate and true law, namely the Law of the Indies. In the academies

[7] J. Chiabra, *La enseñanza de la filosoa en la época colonial* (Buenos Aires, 1911); and E. Martínez Paz, *Una tesis de filosofía del siglo XVIII en la Universidad de Córdoba* (Córdoba, 1919).

annexed to the universities founded by Charles III, the Law of the Indies was taught. In view of this phenomenon, one can explain the preparation which the nucleus of American revolutionists received in the legislation of the Indies, its study and criticism.

Mariano Moreno, for example, who became a doctor in law of the University of Chuquisaca, was acquainted with such philosophers and encyclopedists as Filangieri, Rousseau, Mably, and Raynal. He also had a profound knowledge of Spanish legal codes. By virtue of this preparation he became in his time a noted lawyer and a statesman who took part in the revolution against Spain with a full knowledge of both written and unwritten law.[8]

As we intend to consider colonial medicine in chapter XXI, we shall give here some information concerning the first physicians who settled in Buenos Aires. From the beginning of the seventeenth century, a certificate of competence was required for the practice of medicine. One of the types of doctors allowed to practice was the farrier and veterinary surgeon, who was supposed to prove that he was capable of making "divers cures of diseases and old sores of horses." Despite this, at times physicians did not take up their residence in Buenos Aires, as seems to be proven by the fact that in 1667 the oidor of the royal audiencia of Buenos Aires, Pedro Rojas y Luna, died because of the lack of medical attention and of remedies for his illness.[9]

In order to safeguard the public health, Viceroy Vértiz y Salcedo founded the tribunal of king's physicians. This was a board organized to examine such persons as aspired to the practice of medicine. At that time there was a physician of repute in Buenos Aires, namely, Dr. Miguel de Gorman, whose services Vértiz y Salcedo was able to enlist by giving him all the authority that he needed. The opening of the tribunal of king's physicians was a solemn occasion. Referring to that ceremony, Vértiz y Salcedo said in his official report: "I attended in company with the ecclesiastical and secular cabildos, and the most important citizens in order thus to impress upon the people the respect with which this tribunal

---

[8] Numerous inedited writings of Moreno show that he left the Carolinian Academy with a wide knowledge of the laws of Spain and the Indies.

[9] Preface by E. Quesada to P. Mallo, "Página de la historia de la medicina en el Río de la Plata desde sus origenes hasta 1822," *Anales de la facultad de ciencias médicas* (Buenos Aires, 1897), vol. I.

should be treated by the other doctors, surgeons, apothecaries, and phlebotomists, and the obedience which should be rendered to the decisions that it makes in the exercise of its duties." [10]

Soon after the establishment of this tribunal chairs of medicine and surgery were established. The teaching of anatomy and surgery began in 1801 under the direction of Agustín Eusebio Fabre; the professorship of medicine was inaugurated in the following year by Cosme Argerich with fourteen students.[11] The school of medicine—organized with the two professorships just mentioned—was started with fifteen students.

The champion of the educational cause in La Plata was Manuel Belgrano. He had accepted the doctrines of Campomanes, the great Spanish economist of this age and author of the work entitled *Educación popular* (*Public Education*). The object of this teaching—intended for workmen and young people—was above all professional, technical, and practical. Moreover, Belgrano was an advocate of free public schools.

Among the first institutions created at his initiative were the schools of navigation and design, both founded in 1799. The former of these was placed under the control of a competent technician named Pedro Cerviño, who carried on his duties for some years without any compensation. In his report of 1796, Belgrano declared that one of the means needed to protect commerce was to found a school of navigation and that "no one should be allowed to become captain of a bark on La Plata River unless he knew the principles of navigation; and furthermore that there should be young men available for vessels from Spain in case these came to America without pilots or pilots' mates." [12] And in an address delivered at a public debate in 1802, Belgrano affirmed that the young men who graduated from the school of navigation "as persons accustomed to calculations and to meditation would be excellent professors in all the sciences and arts to which they might apply themselves." [13]

[10] *Revista del Archivo General de Buenos Aires*, III, 290.

[11] Gutiérrez, *Noticias históricas sobre el origen y desarrollo de la enseñanza pública superior en Buenos Aires*, p. 510.

[12] M. Belgrano, *Documentos del archivo de Belgrano* (7 vols. Buenos Aires, 1913-18), I, 79.

[13] *Telégrafo Mercantil* (2 vols. Buenos Aires, 1914-15), III, núm. 12.

With respect to the school of design, its founder said in his report of 1796 that its instruction was indispensable for every artist, carpenter, embroiderer, tailor, smith, and so on. He added: "The benefits arising from a school of design extend to other persons besides artists. Without this knowledge, incipient philosophers will not understand the planispheres of the celestial and terrestrial armillary spheres showing the movements of the earth and other planets in their respective systems, and, in consequence, the designs of electric and pneumatic machines, and many other designs which are now found in their books. To the theologian, to whom some instruction in geography is indispensable, this knowledge will facilitate the use of the map and the compass; to ministers of state and to lawyers this will facilitate the use of the pictorial and surveyor's plans of houses and cultivated lands presented by litigants in lawsuits. And the physician will more easily understand the parts of the human body. . . ." [14] Gutiérrez asserts: "In those days the country did not lack artists capable of teaching the fine arts. At the opening of the revolution a very distinguished Italian painter of real talent was living in Buenos Aires. We know his name and one of his paintings by chance, but if he had not been compelled to collect by legal process payment for one of the portraits painted by him, we would not know that Ángel Campones was the painter of the magnificent canvas representing the miraculous person of the lay brother, Fray José de Zemborain, which hangs in the sacristy of the church of the Dominicans. . . ." [15] But the mother country declared that the academies of navigation and design were establishments "of mere luxury" and on that account suppressed them.

Belgrano also planned to establish schools of agriculture, commerce, and experimental chemistry. One of the causes to which he ascribed the poverty of the farmer was his adherence to custom and his inability either to think seriously about the best course to follow or to make experiments. Hence the necessity for founding an institute of agriculture, a simple and practical plan that Belgrano sketched in one of the reports which he prepared annually

---

[14] Belgrano, *op. cit.*, I, 73.

[15] Gutiérrez, *Noticias históricas sobre el origen y desarrollo de la enseñanza pública superior en Buenos Aires,* p. 28.

in his capacity of secretary of the commercial tribunal. He asserted
that young farmers should be taught "the general principles of the
growth and development of crops, in which they should be taught
to distinguish each kind of land by its natural products, and the
proper tillage of each type, the different kinds of plows available
and the advantages of each for different kinds of soil; the methods
of cultivation; the depth of cultivation according to the nature
of the soil; fertilizers and the time and method of applying them;
the mode of laying drains in swampy land; the quantity and quality
of seed most suitable to this or that soil; the need of preparing
seeds for planting and the process to be used; the proper time to
plant; the care that should be given to planted fields; the manner
of harvesting crops; the methods of preserving grain without risk
or expense. . . ." [16]

He praised the importance of commercial and economic studies
and sketched a plan for the founding of a school of commerce,
"where young men might go for instruction in arithmetic; in the
method of entering accounts and of keeping books; in the calcula-
tion and regulation of exchange; in the rules of mercantile navigation; in insurance, and so on; in the method of establishing and
carrying on mercantile correspondence; in the laws and customs
employed by merchants, and other things where at least the general
principles of geography should be taught and information given
regarding the articles which countries produce or lack, so that
by having a knowledge of these principles they can make their
commercial ventures with the greatest possible certainty." [17]

Because of the report read by Belgrano in 1802 suggesting the
establishment of tanneries, the commercial tribunal conceived the
idea of founding an institute of experimental chemistry to investi-
gate the art of tanning hides. The members of the tribunal, who
formed the project, urged that there should be brought from
Madrid "a chemist with a knowledge of mineralogy so that a practice school and a laboratory sufficient to carry on the investigations
requiring their creation might be established by means of the modest
endowment that should be considered proper." [18] The tribunal ap-

---

[16] Belgrano, *op. cit.*, I, 62-63.

[17] *Ibid.*, p. 79.

[18] Archivo general de la nación, consulado, 1794-1810, expedientes.

proved the entire project and asked the Spanish government for a teacher of chemistry. In 1804, Minister Soler responded in the name of the king denying the petition and directing the commercial tribunal to use "the funds for the objects favored by his ministry and for the expenses of the crown."

During the colonial era, the founding of an institute of mines was also contemplated. In 1779, Escobedo, the visitor, was given charge of the intendancy of Potosí. He carried out an important work in the reorganization of the bank and the mint. Among his significant innovations was that of establishing an academy and practice school in Potosí in order to promote mining. The mineral resources of this region were beginning to decline; the famous hill of Potosí seemed to be exhausted. In order to continue the prudent exploitation of that hill it was necessary to train men in the art of metallurgy. Hence arose the need of founding the institute. In his inaugural discourse Escobedo spoke as follows: "I do not urge that managers of the mining industry should be philosophers, physicians, astronomers, mathematicians, architects, painters, or jurists . . . but I shall be content to demonstrate to you the necessity of their understanding the principles of an art which until the present day have been determined only by custom." [19] The preceding exposition shows that the ideas concerning colonial affairs which prevailed in La Plata did not deal simply with the teaching of theology.

After the signing of the treaty of 1777, which ended the secular dispute between Spain and Portugal, the courts of Madrid and Lisbon appointed boundary commissions which were to try to survey the boundary line that had been agreed upon. The commissioners appointed by Spain were organized into three divisions. The first and the second divisions were in turn subdivided into two parts. The first part of the first division was intrusted to José Varela, a ship captain who was well versed in mathematics. The second part of the first commission was directed by the commissioner Diego de Alvear, who later wrote his *Diario de la segunda partida de la demarcación de límites entre los dominios de España y Portugal* (*Diary of the Second Part of the Demarcation of Boundaries between the Dominions of Spain and Portugal*).

---

[19] Archivo general de la nación, gobierno colonial, Potosí.

In its turn the second division was subdivided into two parts. The chief of the first part was Félix de Azara and its second in command was the engineer Pedro Antonio Cerviño. This group was to start its operations at the Igatime River. Félix de Azara was one of the most eminent scientific men who ever came to La Plata. A scientific observer and naturalist, Azara left in manuscript numerous works that constitute an important contribution to the study of the history, the condition, and the geography of La Plata. With advanced proposals concerning the division of lands and their settlement, he anticipated the ideas of the generation that outlined the course of Argentine development. The second in command of this party, Pedro Antonio Cerviño, was an engineer by reputation. He was the first director of the nautical academy, and his liberal ideas with respect to foreign commerce provoked a sentiment of disapproval among the members of the commercial tribunal.

The second part of the second division was in charge of Juan Francisco Aguirre. He left a *Diario* of his trip, a valuable geographical work, in which are found many "suggestions of travelers and impressions of actual witnesses, and which contains no small amount of informative material that can be used by the true writer who may later try to depict the annals of the colony." [20]

The third division had Rosendo Rico Negrón as its chief. Other important persons figured in the divisions mentioned. For example, in the second part of the first division the geographer, Andrés de Oyarvide, rendered services described in his report in which he noted in detail the events that took place during the proceedings of the boundary commissions.

It is clear that this select group of men exerted an undoubted influence upon the culture of the colony. Such names as Azara, Aguirre, Alvear, Cerviño, and Oyarvide are intimately related to all the manifestations of culture of the last decade of the eighteenth century. They were the persons who diffused among us many principles of astronomical, geographical, historical, and natural science; they scattered the germs of liberal ideas.

Among the instrumentalities that diffused political and philosophical liberalism in La Plata was the University of Chuquisaca

---

[20] P. Groussac, "Noticia biográfica de Don Juan Francisco Aguirre y examen crítico de su diario," *Anales de la Biblioteca* (Buenos Aires, 1905), V, xxix.

where the works of the encyclopedists and writers of the eighteenth
century were expounded.

On the coast, a condition arising from the economic and commercial activity prevailing in the colony provoked a conflict
between those persons who defended the monopolistic interests and
those who pleaded for the adoption of measures of a general
character. This struggle went on everywhere: in the cabildo of
Buenos Aires, in cabildos abiertos, in the periodicals, and above
all in the commercial tribunal. In the discussions of that tribunal
are found the germs of political revolutions. A group of liberal
and enthusiastic men began there the first battles for liberty. Upon
the occasion when the members of the commercial tribunal decided
to ask for the revocation of the royal order regarding commerce
with foreign colonies, Francisco Antonio Escalada denounced
them as being interested in their own personal affairs. In the same
debates, Tomás Fernández and Ventura Miguel Marcó del Pont
displayed a liberal attitude. Pleading for the régime of commercial
freedom, an inhabitant of Buenos Aires named José de María invoked in its favor "the most sensible part of the nation."

The proceedings of Belgrano had been beneficial in various ways.
He was a theoretical preacher of the new principles of political
economy; we have already noticed the significant part which he
played in all the important tasks performed by the commercial
tribunal. Hipólito Vieytes took charge of the periodical which was
to disseminate throughout the country at the opening of the nineteenth century the ideas of liberty cherished by the patriots. In
his post as syndic of the cabildo, Saavedra pronounced his luminous
opinion concerning the existence of guilds by affirming the principle
of the liberty of industry and commerce; in his report, Izquierdo,
the superintendent of the custom house of Buenos Aires, argued
frankly for freedom of commerce; Villalva, fiscal of the audiencia
of Chuquisaca, exposed all the errors of the colonial régime and
advocated the freedom of the Indians; lastly, Moreno represented
the culmination of this process of the diffusion of liberal ideas by
the haughtiness and firmness with which he asserted in his "Memorial of the Landowners" the advent of a new era. To quote
Carbia again:

"With respect to books, it can be shown that despite stringent
prohibitions, many books were read in La Plata which had been

legally prohibited. Robertson's *History of the Discovery of America*, for example, prohibited by the cédula of December 23, 1778, was found in the library of José Antonio Roxas de Mendoza, as well as ninety-five sheets of a Spanish translation of it. The book entitled *Discours sur les principes fundamentaux d'une constitution libre* circulated in Buenos Aires through the instrumentality of Miguel Rubin de Celis whose property had been ordered confiscated by a very secret royal cédula dated December 15, 1792." [21]

In an article on the influence of philosophy in Argentina, Korn states: "By a public proclamation (August 6, 1799) Viceroy Avilés considered it necessary to threaten whosoever perused prohibited readings with severe punishments for he had been 'informed that foreign papers had been introduced with odious accounts of insurrections, revolutions, and upheavals of established and recognized governments.' . . . According to Gutiérrez, the library of Maciel, in its day the best collection in Buenos Aires, contained 1,099 volumes on theology, history, literature, law in general, and some volumes on geography and physical sciences, written in Greek, Latin, Italian, Portuguese, and French, as well as in Spanish. Bayle and Voltaire were represented. . . ." [22]

A suggestive item concerning the spread of liberal ideas in La Plata is that afforded by the citation of Escalada, namely, that Adam Smith, the author of the *Wealth of Nations* was mentioned in the debates of the commercial tribunal exactly twenty years after the publication of that treatise. In 1810, there was published in Buenos Aires by the royal press of the Foundling Hospital a Spanish edition of the *Contrat Social* of Jean Jacques Rousseau with a prologue by Mariano Moreno.

It has been affirmed that America had its literature in the Pre-Columbian era. Nevertheless, in a general view of indigenous civilizations, the literary manifestations discovered are purely choreographic. The first sign of an indigenous dramatic literature has been attributed to the Quechuas of Peru. About the year 1780, that is, in the age of the revolt of Tupac Amaru, the drama entitled "Ollanta" or "Ollantay" was presented to the public. Its theme

[21] Carbia, "La revolución de Mayo y la iglesia," *Anales de la facultad de derecho y ciencias sociales*, XIV, 199.

[22] A. Korn, "Las influencias filosóficas en nuestra evolución nacional," *Anales de la facultad de derecho y ciencias sociales* (Buenos Aires, 1914), XI, 364.

was concerned with an Indian revolt and the restoration of the deposed Inca to his throne. Regarding its pretended Quechua origin an historian has said: "Ollantay is by its content, its form, and by its minor incidents an heroic, swashbuckling drama, both Christian and adventurous, like those created by Lope de Vega and Calderón. It has its king, its old man, its gallant, its lady, its traitor, its confidants of both sexes, its retinues, its love-makings, its pacts, and, in order that nothing should be lacking in that respect, even its amusing squire, and the intimate jester of the gallant. . . . Moreover, all its scenes have a revolutionary atmosphere that indicates the age in which they were written and arranged, and which is repugnant to the political maxims of the absolute government of the Incas, the most absolute that had ever existed." [23]

The first poet born on Argentine soil was Luis José de Tejeda, a native of Córdoba who lived in the beginning of the seventeenth century. He was the author of a poem entitled *El peregrino en Babilonia* (*The Pilgrim in Babylon*) and of numerous mystical poems which were first published only a short time ago.[24] The most intense intellectual literary movement that originated in La Plata in the colonial era was during the administration of Viceroy Vértiz y Salcedo. The founder of the Academy of San Carlos, he was able to surround himself with a select coterie of men: Father Juan B. Maciel, a scholar of great authority among the youth of Buenos Aires, whom he characterized as intelligent and active, and possessed of a noble impatience to learn; Manuel de Basavilbaso, who planned to found settlements on the Río Negro, to establish a hospice for beggars and one of correctional retirement for women in Buenos Aires; and finally Manuel José de Labardén, the highest poetic expression of that age, the author of the tragedy *Siripo* and of an *Oda al Paraná* (*Ode to the Paraná*) which gave him considerable reputation. Labardén became the founder of a small literary school. In another group, Prego de Oliver, the superintendent of the custom-house of Montevideo, an inspired poet, was the leader of a school opposed to that of Labardén.[25]

[23] B. Mitre, *Páginas de historia* (Buenos Aires, 1909), p. 274.

[24] L. de Tejeda, *El peregrino en Babilonia y otras poemas* (Buenos Aires, 1916).

[25] E. García Velloso, *Historia de la literatura argentina* (Buenos Aires, 1914), chaps. 2 and 3; and in *La Nación, 1810—25 de mayo—1910*, pp. 236-41.

Vicente López y Planes commemorated the success of the creole resistance against the English invader by writing a poem entitled *Triunfo Argentino*. Upon the same subject, Dr. Pantaleón Rivarola composed two extensive poems entitled *Reconquista y Defensa* and *Gloriosa Defensa*. As writers of this era should also be mentioned, Manuel Medrano, a poet of only moderate inspiration, Domingo Azcuénaga, author of numerous fables, and Joaquín Araujo who wrote the *Guía de Forasteros* which gives a complete description of La Plata from the administrative, political, and economic viewpoints.

CHAPTER XX

COLONIAL JOURNALISM

COLONIAL JOURNALISM began in the first decade of the nineteenth century. We do not say that it was a revolutionary factor in the society of La Plata, but it contributed powerfully to spread useful knowledge, to promote the study of the country, and to bind together the provinces of the viceroyalty.

The first periodical to appear was the *Telégrafo Mercantil, Rural, Político, Económico e Historiógrafo del Río de la Plata* (*Mercantile, Rural, Political, Economic, and Historical Telegraph of Río de la Plata*) which began publication on April 1, 1801, under the direction of Francisco Antonio Cabello y Mesa, who had edited a periodical in Lima. Among his chief collaborators were José Joaquín de Araujo, who wrote under the pseudonym of "The Patrician of Buenos Aires." Domingo de Azcuénaga, who signed his articles with the initials "D. D. D. A.," and the following gentlemen: Luis José Chorroarín, Juan José Castelli, Juan M. Labardén, Pedro Antonio Cerviño, Manuel Belgrano, and Gregorio Funes. Contributions of great value published in the *Telégrafo* were those of Thaddeus Haenke, the Bohemian traveler and botanist who sent articles from Cochabamba.

The *Telégrafo* carried on an interesting study concerning the condition and the resources of the provinces. Scarcely had fourteen numbers been published, when the public began to pay close attention to the journal and to demand of the editor the information that it wished. The editor replied thus in number fifteen: "Some persons would rather have special information than learned flourishes; others consider such information as trifling and wish that the *Telégrafo* should be filled solely with scientific articles; the merchant seeks information and suggestions concerning his noble business and discounts typical observations and treatises of education . . . (in a word), everyone desires that this periodical should consider no other matters than those which suit his own particular taste and calling." To those asking that he write about the geography and history of these provinces, he responded:

"that such articles should not be written in a hurry and without a very detailed examination of such material as exists in the archives."

The plan devised for studies of every province was realized in part by the coöperation of the delegates of the commercial tribunal in the provinces who transmitted their reports which were published in the *Telégrafo*. These communications of the agents of that tribunal have great historic and geographic value.

Semanario de Agricultura

The *Semanario de Agricultura* (*Agricultural Weekly*) which was first published in 1802 under the direction of Hipólito Vieytes, suspended publication with number 218 on February 11, 1807, as a result of the capture of Montevideo by English forces. It developed a more ample and patriotic program than the *Telégrafo*, for its collaborators not only pleaded in favor of stimulating production but also urged the necessity of opening Buenos Aires to the free exportation of the products of the country. In the prospectus announcing its appearance, the editor said: "Marvel at the truth that, although almost three centuries have elapsed since this important part of the world was discovered, our farmers are accustomed to receive returns from a few grains of wheat or maize that they frequently scatter by chance upon the earth, and that, satisfied with the cultivation of these two crops, they waste the nutritive juices of the most fertile land in the universe, which have been employed up to the present for the most part only in nourishing the thistle and the thorn with which our fields are covered." [1]

description of agriculture in La Plata

As an evidence of the backwardness of our agriculture and the miserable condition of the farmer, the editor said: "If one surveys the vast area of our fields, they show at once the miserable condition of the farmer, who, although the absolute master of a strip of land, which in other countries would be capable of supporting a potentate, makes a bare living from it and finds himself without resources or means with which to make the land productive. . . . He is completely ignorant of any kind of industry; he tills only that portion of land which he considers necessary to his support, and what is worse, he is entirely devoid of the desire which men have of increasing their comforts and their property."

In long articles he advocated the development of the cultivation

---

[1] The *Telégrafo Mercantil* has been reprinted in facsimile by the Junta de Historia y Numismática Americana.

of gardens and the planting of trees; he favored the development
of all industries depending upon fishing and cattle-raising, and
ceaselessly alluded to the necessity of removing all obstacles to
domestic and foreign commerce. The economic creed embraced by
this periodical is indicated by the following paragraph: "Neither
the inexhaustible mines of the hill of Potosí, nor the prolific richness of the enormous masses of solid silver of Guantajaya, nor the
richest gold nuggets of the Tipuani River, could ever be comparable
with the inexhaustible treasure which our extensive fields can
produce."

economic realism.

In May, 1807, the *Estrella del Sud* (*Star of the South*) began
publication at Montevideo; it was issued weekly in English and
Spanish. The part in English was written by one Bradford under
the nom-de-plume of "Veritas," while the Spanish part was written
by Manuel Aniceto Padilla, a native of Cochabamba then living in
Montevideo. It ceased to appear in June of the very year in which
it was founded. A complete file of this journal includes seven
numbers, besides a prospectus, and a special number. The intention
of the English in publishing this periodical was to deaden the resistance of the creoles by convincing them of the advantages of English
domination and of the backward state in which Spanish rule kept
the colony. Its fundamental promise was the freedom of commerce
and industry, and on this point it coincided with the general
aspirations which the creoles had entertained for some time. Differences arose between the English and the creoles, not only with
regard to the fact that the latter refused to accept foreign political domination, but also because English Protestantism was repugnant to the general sentiment of the people who were strongly
Catholic. The *Estrella del Sud* tried to demonstrate the similarity
of the doctrines of the Anglican and Catholic churches, and offered
the assurance that an integral part of the English plan of conquest was to establish liberty of faith and religion. The historian
José M. Estrada declared: "It was the view of the *Estrella del Sud*
that by advocating commercial freedom, as I have already noted,
by criticizing the government, and by displaying to all the decadence of Spain it could greatly promote the progress of the
country." [2]

Estrella del sud

---

[2] Estrada, *op. cit.*, I, 313.

Correo de Comercio

On the eve of the revolution (March 3, 1810) the *Correo de Comercio* (*Commercial Post*), a weekly journal edited by Manuel Belgrano first appeared. It ceased publication on February 23, 1811, after fifty-two numbers had been issued. This new publication followed in large part the plan formed by the *Semanario de Agricultura*. In all of its numbers, Belgrano insisted on the ideas that we have already mentioned concerning such matters as agriculture, industry, and education. "There was a time, disgraceful for humanity," he declared, "in which it was believed that the people should be kept in ignorance, and consequently in poverty, in order to keep them in the greatest state of subjection, but this maxim, injurious to mankind, is now proscribed as a product of the most cruel barbarism." [3]

Almost every issue of the *Correo de Comercio* included a page devoted to the activities of the ports of Buenos Aires and Montevideo. These data are interesting for a study of the commercial movements of the period and for a list of the prices current in Buenos Aires and the other parts of the viceroyalty. They furnish valuable materials for a study relating to the cost of living in that age.

---

[3] Belgrano, *op. cit.*, II, 19.

CHAPTER XXI

COLONIAL SOCIETY

IT IS KNOWN that aborigines, Negroes, and European whites formed the society of La Plata. These races differed by something more than their height or the simple color of their skin. They had different sentiments and manners of living; and they formed distinct civilizations. The three races that intermingled in La Plata also blended their beliefs and their civilizations. The white man or the Spaniard was the civilized European man of the fifteenth century. He introduced, as we have explained, a warlike spirit and also the spirit of municipal organization.

The colonizing streams distributed the germs of rebellion and of an insurgent spirit. The leader of the stream that entered directly by the Río de la Plata ordered the assassination of Osorio, who was accused of being a rebel, upon the coasts of Brazil; in the stream that came by way of Peru, Heredia assassinated Mendoza on the way back; the stream that left Chile conquered Tucumán in sanguinary fashion and violently deflected the colonizing stream from Peru. This warlike spirit provoked a rebellious spirit among those persons of Spanish blood born in the land.

Spain protected the marriages of Spanish settlers in America with the Indians. Such alliances were made from the very beginning of the colonial period. In the Laws of the Indies (book VI, title I, law II) we read: "It is our wish that the Indian men and women should have as they ought to have entire liberty to marry whomsoever they may wish, both aborigines and natives of these our kingdoms or Spaniards born in the Indies, and that no impediments should be put in their way. And we command that no order of ours that has been given or may be given can prevent nor shall it prevent, marriage between Indian men or women and Spanish women or men, and that these shall have entire liberty to marry whomsoever they may wish, and our audiencias shall see that this law is observed and carried out." This fusion of races prepared for the advent of "those born in the land"—creoles, mulattos, or mestizos—who soon formed the vast majority of the inhabitants.

The Negroes, to a minor extent, also influenced the ethnic composition of the population of La Plata. They predominated particularly in Buenos Aires and in Córdoba. In a moral way their influence was great; for Negro slaves played an important rôle in the life of the home; they served as the companions of children and young people. Born in Africa, they were imported in the character of slaves, in order to replace the Indians who were perishing because of the severe labor which they had been forced to perform.

Impelled by sane generosity, Fray Bartolomé de las Casas came to the defense of the Indians. He brought the mistreatment of the Indians to the attention of the court of Madrid and asked it to prevent the hecatomb of thousands of Indians who were being killed by work. But he committed the grave error of advocating the enslavement of the Negroes to replace the Indians; just as though they were not human beings.[1]

The race of mestizos—says Juan de Ulloa—arises in general from the intercourse of white men and Indian women outside the pale of matrimony. Mestizos who spring from the union of Indian men and white women are rare. The progeny of white men and Indian women were exempt from the obligation to pay tribute; but the children of Indian men and white women followed the status of their fathers. This exception favored mixed unions; from it sprang one of the causes of the tendency of an increase in the mixed classes and a decrease in the number of pure-blooded Indians. "It is a fact that pure-blooded Indians are constantly decreasing in all sections, either by the terrible scourge of smallpox or by the use of strong liquor. In the islands of Cuba, Santo Domingo, and Jamaica the same thing happens with regard to the pure-blooded Indians as with regard to gold and silver, so that one may doubt, if there had been any before the conquest." To quote Robertson again: "It is chiefly by this mixed race, whose frame is remarkably robust and hardy, that the mechanic arts are carried on in the Spanish settlements, and other active functions in society are discharged, which the two higher classes of society, from pride, or from indolence, disdain to exercise."[2]

---

[1] See further, R. Altamira y Crevea, *Psicologia del pueblo español* (Barcelona, 1917), pp. 145-46.

[2] Robertson, *op. cit.*, IV, 34.—W. S. R.

In early days, colonial society was centered in the city. The city was everything. Joined to it, the suburbs first, and then the country, were its natural tributaries. The city was everything, first, because it was the government, the official residence of the political, judicial, and communal officials; and, second, because within the city there took place the important phenomenon of the fusion of races, the mingling of the blood of the conqueror and the conquered. The life of this first organic nucleus of the population was in the beginning unfortunate; for the constant invasions of the Indians and the threats of attack imperilled the established order. The people lived ready for hostilities, with spirits alert, prepared to repel threatened invasion, while governors carefully watched over the defense. They prohibited any inhabitant from removing to a distance from the city. In this manner the city was gradually extended; it spread first to the suburbs, and then to the plains. This was the atmosphere that was breathed by the first settlers, and if the native spirit of the Spaniard was in itself heroic and warlike, thanks to the influence of these factors, this spirit was increased and strengthened in his descendants, thus moulding a haughty, courageous, and rebellious spirit.

Within the city the highest class was composed of the nobility of office-holders, while all the rest were the common people, who were composed of the offspring of Spaniards and Indian women. According to the census of 1744, there were in the city of Buenos Aires 10,223 inhabitants, of whom 141 were landed proprietors; in the country there were 6,083 inhabitants, of whom 186 were landlords. Between the nobility of functionaries and the lowest class there was a middle class of artisans and mechanics.[3]

Indians and mestizos lived in the country as well as Spaniards to whom the authorities had made grants of land. The trade of the landed proprietors was concerned especially with the hides of bulls,

[3] By the opening of the nineteenth century the city of Buenos Aires was becoming an important center. More than three hundred merchant vessels anchored every year in its harbor; more than 300,000 hides were exported every year; and in its warehouses there was deposited a consderable quantity of Paraguayan tea, tobacco, cotton, and timber. With regard to its popunlation, Mariano Moreno estimated that in 1806 it had 60,000 inhabitants; the historian Funes asserted that it had 70,000; and Azara estimated that it had 40,000 inhabitants in 1801. According to the best data, it is probable that in 1810 the city of Buenos Aires did not have over 50,000 inhabitants.

steers, and cows which were usually sold at the price of from six to nine reals apiece. In describing the life and labors of the man of the pampas the colonial historian Azara states: "A gang of men gather, who are generally dissolute and wicked, without either law or a king, and go where cattle are to be found. When they find a considerable number of cattle, these men form a semicircle: those on the sides round up the cattle, while those in the center carry a long pole to which is firmly fastened a sharp curved knife with which they hamstring all the cattle without making a pause until they finish with the herd or with those they consider necessary. Then they return by the same road, and those who have done the hamstringing pierce the entrails of each beast with a pike in order to kill it, and the others take off its hide and carry it off in order to stretch it upon a stake.... All the meat is lost, and at best they merely extract some suet." [4]

Estrada said: "Thus the gaucho was the product of a system of government, that gave no stimulus either to agriculture or to commerce, and that was without schools or incentives for civilization. Isolated from the rudimentary civilization of the cities, he was thrust into the pure life of the plains in an open struggle with the desert and with misery. There he became a barbarian: he did not have recourse to science in case of disease; nor in his afflictions did he find either a temple or a home." [5]

Nearer the city were small farms and houses, where produce was raised for urban trade as well as for export.

Until the beginning of the eighteenth century, the life of the colony was poor and simple. The colonial home was always a vast family which was composed of relatives, slaves, Indians, and clients. But during this early period "the house was a bureau or depot of laborers who went out every day to sell their labor on account of the master. As business was plentiful, money could easily be invested and with few risks. With one hundred or two hundred pesos a slave is purchased whose labor yields a profit of eight or ten pesos a month, and whose subsistence costs very little." [6]

---

[4] Azara, as cited by Gutiérrez, "Memorial al ministro D. Diego Gardoqui para los hacendados de Buenos Aires y Montevideo en el año 1794," *La Revista de Buenos Aires*, X, 7-8. See further, M. P. Leguizamón, *El gaucho, su indumentaria, armas, música, cantos y bailes nativos* (Buenos Aires, 1916).

[5] Estrada, *op. cit.*, I, 92.   [6] García, *op. cit.*, p. 85.

With the activity in commerce and the development of the pastoral industry private fortunes began to be formed. This changed the basis of life. In the middle of the eighteenth century there were real fortunes in La Plata: some families lived with all the conveniences of life and occasionally in luxury. Parties and entertainments began to be held frequently, and thus a new social life was initiated. An influence upon the formation of this life was the bureaucratic and administrative organization that was formed in La Plata by the establishment of the viceroyalty. High officials, such as oidors, intendants, councillors, and members of the tribunal of accounts, lived either in Buenos Aires or in interior cities.

In the inventory of the slaves, goods, jewels, and other possessions of a royal official named Gerónimo Matorras there were listed more than a dozen slaves, a "carriage made in Holland with its glass windows, linings, pear-shaped ornaments, iron axles, . . . two pair of mules, and gilded harnesses" (which had cost more than 1,400 pesos), two mate sets with their bowls and drinking tubes, and two trays, "all made of silver with gold adornments" (which cost 700 pesos); "a silver table with feet shaped like those of a goat," a set of diamonds (valued at 700 pesos), two finger rings (worth 100 pesos apiece), a gold chain and its rosary (150 pesos), and other things.[7]

The will of Pedro Altolaguirre, treasurer of the mint of Potosí commences by stating: "In the first place I commend my soul to God, our Lord, and my body to the earth of which it was created;" and ends by asking that upon his death masses should be read "for the persons whom I have injured in honor and estate and whom I have not satisfied." [8]

The Spanish women who accompanied the daring conquerors in the pilgrimage to the New World had their own distinctive traits. When Ovando went to Española in 1502 he took numerous families with him. A few years later, Diego Columbus came with his wife to America and brought with him a number of Castilian maidens. All of them married rich men, "for in truth there was a great lack of such women of Castile, and although some Spaniards married

---

[7] C. Correa Luna, "Don Baltasar de Arandia, antecedentes y desventuras de un corregidor en 1778," *Anales de la academia de filosofía y letras* (Buenos Aires, 1914), III, 44-46.

[8] Archivo general de la nación, hacienda, ley III, expediente, 98.

leading Indian women, yet there were many other Spaniards who under no condition would marry Indian women because of their incapacity and frigidity." [9]

As early as the beginning of the sixteenth century, the king ordered that married men should take their wives with them to America. He forbade the sailing of those men who wished to get away from their homes. A not inconsiderable number of Spanish women undertook to fill political offices of importance in America. In the words of Oviedo:

"It is not extraordinary that Doña María de Toledo should govern as viceroy of the Antilles and appoint subordinate justices in her own name; and that Doña Juana de Zárate should obtain the title of adelantado from the emperor . . . Doña Isabel Manrique and Doña Aldonza de Villalobos became governors of the island of Margarita; Doña Beatriz de la Cueva ruled Guatemala by the choice of the cabildo, and so well liked was she that more public feeling was exhibited at her death than at that of her husband Pedro de Alvarado. . . . Similarly Doña Catalina Montejo became adelantado of Yucatan as successor of her father; the wife of Hernando de Soto ruled the island of Cuba with firmness, . . . and Doña Isabel Barreto, perhaps the only example in the world of a woman who became an admiral, took a squadron to the Philippines with a stricter discipline than that observed by soldiers and sailors." [10]

The cabildo of Buenos Aires in the exercise of its functions as the protector of the people, regularly fixed the price of the articles indispensable for subsistence. At the beginning of the seventeenth century, the cabildo ordered that fourteen loaves of bread weighing one pound apiece should be sold for one peso of eight reals. Subsequently, because of the abundance of wheat, it ordered that sixteen loaves, each weighing a pound and a half, should be sold for one peso. During the same time the wine of these lands could not be sold for more than twelve pesos per arroba, while Castilian wine sold for fourteen pesos per arroba and even more. In 1605, ten

---

[9] According to Oviedo, as cited by C. F. Duro, "La mujer española en Indias," *Memorias de la real academia de la historia* (Madrid, 1910), XII, 172.

[10] *Ibid.*, pp. 182-83. See further, Groussac, "Noticia biográfica de Don Juan Francisco Aguirre y examen crítico de su diario," *Anales de la Biblioteca*, IV, 360, note 1.

pounds of beef were sold at one real. Steers more than three years old were worth six reals, while the smallest were worth four. In 1659, the hide of a cow was worth four reals. An arroba of suet brought the same price. In 1669, because of the quantity produced, a pound of yerba mate sold at two reals per pound. A cartload of wool brought between three and five pesos. In 1673, an arroba of charcoal cost half a peso.

The cabildo also undertook to fix a tariff of prices for articles sold by such artisans as carpenters, smiths, shoemakers, and tailors. For "building a house with a hall having three beams and two rooms of wood, and round pillars made by hand," carpenters could charge twenty-five pesos; for a chair three pesos; for a table with four feet four pesos, and so on. A bridle sold for three pesos; a pair of spurs for two pesos. Tailors could ask six pesos for a cloak, a doublet, and plain trousers. A silk doublet with its trimming was reckoned at four pesos, and so on. Varnished shoes were sold by shoemakers at six pesos a pair; while boys' shoes cost one peso.[11] In the second half of the eighteenth century these prices increased considerably.

The festivals most commonly celebrated in the colony were of a religious character. On the days of Corpus Christi and of Saint Martin, patron of the city, and during holy week, the people solemnly displayed their sentiments. At other times ceremonies were celebrated in order to beseech the aid of the saints against any plague that tormented the city. The Virgin of Luján caused epidemics to disappear; Saints Sabine and Boniface destroyed ants and mice; Saint Martin mitigated the drought in the country and by beneficial rains caused the fields to yield.

Public festivals were developed in connection with taking the oath of allegiance to the sovereigns. On the eve of this ceremony the city was illuminated. Upon the occasion of the oath to Ferdinand VII the following preparatory measures were taken: "The soldiers of the regiment of nobles stationed in Victoria Street erected a beautiful arch in front of their barracks. On its façade were two clasped hands and underneath on both fronts verses were written. All the rest of the arch was illuminated: in its interior

---

[11] A. M. Elflein, "El cabildo y el comercio," *La Prensa*, Buenos Aires, November 10, 1918.

upon a stage with balconies on the sides were placed the musicians of the regiment who for the space of six hours entertained the people with lively sonatas. In the great square, the entire facade of the chapter house and that of the barracks of the Miñones regiment, whose commander was a royal ensign, were illuminated by torches and colored vases which formed a pleasing spectacle. Two orchestras successively entertained the people. One of these was placed under the balconies of the cabildo hall, while the other was upon a stage constructed for that purpose in the square." [12]

The tribunal of commerce had adorned the façade of its building which was illuminated by vases of various colored oil. After Ferdinand VII was proclaimed, the royal ensign gave a banquet.

In 1804, a pompous and solemn festival was held in Paraguay when the Prince of the Peace—Godoy, the minister of Charles IV—accepted the post of the first perpetual regidor of the cabildo of Asunción. After the dispatch was read in which Godoy accepted the post, the news was announced to the public by a triple salvo of artillery and by the ringing of bells. The governor gave a banquet to more than seventy persons. Soon the populace proceeded to the hall of the cabildo; they brought the portrait of the prince in a triumphal car drawn by eight horses. Behind the car, besides the governor, marched the members of the cabildo, the chiefs and officers of the regiments, the high officials of government, and a company of militia. In the central plaza triumphal arches had been erected: in one of these, which symbolized immortality, there was placed the portrait of Minister Godoy. In the evening, a play was presented under this arch, the purpose of which was to give thanks to the prince who had honored Asunción by accepting the post of regidor. Feasts and bullfights and hoop racing were held on the following days, while clothing and plenty of food were given to the prisoners.[13]

The laws styled *Las Partidas* of the thirteenth century already mention bullfights as public amusements. During succeeding centuries this entertainment became more regular and frequent in

---

[12] F. R. de Udaeta, "Proclamación de Fernando VII en Buenos Aires," *La Revista de Buenos Aires* (Buenos Aires, 1868), XV, 165-66.

[13] "Una fiesta en el Paraguay en 1804," *La Revista de Buenos Aires* (Buenos Aires, 1869), XXI, 172-76.

arenas constructed for that purpose. There developed a species of daring men who particularly dedicated themselves to this profession, devotees of a cult of courage.

Whenever the feast of Saint Martin and other religious feasts were celebrated, bullfights took place. The cabildo intrusted the construction of a bullring to an empresario who was given the right to sell admissions to the arena. A description of the ring and of the bullfight is as follows: "An enclosed space was arranged in the square, which was left unpaved; around it were constructed amphitheaters for families and boxes for public officials. A space including a certain number of square yards was reserved for members of the audiencia, for the canons, members of the cabildo, and other personages; the rest of the space was left for the public. The ayuntamiento bore the expense of the refreshments which were ordinarily served to higher officials and their families. . . . Once the officials had taken their seats, everyone took his place, and the bullfighters entered on horseback. They were generally distinguished persons of the city who displayed the greatest luxury in their dress and trappings. They were introduced to the governor or to the superior official there present by the first alcalde, or more frequently by the chief constable of the city. . . . After the ceremony of transferring the key of the bullpen, the professional bullfighters and their assistants dashed into the ring, and then one or more bulls were admitted, according to circumstances. A band of musicians and buglers of the cabildo that heralded the kaleidoscopic changes were complementary factors."

In September, 1790, Viceroy Arredondo authorized the construction of a permanent amphitheater in the square of Monserrat. The contractor was to build the arena at his own expense, and to collect fifty pesos for each bullfight. He was to arrange at least twenty-seven spectacles each year. The cabildo had informed the viceroy concerning the advisability of constructing it, but the act stated that "the season in which bullfights should occur must exclude harvest time, namely the two months of January and February, in order that the bullfights might not serve as a distraction and that there might be harvesters of a grain so necessary for the preservation of life, and as experience has shown that the said entertainment takes farm laborers from their tasks, it has been ordered that during harvest time bullfights should always cease and even more, all public and private works."

Even up to the middle of the eighteenth century the architectural appearance of the city of Buenos Aires was disagreeable. The most important buildings surrounding the main plaza were the royal fortress, the cathedral which was not yet finished, and the hall of the cabildo. The theater had not yet been constructed; the episcopal palace was a very poor house roofed with tile, while the place now occupied by the general archives of the Argentine nation had been acquired by the cabildo as the site for the slaughter-house. To the plaza there came carts laden with meat, fowls, fish, fruit, and other products, which were displayed for sale upon the ground.

Vértiz y Salcedo stimulated the material progress of Buenos Aires by looking after the paving and sanitation of the streets. The lack of grading and the heavy rains at times made the streets impassable. The viceroy asked the opinion of the cabildo and the latter responded by proposing such reforms as the following: (1) that the hauling of heavy bullcarts into the center of the city should be prohibited (they should not proceed east of Monserrat Plaza or north of the New or Yellow Plaza); (2) that two or three markets should be established outside the city walls; (3) that water should be allowed to flow through the streets that ran from north to south; (4) that sidewalks should be constructed at the expense of the landowners; (5) that the sanitary condition of the city should be permanently improved by the use of convicts and handcarts to cleanse the streets of refuse.[14]

From the opening of the nineteenth century one of the aristocratic quarters of the capital city was that which was designated Santo Domingo. Its most central street was that called Rosario, now changed to Venezuela. A not inconsiderable number of colonial structures were still standing in recent times. Among these were the house known as the house of the Abbess (450 Belgrano Street); that of Domingo Basavilbaso, which was one of the most luxurious (in Belgrano Street between Balcarce Street and Avenue Colón); that of Virreyna Vieja (on the corner of Peru and Belgrano streets); and that of Balcarce (Balcarce 161).[15]

---

[14] V. G. Quesada, "La ciudad de Buenos Aires," *La Revista de Buenos Aires* (Buenos Aires, 1967), XIV, 611-12.

[15] On the appearance of other colonial cities, see R. Montero Bustamante,

The prevailing style of architecture was the Andalusian baroque of the eighteenth century. That style of architecture undoubtedly prevailed from Quito to Buenos Aires. This view is supported by numerous architectural details, such as similarity in iron gratings, window embrasures (typical of the Andalusian baroque style), tile roofs, balconies, and other features. But the influence of this style declined at Buenos Aires, which at the end of the eighteenth and the beginning of the nineteenth centuries was affected by a new and degenerate influence that came directly from Spain. On the other hand, Córdoba is the most interesting colonial city, for in that city there was produced a form characteristic of Platean art, namely the fusion of the Andalusian baroque-mudéjar style with elements of Calchaquian architectural technique.

In order to make known a protest against a governmental order, anonymous communications were frequently sent to the authorities and lampoons were circulated. Hence the governors circulated manifestos in which they declared that severe punishments would be imposed on such persons as committed the offense of circulating defamatory lampoons.

In 1776, when the alcabala was increased from four to six per cent, merchants protested and posted lampoons in the streets. One of those caricatured the intendant general, Manuel Ignacio Fernández, and Francisco Cabrera, the accountant of the tribunal of accounts, astride of donkeys headed toward the gallows, and at the foot of the lampoon were various threats. For the same reason, similar incidents occurred in other parts of the viceroyalty. Anonymous sheets, containing allusions to well-known persons or officials, were circulated from house to house. As will be shown further on, the same method of communication was also used to promote revolutionary propaganda. Pillado aptly states:

"It was a common practice in the colony to make wise saws and to apply nicknames to every person or thing. Thus great as well as small men were apt to be given a nickname by popular choice, always obvious and irresponsible. . . . Thus, for example, Governor José de Garro was called 'the Saint,' Viceroy Cisneros, 'the

---

"Arquitectura colonial," *Revista Histórica* (Montevideo, 1909), II, 451-58; and J. B. González, "Córdoba colonial," *La Nación,* Buenos Aires, August 24, 25. 26, and 27, 1916.

Deaf One'; the clerk Eufrasio Boiso, 'Seven Hairs'; Doña Francisca Alfaibar de Viana, 'the Marshal's Wife'; and Señora O'Gorman, 'the Simpleton.' Sites were treated in a similar fashion; when discussing past times, no one will be surprised today to hear such names as the 'Rude Ward,' the 'Corner of the Souls,' the 'Block of the Lights,' the 'Little Street of Sin,' the 'Bridge of the Devout Women.' " [16]

After the opening of the seventeenth century, Buenos Aires had a hospital for men which was managed by the cabildo, and intended for soldiers of the presidio. Efforts were made after 1664 to extend the functions of this hospital; [17] finally, in 1745, the king authorized the founding of a general hospital on the same site as that on which the military hospital was located, which was to be cared for by four or five Bethlehemite fathers. From that time, those fathers took charge of the hospital. As the site was small and unhealthful, they obtained permission from the king to change it and to occupy the site which had been used by the members of the Society of Jesus who were expelled in 1767.

The foundling hospital was established in August, 1779, during the administration of Viceroy Vértiz y Salcedo. It also was installed in a building which had belonged to the expelled Jesuits. This establishment had the humanitarian object of taking care of abandoned infants.

Vértiz y Salcedo found a means of raising funds for the foundling hospital. He had just acquired a printing press that had been left in Córdoba by the Jesuits. From the operation of this press he obtained some money. Its manager was conceded the privilege of selling catechisms and primers, but the price of these was not to compete with that of similar articles imported from Spain. Years later, the king provided that the foundling hospital should be supported by the income from "nine old houses, the annual rent of which amounted to 1,056 pesos, without including another house which produced 250 pesos per annum; by 1,000 pesos that were paid by the managers of the play-house, which it was feared could not continue because of its decadence; and by an annual function given for the benefit of the foundling hospital, the income from

---

[16] José A. Pillado, *Buenos Aires colonial* (Buenos Aires, 1910), p. 205.

[17] E. Peña, ed., *Documentos y planos relativos al período edilicio colonial de la ciudad de Buenos Aires* (5 vols. Buenos Aires, 1910), III, 165.

which was reckoned at 500 pesos. . . ." [18] Even with these funds the needs of the foundling hospital could not be met, and to make good the deficits it was necessary to have recourse to the revenues of the war department. From the year of its foundation until 1802, 2,017 children were received in the foundling hospital. The king had declared that all the foundlings "whose fathers were not known should be considered as legitimate children for all civil purposes generally and without any exception."

Colonial medicine is important and deserves attention, although it is not possible because of lack of space to treat it fully here. It should be observed in the first place that the contact of the conquering race with the aborigines produced a series of epidemic diseases and aggravated endemic diseases. In particular, the Indians were scourged by smallpox, measles, and syphilis.

A physician named Hernando de Zamora came to Buenos Aires with the expedition of Pedro de Mendoza. In 1605, the very year in which the first schoolmaster, Francisco Vitoria, was appointed, the acts of the cabildo of Buenos Aires mention no other surgeon than Manuel Álvarez. The city of Córdoba, founded in 1573, had a physician in 1598 named Telles de Rojo.

In 1619, there was in Buenos Aires a physician of Flemish origin, named Nicolás Xaques. He had been located at Córdoba and enjoyed a good reputation. Despite his presence, the scourge of smallpox that now began in the capital was combatted by religious processions, "in order that God might be pleased to free this land from the evil of the pest." In 1621, the scourge ravaged the growing population in terrible fashion. In 1642, the presence of the physician, Andrés Gedeón, was required, for the city was suffering from a new epidemic in the form of typhoid fever. At all times the quacks were denounced, who without any legal right, exercised the functions of physicians and encouraged prejudices and superstitions among the ignorant people.

In Spanish America, physicians belonging to religious orders excelled, especially the Franciscans and the Jesuits. They devoted themselves to the study of those herbs and plants used by the Indians because of their curative qualities. Among them all, Father

---

[18] V. G. Quesada, "Fundación de la Casa de Niños Expósitos en Buenos Aires," *La Revista de Buenos Aires* (Buenos Aires, 1863), I, 387.

Pedro Montenegro distinguished himself by his work entitled *Materia Médica*, in which are found valuable observations about our medicinal plants.

In 1780, Viceroy Vértiz y Salcedo created the tribunal of king's physicians and appointed Dr. Miguel Gorman the first royal physician, as we have already mentioned. With the advent of Dr. Gorman, the first attempts to prevent smallpox took place, for not only did he use the method of vaccination in order to preserve the population from that scourge, but he proposed the establishment of an isolation hospital in a site removed from the city. In 1793, a new epidemic of smallpox occurred which was handled with success.

The great discovery of the immunizing effects of vaccine made by Jenner in 1798 soon became known in Spain. In 1807, King Charles IV organized a scientific expedition to introduce the new treatment into the Spanish colonies. Because of the long itinerary that it had to follow, the expedition reached Buenos Aires only after considerable delay. Fortunately, in 1805, a Portuguese frigate belonging to Antonio Machado Carvalho brought among a cargo of slaves, "two young negroes bearing fresh vaccines and in excellent condition for the transmission of the desired prophylactic against smallpox." [19] A few days later the first vaccinations were made with good results and soon Dr. García Valdez and Dr. Salvio Gaffarot were able to show to Viceroy Sobremonte the first cases of typhous vaccines seen in our country. In the course of the same month (August, 1805), these cases served for the inoculation of some hundreds of children. The practice of vaccination spread rapidly. In 1810, the junta made it compulsory.

---

[19] E. Cantón, *La facultad de medicina y sus escuelas* ("Historia de la Universidad de Buenos Aires," vol. V, Buenos Aires, 1921), p. 187. [On the expedition sent out by Charles IV, see further R. Altamira y Crevea, *Historia de España* (4 vols. Barcelona, 1900-1911), IV, 354-55.--W. S. R.]

CHAPTER XXII

THE ENGLISH INVASIONS

IN ORDER TO explain the English invasions of La Plata in 1806 and 1807, it is necessary to consider the background of English colonial policy as well as the general course of European policy. English colonial policy had a marked development after the signing of the Treaty of Utrecht (1713), the American importance of which we have noticed in another place. Up to the time of the peace of Utrecht, the English colonies did not have a population of more than 150,000 inhabitants; in 1740, the number had increased to 1,000,000; in 1755, it had reached 1,500,000. In 1763, by the Treaty of Paris, England became mistress of Canada and the French possessions east of the Mississippi. Spain ceded to England the peninsula of Florida in exchange for Havana, which had been conquered by the English during the war, and for Louisiana, which it received from France. During this process of English colonial expansion, Spain discerned the peril of being eliminated as a colonial power by England—a fact that explains the liberal policy of our motherland toward the colonies.

When the thirty-year concession to engage in the slave traffic with the Spanish Indies, which had been conceded by the Treaty of Utrecht to England, had almost expired, that nation declared war on Spain. At this point it is necessary to mention the active measures in favor of Spanish-American independence made by the English. The English sea-dog, Admiral Edward Vernon, who commanded one of the squadrons that attacked Cartagena in 1739, wrote to the English admiralty in June, 1741, in regard to "the necessity of Great Britain undertaking the emancipation of the Spanish establishments in America, in order to open their markets to the merchants of London." [1] The revolt of the Thirteen Colonies against England (1776), which was aided by both France and Spain, had important political and economic consequences for the Spanish-American colonial world, for after that time the opening

[margin note: thirty years after Treaty of Utrecht war again]

---

[1] C. A. Villanueva, _Resumen de la historia general de América_ (Paris, 1913?) p. 190. [See further, Levene's introduction to vols. V and VI of _Documentos para la historia argentina._—W. S. R.]

of the ports of Spanish America was indispensable for British commerce.

When the French Revolution broke out (1789), like the majority of European states, Spain fought on the side of the coalitions formed against revolutionary France. The triumph of the republican armies obliged Spain to sign the peace of Basel (1795) with France. In turn, this event provoked a declaration of hostilities by England against Spain, a condition which lasted until 1802, when the Peace of Amiens was signed. During this period (1796-1802), the measures of England for the emancipation of Spanish America, or rather for the invasion of some of these colonies, became very significant. Miranda, whom we shall consider later, tried to arrange a plan with England for this purpose. In 1797, the viceroy of Buenos Aires wrote to Madrid to ask for reënforcements in men and munitions, for he considered an attack by an English squadron imminent.[2]

The peace signed in 1802 was of brief duration, for in the following year war was again declared between France and England. At the price of a subsidy, Charles IV, king of Spain, bought from Napoleon the right to remain neutral in that war. But, in 1804, England seized four Spanish vessels en route from America to Spain. Spain united its navy to that of France; but, in 1805, their combined navies were vanquished by the English fleet in the naval battle of Trafalgar.

At the same time, an English expedition was dispatched for the purpose of seizing the Dutch colony at the Cape of Good Hope. This squadron was under the command of Sir Home Popham, who took possession of that colony on January 18, 1806. Commodore Popham, who had participated in the preparation of Miranda's plans, then decided to invade La Plata. General David Baird, commander of the army, ordered William Carr Beresford to embark with 1,500 men in the squadron commanded by Admiral Popham.

The Venezuelan general, Francisco de Miranda, is the precursor of the emancipation of the Spanish colonies. After 1790, he was actively engaged in Europe in search of support for the execution of this great plan. But, in 1797, as we have said, because of the

---

[2] Archivo general de la nación, Gobierno colonial, oficios al rey, consejo y ministros, 1768-1787, reservado.

declaration of hostilities by England against Spain, his proposals
acquired practical importance. During this year, there apparently
gathered in Paris various Spanish Americans, who were perhaps
members of a secret society founded for this purpose. They decided
formally to solicit the support of Great Britain upon the basis of
an offensive and defensive alliance. In compensation, they offered
£30,000,000 sterling, besides some commercial and territorial advantages in which the United States should participate on an equality with England. Pitt entertained the idea upon the basis of an
expedition of 10,000 men from the United States, protected by
an English squadron. Indeed, he caused the English secretary of
state for foreign affairs, Henry Dundas, to write to the governor
of Trinidad directing him "to promote the measures most suitable
to liberate the Spanish colonies, and to place them in a position to
resist the oppressive authority of their government, in the certainty that they could count upon all the resources to be expected
from H. B. Majesty; be it with forces, or with arms and ammuni-
tion to any extent, with the assurance that the views of H. B.
Majesty, go no further than to secure to them their independence,
without pretending to any sovereignty over their country or even
to interfere in the privileges of the people, either in their political,
civil, or religious rights."

At the same time, Miranda got into touch with the celebrated
Alexander Hamilton whom he had met in 1784 while making a tour
of the United States. As President Adams (of the United States)
did not decide to promote the enterprise, it was postponed. The
idea reappeared in a different form in 1801, and when the peace
of Amiens was signed it was on the eve of being executed. When
hostilities broke out anew in 1803, the project was again considered by the English cabinet. Upon this occasion the intermediaries
of the cabinet in the negotiations with Miranda were Viscount Melville, first lord of the admirality, and Sir Home Popham. The latter
embraced the plan with ardor and, after a conference with Pitt,
he framed a memoir about it. In consequence, in December, 1804,
after the capture of the four Spanish vessels, it was decided that
Popham should accompany Miranda with the frigate *Diadem* of
sixty-four guns in order to coöperate in his plans concerning
America by "taking advantage of the opportunity offered to secure in the new continent a position favorable to English trade."

Again the project was suspended; but from it there was soon to develop the idea of invading the Spanish possessions of La Plata.[3]

On June 25, 1806, English soldiers disembarked on the coast of Quilmes. On June 27, a column of 1,560 men entered the streets of Buenos Aires and took possession of a city of 55,000 souls.[4]

Viceroy Sobremonte had not attached much importance to a rumor which had reached him some days earlier to the effect that English vessels had appeared on the Platean coast. On the evening of June 24 there had been given in the play-house an entertainment in honor of the future son-in-law of the viceroy who had asked for the hand of his daughter Mariquita. The hall was resplendent. In the central box, which was adorned with the Spanish banner, was the viceroy with members of his family. The entertainment progressed to the great satisfaction of the audience. But at the end of the second act a lieutenant of the viceroy entered his box, and gave him a message from Ensenada advising him of the disembarkation of the English. The audience became aware of the fact, and they all went out of the theater after the viceroy. Consequently everyone became alarmed. Viceroy Sobremonte fled as far as Córdoba, wishing to save his belongings, but in vain; for these fell into the hands of Beresford and were sent to London. In tranquil days the indignation of the people later found expression in the following couplet concerning the flight of Sobremonte:

Al primer cañonazo—de los valientes—
disparó Sobremonte—con los parientes.

(*i.e.*, At the first shot of the cannon from those brave fellows,
Sobremonte vanished, together with his relatives.)

At three o'clock in the afternoon of June 27, Beresford took possession of the fort of Buenos Aires. On the next day he hoisted the English flag. He immediately issued a proclamation which guaranteed to the people of La Plata the following liberties: (1) the administration of justice; (2) the right of private property; (3) the Roman Catholic religion; and (4) freedom of commerce, like that granted to other English colonies.[5]

[3] On the relations between Popham and Miranda, see W. S. Robertson, *The Life of Miranda* (2 vols. Chapel Hill, 1929), I, 257-323.—W. S. R.

[4] J. M. Pueyrredón, *Documentos del archivo de Pueyrredón* (4 vols. Buenos Aires, 1912) I, 83-101.

[5] The decree concerning commerce is found in Levene, *Lecturas históricas argentinas*, I, 250-52.

The people of Buenos Aires realized the gravity of the situation. Various projects were proposed for the reconquest of the city. Some persons wished to explode mines under the fortress where Beresford was living. But this plan did not develop. The creole, Juan Martín de Pueyrredón, led an uprising of the peasantry of Buenos Aires to the number of 1,000, but at the small farm of Perdriel, four leagues from the capital, they were dispersed. They were an army of countrymen, who had never fought, and who could therefore accomplish little against the soldiers of Beresford, who were disciplined veterans. But this movement was significant because it made plain that the people wished to free themselves from English domination.

The honor of successfully reconquering Buenos Aires belongs to Santiago Liniers, a Frenchman by birth but a loyal servant of Spain. Liniers was captain of the port of Ensenada. For the purpose of observing at close range the strength of the invading army, he asked permission to enter the capital city, which was conceded to him because he was a foreigner. Then he proceeded to Montevideo, where the governor, Ruiz Huidobro, placed 1,000 men under his orders. Taking advantage of a dark night, in order to elude the vigilance of the English, Liniers disembarked with his army at Tigre. In San Fernando, he was joined by the valiant contingent of Pueyrredón's peasants, who had been routed at Perdriel, and marched upon Buenos Aires. The entire population welcomed his approach, and young men swelled his ranks. On August 10, Liniers reached Corrales de Miserere (now Plaza Once de Septiembre, the Plaza of September 11). Then he occupied the Plaza de Toros (Retiro). He attacked the city on August 12. Liniers divided his army into two columns: one entered the city by San Martín Street and the other by Reconquista Street (this name commemorates the event). Liniers' triumph was complete, and Beresford was imprisoned at Luján. During the engagement the English lost about 300 men, dead and wounded; they surrendered 1,200 soldiers, who became prisoners of war, and gave up their flags and standards, 35 cannon, and 1,600 muskets. The army of Liniers had 200 men dead and wounded.

On the day following the reconquest, as the government was without a head, the cabildo invited a number of members of ecclesiastical, civil, and military organizations to a meeting of the cabildo abierto or general congress, which was to meet on August 14, in order "to insure the victory." The members of the open council decided that the command of military affairs, according to the Law of the Indies, was a special prerogative of the viceroys; but they resolved that "that law left an opening by which the desires of the soldiers and of the people might be satisfied. They declared in favor of Santiago Liniers whom they named as lieutenant of the most excellent viceroy." [6] In order to respond to the insistent requests of the people, the cabildo abierto appointed a committee of three members who left the capital to have a conference with the viceroy. When they met Sobremonte, he "affirmed that there was no authority whatever, except that of the Spanish king, which could deprive him of his prerogatives." The bases for a conflict were thus laid: the cabildo was obliged to accept the reasons set forth by Sobremonte, in opposition to those of fact and of force which had impelled the general congress to reach its decision. Other events that occurred later obliged the people to adopt an energetic and radical resolution.

"Few people have suffered such attacks or have repulsed them with so much glory," wrote Mariano Moreno concerning the people of Buenos Aires.[7] He alluded to the constant invasions of Indians, to the struggles with corsairs and pirates, and to the war with the Portuguese—all of which were endured by the people with dignity. In the beginning of the nineteenth century, the number of veteran soldiers stationed in the viceroyalty of La Plata did not exceed 2,400.[8]

In consequence of the successful repulse of the English, the military spirit became strong among the people. The ineptitude of the rulers and the lack of an army were supplied instantaneously by general patriotic coöperation. Thus there was formed by the heat of a new sentiment, the citizen militia, the first training-school of a creole army. The enlistment was ordered within four days of all inhabitants between sixteen and fifty years of age. The recruits

---

[6] *Documentos referentes á la guerra de la independencia y emancipación política de la República Argentina,* I, 389.

[7] Mariano Moreno, *Colección de arengas en el foro y escritos del Doctor Dn. Mariano Moreno* (London, 1836), p. 31.

[8] M. R. García, "Estudios sobre el período colonial," *Revista del Río de la Plata* (Buenos Aires, 1872), IV, 354.

were required to attend "the instructional exercises which take place from six to eight in the morning"; and a warning was given that otherwise "action would be taken against them as persons suspicious to the state." [9] To these recruits a democratic military organization was given, for they had the power to appoint their own officials by majority of the votes cast in a direct election. These elected officials were to choose their commanders in the same manner.

Five battalions of creoles were formed: four of nobles residing in Buenos Aires (one of them composed of colored or swarthy people), and one of Arribeños (*i.e.*, men from the hinterlands, who live or travel along rivers), in which were included the natives of interior provinces. To these were added squadrons of cavalry, a battalion of provincial grenadiers, one of hunters of the province of Corrientes, and a corps of artillery. The Spaniards also formed corps of soldiers who were called Andalusians, Catalonians, and Galicians. The commander of the body of nobles was Cornelio Saavedra. In the ranks of this regiment were included many young men who later played an active part in the May Revolution. Among them were Manuel Belgrano, Juan Viamonte, Eustaquio Díaz Vélez, Feliciano Antonio de Chiclana, and others. In October, 1806, the total number of veteran soldiers and militia in this capital was 8,151, of whom only 3,000 were Spaniards, while the remaining 5,100 were creoles.

Great was the rejoicing of the English people, when they learned that the city of Buenos Aires had fallen into the hands of Lord William Carr Beresford. Soon afterward, the property which had been taken from Sobremonte reached London. In order to insure the conquest, the English government dispatched Samuel Auchmuty at the head of an army to reënforce Beresford. It sent another army under the command of Craufurd to conquer Valparaiso. At that port he was to serve as a defense to Buenos Aires by making it impossible for that city to receive aid from Peru. But soon the news of the expulsion of the English from Buenos Aires was received. Craufurd was then ordered to place himself under the orders of Auchmuty; and Stirling was made admiral of the squadron to replace Popham.

---

[9] Archivo general de la nación, Real audiencia: Buenos Aires, 1806-1809.

General Baird had sent 1,300 men from the Cape of Good Hope who seized Maldonado. The forces of Auchmuty soon arrived and in conjunction with those sent by Baird they captured Montevideo on February 3, 1807. Sobremonte, who was in charge of the fort, repeated the cowardly conduct he had displayed at Buenos Aires, and abandoned the city. The people of Buenos Aires instituted a suit against him and deposed him.

In the meantime, Craufurd had reached Buenos Aires, and soon afterward General John Whitelocke arrived. The English forces formed a total of 12,000 men, with three brigades of artillery, a brigade of engineers, twenty warships, and ninety transports.

After the occurrence of the events which we have just mentioned, grave differences arose between the cabildo and the audiencia in regard to the policy which should be adopted. Santiago Liniers took the reins of government and convoked a junta of war which assembled in the fort of Buenos Aires on February 10. This so-called junta of war was essentially a cabildo abierto, which was attended by the members of the audiencia, members of the superior tribunal of accounts, of the cabildo, of the commercial tribunal, and of the junta of the royal treasury, in conjunction with the leaders and commanders of the soldiery, as well as some leading inhabitants. The difference between this gathering and other open councils lies in the fact that the council which met on February 10 was convoked by the military commandant and took place in the fortress. The members of the cabildo, the military commanders, and the citizens present voted in favor of the suspension from office and imprisonment of the viceroy, which was the policy decided upon with the addition that the royal audiencia should assume control of the government. The judges had no other recourse than to address Sobremonte "making known that it would be advantageous to the service of his Majesty for him to delegate all his powers to this royal audiencia as though the circumstance had come to pass which was contemplated by law XLVIII, title XV, book II of the *Recopilación*." The Law of the Indies thus cited referred to viceroys who fell ill "in such a manner that they were entirely unable to govern." And thus, yielding to the pressure of circumstances, the judges justified by a simple juridical fiction the revolution which had occurred—the viceroy was sick. It was a fragile and inefficient theory, flung like a feather to all the winds. . . .

The crisis of Spanish-American public law had begun, and the agitation was profound. The first spark of the juridical revolution of Spanish America had just been lighted in Buenos Aires.

Whitelocke prepared to attack that city. He organized his forces in four grand divisions under the command of generals Craufurd, Auchmuty, Lumley, and Colonel Mahon. The army of Buenos Aires did not number 8,600 men, who had to face 11,000 English soldiers. Whitelocke had left 1,000 men to defend the fort at Montevideo. Liniers mistakenly believed that the army of Buenos Aires could meet the English in a pitched battle and little anticipated a defeat.

On June 28, 1807, the English army disembarked twelve leagues from the capital. The creole soldiers numbering 7,000, commanded by Liniers, stationed themselves to the south of Riachuelo de Barracas. One thousand six hundred creoles had remained to defend the city which had not been fortified. With regard to this maneuver Mitre makes the following comment: "This sally (of Liniers) was imprudent, and the selection of a position was an error that reflected little credit upon the military skill of Liniers; for it would have produced as an inevitable result the loss of the capital, and with it in all probability the loss of La Plata, if mistakes of the enemy had not offset it, and if other Platean commanders had not compensated for the deficiencies of the viceroy. It is not possible to suppose that with forces so inferior in number and quality, he could triumph over an enemy so superior in all particulars; and, even conceding the wisdom of the sally, it was a mistake to lose the advantage furnished by the Río de Barracas, to relinquish that vantage ground to the enemy and to leave it on his flank with the grave risk of losing everything in case of a defeat, for retreat was impossible, as the city had been left practically defenseless with only a battalion of organized nobles, and some artillerymen and marines." [10] The army of Liniers was routed by the division commanded by General Gower, who took possession of the Plaza Once de Septiembre and, in accordance with superior orders, did not advance. Meantime, dismay had spread in the city at the news of Liniers' defeat; but at this critical moment the alcalde, Martín Alzaga, fortified the city. General Whitelocke attacked it on

---

[10] Mitre, *Historia de Belgrano,* I, 133.

July 5, according to a plan that gave the following result: Colonel Pack was routed in his attempt to gain possession of the Temporalities; Craufurd was also vanquished at Santo Domingo; the creole soldiers completely triumphed at San Miguel and La Merced; but Auchmuty succeeded in capturing the Plaza de Toros.

In this wise the English army had been vanquished because of the decision of Alzaga that he could in time fortify the city.[11] General Whitelocke surrendered by accepting the capitulation offered by Liniers by which the English agreed at once to evacuate Buenos Aires and to relinquish the fortress of Montevideo.

The reconquest of Buenos Aires was, as we have said, the result of the efforts of the people, headed by Santiago Liniers. The defence of Buenos Aires was also a victory won by the strength of its people and those of the vicinity. This is perhaps one of the finest pages in the history of Buenos Aires, because of the valor, decision, and patriotism that its sons displayed in the defense of the capital. The best praise was, indeed, that given by General Whitelocke in the defense that he presented to the court in England. The English general said: "I have before stated that it was understood the tops of the houses would be occupied, and from the known hostility of the inhabitants, it was supposed that many of them would take part in the defence, and that their post would be on the roofs of the houses, while the Spanish troops offered a resistance in the streets, and defended the fort, and such defences as they might have prepared in the streets of the town. We, therefore, looked for a vigorous resistance: but I will ask the Court and every individual member of it, whether from any experience in modern times, from anything handed down to us in military history, since the modern system of warfare, and the use of firearms have prevailed, or even from any information we had received, or observation we had made, as to the hostility of the inhabitants, anything but the actual result could lead us to form a just estimate of the resistance made. A multitude of instances might be mentioned, in which a certain proportion of the young and active population has increased the strength, but in which the general population has always impeded, instead of assisting the efforts of the defending army. Not one can, I will venture to say, be produced

---

[11] On the tactics of Liniers, see P. Groussac, *Santiago de Liniers* (Buenos Aires, 1907), p. 132.

like the present, in which it is no exaggeration to say, that every
male inhabitant, whether free or slave, fought with a resolution
and perseverance which could not have been expected, even from
the enthusiasm of religion and national prejudice, or the most in-
veterate and implacable hostility." [12]

The English invasions were an important event in the destinies
of the viceroyalty of La Plata. We have already said that, with
the viceregal period there began an important historical evolution
—economic, political, and intellectual—which led toward the revolution, a process that we have seen developing slowly and gradually. When the English invasions took place in 1806 and 1807, this
historic evolution was stimulated and precipitated. The city of
Buenos Aires, which was the head of the viceroyalty, caused an
event that accomplished a profound transformation in its breast.
In fact, the people were revealed in all the integrity of their
strength and valor. The reconquest and the defense had been the
result of popular force; the people, therefore, acquired in the decisive ordeal of the struggle, a knowledge of their own strength.
They had vanquished the English army, powerful because of its
numbers and discipline; and the victorious force might be employed, if opportunity arose, against the Spaniards. Woodbine
Parish, who later served as English consul general at Buenos Aires,
said of the colonists: "Their successful resistance of the British
invasions of Buenos Ayres in 1806 and 1807, the issue of which
could have surprised no one more than themselves, roused the people from their slumbers, and taught them for the first time their
own power, and all the weakness of the mother country, then in
fact reduced to little better than a dependency of France. In reply
to their request for military aid, after General Beresford's first
attack, and under the certainty of its being repeated by a more
imposing force, they were told they must defend themselves as they
could, for Spain could send them no help." [13] To quote Mitre again:
"The sons of the country raised their heads with pride; and upon
proclaiming themselves the equals of the Spaniards in spirit, in
patriotism, and in force, they, indeed, realized that this equality

---

[12] *The Trial at large of Lieut. Gen. Whitelocke* (London, 1808), p. 544.
—W.S.R.

[13] W. Parish, *Buenos Ayres and the Provinces of the Río de la Plata* (London, 1852), p. 70.—W. S. R.

was a transitory concession, and that what would require it in essence was the authority, the government, and the superiority of the land of their birth." [14]

The results of the English invasions may be classified as commercial and political. The political results of the English invasions are concerned with the knowledge that the creoles acquired of their own strength. These forces crystallized and took on two democratic forms: one, by organizing itself into a party—the creole party led by Liniers—and the other, by organizing itself into the army corps formed by people who would serve as the center from which they could successfully demand their rights in the hour of revolution. There should also be noticed the special political value of the English occupation of Buenos Aires, for this made known among the creoles the ideal of emancipation—a topic which we shall consider with care in a separate chapter.

The economic results of the English invasions were also important. The English disseminated in La Plata the ideas of free commerce of which they were the heralds. We should notice that during the few days of Beresford's rule in Buenos Aires he issued a proclamation by which he conceded, among other liberties, freedom of commerce like that granted to English colonies. The occupation of the fort of Montevideo by the English served to disseminate economic doctrines. English prisoners who were kept in Buenos Aires also carried on a propaganda, for they suggested to the creoles the notion of independence under an English protectorate. Besides, in May, 1807, the English published in Montevideo a journal named the *Estrella del Sud* (*Star of the South*), written in English and Spanish, which they used as an organ for the propagation of their liberal ideas. It is accordingly clear that the spirit of the economic doctrines desseminated by the English reenforced the work which Belgrano, Vieytes, Escalada, Castelli, and others had accomplished in the commercial tribunal and in journalism by advocating freedom of commerce in opposition to the form of political economy which then prevailed.

[14] López, *op. cit.*, II, 173-74.

CHAPTER XXIII

THE PRECURSORS OF THE REVOLUTION

SOME YEARS before 1810 a nucleus of patriots embraced the idea of emancipation. In the light of new documents it can be affirmed that the idea of a revolution against Spain had been entertained in the provinces of La Plata even before the English invasions occurred. In fact, in April, 1805, Viceroy Sobremonte addressed the oidor of the audiencia, Juan Bazo y Berri, and in a most secret manner instructed him to make an investigation concerning "the circulation of news and of extraordinary reports that for some time past had been spread among the people announcing upheavals and changes in our government." The inquest of Bazo is of great interest, for in July, 1805, he said to the viceroy that he did not wish to commit to writing the tales in circulation which he had collected, "for they were unworthy of being transmitted to posterity even in most secret documents."

After the English invasions took place the revolutionary propaganda became more intense and its authors became visible, that is, those persons who have already been designated as precursors. Saturnino Rodríguez Peña was the patriot who initiated in La Plata the negotiations for independence under an English protectorate as an agent of the plan that Francisco de Miranda, precursor of Spanish-American independence, had developed in London. Until the year 1804, the proposed object of English policy was not to conquer Spanish America, but to promote its independence in order that England could freely trade with the Spanish-American ports.

These ideas were expressed in 1804 by Admiral Popham and Francisco de Miranda to Lord Melville, first lord of the English admiralty. Subsequently, there developed the strange policy of England, involved in the invasion of La Plata in 1806. But soon after this attack was repulsed, General Beresford, who was confined in Luján, began to disseminate revolutionary ideas. He conveyed the impression that England's plan was to aid in the emancipation of the Spanish-American colonies. Saturnino Rodríguez Peña undertook to spread this idea; he conferred about it with

Martín de Alzaga, who at that time was chief alcalde and a man of great influence. These activities became known to the authorities. The viceroy commanded that General Beresford should be interned at Catamarca, but Rodríguez Peña and his friends helped him to escape.

The intrigues of Saturnino Rodríguez Peña did not end with those that have been narrated, but he went to Rio de Janeiro, to which capital the Portuguese court had been transferred, and became the champion of a plan for the independence of La Plata under the rule of Princess Carlota. The arrival in Brazil of the reigning family of Portugal had caused much uneasiness in that capital. The fears were well-founded for that nation was attached to England which had been very hostile to Spain. After reaching Rio de Janeiro, Princess Carlota, sister of the captive king, Ferdinand VII, pursued a contradictory and inexplicable policy toward the authorities of Buenos Aires. Thus, on April 26, a secret dispatch, dated March 13, was received by the cabildo of Buenos Aires from the Portuguese minister, Souza Coutinho, in which he offered the protection of the Portuguese against any attack, with the stipulation that, if this friendly proposition were not accepted, "her Royal Highness will consider it necessary to make common cause with her powerful ally, England, against the people of La Plata." This threatening proposal was declined in a dignified manner by the cabildo. Almost at this juncture there arrived at Montevideo the Portuguese commissioner, Joaquim Javier Curado. However, it was necessary to dismiss him because he had the temerity to propose that the Banda Oriental should be annexed to the Brazilian dominions.

In Rio de Janeiro, Saturnino Rodríguez Peña negotiated with Princess Carlota for her transfer to Buenos Aires, where she might be crowned by virtue of her status as the eldest sister of the king of Spain, Ferdinand VII. To promote the success of his plan, Rodríguez Peña wrote to numerous families of Buenos Aires, to his brother Nicolás, to Juan José Castelli, to Martín Alzaga, and to others. Rodríguez Peña advised such persons as became implicated in his project to promote it "with a haughty air as the plan would be realized despite the slight opposition that it may encounter," that it should be advocated among "the priests who have an incomparable influence, especially among the lower classes, who la-

bor under a heavy yoke imposed by the peninsular Spaniards";
and that a propaganda should also be carried on among the commandants and officials of the militia, in the belief that one "could
count upon generous support." The plan of Rodríguez Peña was
based upon the idea that Carlota should be proclaimed ruler of
La Plata by an assembled congress and upon the basis of establishing the independence of the country. However, the princess soon
denounced the activities of Rodríguez Peña to the authorities of
Buenos Aires. Why did Princess Carlota take this step, if she had
ambitions to rule over La Plata?

As the same interested party declared, the letters of Rodríguez
Peña were "full of revolutionary principles subversive of the present monarchical order and tending toward the establishment of a
fanciful and visionary republic." As is seen, Carlota did not accept a revolutionary plan that weakened the doctrine of her divine
right to succeed to the throne.

The cabildo abierto of 1806 decided to send an agent to Spain
to inform his Majesty of the credit gained by the city during the
days of the reconquest. The nomination fell upon the victor of
Perdriel—the man who had organized the first creole defense
against the English attack. Pueyrredón was absent from La Plata
three years and witnessed the progress of the convulsion that agitated Spain, in particular the spasm that followed the Napoleonic
invasion.

With the exception of the news of Europe that Belgrano brought
in 1795, Pueyrredón was the first creole of importance who spoke
to the South Americans about the results and new events that flowed
from the revolution of 1789. Forgetting his mission, Pueyrredón
sent seditious messages from Spain to the cabildo and to his friends.
He avowed in them that Spain was in an anarchical condition, divided into as many governments or juntas as it had provinces. He
added that "all these wish to inherit this rich territory [meaning
the Spanish Indies], and that in such a situation I believe that a
prudent delay is the policy which reason recommends." Upon his
return Pueyrredón was made a prisoner and put on a vessel destined for Spain. But he escaped, sojourned some months in Rio de
Janeiro, and in June, 1809, returned to Buenos Aires.

In the middle of 1809, Buenos Aires was the scene of intense
political agitation. After the revolution of January 1, 1809, in

which the cabildo planned in vain to depose Liniers, the entire colonial political framework was tottering. In Upper Peru, the revolts in Chuquisaca and La Paz demonstrated that unrest was spreading throughout the entire organism.

After 1809, the plan of emancipation, which hitherto had made headway in La Plata, either in the form of an English protectorate or the candidacy of Carlota, became identified with the revolutionary and republican theory with which independence was accomplished—the principle that juntas should be formed for self-government. In June of that year frequent secret meetings were held in order to plan to resist the arrival of Cisneros, who had been appointed viceroy of La Plata. In the book containing the acts of the cabildo is found an account of its meeting of July 13 in which the patriots proposed to solicit the establishment of juntas. The account contained this decisive declaration: that it was necessary "to display now in a clear light the sole and true object of the patriots; and that to take such a step (to establish juntas) could have no other object than to elude Spanish domination and to aspire to the complete independence of these dominions." Thus it was that almost a year before May 25, 1810, the cabildo, which was the bulwark of the royalist party, proclaimed that the object which animated the patriots to resist Cisneros or to desire the establishment of juntas was "the complete independence of these dominions."

Toward the end of 1809, an anonymous communication was delivered to Cisneros. As has been stated, this was the ordinary mode of carrying on a propaganda during the colonial age: anonymous communications also served the ends of the struggle of the patriots against the government and promoted the spread of subversive plans. The anonymous billet given to Cisneros contained among other things the following statement: "A system of colonial government without a motherland and without an effective governor to whom recourse can be had as a center of unity is an absurdity that shocks every principle of sane policy and is real anarchy."

As the atmosphere was charged with revolutionary menace, Cisneros decided to create the court of political vigilance in order to prosecute "those persons who promoted or sustained the detestable maxims of the French party and of any other system contrary to the preservation of these dominions in union with and dependence upon the motherland." For this purpose, the viceroy appointed Antonio Carpe to be criminal fiscal. It will be remembered that Viceroy Sobremonte had intrusted a similar function to the oidor Bazo y Berri.

Philadelphia and Rio de Janeiro were two great centers in which a not inconsiderable number of patriots and foreigners carried on a revolutionary propaganda in favor of La Plata. So large was the number of suspicious foreigners who embarked in North America with the Spanish colonies as a destination that the minister plenipotentiary of Spain in the United States hit upon a device to check this inroad—namely, a countersign on the passport.

The most active revolutionary center which was in immediate communication with Buenos Aires was Rio de Janeiro. The Spanish minister at that court, the Marquis of Casa Yrujo, who had arrived there in the middle of 1809, informed the viceroy of Buenos Aires that frequent meetings of large numbers of revolutionary patriots took place in the house of Madame Perichón, the former mistress of Liniers, and that such reunions occurred especially in Pueyrredón's house. The Spanish minister initiated negotiations with the Portuguese government in order to have Saturnino Rodríguez Peña and other persons placed at the disposal of the government of Buenos Aires.[1] The Portuguese minister did not grant this request because the patriot in question was under the protection of England, a power which paid him an annual subsidy for spreading revolutionary doctrines.[2]

---

[1] The topic surveyed in this chapter is treated in detailed and documented fashion in R. Levene, "Causas criminales sobre intentada independencia del Perú, 1805-1809," *Anales de la facultad de derecho y ciencias sociales* (Buenos Aires, 1917), XVII, 519-628.

[2] An undated memorandum in the archives of the English government shows that a pension of £300 per annum was being paid by that government to Saturnino Rodríguez Peña because of his services to the English forces at the time of the invasion of La Plata, Public Record Office, War Office, misc. series, vol. 1121.—W. S. R.

CHAPTER XXIV

PROLEGOMENA OF THE REVOLUTION

DURING THE viceregal years of La Plata, there was a tendency in colonial society toward independence. An historic revolution that fundamentally changes the government in principle and laws is not improvised. Neither is it the work of a political chieftain or of a group. In this sense, an historic revolution is a natural phenomenon that takes place at the precise moment determined by social, economic, and political conditions. We say that the causes which provoke a revolutionary movement, are not improvised, but that they do their work slowly and gradually by preparing and elaborating events. We also affirm that a revolt like the May Revolution of Buenos Aires is not the result of the wish or decision of one man or of a group. It is an historic process, the logical consequence of more profound causes—economic and political—so that its leaders are the revolutionary organs and agents of a general sentiment which is dominant in society.

The May Revolution was in preparation during the age of the viceroys when it was morally transforming society, which was advancing by slow but firm steps toward a renovation. There was a moment, after the English invasions, when this renovation and evolution of society was accelerated. We have studied the important political and economic consequences that followed the defeat of the English invasions. The people—up to that time a vague entity that was beginning to take form—conscious of its strength, performed acts of sovereignty, such as the choice of a military chieftain in the person of the hero of the reconquest, Santiago Liniers, which demonstrated the state of mind of the epoch that was disposed to emancipation. The English had come to offer the creoles commercial and other liberties of all sorts that the Spaniards had not conceded. The prevailing sentiment did not approve the proposal of the English; it hoped for more auspicious times to achieve true and complete emancipation. But from that time a dividing line began to be drawn between creoles and Spaniards. A large number of patriots strongly supported Liniers who was, as it were, a personification of their glory. A certain part of

the Spanish party recognized as leader the chief alcalde, Martín
Alzaga, who was an energetic and haughty person. Up to this
juncture, the creoles had moved in a lower plane of society; for
the Spaniards occupied all the higher offices in church and state.
The creoles, feeling that they were masters of the situation,
aspired to reject the rule of the motherland, especially after the
news arrived from the Spanish court that the selection of Liniers
as viceroy, which had been consecrated by the popular will, had
been confirmed.

It is an error to affirm that the English invasions started the
emancipatory movement in the colony of La Plata, for this movement had its origin in the first days of Spanish colonization (as we
have seen on studying the revolutionary and democratic movements that occurred after the sixteenth century) and it became
more definite and strong during the age of the viceroys. The
English invasions, like the events that occurred in Spain, only
accelerated the preëxisting tendency toward emancipation.

In the beginning of 1808, two European events took place that
were destined to have a great repercussion in La Plata: the arrival
in Brazil (on January 23) of the Portuguese royal family; and
the scandal of Bayonne (April 20-30). From the beginning of
1807, the strong and sovereign will of the chief alcalde, Martín
Alzaga, who had been the soul of the military junta of February
10 which deposed Viceroy Sobremonte and ordered his arrest,
controlled the cabildo of Buenos Aires. The relations between
Alzaga and Liniers apparently remained without alteration until
the middle of 1808. At a certain moment (month of April), faced
by the threat of a new English invasion, these relations became
cordial.

On May 13, the appointment of Liniers as provisional viceroy
became known; and in July, because of the appointment of an
emissary who should represent the viceroy before the prince regent
in Rio de Janeiro, the cabildo protested; but the viceroy retorted
in energetic and facetious words to point out that the functions
of the cabildo should be limited to such matters as police, the
supply of provisions, and the promotion of arts. Liniers, who had
recently been appointed viceroy, desired that the cabildo which
had been everything and had done everything should confine itself
to these affairs—just as the shoemaker of the story should stick

to his last. Up to the month of April, Alzaga had held the reins of all serious matters affecting the colony and in July the viceroy wished to tear them from his hands. A simple statement of the facts indicates the imminence of the conflict.

Napoleon dominated all Europe, excepting England, a nation which he had not been able to subjugate. As Portugal wished to open its ports to English commerce, which Napoleon had prohibited by declaring a continental blockade, the French emperor decided to occupy the city of Lisbon with his soldiers. In order to carry out this plan, he solicited and obtained from Spain, his faithful ally since 1795 (peace of Basel), permission for his soldiers to march across Spanish territory and thus to reach Portugal. But the armies of Napoleon remained in Spain, and upon obtaining the abdication of its sovereign and of the heir to the throne they made Joseph Bonaparte, brother of Napoleon, king of Spain. All Spain rose in indignation as one man, and armies were organized in its territory which waged a guerrilla warfare against French domination and which maintained popular juntas of government.

On July 29, 1808, the audiencia of Buenos Aires learned of the cédulas announcing the accession to the Spanish throne of Ferdinand VII, as a result of the abdication of Charles IV on March 19. A little later it received a paper in which Charles IV declared his abdication null and void. The audiencia decided not to change its program for the ceremony of an oath of allegiance to Ferdinand VII because the paper announcing the withdrawal of his abdication by Charles IV had not been transmitted through the legitimate channel of the Council of the Indies. Public disquietude reached a climax when, on August 13, the Marquis de Sassenay, an emissary of Napoleon, disembarked with dispatches from the emperor.

These dispatches were opened before a junta that had been summoned as a precautionary measure by Liniers.[1] It thus became aware of the renunciations of Charles IV, Ferdinand VII, and the infantes in favor of the emperor. The junta also learned of the dispatches of the minister of foreign affairs of France in which he announced the selection that Napoleon had made of his brother

---

[1] A vivid description of this scene has been given by Groussac, *Santiago de Liniers,* pp. 207-11.

Joseph as king of Spain and the proposal to convoke a cortes at Bayonne in order that the nation should give its consent to this change. In describing the events of those days, the audiencia of Buenos Aires declared that "the surprise caused by this news cannot be exaggerated."

On August 15, Liniers signed a proclamation addressed to the inhabitants in which he made known the events that had occurred and announced the ceremony of the proclamation of Ferdinand VII as king and the taking of an oath to support him. In commenting upon this announcement, Javier de Elío, governor of Montevideo, gave it a suspicious connotation. Henceforth, a lack of confidence in the conduct of the viceroy spread; and even his partisans recognized the gravity of this fact.

The plot against Liniers was hatched between a nucleus of Spanish opponents, who resided in Buenos Aires (led by Alzaga) and a similar group in Montevideo (headed by Elío). On September 10, a regidor of the cabildo of Montevideo brought secret dispatches to Buenos Aires. On the envelope of one of them there was written that it "should not be opened in the presence of the viceroy for it was concerned with his person, but that it should be opened by the audiencia and the cabildo in the presence of the reverend bishop and the military inspector. . . ." [2] The dispatch was from Elio and was also signed by four regidors; it contained the accusation that the conduct of Liniers was suspicious. In view of the gravity of the charge, the assembled junta decided to summon before it the governor of Montevideo, so that he could present the documents supporting the accusation. Elío declined to proceed to Buenos Aires; Liniers then appointed Juan Ángel Michelena to relieve him of his command. The cabildo of Montevideo recognized Michelena in that character, but the governor and his partisans incited an uprising and Liniers' agent was compelled to return to Buenos Aires.

A few days later, copies of another Montevidian manifesto were received in the city of Buenos Aires "which announced that, following the example set in that city on August 14, 1806, a cabildo abierto had been held which had decided to establish in imitation

---

[2] *Documentos relativos á los antecedentes de la independencia de la República Argentina* (Buenos Aires, 1912), p. 74.

of the juntas of Spain, a junta subordinate to that of Seville." [3]

On October 15, the audiencia of Buenos Aires formulated a decision in which, rejecting as rash and unjust the suspicions regarding the conduct of Liniers, it ratified his decision to dissolve the junta of Montevideo. Meantime, the members of the cabildo prepared an armed movement. On October 3, the commanders of the corps that sympathized with Liniers had made known to him the hostile attitude of certain officials. In this communication, many officers offered him their support. The insurrection of the Spaniards was scheduled for October 17, two days after the audiencia reached its decision. At five o'clock in the morning of that day a gathering of the Biscayan soldiers took place, but Liniers was warned in time and was able to ward off the blow. [4]

In the last days of December, the eldest daughter of Liniers was married without royal permission, thus violating a provision of the Laws of the Indies. The cabildo maintained that the viceregal authority had in fact ceased to function, and that, therefore, this authority was not able to ratify the nomination of the new regidors which was to take place on January 1. But the audiencia informed the cabildo that only the Council of the Indies could punish the viceroys.

On January 1, the cabildo met in order to elect its new members. Soon it heard the bell summoning to the plaza a crowd that wished to depose the viceroy and to establish a junta. The viceroy gave his approval openly and frankly to the nominations. In the plaza, a general clamor kept on repeating the phrases: "We desire a junta! Down with the Frenchman Liniers!" The regidors then resolved promptly to assemble a cabildo abierto, in which the decision was reached to install a junta like those existing in Spain. For this purpose, successive delegations were sent to the viceroy. The bishop of Buenos Aires, who was one of the most active emissaries, declared that in the end Liniers agreed that a junta should be established, and that for this purpose the regidors and the important inhabitants should meet in the fortress in order to determine the nature and mode of establishing the new government. In

---

[3] *Ibid.*, p. 75. The views of Mitre on the significance of this event are found in *Historia de Belgrano*, I, 188.

[4] Groussac, *Santiago de Liniers*, pp. 274-75 and note 1; and also the archivo general de la nación.

this meeting, which occurred immediately afterward, Liniers opposed the establishment of a junta; but, in order to calm the public excitement, he nevertheless offered to relinquish the command.

Suddenly, the aspect of the scene unexpectedly changed. Just after the commanders of the troops faithful to Liniers entered the meeting, Cornelio Saavedra said: "Let Liniers come with us, let him appear before the people, and if they should reject him or say that they do not wish him to remain in command, I and my companions will sign the act deposing him." [5] Liniers and his companions proceeded to the plaza where the crowd, which was now composed of citizens belonging to the creole soldiery, cried out: "Long live Liniers!"

The regidors were detained in the consultative hall of the fort until the morning of January 3 when they were conducted on board different vessels and exiled to Patagonia. Thus ended the political tumult of January 1, which trained its authors in the knowledge and management of instruments, means, and men with which in the immediate future they might essay a revolution of great historical significance.

The invasion of Spain by the French and the imprisonment of Charles IV and Ferdinand VII produced the great crisis of Spanish public law. On January 22, 1809, the central junta that governed Spain in the name of the captive king issued the famous royal order of emancipation, as it was called, of the colonies, which affirmed that the colonies were an integral part of the nation and that all the provinces of the monarchy were equal. By another decree of the same junta, dated May 22, 1809, a general cortes was convoked in Spain, which was to have supplementary representation from the Indies. There attended this cortes twenty-six delegates for America, the Windward Islands, and the Philippines. The events of the war with Napoleon obliged them to postpone the meeting of the cortes that should have opened on March 1, 1810.

In the course of the perils through which Spain was passing, it sought the means of linking to its own destiny the fate of its colonies.[6] Remember that since the year 1519 it had been declared

[5] A. Zimmermann Saavedra, *Don Cornelio de Saavedra* (Buenos Aires, 1909), p. 353.

[6] E. del Valle Iberluca, *Los diputados de Buenos Aires en las Cortes de Cádiz y el nuevo sistema de gobierno económico de América* (Buenos Aires,

that the provinces of the Indies were "annexed" to the crown of Castile and León. Now the central junta of Seville wished to maintain that the colonies formed an integral part of "the nation." We saw that, in the beginning of 1809, a popular movement took place in Buenos Aires which sustained the authority of Viceroy Liniers. On May 25 and July 16 of the same year, two other important movements took place, one in the city of Chuquisaca, and the other in La Paz. The same phenomenon of political and institutional decomposition occurred in Chuquisaca that had undermined the entire viceroyalty and had produced violent changes at Buenos Aires. If struggles had broken out in that capital among the viceroy, the cabildo, the audiencia, and the military organization, in the distant, erudite city of Chuquisaca the principal parties were the president, the archbishop, and the audiencia. Because of the dispositions that it had made for the defense of the frontier against the Indian menace, trifling incidents and futile pretexts in the beginning had since 1804 put the high court of justice on bad terms with its president Garcia Pizarro.

The fundamental event in this domestic quarrel took place because of the arrival of José Manuel de Goyeneche, a commissioner of the junta of Seville. The audiencia did not recognize him in that character; while Archbishop Moxo, taking the side of the president, commanded the clergy to yield obedience to the junta of Seville. By resolutions of September 18 and 23 the audiencia declared that the credentials of Goyeneche, as representative of the supreme junta of Seville, were not in proper form. When Goyeneche arrived in Chuquisaca, an unexpected complication ensued because he bore dispatches from Brazil offering to Upper Peru the protectorate of the prince regent of Portugal and Carlota. Among the clergy, the people, and the members of the audiencia, the rumor spread that the secret plan embraced by Goyeneche, the president, and the archbishop provided for the transfer of Upper Peru to Portuguese rule. The Portuguese court did not cease to covet New Toledo (Charcas, Cochabamba, Potosí, and La Paz), especially after it had been checked in its purpose of expansion

---

1912), takes the view that the American revolutionists mistrusted the proceedings of the Cortes because they considered it an illegal body and because they believed that the time had come for separation from Spain.

toward the Banda Oriental of the Río de la Plata.

As a result of certain violent acts, García Pizarro relinquished his office on May 25, after having vainly awaited the military support of Paula Sanz, and the audiencia assumed command. It appointed as commandant general the delegate of Yamparaez, Lieutenant Colonel Juan Antonio Álvarez de Arenales. The incident at Chuquisaca was simply a violent assault which precipitated the downfall of colonial institutions, and was intimately related to previous tumults that took place in Buenos Aires.

In the intendency of La Paz—where revolutionary threats were made in 1798, 1800, and 1805—the uprising was stimulated on March 30 (1809) when news was received that Alzaga had been guilty of sedition in Buenos Aires and that independent juntas would be established. But the more exact news that the tumultuous crowd had failed to accomplish its purpose in the capital of the viceroyalty delayed the blow. The commotion of May 25 in Chuquisaca had its logical repercussion in La Paz. It is, however, necessary to notice that there was a profound difference between the character and results of the two movements.

Under the direction of Pedro Domingo Murillo, the commandant of the fort, and Colonel Juan Pedro Indaburu, everything was ready for July 16. After the governor and the bishop had been compelled to relinquish their posts, the cabildo took charge of the government. Later, it constituted itself as a junta in the character of a consultative body. On July 22, a "plan of government" was approved that was composed of ten articles in which, besides an exposé of the motives and bases of the revolution, regulations were included concerning the operations of the junta which was to represent and protect the rights of the people in order that "they should become tranquil and duly subordinate themselves to the constituted authorities"; a delegate was to be sent to each district in order to persuade the Indians of "the sacred objects which this people contemplate"; besides an Indian from each district of the six subdelegations should be included in a congress of the people, and so on. On July 27, the protective junta issued a proclamation containing the following passage: "Now is the time to organize a new system of government, founded upon the interests of our country which is greatly depressed by the bastard policy of

Madrid. . . . Now is the time, in fine, to raise the standard of liberty in these unfortunate colonies. . . ." [7]

José Manuel Goyeneche, who was now in Cuzco, was directed by José de Abascal, viceroy of Peru, to crush the movement at La Paz. He did this easily and with obvious cruelty. The insurrectionary leaders were subjected to "exemplary punishment." After being beheaded, their bodies were exhibited as a warning.

Feeling that perilous agitations were taking place in society, the president of the audiencia of Charcas ordered the imprisonment of the leaders. The people then revolted, attacked the palace of the president, cast him into prison, and turned over the government to the royal audiencia. This revolution at Chuquisaca had an immediate effect in La Paz where, on July 16, the people formed a junta of government and mobilized soldiers to support it. From Buenos Aires the new viceroy, Cisneros, sent an army of 1,000 men, while the viceroy of Peru entrusted a similar commission to Goyeneche who marched at the head of a column of 5,000 men. Prominent among the revolutionists were the creoles Arenales and Monteagudo; but they were vanquished, and many of them were condemned to exile or to die either on the scaffold or by the garrote. Among those who fell was the valiant Murillo who was executed in the public plaza. Addressing himself to the Spanish Americans, before he died, Murillo exclaimed: "The torch that I have set on fire will never be extinguished."

In mentioning the revolution of La Paz, an anonymous production of a citizen of Buenos Aires avowed "that heroism and patriotism are virtues that the Spanish American wisely conceals in order to display them opportunely: he also makes manifest that the people of South America are also aware of the rights of which they are defrauded and that if they have not claimed them until the present, it was not because of lack of intelligence but because of excess of fidelity; he has made clear that the Americans are free men . . . who know their inalienable rights and also the usurpation that they have endured and which it is now desired to restore." [8] The uprising in La Paz had an important political

---

[7] Levene, *Ensayo histórico sobre la revolución de Mayo y Mariano Moreno*, I, 364.—W. S. R.

[8] M. M. Pinto, *La Revolución de la intendencia de La Paz* (Buenos Aires, 1909), apéndice, núm. II, A, pp. xxvi-xxvii.

character and is moreover clearly an emancipatory movement. In the words of Ramos Mejía, "the crowd appears with a more personal temperament, for even in its component elements, it is native and, one might almost say, national." [9]

The efforts that the junta of Montevideo had made to depose Viceroy Liniers met with success in Spain, where the central junta named Don Baltasar Hidalgo de Cisneros in order that he might take charge of the government of the viceroyalty in place of Liniers. In these circumstances there circulated in Buenos Aires the rumor of an active hostility toward the new viceroy, a fact that we have mentioned in the previous chapter. Once in office, Viceroy Cisneros undertook to soothe the people and showed himself a capable ruler. In that rôle, he took certain steps: for example, he granted an amnesty to those persons who were implicated in the uprising of January 1; he left the nobles in their posts, and although he approved the measures taken by the junta of Montevideo during the period when it was separating from Buenos Aires, nevertheless he dissolved it; in a junta of residents he framed the famous decree concerning trade with the English and signed a resolution which established compulsory primary education.

During the year 1809, various events occurred which gave public notice of the revolutionary intentions of the patriots. Thus, on January 1 of that year, the popular party supported the authority of Viceroy Liniers, whom the Spaniards, led by Martín de Alzaga, had tried to depose; on May 25 and July 16, 1809, there also took place the two important revolutionary movements of Chuquisaca and La Paz; in August, when the central junta of Spain designated Cisneros to replace Liniers, the patriots planned to start a revolution.

It may, therefore, be affirmed that revolution was in the air, and that the minds of men were disposed to serve it. A propitious air pervaded university halls, the clubs, judicial courts, and the militia, and a new spirit animated their members. Early in 1810, the revolutionary agitation was directed by a secret society. Among its members were the patriots Nicolás Rodríguez Peña, Belgrano, Paso, Vieytes, Agustín Donado, Alberti, Terrada, Darragueira,

[9] J. M. Ramos Mejía, *Las multitudes argentinas* (Madrid, 1912), p. 60.

Chiclana, Castelli, and the young enthusiasts, French, Berutti, Viamonte, and Guido. The patriots gathered in the house of Vieytes, in that of Rodríguez Peña, or in the villa of Orma. Cornelio Saavedra, commander of the regiment of nobles, had also placed himself at the service of the same cause, and offered the support of his forces for the opportune moment which would be when the junta of Seville, the last Spanish junta that represented the authority of the captive king, would fall into the power of the French.

The French armies penetrated into Spain as far as Andalusia and entered Seville. They abolished the central junta that ruled in the name of King Ferdinand VII. The propitious moment for the revolution had arrived. On May 13, an English vessel brought to Montevideo the news of the downfall of the last Spanish junta. A little later these alarming reports were circulating in Buenos Aires, and for several days longer, Viceroy Cisneros, who was in a difficult position, strove to keep the news secret. But the situation was untenable; Cisneros was aware of the noiseless agitation that pervaded the atmosphere and owed a satisfaction to public sentiment. Finally, he decided to frame a manifesto on May 18 publishing "in proper form" the last news from Spain, and recommending obedience and order.[10] But the object of the viceroy was to give himself time and to prevent any popular demonstration. For this reason he refused, but without avail, to grant permission to assemble a cabildo abierto.

In this solemn moment the patriots acted with energy and rapidity. They hastened towards the cabildo, in order to secure the convocation of a cabildo abierto. For this purpose, Cornelio Saavedra and Manuel Belgrano had an interview with the chief alcalde, Juan José Lezica, who was a creole, to ask that "a cabildo abierto should be held without delay, in order that the people in a general assembly might decide whether or not the viceroy should give up his office, and whether a superior junta of government should be erected that would improve the condition of the country." On May 20, the alcalde Juan José Lezica transmitted to Viceroy Cisneros the request which had been formulated by the patriots. The viceroy was alarmed at this request and, in order

---

[10] *Días de Mayo; actas del cabildo de Buenos Aires.*—W. S. R. See further, Zimmermann Saavedra, *op. cit.,* pp. 359-60.

to make known the gravity of the situation, he summoned the military commanders to meet at the fortress on the same day at seven o'clock in the evening. In this conference, Cisneros said "that the situation was perilous and the desires of those groups that designated themselves the people were stormy and disordered; that in virtue of the protests and oaths which they had taken to defend his authority and to support public order, he counted upon them (the military commanders) to restrain those agitators who desired a cabildo abierto. He concluded by exhorting them to exercise their fidelity in the service of their king and country." A Spanish commander of a regiment declared that he would support the authority of the viceroy. Commandant Martín Rodríguez, a creole, said: "That will be seen tomorrow." And Cornelio Saavedra said in a loud voice: "Your Excellency, do not count upon me, nor upon the regiment of nobles for this: the government that gave authority to your Excellency to command us no longer exists; this is a matter of assuring our fate and that of Spanish America, and because of that the people wish to reassume their rights and to preserve these for themselves." Great was the surprise of Cisneros upon hearing these words from the lips of Saavedra; he wavered and did not dare to make a decision.

On the evening of the same day of May 20, there gathered in the house of Rodríguez Peña the members of the secret society who resolved to send Castelli and Martín Rodríguez to see the viceroy and to demand the convocation of a cabildo abierto. Castelli and Rodríguez entered the hall of the viceroy whom they found playing cards with other gentlemen. It was ten o'clock at night. Mitre said: "The two emissaries of the revolution, who came to announce to the viceroy that the last hour of his power had struck, approached him with gravity and respect. Castelli began to speak and said that he came in the name of the people and of the army that was in arms to request that as his rule over the viceroyalty had of right ceased, it was the duty of the people assembled in congress to deliberate concerning his fate. The effect of these words was terrible. The men all rose to their feet, and Cisneros with sparkling eyes and menacing air, as when he fought valiantly at Trafalgar, addressed himself to Castelli thus: 'What foolhardiness is this? Why do you thus insult the person of the king through his representative?' Castelli meekly replied 'that there was no reason for becoming excited, that the matter could not be helped.' More impatient than Castelli, Rodríguez added: 'Excellent sir, five minutes is the time allotted us to return with your Excellency's reply.' Cisneros went into an adjacent room to confer with his companions, and soon with a more tranquil air said to the emissaries in a resigned tone: 'Gentlemen, much do I regret the evils that will come upon this people as a result of this step! But inasmuch as the people do not desire me to rule, and as the army abandons me, do what you will.' The emissaries departed to report the result of their mission. Upon learning that the viceroy had at last yielded, all the patriots began to embrace each other and to throw their hats into the air." [11]

On the following day, May 21, the people gathered in the plaza and demanded the convocation of a cabildo abierto. The viceroy granted the request and summoned it to meet on May 22.

[11] Mitre, *Historia de Belgrano,* I, 239-40.

CHAPTER XXV

THE REVOLUTION

IN ACCORDANCE with the request of the patriots Viceroy Cisneros finally decided to convoke the cabildo abierto for May 22. Four hundred and fifty citizens were invited to the meeting. To quote Mitre: "In the popular assembly of May 22 three parties met face to face. The loyalist party favored the continuance of the viceroy in his post with only the innovation of associating with him in the government the chief members of the audiencia of Buenos Aires. That audiencia was at the head of the loyalist party, and its organs were the oidors of the audiencia, supported by the moral authority of the bishop and the phalanx of Spanish officials. As already indicated the party of reconciliation, which was under the influence of the chief municipal alcaldes and regidors, and which counted upon the support of the influential Spanish general, Pascual Ruiz Huidobro, wished to harmonize the demands of the two extreme parties with the exigencies of the situation and to settle the dispute by having the cabildo temporarily assume the supreme command until a provisional government should be organized that would remain dependent upon the supreme authority of the Peninsula. This party had the support of some patriots; among others Nicolás Rodríguez Peña, Feliciano Chiclana, Vieytes, Viamonte, and Balcarce. The majority of the patriot party stood merely for the deposition of the viceroy and the formation of a suitable government invested with power conferred by the people. This party was divided into two factions: one which wished to delegate to the cabildo the duty of organizing a new government, and the other which desired that this should be done as the result of a popular vote. Cornelio Saavedra, who was one of the outstanding leaders of the revolution, belonged to the first faction, while Castelli and other more impetuous or farsighted citizens belonged to the second." [1]

The cabildo abierto opened its sessions at nine o'clock in the forenoon with 251 persons in attendance. Only 224 of them voted.

---

[1] Mitre, *Historia de Belgrano*, I, 241-42.

According to Groussac: "The chief social classes were represented in the following proportions: military and naval officials, 60; civil employees (including alcaldes and members of the commercial tribunal), 39; clerics and friars, 25; liberal professions (of whom the majority were lawyers), 26; merchants, landowners, and other persons, 94.[2]

The suggestive absence from the meeting of more than 200 residents of the city and the participation in it of many other persons who were not residents, have been explained by Cisneros and by the audiencia. The former in his report to the king mentioned the partiality of the soldiers stationed at the entrance to the plaza who blocked the progress of persons who had been invited to the meeting and permitted the passage of the plotters, even providing them with "copies of the billet of invitation bearing no name." "In a city containing 3,000 inhabitants of distinction"—added the viceroy—"only 200 came to the cabildo abierto, and many of these were shopkeepers, some were militiamen, while others were minors. . . ."

On its part, the audiencia later declared that in the cabildo of May 22 the absence was noticed of "many residents of distinction and heads of families, while very marked was the attendance of soldiers belonging to the regiment of nobles; among them was a considerable number of officials belonging to that regiment, as well as minors who were not even residents of the city.[3]

The secretary of the cabildo opened the proceedings by inviting the people present freely to express their opinions, and advising them at the same time to refrain from perilous innovations. Bishop Lue immediately arose to speak. He was a haughty person whose character is aptly illustrated by an anecdote. According to this story, at a feast of Corpus Christi he trampled upon the Spanish standard because its bearer had not done him ample reverence. Such was the man who first asked to speak in that great popular assembly in order to decide the destinies of La Plata and of Spanish America. He supported the following proposition: "That while there should remain in Spain a bit of land governed by Spaniards,

[2] Groussac, *Santiago de Liniers*, pp. 338-39. In the *Revista Nacional*, vol. XLIII, núms. 1 and 2, is printed a list of the members of congress.

[3] Levene, *Ensayo histórico sobre la revolución de Mayo y Mariano Moreno*, II, 51.

that bit of land ought to rule Spanish America; that as long as there was a single Spaniard in the Indies that Spaniard should rule the Spanish Americans; and that the control of Spanish America could only pass to the sons of the country when there was no longer a single Spaniard in it." These words caused real indignation in the assembly. The patriot Castelli then arose and spoke with fiery eloquence; he rebutted the argument of Bishop Lue and made his argument center around the crisis that had occurred in Spanish public law. He pointed out that a revolution had occurred in the Peninsula by virtue of which the supreme power, "the sovereign power," had reverted to the people in Spain and America. The argument of Castelli was decisive; it enthused the patriots who considered it as the true expression of public sentiment.

Then a clever jurisconsult, the fiscal, Dr. Villota, refuted the views of Castelli. He declared that he accepted the hypothesis which held that as the monarch had ceased to rule, his representatives in America had also ceased to rule, and that governmental authority would accordingly reside in the sovereign people; but he pointed out that in the cabildo which was in session, there were present only the representatives of the municipality of Buenos Aires, who had neither the power nor the right to decide matters which concerned the entire Spanish monarchy, and concluded by arguing that the question should be postponed until a decision could be reached upon the matter "in conjunction with the entire national representation." The patriot Paso, who spoke next, emphasized the necessity of removing the viceroy and of establishing a junta because "Buenos Aires urgently needs to protect itself against the perils that threaten it on account of the power of France and the distracted condition of the peninsula." [4]

The cabildo abierto of May 22 may be considered as the first Argentine congress in order of time; for in its midst the most representative patriots of the revolution scored a triumph for the cause of emancipation. The first step taken by the government cabildo on the morning of May 23 was to revoke the order calling a meeting of the general congress for three in the afternoon in order to scrutinize the votes cast. It, therefore, arranged that the act should not bear the signatures of the members of the open

[4] *Días de Mayo; actas del cabildo de Buenos Aires.*—W. S. R.

council, that the ballots which had been duly signed should be deposited in the archives for consideration in view of "whatsoever doubt that may arise," that two regidors should "be ready to inform those persons who had been present that they retire until a new invitation was received," while the cabildo voted itself to the task of certifying the ballots "by the most careful scrutiny."

This was a system of preliminary measures which would promote the purpose of the cabildo—formed in anticipation of reactionary plans—to frustrate the will of the majority of May 22. An inspection of the votes is a demonstration of the audacious jugglery that was performed. "More than a majority," said the cabildo, desired that (1) the viceroy should relinquish his command; (2) the government should be reassumed by the cabildo with a vote by the syndic until the establishment of the junta that would be formed "in a manner that is considered convenient"; (3) the junta should assume command "until deputies had assembled who were to be convoked from the interior provinces to establish the proper type of government."

With the exception of the first point—the deposition of the viceroy—and the temporary delegation of authority to the cabildo, the regidors fraudulently announced as the result of a plurality of ballots the decision of two other important questions. A plurality of ballots had not decided in favor of authorizing the cabildo to establish a junta in the manner and form that it might judge convenient and a plurality had not decided upon the convocation of delegates from the interior provinces.

An impartial scrutiny—a recount and careful consideration of the ballots—gives the following result:

For the continuation of the viceroy in command, either
    alone or associated with other authority 69
For the deposition of the viceroy 155
                                         ————
    Total 224

The 155 votes cast for the deposition of the viceroy considered the authority that would be established in his place and may be analyzed thus:—the formula of Ruiz Huidobro: that the authority should be temporarily reassumed by the cabildo pending the formation of a provisional government; the formula of Chiclana contained the addition that the syndic should have a vote in the cabildo—25 votes; the formula of Pedro Andrés García and José Luis Chorroarín: the authority should be provisionally reassumed by the cabildo until "the manner and form of government that shall be constituted is decided," as the first proposition states; meantime, "the erection of a junta of government should be arranged," as stated in the second proposition—20 votes.

The formula of Saavedra included the temporary delegation of authority to the cabildo until the corporation or junta is formed "that should exercise the government; the formation of this junta should be after the form and manner desired by the cabildo and there is no doubt that it is the people who confer the authority or command;" this covered the formula of Castelli, and also those persons who cast their ballots with an addition in favor of the syndic proctor—87 votes. The formula of Juan Nepomuceno Sola comprised the following: the government should be provisionally vested in the cabildo, including the syndic, until the election of the junta with deputies from the viceroyalty—19 votes. The formula which provided that as the viceroy had ceased to rule he should be replaced by the cabildo—4 votes. This made a total of 155 votes.

It should be noticed that only the 25 votes cast for the Ruiz Huidobro-Chiclana formula had delegated to the cabildo the power to constitute the provisional government; that the 20 votes of the formulas García and Chorroarín explained that the government of the cabildo was provisional until it was decided to establish a new government without delegating to the ayuntamiento the power to establish it; and that the 87 votes of the formula Saavedra expressly stated that there should be no doubt that the people are the entity that should confer the authority upon the junta to erect itself as a governmental authority. Finally, it should be noticed that only 19 votes stated that the election of the junta should take place with the participation of delegates from the viceroyalty. There may be added to these 6 votes that were cast for the retention of the viceroyalty, and with a qualification that if any change took place, it should be carried out by convoking delegates from the capitals and other cities of the interior.

Hence, after analyzing the votes "by a most detailed examination," it is seen that "more than a plurality" is as follows: (1) that the viceroy should cease to rule—155 votes; (2) that the cabildo, including the syndic, should temporarily assume the government until the establishment of a junta in a form and manner to be determined by the cabildo, there being no doubt that the people should confer the authority—87 votes. Accordingly, the two alleged resolutions attributed to the general congress of May 22, namely, that the cabildo should decide upon the manner of erecting a junta (which only obtained 25 votes), and that this junta should be intrusted with the governmental authority until the delegates from the interior provinces assembled (which only received 19 votes were null and void because they were fraudulent.

The cabildo mocked the wish of the cabildo abierto by attributing to itself the right to establish a patriotic junta of government that should govern in the name of Viceroy Cisneros. The Spaniards took advantage of this circumstance in order to thwart the revolutionary proposals by arranging that the cabildo would not fulfil the mandate of the people. In fact the cabildo put itself in accord with the royalist party, and in the session of the forenoon of May 23 it resolved that, "although a plurality of votes in the cabildo abierto favored the deposition of the viceroy, yet he should not be entirely deprived of authority, but should be named with other persons to exercise the rule until the deputies of the viceroyalty assembled. By this measure the cabildo mocked the popular will that had been decisively manifested in the cabildo abierto on May 22, for it undertook to maintain Viceroy Cisneros in power.

The patriots were informed of the pretensions of the cabildo that remained in session, while the people who were assembled in the plaza and the street impatiently awaited the deposition of the viceroy. In the character of representatives of the people, the patriots Saavedra and Castelli approached the regidors in order to inform them that the crowd expected the nomination of a junta of government. Upon the following day, May 24, the cabildo appointed the junta of which Cisneros was made president, while Sola, Inchaurregui, Saavedra, and Castelli were made members.

Clothing so great an abuse in legal phraseology, the cabildo issued a constitutional charter composed of thirteen articles which contained some notable stipulations (such as that members of the junta could not exercise judicial authority, that an account of the royal treasury should be published on the first days of the

month, that no order of the viceroy should be obeyed unless it
was countersigned by the other members and so on) ; but the majority of its provisions show that the cabildo intended to keep
the nascent junta in complete subordination.

Upon this occasion the people expressed their dissatisfaction,
for they were resolved not to allow Viceroy Cisneros to remain
on the governmental junta. The young men, who were led by French
and Berutti and organized under the name of "Chisperos," took
an active part. The decision of their proposals and the determined
energy which they put into this movement reached, indeed, such
a point that the Spanish party realized that it was not easy to
support the junta which the cabildo had formed. The patriots
assembled in the house of Rodríguez Peña determined to take up
arms in order to carry out the popular will. In the evening Saavedra
and Castelli, who had been selected as members of the junta presided over by the viceroy, appeared before Cisneros, presented their
resignations, and requested that he should relinquish the command.
Cisneros then signed his resignation as the "only way of allaying
the agitation and effervescence again being aroused among the
people." In conjunction with the viceroy, the other members of
this junta resigned.

On the next day—the symbolic date of May 25—the cabildo,
which had been in session since an early hour, considered the resignation of the viceroy and the members of the junta. It was a cold
and rainy morning. The people hoped that once and for all the
cabildo would accept the resignations and would constitute the
first patriotic junta of government. The young men, French and
Berutti, distributed among the patriots badges of white and sky-
blue—the colors used by the regiment of nobles during the English
invasions. As the cabildo continued in session with closed doors,
the people knocked on the door of its hall and said: "The people
wish to know what you are doing."

A delegation from the people ascended to the cabildo to present
a "written petition" which stated that the popular will desired
the success of a list including Saavedra, Castelli, Belgrano,
Azcuénaga, Alberti, Matheu, Larrea, Paso, and Moreno. Nevertheless the cabildo refused to yield. "After a long interval of suspense"—one reads in the proceedings of the cabildo dated May 25
—"the persons mentioned above presented the proffered petition

which was signed by a considerable number of citizens, clerics, commandants, and other military officers, and which embodied the same sentiments that they had expressed verbally. And the members of the cabildo declared that the people should assemble in the plaza, for, in order to reach a decision the cabildo should listen to the people, if it approved the sentiments expressed in the paper. After agreeing to act thus, the members of the cabildo retired. After the lapse of considerable time, the honorable cabildo went out on the principal balcony of its hall, and the syndic proctor (Dr. Leiva), seeing a small number of people, in comparison with what he had expected, inquired 'where are the people'? and after various replies given by the persons present, and reproaches made by the syndic, among others, voices were heard to the effect that 'if up to this juncture they had proceeded with prudence, in order that the city might not suffer disaster, it was now time to use violent measures: that as it was an inopportune hour the people had retired to their houses; let the bell of the cabildo be rung and let the people gather there in order to satisfy the ayuntamiento; and if, because of the lack of a clapper, the bell could not be used, they would direct drums to be beaten; and let the barracks be opened, in which case the city would suffer what up to that time it had been possible to avoid.' "

So strong was the popular passion that the cabildo finally yielded and consecrated the first patriotic junta of government in the name of the people. It was thus constituted: Cornelio Saavedra as president, Mariano Moreno and Juan J. Paso as secretaries; and as other members, Belgrano, Castelli, Matheu, Alberti, Azcuénaga, and Larrea.

The membership of the junta of 1810 had sprung from the popular will. We have seen that will energetic during the May days and stimulated by a lofty spirit. Thus, the Revolution of 1810 had a popular origin; and the sovereignty and force of this popular entity were not of sudden growth but were an historical resultant. From the early days of conquest and colonization, democratic movements had occurred; during the three centuries of colonial history revolutionary explosions took place which were forming this anonymous entity, the great popular mass that did not govern according to the law, but which felt impulse and strength enough within itself to govern and to emancipate itself. The May Revo-

lution was so democratic that it did not have chieftains (caudillos)
but inspirers and directors of the popular will. But even further,
the people keenly realized the gravity of the situation; we have
seen that on the day following May 22, it was the people scattered
throughout the plaza, the street, and the barracks, who did not
accept the conciliatory formula proposed by the cabildo, that is,
that the junta which was to govern should be presided over by
Cisneros.

The revolution was carried out in the name of Ferdinand VII.
Was this the truth? Historic revolutions are produced as natural
phenomena at the precise moment determined by historic and
social conditions. They are produced; they come to life; and, in
the milieu of reality which surround them, and which is their
atmosphere, they live or die. If they triumph, reality and social
conditions nourish them; they grow; and they do their work. The
Revolution of 1810, born as a popular, democratic, and spontaneous movement, gathered strength; it extended its influence
powerfully and triumphed. Because of that, though promoted in
the name of the king, it acted against him, because it was stronger
and because it was a social revolution. The invocation which the
patriots made of the name of the captive king has been appropriately styled the "mask of Ferdinand." It is known that the idea
of emancipation had been formulated in organic and explicit terms
some years earlier by a nucleus of patriots which gradually enlarged
from the time that they embraced the plan of independence under
an English protectorate or the coronation of Princess Carlota
as monarch of La Plata until they secured the meeting of the
cabildo abierto of May 22.

The causes of the May Revolution may be classified as internal
and external. The internal causes, as the name indicates, are those
elaborated and prepared within the colonial society; and the external causes are those influences and events that affected conditions from without and coöperated in the movement of May.

The internal causes include the economic, political, and intellectual antecedents and also the English invasions. By an economic
cause is meant the condition of richness and commerce in the
colony as a result of the prevailing régime. During the last years
of Spanish domination there took place at the same time, on the
one hand, active movements of the monopolistic merchants, for

the purpose of obtaining concessions and special privileges for
their commerce, and, on the other hand, movements of the landowners, laborers, national merchants, and foreigners domiciled in
the country who pleaded for the free exportation of its products.
The documents of this last category in the seventeenth century
are characterized by opposition to the monopolistic economic
policy of Peru, and at the end of the eighteenth century, after the
promulgation of the regulations concerning free commerce between
Spain and the Indies (1778), the struggle is interpreted in Buenos
Aires as one of opposing interests against the monopolistic clique.
Let one remember the *Representación de los Labradores* (*Memorial
of the Farmers*) of 1793 asking for free trade in grains; the representation of the landowners of Buenos Aires and Montevideo in
1794 with regard to the means of promoting the exportation of
beef; the debates that took place in the commercial tribunal because of the petition to obtain the revocation of the privilege of
commerce with the colonies of other nations than Spain, in which
Marcó del Pont, Escalada, Fernández, and others defended national
interests; the memorials of Belgrano; the liberal reports of the
administrator of the customs, Ángel Izquierdo; and the subsequent
representations that were made whenever the conflict started: a
struggle of opposing interests which had its most complete expression in the report concerning the free admission of English
goods, and in which there figures Moreno's *Representación de los
Hacendados*.

On its part after the reconquest, the old group of monopolists,
which was represented by a nucleus of Spaniards, with seats in
the cabildo and the commercial tribunal and with trade relations,
tried to utilize the benefits of the victory for itself and against
Platean interests by making use of that prestige before the king.
In fact the cabildo had already appointed Pueyrredón its deputy
in Spain and, among other instructions, he was directed to solicit
an absolute and general prohibition of trade with foreigners. In
addition, the monopolistic merchants, assembled in a general junta,
selected for the same purpose José Fernández de Castro, who was
to make clear to the court the grave evils that resulted to Spanish
America from "allowing the colonies freely to engage in foreign
commerce, from allowing the slave trade, and from special concessions." The peculiar fact in regard to this last mission is that

toward the end of 1809, Fernández de Castro continued to solicit in Spain the revocation of the privileges granted to foreign commerce while in Buenos Aires, by virtue of an act of November 6, 1809, such commerce was actually permitted.

As may be deduced from these data, the question of free commerce or monopolized commerce agitated the merchants of Buenos Aires, and divided them into factions even during the early years of the nineteenth century. Further, the act of November 6, 1809, had not fully decided the question; in 1810, Da Silva Lisboa, the Brazilian economist and jurist translated and published in Rio de Janeiro the *Representación de los hacendados* in order to combat the monopolistic pretensions of the Portuguese merchants.[5]

The second internal cause of the May Revolution is political in character. Just as reactions took place in the economic order against the prevailing commercial system by divers facts which we have just mentioned, so, too, various reactions of the people took place against the governmental régime during the colonial era. These reactions occurred in the form of revolutionary explosions, scattered throughout the sixteenth century, but were of a more organic and definite nature during the seventeenth and eighteenth centuries. During the age of the viceroys, we can also distinguish the following stages of reaction against the prevailing political régime: (1) after the English invasions, the people had brought about the reconquest and the defense of Buenos Aires by their own strength, and they then appeared as a powerful entity; (2) in the cabildo abierto of August 14, 1806, and the junta of war of February 10, 1807, the people, declaring themselves to be sovereign, forced Sobremonte to cease ruling and designated Liniers, the hero of the war with the English, as commander of the troops; (3) on May 25 and July 16, 1809, two important revolutionary movements occurred at Chuquisaca and La Paz; and lastly in the cabildo abierto of May 22, 1810, the people ordered that Viceroy Cisneros should cease to rule.

The episode of a political character which should be considered is the Napoleonic invasion of Spain. As a result of this fact, a fundamental political revolution took place in Spain that soon extended to the New World. I refer to the reversion of power to the

---

[5] Levene, "La traducción y publicación portuguesa de 1810 de la 'Representación de los hacendados de Moreno,' " *Nosotros*, XXIX, 498-525.

people when the king was a prisoner, and from the breast of the people the power was constituted in the form of juntas. The supreme junta of Seville succeeded in making itself superior to all the other peninsular juntas and to the authorities of the Indies. When it was dissolved because of the advance of the French armies, the people of Spanish America claimed the right to form juntas as had been done in Spain—such was the pretext for the revolution throughout Spanish America. Upon the fall of the junta of Seville, juntas of government were established at Buenos Aires, Caracas, Mexico, and Santiago de Chile. In the cabildo abierto of May 22 in Buenos Aires, the patriot Castelli developed the theory of a crisis in Spanish political law and the doctrine that the *poder magestas* had reverted to the people.[6]

From this viewpoint the Revolution of 1810 should be explained as a stage in the disintegration of the Spanish monarchy. The intellectual antecedents of the movement include the diffusion of liberal ideas mentioned in chapters XXII and XXIII and the formation of the revolutionary conscience. The economic, political, and intellectual causes are thus the fundamental causes of the May Revolution that can be explained as the historical resultant of the events and the antecedents which determined its outburst.

The English invasions should also be mentioned among the internal causes of the revolution; for they defined and reënforced the preëxisting sentiment in favor of independence. After 1806 and 1807, event followed event in rapid succession, and the progress of the revolution was accelerated. In another chapter have been explained the important economic, political, and military consequences of the war with the English.

The external causes of the May Revolution were the North American Revolution and the French Revolution. The first began in 1776. Its immediate cause was the attempt of the English parliament to lay duties upon tea, glass, and stamped paper payable by the North American colonists. These colonists then pleaded a principle of English public law by virtue of which the people

---

[6] A Venezuelan patriot, Juan G. Roscio, in a letter to Andrés Bello on June 29, 1810, presented the constitutional argument that the dethronement of the Spanish king had broken the connecting link between Spain and its colonies. See M. L. Amunátegui, *Vida de Don Andrés Bello* (Santiago de Chile, 1882), p. 85. The term "poder magestas" (magestatis), apparently a mixture of Spanish and Latin, is perhaps best translated by "sovereign power."—W. S. R.

should only pay the duties voted by their representatives. The colonists rose in arms, and a few years later as the revolution triumphed, they were emancipated. The North American Revolution had an influence on the May Revolution and on the emancipation of all the Spanish colonies in America for three reasons: (1) because it furnished an example for the Spanish-Americans to imitate; (2) because Spain coöperated in the emancipation of the colonies of North America without considering that it was the mistress of other colonies that might follow the example of the Thirteen Colonies; (3) as a consequence of the aid that Spain furnished to the North American colonies, England waged war upon Spain (1779-1783), an event which produced grave economic disturbances in Spanish America. As a result of such events, England intensified its campaign, with the idea of promoting the emancipation of the Spanish colonies.

In fact, there had occurred in Spanish America many events which presaged the approaching movement of emancipation. Some historians believe that the minister of the king of Spain, Count Aranda, had proposed to his sovereign that in order to dominate that movement and to prevent the absolute loss of the colonies—so extensive and so distant from the motherland—it would be convenient to found three monarchies (in Mexico, Peru, and La Plata) headed by princes of the reigning Spanish dynasty. But King Charles III did not attach great importance to these events, and soon afterward the revolution broke out which Count Aranda had foreseen and tried to avoid.[7]

Another external cause of the May Revolution is the French Revolution of 1789. The influence of this revolution was universal, for it formulated "The Declaration of the Rights of Man," which included liberty, equality, property, and the sovereignty of the people. The ideas of the French Revolution spread throughout

---

[7] Levene here refers to a so-called secret memoir first published in 1827, which is of doubtful authenticity. Certain writers have assumed that the Spanish minister, Count Aranda, presented this memorial proposing the establishment of appanages in the Spanish Indies to King Charles III just after the Treaty of Peace had been signed in 1783 between England and the Thirteen Colonies. The text of this memoir, which was printed from a copy found by the translator among documents of a much later date, is found in the *Boletín del instituto de estudios americanistas de Sevilla,* año 1, núm. 2, pp. 52-57. See further, M. Danvila y Collado, *Reinado de Carlos* III (6 vols., Madrid, 1890-91), V, 470-71.—W. S. R.

the world, through its writers and philosophers. To the distant colony of La Plata those ideas of liberty and sovereignty also came. Thus, in the University of Chuquisaca the patriots studied the jurists and historians of the Indies and the French philosophers: Moreno republished a translation of Rousseau's *Social Contract*.

The Argentine Revolution of 1810 is a milestone in the history of free peoples. Like the French Revolution and the Revolution in North America, the May Revolution was a revolution of principles; it overthrew one régime to supplant it by another, which proved to be liberal in its laws and guarantees. It began in Buenos Aires on May 25, 1810, and spread throughout the entire viceroyalty; on July 9, 1816, it became general for all the United Provinces of La Plata; and, in 1817, the cause of the revolution was Americanized, for it was extended to Chile, Peru, and Ecuador. The May Revolution, born in Buenos Aires in 1810, was accordingly continental and American in its ends and great consequences.[8] We may affirm that this revolution had its "declaration of rights"; for it proclaimed and made effective the rights of political, intellectual, and commercial liberty and guaranteed the principles of equality among all men and justice founded upon law.

---

[8] E. Quesada, "La evolución social argentina," *Revista argentina de ciencias políticas* (Buenos Aires, 1911), II, 639-40.

CHAPTER XXVI

INDEPENDENCE

MAY 25, 1810, marks the beginning of the second period of Argentine history, the period of emancipation. That period includes both the movement for independence and the process of national organization.

The separatist movement in the United Provinces of La Plata extended from 1810 to July 9, 1816, when the congress of Tucumán confirmed and consecrated the work of the May Revolution. In reality, in 1816, the revolution had extended throughout all of the former viceroyalty of the Río de la Plata. In 1817, the revolution became an American revolution. It was General San Martín who extended it triumphantly into Chile, Peru, and Ecuador. So far as the destinies of Spanish America are concerned, the period of emancipation closed in 1824 with the battle of Ayacucho, which was the last battle fought by the patriots against the Spanish armies on the American continent. For the United Provinces of La Plata the period of emancipation accordingly includes a span of six years, from 1810 to 1816, during which the fate of the nascent revolution was sometimes happy (as at Suipacha, Las Piedras, San Lorenzo, Tucumán, and Salta), and at other times unfortunate (as at Huaqui, Tacuarí, Vilcapugio, Ayohuma, and Sipe Sipe), until at last the patriots triumphantly consecrated their fate in the congress of Tucumán.

The independence of the country once assured, there was next to be solved the difficult problem of national organization. In truth, after 1810, governmental questions had provoked various conflicts among the patriots. As the first patriot government was the fruit of the revolution, the logical result was that the patriots were concerned about the form of government which should be adopted by the new nation.

Accordingly, after 1810, there proceed two lines of progress which form the warp and the woof of our national history: one line represents the external action of the revolution and has as its object independence; while the other represents internal action and has as its object national organization. The federalization of the city of Buenos Aires in 1880 was the fulcrum of the lever in the work of consolidating order. It inaugurated the era of economic, intellectual, and cultural progress in the republic. The establishment of a country's independence is a task that requires the patriotic consecration and the generous efforts of its sons. The fate of such a movement is determined on the field of battle. Military men and men of action are the directors and chieftains of a movement for liberation. Among all free peoples, history has consecrated the romantic figures of self-denying military commanders who at the head of nameless legions have at critical moments offered the homage of their lives.

The problem of the political organization of a country is of a different character. The solution is not found on the field of battle, but in the serene and mature thought of politicians and statesmen. In order to organize a country politically, it is not sufficient to conceive a constitution of an advanced type in accordance with a perfect ideal. It is necessary that this political code should be suited to the social and economic conditions as well as to the capacity of the people who are to respect it and to cause it to be obeyed. In order to frame a constitution adapted to a particular country, there is necessary a profound observation of historical and social facts and of geographical and historical influences without forgetting the political ideal as indicative of the course of progress.

If the task of the emancipation of a country requires the patriotic sacrifice of its sons, the task of constitutional organization demands the study and meditation of its statesmen. Let us notice some examples of this truth. The English colonies in North America freed themselves from their motherland after a brief period of struggle. The organization of the United States of America into a federal republic was relatively easy because of the fact that, during the colonial period, England had conceded to its colonies in North America economic and political liberties which prepared the genius of the people for self-government. Yet, despite this favoring circumstance, there were moments in which it seemed that the union of the United States was about to dissolve, for a number of the former colonies threatened to separate from it. In 1789, the French people revolted against an absolute king and when the monarchy was overturned they tried to give France a republican constitution, which a few years later was superseded by another, and this constitution in turn by another, and that by still another in a giddy succession of written constitutions that did not faithfully reflect the social and political conditions of France— constitutions that were rejected by revolutionary movements.

Spanish America furnishes us with an eloquent example of the difficulties and complications inherent in the problem of the political organization of a country. In the viceroyalty of La Plata, the revolution broke out in 1810 and was consecrated in 1816, but only in 1853 did the Argentine nation begin to inaugurate constitutional presidents. That is to say, that we devoted almost a half-century to the solution of the political and constitutional problem of our organization. During this period, each attempt or essay to constitute or to organize the country was followed by civil wars and schisms between sister provinces. The general constituent assembly of 1813 framed several partial organic laws. Although it gave to a commission of its members the task of formulating a constitutional project, yet it did not promulgate a constitution. The congress of Tucumán of 1816 considered the question of the political organization of the country, and the majority of its members were so inconstant as to favor a monarchical form of government. However, this congress did not adopt a constitution until the year 1819 when it promulgated one of a unitarian or centralistic type that the people and the political chieftains disobeyed. The constituent congress of 1824 also promulgated a centralistic constitution in 1826 which in turn was also resisted. In 1853, the constituent congress of Santa Fe approved the federal constitution which is now in force, but it was not put into operation throughout Argentina until after the battle of Pavón (1861).

The history of national organization might be divided into five distinct eras: that extending from 1810 to 1820; one from 1820 to 1829; one from 1829 to 1852; another from 1852 to 1880; and the last, from 1880 to the present time.

The first period includes the successive, violent crises of patriot governments that, with the exception of the directory of Pueyrredón, did not endure for the time set by the constitution or by a particular law. Thus the junta of patriotic government established on May 25, 1810, was replaced by the great junta because of the differences between President Saavedra and Secretary Moreno.

The revolution of April 5 and 6, 1811, dislodged from the great junta the followers of Moreno who belonged to it; after the rout of the army of the north at Huaqui, it dissolved and formed the first triumvirate. By a coup d'état this new body disrupted the junta of observation, a legislative body composed of the deputies who belonged to the great junta. The first triumvirate was overthrown by the revolution of October 8, 1812, and the second triumvirate was installed. The new body dissolved in 1814 and the directory was organized, which represented unipersonal executive power. The first director, Gervasio Posadas, had to give up his post before completing his term of one year. His successor, Alvear, was overthrown by the revolution of Fontezuelas of 1815 which was of historical significance because, for the first time, the national government was interrupted in a transitory fashion. When the congress of Tucumán assembled, it designated as supreme director, Juan Martín de Pueyrredón, who ruled for three years and restrained the outbreak of anarchy with an iron hand. After the constitution of 1819 was promulgated, Pueyrredón resigned, and anarchy broke out.

The second era (from 1820 to 1829) includes a study of political anarchy and of political chieftainship (*caudillismo*) as its expression. During this era the national government was suspended, with the exception of the presidency of Rivadavia, which lasted only a short time, and the provinces were delivered up to the personal government of their political chieftains. The governments of Martín Rodríguez, Las Heras, and Dorrego in the province of Buenos Aires accomplished much in the work of reorganizing that province. The government of Dorrego was interrupted by the military insurrection of Lavalle, who ordered that Dorrego should be shot, and prepared the way for Juan Manuel de Rosas, who may be designated as the avenger of that murder.

The third era (from 1829 to 1852) comprises the twenty years of the rule of Rosas. This era represents an important stage in Argentine political and social evolution, because the political parties with principles (federalists and centralists) caused a crisis, owing to the peculiarities of social psychology and public spirit, and the international problems that arose.

The fourth period (from 1852 to 1880) includes the downfall of Rosas at Caseros and the conflict that began between the prov-

ince of Buenos Aires and the Argentine Confederation, represented
respectively by Mitre and Urquiza, and which for almost ten years
kept the problem of national organizations in suspense. In the
year 1853 the congress of Santa Fe promulgated the Argentine
constitution and constitutional presidencies were begun.

After the revolts of 1874 and 1880 were suppressed, national
organization was definitively accomplished, the city of Buenos
Aires was declared to be the capital of the republic and the seat
of the national authorities. From that time forth the nation made
surprising progress along economic, political, and cultural lines.[1]

---

[1] See further the author's discussion of interpretations of his country's history by Argentine scholars, *infra.*, pp. 526-27.

CHAPTER XXVII

THE FIRST PATRIOT GOVERNMENT

On May 25, 1810, the popular will had triumphantly consecrated the establishment of a patriot government. Thus, there was born the first governmental junta composed of the following members: Saavedra as president, Moreno and Paso as secretaries, and Castelli, Belgrano, Azcuénaga, Alberti, Larrea, and Matheu.

The deposition of Viceroy Cisneros and the formation of the patriotic junta of government was not a mere substitution of names and persons but a change of régime. The new government was the expression of the popular will and had an historic mission to fulfil. After May 25, two great problems formed the essentials of our history: the assurance of independence, and the organization of the country. In order to assure independence and to extend it over the entire viceroyalty, the governmental junta ordered the departure of three armies with a definite destination: one to Upper Peru; another to Paraguay; and a third to Montevideo.

Without losing a moment in the extension of the revolution, the governmental junta arranged the departure of an expedition of 1,150 soldiers destined for the interior provinces under the commandant of the forces from the upper provinces, Francisco Antonio Oritz de Ocampo. This expedition was composed of volunteers and had been financed in part by contributions of the patriots. Antonio González Balcarce was second in command, while Hipólito Vieytes was auditor of war and representative of the junta.

Although the political proposal of independence had been concealed by invoking the name of the captive king, Ferdinand VII, yet there was a rude and violent shock between the directors of the revolution, on the one hand, and the royalists on the other. This collision further proves that a general conviction had been formed to the effect that the revolution aimed at the independence of La Plata. Proof of this fact is found in a document emanating from the Spaniards themselves. In July, 1809, because of frequent secret meetings of patriots to prepare the blow and to resist the accession of Cisneros to power, the cabildo of Buenos Aires framed several resolutions to thwart that plan. In its act embodying a resolution

of July 13 of that year, is found this concluding declaration:
namely, that "it was incumbent to withdraw the veil of simulated
opposition to the sovereign mandates of the supreme junta of
Spain and presently to manifest clearly the sole and true object of
this opposition; that it could have no other object in such a case
than to escape from Spanish domination and to aspire to the
complete independence of these dominions." Thus, almost a year
before May 25, 1810, the cabildo, which was the bulwark of the
royalist party, proclaimed that "the sole and true object" which
animated the patriots to resist Cisneros or to try to form juntas
was "the complete independence of these dominions." [1]

In view of this document, there is no truth in the statement made
by a contemporary, Tomás Manuel de Anchorena, years after the
events, according to which, when the revolution occurred "all the
official documents not only exhaled enthusiastic obedience to Ferdinand VII, but did so with such sincerity in the judgment of
patriots of good faith that Dr. Zavaleta in a sermon which he
preached in the presence of the first governmental junta to celebrate its installation, when speaking of the imputations cast upon
us by our enemies who avowed that all these protests of obedience
and submission to Ferdinand were feigned and that our intention
was to revolt against his authority, replied to them by the emphatic phrase, 'they lie.' " [2]

Another conclusive document is the communication dated June
12, 1810, of the commander of the royal navy at Montevideo, José
María Salazar, to the Spanish secretary of state in which he avowed
that "the disturbers of Buenos Aires were moving openly toward
independence." [3] When we study the political program of the new
government and the diplomacy of the revolution, we shall cite new
documentary proofs concerning the definite proposal of independence which was accepted by the patriots who took part in the
revolution of 1810.

It has been explained that the first patriot government was imposed by the will of the people. In this designation we include that

---

[1] *Acuerdos del extinguido cabildo de Buenos Aires,* libro LXIV, f. 101.

[2] Saldías, *La evolución republicana durante la revolución argentina* (Buenos
Aires, 1906), apéndice, p. 381. See further, Levene, "Causas criminales sobre
intentada independencia del Perú, 1805-1809," *Anales de la facultad de derecho
y ciencias sociales,* XVII, 519-628.

[3] P. Torres Lanzas, *Independencia de América* (6 vols. Madrid, 1912), II, 236.

large group of citizens who signed the written petition addressed
to the cabildo which embodied the reiterated proposition that the
patriotic junta of government should assume the command in place
of Viceroy Cisneros.[4] But the formula which was adopted, consistent in invoking the patronage of King Ferdinand VII, was a
serious obstacle to the rapid spread of the revolution in society.
The Spanish governors of interior provinces and the majority of
their cabildos—as bodies representative of the burghers of the
cities—declared against the patriot doctrine; for the people were
unacquainted with the political theory that had been enunciated,
that is, the theory of establishing juntas of self-government during
the captivity of the monarch. Thus it was that the new governors,
in the same manner as those whom they had replaced, invoked the
name of the king. In principle, to the eyes of the people one set of
rulers seemed as good as the other. If in reality they were not equal,
time would tell. In truth, time was the great ally of the developing
cause; for to the same degree that the revolution was unfolding
and publicly carrying out its program of government, it was also
becoming very popular.

From the very beginning, the provisional governmental junta
discerned the magnitude of the peril that encompassed it. With
the single exception of the viceroy, the colonial administrative
framework remained intact. The governmental junta was like an
extraneous organization, which, besides, was dependent upon the
cabildo; for the act of May 25 gave to the latter institution the
entire function of closely watching the proceedings of the members
of the junta. In the general meeting of May 22 the oidors of the
audiencia had voted in favor of the retention of the viceroy in
command, while the cabildo had wished to form a junta with Cisneros as president. The deposed viceroy entertained hopes of re-
assuming the government by virtue of the "provisional" character
of the junta, and confided in the arrival of provincial deputies
who were to decide everything regarding the new political organization that was to be established in the viceroyalty. But these hopes
soon disappeared. Then the audiencia, the cabildo, and the former
viceroy conspired against the junta. The high tribunal of justice
urged upon the patriot government the necessity of taking an oath
to support the regency installed at Cadiz in the beginning of 1810,

---

[4] *Días de Mayo; actas del cabildo de Buenos Aires.*

which was taking the place of the defunct junta of Seville. The pretensions of the audiencia were completely destroyed by the solid argumentation of Moreno.

All the interior region with the intendancy of Córdoba in the lead had risen against the junta. The same attitude was taken in Montevideo and in Paraguay. Meantime, the house of Cisneros, to whom "all the honors, distinctions, and privileges" of viceroy had been assured, had been converted into an active center of criticism directed against the government and of protests on account of the activity of the patriots.[5]

Saavedra aptly mirrored the distracted feelings that agitated those persons responsible for the revolution when he affirmed in his *Memoria Póstuma:* "In Buenos Aires itself there were not lacking creoles who viewed our enterprise with loathing; some believed that it could not be accomplished because of the strength of the Spaniards; others judged it to be the madness and delirium of untrained leaders; others, in brief—and these were the most pious—viewed us with compassion, not doubting that in a few days we should be the victims of Spanish power and fury in castigation of our rebellion and infidelity against the legitimate sovereign, lord, and proprietor of America. . . . ."[6] Cisneros was preparing to start a vast conflagration in the new system. The junta got hold of some secret communications in which the ex-viceroy incited his followers to support the king's rights until they shed the last drop of their blood.[7] Placing Cisneros and the oidors of the audiencia on board an English vessel, the patriot government insured their departure from La Plata.

It was the governor of the intendancy of Córdoba, Colonel Juan Gutiérrez de la Concha, who in conjunction with Santiago Allende and General Liniers, prepared to resist the liberating expedition that was to leave Buenos Aires. The bishop of that diocese supported the counter-revolutionary plan. Dean Gregorio Funes resolutely refused to support it. By the aid of new documents it can be shown that the plan of a counter-revolutionary conspiracy had gained adherents throughout all the interior. In order to thwart

[5] Archivo general de la nación, archivo de gobierno de Buenos Aires, 1810, vol. XLII, cxxi-cxxix.

[6] Zimmermann Saavedra, *op cit.,* apéndice, p. 366.

[7] Archivo general de la nación, Archivo de gobierno de Buenos Aires, 1810, vol. XXVII, caps. xlvii and xlviii.

this plan the rapidity of execution and the restless energy of the junta of Buenos Aires were necessary. Intendant Gutiérrez de la Concha undertook to secure immediately the coöperation in the reactionary cause of Mendoza where a not inconsiderable number of inhabitants pledged their adhesion to him.[8]

In Salta, Nicolás Severo de Isasmendi, whose post had been declared vacant by Viceroy Cisneros, returned to take charge of the governorship. But after the junta of Buenos Aires was installed, with all speed Isasmendi undertook to gather a few residents who were attached to him in order that he might be recognized and named a deputy. However, after the junta named Chiclana as governor of the intendancy of Salta, Isasmendi offered to serve as a spy; thus he made the royalists believe that he was conspiring against the revolution.

In a letter dated August 11 of Francisco de Paula Sanz, governor-intendant of Potosí, to Gutiérrez de la Concha, which was opportunely intercepted, the former mentioned the expeditions that were to leave Potosí and Chuquisaca in order to unite with the men of Porco and Chichas in Tupiza. "Whence," continued Paula Sanz, "they will proceed to Jujuy in the hope of receiving advice from you to assemble in any event. In place of these troops I believe there will come immediately six hundred men of Cochabamba and Santa Cruz, besides another six hundred who will not be long in arriving from Arequipa and Puno where Goyeneche ordered them to assemble and where they are now quartered; whence I suppose they must by this time have departed. . . . In addition there are being sent me five hundred muskets and an ample supply of cartridges." [9]

In a letter of Vicente Nieto, president of La Plata, also addressed to the same governor, Gutiérrez de la Concha, a reference was made to the latter's plan to place himself in communication with Montevideo, from which city he had asked the aid of five hundred seamen armed and equipped with munitions. In case that he had not gathered a force strong enough to show fight, Nieto advised Gutiérrez de la Concha to fall back upon Jujuy without undertaking any engagement until he joined forces with General

---

[8] *Ibid.,* vol. XV, cap. lxxi, primera parte.

[9] *Ibid.,* vol. XXII, cap. lxxxiii, parte tercera.

José de Córdoba. The officials of the government at Buenos Aires were in possession of all the clues to the military and political plan formed against them. Under date of August 17, Moreno said to the junta of the committee of the patriot army: "As one of the first objects of the expedition is to surprise the people of Peru before reënforcements from Lima can put them into a strong defensive condition, it would perhaps be advisable for a detachment of four hundred men under the command of General Balcarce with four pieces of artillery and one hundred cavalrymen to advance to Tupiza, where they should station themselves until the arrival of the main body of the army. The distance which separates Potosí from Tupiza would safeguard this force from attack, provided that it takes precautions and fortifies itself as military art requires." [10]

When news reached Córdoba of the impending arrival of the liberating expedition of Ocampo, the insurgents disbanded; and many of them went in a northern direction with the intention of joining the Spanish forces in Upper Peru. But General Balcarce overtook the fugitives, and captured Liniers, Gutiérrez de la Concha, Bishop Orellana, Colonel Allende, the treasurer Rodríguez, and the paymaster Moreno.

On July 13, the junta informed the committee of the army that it should "destroy the conspiracy of Córdoba and make its promoters prisoners." [11] As has been indicated, nothing had yet been said of their execution. But on July 19, and before receipt of the alarming reports regarding acts of violence committed in Mendoza, the junta again wrote to the committee of the army and in conclusion alluded to the "exemplary punishment" which would be inflicted upon the revolutionists of Córdoba. The decree that they should be shot is dated July 28 and is in the handwriting of Mariano Moreno. The junta directed that the conspirators mentioned were to be shot "at the very moment when one or all of them may be captured; whatever may be the circumstances, this decision will be carried out, without affording time for supplications and reports that might compromise the fulfilment of this order and the honor of your Excellency. This chastisement should serve as the basis for the stability of the new system and as a lesson for the leaders

[10] *Ibid.*, vol. XXXVI, cap. cxii.   [11] *Ibid.*, vol. XXXVI.

of Peru, who are indulging in a thousand excesses in the expectation that they can do so with impunity." [12]

When this order for capital punishment of the chief conspirators became known, a panic spread through the entire population of Córdoba and its principal inhabitants petitioned that it should not be carried out. Ocampo, the commander of the liberating expedition, and Hipólito Vieytes, the representative of the junta, delayed the order of execution, forwarding the request to the junta of Buenos Aires. In response to this request it dispatched a new note dated August 18 which repeated the order for the execution of the conspirators. To accomplish this order it sent one of its members named Castelli and declared "that the chiefs of that expedition had violated the orders of the junta by entertaining representations which it had previously commanded should not be heard." [13]

On August 26, at a place called the Tiger's Head, Liniers and his companions were shot, with the exception of Bishop Orellana, who was spared because of his ecclesiastical character.

Rightly to judge this decisive resolution of the junta of Buenos Aires one must keep in mind the following facts: (1) In view of the conspiracy that was being formed in Córdoba, the junta had written to Governor Gutiérrez de la Concha on June 27 and earnestly warned "him to leave the path on which he had started, in the opinion that he will himself become a victim of evils that will occur without his being able to plead ignorance." [14] That is to say, the junta had warned the conspirators and had invited them to maintain order and concord. (2) The authors of the counter-revolution had availed themselves of the most reprehensible measures in order to make their cause triumph and they were the first persons to threaten the patriots of Buenos Aires with death. (3) The resistance of Córdoba does not appear as an isolated event but as associated with the resistance which was displayed at the same juncture in Montevideo and Upper Peru. There is no doubt that the order for the execution of the insurgents of Córdoba was lamentable. Considering the facts, after the lapse of a century, it is possible to believe that the punishment was excessive. But at that moment, when

---

[12] A facsimile of this document is printed in A. Rosa, *Medallas y monedas de la República Argentina* (Buenos Aires, 1898), pp. 34-35.

[13] Archivo general de la nación, Archivo del gobierno de Buenos Aires, 1810, vol. XXXVI.　　　　[14] *Ibid.*, vol. XXIV, cap. xli, primera parte.

the revolution was menaced by serious perils to which it might have
succumbed, it appears that the decision of the junta was in response
to a high patriotic inspiration.

Immediately after the execution at Tiger's Head, the liberating
expedition proceeded in a northerly direction and in a short time
it came under the command of Balcarce and Castelli, the latter
being the representative of the junta. They advanced as far as
the ravine of Humahuaca, and received the important contingent
sent by Martín Güemes. On October 27, at Cotagaita, the first encounter of the royalists and the patriots occurred. In this engagement, Balcarce was defeated, but he was able to reform his forces
and with fresh reënforcements received from Jujuy, he awaited in
Suipacha the Spanish army under the command of Generals Córdoba and Nieto. The patriots completely routed the Spanish army
from which they took all its artillery and equipment. The battle,
which took place on November 7, 1810, did not last more than half
an hour, but it was decisive. Generals Córdoba and Nieto and the
intendant, Paula Sanz, were shot by order of Castelli, in accordance with the instructions of the junta.

The battle of Suipacha had two important results for the cause
of the revolution: one result was of a moral character, for that
combat was the first triumph of the Argentine army and gave spirit
and enthusiasm to the patriots; the other result was of a political
character, for the four intendancies of Upper Peru declared in
favor of the revolution. Regarding the victory of Suipacha, the
secretary of the governmental junta, Mariano Moreno, wrote in the
Gaceta de Buenos Aires as follows: "The valor, energy, and constancy displayed by our soldiers struck terror into our enemies.
When these soldiers march through our streets we shall say to them:
'To you we owe the happiness that we are enjoying!'"

The triumph of Suipacha gave the patriots possession of Upper
Peru. The army of Castelli advanced to the river Desaguadero—
the boundary between the viceroyalty of La Plata and the viceroyalty of Peru. Upon the opposite bank was encamped the army of
Goyeneche. On May 13, Castelli and Goyeneche agreed to an armistice for a period of forty days; but General Goyeneche, violating
this truce, surprised the patriot army at Huaqui on June 30, 1811,
and routed it completely. On receiving notice of this reverse, the
president of Chuquisaca, Juan Martín de Pueyrredón, marched

rapidly to Potosí, where he seized the property that was in the mint, and undertook a retreat to Jujuy (which someone has likened to "the retreat of the ten thousand" from Asia) and thence to Tucumán.

The disaster of Huaqui signified the loss of Upper Peru, the possession and control of which had been assured by the triumph at Suipacha. From that base the Spaniards were able to offer a strong resistance; besides they could threaten to invade the Argentine provinces of the north. Such a disaster also caused a serious commotion in the revolutionary government at Buenos Aires: the governmental junta dissolved, and the first triumvirate was formed.

CHAPTER XXVIII

THE EMANCIPATION OF PARAGUAY AND URUGUAY

AFTER THE revolution had begun, the junta of government addressed notes to the intendants and cabildos which invited them to send deputies to the general congress that was to assemble at Buenos Aires. The governor-intendant of Paraguay, Colonel Bernardo de Velazco, summoned a general assembly of residents for July 24 in order to decide upon the relations that were to be maintained with the junta of Buenos Aires. The two hundred persons who attended this congress resolved: (1) to swear obedience to the council of regency set up in Spain; (2) to maintain a fraternal solidarity with Buenos Aires, but without recognizing its superiority; (3) to form a junta of war that should have in its charge the defense of the intendancy of Paraguay. In the assembly of July 24, appeared Dr. José Gaspar de Francia, who, according to some writers, suggested the idea of the absolute independence of Paraguay. In every quarter there were disseminated "the revolutionary ideas of Dr. Francia; by some persons, in the radical meaning inspired by him, and by other persons, with the intention of adopting the system of Buenos Aires and of forming a federative state with the other provinces of the viceroyalty.

"As a result of this divergence of opinion, three parties were formed that differed concerning the guidance of the revolutionary cart. The 'royalists,' headed by Velazco, subordinated all their acts to the interests of the motherland; the 'porteños,' deluded by Somellera, yielded to the tendencies and proposals of Buenos Aires; while the 'natives,' inspired by Francia, aimed at absolute independence." [1]

Immediately after the Paraguayans had adopted the resolution of July 24, the governmental junta directed that Manuel Belgrano should lead an expedition intended for Asunción. Two hundred men of the garrison of Buenos Aires were selected to serve as the nucleus of this new army; and to these soldiers were added some militia of Paraná, of the mission district, and of Corrientes. Belgrano had

---

[1] C. Báez, *Resumen de la historia del Paraguay desde la época de la conquista hasta el año 1880* (Asunción, 1910), p. 40.

357 men under his command at San Nicolás de los Arroyos; from that place he proceeded to Santa Fe, and thence he soon marched to the town of Bajada del Paraná. Such was the enthusiasm for the revolutionary cause that Belgrano was received with many demonstrations of sympathy and all the people offered their support. Señora Gregoria Pérez wrote a letter to Belgrano in which she said: "I place at the disposition of your Excellency my haciendas, my houses, and my servants, from the river Feliciano to the post of Estacas. Within these bounds your Excellency is master of my small properties, in order that you may aid with them the army under your command without the payment of any material consideration whatever."

Belgrano assembled an army of 950 men, one-half composed of cavalry and one-half of infantry. About the end of October the expedition began to march toward Curuzú-Cuatiá; it crossed the Paraná River at Candelaria in the middle of December and encamped on the banks of a stream called the Paraguary (January 19, 1811), it met the army of the enemy. In the ensuing battle, Belgrano was repulsed; he sent a letter to the junta asking for reënforcements, for the Paraguayan army under command of the governor-intendant, Velazco, numbered 8,000 men. The junta sent 600 soldiers who embarked on three warships under the command of Azopardo, who was to go to Santa Fe and there to await orders from Belgrano. But at San Nicolás, a Spanish squadron sent from Montevideo commanded by Jacinto Romarate attacked Azopardo, who fell covered with wounds. In the meantime, General Belgrano remained isolated: the Paraguayan army took him by surprise and another battle occurred at Tacuarí. Fate was again adverse to Belgrano, but he was able to negotiate a convention with Colonel Cabañas, who was at the head of the Paraguayan army, by virtue of which Belgrano's army was pledged immediately to leave Paraguay.

From the military point of view the expedition of Belgrano was a fiasco. The Paraguayan army was composed of veterans and was strong because of its numbers. Further, Belgrano was an improvised military leader, a sincere and enthusiastic patriot, but destitute of the military talent that was required to direct a campaign in the province of Paraguay. He was not even acquainted with the Paraguayan terrain. From the moral point of view and from the viewpoint of revolutionary propaganda the expedition of Belgrano helped to promote the independence of Paraguay. The viceroyalty of La Plata suffered the first revolutionary dismemberment that took place in South America, but Paraguay did not become, like Upper Peru and the Banda Oriental, a center of Spanish resistance.

The emancipation of the intendancy of Paraguay was not, as might be supposed, a mere result of Belgrano's expedition. This invasion doubtless influenced the separatist tendency, but did not directly cause it. The notion of independence had its roots in tradition. In truth, during the long colonial epoch the province of La Guayrá or Paraguay witnessed numerous revolutionary movements which revealed the lofty and warlike spirit of its people. In the first half of the eighteenth century that province had been the theater of the famous revolt of the "comuneros" led by Antequera and Mompó—one of the revolutionary movements that presaged the emancipation of Spanish America.

Aside from the existence of this vigorous provincial sentiment, the intendancy of Paraguay had carried on continuous conflicts with the city of Buenos Aires. In 1680, a royal order imposed a duty of half a peso upon every arroba of Paraguayan yerba mate unloaded at Buenos Aires,[2] while a duty of one peso was imposed upon every arroba of yerba transported to Tucumán or to Peru. Again, the products of Paraguay could not be transported directly to Buenos Aires. Santa Fe was a necessary port of transhipment: in that place Paraguayan yerba had to be unloaded; thence it was conveyed overland to Buenos Aires.

Paraguay had repeatedly protested against these exactions. Now and then the cabildo of Asunción had asked to be allowed a part of the impost duty for aid in its defensive campaigns against the Indians. The council avowed that it was "only claiming a part of what was its own, for it was not just that the other cities should be supported by the imposts on Paraguay."[3] In view of such antecedents, the autonomous sentiments of the Paraguayans are explained. On June 19, 1811, a junta of self-government was formed in Paraguay, in which prevailed the views of one of its members,

---

[2] An "arroba" weighed twenty-five pounds.—W.S.R.
[3] F. R. Moreno, *Estudio sobre la independencia del Paraguay* (Asunción, 1911), I, 57.

Dr. Francia, who wished to transform his province into an independent republic.

Since colonial times the geographical position of the Banda Oriental and a combination of economic and moral factors had prepared the way for the emancipation of Uruguay. In the words of Bauzá: "The Charruan Indians acknowledged no authority superior to their own within their tribal jurisdiction, and the Spanish conquest confirmed this physical truth which was made clear by the form of government of the aborigines and the peculiarity of their resistance. In a sense, the persistent attacks of the Portuguese upon the Banda Oriental served as a confirmation of that acknowledged independence, for Uruguay maintained autonomy in its territories by its own force, being acknowledged as a special region and as the sole object of Portuguese covetousness. This tendency was later reënforced by the creation of a distinctive government which, although dependent on the viceroy of Buenos Aires, possessed sufficient authority to function within a considerable sphere." [4]

The resistance of Uruguay against Buenos Aires was in germ in 1776. The two banks of the Río de la Plata had economic interests that were not harmonious. Viceroy Cevallos sent word to Spain of the injury caused to the commerce of Buenos Aires by the fact that registered ships had to touch at the port of Montevideo and could not proceed directly to Buenos Aires. In 1799, the advocates of the merchants and proprietors of Montevideo addressed a petition to the king to protest against the "oppression and fatal dependence upon the commercial tribunal of Buenos Aires" and to recommend the erection of a tribunal of commerce in that port. The commercial tribunal of Buenos Aires opposed the establishment of a sister tribunal at Montevideo.

At the opening of the nineteenth century a new cause for difference arose. Labardén had composed a memoir advocating the necessity of establishing a port at Ensenada and extolling its advantages as compared with Montevideo. This proposal provoked an impassioned polemical discussion.[5]

After the English invasions of La Plata in 1808, the governor

---

[4] F. Bauzá, *Historia de la dominación española en el Uruguay* (3 vols. Montevideo, 1895-97), II, apéndice crítico, pp. 659-60.

[5] *Telégrafo Mercantil,* vol. I, núms. 3, 4, 5, 8, 9, and 10.

of Montevideo, Javier de Elío, in connivance with the Spaniards of Buenos Aires, rose against the authority of Viceroy Liniers and formed a junta of government. The medium employed on the adjacent bank of the river, that is, the open revolutionary council, became known in the city of Buenos Aires where, on August 14, 1806, and on February 10, 1807, the assembled citizens had resolved upon the deposition and arrest of Viceroy Sobremonte. Indeed, it may be said that Martín Alzaga, who was the inspirer of these acts, suggested that medium to Javier de Elío, his associate in the cause. But the doctrine, which embodied the principle of a junta of government in imitation of the juntas existing in the Spanish Peninsula, was new in America, and when it had once triumphed in Montevideo, on January 1, 1809, Alzaga and Elío wished to impose it on Buenos Aires.

It was this same principle, advocated by creoles, however, and therefore, for a different purpose, that was adopted on May 25, 1810. Accordingly, when the revolution of Buenos Aires began, the Banda Oriental had been separated from the viceroyalty of La Plata for almost two years.

From the end of 1809, a nucleus of Uruguayan patriots labored for the independence of Uruguay from Spanish domination. The agents of this plan were Mateo Gallegos in Montevideo and Francisco Javier de Viana in Buenos Aires. "At the isolated farm of Dr. Manuel Pérez, Larrañaga, Barreiro, Monterroso, the brothers of José Artigas, Otorgués, and other persons assembled, in order that they might converse about independence. They soon showed that they desired José Artigas to assume the direction of the movement." [6]

In 1797, José Artigas had become a private in the regiment of lancers, which had as its chief function to police the rural districts.[7] His merits won him the post of captain of the militia in the Montevideo regiment of cavalry. Later, he joined the expedition of Santiago Liniers which accomplished the reconquest of Buenos Aires which had been invaded by the English. When the second English invasion took place, he also distinguished himself in the defense

---

[6] E. Acevedo, *Manual de historia uruguaya* (5 vols. Montevideo, 1916-23), I, 119-20.

[7] R. Llambías de Olivar, "Ensayo sobre el linaje de los Artigas en el Uruguay," *Revista Histórica* (Montevideo, 1925), XI, 1054-1159.

of Montevideo. In February, 1811, Artigas came to Buenos Aires where the government incited him to start a campaign in Uruguay against the Spaniards. Under the command of Viera and Benavídez, but under the influence of the action of Artigas, on February 28, 1811, on the coast of Arroyo Asencio, a nucleus of Uruguayan patriots began the rebellion. A few days later, the revolutionists took possession of the towns of Mercedes and Soriano.

The junta of Buenos Aires immediately ordered that the remnant of the expedition which had been dispatched to Paraguay should proceed under the command of Belgrano to the Banda Oriental, with José Rondeau as second in command. But Belgrano came to Buenos Aires because of the suit initiated on account of the defeats administered to his army in the Paraguayan campaign, and intrusted the army to Rondeau. In a letter written in April, 1811, Artigas wrote as follows to the junta of Buenos Aires: "I am awaiting the orders of his Excellency, Manuel Belgrano, to proceed to Montevideo with as little delay as possible, and your Excellency can place confidence in the strength of these patriot legions that will know how to break the chains of slavery and assure the happiness of our country."

On May 18, 1811, at the head of one thousand soldiers composed of infantry and cavalry, José Artigas triumphed at Las Piedras over the royalist army composed of more than one thousand two hundred men. In this battle, Artigas made almost five hundred prisoners, many of whom later adhered to the insurgent cause. The news of this triumph reached Buenos Aires on May 24 and was worthily celebrated on the following day, which marked the first anniversary of the opening of the revolutionary movement. After the battle of Las Piedras, Artigas marched to Montevideo and demanded the surrender of that city. Soon afterward, the army of Rondeau joined him. The siege lasted until October 20 of that year, when an armistice was signed between Viceroy Elío and the junta of Buenos Aires. Elío caused the Portuguese soldiers that had marched to his succor to withdraw from the Uruguayan frontier.

CHAPTER XXIX

TENDENCIES OF THE REVOLUTION

"OUR HISTORIANS have preferred to study the military achievements and outstanding actions of the men who occupied the stage after May 25, 1810. They have neglected the thoughts and tendencies of those men as revealed in various documents and also certain measures which were adopted without ostentation, but which involved immense consequences." These words were penned by Luis V. Varela, author of a constitutional history of Argentina.[1]

After the first days of the revolution there became apparent in the governmental junta two great political tendencies, which may be likened unto historic forces, the initial impulses of which determined later political evolution. These were a tendency toward a turbulent democracy, which made necessary the formation of a strong government to maintain order and to insure the cause of emancipation; and a tendency toward a federal democracy, that is, the feeling that the provinces were autonomous entities with the right to representation in the government. These two forces which became manifest after 1810 had their origins in the colonial epoch. During the three centuries in which Spain dominated the colony of La Plata, persons born in that region did not cease to start insurrections and rebellious movements against the dominant economic and political régime. Continuous revolutions breaking out during the sixteenth, seventeenth, and eighteenth centuries produced a common and predominant sentiment among the mass of the population which favored the organization of a turbulent democracy.

The vast territorial extent of the viceroyalty favored the formation of autonomous nuclei whose visible heads were the cities which were self-supporting and between which it was difficult to establish frequent communication because of the lack of roads or because of the intervening distance. The existence of a turbulent democracy made the establishment of a strong government necessary in order to insure the cause of the revolution. Popular passion succeeded in making of that government a powerful war machine; it was vested

---

[1] L. V. Varela, *Historia constitucional de la República Argentina* (4 vols La Plata, 1910), I, 229.

with large powers because the cause of emancipation required this
to be done. In this wise the junta, proceeding energetically, ordered
the execution at Tiger's Head of the counter-revolutionists of
Córdoba, for "this punishment was to serve as the basis for the
stability of the new system"; in the same manner, after the victory
of Suipacha, it ordered the execution at Potosí of Paula Sanz, and
Generals Córdoba and Nieto.

The governmental junta took severe measures in regard to internal order. Thus, "it declares any person who does not report
any project or conspiracy against the authorities or against the
safety of particular persons to be responsible to the government";
"the property of every person who absents himself from this city
without a license from the government shall be confiscated, without
the need of any other process than the simple proof of his departure." In the month of June, the junta ordered the exile of ex-Viceroy Cisneros and the oidors of the audiencia, who were accused of
being conspirators against the new régime. By the regulations of
May 24 and 25, it had been decided that there pertained to the
cabildo "the authority of supervising" the operations of the junta
and "in the unexpected contingency that it should fail in its duties
the cabildo, for that sole reason, was to proceed to dismiss it," and
only in that case to reassume the authority conferred upon it by
the people." The cabildo obstructed the freedom of action of the
governmental junta; the junta issued a decree dismissing the members of the cabildo, for "public security requires the removal of
those persons who composed the honorable ayuntamiento because
of the repeated outrages that it had caused to the rights of the
people, and as there was vested in this junta a direct representation of the people who had constituted it a legitimate organ of its
will, it has released the members of the cabildo from their duties as
councillors with the express declaration that they will never be
able to exercise a councillor's post in this city nor in any other city
within its jurisdiction." [2]

As already indicated, the first definite object of the revolution
was independence; aside from this high purpose, the revolution had
a fundamental political program. The principal features of this

---

[2] *Registro oficial de la República Argentina*, I, 35, 58, 17, 79.—W. S. R. See
further, López, *op. cit.*, I, xxxiii, for the view that the use of military force by
the colonists was necessary.

plan, which were made clear in secret instructions transmitted by the junta to the governors of interior provinces were as follows: the guardianship and protection of the Indians; the promotion of public improvements; the grant of privileges to agriculture, industry, and commerce; the preservation of tranquility; the holding of public offices by creoles, and so on. Even in the very year in which the revolution took place this plan began to develop in all its parts.

In order to disseminate the principles proclaimed by the revolution, the junta sent diplomatic representatives to provinces and nations. Dr. Juan José Paso went to Montevideo on June 9 where he explained "the purpose of his mission with energy and dignity." As has been shown, this neighboring city was in the power of the royalists and constituted a serious peril for Buenos Aires. The mission of Paso had no result. On August 13, 1810, the junta announced that all correspondence and communication with the Banda Oriental was cut off; it prohibited any person from going to that region.

Matías Irigoyen was dispatched to Spain and England. This envoy relinquished his purpose of landing in Spain, for the council of regency had been established there. On August 6, he was received by Lord Wellesley, the English secretary of foreign affairs. Irigoyen's purpose was to solicit the friendship and protection of his Britannic Majesty. In the beginning of 1809, England had signed a treaty of alliance with Spain; hence Lord Wellesley declared to the Argentine diplomat that he could not give his approval to the May Revolution at Buenos Aires. Wellesley inquired whether that movement implied the independence of the colony of La Plata from Spain. To this question, Irigoyen replied in the negative, but in a report that he soon sent to the junta of Buenos Aires, in commenting upon this part of the interview, he added that although he was not advised of the meaning of the revolution of 1810, yet he made this response because he deemed it convenient and diplomatic.

In November of the same year, the junta sent Antonio Álvarez Jonte to Chile for the purpose of "maintaining and stimulating the relations that naturally should exist between the provinces of the Río de la Plata and the provinces of that kingdom of Chile to the mutual advantage of both countries and to consolidate the glorious system that this portion of America has embraced."

In the beginning of 1811, credentials were prepared for a mission by Mariano Moreno to Brazil and England. The instructions which Moreno was given concerning his proceedings in Rio de Janeiro dealt with the negotiations that he was to undertake with Princess Carlota in order to persuade her that her contingent rights to the Spanish throne were viewed with much respect in Buenos Aires. In an interesting paragraph of Moreno's secret instructions the following statement is made: "All these negotiations are to be very secret and shall be managed with such dexterity that they do not compromise the junta with the Infanta Carlota; and if she should wish to strengthen relations with Buenos Aires by a decisive compact, he shall resort to the plea that he lacks instructions on that point, and shall ask for time to consult the junta. With the English minister he shall pursue a more frank and intimate policy, and with regard to the rights of the infanta he will show that he is indecisive, skilfully allowing the minister to perceive indirectly the repugnance of the people to all foreign domination." [3]

In England he was to negotiate for the recognition of the government at Buenos Aires. In order to promote the success of his negotiations he should offer as an inducement a treaty of commerce with Great Britain. In case the English government should insist upon the necessity of recognizing the Spanish council of regency, or if this fact should prevent a public declaration by England, the agent was to undertake "a secret negotiation under the faith and protection of which, the government of these provinces could make its calculations." Moreno was not able to perform the mission which was intrusted to him after he renounced the post of secretary of the junta, for he died on the voyage to England.

The governmental junta represented the executive authority and its mission was, therefore, to act, "to execute." Among its members, two personalities stood out: Saavedra and Moreno. Cornelio Saavedra was the effective man of the revolution. Serene, but determined, his participation had been decisive in the days that preceded May 25. Let us recall the scene that took place in the fort on May 20 when the regimental commanders were summoned by Viceroy Cisneros. Upon that occasion Saavedra, who was the commander of the regiment of nobles by the free choice of its officers, told the viceroy that the latter could not count upon his support, because

---

[3] F. F. Outes, "La diplomacia de la revolución," *Revista de la Universidad de Buenos Aires* (Buenos Aires, 1911), XV, 509.

he was on the side of the people and of the revolution. On May 25, when the popular wish selected the first list of officials for the patriot government, the name of Saavedra was spontaneously presented for the position of president.

Mariano Moreno was endowed with brilliant talent and great energy. As a scholar, he had won a leading position among the young men of his generation. It was easy to anticipate the important rôle which he would play in the governmental junta. As Saavedra was the equilibrating thought, so Moreno was the dynamic genius, who with admirable intuition discerned the future of his country.

A difference developed between these two personalities: at first it was personal; later it became one of principles. The activity of Moreno was expansive, like the generous enthusiasm which inspired him, and it tended to absorb and to preponderate by natural force. The poised temperament of Saavedra impelled him to maintain and preserve the existing state of things. Moreno wished to accomplish a rapid and energetic reform, a faithful expression of his own temperament. Possibly Saavedra aspired to the same end, but he clung to the principle of the slow evolution of things and events.

A conflict between these two men was inevitable. On the occasion when the triumph of Suipacha was being celebrated, there was held on December 5, 1810, in the barracks of the regiment of nobles, an entertainment in honor of Cornelio Saavedra. Mariano Moreno wished to attend it; but the sentinel on duty did not recognize him, and, as Moreno did not make himself known, he was not allowed to enter. Two hours after this misadventure, Moreno was informed that during the entertainment, a captain of hussars named Atanasio Duarte, a person of dissolute habits, had offered a toast in which he avowed that America impatiently awaited the proclamation of Saavedra as emperor. Already prejudiced because of the mishap with the sentry, Moreno was vividly impressed by the news of this episode. He accordingly composed a "decree concerning honors" in which he declared that it was not a function of the president of the junta to receive honors and homage individually but that this pertained to all the members of the junta collectively; that the wives of public officials were not participants with their husbands in these ceremonies; that as Captain Duarte had given a toast which offended the decorum of both the president and the members of the junta, he was condemned to death, but that as he had been drunk, this penalty would be commuted into exile from La Plata; "for no Argentinian, whether sober or drunk, should entertain views antagonistic to the liberty of his country." Upon the following day, Moreno took this decree to the president for approval, and Saavedra signed it.

This incident widened the breach between Saavedra and Moreno. The members of the governmental junta joined one or another of these two groups—the Saavedristas or the Morenistas. In its origins this difference was one of temperament and purely personal; later, when a problem arose regarding the provincial deputies, it became a matter of principles.

The open council of May 22 had approved a procedure which provided for the formation of a suitable government and the convocation of a general congress. In the act of May 25, it was further resolved that the governmental junta should send a circular to the cabildos of the cities asking that deputies should be selected to form a general congress, which should consider what form of government would be most suitable for La Plata. According to the circular of May 27, the deputies chosen by the cabildos were to be incorporated in the junta upon their arrival in the capital. On November 1, Moreno began to publish in the *Gaceta de Buenos Aires* his memorable articles "Sobre las miras del congreso que acaba de convocarse y constitución de estado" ("Concerning the Constitution of the State and the Views of the Congress which has just been convoked"). These articles of Moreno were composed hastily, for urgency was demanded by the need of promoting an exchange of ideas on the eve of the day when congress was to enter upon the execution of its constitutional functions.

Let us notice some of the points explained by Moreno in the articles which engage our attention: "Can Spanish America establish a stable constitution worthy of being recognized by other nations during the life of Ferdinand VII whom it recognizes as its monarch?" On this point Moreno made a brilliant juridical demonstration of the right of Spanish America to frame its own constitution. When that fundamental question had been elucidated, the publicist inquired: "Can a part of Spanish America by means of its legitimate representatives establish the legal system which it wishes and which it so much needs or should it await a new assembly in which all Spanish America shall enact its own laws?" In view of the social differences existing among the various peoples of Spanish America and also because of the differences imposed by nature, Moreno completely shattered the scheme of assembling one Spanish-American legislature.

Moreno had invited all the deputies to publish their ideas in regard to the constitutional organization which they desired. Funes responded to this invitation and wrote three articles for the *Gaceta*. In the middle of December, nine deputies had arrived in the capital but no other citizen had made a declaration concerning his political principles. A perusal of the instructions of the deputies, which are documents of great importance, do not warrant us in concluding that the representatives were imperatively directed to decide upon the form of government to be adopted nor in general upon any constitutional matter, if indeed they were sent to form a part of congress.[4]

The deputies from the provinces, headed by Dean Gregorio Funes, the representative for Córdoba, and by Felipe de Molina for Mendoza, demanded that they should be incorporated in the junta. They got into touch with President Saavedra who supported their demand. To this pretension Moreno was resolutely opposed. Under these circumstances a fundamental disagreement became evident.

On December 18, a general conference was held which was attended by the provincial deputies as well as by the members of the governmental junta. In it, Dean Funes explained the reasons which justified the petition. He affirmed "that the deputies felt compelled to claim the right which belonged to them of being incorporated in the provisional junta and of taking an active part in the management of the provinces until the meeting of the congress that had been convoked; that this right, besides being undisputed by the people, their constituents—for the capital city did not have the legitimate right by itself to elect rulers whom the other cities ought to obey—had been acknowledged by the junta itself for, in the official circular of the convocation, it had expressly pledged the delegates that as soon as they arrived they would take an active part in the

---

[4] Hitherto inedited documents concerning this congress are published in Levene, *Ensayo histórico sobre le revolución de Mayo y Mariano Moreno,* vol. II, apéndice.

government and would be incorporated in the junta." According to the minutes of this conference all the members of the junta who were present attacked the argument of Funes and adduced the following reasons: (1) that in regard to the question of right, no one considered it as acceptable, for the purpose of the convocation of the deputies had been to hold a national congress; (2) that the deputies should not be incorporated in the junta, for that body had only been created provisionally, "and the end of it should mark the beginning of the functions of the deputies"; (3) that the clause of the circular of May 27 invoked by Funes was the result of inexperience which time "had later shown to be entirely impracticable," and that, besides, the credentials of the deputies stated explicitly that they were destined "to form a national congress and to establish in it a solid and permanent government"; and (4) "that the recognition of the junta which had been accorded in all the towns repaired the lack of their participation in its installation."

The arguments set forth by Funes were entirely destroyed; and yet, upon proceeding to a vote, the majority of the members of the junta were in agreement with the dean of Córdoba. Only the secretaries, Paso and Moreno, voted against his proposal. The explanation of this change lies in the well-founded opinion of Cornelio Saavedra who said "that the incorporation of the deputies in the junta would not be according to right but that he would agree to it because of public convenience." The public convenience to which the president alluded was the pretended popular agitation that had been produced by the decree of December 6 by which the honors allowed to the president were abolished.

The personal situation of Moreno was strained and delicate. During the conference of December 18 allusions had been made to him; loyal to his convictions and firm in character, he resigned his position as secretary of the junta. Mariano Moreno is a lofty expression of our democracy. From May 25 to December 18, when the conference was held with the provincial delegates, not a single day passed that was not marked by the unmistakable seal of his personality in the drafting of a decree, the planning of a work, or the strengthening of a democratic institution. After leaving the University of Chuquisaca his intellect had been trained by alternating the study of the classics with that of the writers and philosophers of the eighteenth century. Broad in his culture, he was a

sagacious observer of political and social events and well versed in
the history and law of the Spanish Indies.

The beginning of the public life of Mariano Moreno must be
traced back to the year 1802 when he composed the study entitled
*Disertación jurídica sobre el servicio personal de los Indios en
general* (*A Juridical Dissertation concerning the Personal Service of the Indians in general*) which he read before the Carolinian
Academy of the city of Chuquisaca. In this splendid essay, Moreno
protested against the régime of brutal exploitation to which the
aborigines were subjected and compared the evils that they suffered
with the punishments imposed in ancient Rome upon the wicked and
the delinquent. That dissertation of the illustrious patriot is his
youthful confession of faith: for in its adolescent pages vibrate
the passions that dominated his entire life—justice and liberty.[5]
Having been granted the degree of doctor in law, in 1805 Moreno
returned to his native city, where he played a very important rôle
as a lawyer. On January 1, 1809, his name appeared in a list of
members of the proposed junta which Martín Alzaga tried to impose upon Liniers. He did not actively participate in that movement; but the fact that his name appears, shows that he was an
advocate of the novel principle that juntas of government should
be established, a principle which was to be proclaimed by the revolution in 1810.

In the same year, Moreno signed two important documents. One
of these, prepared jointly with Julián de Leyva, was the report
giving a legal opinion to the viceroy concerning the suits against
the promoters of the revolution of January 1, in which they advised
a general pardon. The other was the *Representación de los Hacendados,* the content and significance of which we have already considered. But the salient features of this personality became clear
during those months of 1810 in which he served as secretary of the
junta and was intrusted with the management of affairs of government and war. If we were to describe in a single phrase the distinctive trait of his personality, we should say of Moreno that he was
an "organizer of democracy." His initiative and his reforms prove
this, capable as he was of ample and panoramic vision, and with a
constructive aptitude and genius, par excellence.

[5] R. Levene, "Iniciación de la vida pública de Mariano Moreno." *Anales de la
facultad de derecho y ciencias sociales* (Buenos Aires, 1917), XVII, 464-518.

Comprehending the unavoidable necessity that the new government should have an organ of publicity, which would keep it in direct touch with public opinion, he accordingly founded the periodical designated the *Gaceta*, and wrote as follows in the number of that gazette dated June 7, 1810: "The people have the right to be informed concerning the conduct of their representatives, and their honor is concerned that all should know the execration with which the people view the secrets and mysteries invented by power to conceal its misdeeds. . . . In order to fulfil such just desires the junta has decided that there shall issue from the press a new weekly periodical entitled the *Gaceta de Buenos Aires*, which will make known to the people the domestic and foreign news that they ought to peruse with interest. In it there will also be made public the relations of the junta with the other commanders and governments, the condition of the royal treasury, and the measures necessary for its improvement. The junta will frankly make known the motives that determine its principal measures, it will open the door to the suggestions that anyone may wish to make who can contribute by his talent to the security of the result." As indicated, a fundamental principle of democratic government was announced in this notice, namely, that decisions and political acts should be given publicity. As only a small edition of the *Gaceta* was published, after they celebrated high mass, the priests were to read that journal to the communicants. In this manner, the people were to be informed of the progress of revolutionary events and their spirits were to be educated in democracy.

Another memorable innovation of Moreno was the public library of Buenos Aires, for the purpose of encouraging reading and to instruct the people. On this occasion, and to explain this innovation, he wrote a beautiful page for the *Gaceta* which alone would be enough to consecrate the new institution. He reasoned thus: "The people purchase at an increasing price the glory of arms; and the blood of citizens is not the only sacrifice which accompanies triumphs; the terrified muses flee to more tranquil regions; and men, who have become insensible to everything except desolation and clamor, forget those establishments which they should encourage in happy times in order to promote science and art. If the magistracy does not pledge its authority and zeal to prevent the fatal

culmination to which such a perilous condition steadily leads, to
pleasant customs there will succeed the ferocity of a barbarous
people and the rudeness of the sons will dishonor the memory of the
great achievements of the fathers. Buenos Aires is threatened with
such a terrible fate; four years of glory have silently undermined
the enlightenment and the virtues that produced it. Necessity made
it imperative to assign provisionally the Academy of San Carlos
as a barracks for soldiers; the young men of Buenos Aires began
to taste a liberty as perilous as it was agreeable; and, attracted
by the luster of arms produced by our glories, they wished to become soldiers before they were ready to become men." This is an
epigrammatic page, which reveals the nature of that historic moment: the Academy of San Carlos had been transformed into a
military barracks! It was necessary to check the fatal dénouement toward which such a perilous state of war was leading, and
Moreno proposed the founding of the library. Education was a
formula for social improvement.

Admirable is also the prologue that Moreno wrote for the edition of Rousseau's *Social Contract* with the publication of which he
proposed to initiate a series of remarkable works concerning politics, law, and history destined for the education of the people. When
the provincial deputies arrived at the capital, Moreno published in
the columns of the *Gaceta* his notable articles "Regarding the Constitution of the State and the Views of the Congress that has just
been Convoked" to which we have alluded.

Moreno asked: "Where shall the depository of the supreme
power of these provinces look for the rule of its operations? The
Laws of the Indies were not framed for a state, and we are presently to organize one. The supreme power that is to be erected
should treat with nations, and the people of the Spanish Indies
would have committed a crime, if they had done this earlier. In a
word, the power, which has displaced the person of a king who is
prevented from ruling it, by the election of a congress, has no rules
for its guidance, and it is necessary to determine them. That authority should promote our felicity, and it is necessary to show it
the way. That authority should not be a despot, and only a well-
defined constitution will prevent this. We agree then, as a basis for
further propositions, that congress has been convoked in order to

establish a supreme authority which will supply the lack of Ferdinand VII and to form a constitution which will relieve the people
from the unhappiness that they suffer."

We have said that, when the motion of Dean Funes to the effect
that the provincial deputies should be incorporated in the junta
was approved, Moreno, as a result of his convictions, resigned absolutely his position as secretary of the junta. This resignation contained a paragraph which is proof of the civic spirit and self-abne-
gation animating him. It ran thus: "I relinquish my position . . .
and hope that some day I shall enjoy the gratitude of the very
citizens who have persecuted me. From my heart I forgive them,
and I even view their erring conduct with a species of pleasure;
for, above the estimation in which I may be held, I prefer that the
people should begin to think about the government, even though
they should commit errors which they will later remedy." After his
resignation Moreno left upon a diplomatic mission in order to petition England to interpose its influence in favor of the independence
of the provinces of La Plata.[6] He embarked on the ship *La Fama*:
the voyage was stormy; and at dawn on March 4, 1811, he expired,
having scarcely attained the thirty-third year of his age.

One of the militant personalities of the revolution was Dean
Funes. A native of Córdoba, he became prominent in that city as
rector of the university. He was responsible for the proposal to
introduce the teaching of mathematics into the curriculum of the
University of Córdoba. His activity was checked at the moment
when the news of the revolution which broke out in Buenos Aires
reached Córdoba. When the governor-intendant of the province
invited Dean Funes and other citizens to oppose the revolution of
Buenos Aires and the liberating expedition of the North which
was about to leave under the command of Ortiz de Ocampo, Dean
Gregorio Funes declared himself emphatically in favor of the cause
of the revolution and informed the junta of the counter-revolution
that was being prepared in Córdoba.

A little later, the cabildo of Córdoba elected Funes its deputy,
and once in Buenos Aires, as a personal friend of Moreno and soon

---

[6] Extracts from official documents of the junta that indicate the purpose of
Moreno's mission are found in W. S. Robertson, *Rise of the Spanish-American
Republics* (New York, 1918), pp. 164-66. Translations of original documents
concerning this mission are found in the Public Record Office, Foreign Office,
Portugal, 102.—W.S.R.

as a partisan of Saavedra, he took an active part in matters of internal policy. In the conference held on December 18, it was Dean Funes who defended the provincial deputies and maintained that they should be incorporated with the governmental junta. After Moreno's resignation, the dean of Córdoba occupied one of the first posts in the junta, for in addition both Castelli and Belgrano were absent. The activity of Dean Funes in Argentine politics continued many years longer. On April 20, 1811, he had the freedom of the press established for the first time in La Plata, while the right of censure was reserved only over writings of a religious character.[7] In 1816 and 1817 he published the work entitled *Ensayo de historia civil* (*Essay on Civil History*), which, considered with respect to the time of its publication, is the first history written by an Argentine author. Dean Funes dedicated this work to his native land.

The incorporation of the representatives of the provinces in the governmental junta postponed the assembling of congress. In order to furnish the provinces an active participation in the government, the junta, on February 10, 1811, promulgated a decree relative to the constitution of provincial juntas which had been framed by Dean Funes. This decree provided that the citizens of each provincial capital should elect two representatives in cabildo abierto who in conjunction with the governor should constitute the provincial junta until the meeting of the general congress. Among the proper functions of this junta were the following: to collect the revenues, to watch over the fulfilment of the obligations of all citizens who should enroll in the army, and to execute the orders of the central government. The head of each province, or the intendant governor, was named by the governmental junta. The creation of the provincial juntas accentuated the federal and democratic character of the revolutionary government.

An immediate result of the differences that had developed among the members of the junta was the revolution of April 5 and 6. After the resignation of Moreno, there remained within the junta, as well as outside of it, many partisans of his ideas. Enthusiastic young men led by the fiery French were Morenistas and disseminated their ideas through the *Gaceta* which was now edited by Dr.

---

[7] See further, M. de Vedia y Mitre, *El Deán Funes en la historia argentina* (Buenos Aires, 1910).

Agrelo. All these elements were united in a popular club that assembled in the café of Marcos and had as a device a bow of blue
and white ribbons. The Saavedristas viewed this club as a threat;
and, for the purpose of destroying it, they planned, without notify-
ing their leader, Cornelio Saavedra, to start a revolution themselves. Accordingly, at eleven o'clock on the night of April 5, there
gathered in the Corrales de Miserere men from the suburb who were
commanded by the alcalde, Tomás Grigera. The revolutionists
advanced to the square where the soldiers belonging to the regiments of Patricios, Arribeños, Pardos, and Morenos supported the
movement. The junta was deliberating under the presidency of
Saavedra, who appeared surprised by this event. The crowd was
led by Colonel Martín Rodríguez and Dr. Joaquín Campana. At
dawn a deputation presented a request from the people signed by
the alcaldes of the district and by the commanders of the military
corps in which they asked that Nicolás Rodríguez, Hipólito Vieytes, Miguel Azcuénaga, and Juan Larrea, should be dismissed from
the governmental junta. They also asked that various members of
the Marco Club should be deported from La Plata and that the
president of the junta, Cornelio Saavedra, should retain the military command. The junta sanctioned this subversive movement by
granting this unusual petition.

Such was the revolution of April 5 and 6. This movement has
unusual importance in our internal political history. It was a revolution without a flag or a principle, which was animated by passions
and special interests. It was the first of a series of commotions of
the patriot governments. Dean Gregorio Funes has appropriately
said in referring to the April Revolution "that in the procession of
parties one revolution engendered another of its kind, for once
in power each clique regulated its justice according to its own
interests."

It has been explained that near the end of 1810 two series of
events were under way: one series followed the line of the external
action of the revolution and made for emancipation from Spain;
the other referred to the internal action of the revolution and made
for the consolidation of the patriot government and the organization of the nation. But both series of events were rooted in the
very society that produced them and they exercised reciprocal
influences. The events of emancipation had an immediate and in-

tense repercussion in the internal affairs of government and organization. Thus the disaster of Huaqui, which occurred on June 20,
1811, produced a fundamental change in the second governmental
junta. President Saavedra departed for Peru to inspect the troops;
the junta of Buenos Aires sent a circular to the provinces announcing the appointment of Saavedra on a mission to the juntas and
cabildos of the interior provinces. A week after the arrival of Saavedra at Salta, he was notified of his dismissal from the government
and from the presidency of the junta. On September 23, 1811, this
body, presided over for the time being by Domingo Matheu, "having in view the celerity and energy with which the affairs of their
native land should be managed," issued a decree creating the triumvirate, an executive authority composed of three members.[8]

With the first misfortune, namely, the disaster of Huaqui—the
responsibility for which the people ascribed to the junta—and
before a year had expired since the resignation of Moreno, the
course of events tended to justify the deceased secretary. Later
Dean Funes came to accept Moreno's ideas.

Cornelio Saavedra was, as we have indicated, the effective leader
of the revolution in its first phase. In the days preceding May 25
his activity was exceptional; the regiment of nobles, which acknowledged him as leader, was the armed institution that supported the
principles and the ideas of the revolution by virtue of force. In
the government junta, the scene of the first political conflicts,
Saavedra typified the opposite pole from Moreno. In this disagreement, Moreno was great and preserved the integrity of his character; loyal to his convictions, he relinquished his post. On the
other side, Saavedra was lacking in clear vision of events and a
comprehension of the future. We have already noticed that the
incident of the barracks of the regiment of nobles, provoked by
a drunken officer who offered Saavedra an imaginary crown, had
no significance whatever. On the following day, the president of
the junta placed his signature at the foot of the decree framed by
Moreno that "suppressed the custom of observing honors." Upon
Saavedra has been placed the entire responsibility for the revolu-

[8] In November, 1811, Vicente Pazos Silva was made director of the *Gaceta*
in place of Agrelo. See J. Canter, Jr., "Monteagudo, Pazos Silva y El Censor
de 1812," *Boletín del instituto de investigaciones históricas* (Buenos Aires,
1923), II, 65-105, 145-69.

tion of April 5 and 6, but it is certain that he did not promote this uprising, which soon discarded him. His fault consists in the fact that he did not have foresight and energy enough to prevent it.[9]

After the disaster of Huaqui, Saavedra left the governmental junta, over which he had presided from May 25, 1810, to August 26, 1811. From this last-mentioned date his exile began; he resided first in San Juan, and afterward had to emigrate to Chile. In Buenos Aires, the new government, the triumvirate, was antagonistic to him; in the *Gaceta*, Bernardo Monteagudo published articles criticizing Saavedra's administration. The assembly of 1813 instituted a suit against him with the intention of holding an inquest upon the proceedings of all the earlier governments. In the judgment by the assembly, the view was taken that Saavedra had had secret communications with Princess Carlota and that he had desired to perpetuate himself in office. "Upon his return from Chile, Saavedra lived in exile amid the icy cordilleras, accompanied by a son and a faithful servant, under the protection of Providence, which he said briefly had never abandoned him. At intervals of three days his servant went to buy meat from a distant village and the noble exile remained with his child, alone and defenceless. . . . And, stoic though he was, his heart must have been filled with bitterness at the thought that history might consider him capable of delivering the land of his children to a foreigner, and of exciting an uprising among the people because of a thirst for command."[10]

In 1818, he appeared before the congress of Buenos Aires to appeal for a revision of the judgment which had been pronounced against him at the instance of the assembly of 1813. A committee of congress considered the appeal; it declared null and void the exile of the ex-president of the junta and reinstated him in the grade and position of general. Thus, after having suffered many years in exile, during his life Cornelio Saavedra was able to assist in his own historic justification.

---

[9] J. Canter, Jr., "La formación del primer triunvirato," *Boletín del instituto de investigaciones históricas* (Buenos Aires, 1922-23), I, 7-20.

[10] Zimmermann Saavedra, *op. cit.*, pp. 98-99.

CHAPTER XXX

THE TRIUMVIRATE

UPON THE dissolution of the great junta, there was formed the first triumvirate composed of the following members: Feliciano Chiclana, Manuel de Sarratea, and Juan J. Paso, with José J. Pérez, as secretary of government, Bernardino Rivadavia, as secretary of war, and Vicente López, as secretary of the treasury. The triumvirs were to be renewed every six months; the members selected to act in that capacity were to take office on September 23, 1811; on March 23, 1812, the term of office of one of the triumvirs was to expire, and Pueyrredón was designated as his successor.

The triumvirate constituted the executive power; while the members of the great junta, the majority of whom were deputies of the provinces, were transformed into the junta of observation, which composed the legislative power. That body framed a "provisional regulation" which aimed to reserve to itself the greater proportion of powers and functions. In order to check its advances, the triumvirate in its turn framed a "provisional statute" which limited the functions of the junta; but this body intended to promote an uprising, and the triumvirate then ordered the deputies to leave the capital and return to their respective provinces within twenty-four hours. The coup d'état by which the triumvirate dissolved the junta of observation was a grave measure. The deputies returned to their homes to stimulate the nascent rivalries that began to form between the provinces and Buenos Aires.

The first triumvirate inaugurated important institutional foundations, which in large part were inspired by Rivadavia who was the soul of that body as Moreno had been the soul of the junta. The following measures deserve to be mentioned: the commission of justice whose duty it was to proceed against vagrants and delinquents; the extension and promotion of the national library; the establishment of numerous schools which displayed the modest but fruitful labor of Rufino Sánchez, who was the schoolmaster of several generations. In addition, the triumvirate directed that a "History of the Revolution" should be written and intrusted this task to Father Julián Perdriel; it announced the emancipation of Negro slaves which was supplemented by a measure later enacted by the assembly of 1813 providing that children born of slave parents should be free; and finally, it enacted a decree establishing a junta to guard the liberty of the press. For the concession of this great privilege it was inspired by the initiative that had been taken in April of the same year by Dean Gregorio Funes.

Until this stage of the revolution, the end of 1811, Argentinians and Spaniards had struggled against each other in battle under the protection of the same banner. To Manuel Belgrano belongs the honor of having unfurled for the first time the Argentine flag which bore the same colors that had been adopted by the regiment of nobles during the English invasions, and which on the morning of May 25 the patriots used as a distinctive insignia. The triumvirate had directed that batteries should be constructed on the banks of the Uruguay and the Paraná, with the intention of closing those rivers to Spanish vessels. In charge of the battery on the Paraná was General Belgrano. Near the ravines of Rosario, that general christened two batteries with the symbolic names of "Liberty" and "Independence." On February 27, 1812, the colors of the Argentine flag were hauled to the top of those batteries.

Nevertheless, the triumvirate disapproved of the conduct of Belgrano in a note couched in the following terms: "The present situation, as the consequence of principles to which we are bound, demands of us that we should conduct ourselves with the greatest circumspection and moderation in matters of the first importance to the state. Because of that necessity, the demonstrations with which you have excited the soldiers under your command, namely, by unfurling a white and blue flag as indicative of the colors which should be our future device, are believed by this government to be an influence capable of destroying the bases upon which we justify not only our operations but also the protests which we have made so often and which constitute in our external communications the political maxims adopted by us. In view of this and of all the other circumstances which are involved in this grave affair, this government has resolved that if your Excellency subordinate your own notions to the principles which guide its actions, it will pass over as a burst of enthusiasm the affair of the unfurling of the white and blue banner, on condition that you quietly conceal that banner and replace it by the standard which is sent you—the one that has been used up to this time in this fortress which is the center of the State. In the future, you are not to anticipate the decisions of the government in a matter of such importance, or in any other matter, which when once executed does not allow freedom for its approbation, and which at least produces inevitable evils that are difficult to overcome successfully." [1]

It is seen that the government was endeavoring in this note to conceal its intention which was manifestly to consolidate the independence of the provinces of La Plata by discreet and prudent measures. Belgrano was not informed of the note which we have quoted; for he had been appointed commander of the Army of the North. Hence in the city of Jujuy, he unfurled the flag of Argentina for the second time. This was on May 25, 1812. In place of the standard of Ferdinand VII, Belgrano had brought the banner of his native land to the church at the solemn hour of the mass of *Te Deum*. The canon, Dr. Gorriti, saluted it upon that occasion in an eloquent discourse. In the afternoon Belgrano took the flag in his hand and in the center of the plaza surrounded by soldiers and by an immense crowd he said: "Soldiers, worthy sons of our native land, my comrades: two years have passed since there first resounded in these regions the echo of liberty which was repeated until it penetrated the most hidden caverns of the Andes; for it is not the work of men but of God Almighty which offers us the opportunity of entering upon the enjoyment of our rights. May 25 will be forever memorable in the annals of our history; and you will have an additional reason for remembering it, when upon that day you see for the first time in my hands the national flag which now distinguishes you from the other nations of the world, in spite of the efforts made by the enemies of the sacred cause which we defend to cast us into chains and to make them heavier than those which burden us. But we must maintain this glory in a manner worthy of the union, the constancy, and the exact fulfilment of our obligations toward God, toward our brothers, and toward ourselves, to the end that our country may have the pleasure of sheltering in its breast such worthy sons and that it may present them to posterity as models for emulation in order that it should be preserved free from enemies and full of happiness. . . ." [2]

[1] J. M. Eizaguirre, *La bandera argentina* (Buenos Aires, 1900).
[2] *Archivo capitular de Jujuy*, II, xxiv-xxv.

"We are not certain whether or not Belgrano took with him on his journey to the north the same flag which he had already unfurled. That is a secondary question and almost devoid of importance. The fundamental matter is to determine the priority of the oath taken in Jujuy on May 25, 1812, and the Argentine amplitude in that initial ceremony. In Rosario, the flag was unfurled as a military symbol; the name of that city is linked to this glory. There it was created, in front of the waters of the Paraná that appeared to consecrate that flag in each cloud when its vapor turned blue and floated over the turbid and troubled waves as over a multitude upon the march. . . . The glory of Jujuy consists in having sworn allegiance to the flag earlier than any other city, with all its social classes—clergy, militia, and common people— united in a bold and universal agreement, in the face of a hostile army, and in having sworn allegiance to it as a symbol of nationality." [3]

In a session of July 20, 1816, the congress of Tucumán consecrated the blue and white banner as the emblem of the new nation, whose declaration of independence was adopted and sworn to on July 9. Until that time no significance had been attached to the banner. In the year 1818, the deputy of Buenos Aires, Señor Chorroarín, proposed to congress "that the only national flag should consist of the two colors white and blue in the form and manner hitherto used, and that, as a device peculiar to the battle flag, a sun should be represented in the midst of those colors." This proposal was approved. The emblem of the sun was the symbol of the Incas.

In the middle of 1812, the plan for independence was threatened with serious perils. Among these was the secret conspiracy formed by the Spaniards to smother the revolution in its cradle. Another peril was the defeat administered to the patriot army at Huaqui, which opened the gates of the north to invasion by the Spaniards.

The conspiracy of Alzaga was not an isolated movement. It was under the patronage of Princess Carlota of Brazil, the sister of King Ferdinand VII, who desired to be crowned in the provinces of La Plata. The princess pledged herself to furnish aid to the head of the conspiracy, Martín Alzaga, in men, arms, and money. At

[3] *Ibid.*, p. xxxiii.

this juncture, Buenos Aires was almost without a garrison; many of the battalions had marched to join the Army of the North, and other battalions were in Montevideo. In the capital city, there remained scarcely three hundred militia under the orders of Ortiz de Ocampo. As a consequence, the government was able to oppose the conspirators, who cherished the project to redeem Buenos Aires, in order that they might deliver it anew to the government of Spain with only a very small force. On the other hand, the conspiracy was strong, not only because it had considerable support but also because it had on its side the Portuguese soldiers as well as the troops who defended the fort of Montevideo.

About the end of June, 1812, everything was ready for the blow. Martín Alzaga, who was the chief of the conspiracy, delayed the pronunciamiento some days in order to satisfy his own personal pride. He was desirous for the counter-revolution to begin on July 5, the anniversary of the defense of Buenos Aires against the English invasions, an exploit in which he had been the hero. This delay caused the uprising to fail and saved the cause of the revolution. In fact, on July 2, the triumvirate received a secret denunciation of the conspiracy. At once it proceeded to imprison the conspirators and appointed four judges who were to draw up accusations against them. The members of this commission were Monteagudo, Chiclana, Vieytes, and Irigoyen, with Pedro J. Agrelo as fiscal. Alzaga, who had succeeded in concealing himself, was not arrested until July 4. All the conspirators were condemned to death; on July 5, the leader of the conspiracy was shot. The energetic activity of the triumvirate was due to the initiative of Rivadavia.

After the rout at Huaqui (June 20, 1811), Juan Martín de Pueyrredón was intrusted by the government with the reorganization of the Army of the North which had retired to the province of Salta. Goyeneche, the commander of the royalist forces, who had entered triumphantly into the provinces of Upper Peru, decided to invade the province of Salta, placing Pio Tristán at the head of an army of 3,000 men. Pueyrredón proceeded to Tucumán, and at a place called Yatasto, he gave the command of the patriot army to General Belgrano who marched to Jujuy with 1,000 men. The situation was delicate in the extreme. The Spanish army intended to march to Tucumán, and then, in conjunction with the royalist forces at Montevideo, to attack Buenos Aires. Further, the patriot Army of the North was demoralized and without arms. If one adds to these circumstances, the fact that internal dissensions had already divided the patriots into contending bands, one will have an idea of the difficult situation that confronted the revolution. Justly alarmed, the government of Buenos Aires ordered General Belgrano to retreat and to withdraw to Córdoba with his army. Belgrano obeyed, and on crossing the Río Piedras the rearguard of the patriot army had an engagement with the vanguard of the royalist forces. This encounter, which did not have much military importance, had a high moral significance; for the patriot army, which triumphed at the Río Piedras, regained enthusiasm and calmed its spirit. Belgrano reached Tucumán where he received a new order from the government to the effect that he should not give battle but should carry out the order immediately to march to Córdoba. But the people of Tucumán urged Belgrano not to abandon them; they offered him their aid and placed a contingent of gaucho cavalry under his orders. These cavalry were not soldiers by profession, but they were brave men and they knew how to fight; in place of arms they were equipped with daggers fastened to poles. This was the terrible gaucho cavalry which played so brilliant a part in the battle of Tucumán. Encouraged by such patriotic support, Belgrano disobeyed the order of the government of Buenos Aires and waited for Tristán's army.[4]

Thus occurred the battle of Tucumán which has a double importance in our history: military and political. It has a military importance, because General Belgrano was able to thwart Tristán's plan of attack in an intelligent manner by valiantly assaulting the flank of the enemy's army when it tried to perform an enveloping movement; and further, because the main body of the Spanish army exceeded the number of the patriot army by one half. This battle has a political importance because the triumphal march being developed from the north by the enemy was checked. The government of Buenos Aires could now be tranquil; the Spanish army undertook to retreat to Salta, and the immediate peril of an invasion was over. Because of the disobedience of General Belgrano, the battle of Tucumán, which took place on September 24, 1812, was fought in violation of the orders of the government of Buenos

---

[4] See further, Mitre, *Historia de Belgrano,* II, 73-85.

Aires. We emphasize this fact because the action of Belgrano was the salvation of our country. Mitre declared:

"On March 9, 1812, there arrived at the port of Buenos Aires from London the English frigate *George Canning*. Under the auspices of that name the Old World was later to recognize South-American independence—an independence which one of the obscure passengers transported on that vessel was to insure by the force of his genius. This passenger was Colonel José de San Martín, 'the greatest creole of the New World,' as he has been designated in truth and with posthumous justice. It was twenty-six years since, while still a child, he had left his native land. He returned to it at that time in the full force of virility, possessed of an idea and animated by a passion. His intention was to offer his sword to the South-American revolution, which had been going on for two years, and which at this juncture was passing through an ordeal. Tempered in the struggles of life, trained in the military art, initiated into the mysteries of secret societies which were disseminating the new ideas of liberty, with his character formed and his reason matured in the austere school of experience and of labor, the new champion brought as a contribution to the American cause, the maxims of tactics and discipline applied to politics and to war; and in germ, a vast plan for a continental campaign which embraced one-half a world, and which was to furnish as a concrete result the triumph of its independence." [5]

San Martín had been born at Yapeyú, one of the pueblos of the mission district probably on February 25, 1778.[6] He was the son of Juan de San Martín and Jerónima Matorras. Under the Jesuit régime, Yapeyú had been a flourishing settlement; at the time of the birth of José de San Martín it had begun to decay. To quote Mitre again: "The scenes of his early youth faded from the memory of the creole child who was born in the shade of indigenous palms, but he could never forget that he had been born on American soil and that he owed his existence to it. Of undoubted aid in indelibly fixing these recollections were the impressions which he received during the receptive age of intuitive reason. He frequently heard

[5] B. Mitre, *Historia de San Martín* (3 vols. Buenos Aires, 1887-88), I, 113-14.

[6] Some historians do not accept this date, which is the one mentioned in San Martín's death certificate. The certificate of his baptism appears to have been destroyed in 1817. See *ibid.*, I, 122-24; and Leguizamón, "Las ruinas del solar de San Martín," *La Nación*, Buenos Aires, September 2, 1923.

his parents tell the history of the recent wars on the frontier against the Portuguese, who were destined later to reduce to ashes the very town where he had been born. His infant dreams were frequently disturbed by alarms caused by the savage Indians who devastated the neighborhood. The companions of his infancy were little Indians and mestizos by whose side he began to study the alphabet in the democratic school of the pueblo of Yapeyú. . . . Some years later Yapeyú was a heap of ruins; San Martín no longer had a birthplace; but, on the very day and hour when this took place, Spanish America was free and independent by virtue of the efforts of the greatest of her sons, and the palms still flourished under the shade of which he had been born and raised." [7]

He soon went to Spain with his parents. He enrolled as a student in the Seminary of Nobles in Madrid, which, as its name indicates, was an aristocratic school. In this institution he remained two years, and when he was scarcely twelve years of age (July, 1789), he enlisted as a cadet in the regiment of Murcia. San Martín began his military career by fighting against the Moors in Africa. He later joined the army of Roussillon which fought against the French Republic under the orders of General Ricardos, a commander of great tactical and strategic ability.

At twenty-one years of age he proceeded to Madrid, and thence to Seville, in order to join the army of General Castaños. San Martín was constantly trained under the orders of distinguished Spanish military commanders who were contending with the French armies that had invaded the Iberian Peninsula. He took part in the battles of Bailén and Albuera, and in the last-mentioned battle he was adorned with the aiguillettes of a commandant. After the revolution of May 25, 1810, began at Buenos Aires, it became the passion of San Martín to place himself at its service. When the opportunity arrived, before undertaking the voyage to Buenos Aires, he went to London, the city in which the precursor of South-American emancipation, Miranda, had founded a secret lodge.[8] At London, he embarked in the *George Canning* with Alvear and

---

[7] Mitre, *Historia de San Martín,* I, 123-24.

[8] No evidence has yet been found to show that San Martín ever met Miranda. Neither has it been demonstrated that Miranda was the founder of the Lautaro Lodge, which became an influential factor in the revolution in southern South America. See Robertson, *The Life of Miranda,* I, 199-200.— W.S.R.

Zapiola and voyaged toward his native land, which expected and needed his aid.

Carlos de Alvear—born in the eastern mission district on October 25, 1789—had also proceeded to Spain as a child, and entered upon a military career by fighting against the army of Napoleon. He distinguished himself in the battles of Talavera and Ciudad Real and earned the grade of ensign. Desirous to lend his aid to the revolution at Buenos Aires, he sailed for that purpose.

Seven days after his arrival at Buenos Aires, at the suggestion of San Martín himself, the government intrusted him with the organization of a regiment of mounted grenadiers. Mitre said: "The first squadron of mounted grenadiers was the rudimentary school in which a generation of heroes was educated. In this mould, San Martín cast a new type of soldier who was animated by a new spirit. After the manner of Cromwell in the Puritan revolution, he began with a regiment in order to create the pattern of an army and the decisive factor of a situation. Under an austere discipline which did not diminish individual energy but rather retempered it, San Martín fashioned soldier after soldier, official after official, and inspired them with a passion for duty; he inoculated them with that cold fanaticism of courage which holds itself invincible, and is the secret of victory. The sensible and original means which he used to promote this end, demonstrated that San Martín knew how to manage both swords and wills with equal tact and dexterity." [9]

He instituted an academy of military instruction and elevated the personal dignity of both soldiers and officers. In this stroke may be discovered the secret genius of this superior man. San Martín was endowed with marvelous patience. And as he displayed it in training the first detachment of mounted grenadiers, so he again used it in the city of Mendoza in the year 1816, when he also patiently prepared the emancipating army of South America, which covered itself with glory upon the equatorial line in the battle of Pichincha, after having triumphantly crossed half a continent.

[9] Mitre, *Historia de San Martín,* I, 157.

CHAPTER XXXI

THE CONSTITUENT ASSEMBLY OF 1813

THE FIRST triumvirate soon lost the confidence and support of the people. There had been formed in the city of Buenos Aires the Sociedad Literaria (Literary Society) to which belonged San Martín, Monteagudo, Alvear, and many other patriots. This society represented opposition to the triumvirate; among other objections the charge was made that it governed despotically, because it had not convoked congress. Further, it had completely neglected the Army of the North commanded by Belgrano, the defeat of which was believed to be imminent. The news of the victory of Tucumán, which reached Buenos Aires some days later, helped further to lower the prestige of the government that had ordered General Belgrano not to offer battle. The general discontent became more and more evident, and on October 8, 1812, the revolution began. On the forenoon of that day there appeared in the Plaza de la Victoria the regiment of mounted grenadiers under the command of its leaders, San Martín and Alvear, the regiment of nobles, and the artillery. In the name of the people they asked for the resignation of the triumvirs, the selection of others by the people, and the convocation of a general congress.[1]

In this manner, the second triumvirate, composed of Juan J. Paso, Nicolás Rodríguez Peña, and Juan Álvarez Jonte, was organized. A few days later, on October 24, the new government issued a decree inviting the people to participate in elections. These elections were based upon the principle of universal suffrage, that is to say, all citizens could vote: they were to name an elector for each district, and then the assembled electors were to designate the representatives or deputies. After a summons for the elections, the people of the United Provinces chose the representatives who were to compose the general constituent assembly.

In reality, this assembly was not "constituent," for it did not frame a constitution, but, nevertheless, it appointed a committee

[1] Mitre's observations on the movement of October 8, 1812, are found in *Historia de San Martín,* I, 172-73. See further, G. Rodríguez, *La patria vieja* (Buenos Aires, 1916), pp 94-113.

which was intrusted with the task of framing a project of constitution. The committee composed of Valentín Gómez, Manuel José García, Pedro José Agrelo, Pedro Somellera, Nicolás Herrera, Hipólito Vieytes, and Gervasio Posadas, executed its task. The project drawn up by it affirmed the existence of the provinces of the Río de la Plata "as a free and independent republic." At the same juncture, the second triumvirate had invited the Sociedad Patriótica (Patriotic Society) to coöperate in the government by framing a project for a constitution. This new project was presented in the year 1813, and by its terms a unitarian or centralistic government was to be established.[2] On the other hand, although the project of the official committee said nothing explicit about the form of government that should be adopted, yet it tended to strengthen the federal régime.[3] Neither of the two projects was considered in the deliberations of this assembly.

But if this assembly did not take the formal step of adopting a constitution, yet on the other hand, it passed numerous special laws which taken together form a solid organic work to the extent that the assembly of the year 1813 may without disadvantage be compared with other great assemblies: namely, the cabildo abierto of May 22, 1810, which decreed the downfall of the Spanish government, the congress of Tucumán which adopted a declaration of independence, and the constituent congress of Santa Fe which in 1853 sanctioned the constitution that now rules us.

The assembly of 1813 passed, as we have stated, numerous laws that tended to assure independence. It ordered that the coat-of-arms of Spain should no longer be used and that the effigies of the former monarchs should be effaced from the coins. It substituted for these the seal of the United Provinces which was composed of a sun and a liberty cap with its border a laurel wreath. Henceforth, in public documents the invocation of the sovereign, the King of Spain, was suppressed and replaced by a declaration of the supreme sovereignty of the people, whose wishes the deputies represented. The assembly also enacted a law concerning the freedom of children who were born slaves. According to the guarantee of

---

[2] D. Peña, *Historia de las leyes de la nación argentina* (2 vols. Buenos Aires, 1916) II, 701.

[3] C. L. Fregeiro, "Primera constitución argentina," *La Biblioteca* (Buenos Aires, 1896), I, 369-85.

this law, all persons born within the dominions of the United Provinces were to be free and equal and all slaves who entered the country were also to be free. The assembly also suppressed titles of nobility, the mita system, and the system of encomiendas. It prohibited anyone from taking the vows of a priest before he had reached the age of thirty years. Lastly, it declared the glorious date of May 25 to be a civic feast day, directed two of its members, Vicente López y Planes and Fray Cayetano Rodríguez, to compose the hymn of the Argentinians, and provided that the poetic compositions were to be heard in congress on May 11. On that day, López y Planes read before the members of the assembly the hymn that henceforth was sacred to all Argentinians.

The deputies were recognized as "deputies of the nation in general," thus establishing the inviolability of their mandates. "That declaration implied the consecration of national Argentine unity, as an indestructible entity."[4] If this assembly did not make an explicit declaration of independence by implication it assured such a declaration by its fruitful organic and legislative activity.[5]

In the middle of the year 1813, a political event happened which was of great importance for the provinces of the Río de la Plata; namely, the rejection by the assembly of the delegates from the Banda Oriental. In order to proceed to the recognition of the assembly and to swear obedience to it, Artigas summoned a local congress. The province of the Banda Oriental selected five deputies to the assembly of Buenos Aires, because there existed five cabildos within its limits. These deputies came to Buenos Aires supplied with instructions which made the following imperative demands: (1) a declaration of absolute independence from Spain; (2) a constitution for the country providing for a system of confederated states; (3) each province was to have its own government, and the Banda Oriental would accordingly preserve its sovereignty; (4) the national government should be republican in form and should assure autonomy to the confederated states.[6] However, the assembly of 1813 committed the impolitic act of refusing to admit

---

[4] J. A. González Calderón, *Derecho constitucional argentino* (3 vols. Buenos Aires, 1917-23), I, 61.

[5] See the autobiography of Agrelo in Levene, *Lecturas históricas argentinas,* II, 171-75.

[6] J. Artigas, *Artigas: estudio histórico* (edited by C. L. Fregeiro, Montevideo, 1886), pp. 167-69.—W.S.R.

the delegation from the Banda Oriental. In order to justify so unusual a measure, it alleged that the deputies had not been selected according to the method stipulated by the summons.

After the triumph of Las Piedras, the patriot armies of Artigas and Rondeau advanced upon Montevideo, thus beginning the first siege of that city. Viceroy Elío called the Portuguese to his aid. In Buenos Aires, news was received of the defeat of the Army of the North at Huaqui, and because of this, fearing a fresh disaster, an armistice was signed by virtue of which the Portuguese army and the army of the Banda Oriental under Artigas agreed to abandon the siege of Montevideo, which remained in the hands of the Spaniards. Artigas did not abandon his native land, but withdrew with his soldiers to the north of the Río Negro.

About the end of 1812, the government of Buenos Aires ordered Manuel Sarratea to march against Montevideo which was governed by General Gaspar Vigodet, who had been appointed in place of Viceroy Elío. The command of the vanguard was confided to Rondeau who advanced to El Cerrito, a hill northeast of the capital, and began the second siege of Montevideo, which lasted almost two years. On December 31, 1812, the battle of El Cerrito took place between the besieging forces of Rondeau and the Spanish army commanded by Vigodet. The patriots won a victory.

Montevideo was so closely invested by the army of Rondeau that the Spaniards had to get supplies by sea. A small royalist squadron frequently sailed from Montevideo in the direction of the Paraná River. Its crews pillaged the river banks and carried off cattle. An expedition composed of eleven ships which had left Montevideo for this purpose was pursued on land in a parallel course by the colonel of mounted grenadiers, José de San Martín, with one hundred and twenty-five men of his regiment. The forces of San Martín marched to a point near the post of San Lorenzo which was situated twenty-six kilometers north of Rosario. At that point was located the monastery of San Lorenzo in which San Martín and his grenadiers concealed themselves in such a manner that they could not be perceived by the Spanish squadron. On February 3, 1813, when the Spaniards disembarked, the grenadiers with sword in hand, attacked them and obliged them to flee in terror. From its banks some of the invading party threw themselves into the river and were drowned. In the pursuit the horse of

San Martín fell and pinned one of his legs to the earth. An enemy tried to stab him with a bayonet but at that very moment the patriot, Sergeant Juan Bautista Cabral, interposed; he saved San Martín, and with him, as has been aptly said, the liberty of half a continent.

At the very time when the mounted grenadiers won the triumph of San Lorenzo, General Belgrano, increasing his army with fresh recruits, marched across the province of Tucumán in the direction of Salta where General Tristán had halted his march and reorganized his army with the aid of forces sent to him by General José Manuel Goyeneche. The army of Belgrano spent a month in traversing the province of Tucumán, and upon crossing the Pasaje River it performed the ceremony of swearing obedience to the general constituent assembly which had just met in Buenos Aires.

On February 20, 1813, was fought the battle of Salta, which lasted three hours. The right wing of the patriot army was commanded by Díaz Vélez and the left wing by Martín Rodríguez. After a bloody struggle, convinced of the futility of his efforts, Tristán decided to ask for terms of surrender at the very juncture when Belgrano was disposed to summon him to capitulate. Tristán gave up all his arms and other military supplies, and after he and other prisoners belonging to the vanquished army took an oath that they would never again take up arms against the patriots, Belgrano granted them their liberty. The prisoners numbered 3,000 men; but the generosity of Belgrano annulled the triumph of Salta; for the Spaniards returned to fight against the army of Belgrano which soon suffered the defeats of Vilcapugio and Ayohuma.

In recognition of the triumph of Salta, the assembly decided to reward Belgrano with 40,000 pesos. The self-denying patriot again revealed his noble and disinterested soul by refusing the gift in a letter—honorable for the moral history of Argentina—in which he said: "I believe it conformable to my honor and to my ardent desire for the prosperity of my country, to decline the specified 40,000 pesos, and to assign them for the establishment of four elementary public schools in which there shall be taught reading, writing, arithmetic, Christian doctrine, and the rudiments of the rights and obligations of man in society."

Victorious at Salta, in order to assure the success of the patriots in the provinces of Upper Peru, General Belgrano advanced at the head of 5,000 men to Potosí. General Pezuela had placed himself at the head of the royalist army which numbered no less than 4,500 men. On October 1, 1813, he gave battle on the fields of Vilcapugio, a battle which is mentioned in Argentine military annals as one of the most sanguinary battles of the war for independence. In the words of the historian Pelliza: "The waters of the rivulet that crossed the field of battle were dyed red." The patriot army was completely routed, and began to retreat in scattered detachments. Before it had sufficient time to reorganize, on November 26, the armies clashed again on the pampa of Ayohuma, where Belgrano suffered a fresh calamity.[7] Henceforth, the Peruvian frontier was defended by the famous gauchos of Salta led by the caudillo Martín Güemes.

---

[7] J. Beverina, *El general José María Paz, sus campañas y su doctrina de guerra* (Buenos Aires, 1925), p. 62.

CHAPTER XXXII

THE DIRECTORY

DURING THE captivity of Ferdinand VII, the Spanish people had promulgated the liberal constitution of 1812. Upon the return of the king to his throne in 1814, his first act was to disavow the constitution. With respect to the American colonies, he cherished the thought of sending an expedition of 10,000 men under the command of General Morillo to the Río de la Plata. This expedition came to America, but it was directed against Venezuela.

In such a delicate situation, the government of Buenos Aires opened diplomatic negotiations with England and Spain in order to secure the recognition of the independence of the United Provinces and the founding of a constitutional monarchy. Director Posadas intrusted this mission to Belgrano and Rivadavia. In the secret instructions furnished to the commissioners, they were advised that the prime object was "to assure the independence of America," and that the agreement would be submitted to "the examination of all the provinces in an assembly of their representatives." The commissioners were to confer with Lord Strangford in Rio de Janeiro in order to secure the support of the English government. About the end of December, Belgrano and Rivadavia left Buenos Aires bound for Rio de Janeiro, where they were joined by Manuel J. García who had just been appointed confidential envoy to the court of Brazil. García had been intrusted by Director Alvear, the successor of Posadas, with the special task of securing the protection of the English government.[1]

Belgrano and Rivadavia continued their voyage to Europe to seek the support of the English government in order to negotiate

---

[1] Belgrano and Rivadavia arrived at Rio de Janeiro on January 12, 1815. In a confidential letter to Strangford on March 3 following, García asked that England would assist the provisional government at Buenos Aires: "it has sent me to lay before you the state of its affairs, and to request you to inform me verbally whether it may hope for such timely assistance as is necessary to preserve the Country from the Evils that threaten it, or whether the Determination of His Britannic Majesty being yet unknown, it must still continue to depend for some time longer on its own Means." Translation, inclosure in Strangford to Castlereagh, March 14, 1815, Public Record Office, Foreign Office, Portugal, 181.—W. S. R.

with the court of Spain. Upon their arrival in Europe, they decided
that Rivadavia should proceed to Madrid, while Belgrano should
remain in England conjointly with Sarratea who had proceeded to
Europe but without a diplomatic mission. Nevertheless, using Count
Cabarrús as an intermediary, Sarratea had undertaken to negotiate with Charles IV, who was in Rome, for the coronation in
Buenos Aires of the infante, Francisco de Paula. Charles IV rejected the proposal, and stated "that his conscience directed him to
do nothing which was not favorable to the king of Spain." In the
face of this reply, Cabarrús and Sarratea undertook to plan the
kidnapping of the prince, in order to transport him secretly to
Buenos Aires and there to proclaim him king of La Plata. But
Belgrano and Rivadavia very prudently opposed this design. Belgrano decided to return to Buenos Aires, leaving Rivadavia to continue the diplomatic negotiations. The Spanish minister Cevallos
gave Rivadavia an interview, but as they could reach no agreement
about an acknowledgment of the independence of the United Provinces, the agent was obliged immediately to leave the soil of Spain.[2]

In regard to the mission of García, which had been arranged
by Director Alvear, we have already stated that it had as its object
the securing of a protectorate by the English government. In the
letter that García was intrusted with for the English secretary
of foreign affairs, Alvear declared that the provinces of the Río
de la Plata were incapable "of governing themselves, and that they
needed a foreign hand to direct them into the realm of order, lest
they should precipitate themselves into the horrors of anarchy.
These provinces desire to belong to Great Britain, to receive its
laws, to obey its government, and to live under its powerful influence. Without any conditions whatever they resign themselves
to the generosity and good faith of the English people; and I
am resolved to support so just a request, in order to free them from
the evils with which they are afflicted. It is necessary to take advantage of the occasion; let soldiers be sent to restrain wayward
inclinations, with a commander fully authorized to give the country
the form of government that pleases the king and the nation.
With this in view, I expect that your Excellency will give me his
advice with the secrecy and promptness that will opportunely

---

[2] C. Correa Luna, *Rivadavia y la simulación monárquica de 1815* (Buenos
Aires, 1929), chaps. I-XII.

prepare the way for the execution of this project." García also carried a letter for Lord Strangford which mentioned the diplomatic mission that Director Posadas had earlier intrusted to Belgrano and Rivadavia. In this note, Alvear said: "All the prudent policy and the ascendancy of the existing government has been necessary to sooth the irritation provoked in the mass of the people by the dispatch of agents to the Spanish king. The simple idea of a reconciliation with the Spaniards excites them to fanaticism; all the people avow in public and in secret that they would die rather than submit to the Spaniards. Under these circumstances, only the generous English nation can furnish an efficacious remedy for such evils by opening its arms to these provinces, which will obey its government and accept its laws with pleasure; for they know that this is the only means to prevent the destruction of the country. . . . "[3]

We have described the development of the diplomatic negotiations of Belgrano, Rivadavia, and García in order to emphasize their great importance. The patriot governments, the directive nucleus, intended to organize the provinces of the Río de la Plata in the monarchical form. Intrigues for the establishment of a constitutional monarchy had been initiated in the year 1808 with Princess Carlota of Brazil, sister of King Ferdinand VII, by a proposal to transfer to her the government of these provinces. This proposal was repeated, as we have just seen, in 1814. In 1816, in the congress of Tucumán, monarchical plans reappeared with the support of San Martín and Belgrano. Nevertheless, in this early stage of the revolution there appeared an enthusiastic and representative democrat, Mariano Moreno.

To give an exact account of these events one must distinguish between the diplomatic labors of the directive nucleus (Posadas, Alvear, Belgrano, Rivadavia, García, San Martín, and Pueyrredón), and the historic reality, the predominant, collective sentiment which was essentially democratic. The democratic instinct of Argentine society has its roots in the colonial past; it had been expressed in constant revolutionary movements in favor of liberty,

---

[3] C. A. Villanueva, *Bolívar y General San Martín* ("La Monarquía en America," vol. I: 4 vols. Paris, 1911-14), p. 28. See further, the new evidence in G. F. Rodríguez, *Contribución histórica y documental* (3 vols. Buenos Aires, 1921-22), I, 87 ff.

had been consolidated by the fusion of the Spaniards with the indigenous race, had been influenced by the geographic situation that established a common equalizing gradation which increased with the progress of time and events. The patriot governments had recourse to the expedient of founding a monarchy in La Plata, as a means of saving the revolution which was threatened by numerous internal and external perils; external perils, because the war for emancipation had not yet terminated, and, restored to his throne, the Spanish king threatened to send a formidable expedition to the Spanish-American colonies; internal perils, because the patriot governments had not been able to maintain themselves in power, and they had fallen one after another as the result of violent and successive crises. In this distressing situation, the officials of the government aspired to save the revolution by the establishment of a monarchy, but they forgot that the revolution had been proclaimd to be against the king, and that the only doctrine by which it could be saved was democracy.

The constituent assembly approved a project for the modification of the executive power in order to vest it in a single person with the title of supreme director of the United Provinces.[4] The director was to exercise his functions for two years, and was to consult with a council of state composed of nine members. As supreme director the assembly appointed Gervasio A. Posadas who assumed the office on January 31, 1814. As minister of government he appointed Nicolás Herrera; as minister of war, Colonel Francisco J. Diana; and as minister of the treasury, Juan Larrea.

The chief aim of Director Posadas was to end the siege of Montevideo, which for two years had been beleaguered by the patriot army. The Spaniards of Montevideo maintained egress to the sea. Posadas realized that it was necessary to equip a squadron in order to blockade the port, and then to conquer the city. Minister Larrea took charge of preparing the squadron. He secured some merchant vessels which he equipped for war by the financial aid of a citizen of North America named William White, who had become known in Buenos Aires in the days of the English invasions.

---

[4] A detailed study of the directories of Posadas and Alvear is found in G. F. Rodríguez, *Historia de Alvear con la acción de Artigas en el período evolutivo de la revolución argentina de 1812 á 1816* (2 vols. Buenos Aires, 1913), pp. 181 ff.

The nascent armada was placed under the command of the Irish seaman, William Brown.

Artigas, the chief of the soldiers of the Banda Oriental, abandoned the army besieging Montevideo because the assembly of Buenos Aires had refused to seat the deputies of that region. Irritated by this event, Director Posadas issued a decree by which he declared that José Artigas was infamous, shorn of his offices, beyond the pale of the law, and an enemy of the country. The third article of the decree contained the following announcement: "Whoever delivers up the person of José Artigas, dead or alive, will be rewarded by six thousand pesos." The only effect of such an extreme measure was to open a schism between the government of Buenos Aires and Artigas, who, upon learning of the decree of Director Posadas, broke camp and excited to rebellion the inhabitants of Entre Ríos, Corrientes, and the Banda Oriental.

Meantime, the Argentine squadron undertook to blockade the port of Montevideo. Brown proceeded to the island of Martín García where the Spanish squadron under Romarate was stationed. Because of the narrowness of the channel the patriot ship *Hercules* was stranded, and, being attacked by the Spanish squadron, suffered many losses. In the afternoon, the level of the river rose, and Brown was able to maneuver easily. He repaired the injuries, and then attacked the enemy with so much success that Romarate was forced to take refuge in the Uruguay River. A victor at Martín García, Brown then went to Montevideo. He first feigned a retreat, and then he entered into a stubborn combat in which the patriot ships completely vanquished the Spanish squadron. While the naval blockade of Montevideo was being undertaken, the director appointed Alvear commander in chief of the besieging army at the very juncture when the Spanish squadron was routed and the surrender of Montevideo became necessary. A capitulation was signed which provided that the fort should be delivered to the patriots. The triumph of the army and of the patriot armada put an end to Spanish domination on the adjacent banks of La Plata River.

Alvear appeared as the glorious victor of Montevideo. The director appointed him commander of the Army of the North, which was under the orders of Rondeau, but the commanders and officers of this army declared themselves against Alvear. When he learned of the uprising at the port of Santa Cruz in the province

of Córdoba, Alvear returned to Buenos Aires. The government of
Posadas was vacillating because of the recent insurrection in the
army of Rondeau, and the failure of the diplomatic mission of Belgrano and Rivadavia. Because of such conditions, Posadas presented his resignation to the assembly, which accepted it and appointed Alvear to take his place.

The principal measures of Alvear's directorship were to promote
a peaceful adjustment with Artigas, and, as we have noticed, to
send Manuel J. García to negotiate with Lord Strangford in Rio
de Janeiro for a protectorate by the English government. But
Alvear could not depend upon the support of public opinion. His
downfall was consequently imminent.

The chieftain Artigas, with the title "chief of the people of
the east and protector of the free people," had overrun the provinces of Entre Ríos and Corrientes. He crossed the Paraná River,
occupied Santa Fe, and threatened to attack the capital. Director
Alvear left the city at the head of part of the army, but upon
arriving at Fontezuelas, a district in the province of Buenos Aires,
his troops mutinied under the lead of Colonel Ignacio Álvarez
Thomas. On April 15, 1815, an uprising took place in the capital
city, and the civic corporations became disaffected. The cabildo
announced the downfall of Director Alvear and the dissolution of
the assembly. This revolution manifestly had a national character.[5]
The uprising at Fontezuelas was supported by the armies of
Artigas on the coast, by the army of Rondeau in the north, and
by that of San Martín at Mendoza.

Upon the fall of the directory, the national government was interrupted for the first time. In 1815, having been deprived of its
moral authority, the general constituent assembly of 1813 was also
dissolved. The cabildo of Buenos Aires assumed the command and
created the junta of observation which was intrusted by the people
with the special task of convoking a national congress. On May
5, 1815, that junta promulgated the "provisional statute" which
tentatively regulated the exercise and the functions of the organs
of government. It arranged that the director should depend absolutely upon the superior authority of the junta, in this manner

---

[5] In the introduction to vol. VIII of *Documentos para la historia argentina*,
pp. xxv-xxvi, Correa Luna takes the view that the terms "Unitarian" and
"Federalist" were not current in La Plata in 1815.

making imminent a clash between the two authorities. Rondeau was appointed supreme director; as he was absent, Colonel Álvarez Thomas, the leader of the insurrection of Fontezuelas, was named to take his place temporarily.

Provisional Director Álvarez Thomas was not the statesman to cope with a difficult situation. Making himself an instrument of partisan passions, he organized two commissions, one civil and the other military, which were to institute suits against those members of the assembly who had accompanied Alvear.

The government of Álvarez Thomas lasted only a short time. His downfall was the result of a military uprising. In order to check the advance of the army of Artigas, the director had sent General Eustaquio Díaz Vélez to Santa Fe with the soldiers the latter had in San Nicolás and Colonel Francisco Pico with the soldiers of the frontier. This army was to place itself under the orders of General Belgrano who had just returned from Europe. But Díaz Vélez refused to transfer the command of the army and signed the pact of Santo Tomé, in accordance with which Belgrano agreed to withdraw to Buenos Aires, the army was to remain in charge of Díaz Vélez, and Supreme Director Álvarez Thomas was to be deposed. Balcarce, who was selected to replace Álvarez Thomas, counted upon the support of those chiefs who had refused to obey Belgrano at Santo Tomé.

The Army of the North was under the orders of Rondeau. We have already spoken of the uprising of this army, upon the occasion when Director Posadas appointed Alvear to the position of commander. Confirmed in his command by the good will of his officers and soldiers, Rondeau resolved to open a campaign against the army of General Pezuela who in April, 1815, had suffered the check of Puesto del Marqués. The Argentine commander advanced to Potosí, while the army of Pezuela stationed itself at Torazora, with its vanguard at Venta y Media. At the latter place, in the belief that the royalist army was composed of only a few men, the patriots offered battle under the direction of General Rodríguez, but they were defeated. This disaster induced Rondeau to retire to Cochabamba, but on November 23, Pezuela attacked Rondeau at Sipe-Sipe where he completely routed the patriots.

The battle of Sipe-Sipe created a perilous situation for the patriot government. Upper Peru returned to the hands of the

Spaniards, who, because of this victory, threatened to invade Argentine territory from the north. The news of the rout of the patriot army at Sipe-Sipe was celebrated in Spain as the definitive victory over the revolutionary armies of Spanish America; for of all the Spanish continental dominions there remained unconquered only the provinces of La Plata. However, the condition that confronted the patriots was not quite so grave. In the northern part of those provinces, Güemes and his famous gauchos kept up the defense on the frontiers, while, in the west, San Martín was preparing the liberating army of the Andes.

Martín Güemes was the spontaneous personification of the popular chieftain. Appointed commandant-general of militia at the opening of the third campaign in Upper Peru, he had participated in it with two squadrons, had been present at the engagement of Puesto de Marqués, but returned to Salta because his soldiers who were cavalry had no duties to perform in the war. On being appointed governor of the province of Salta, he transformed the organization of the militia. He explained to the entire population in an assembly that he had adopted the squad as the type of military organization. In this scheme, each twenty or thirty inhabitants constituted a squad under the charge of an official who directed the military exercises. These exercises were sham battles: tournaments of cavalrymen armed with lances, muskets, or carabines, "which made menaces of disordered charges like Cossacks, discharged volleys into the air like Arabs, or jumped to the ground, and now forming groups of infantry, now dispersing as sharpshooters, now mounting quickly on horseback, now concentrating rapidly with savage alacrity, like the Indians of the pampas. . . . Primitive tactics, suited to the character of those simple men, they moved the imagination of the gauchos, promoted their warlike instincts, stimulated individual spontaneity, and created a new spirit which they identified with the defense of their territory and with the supreme authority of their chieftain. . . . Their system of government was as elementary as their tactics. It was composed of an authority personal and irresponsible, which could dispose of purposes, lives, and properties, without any check or corrective upon the man who was absolute magistrate, the one who by natural selection was the general, the prophet, and the judge, without any other civil institutions than the cabildos, to which he left a certain liberty of action in administrative and judicial affairs." [6]

Pezuela, who had been appointed viceroy of Peru in place of Abascal, had delegated the supreme command of the army to José de la Serna, to whom he had given orders to take advantage of the disorganization of the patriot army and to invade its territory. Although the army of La Serna was formed of capable and disciplined soldiers, the opposition that Güemes and his gauchos were able to offer him was invincible. In this wise, conjured by the peril of the north, San Martín was impelled to consecrate all his powers to the organization of the Army of the Andes in order that he might execute the far-reaching plan of marching into Chile, of proceeding thence to Peru, and of smothering the powerful Spanish resistance at its base of operations.

As we have already explained, the federal revolution of April 15, 1815, which had overthrown Director Alvear and dissolved the assembly of 1813, had interrupted the national government, for by an article of the provisional statute of 1815 the provinces were vested with the power to name their governors and to rule themselves by their own institutions. The situation accordingly imposed the need of convoking immediately a general congress, and in order not to arouse emulation and jealousy among the provinces, this congress ought to meet in a central province. While this plan was being carried out by the men of Buenos Aires, the Uruguayan chieftain Artigas, convoked a congress at Paysandú which was attended by delegates from the Argentine provinces of Entre Ríos, Corrientes, Santa Fe, and Córdoba. The province of Cuyo, of which San Martín was intendant, sent its representatives to the congress of Tucumán. The same procedure was followed by émigrés from Upper Peru whose territory was occupied by the Spanish army. A little later Córdoba sent its deputies to this congress— an example that was immediately followed by the province of Salta.

At the beginning of 1816, the provincial deputies began to arrive at Tucumán. When two-thirds of them had appeared, they fixed upon March 24 as the date for the formal opening of congress. According to Mitre: "The men whom the people had selected as the delegates of their sovereignty were generally among the most worthy and respectable inhabitants of their respective prov-

---

[6] Mitre, *Historia de Belgrano*, II, 317.

inces, and the most distinguished among them for their adhesion to the American cause. . . . In the front rank of the priests in attendance there figured the following members: Antonio Sáenz, who joined to the clearest understanding a cleverness and a will strong enough to aid in the deliberations of an assembly; Fray Justo de Santa María de Oro, an angelic soul in whom the endowments of heart and head were harmoniously balanced; Fray Cayetano Rodríguez, whom we already know, and who was destined to be the chronicler of the congress; and lastly Fray Pedro Ignacio Castro Barros, whom we have seen appear for the first time in the assembly of 1813, who still carried on with the same fanaticism his noble political and religious propaganda. In the front rank of the lawyers were found Doctors Juan José Paso and José Mariano Serrano, who at the same time were the two most notable writers and orators of this assemblage. After them came Pedro Medrano, who was an imitation (at times somewhat grotesque) of his two colleagues. Then there were other members whose names were preserved because they were inscribed on the declaration of independence. Among those who could display no university degree, but who were destined to exercise a decisive influence in congress, were the following delegates: Francisco Laprida, a fine character who was an honor to that nascent democracy. . . . Tomás Godoy Cruz, a man with common sense, philanthropic, intelligent, and persevering, who was a good judge of men and of the practical needs of his time; Eduardo Pérez Bulnes, a notable citizen of Córdoba, who was endowed with the gift of felicitous expression and discerning intelligence; José Ignacio Gorriti, with a virile character and elevated common sense that commanded the confidence of his fellow citizens; and, lastly, Tomás Manuel de Anchorena, the former secretary of Belgrano."[7]

At the juncture when this congress assembled the general situation of the country was precarious. The congress of Tucumán represented a country in a condition of anarchy; and it had to solve difficult governmental problems. On May 3, 1816, it appointed Juan Martín de Pueyrredón as supreme director. This appointment was suitable and it was well received by the public opinion of the country. As we shall see in due time, the work of this government was distinctive; for it was able to give stability to public authority

---

[7] *Ibid.*, II, 274-76. See further, the introduction by Correa Luna to *Documentos para la historia argentina*, VIII, 43-45.

and to restrain national dissolution and political anarchy. In fact, Pueyrredón remained at the head of the government for three years. During the period from 1810 until 1816 he was the only executive who remained in the exercise of his functions for the term set by law.

Two eminent leaders of the revolution, San Martín and Belgrano, exercised a decisive influence upon the members of this congress. In order to elevate the public spirit and to incite the revolutionary armies, it was the intention of all the members of congress to make a solemn declaration of the independence of the United Provinces of the Río de la Plata. With this object General San Martín took action in order that congress should hasten to frame the declaration. He wrote thus to Tomás Godoy Cruz, the delegate for the province of Cuyo: "How long should we wait before declaring our independence? Does it not indeed appear ridiculous to coin money, to have a flag and a national cockade, and, lastly, to make war on the sovereign, on whom it is believed that we are in a state of dependence, and still to remain a ward of the enemy? What more have we to decide? By a declaration of independence the State will make a gain of fifty per cent; and if you run risks, remember that it is only by men of courage that enterprises have been accomplished." Godoy Cruz replied to San Martín explaining that the formulation of a declaration of independence was not so simple a matter. In turn, San Martín replied thus: "I notice you tell me that to declare independence is not so easy to do as it seems to be; and I reply that it is a thousand times easier to decide upon independence than to decide many other matters that seem much simpler."

General Belgrano arrived at Tucumán in the beginning of July, and exercised an influence upon the members of congress both in favor of a declaration of independence and in favor of the adoption of a monarchical form of government. The congress of Tucumán also occupied itself with the difficult task of national organization and considered what would be the most suitable form of government for the United Provinces. The majority of its members were monarchists, and such ideas were also entertained by San Martín. Congress decided to listen to Belgrano in secret session, and for this purpose it assembled on July 6. Belgrano sketched the condition of dissolution and anarchy that prevailed in the country as well as the situation of Europe. He pointed out that in the old continent a complete change of ideas had taken place in what concerned the form of government: that, just as the general spirit of the nations in previous years was in favor of republicanism, at that time the spirit was in favor of monarchy. The discussions concerning the form of government were, however, postponed in order to give way to the most important subject that glorified this congress—the declaration of independence.

Among other important centers of Spanish America, the revolution had broken out in 1810 in Caracas, Buenos Aires, Santiago de Chile, and the city of Mexico. In 1816, the cause of Spanish-American emancipation seemed lost; in 1814, the king of Spain, Ferdinand VII, had been restored to his throne, the revolution had been gradually subdued in all the colonies, except La Plata. Mexico, Venezuela, and Chile had been conquered, and after the disaster of Sipe-Sipe the United Provinces of La Plata also seemed to be subjugated.[8]

In 1816, the government of the United Provinces was surrounded by perils. To the east the caudillo Artigas had revolutionized the Banda Oriental and the provinces of the Argentine littoral. To the north, Upper Peru had been definitively lost after the rout at Sipe-Sipe, and the Spanish army threatened an invasion from that point. To the west, the patriots beyond the Andes had been vanquished at Rancagua, and Chile had been reconquered by the Spaniards whence they also threatened invasion of Argentine territory. Aside from all these grave external perils, a grave internal evil was undermining the political organism: this was anarchy, which weakened but did not break the bonds of union between the provinces.

The members of congress realized that in order to save the revolutionary cause at this moment, in which internal and external perils seemed to throttle it, an explicit and solemn declaration of independence was needed to temper the public spirit. On July 9, a numerous crowd of people attended the session of congress. The secretary submitted the following proposition to the delegates: "Did they wish that the provinces of the union should form a nation

---

[8] The fact that La Plata was not reconquered by the Spaniards has been attributed by one Argentine historian to the absence of aboriginal and aristocratic elements in the population. See Groussac, *Santiago de Liniers*, pp. 160-61.

free and independent of the kings of Spain?" They all rose to their feet and replied by acclamation that they so wished. Immediately afterward the act was framed in which congress solemnly declared that "invoking the God who presides over the universe, in the name and by the authority of the people whom we represent . . . it is the unanimous desire of the United Provinces of South America to sever the oppressive bonds which connected them with the kings of Spain, to recover the rights of which they were deprived, and to assume the exalted position of a nation free and independent of King Ferdinand VII, of his successors, and of the mother country, and to remain in consequence, by fact and right with full and ample power to give themselves the political organization which justice demands and which is required by the present concatenation of circumstances. Each one and all of the provinces thus make public, declare, and ratify this act and on our part we pledge ourselves to the fulfilment and maintenance of their wish under the security and guarantee of our lives, our property, and our honor." [9]

Several days later, in the session of July 21, a delegate named Medrano proposed that the following clause should be added to that part of the declaration which asserted the proposition of independence of King Ferdinand VII, of his successors, and of the mother country, "and of any other foreign domination, even with life, honor, and fortune," in order to discredit the rumors which had been circulated to the effect that negotiations had been initiated for the coronation of a prince of the house of Braganza. The congress agreed to Medrano's proposition. May 25, 1810, opened the period of independence which closed with the declaration of the congress of Tucumán.

On the first-mentioned date, the revolution, which was ostensibly communal in form, was made popular in origin and national in spirit. In 1816, the revolution was in effect national; for first the armies, and then a popular and spontaneous propaganda had extended it throughout the entire territory of the United Provinces. These two dates supplemented each other. The revolution of 1810 had for its object emancipation, even though it concealed its pur-

---

[9] *El redactor del congreso nacional* (edited by D. L. Molinari, Buenos Aires, 1916), núm. 6, p. 4.—W.S.R.

pose by invoking the name of the captive king, "the mask of Ferdinand." After that date the revolution marched secretly but resolutely toward independence.

Upon framing the declaration of independence, the congress of Tucumán simply sanctioned a state of affairs that had existed since 1810 and that subsequent events confirmed.

CHAPTER XXXIII

THE CAMPAIGN OF THE ANDES

THE REVOLUTION of May 25, 1810, communal in its origins, was, as we have said, continental in its objects. In fact, six years after it had been started and announced, the revolution had extended throughout the territory of the former viceroyalty, and in 1817 the genius and the activity of San Martín, who carried out his plan of proceeding to Chile and thence to Peru, made the movement continental, that is to say, Americanized the revolution. In the year 1810, the revolution had begun in Spanish America, from Mexico to Buenos Aires. This was an historic movement, which has been rightly designated as the most important event of the first half of the nineteenth century.

But if the revolution occurred simultaneously in various centers, it did not have the same significance and progress in all of them. Various influences caused those movements to have local tendencies and objects. Only the revolutions which began at almost the same time in Buenos Aires and Caracas acquired continental proportions. The Argentine revolution crossed the Andes and insured the freedom of Chile and Peru, and upon the equatorial line an army containing Argentine soldiers fought the battle of Pichincha, thus insuring the freedom of Ecuador. The Venezuelan revolution had an analogous evolution: it crossed the Andes, dislodged the royalists from Colombia, and met the Argentine revolutionary movement in Ecuador. This conjunction of two continental movements is personified in the historic interview of its two glorious representatives, San Martín and Bolívar. Henceforward, the destiny of Spanish America was assured. San Martín withdrew from the scene, and prepared the way for the advance of the victorious army of Bolívar, to whom fate allotted the task of sealing at Ayacucho in 1824, through his able lieutenant, General Sucre, the independence of the Spanish-American colonies.

After the defeat of Ayohuma, the government of Buenos Aires appointed General San Martín military commander of the north, and he led the remainder of the army to the citadel of Tucumán. It was at this historic opportunity that San Martín began to

conceive a vast plan of campaign. After Tucumán had been fortified, his task had been limited to an effort to prevent the victorious
Spanish army from invading Argentine territory. He had time to
meditate concerning the vacillating fortunes of the patriot armies
that had marched into Upper Peru: the first army under the command of Balcarce had been victorious at Suipacha and defeated
at Huaqui; and the second army had been successful at Tucumán
and Salta, but about the end of 1813 had suffered the disasters of
Vilcapugio and Ayohuma. San Martín gathered data from the
military officers who had accompanied Belgrano and who realized
the uselessness of force and the military error that would be committed, if he insisted upon the same plan of campaign. He realized
that the strong and powerful resistance to South-American independence was in Peru and that the triumphs which had been always
fleeting in the Platean field of battle signified nothing; for the bulk
of the Spanish army was on the Pacific coast. In fine, he affirmed
that it was necessary to proceed directly to the very center of Spanish resistance by marching to Chile, and thence proceeding at once
by sea to Peru. Dominated by this great thought, with the patriotic
desire of realizing it, he resigned the command of the Army of
the North, and retired to the province of Mendoza because of his
health. "At the beginning of the autumn (of the year 1814)," said
General Paz in his memoirs, "it was rumored in the army that a
disease of the chest afflicted San Martín; he did not leave his quarters for a considerable time; the tattoo did not resound at his
door for fear that the noise would inconvenience him; and utter
silence was requested of those persons who came to inquire concerning his health or for other reasons. A little later he left the camp,
and after spending about a month on a farm, he departed for
Córdoba on the pretext that he was still seeking a climate adapted
to his health." [1]

On September 18, 1810, there began in Santiago de Chile the
revolution that deposed the Conde de la Conquista, who was the
governor of Chile, and transferred the command to a governmental
junta of seven members. Said Mitre: "The revolutions of Santiago

---

[1] J. M. Paz, *Memorias póstumas del general José Maria Paz* (second edition,
3 vols. La Plata, 1892), I, 188. On San Martín's plan see further, L. L. Domínguez, "El paso de los Andes y el general Guido; rectificaciones históricas," *La
Revista de Buenos Aires* (Buenos Aires, 1864), IV, 78.

and Buenos Aires had the same formula to the effect that they resumed their own rights without immediately severing relations with the motherland and avowed their loyalty to the legitimate sovereign. With ramifications that were less extensive than those of Buenos Aires the first of these revolutions was aristocratic and conservative according to the disposition of the people, while the second was democratic and radical. However, both were essentially American and obeyed the same historic law. In the beginning neither revolution had chieftains; neither did they subordinate themselves to any personal interest. In Chile, the program of the revolution was formed by the word of its tribunes, José Gregorio Argomedo and José Miguel Infante, who were the interpreters of the law and of opinion. In Buenos Aires, the progam was formed by the voices of Paso and Castelli, who in the arena of discussion vanquished by arguments the representatives of the senile colonial authority. The two salient personalities who typified respectively the advanced ideas of the respective revolutions were two civilians of high intelligence who gave the revolution direction and moulded its political character. Doctor Mariano Moreno, jurisconsult and publicist, was the inspiration of the May Revolution in Buenos Aires. Juan Martínez Rosas (an Argentine who had been born in Mendoza) was from the very beginning the inspirer of the renovation of Chile.[2]

News of the triumph of the revolution in Chile was received in Buenos Aires by a salute of twenty-one guns; and in the *Gaceta de Buenos Aires* there was published an article which began thus: "Chile has been restored to the exercise of the sacred rights which were scandalously usurped; a breath of the genius of its illustrious people was enough to break the weak fetters which had been forged by ignorance and desperation."

During the progress of the Chilean revolution there appeared two parties: one was moderate, while the other was radical. José Miguel Carrera, representing the latter, was at the head of the army. A little later he was replaced by Bernardo O'Higgins. But Carrera and his brother Luís deposed Director O'Higgins and formed a junta. A civil war broke out between O'Higgins and Carrera which only ceased when the viceroy of Peru appointed Osorio president of the captaincy general of Chile. Confronted by this

[2] Mitre, *Historia de San Martín*, I, 303.

common peril, the patriots who belonged to conflicting political camps united, but at the end of 1814 they were completely routed by the royalist army at the battle of Rancagua. In this wise, the Chilean revolt was suppressed; the disheartened patriots crossed the Andes and emigrated to Mendoza where San Martín was preparing his project to carry the war directly into Peru by way of Chilean territory.

On August 10, 1814, the government of Buenos Aires appointed San Martín to the post of governor intendant of Cuyo, a jurisdiction that comprised the provinces of Mendoza, San Juan, and San Luis. After the defeat at Rancagua, Chilean patriots placed their hope for independence in the realization of the continental plan of San Martín. O'Higgins placed himself and his soldiers at the disposition of the intendant of Cuyo; and from that day the two eminent leaders of the Argentine revolution and the Chilean revolution sealed an indestructible friendship.

The defeat at Rancagua created a compromising situation for San Martín, for the triumph of the Spanish army in Chile was a menace. In order to guard the western frontier, the government of Buenos Aires decreed the creation of a regiment of infantry of the line (number eleven which was under the orders of Las Heras), and a squadron of cavalry. In Mendoza, there were only two battalions of militia—one composed of white persons and the other of mixed classes—and a picket of lancers. In December, 1814, the government of Buenos Aires sent new forces to Mendoza, in order to defend the province against possible invasion by Chilean royalists.

After Juan Martín de Pueyrredón was elected supreme director by the congress of Tucumán, he was invited by San Martín to meet him in a conference in the city of Córdoba. This was an historic interview, and when they reached an agreement, San Martín returned to Mendoza, while Pueyrredón proceeded to the capital whence he began to send San Martín soldiers, munitions, and money for the formation of the Army of the Andes.

With infinite patience, San Martín consecrated himself to this task. The provinces of Cuyo made self-denying and patriotic sacrifices. Near the city of Mendoza a camp was established; later a park and an armory were provided, as well as a nitrate laboratory, and a cloth factory to prepare uniforms for the soldiers. To aid him in these labors San Martín had the support and coöperation of the people. In this enterprise there are incidents that flatter our patriotism. Thus, in a critical moment, when the treasury of the province of Cuyo was empty, the women of Mendoza, acting as a committee, proceeded to the hall of the cabildo where María de los Remedios Escalada de San Martín, the wife of the general, said to him that the ladies of Mendoza who were present would offer their jewels as a contribution to the success of the cause. And at that very moment all the ladies stripped themselves of their jewels.

Before beginning his march, San Martín noticed that one of his squadrons lacked its quota of recruits. Hence he issued a proclamation to the people of Mendoza which made this appeal: "I have one hundred and thirty sabres stored in the barracks of the mounted grenadiers for lack of brave men to wield them. The cordillera is about to open. Let him who loves his country and his honor come and take up arms." The sabers were seized by one hundred and thirty volunteers.

During the entire preparatory period of the campaign San Martín carried on what he denominated the "war of trenches."[3] This consisted in deluding General Osorio, who was in command of the royalist army on the other side of the Andes, by sending emissaries who were to deceive him in regard to the plan of invasion. San Martín had also to become acquainted with the passes of Los Patos and Uspallata through which he intended to cross the mountains. For this purpose, he commanded Álvarez Condarco, the engineer of his general staff, to give to the president of the captaincy general of Chile, Marcó del Pont, the declaration of independence which had been adopted by the congress of Tucumán. Álvarez Condarco crossed the Andes by the pass of Los Patos and carefully observed all the features of that pass. He reached Chile and delivered the declaration to Marcó del Pont, who at first proposed to have the messenger of San Martín shot; but soon decided instead to burn the act of independence in the presence of a large crowd

[3] In the secret instructions of the Platean government to San Martín for the campaign in Chile, any intention of annexing the liberated country was disclaimed. The motives for the expedition of liberation were declared to be as follows: the establishment of Spanish-American independence, and the glory of participating in that enterprise. See J. de San Martín, *Documentos del archivo de San Martín* (12 vols. Buenos Aires, 1910-11), III, 402-3.

in the great square of Santiago. Marcó del Pont wrote a reply, which Álvarez Condarco was to take, in which the declaration of independence of the congress of Tucumán was stigmatized "as an act of perfidy and treason." San Martín's messenger returned to Mendoza by the Uspallata pass.

"It is not the opposition which the royalists can offer to my soldiers that disturbs my sleep," said San Martín, "but the passage of these immense mountains." [4] The great mountain chain had peaks like those of Aconcagua which reached 22,860 feet above the level of the sea. The roads across the Andes rose to more than 9,000 feet and were impassable during the winter when they were covered with snow.

Everything was ready for the march. The Army of the Andes included 4,000 men, besides 1,200 auxiliary militiamen who were to be used to transport provisions and munitions. The army was divided into two great columns: one was to cross the Andes by the pass of Los Patos; its vanguard was under the command of General Miguel Estanislao Soler, and its reserve was under O'Higgins. The other column was under the command of Las Heras; it was to march by the road of Uspallata and to transport the munitions and artillery, which could not be taken by the pass of Los Patos. These two large columns were the main bodies of the army. Two small divisions, in the form of wings, one to the north and the other to the south of the main bodies, completed the plan of campaign. The small division of the north was composed of sixty infantry of the line, eighty militiamen of San Juan, and a legion of Chilean émigrés under the orders of commandant Juan Manuel Cabot. This detachment was to march from San Juan and to capture Coquimbo at the same time that a detachment from La Rioja under the orders of Commander Francisco Celada, and his second in command, Captain Nicolás Dávila, was to occupy Copiapó and Huasco. The small division of the south, under the orders of the Chilean, Captain Freire, was to penetrate Chile via Planchón and to capture the city of Talca. The two great central columns of the army and the small detachments on the wings were instructed to appear in Chilean territory at the same time, that is, between February 6 and February 8, 1817.

In fine, the plan consisted in invading Chile by the passes of

---

[4] Mitre, *Historia de San Martín*, I, 504.--W.S.R.

Uspallata and Los Patos, thus leaving Marcó del Pont in doubt as to the place where San Martín's army would appear, in order thus to keep the royalist forces divided and scattered. The pass of Uspallata is a shorter route than the pass of Los Patos, for at that place the Andes are not so wide and the Uspallata route leads directly to the valley of Aconcagua where the village of Santa Rosa de los Andes was located. The pass of Los Patos, which was larger, led to the valley of Putaendo. In this manner the column of the army that marched via Uspallata under command of Las Heras would meet the enemy first and would act as the vanguard. The main body of the army that proceeded by the road of Los Patos, which was commanded by General Soler and O'Higgins under the supervision of San Martín, was to serve as the rearguard. Everything was calculated with mathematical exactness. Chacabuco was the point where the patriots were destined to measure themselves with the opposing forces and to decide the result of this great campaign.

The division of the north, which was under the command of Cabot, left San Juan on January 12, 1817; it crossed the cordillera of Coquimbo, reached Chile on February 8, and two days later fought a successful engagement at Salala. At the same time, the expedition of La Rioja commanded by Captain Dávila took possession of the city of Copiapó. In this way all the northern part of Chile fell into the hands of the patriots.

The division of the south, which was under the command of the Chilean, Captain Freire, had left Mendoza on January 14, 1817, had defeated an enemy force in the engagement of Vega de Campeo, and had occupied the city of Talca. By this time the two small divisions of the north and the south had fortunately realized a part of the vast plan that had been conceived. This was important; for these light wings served to deceive Marcó del Pont by inducing him to believe that the main body of the army would invade Chile by these routes. Thus he was induced to divide his forces and to maintain them in echelon along the Andes.

After the expeditions of the north and the south had been dispatched, San Martín decided to begin the principal part of the campaign with the division of Las Heras composed of eight hundred men, which was to cross the Andes by the Uspallata road. Four days later the main body of the army started up the road to Los

Patos. The two divisions followed a parallel course. The army crossed the mountains in eighteen days. On February 4, in the pass of La Guardia, the division of Las Heras had an encounter with the enemy and took possession of Santa Rosa de los Andes. At the same time the vanguard of Soler entered the valley of Putaendo and took possession of San Felipe de Aconcagua. In this manner the remobilization of the Army of the Andes took place to the west of the cordillera on the very day set by San Martín. The most difficult, most daring, and most characteristic part of the campaign was thus successfully executed, that is, the passage of the Andes and the concentration of the army on the Chilean side of the mountains. With his natural simplicity, San Martín gave an account of the campaign in a note which ran thus: "The passage of the Andes has been a triumph in itself. The soldiers of the army with supplies for almost a month, with armament, munitions of war, and baggage have marched a hundred leagues along a road which crossed craggy peaks, defiles, folds, and deep, narrow chasms—a road intersected by four mountain ridges, where the ruggedness of the terrain competes with the harshness of the atmosphere. If to overcome these obstacles has been to gain a victory, it is no less a victory because it has frightened the enemy."

The passage of the Andes elevates the military figure of San Martín to the plane of the great generals of history. He has been compared with Alexander, who in olden times consummated the conquest of Asia; he has been compared with Hannibal, who crossed the Ebro, the Pyrenees, the Rhone, and the Alps to descend upon Italy; and he has been compared with Napoleon, who was the most inspired and colossal genius of war. "If the passage of the Andes," said Mitre, "is compared as a human victory with the victories of Hannibal and Napoleon, one of whom was animated by vengeance and cupidity and the other by ambition, it will be seen that the enterprise of San Martín, which in itself was great from a military viewpoint, though less important as a classic model, is more important in the matter of human destinies; for it had as its object and as a motive the independence and liberty of a republican world, whose glory has been and will be more fruitful through the ages than the sterile campaigns of Trebbia and Marengo. From this viewpoint, the only mountain march which is comparable with that across the southern Andes by San Martín is that which Bolívar accomplished two years later (1819) over the equatorial Andes, which had as its result the American victory of Boyacá (1819)—a complement to the victory of Maipú (1818)—and the reconquest of New Granada—a complement to the reconquest of Chile at the south (1817). Both of these operations were equally fruitful and decisive and memorable as military exploits. The Andean campaign of the Colombian Liberator possessed the greater instinctive promptings of genius, but lacked the admirable foresight and precise regularity of the strategic combination of the Argentine general. Both generals typified a human victory; but there belongs especially to San Martín the initial glory furnished by his passage of the Andes, which was the first signal achievement of offensive war in the struggle for South-American emancipation. He bequeathed to the military history of the New World and the Old the most consummate lesson of its kind." [5]

When the patriot army reassembled on the other side of the Andes, Governor Marcó del Pont, surprised by the rapidity of San Martín's operations, assembled his soldiers on the hill of Chacabuco under the command of General Maroto. San Martín divided his army into two wings; he intrusted the right wing to Soler, and the left wing to O'Higgins. The commander himself was in charge of the reserve. The plan of battle was simple: Soler was to attack the enemy on the flank and to envelop it, thus starting the battle; at the same time O'Higgins was to attack the enemy's front. Soler's column could not rapidly execute the flank movement, while the division of O'Higgins dashed imprudently to the front and started the battle. This move of O'Higgins compromised the battle; for he had to retire in disorder under the fire of the Spanish infantry. In the words of Pelliza:

"When San Martín saw that the movement of O'Higgins, which anticipated the attack, had imperiled the outcome of the battle and that the impetuous charge of the Spanish cavalry might disrupt and destroy battalions seven and eight which were commanded by that general, and without knowing what had happened to his right wing, he saw no other recourse to prevent an imminent disaster to his left wing than to place himself at the head of three squadrons of grenadiers commanded by Zapiola. Unsheathing his sword, he fell like a thunderbolt upon the enemy cavalry, beat it back at the

---

[5] *Ibid.*, pp. 551-52.

point of the saber, and took from it a large part of the field of battle, thus giving O'Higgins time to reform his division." [6] In the moment of greatest peril, Soler appeared on the scene, and the surprised Spaniards beheld transformed into a disaster what seemed at the beginning to be a royalist victory. O'Higgins was able to unite his two battalions and to make a bayonet charge. The Spanish army was surrounded and, after a long and valiant struggle, it fled leaving six hundred soldiers as prisoners, besides many commanders and officials. February 12, 1817, marks in American history the glorious victory of Chacabuco. Forty-eight hours after the battle General San Martín entered the city of Santiago.

The battle of Chacabuco has both military and political significance. From a military viewpoint it was a result of the foresight and tactics that had inspired the campaign of the Andes, of which it was the logical and natural consequence. Mitre remarks: "As a political event and in relation to American destinies, its importance is even greater, as has been recognized by prominent historians and even by the vanquished enemy. That battle gave the first sign of the offensive war for South-American independence, and permanently secured for it a solid base of operations on the coasts and in the waters of the Pacific. Above all, the battle of Chacabuco furnished a precedent for the plan of a continental campaign to the movement for the emancipation of the New World by confining Spanish power in America to the narrow region of Peru, where it bade fair to be vanquished within the passage closed by the initial force of the revolution. Chacabuco saved the Argentine revolution from ruin, checked the invasion which threatened it from Upper Peru, thus suppressing a perilous enemy that menaced it on the flank, and gave it a chance to expand, without which it would perhaps have been smothered in its cradle. It was the first battle in Spanish America that had far-reaching historical results. Pezuela, the Peruvian viceroy, admitted that this battle marked the moment when the cause of Spain in America began to retrogress, and when its power was shaken to its very foundations." [7]

On February 14, the patriot army triumphantly entered the

[6] M. A. Pelliza, *Historia argentina desde su origen hasta la organización nacional* (2 vols. Buenos Aires, 1910), I, 410.

[7] Mitre, *Historia de San Martín*, II, 20-21.

city of Santiago amid the acclamations of the people. They gave
expression to a desire that General San Martín should take charge
of the government. But faithful to the norm of conduct which he
had adopted for himself, he declined that honorable invitation,
saying that his armies did not fight battles to conquer governments
but to liberate peoples. The request to occupy the position of
supreme director then passed to O'Higgins. With the intention of
promoting the plan which he had conceived, San Martín decided
to go to Buenos Aires in order to arrange with Director Pueyrredón the formation of a squadron that should plow the Pacific and
liberate Peru.

Meantime the Spaniards had concentrated their forces in the
southern part of Chile, where Las Heras won the triumphs of Cura-
paligüe and Gavilán. The main body of the royalist forces, under
the command of Colonel Ordóñez, had fortified itself on the peninsula of Talcahuano. In order to reënforce the army of Ordóñez
and to undertake the reconquest of Chile, the Peruvian viceroy dispatched a new army which he intrusted to General Mariano Osorio.
The combined royalist forces thus amounted to 5,000 men. Las
Heras was directed to attack Ordóñez, and after occupying the
city of Concepción, he besieged Talcahuano. As the siege proceeded
slowly, O'Higgins marched to the aid of Las Heras, with the resolution to take the fort by an assault which should be led by a French
officer named General Brayer. In the assault the patriot forces
were repulsed. Then O'Higgins raised the siege of the fort and
marched northward to join San Martín who had returned from
Buenos Aires. The patriot army pursued the royalists stationed
in the city of Talca in the vicinity of which there was a plain called
Cancha Rayada. Late in the afternoon of March 19, 1818, the
Spaniards intrenched themselves in the city and the patriot army
encamped for the night in two parallel lines. Suddenly, San Martín
received warning that the Spaniards were leaving the city, and,
without affording time for the patriots to defend themselves, the
Spanish army fell upon them by surprise. Great confusion occurred
and a panic threw the patriot ranks into disorder. But General
Las Heras, who knew the plan of the Spanish general to surprise
the patriots, was able to save the entire division of 3,000 men under
his command.

The disaster of Cancha Rayada seemed to signify the loss of

Chile to the patriots. O'Higgins had been wounded and San Martín believed him to be dead. With admirable rapidity, the latter genius was able to proceed to reorganize the army by using as a base the division of Las Heras. San Martín immediately convoked a council of war composed of citizens and the chief leaders of the army. "The conference opened," says General Espejo in the unpublished biography of Commandant Bertrand, "by a description of the circumstances in vivid colors which it would not have been prudent to conceal. Although he had already decided the matter in his own mind General San Martín, who realized the crisis that had been reached, and wished to discover the prevailing attitude of mind, asked the council the two following questions: 'Is it advisable to concentrate the army in the capital and to defend it at all costs, or is it better to continue the retreat to the valley of Aconcagua in order to reorganize the forces and to await an opportunity to challenge the enemy to battle?' After a brief interval that followed this inquiry a member of the council said that before reaching any decision it would be proper to know what was the condition of the artillery department and upon what resources it depended."

Upon being informed that his presence was desired in the council, the head of that department, Commandant Bertrand, appeared at once. After informing him concerning the two questions that he had just propounded, San Martín concluded by saying: "The members of the junta desire to know from you how well we are supplied with munitions." To which Bertrand resolutely responded, raising his right hand to give more emphasis to his words, "Up to the roof, gentlemen."

The council of war then resolved to defend the position. The decisive battle was to take place which would decide the fate of Chile and the liberty of our country. In the ranks of the Spanish army there were doubts about the operations that were to take place. General Osorio did not have the intrepidity of the Argentine general; finally, after seventeen days, he took up a position on the plains of Maipú. San Martín had carefully studied the strategic possibilities of the field. About noon on April 5 the armies clashed. San Martín attacked the royalists in front with patriot forces; the right wing was under the command of Las Heras; and the left wing was commanded by Alvarado. Balcarce had charge of the infantry, and Zapiola was at the head of the cavalry on the right.

The battle lasted six hours, and, after a bloody struggle, victory was on the side of the Americans. Two thousand corpses remained on the battlefield, and the patriots took three thousand prisoners. In a brief communication to the director of Chile San Martín thus reported the victory: "We have completely won the battle. A small remnant of the enemy is in flight; our cavalry will pursue it to the end. Your country is free."

Supreme Director O'Higgins, who was wounded, proceeded to the battlefield and there embraced San Martín. The battle of Maipú definitively consecrated the liberty of Chile, and in that sense it confirmed the triumph of Chacabuco. Besides assuring and consolidating the liberty of Chile, the battle of Maipú had continental consequences; for the royalists took refuge in Peru, their last bulwark in Spanish America, where they were to be surrounded and attacked by the liberating armies of San Martín and Bolívar.[8]

Six days after the battle of Maipú, San Martín addressed dispatches to Viceroy Pezuela of Peru in which he proposed the cessation of the war, with a view to the welfare and liberty of the Spanish-American people. This was a memorable communication. San Martín began by stating that the fortune of arms had placed the entire army of the enemy in his hands and that the right of reprisal would justify him in executing upon the prisoners the horrible treatment that they had arranged for his soldiers in case of victory according to the barbarous orders of their commander. But influenced by humane motives he had respected the rights of the vanquished, and all the prisoners—the greater part of the commanders, almost 200 officers, and 3,000 soldiers—had received hospitality and aid in their disgrace.

In another dispatch of the same date, San Martín informed Viceroy Pezuela that Chile and the United Provinces of la Plata desired a liberal constitution and reasonable liberty. "To attempt to restrain by the bayonet," he said in an eloquent passage, "the general course of opinion in Spanish America is like attempting to enslave nature. Examine with impartiality the result of the policy of the Spanish government in recent years, and without lingering upon the ephemeral triumphs of the royal arms, you will discover

---

[8] On the significance of the battle of Maipú, see further, López, op. cit., VII, 195; and The Times, August 1, 1818.

their impotence against the spirit of liberty." [9] In conclusion, San Martín proposed that the people of Peru should be convoked to decide upon their own destiny. The propositions of San Martín were rejected by Pezuela.

---

[9] *Gaceta de Buenos Aires,* April 29, 1818.

CHAPTER XXXIV

THE LIBERATION OF PERU

THE VICTORY of the Argentine army in Chilean territory was the first step toward the definitive emancipation of all Spanish America. In the campaign of the Andes the war against Spain had assumed an offensive character. Routed in Chile, the royalist armies had been concentrated in Peru, which was the last bulwark of Spanish resistance. In the far-reaching continental plan of San Martín, the campaign for the liberation of Peru crowned the work that he had started in 1817.

After the battle of Maipú, San Martín returned to Buenos Aires where he was acclaimed by the people. The poets Esteban de Luca, Vicente López y Planes, Juan Crisóstomo Lafinur, and Fray Cayetano Rodríguez, sang his praises; and the government granted him the grade of brigadier-general, which he modestly declined to accept. He had not journeyed to Buenos Aires to receive homage but to insist upon the realization of an ideal. The new campaign required a squadron that would dominate the Pacific Ocean. For this purpose, he asked for an allowance of 500,000 pesos for the Army of the Andes which should be raised by means of a loan.

Once this matter was arranged, he departed incognito as he had arrived. Upon reaching Mendoza, confidential letters from Pueyrredón informed him that the loan of a half million of pesos would not be realized. In a characteristic manner, San Martín thus replied: "Determined to sacrifice my life, I marched to take charge of the united army, in spite of the fact that the physician, William Colisberry, who also attended me during my illness in Tucumán, assured me that I would not live six months. Nevertheless, I risked everything in the supposition that this army would operate outside of Chile; but, as circumstances have changed, I ask that you accept the resignation which I make of said command." A fortnight after this resignation was presented, the government wrote to San Martín asking that he withdraw his resignation; for by dint of sacrifices the floating of the loan would be assured.

The plan that had been projected began to be realized. At the same time, in the northern part of South America, Bolívar, the

Liberator of the North, had crossed the equatorial Andes, had fought at Boyacá a battle—like that of Maipú of South American significance—which insured the liberty of Colombia, and, like San Martín, was marching toward Lima. In this fashion the Spaniards, who were vanquished at both extremes of the continent, took refuge in Peru, which San Martín was destined to reach first.

In the beginning of 1819, San Martín, firm in his convictions, addressed the following proclamation to the Peruvians: "Inhabitants of Peru: the independent states of Chile and the United Provinces direct me to enter into your territory in order to defend the cause of your liberty. My announcement is not that of a conqueror. The force of events has prepared this great day of your emancipation. The union of three independent states will finally convince Spain of her importance. The annals of the world do not record a revolution more holy in its object or more fundamentally necessary."

In February, 1819, a treaty of alliance was signed between the governments of Buenos Aires and Chile "in order to put an end to Spanish domination in Peru by means of a joint expedition financed by the two nations, in response to the wishes manifested by the inhabitants of the dominated country, in order to establish by the free will of the Peruvians a government more adapted to their physical and moral condition, which would mutually guarantee the independence of the new state."

"San Martín had assumed three great duties," declared Mitre. The first, concerning Spanish America, was to persevere in his plans for its liberation; the second, as a soldier, was to support the legal order which was threatened by civil war; the third, was to act as an Argentinian, in the face of an imminent Spanish expedition to the Río de la Plata. With respect to the first, his formula was this: 'If the expedition to Peru were not carried out, everything would go to the devil,' both Spanish America and Argentina. With respect to the second, he felt an unconquerable repugnance to taking sides in an internal question. . . . With respect to Spain, whether it was a matter of vanquishing her last army on the Pacific slope or of repulsing her last expedition to La Plata, in both cases he would be opposing her objective and her passion. . . ." [1]

Such were the fundamental norms of his character that circum-

_____
[1] Mitre, *Historia de San Martín,* II, 320-21.

stances and destiny put to the proof. In the end of 1819, the interior political condition of the United Provinces was that of anarchy and dissolution. The congress assembled in Buenos Aires had promulgated the unitarian constitution of 1819. The supreme director was still Juan Martín de Pueyrredón, whose government had succeeded in energetically and decisively restraining the torrent of anarchy that since 1810 had become apparent during the successive crises of revolutionary governments. The constitution of 1819 was rejected by the people; and wearied by the prolonged struggle necessary to keep himself in office, Pueyrredón presented his resignation. A cloud obscured the horizon: the chieftains and the revolutionary cavalry threatened to attack Buenos Aires. The new director, Rondeau, ordered, as indeed Pueyrredón had done, all the troops to be concentrated in Buenos Aires in order to defend the city: the Army of the North, under the command of General Belgrano, was disposed to carry out the orders of the director, but an uprising took place at Arequito. In such a critical emergency, San Martín, who had been ordered to march with the Army of the Andes to Buenos Aires was forced to vacillate. He was confronted with two duties: either to intervene with his army in the civil war in order to support the government, or to disobey the command so that he might pursue his campaign of liberation. He reasoned that the independence of his country was not yet established; that the Spanish resistance in Peru, where he ought to go in order to consolidate the emancipation, was still powerful. On the other hand, if he went to Buenos Aires with his army, could he be certain that he went to mitigate the anarchy? Anarchy was a political phenomenon that sprang from the nature of the people, and an army would certainly not be the most adequate means of restraining the mighty force and reality of an historic evolution. He disobeyed Rondeau's order. One may designate this the characteristic disobedience of San Martín; for in this manner he could undertake the expedition for the liberation of Peru, which would assure forever the emancipation of his country.

When the Spanish-American colonies revolted against the motherland in 1810, the viceroyalty of Peru remained apart from that movement. Two chief causes explain that phenomenon: first, the heterogeneous character of its population which was composed of aborigines, Negro slaves, and mestizos resulting from the admixture of Indians, Africans, and Spaniards. The cohesion which the fusion of races had caused in the provinces of La Plata, and which early produced among us the phenomenon of a spontaneous democracy did not, therefore, exist in Peru. A second cause was due to the powerful Spanish resistance in Peru. Its viceroy at this time was General José de Abascal, a man of military and political talent, of whom it has been said that, if the Spanish-American revolution could have been suppressed, he would have done so. In fact, Abascal suppressed the insurrection of Quito, triumphed with his armies in Upper Peru, threatened to invade Argentine territory, and by the battle of Rancagua reconquered Chile—thus he subjugated all the revolutionary colonies with the exception of Buenos Aires and Venezuela. Such was the military preponderance of Peru through the influence of Viceroy Abascal, that he was able to form there an American royalist party and to organize a colonial army among the inhabitants of the sierra to defend the cause of Spain.

In 1820, the royalist soldiers in Peru numbered 23,000 men, who were organized in two great divisions: the army of Lower Peru that defended Lima, and the other army that defended Upper Peru. The liberating army of San Martín included over 4,000 men. In addition to the numerical superiority of the Spanish forces, Peru had distinguished military leaders. In the place of Abascal was General Pezuela, victor at Vilcapugio, Ayohuma, and Sipe-Sipe. General José de la Serna, a trained soldier, with a large experience in war, commanded the army of Upper Peru. Among others, General José Canterac, a Frenchman by birth, was chief of the general staff. Against this royalist position in Peru, strong and consolidated in both its military and political aspects, the expedition of San Martín was to precipitate a struggle.

The expeditionary army was designated as the "Liberating Army of Peru." It was composed of 4,450 men, of whom 2,313 belonged to the Argentine Army of the Andes, while 1,805 were Chileans. The commander in chief of this expedition, San Martín, appointed General Juan Gregorio de las Heras chief of the general staff to which there belonged the generals of division Juan Antonio Álvarez de Arenales, and Toribio Luzuriaga, the ex-governor of Cuyo.

Chile had coöperated by furnishing the contingent of the army which we have just mentioned and also by furnishing the naval squadron. This was composed of eight vessels of war that were manned by 1,600 soldiers and sailors, of whom 1,000 were Chileans and the rest English seamen. In addition there were sixteen transports which carried provisions sufficient for four months for the army that was to fight on land. The squadron was under the orders of Lord Cochrane, an English seaman who had been engaged especially for that purpose. In February, 1819, Cochrane had bottled up the royalist squadron in the Bay of Callao and thus dislodged the Spaniards from the Pacific coast.

The liberating army of Peru weighed anchor from the port of Valparaiso on August 20, 1820. Admiral Cochrane sailed on the ship *O'Higgins,* which was followed by the *Lautaro* and the *Galvarino.* The soldiers to be landed filled twelve transports. The general staff and the generalissimo sailed in the *San Martín.*

On September 7, the squadron arrived at the Bay of Paracas, three leagues south of Pisco, where San Martín ordered the landing of a division under the command of Las Heras which marched toward that port. In this wise the rest of the liberating army could land in Pisco Bay. After landing on Peruvian soil, San Martín issued the following proclamation to his soldiers: "We have now arrived at our destination, and only valor is needed to consummate the work of constancy. Remember that your great duty is to console America and that you come not to make conquests but to free peoples. The Peruvians are our brothers: embrace them and respect their rights as you respected the rights of the Chileans after Chacabuco."

With the intention of inciting the people of Peru to rise in favor of the principles of the revolution, a division of more than 1,100 men marched into the interior under the command of Álvarez de Arenales. He marched to Ica, which was abandoned by the royalists, crossed the Andes by a defile, and reached Jauja and Junín. On December 6, 1820, the battle of Pasco took place between the patriot army of Arenales and the royalist army of General O'Reilly. Victory was the reward of the patriots: the royalists were completely dispersed. General O'Reilly was taken prisoner. The battle of Pasco, and the engagement which Arenales had shortly before fought at Nazca, had spread the spirit of revolution among the Peruvian people.

The success of the liberating expedition of San Martín seemed assured. In the royalist army there began to appear the first dissensions and defections. Soldiers, officers, and commanders passed over to the ranks of the liberating army; thus the battalion of Numancio mutinied, and the royalist chief José la Mar surrendered the fortress of Callao. In addition, anarchy began to spread among the enemy commanders. Viceroy Pezuela was deposed by a conspiracy of commanders and officials who named General La Serna in his place. The patriot forces had triumphed at Paracas, Pisco, Nazca, and Pasco; the situation of La Serna became hazardous and on July 6, 1821, he resolved to abandon the city of Lima.

As a result, San Martín entered that city on July 8. As he had indicated in his proclamation, he entered as a liberator and not as a conqueror. Representatives of the cabildo received the generalissimo; and all the people placed themselves under his protection. The first act of San Martín was to convoke "a general junta of citizens of known probity, patriotism, and intelligence who as representatives of the inhabitants of the capital should decide whether or not the general opinion was in favor of independence and whose decision was to justify a proclamation or whatever step that body might dictate." When the junta assembled, its members declared that the Peruvian people wished that their independence from Spain should be proclaimed.

On July 28, 1821, the act of proclaiming the independence of Peru was performed with due solemnity. On that day there left the palace of the viceroys in Lima a cavalcade led by the University of San Marcos with its four colleges, the religious corporations, the military officers, the oidors, the ayuntamiento, and the principal representatives of the native nobility. Then followed the liberator with his general staff, accompanied by the political governor of the city. In the rear marched the civil guard, the halberdiers of Lima, and the generalissimo's escort of huzzars. At the end of the procession came battalion number eight of the Army of the Andes, the victor at Chacabuco and Maipú, which bore the flags of the United Provinces of the Río de la Plata and of Chile. Farther to the rear came the artillery with the cannon which were to salute the advent of the new nation. San Martín mounted a stage that had been erected in the main square, and unfurled for the first time the national flag of Peru which he had designed at Pisco. He was greeted by tremendous applause. When the tumult was stilled for a moment, the liberator exclaimed in a firm and sonorous voice: "From this moment Peru is free and independent, by the general wish of the people and by the justice of its cause, which may God defend!" After saluting the flag three times, he exclaimed: *"Viva la patria! Viva la libertad! Viva la independencia!"* [2] The people repeated these phrases amidst the thunder of cannon.

Meantime, the forces of General Simón Bolívar were pursuing a campaign of liberation in Venezuela and Colombia which he triumphantly maintained. His army approached the line that had been reached by General San Martín and his host. Nevertheless, in Ecuador the royalists dominated everything. Against them Bolívar sent a strong division under the command of General Sucre. When the moment arrived for a decisive battle, Sucre realized that the royalist army was more powerful than his own, and that this fact might create a difficult situation if he began a battle. At this juncture, San Martín placed under his orders a division of the Argentine army of more than 1,000 men under the command of General Santa Cruz. A little later, on May 24, 1822, Sucre fought the battle of Pichincha in which victory crowned the efforts of the combined Argentine, Colombian, and Venezuelan armies. The battle of Pichincha assured the emancipation of Ecuador. It was the last struggle within the vast arena that the Venezuelan revolution had up to this time embraced.

It has been asserted that the conference which José de San Martín and Simón Bolívar held in Guayaquil shortly after the victory at Pichincha is a mystery that history has not been able to solve. This assertion is not correct. By the use of important documents, history can reconstruct the scene of the interview. It has also been said that the conference was concerned with three points: namely, to determine the definitive status of Guayaquil: to fix the norm of government that would be given to the new states; and to decide upon the best means of terminating the war in Peru against the royalists. These matters were considered, but the chief object of that historic interview was to decide upon the manner in which the war in Peru should terminate. The letters of San Martín allow us to discern in an unequivocal manner that the dominant thought in his mind was to ascertain from General Bolívar "the aid which he would be able to furnish in order to end the war in Peru."

---

[2] San Martín, *Documentos del archivo de San Martín,* XI, 373.—W. S. R.

The affirmation that General San Martín wished to set foot in Colombian territory and to bring the territory of Ecuador under the dominion and jurisdiction of Peru is in manifest contradiction with the character and actions of the liberator of the south. He had already said and proved by deeds that he was not a conqueror but a liberator. He had declined the position of supreme director of Chile which the people had offered him, and had accepted, in a provisional character, and until the war should terminate, the post of protector of Peru. It was inconceivable that with such an invariable norm of conduct proven and sustained by incontrovertible and suggestive facts, he was about to precipitate a paltry and purposeless dispute about a portion of the territory of Ecuador.

Neither is it correct to say that the fundamental difference between the two liberators was due to the problem of the form of government for the liberated colonies. This point was indeed treated incidentally at the conference. San Martín believed that the first task was that of emancipation, and holding firmly to this conception, he had carried out the campaign in Chile and in Peru. If San Martín was a partisan of the monarchical form of government, while Bolívar was not a partisan of that form, this question was of minor importance in the face of a more serious issue that had a prior claim, namely, the termination of the work of emancipation which would assure liberty to all of Spanish America; for it was necessary to cope with the royalist army that had evacuated Lima but which was powerful and was still on Peruvian soil. Precisely this was the great question, and from it, and from nothing else, the disagreement arose.[3]

The interview of San Martín and Bolívar included three conferences: one took place on the forenoon of July 26, and lasted scarcely an hour and a half; another took place on the afternoon

---

[3] The most illuminating documents on the interview at Guayaquil are in J. M. Goenaga, La entrevista de Guayaquil (second edition, Rome, 1915), pp. xx-xxvi, who published the letters of J. G. Pérez, Bolívar's secretary, to the Colombian secretary of foreign relations. See also San Martín, Documentos del archivo de San Martín, VI, 500, 503-4; San Martín; su correspondencia (second edition, Madrid, 1910), pp. 72-73; G. Lafond, Voyages autour du Monde et naufrages célebres (8 vols. Paris, 1870), II, 138-41; Mitre, Historia de San Martín, III, 622, 818-20. Many salient documents are printed with comment in E. de la Cruz, La entrevista de Guayaquil (Madrid, 1920). A description in English of the interview, with translations of important documents, is found in W. S. Robertson, Rise of the Spanish-American Republics, pp. 252-61.—W. S. R.

of that day and did not last more than half an hour; and the third, the real conference, took place on July 27 and lasted from 1 to 5 P.M. In this interview, San Martín requested of General Bolívar "the active and efficacious coöperation of all the forces of Colombia" in order to terminate with success the war in Peru. Bolívar replied that the aid which he could offer would be 1,070 men who would not be placed under the command of San Martín but would be subject to special instructions.

An attempt has been made to explain the refusal of Bolívar to aid San Martín with the full force of Colombia by the consideration that he could not leave its soil without the authorization of its congress. This reasoning is inconsistent. This was not the moment for Bolívar to raise a question of method, which he did not take into account later when he proceeded with his armies to Peru. Still, an attempt has been made to maintain this view by considering the grave problem of the leadership of the army. We now know what a noble and beautiful solution was offered by San Martín—in the belief that that constituted the difficulty which restrained Bolívar from offering all his support—namely, to place himself and his army under the orders of the liberator of the north. But Bolívar did not accept this offer.

Having discarded as unjust the allegation that General Bolívar limited himself to the offer of 1,070 men because San Martín did not possess the moral authority to undertake the campaign, having discarded as puerile the view that the army of Colombia could not leave its territory wthout the authorization of congress, a problem arises concerning the command of the army in conjunction with the offer of San Martín to place himself under Bolívar's orders. What causes can explain the attitude of Bolívar, who after having terminated the campaign in Venezuela, in Colombia, and in Ecuador, confined himself to offering a number of men equal to those that San Martín had loaned him when he was in the difficult position of struggling against the enemy? The reply issues spontaneously and naturally: Bolívar, radiant in glory, wished to terminate the campaign himself.

In the conference at Guayaquil the problem of the organization and form of government of the new states was treated incidentally. Upon that occasion, San Martín stated his opinion, namely, that in order to establish the independence on a firm basis it was not possible to adopt the republican régime at that juncture. Bolívar's general secretary reported San Martín as saying that "the government should not be democratic in Peru, for such a system did not suit that country; and that a prince should be sent from Europe to take complete charge of that state. His Excellency, Bolívar, replied that the introduction of European princes would not suit America or Colombia, for they were so different from our peoples: that for his part he would oppose this, so far as he was able; but that he would not object to the particular form of government which each state wished to establish for itself. On this point, Bolívar added his view on the character of governments, making a reference to the congress of Angostura. The protector of Peru replied that he would never agree to allow such princes to be enthroned in America; that he would prefer to invite General Iturbide to accept the throne, in order that no Bourbons, or Austrians, or members of any other European dynasty should come to America." [4]

The conference of the two liberators had ended. In the evening a banquet was served in which Bolívar offered the following toast: "To the two greatest men of South America: General San Martín and myself." San Martín responded with the following toast that embodied the beautiful ideal of his life: "For the speedy termination of the war, the organization of the different republics of the continent, and the health of the liberator of Colombia." [5]

As he had promised, upon the day when the constitutional congress of Peru assembled, September 20, 1822, General San Martín presented his irrevocable resignation of the office of protector. Upon relinquishing the command and retiring from the South-American

[4] An extract from the letter of J. G. Pérez describing the interview has here been substituted by the translator (who has seen the original letter) for Levene's quotation, see Goenaga, *op. cit.,* pp. xxii-xxiii. The political plans of San Martín and Bolívar have been the subject of much discussion by Spanish-American historians. Villanueva in his volume entitled *Fernando VII y los nuevos estados* ("La Monarquía in América." vol. II: 4 vols. Paris, 1911-14), pp. 255-56, ascribes monarchical designs to Bolívar. This view has been vigorously criticized in Venezuela; see L. Vallenilla Lanz, *Un detractor contumaz* (Caracas, 1914).—W. S. R.

[5] Such, at least, is the story told by Mitre, *Historia de San Martín,* III, 621, basing his account in part on unpublished material.—W. S. R. See further on Bolívar and San Martín, Levene, "Sobre la personalidad moral de San Martín," *Revista de la Universidad de Buenos Aires* (Buenos Aires, 1919), XXXVIII, 511-28.

stage, he addressed to the Peruvians a famous farewell which with much reason has been compared with Washington's farewell address. The proclamation of San Martín said: "I have witnessed the declarations of independence of the states of Chile and Peru. I hold in my hand the standard which Pizarro brought to enslave the empire of the Incas; and I have ceased to be a public man. Thus I am recompensed with usury for ten years employed in revolution and in war. My promise to the countries for which I have fought is fulfilled: to secure their independence, and to leave them to select their own governments. The presence of a fortunate soldier, however disinterested he may be, is dangerous to newly established states."

This incident forms a beautiful page in the moral history of peoples. Upon few occasions have self-denial, greatness of soul, the force and superiority of an ideal as the guiding principles of a life, reached so elevated a plane. San Martín realized that he had been the fighting arm of independence and that because of this very fact he constituted a peril for the "newly established states." A victorious military commander absorbs by natural attraction all the energies and collective sentiments of a people, and upsets the political and social equilibrium, as did Napoleon in France after the campaigns of Italy and Egypt.

The historic personality of San Martín has a profound moral significance.[6] His own life as a military man is an expression of morality. The historian Mitre has appropriately said in passing judgment upon the crossing of the Andes that if that campaign could be excelled as a classic model, it is nevertheless more important in the order of human events, because it had as its object and motive the independence and the liberty of a republican world, the glory of which has been and will be more fruitful in the course of time than the sterile marches of Trebbia and Marengo in which Hannibal and Napoleon triumphed.

He placed his life at the service of the cause of emancipation, and formulated the irrevocable decision of not becoming involved in the internal politics of his country. In the revolution of October 8, 1812, when he had scarcely begun his public career, he intervened in order to overturn the government by a movement that

---

[6] The morality of San Martín is suggested in his letter to General Miller published in *San Martin; su correspondencia,* p. 80.

had been in preparation, and which had resolved upon an insurrection before his arrival at Buenos Aires; but later in 1815 from the intendancy of Cuyo he loaned his moral and military support to the federal revolution which deposed Director Alvear. In both cases he supported a just and popular cause: in the first case against the incompetence of the triumvirate, and in the second case against the improvised dictatorship of Alvear. In neither of these cases did he realize a personal political ambition, for he declined the executive posts that were offered him. From this moral viewpoint much more can be affirmed in regard to San Martín: he never cherished a personal ambition. If patriotism consists in accomplishing a great and generous work for others, with forgetfulness of one's own interests, San Martín can be cited as a singular type of patriot.

Henri Lorin, a professor in the University of Brussels, has said that San Martín was "an organizer of victory," and has asserted that all his military achievements were based upon cool calculations and supreme patience. We are able to say that, in fact, San Martín's entire life confirms the judgment of the Belgian professor as to his personality. His decision not to accept executive positions either in the second triumvirate or in the directory of his country; his refusal of the post of supreme director of Chile; his consecration to the task of forming the Argentine-Chilean army that was to liberate Peru; his entry into the city of Lima, where he accepted the provisional magistracy of protector in order to terminate the war; his interview with General Bolívar, which caused his abdication to be viewed as a sign of weakness of character and not of greatness of soul; his farewell address to the Peruvian people; his ostracism, his physical and moral anguish—all reveal in General San Martín a consistent life possessing harmonic unity, which was guided by unquenchable ethical ideals.

The historian Lavisse wrote: "Napoleon caused the death of two million men and fifteen years of suffering to the peoples of Europe. Who profited by these wars?" The military heroism of San Martín had a high moral inspiration: he was a liberator.[7]

---

[7] In the fifteenth edition of this work the author intercalates with the above tribute some additional passages concerning San Martín, Levene, *Lecciones de historia argentina* (2 vols., Buenos Aires, 1934), II, 179-89.—W. S. R.

CHAPTER XXXV

THE GOVERNMENT OF PUEYRREDON

AFTER SWEARING to support independence, the congress of Tucumán had busied itself with national organization. As a result of the influence of Belgrano and San Martín, the monarchical idea prevailed among its members. Belgrano had advocated the project of restoring the dynasty of the Incas in the provinces of the Río de la Plata. Deputy Acevedo proposed that congress should begin a discussion concerning the form of government to be adopted. He declared himself in favor of a limited monarchy, which would restore the dynasty of the Incas, and designated the city of Cuzco as the prospective capital. Deputy Serrano also expressed himself in favor of a limited monarchy, "which, reconciling the liberty of the citizen and the enjoyment of the principal rights of man with the salvation of the country, would make a monarchical régime preferable to any other form of government in the crisis in which they found themselves involved." In his turn, Deputy Castro Barros declared that "the system of a constitutional monarchy was that which God gave to the people of Israel, that which Jesus Christ established in the Church, the system most favorable to the preservation and progress of the Catholic religion."

Deputy Anchorena opposed the monarchical system; for according to him, there existed an antagonism between the inhabitants of the plain and the inhabitants of the mountain, the last-mentioned type being those who were most attached to the monarchical form, while the first-mentioned were those who were most opposed to it. Anchorena argued that in order to provide a frame of government suitable alike to the inhabitants of the plain and of the mountain, the federal system should be adopted. But the voice which was most energetically raised in congress against the monarchical system of government was that of Fray Justo Santa María de Oro, who maintained that in order to determine upon the form of government to be adopted, the people ought to be consulted beforehand, and that, if this mode of procedure was not followed, he would ask for permission to withdraw from congress.

While congress engaged in such a sterile discussion, the provinces were in the convulsions of civil war. Supreme Director Pueyrredón was living in Buenos Aires, and the congress of Tucumán, feeling that it had no greater support than he, decreed that it should be transferred to that capital. Meantime, it named a committee of its members which, acting in conjunction with the director, should frame a treaty with Brazil based upon the recognition of the independence of the provinces of the Río de la Plata. In order to secure this end the committee was empowered to make known to the court of Brazil that the Argentine people had relinquished the idea of organizing themselves in a democratic and republican form, that they would accept a constitutional monarchy, and that a prince of Brazil might become the monarch.

The selection which the congress of Tucumán had made of Juan Martín de Pueyrredón as supreme director was fortunate: for the new executive had the qualities of intellect and character that were required to guide the destinies of the country in such trying times. The internal political situation of this period, which was becoming more and more complicated, may be characterized by the following facts: (1) the opposition of the provinces to Buenos Aires and the opposition of Buenos Aires to the provinces; (2) the civil war in which the provinces were engaged, each of them governed by its respective chieftain; and (3) the monarchical spirit of the leading men and of congress, which stimulated and furnished a pretext for the uprising of the provinces and the peoples.

In both the province and the city of Buenos Aires a provincial party had been formed which refused to recognize the authority of the new director, Pueyrredón. It championed the absolute autonomy which the province had enjoyed after the federal revolution of 1815. This party became still stronger when the congress of Tucumán informed the provisional director, Balcarce, that he should confine himself to executing the acts of which he was notified, without going beyond these by governmental measures in matters relating to national affairs. But Deputy Sáenz arrived at Buenos Aires and gave explanations that tended to secure the support of that city for the government designated by congress. Though the cabildo of Buenos Aires and the junta of observation accepted the proposals made by Sáenz, yet in both the city and the country manifestos and petitions were framed declaring "that the town of Buenos Aires strongly and publicly desires to be reduced to the

status of a province like the other provinces, that it refuses to be
the capital, and wishes, as they all had wished and still wish, to be
reduced to the status of a single province to be governed as such
in its internal administration, which acknowledges and obeys the
supreme executive power appointed by the sovereign congress
wherever it may fix its residence, provided that congress recognizes
this determination and the governmental regulations that are to
be formed for the management of the province." Such importance
did this autonomist movement acquire that its promoters desired
to summon a popular assembly, but as a difference developed between the provisional director, Balcarce, on the one hand, and the
local authorities, the junta of observation, and the cabildo, on the
other hand, the desire weakened and on learning of the arrival of
Pueyrredón, everyone sallied forth to greet him.

In the provinces civil war had begun to have a disorganizing
effect. In the province of Córdoba, which was governed by Ambrosio
Funes, who had been appointed to that post by the congress of
Tucumán, Juan Pablo Bulnes had led a revolutionary movement
that aimed to depose the governor, but this was checked in time
by a division of Belgrano's army. This insurrection of Córdoba was
combined with another which was to have been led by commander
Juan Francisco Borges in the province of Santiago del Estero and
which had as its object to transform this province into an autonomous political entity. But deserted by his partisans, and delivered up to General Belgrano, Borges was executed.[1] A little later
we shall refer to this theme which is related to the monarchical
spirit of the leading men.

In the month of June, 1817, Director Pueyrredón issued a decree that reëstablished the extinct Academy of San Carlos, thus
creating the Academy of the Union of the South. A year later that
academy was opened with forty-seven students who held scholarships. For the maintenance of this educational institution there
was set apart the revenue accruing from the tax on collateral in-
heritances. Its first rector was Dr. Domingo Achega. The Academy
of the Union of the South furnished a curriculum more ample than
that offered by the Academy of San Carlos. Subjects were now
studied in the former institution which had hitherto not been taught.

---

[1] Suggestive observations concerning party struggles in the Platean provinces
are found in López, *op. cit.*, V, 447-51.

Among them may be mentioned the living languages (English, French, and Italian) which had been required little by little until they became a need which was the more keenly realized as the relations with foreign lands developed, and as the number of foreigners increased who came to settle in the country. Worthy of special mention also was philosophy, the chair of which was filled by competition in 1819 in the person of Juan Crisóstomo Lafinur. Lafinur signalized the transition in La Plata from scholasticism to the new doctrines which began to be disseminated at this time and which were accepted by the chief philosophers of the age. He completely abandoned the old theories and drew inspiration from the newest ideas and from the writings of those thinkers who preconized them, such as Condillac, Locke, Destut de Tracy, and Newton. As has rightly been said, "Before the advent of Lafinur the professors of philosophy wore cassocks; he, attired as a simple citizen and man of the world, first secularized the lecture room and then secularized the fundamentals of teaching!" [2]

At this epoch the periodical press became noteworthy, and should be considered as an important element in public opinion. The chief periodicals were the following: *El Censor*, the organ of the cabildo of Buenos Aires; *La Gaceta*, the organ of the director; and *La Crónica Argentina*, which was edited by Doctors Agrelo and Manuel Moreno, Colonel Dorrego, and the proprietor of the journal, Pazos Silva. In its propaganda *El Censor* inclined to treat the problems of the province of Buenos Aires as distinct from the political questions of the other provinces. Its viewpoint was accordingly federalistic. "Let it never be said," this periodical avowed in an article, "that we wish to cast off the abominable yoke that symbolized the Spanish domination, and that we wish at the same time to impose that identical yoke upon our brothers." In this periodical there was also supported the project of Belgrano to establish an Incaic monarchy, as a means of compensating for the despoliation that had been suffered by the Quechua sovereigns during the Spanish conquest.

La Gaceta defended the centralistic government, and replied to the assertions that Buenos Aires wished to absorb all the life of

---

[2] N. Piñero and E. L. Bidau, "Historia de la Universidad de Buenos Aires," *Anales de la Universidad de Buenos Aires* (Buenos Aires, 1888), I, 34. See further, Korn, *op. cit.*, XIV, 415-17.

La Plata in the following words: "Is it urged that Buenos Aires should make an allotment of its port upon the ocean among the Platean people? Is it possible that with this single advantage, prosperity, aggrandizement, and fortune will redound to the favor of the interior provinces? No matter what fluctuations may take place in politics, no province can ever leave its local position." And as evidence that the porteños were not engrossing the executive positions, it said: "Among four supreme directors, only one has been from Buenos Aires. In the government of Gervasio Posadas, the three secretaries of state were provincials: in a word, one should talk about good faith, if in Buenos Aires, whenever an office is filled, one inquires whether the person destined to fill it was born there or in the interior provinces." [3]

In the columns of *La Crónica Argentina* the project of Belgrano to found an Inca monarchy was severely criticized. Its editors formed a party of opposition to Director Pueyrredón which championed the principles of federal government. "These are very serious and grave questions"—the ones concerning the government— said *La Crónica*, "that cannot and should not be decided by the generals, but by reason and by the free vote of the citizens."

The position of Director Pueyrredón became even more complicated by reason of the invasion of the Banda Oriental by the Portuguese; for the party that opposed the administration demanded a declaration of war against the government of Portugal and asked that the Army of Cuyo should be transferred to Buenos Aires. Ill advised by its own passions, however, this party indulged in excessive and unjust criticism.

Confronted by the necessity of opposing resistance to the invasion of the eastern guerillas into Brazilian territory, the Portuguese army under the command of General Lecor, invaded the territory of the Banda Oriental in September, 1816. Artigas and Rivera went out in defense of the autonomy of that region, but they were defeated. This event aroused excitement in Buenos Aires, which demanded immediate intervention by the director, and requested that, if necessary, a declaration of war should be made against Portugal.

On January 20, 1817, General Lecor and his army entered the

---

[3] Porteño was the name given to a person born in the port of Buenos Aires. —W.S.R.

city of Montevideo. Director Pueyrredón sent him various notes to protest against this foreign invasion of an Argentine province. Brazil replied by declaring that if the Banda Oriental was an Argentine province, the government of Buenos Aires should prevent the invasions which Artigas and the guerrillas were making into Brazilian territory. As the Argentine government did not assume an energetic attitude, the Portuguese army remained in possession of the territory on the lower east bank of the Uruguay. Nevetheless, the Uruguayans, led by Rivera and Artigas, defended their native land, and won some successes.

We have stated that the monarchical spirit of the leading men and of congress furnished a stimulus and a pretext for the uprising of the towns and the provinces against the capital. The party of opposition, assuming the character of a democratic party, carried on a campaign of criticism against the government of Pueyrredón based on the belief that he intended to bring over a foreign prince to govern the country. This censure went so far that the supreme director decided to exile Manuel Dorrego, with the explanation that, despite the personal merits and talents which Dorrego had displayed, the government exiled him because his presence during a discussion of the political problems of the age was perilous. As the editors of *La Crónica Argentina* continued their campaign against the government, Pueyrredón was authorized to deport Agrelo, Feliciano A. Chiclana, Manuel Moreno, General French, and Colonels Pagola and Valdenegro to North America.[4]

The struggle between monarchical and republican ideas was carried on from opposite camps. The monarchists were the leading members of the government and of congress who advocated this program as a means to guarantee peace and to promote the organ-

---

[4] The most striking illustration of monarchial tendencies in Buenos Aires is found in the secret mission to Europe of José V. Gómez, which was authorized in October, 1819, by Director Pueyrredón. To the French minister of foreign affairs, Baron Dessolle, Gómez broached the project of establishing a monarchy in La Plata under a prince of an European dynasty. It seems that Dessolle favored placing the Duke of Lucca upon a throne at Buenos Aires. In November, 1819, the congress of La Plata decided to accept Dessolle's proposal on certain conditions, but meanwhile, this French diplomat had changed his mind and the scheme was abandoned. See C. A. Villanueva, *Historia de la República Argentina* (2 vols. Paris, 1914), I, 161-65; and Dessolle to D'Osery, May 22 and August 6, 1819, Archives du ministère des affaires étrangères, correspondance politique, Russie, vol. 159.—W. S. R.

ization of the country. The democratic party had no definite form, but it was latent in society; all were democrats, perhaps without having a clear and consistent idea concerning the democratic form of government, but with the instinct and the sentiment of democratic organization. The people believed that the complement of the work of 1810 was the establishment of a republic; and the motive of the revolution was explained only for the purpose of dethroning a king, in order to declare themselves sovereign, and not for the purpose of enthroning another king. The propaganda carried on by the editors of *La Crónica Argentina* was supported by popular sentiment. From this fact sprang the unpopularity resulting from the act of Director Pueyrredón who had decreed the exile of the leading chiefs of the opposition.

In the year 1814, Director Posadas gave the status of autonomous provinces to the districts of Corrientes and Entre Ríos, which up to this time, in conjunction with the Banda Oriental, had formed the eastern province of the Río de la Plata. In the autumn of 1818, when Estanislao López was governor, the district of Santa Fe had declared itself autonomous. These three provinces responded to the direct influence of the caudillo, Artigas, who was designated the "protector of the free peoples." In conjunction with Córdoba, they had opposed the convocation of the congress of Tucumán and had sent their representatives to a congress which had been assembled by Artigas in the city of Paysandú.

In 1817, in the province of Entre Ríos, the chieftain Eusebio Hereñú, who was under the influence of the partisans of Artigas, rose against the protector. But the leading chieftain of Entre Ríos was Francisco Ramírez, who on various occasions routed the army of Buenos Aires. In the province of Corrientes the ascendancy of Artigas was also manifest. The supreme director tried to destroy this influence but without success. Lastly, in the province of Santa Fe, a civil war had also begun, for the reason that Buenos Aires to which it had been subordinated would not acknowledge the autonomy of the province. Armies under the command of Viamonte and Díaz Vélez had left the capital city for the purpose of subjugating the insurrection, but as they were defeated by the soldiers of Santa Fe, the province realized its aspiration of becoming autonomous and designated Estanislao López as governor.

In the face of this anarchy in the Argentine littoral, the director

asked General San Martín to bring to Buenos Aires the army with
which he had won the victory of Maipú; but San Martín disobeyed
the order, determined as he was to consecrate his forces to the task
of independence. The director also summoned to his aid the army
of Belgrano in order that it might attack Santa Fe in conjunction
with General Balcarce and the chieftain, Juan Bautista Bustos,
of Córdoba. Estanislao López defeated Bustos at Fraile Muerto,
and the civil war continued until 1819 when a peace treaty was
signed.

In the beginning of 1817, after the congress had uselessly discussed in Tucumán a monarchical form of government, it decreed
that the government should be transferred to Buenos Aires. In the
end of that year it promulgated a "provisional regulation for the
direction and administration of the state." As congress proposed
to frame a constitution, it announced that until that fundamental
law was sanctioned the provisional regulation should be in force.
In this statute it was provided that the executive power should
be vested in a director of state who should be chosen by the outgoing
director from lists of persons prepared by the cabildos of each
province. The provisional regulation of 1817 embodied many of
the provisions contained in the provisional statute of 1815.

On April 22, 1819, congress promulgated a constitution which
was sanctioned with patriotic enthusiasm on May 25 of that year.
This constitution was of a unitary character, that is to say, it
organized a centralistic government to which the provinces were
to be subordinated. In addition, the government had an aristocratic
tendency. This double character is explained if it is borne in mind
that the majority of the members of congress were monarchists
who although they professed monarchical ideas had discarded that
system of government in view of the violent opposition which it had
provoked and had sanctioned a constitution, which if it was not
monarchical, was not democratic, and hence could not satisfy the
general aspirations.

The executive authority created by the constitution of 1819
was exercised by a director, who was elected by the two houses of
the legislature acting jointly. The director was to exercise his
functions for five years, and might be reëlected once. The legislative department was bicameral: the house of representatives was to
be composed of deputies elected in the ratio of one for every 25,000

inhabitants or a fraction of not less than 16,000; the senate was to consist of a member for each province, three military officers who at least enjoyed the rank of colonel, a bishop and three priests, and a member for each university. The littoral provinces refused to swear obedience to the constitution. The fact that a unitarian constitution had been promulgated which was at variance with the federalistic tendencies of the provinces became the pretext for civil war and anarchy.

In the same year as that in which congress undertook the task of framing a constitution for the country, Argentine society was afflicted by grave evils.[5] It was thrown into anarchy by a movement of inorganic democracy, which broke out as an explosive and disintegrating force without any clear, conscious, or definite aspiration—a natural and spontaneous movement which it was impossible to avoid because of the nature of the constitution. In fine, it was federalism in fact, which existed as a social force, and which had to be recognized in any project of political organization. All the provinces were agitated and impelled by an autonomist sentiment; Santa Fe, which was a dependency of the province of Buenos Aires, had aspired to become a province and had revolted several times before being acknowledged as such in 1818. The province of Córdoba had declared its independence and had joined the federal league of Artigas. La Rioja, which was a dependency of Córdoba, had likewise seceded and established its autonomy; Salta enjoyed its autonomy, incarnated in Güemes; Upper Peru had been lost after the defeat at Sipe-Sipe; while Entre Ríos and Corrientes had yielded to the sway of Artigas, and, with the Banda Oriental, formed a confederation of states.

Such was the political condition of the country that demanded a federalistic régime at the very juncture when congress assembled in Buenos Aires sanctioned a unitary and aristocratic constitution. From 1813 to 1820, the political organization of the country was notably altered. Within the pre-existing divisions, new organic entities were created that became the basis of the existing provinces.

After the separation of Paraguay from the viceroyalty of La Plata in 1811, the first decree regarding the creation of new provinces was promulgated in 1813, and was signed by the triumvirate.

---

[5] Regarding the anarchical effects of the early revolution upon society in the former viceroyalty of La Plata, see Mitre, *Historia de Belgrano*, III, 29-31.

This decree provided that the provinces of Mendoza, San Juan, and San Luis, which had formed part of the intendancy of Córdoba, should constitute a separate intendancy with its capital at Mendoza. This political reform was not based on the problems relating to federalists and unitarians, which developed subsequently, but arose from the necessity of organizing at Cuyo a government vested with authority ample enough to guard the frontier.

On March 7, 1814, Director Posadas created the eastern province in the belief "that the territory of the Banda Oriental, because of its extent, fertility, topographic condition, and increased population, should form by itself a constituent part of the state." Several months later—in October of the same year—Posadas created the provinces of Entre Ríos and Corrientes (the last-named included the towns of the mission region) by separating them from the intendancy of Buenos Aires. This reform was in response to the need of opposing an energetic opposition to the influence of the partisans of Artigas, which was in conflict with the national authority in the littoral provinces.

On October 8, 1814, the intendancy of Salta was divided into two parts: the province of Tucumán was formed by including the territory under the jurisdiction of the cities of Tucumán, Santiago del Estero, and Catamarca; while the province of Salta retained the cities of Salta, Jujuy, Orán, Tarija, and Santa María. In addition, mention must be made of the resolutions of the cabildos of the respective cities which transformed the former dependencies into separate provinces. "This transformation," says González, "was in progress from 1817 to 1820, at the end of which period Santa Fe, Santiago, San Luis, San Juan, Catamarca, and La Rioja remained definitely separated, with their own officials and laws. The province of Jujuy was organized in 1834. But it should be remembered that in the acts of separation of each one of these provinces the intention was expressed that they would continue to form a part of the Argentine nation, free, independent, and regulated by a constitution that should be the result of the will and the sentiment of all the towns that formed a part of it." [6]

---

[6] J. V. González, *Manuel de la constitución argentina* (Buenos Aires, 1897), p. 53.

CHAPTER XXXVI

ANARCHY

LATENT CIVIL WAR existed on the coast of Argentine territory. We have noticed that, stimulated by the influence of the chieftain Artigas, the provinces of Entre Ríos, Corrientes, and Santa Fe manifested a spirit of opposition to the government of Buenos Aires. In such a delicate situation, Director Pueyrredón had been obliged to ask the support of the army of San Martín that was in Chile, and of the army of Belgrano that was in Tucumán. Nevertheless, in April, 1819, a treaty of peace had been signed with the chieftain López of Santa Fe, which indicated for a moment that peace would not be broken.

But it was not so. At this juncture the Chilean, José Miguel Carrera, returned from the United States, and desired Director Pueyrredón to support his project of organizing an army for the liberation of Chile. Pueyrredón properly declined to support Carrera, as the Argentine Army of Liberation under the command of San Martín had already crossed the Andes. This decision enraged Carrera and he thereupon made overtures to the Argentine general, Carlos de Alvear, who, exiled since 1815, desired to get control of the government of Buenos Aires. These two men set on foot a movement of hostility and of resistance to the government of Pueyreedón. They proceeded to Entre Ríos where they converted the chieftain Francisco Ramírez to their views; next they converted López of Santa Fe. They induced both of these leaders to decide in favor of war.

As the constitution of 1819 had been sanctioned, and, as he felt that he did not have enough energy to dominate the anarchy that distracted the country, at the end of his term of office Pueyrredón presented his resignation. Congress did not at once accept it; but as the director expressed his desire to resign a second and a third time, the resignation was accepted on June 11, 1819, and General Rondeau was appointed provisional director. The chieftains of the riparian provinces were ready to declare war on Buenos Aires. In the month of October, 1819, a wagon caravan dispatched by the government of Buenos Aires, and conducted by Marcos Balcarce and other commissioners of that government, crossed the province of Santa Fe. The chieftain López adopted a hostile attitude and seized the commissioners. Moved by the same spirit, Ramírez supported the proceedings of López, and war was declared upon Buenos Aires.

This war of the guerrillas of the riparian provinces against Buenos Aires was the result of both incidental and fundamental causes. The fundamental causes consisted in the division existing between the provinces and Buenos Aires, in the opposition between provincials and porteños that had a circumstantial basis, namely, the fact that the government of Buenos Aires wished to deliver the country to foreign princes, thus thwarting one of the objects of the May Revolution which was the formation of a republic. Another fundamental cause of the war was the unitarian charter which congress had just promulgated, a constitution that ignored the autonomistic tendency of the provinces which was consecrated to a *de facto* federalism. The chieftain, Ramírez, addressed a proclamation to the people in which he declared that the war against Buenos Aires had for its object the removal of despots from the government, in order to reëstablish the liberty of the people and the equality of the citizens, and also to put an end to the Portuguese invasion of the Banda Oriental.[1] The chieftain, López, made a similar exposé of his motives. And the interior provinces of Córdoba, San Luis, San Juan, and Mendoza adhered to this movement headed by the riparian provinces, thus rejecting the unitarian constitution of 1819.

The incidental causes of this conflict were owing to the mistaken policy of conciliation which Buenos Aires had followed in regard to Santa Fe and Entre Ríos, as well as to the revolutionary agitation which Carrera and Alvear had provoked by getting the support of López and Ramírez. Equipped for war, the army of guerrillas numbered 1,500 men under the command of Ramírez who stationed himself near a stream named Pavón.

Provisional Director Rondeau directed General San Martín, as Pueyrredón had done previously, to bring his army to the defense of the capital. Rondeau made the same request with regard to the army of Belgrano which was at Tucumán. San Martín repeated

---

[1] An iconoclastic article on Ramírez by M. Leguizamón entitled "El caudillo Ramírez," is found in *La Nación*, Buenos Aires, September 23, 1923.

his disobedience; for he had devoted his energies to the higher task of establishing independence. The army of Tucumán obeyed the order but, because of the illness of General Belgrano, it marched under the command of General Cruz. At the post named Arequito, on the boundary of the province of Córdoba, an uprising occurred which bears the name of that post. This uprising was led by General Bustos and the commandant, José M. Paz, who proceeded with the troops to the city of Córdoba where the former had himself proclaimed governor. From this mutinous army there emerged Ibarra, who soon became the chieftain for life of Santiago del Estero. To justify the uprising of Arequito, an assembly of deputies in the city of Córdoba declared "that as a free and sovereign province, Córdoba did not acknowledge dependence on, nor subordination to, any other province; that it considered as one of its chief duties the fraternity and union of all the provinces and the closest relations with them all, until, assembled in a general congress, they might frame the treaties of a true federation in peace and war to which they aspired in conformity with the people of the other provinces."

The provinces of the interior supported the uprising of Arequito, and announced that their political relations with the capital were dissolved. After the revolt of the Army of the North at Arequito, Director Rondeau, aided by the city of Buenos Aires and the adjacent country, gathered an army of 2,000 men, which he stationed in the glen of Cepeda. On February 1, 1820, occurred the battle of that name, which was of great influence in the civil war. The army of Buenos Aires was vanquished. A division of one thousand men commanded by General Balcarce escaped, for he succeeded in withdrawing with it in safety to San Nicolás de los Arroyos.

The battle of Cepeda broke the last bond that existed between the interior provinces and the province of Buenos Aires. After the disaster, in the absence of Rondeau, the congress of Buenos Aires had named as his substitute Juan Pedro Aguirre, who merely summoned the militia of the capital and the adjacent country, which he placed under the command of General Soler. In this manner 3,000 men were gathered who were stationed at the bridge of Márquez, seven leagues distant from the city. After their triumph, the chieftains Ramírez and López were ready to enter into negotia-

tions for peace with the capital but on the condition that congress
and the directory should be dismissed. As a necessary result of this
demand, the national political régime was swept away. It is thus
clear that the war of Ramírez and López did not contemplate acts
of rapine; for if such had been their intention they would have
advanced to the capital. In order to justify his conduct, Ramírez
also demanded as a condition of entering into peace negotiations,
that the secret acts of congress should be published. When this request was fulfilled, it was discovered that congress had supported
the project of founding a monarchy in the Río de la Plata, not by
the coronation of a prince of the Braganza dynasty, as the chieftains (caudillos) had believed, but by the coronation of a member
of the House of Bourbon, the Duke of Lucca. In regard to the incident Pelliza makes the following comment: "For this service, the
democracy is indebted to the rude guerrillas of the littoral provinces. The directorate and the congress, which included the persons
most distinguished in the country for their intelligence, carried on
the mysterious policy that the publication of the secret acts made
known to the people, and without that struggle which thwarted
the plans of the legislature, nothing would have checked its members in their erroneous and fatal policy of establishing a monarchy." [2]

Upon the abolition of the directorial régime and the dissolution
of congress, the cabildo was invested with authority until such time
as a governor of the province should be designated. For this purpose the cabildo summoned the citizens to meet in its hall at five
o'clock on the afternoon of February 16. At the time set there
assembled in cabildo abierto three hundred persons, including the
best citizens of the neighborhood. The object of the meeting was
"to elect a provincial government which, having been chosen by a
free election, would enjoy the public confidence demanded by the
circumstances and by the treaties that were being arranged with
the federal army." Aguirre, the alcalde of the cabildo, was chosen
to preside over the popular assembly. One of the citizens present
proposed that, in order to designate the governor, each citizen
should vote for twelve candidates and that those persons who re-

---

[2] Pelliza, *op. cit.*, I, 478. [By the term "littoral provinces" Argentine writers
concerned with this period of their history generally mean the provinces of
Buenos Aires, Santa Fe, Entre Ríos, and Corrientes.—W. S. R.]

ceived the majority of votes should constitute "the junta representative of the people." The functions of this junta should be to appoint the governor of the province, and to propose the measures which would lead to an honorable pacification. "Thus it was," said the historian Mitre, "that the right of representation was inaugurated under the auspices of a *de facto* federation." Two hundred and twenty-two citizens took part in the election which resulted in the choice of the junta of representatives composed of twelve electors who had received the largest number of votes. This junta assembled on the following day to choose the governor. It selected Manuel Sarratea who was proclaimed as the first governor and captain general of the province of Buenos Aires.

At the place called Pilar a treaty of peace was framed between Governor Sarratea and the chieftains of the riparian provinces, López and Ramírez. Article I provided that in sixty days the deputies of the three contracting provinces should assemble, and that they should invite the other provinces to send deputies to the congress which was to form a federal scheme of government. Article IV established the free navigation of the rivers Paraná and Uruguay for the three signatory powers. Article V offered amnesty to political offenders. Article VII declared that the members of the preceding administration must answer for their conduct in a public hearing before a tribunal appointed for that purpose. Lastly, it was agreed that the small squadron of the Paraná, a large quantity of accoutrements, and 250,000 pesos should be transferred to Ramírez.

This treaty further enunciated two fundamental principles: (1) the signatory provinces were recognized as autonomous, and hence accepted the principle of "federalism"; (2) these provinces considered themselves as an integral part of the nation; they agreed to send deputies to a national congress, and thus they accepted the principle of "nationality."

The Treaty of Pilar was not altogether favorably received by the public opinion of the province of Buenos Aires. The first person to rebel was General Balcarce, who, as we know, had saved his division of the army at the battle of Cepeda. Balcarce and his friends violently protested against the convention. They congregated in the Plaza de la Victoria and asked for the convocation of a cabildo abierto which was granted to them. After that assembly had discussed the conduct of Governor Sarratea, it resolved to remove him from office. Assuming the functions of the junta of representatives, to which pertained the right to designate Sarratea's successor, the people named Colonel Juan Ramón Balcarce as governor.

Upon hearing that Sarratea had been deposed and that Balcarce had been made governor in his place, the chieftain Ramírez assumed a hostile attitude. Ramírez notified Balcarce that he would precipi- tate a civil war without any delay, and that the federal provinces would recognize no other governor than Sarratea. The latter was in Ramírez's camp whence he addressed a summons to the militia of the country. Balcarce, who was preparing to make a defense of the city, published a manifesto inviting the people to assemble in the Plaza de la Victoria. But the federal army was more power- ful, not only because it was led by López, Ramírez, and Sarratea, but also because General Soler supported it. On March 11, this army marched to the Plaza de la Victoria, and the deposed Sarra- tea again assumed the duties of governor.

Carrera had succeeded in assembling six hundred Chilean soldiers with whom, after the restoration of Governor Sarratea, he had encamped at Chacarita for the purpose of engaging in a campaign for the liberation of Chile. On the night of March 25, in conjunc- tion with Carrera, Alvear ordered Generals Soler and French, and Colonel Berutti, the chief leaders who supported the authority of Sarratea, to be seized. After this coup, General Alvear sent a note to the chieftain (caudillo) Ramírez asking for his protection in the position of general in chief of the army of Buenos Aires. Meantime, the cabildo had assembled and decided that, without losing a moment, Governor Sarretea should "force the revolting chieftain (Alvear) to lay down his arms; it ordered that he should leave the province as the only mode of compensating for his enor- mous errors." Realizing that he was without support, Alvear fled to Carrera's camp. On the following day, General Soler was re- stored to the command of the army of the city.

When he became aware of the tumult which we have mentioned, General Alvear had joined hands with Carrera and López. In the face of this new league of chieftains against the city of Buenos Aires, the situation of Governor Sarratea became difficult. Be- cause of the suit instituted against the members of the directorial government, the junta of representatives asked for the resignation of Governor Sarratea. When this was presented, the junta accepted it and appointed Ildefonso Ramos Mejía as provisional governor of Buenos Aires. Soler, who was the commander of the forces, believed for a moment that the junta would designate him as governor, and as it did not do so, he prepared for a new struggle. Irritated at finding that he was excluded from political office, and that military authority was being decreased in the army under his command, Soler presented his resignation. When this was accepted, and when Martín Rodríguez was selected to replace him, Soler refused to turn over the army; and the cabildo of Luján declared "that it was the general wish of all the country that he should be restored to the command of the army as captain general and that he should be accepted and recognized as governor." This petition was addressed to the junta of Buenos Aires at the same time that a delegation was sent to the cabildo of that city for the purpose of framing an agreement.

Governor Ramos Mejía who, because of the actions of Soler could no longer count upon the moral support of public opinion, now presented his resignation. The junta neither accepted nor rejected this resignation, but arranged that he should deposit the baton of command with the cabildo. "This was the famous day in the annals of anarchy of the year 1820," said the historian Mitre, "which has become known as 'the day of the three governors,' although no one of the three men was governor either in law or in fact." In truth, on June 20, the government of the province was managed by Ildefonso Ramos Mejía, General Soler, and the cabildo. By a melancholy coincidence, upon this day which marked one of the most critical junctures of Argentine anarchy, Manuel Belgrano died in Buenos Aires.

General Soler took charge of the government of the province on June 23. In his turn, as General Alvear counted on the alliance of López and the aid of Carrera, it did not seem to him difficult to seize the government of Buenos Aires. These two caudillos and General Carrera penetrated into the province of Buenos Aires. General Soler prepared to resist the invasion; on June 28, the soldiers of the riparian provinces advanced up to the glen of La Cruz where a battle took place. The result was disastrous for the army of the capital, and the vanquished Soler handed in his resignation as governor. In the town of Luján the victors assembled the representatives of the people of the north and designated General Alvear as governor.

The junta of representatives then chose Manuel Dorrego as governor and captain general. In consequence of the recent defeat at La Cruz and the earlier defeat at Cepeda, the army of the city was disorganized. Because of those defeats, the chieftains felt certain of the outcome. Dorrego reorganized the municipal forces, and advanced until he met the allied army of López, Carrera, and Alvear. At this moment, Juan Manuel de Rosas appeared at the head of six hundred cavalry and gave his valuable support to Colonel Dorrego. On August 2, in the city of San Nicolás, the first engagement took place between the forces of López and Dorrego, and the victory remained with Buenos Aires. Ten days later, on the banks of the rivulet Pavón, the guerrillas of López suffered another check. Negotiations for a reconciliation were initiated which gave López time to reorganize. On September 2, on the field of Gamonal, near Pavón, Dorrego was defeated and obliged to retire.

After the rout at Gamonal, alarm again spread among the people of Buenos Aires. On September 26, the junta of representatives designated Martín Rodríguez as governor, for the purpose of avoiding a new and bloody war with López and in order to celebrate a friendly treaty with the chieftains of the riparian provinces. On October 1, the troops of the garrison mutinied and imperiled the authority of the governor.[3] He summoned Commandant Rosas to his aid, who, at the head of a body of militia formed from the squadron of *Colorados del Monte,* marched toward the capital. The uprising was suppressed and General Rodríguez was able to count upon the aid of Rosas and Dorrego in operations against the caudillo López.

It was not difficult to bring about a pact of union between the provinces of Buenos Aires and Santa Fe; for everyone desired the termination of so fatal a war. On November 24, 1820, representatives of both provinces signed a treaty of peace by which those provinces agreed to promote the convocation of a congress in the province of Córdoba. General Bustos—a mediator between Rodrí-

---

[3] On this mutiny and the resulting movements, see C. Heras, "Iniciación del gobierno de Martín Rodríguez; el tumulto del 1° al 5 de Octubre de 1820," *Humanidades* (La Plata, 1923), VI, 263-86.

guez and López—had won from the treaty of peace the advantage
that the national congress was to assemble in the city of Córdoba.
At last Buenos Aires became tranquil. Governor Martín Rodríguez
was able to turn his whole attention to the maintenance of peace,
thus making possible the convocation of a national congress.

The Treaty of Pilar signed by Sarratea, governor of Buenos
Aires, and the chieftain Rodríguez had given the latter a great advantage. Artigas disapproved of the treaty. At the same time, he
fought the battle of Tacuarembó against the Portuguese forces
in the Banda Oriental. After the eastern chieftain was routed, he
took refuge in Entre Ríos with his scattered army which vanquished the army of López Jordán and Hereñú. Francisco Ramírez
passed rapidly to Entre Ríos to defend it against Artigas. At
Gauchas, Ramírez met a check; Artigas crossed the Gualeguay and
returned to attack Ramírez, but the latter defeated him and won
a fresh victory at Sauce de Luna. On July 29, Artigas was defeated
in a new battle and was obliged to flee to Paraguay where he was
confined by Francia.

The triumphs of Ramírez over the forces of Artigas had made
him so proud that he decided to attack Buenos Aires. Ramírez
asked permission of López to march through the province of Santa
Fe, which the latter denied because of a peace treaty that he had
signed with Governor Martín Rodríguez. This refusal caused war
between López and Ramírez. The chieftain of Entre Ríos crossed
the Paraná River and defeated La Madrid, who was marching to
join the army of López. But, at a town called Coronda, López defeated Ramírez, who, in conjunction with Carrera, proceeded to
Córdoba with the intention of attacking Bustos. The chieftain and
the governor of Córdoba then defeated Ramírez and Carrera at
Fraile Muerto. Ramírez retreated across the province of Córdoba,
but being pursued by the forces of López was again routed at San
Francisco near the River Seco. An enemy division overtook him,
and the chieftain of Entre Ríos lost his life.

Upon the death of Ramírez, Ricardo López Jordán assumed command of the province of Entre Ríos. López Jordán desired to
continue the policy of his predecessor. As a condition of peace the
government of Buenos Aires demanded of López Jordán that he
should return the squadron that the governor of the province of
Entre Ríos had retained, which would have ended his influence in

the province of Corrientes and opened the navigation of the Paraná River. López Jordán would not agree to such a demand, but Colonel Lucio Mansilla led an uprising in September, 1821, and was made governor of the province. Mansilla also strove to initiate a régime of freedom in the province of Corrientes. Under this salutary influence, the people of that province first selected Ramón de Atienza as their governor and then Juan José Blanco. The death of Ramírez and the political triumphs of Lucio Mansilla in Entre Ríos and Corrientes formed a basis for the pacification of the riparian provinces.

CHAPTER XXXVII

THE ECONOMIC LIFE OF THE PROVINCES

AT THE BEGINNING of the revolution the decree of Cisneros of November 6, 1809, opening the port of Buenos Aires for the exportation and importation of foreign products was in force. The revolutionary wars with Peru, Uruguay, and Paraguay had important economic consequences for that port. Thenceforth, the exchange of products of La Plata for the metals of Potosí and for the yerba mate and tobacco of Paraguay was interrupted.

On June 5, 1810, the junta framed a new scale of customs duties, in order to promote the exportation of hides. It levied a tax of four per cent in the nature of an alcabala, while various other imposts amounted to one and one-half per cent, besides one-half of one per cent as a war tax, that is to say a total of six and one-half per cent. Tallow and other pastoral products were to pay duties aggregating twelve per cent. The first report of the treasury was published in the *Gaceta* of July 19, 1810. It contained an account of the income and expenditures of the treasury from May 25 to June 30 of that year. The total income amounted to 615,394 pesos, and the expenditures came to 391,120 pesos, leaving a surplus of 224,274 pesos. Among the first liberal economic measures of the junta mention should be made of one that allowed the exportation of specie which had been prohibited.

During the year in which the revolution began, a financial deficit occurred in the public treasury, in consequence, on the one hand, of the heavy expenses which the government had to meet in order to promote the success of the movement, and on the other hand, of the interruption of commercial intercourse with certain provinces. This explains why on May 1, 1811, an order was promulgated providing for a forced loan to be raised from the Spaniards owing to the fact that Viceroy Elío had declared a blockade of the port of Buenos Aires. Further, at the end of that year, a reduction was ordered in the salaries paid to civil and military employees, which, in the latter class, affected those who were not in active service.

On September 4, 1812, the triumvirate signed a notable decree concerning immigration and colonization. "The government offers its immediate protection"—so this act declares in the explanatory phrases—"to persons of all nations and their families who wish to fix their domicile in the territory of the state and assures them the full enjoyment of the rights of man in society. . . ." To those foreigners who were engaged in the cultivation of the fields, the decree provided that "they shall be given sufficient land; they shall be given aid for their first rural establishments; and in the exchange of their products they shall enjoy the same privileges as the natives of the country." Finally, the vacant lands would be distributed gratuitously to those who should devote themselves to the mining industry, and they would be allowed the free importation of the implements necessary for the exploitation of minerals. This decree bears the signatures of Chiclana, Pueyrredón, and Rivadavia.[1]

The assembly of 1813 passed some measures of an economic character in order to combat the practice of extensive indivisible rural land holdings. For this purpose it suppressed entail and granted authority to the executive to distribute the public lands in "the manner that it judged the most convenient for the benefit of the state." In the year 1818, Director Pueyrredón minutely regulated the distribution of land. Vacant lands inside the frontier were granted to prospective settlers on condition that they should be settled within four months after the land was acquired. The extent of land granted was to be proportioned to the ability of the grantee to settle it. The government promised to protect the new proprietors against invasions by Indians. The congress of 1819 passed a law providing for the disposal of unoccupied lands in the provinces of Salta, Cuyo, Jujuy, Santiago, Catamarca, and Córdoba. Of such lands, Cárcano wrote: "These grants gave rise to many abuses. Extensive areas were claimed even within frontiers that were entirely safe. In the majority of cases the terms of settlement specified by the government were not fulfilled. . . . In the first period of independence the government was not able to use any other method than that of land grants for the settlement of its territories, especially on the frontier. The forces which it had available to check the Indians on three extensive frontiers were very small, while military police and the judicial system were not strong enough to compel respect for the law which was not enforced there." [2]

---

[1] *Registro oficial de la República Argentina,* I, 178.—W. S. R.

[2] M. A. Cárcano, *Evolución histórica del régimen de la tierra pública* (second edition, Buenos Aires, 1925), pp. 30-31.

In the middle of 1812, still under the influence of the heavy blow inflicted at Huaqui, the revolutionary government provided for an extraordinary tax upon capital in order to meet the pressing needs of the State. With this object it invoked the disinterestedness of the people, reminding them that without their financial support "the death of the country would be inevitable." The total contribution amounted to 638,030 pesos, distributed as follows:

Merchants, shopkeepers, and artisans, including
foreigners 228,000
Resident proprietors 163,579
Warehouse keepers, grocers, and so on 100,000
Bakers 37,200
Upon wheat 40,000
Apothecaries and druggists 3,000
Four reales upon each head of cattle consumed 54,250
Cafés, billiard halls, confectionaries, taverns, inns,
pastry shops, and chocolate shops .... 12,000[3]

After the victory of Salta, which brought as a consequence the reconquest of a part of Upper Peru, the assembly of 1813 ordered that money of gold and silver, bearing new inscriptions, should be minted. On one side the coins were to be stamped with the seal of the assembly with the following inscription: "Provinces of the Río de la Plata" and, on the other side, the coins were to bear a sun with the legend "in union and liberty." In addition, the gold coins were to bear military trophies. At first, the people were inclined to oppose the circulation of the new money, either because of economic or political motives. Hence, the government issued another decree providing penalties for those persons who refused to accept the new coins.

In July, 1813, the assembly decreed that a forced loan should be raised for the purpose of constructing and arming ships of war. According to this decree, the capitalists were to furnish the sum of 500,000 pesos by way of a loan. To each contributor there should be given a promissory note bearing the seal of the state and signed by the government. After two months, these notes were to be accepted in the payment of debts, and at the end of six months they were to be received as if they were actual money. At the expiration

[3] E. Hansen, *La moneda argentina* (Buenos Aires, 1916), p. 144.

of a year, they were to be redeemed upon presentation. "This law was noteworthy, . . . because it contained the true germ of a paper currency, and it was the embryo of the fiduciary currency that played so important and interesting a rôle in Argentine evolution." [1]

About the end of 1818, there was created the funding bank of South America which was the basis of the banking institutions of the country. This bank had a capital of three million pesos. It received on deposit notes of amortization or certificates of the treasury, paying a high rate of interest. In exchange for these deposits were issued certificates that were evidences of permanent debt, for no provision was made for their amortization. As is clear, the object of this establishment was to unite and consolidate the numerous certificates of indebtedness which the government had issued to individuals in the course of the forced loans, transforming them into a long term debt. In 1821, the funding bank of South America was suppressed and the bank of discount was founded.

We have already explained that the provinces of the viceroyalty had developed their own resources and industries. With the opening of the port of Buenos Aires to commerce, the interior of the country was much injured, for its manufactures could not compete in price with foreign products. Wines from the provinces of Cuyo did not reach the markets of the coast where foreign wines, which sold at lower prices, were consumed. The rice industry of the province of Tucumán was seriously injured because of the competition of Brazil with the sugar industry of Jujuy. The cloth manufactures of Córdoba, Catamarca, and Corrientes were easily driven from the markets by English goods. In 1817, Bishop José Eusebio Colombres founded the sugar industry in Tucumán.

On their part, Buenos Aires and the coast aided in the appraisement of the products of pastoral industry. In 1812, the government declared that the exportation of meat should be free of duty, which promoted the industry of salting meat. "Thus it happened," asserted Álvarez, "that the most important part of the steer was its flesh, and the issue was raised whether the gauchos of the riparian provinces should continue to consume it gratis or whether it should be sold, for the profit of the ranchers, to the slaveowners of Brazil, Africa, and the Antilles. The custom of hunting cattle

---

[1] *Ibid.*, p. 163.

without any other charge than that of giving the hides to the owner of the ranch, came to be replaced by that of laboring some months in the meat-salting establishments and of purchasing meat with the wages at the price set by foreign consumers. The business of salting meat became a capitalistic enterprise and the entrepreneurs did not think of recognizing the gauchos as partners." [5] As the years passed the unprecedented rise in the price of meat reached such a point that during the age of the directorate Pueyrredón decreed that the meat-salting establishments should be closed.

The problem of the Indians and their penetration into the territory colonized by the Spaniards had been serious during the entire colonial era. The viceroys listened to the appeals of the ranchers and took steps to protect their property. Viceroy Melo de Portugal commissioned Félix de Azara to make a study of the frontiers of the viceroyalty, in order to restrain the frequent irruptions of the barbarous Indians. Azara concluded that it was not necessary to increase the number of forts and posts upon the frontiers and that the only efficacious means to assure the tranquillity of the settlements was "to divide the landed estates." [6] In order to supplement this report, we should mention that the census of 1778 showed that La Plata had a rural population of 12,925.

Despite the numerous and urgent problems that it had to solve, the first patriot government considered the agrarian problem with much care. In the general archives of the Argentine Nation there exists a decree in the handwriting of Mariano Moreno directing Colonel Pedro Andrés García to lead an expedition to the frontier. It was stated in that document that the object of this mission was not purely military but also economic; for it was to propose measures that would promote the distribution of lands as well as their settlement.

About the end of 1811, Colonel García made a report to the effect that the forts did not perform any function whatsoever, and that settlement had already extended from twenty to sixty leagues farther south. In order to safeguard the defenseless situa-

---

[5] J. Álvarez, *Estudio sobre las guerras civiles argentinas* (Buenos Aires, 1914), p. 98.

[6] Angelis, *op. cit.*, V, 57-87, prints the diary of Azara's tour of the frontier of the viceroyalty.

tion in which so many settlers found themselves, García proposed that a new frontier line should be drawn. In this very year, numerous Indian chiefs had been received in Buenos Aires by the triumvirate as a sign that the new government was disposed to maintain peaceful relations with the aborigines. Colonel García made subsequent studies of the frontier. All of these emphasized the necessity of pushing the frontier southward to the Río Colorado or to the Río Negro.[7]

---

[7] On the need of frontier defense at this time, see further, V. G. Quesada, "Las fronteras y los Indios," *La Revista de Buenos Aires* (Buenos Aires, 1864), V, 197-98.

CHAPTER XXXVIII

ANARCHY

THE ANARCHIC dénouement of the events of 1820 has been studied; and it is now necessary to point out some of the features of so dramatic and suggestive a picture. In the ten years that had passed since the May Revolution took place, Buenos Aires had been the scene of successive and violent convulsions of internal politics. Though some attempts at national organization had been made, yet in 1820 the country was in a state of social and political decomposition. If one desires to discern the nature of the phenomena that agitated society at this time, he must observe that the anarchy of the government and of the parties or factions that were struggling for power was merely an external manifestation, and that in the background of this epoch there was profound economic, moral, and political anarchy. As one author asserted:

"The torment which had been caused by the influence of the democratic and republican spirit, the social semi-barbarism of our country districts, the immense distances separating the capital cities of the provinces, and the poverty they suffered, were in sharp contrast with the concentration in the city of Buenos Aires of all the resources and leaders that could give direction and power to the revolutionary movement. Because of the fatal necessity of the situation, and because of the effect of that constitutional vice which still hindered the emancipation and the development of the life of the republic, Buenos Aires had to usurp, so to speak, the sovereign function of directing the other peoples and of imposing a tyrannical military government, in order to unite them in a common effort against the repeated attempts of Spain to regain the lost empire of its colonies." [1]

In truth, after 1810, Buenos Aires tended to absorb the entire life of the country. This policy of predominance was the result of two facts: one fact was economic, for Buenos Aires possessed the port of entry and exit of all the products, thus assuring its wealth and commercial superiority. The other fact was political, for Buenos Aires had produced the revolution; and that city had to

---

[1] V. F. López, "El ano XX," *Revista del Río de la Plata* (Buenos Aires, 1872), IV, 580-81.

Upper, Gauchos of Tucumán.   Lower, The Great Square of Buenos Aires.
Both from Vidal, *Picturesque Illustrations of Buenos Aires
and Montevideo.*

spread it throughout the entire territory of the viceroyalty and to assure independence, for which a strong public and military power had to be established. For their part, the provinces had possessed their own traits and life since the colonial era. When the revolution began they were imbued with the spirit of sacrifice, once they became aware of its finality; thus they were autonomous entities that also possessed the right of self-government. And from the shock of this collision between the preponderance of Buenos Aires and the provincial autonomies, there resulted the political crisis and the anarchy of 1820. The battle of Cepeda, which was won by the chieftains López and Ramírez against Supreme Director Rondeau, signified the triumph of the provincial autonomies, of federalism *de facto*, in opposition to the directorial régime of Buenos Aires.

The domination of Buenos Aires over the provinces was imposed by circumstances and by the necessity of assuring the definitive emancipation of the country. When the governments of Buenos Aires felt themselves shaken to their foundations by the resistance set up by the provinces, its thinking men had the fickleness to believe that the only way to secure internal peace and political organization was to crown a king. The resistance of the parties and factions of the provinces, of the social mass which did not think but which felt, thus became more powerful and irresistible; civil war broke out, and the directorial and monarchical government of Buenos Aires was defeated at Cepeda. This is the other significance of the battle fought between the riparian chieftains and Director Rondeau; Cepeda represents, besides the triumph of the provinces over Buenos Aires, the triumph of the sentiment and democratic instinct of the mass over the monarchical formula of government proposed by the directing nucleus of the country.

The democracy, accordingly, emerged victorious in 1820. It emerged "barbarous but fecund," said the historian Estrada. "Fecund, I say, because it was an assertion of democracy as the immutable formula of our political being; barbarous, because the social nucleus which produced it was barbarous, because its methods were barbarous and the roads into which it drove the people were bloody." [2]

---

[2] J. M. Estrada, *La política liberal bajo la tiranía de Rosas* (Buenos Aires, 1917), pp. 30-31.

To discover the origin of the problems arising from the political organism of the country, it is necessary to revert to the colonial era. In fact, as we have already explained, rooted in the three centuries that had passed were two powerful historical forces which were active after 1810: the democratic current, and the federal current. The democratic current was formed by the prevailing sentiments of colonial society: "the cult of courage," which was the sentiment of force and self-defense, and "a disdain for the law" which was the instinct of rebellion against established authorities.[3] The federal current was also rooted in the colonial period. The territory of La Plata was very extensive, and within its limits the colonists founded the first cities, which were widely separated, and without means of communication or contact. Thus, these cities grew up by themselves; they were nourished by their own vigor; and by their own force they defended themselves against the frequent invasions of Indians. The cities had their own authorities, and among all those organs that aided in the formation of the nascent peoples the cabildo was the most expressive. In this manner the foundations of Argentine federalism were laid, that is to say, the basis of an autonomy in which the early history of the provinces was rudimentary and purely *de facto*.

After 1810 these two historical currents, the turbulent democracy, and the federal democracy became stronger and stronger. The federal current made more definite the profile of the provinces; it also created new provinces. All the provinces refused to delegate the supreme authority to Buenos Aires. The sentiment of autonomy was the impulse that moved the provinces to disobedience and resistance, when the congress, which had assembled in Buenos Aires, adopted the unitarian constitution of 1819. After 1810 the current of turbulent democracy produced successive and violent crises of the patriot governments. Such crises were the precursors of the political anarchy of 1820; they were less intense but they are historical antecedents which illustrate and explain events that happened later.

The crises of the patriot governments from 1810 to 1820 were as follows: (1) the conference of December 18, 1810, from which resulted the incorporation of the provincial deputies into the governmental junta, in opposition to the ideas of Mariano Moreno

---

[3] García, *La ciudad indiana*, p. 11.

who had supported the view that the provincial deputies should constitute by themselves the legislative authority. (2) The uprising of April 5 and 6, 1811, in which the populace of the suburbs thronged to the Plaza de la Victoria to demand and to secure the removal of the morenista deputies who belonged to the junta. (3) After the battle of Huaqui the great junta was dissolved; its members then constituted the junta of observation; and the triumvirate was organized which represented the executive authority. That authority executed a coup d'état and dismissed the junta of observation, whose members were obliged to leave the capital within twenty-four hours. (4) The revolution of October 8, 1812, inspired by the Sociedad Literaria (Literary Society), which came to an end with the first triumvirate. (5) In 1814, the triumvirate was dissolved and a one-man executive power was constituted with the title of supreme director. Posadas, the director, resigned his position before the expiration of a year, in the midst of insuperable difficulties, among which the most important was the uprising of the Army of the North commanded by Rondeau. (6) After Posadas came Alvear. During his administration occurred the federal revolution of 1815 which was headed in Buenos Aires by Álvarez Thomas, the commander of the soldiers of the capital, a movement that was supported by the forces of the riparian provinces under the command of Artigas, by the forces of the north, under the command of Rondeau, and by the training school of the Army of the Andes under San Martín. The downfall of Director Alvear constituted the first interruption of the national government. The provisional statute promulgated in 1815 left to the provinces the authority to select their own officials and to govern themselves by their municipal régimes. This authorization, as may be imagined, was one of the most important and noteworthy provisions.

(7) In March, 1816, the national authority was recognized with the convocation of the congress of Tucumán and the selection of Pueyrredón as supreme director of the provinces of the Río de la Plata. Pueyrredón remained in office for three years. He aimed to put down political anarchy. In this he succeeded in a transient fashion, but it broke out violently after he left office. As we have thus explained, the political anarchy of 1820 was not an inexplicable event, but it has historical antecedents that explain it, enabling us to understand its true portent, which is that of an his-

torical phenomenon—the resultant of two powerful currents originating in the colonial epoch: the current of turbulent democracy, and the current of federal democracy. Let us quote Mitre again:

"The noisy fall of congress and the directorate stripped from the general government of the United Provinces the borrowed apparel in which it was clothed, and left naked the skeleton of the colonial régime whose flesh had been consumed by the fires of ten years of revolution. All vestiges of legal authority had disappeared. Not a single coherent institution remained intact. No principle of public law survived in the midst of that great shipwreck. All that was left was a nation independent in fact; a geographic and social constitution that was anterior and superior to written laws; a people who were politically disorganized, ruled by their instincts and by historical traditions or customary rules; a political association in embryo; a rudimentary federation. . . ." [4]

On that occasion, anarchy made evident the absolute absence of organic and progressive institutions. In ten years of free life, it had not been possible to create and consolidate the internal political régime. In this particular, the important bases had been laid by Mariano Moreno; by the first triumvirate, which enacted laws concerning personal guarantees, inviolability of property, and the promotion of agriculture, commerce, and public instruction; and by the general constituent assembly of 1813, which though it did not frame a constitution, did promulgate partial organic laws. Yet all these measures had failed to put the people into tranquil possession of their rights and their sovereignty. Without established institutions, created in the heat of new principles; without laws that disciplined the social instincts and sentiments; without a constitution that was adapted to the historic and geographic conditions of the country, it was natural and explainable that the anarchic movement of 1820 should demolish everything, should leave nothing in sight but a skeleton, and should throw to the winds authority and the national government.

The May Revolution was more intent upon destroying the colonial past than upon constructing the future. The political and administrative system founded in America by Spain was disturbed by the fierce wind of the Revolution of 1810 which aimed to uproot colonial institutions. It was necessary to undertake the urgent and

---

[4] Mitre, *Historia de Belgrano*, IV, 124-25.

difficult task of improvising institutions that would harmonize with the new spirit proclaimed by the revolution. But in the ten years that passed prior to 1820, the revolution had not been able to lay any better foundations; for it was disturbed by the pressing and grave question of independence. Thus, when the anarchy of 1820 broke out, the country found that the colonial régime, that is the economic and judicial institutions and, in part, the political institutions, was still intact. It further realized that the ethnographic composition of society had remained unaltered.

The new institutional and organic task announced by the revolution had been postponed. To this task the provincial governments applied themselves. In particular, the government of the province of Buenos Aires did so during the administration of Martín Rodríguez.

We have said that the federal current found its sources in the colonial era; for during its three centuries the regional autonomies were outlined. These historical antecedents formed the bases of a *de facto* federalism, that is to say, a condition in which the provinces constituted themselves by force of events as autonomous entities. When the guerrillas of the coast triumphed at Cepeda over the cultured city of Buenos Aires, all the provinces had their respective governors or chieftains, some of whom had been freely elected and others imposed by violence; but such governors were political exponents of provincial autonomy.

Upon the basis of this federalism *de facto*, there began to emerge at the opening of the revolution, a doctrinal federal party, that is, a party that advocated a federal government as a principle and device of national organization. The chief representatives of federalism were Manuel Dorrego and Manuel Moreno. Discussions of the theories and principles of federalism, which maintained that the country should be organized upon the basis of the autonomy of the provinces, and discussions concerning unitarianism, which maintained that the country should be organized upon the basis of the founding of a central government, took place, especially in the constituent congress which assembled at Buenos Aires in the end of the year 1824.

The anarchy of 1820 razed the few existing institutions and destroyed the national government. But in the midst of this political chaos, amid the commotion which the colonial past suffered by being displaced by a future that had to be reckoned with, even in the breast of this dissolving society, there existed latent, but powerful, the sentiment of nationality. This sentiment had been strengthened during the war for independence. Whatever was the condition of the interior, whatever the disputes and struggles between parties and factions, Buenos Aires and all the provinces devotedly cherished the ideal of independence. Aptly did San Martín speak, when he wrote to a deputy of the congress of Tucumán and affirmed that to declare the independence of the provinces of the Río de la Plata was easier than to decide many other matters which seemed much simpler. The doubts and fears of the first year of the revolution had vanished, and the sentiment in favor of independence had spread, despite the sacrifices and weariness of the people who were confronted by war.

In the beginning, the spirit of nationality consisted of the sentiment in favor of independence from Spain. The moral bond that linked together the inhabitants of the provinces of La Plata was composed of more than the desire for independence. This bond was the common organization; for all the provinces recognized that they were an integral part of the same state. An example that illustrates this statement is the Treaty of Pilar, framed immediately after the battle of Cepeda, in which the contracting parties, that is, the signatory provinces, agreed that as the civil war had terminated they should assemble in a congress to organize the country. Thus, in the very midst of the catastrophe which dissolved political society in 1820, there existed the feeling of nationality which was based upon the sentiment of independence and the existence of a common organization.[5]

---

[5] See J. N. Matienzo, *El gobierno representativo federal en la República Argentina* (Buenos Aires, 1910), pp. 47-48, where Napoleon is classed as a caudillo with Rosas.

CHAPTER XXXIX

THE GOVERNMENT OF RODRÍGUEZ

AFTER THE unusual changes which occurred in the government of Buenos Aires during the year 1820, and with the assurance of order and internal peace, Governor Martín Rodríguez was able to undertake the task of reorganizing the province which was under his command. A sign of the broad spirit animating the new governor was his appointment of Bernardino Rivadavia and Martín J. García as ministers. During this administration, and under the inspiration of its ministry, numerous organic reforms were undertaken, all of which tended to develop the political and institutional progress of the province. Such a reorganization of the province of Buenos Aires was significant because it initiated the plan of reconstruction which served as an example to the other provinces. Solid bases were thus laid for the future organization of the entire country.

Ministers Rivadavia and García performed an important work by attending to all the tasks of government. They constituted a real ministerial power. The majority of these reforms were due to the initiative of Rivadavia. This illustrious patriot had returned to his native soil after eight years of residence in Europe. He had been impressed by the spectacle offered by the Old World, where the parliamentary régime had triumphed, that is to say, a political régime according to which the ministers who formed part of the executive authority, in order to remain in power, had to have a majority of the votes in the legislative chambers that directly represented the people. Full of patriotic enthusiasm, Rivadavia had desired to bring about a radical change in the society and government of the country, in order to place it upon a level with the most cultured and progressive nations.

The reforms undertaken during the administration of Martín Rodríguez may be classified as political, economic, military, ecclesiastical, educational, and social. In the front rank of the political reforms should be mentioned the organization of the junta of representatives. In the course of the revolutions of 1820 the government had been invested with extraordinary powers. When the province was restored to its normal condition, the government relinquished this authority. It proposed an electoral law increasing the number of representatives of the people upon the basis of universal suffrage and direct elections. It also arranged that the junta of representatives should have an "extraordinary and constituent" character.

One of the most generous laws enacted during this administration was "the law of amnesty." A complete forgetfulness was granted for all the passions and hatreds provoked by the heat of party struggle which had caused the exile of some Argentine citizens during the administration of Pueyrredón. Under the protection of this law those exiles were able to return to their country. The draft of this bill presented to the junta was preceded by a note which ran thus: "The people of the continent are independent: that they should be free and happy is the wish of this province. But in the meantime it appears that the province owes it to itself to terminate forever the era of revolution on the very day upon which the first attempt took place. In order to enjoy such melancholy sacrifices in the most complete fashion, they must be forgotten; the ingratitudes, the errors, or the weaknesses that degraded men or afflicted the people in so serious and famous an enterprise must no longer be remembered. On this account the government believes that it would be acting worthily in proposing upon this occasion the accompanying project of a law of amnesty." This law is one of the most glorious deeds of Minister Rivadavia.

For the purpose of insuring peace and union with the other provinces, in January, 1822, Governor Martín Rodríguez arranged a quadruple treaty with the provinces of Entre Ríos, Santa Fe, and Corrientes. According to the terms of this treaty the contracting provinces agreed to render mutual aid to one another and to influence the other provinces to enter the pact. In this "quadruple treaty" there was once more affirmed the two fundamental principles embodied in the Treaty of Pilar signed in 1820; first, the principle of federalism, for the signatory provinces were recognized as autonomous; and second, the principle of nationality, for the provinces were recognized as being an integral part of the same nation. A new collection of documents gives an account of the multiplicity and importance of the relations which the province of Buenos Aires maintained with the other provinces, thus keeping alive the sentiment of the unity of the nation.[1]

By another decree, Rivadava abolished the cabildo. He based this measure upon the fact that the disturbances and revolutions that occurred during the anarchy, had had this municipal institution as their stage. The cabildos had a secular tradition; during the colonial era they had exercised the important function of aiding the development of the towns. They had also served as an organ for the expression of the general will.

Near the end of the age of the viceroys, the cabildo began to acquire a great political preponderance over the other authorities. On February 10, 1807, the cabildo of Buenos Aires decided upon the arrest and expulsion of Viceroy Sobremonte. During this year and until the middle of 1808, a period in which Liniers had not yet been named viceroy, it was in reality the cabildo that exercised all the important governmental functions in the viceroyalty. On January 1, 1809, the regidors of the city of Buenos Aires proposed to depose Viceroy Liniers. In the days of the famous week in May, the cabildo considered how the nascent revolutionary movement might be suffocated. When, on May 25, in the face of popular pressure, it agreed to allow the establishment of the governmental junta, it reserved for itself a mass of attributes by virtue of which the new government was subjected to the vigilance and control of the cabildo. A few months after the May Revolution occurred the cabildo conspired against the junta and its members secretly swore to observe fidelity to the council of regency that had been formed in Spain. This action provoked Mariano Moreno to institute a criminal suit against the regidors which resulted in the imposition of fines and their exclusion from office. In all the subsequent political episodes (the revolutions of April 5 and 6, 1811, of October 8, 1912, of Fontezuelas in 1815, and during the scandal of 1820), the cabildo had intervened in an energetic and dominating manner. These reasons influenced Rivadavia to abolish the institution of the cabildo, which doubtless could have served as the basis of modern municipal life, had it confined itself to represent and to watch over the interests of the city. In Rivadavia's opinion the existence of the cabildo was incompatible with the existence of the

---

[1] *Documentos para la historia argentina,* XIII, *passim.*

junta of representatives; besides, in consequence of the general reform, he argued in favor of the separation of the police from the judicial authorities of the first instance.[2]

The economic reforms accomplished during this administration gave vitality and richness to the province of Buenos Aires. A loan of three million pesos fuertes was ordered to be floated in the London market for the purpose of constructing the harbor of the capital, establishing a municipal water supply, and founding three cities in harbors of the southern coast and of Patagonia. In order to guarantee the amortization and the payment of the interest of this loan the government encumbered the public lands. But in order that they should not be left sterile and unoccupied, the government conceived the system of emphyteusis, by virtue of which this land was leased for long terms.

Emphyteusis began to be used in 1822; and the national congress of 1826 enacted a suitable law. In the first place a prohibition was laid on the alienation of public land. Soon the idea was conceived, nevertheless, of placing it under cultivation. The law of 1826 provided that an emphyteutic contract should run for at least twenty years, that the lands should be appraised every ten years by juries composed of three or five residents, and that the rate or amount of rent which the lessee had to pay should be either eight per cent or four per cent of the appraisement, depending respectively upon whether the land was to be used for pastoral purposes or for the raising of cereals. According to this system the state always remained the owner of the land, but its function was only that of leasing a part of the land to an individual who might file legal notice of his desire to rent it. Finally, the agrarian policy practiced until the present was developed, that is, the sale or grant of land which had been evolved on a great scale by the latifundian system. Shortly after the introduction of the emphyteutic system, a very important economic and moral reform began in the plains of Buenos Aires. Some writers have even ventured to assert that the revolution of the south against Rosas was one of its effects.[3]

---

[2] C. Heras, "La supresión del cabildo de Buenos Aires," *Humanidades* (La Plata, 1925), XI, 445-85.

[3] On the system of landholding in Argentina, see the views of Tejedor and Mitre in Cárcano, *Evolución ristórica del régimen de la tierra pública*, pp. 68-69. See further, Coni, "Rivadavia y su obra colonizadora," *La Nota*, Buenos Aires, August 30, 1918.

In June, 1822, a law was passed creating the bank of discount. This institution began with a capital of 300,000 pesos. Its function was to attend to the needs of commerce and industry. Two years later, the activities of this bank began to be resented because of the extraordinary expenses caused by the war and because of the unfavorable commercial balance, that is, the excess of the total imports over the total exports, a condition that made necessary heavy exportation of gold. In 1826, the national bank was founded, which continued the functions of the old bank of discount. It carried on these functions, however, only with great difficulty. In 1836, during the reign of Rosas, the national bank was converted into the *casa de moneda* which had limited banking functions.

During the period of the war for independence and of the civil war important events had occurred in the army—the instrument of those wars—which demanded the attention of the government. Numerous chiefs and officers were retired from active service and pensioned, and thus inefficient or insubordinate soldiers were eliminated. The law concerning the pensioning and retirement of military men not only benefited them but left the government at liberty to organize the army with men of merit and culture.

After 1810, the Argentine clergy had remained without any immediate and superior authority. A large number of the members of the Hispanic-American Church embraced the cause of independence and enrolled in the revolutionary ranks. In the provinces of La Plata not only might there be mentioned many ecclesiastics who played prominent rôles in the revolution, but also a humble legion of clerics who carried on a silent work in favor of the revolutionary cause. These were the parish priests who, after performing mass, were accustomed to read to the communicants the articles that embodied the principles and ideals of independence.

In 1814, King Ferdinand VII was restored to the throne of Spain. Certain sovereigns of Europe formed the Holy Alliance. The object of this alliance was mutual defense against liberal and revolutionary movements by the people. With respect to Spain, the sovereigns promised to work together so that it should regain its lost American colonies.[4] At this juncture, the pope carried on a

---

[4] Although the king of Spain did address through France an appeal to the Holy Alliance to aid him in restoring his authority over the revolted colonies in America, yet no evidence has been found to show that the Holy Allies ever

propaganda by means of the Church; he ordered that Spanish-American priests should embrace the cause of the king under pain of excommunication. Many members of the American Church did not heed this mandate of their superior; hence they were excommunicated and loosed from pontifical authority. In this wise, without dependence upon either the pope or the temporal authority, members of the clergy became corrupt. For the welfare of the Church, it was necessary to purify the morals of the clergy. The sincere and energetic spirit of Rivadavia was dedicated to this work of regeneration.

The "ecclesiastical fuero" was abolished. This was the privilege enjoyed by members of the clergy by virtue of which crimes committed by a cleric were tried by ecclesiastical judges and not by civil judges. The tithe, the impost laid for the support of the clergy and the maintenance of the Church, was also abolished. By the ecclesiastical reform, persons less than twenty-five years of age were prohibited from taking religious vows. The number of friars in each monastery was set at thirty as a maximum and sixteen as a minimum. The monasteries belonging to the Bethlehemites were suppressed, and their real and personal property was confiscated to the State.

The reform of the Church provoked a strong protest from the clergy. A Catholic party began to be formed to oppose Rivadavia. The head of this party was Father Castañeda.[5] Nevertheless, Rivadavia had as collaborators in religious reform such ecclesiastics as Dean Funes and Agüero. In the press, Juan Cruz Varela carried on a propaganda in support of Rivadavia's ideas. The opposition party eventually brought together men of diverse political complexions and, led by Dr. Gregorio Tagle, they set on foot a conspiracy. The government learned of the move and undertook to thwart it, but before this was accomplished a clash occurred in the Plaza de la

---

entered into an agreement to subjugate Spanish America. The archives of the French government do not contain any trace of the so-called "Secret Treaty of Verona" which has been used to lend color to the view that in 1822 Austria, Prussia, Russia, and France intended to intervene in Spanish America. Among other places, the spurious treaty is found in Kosta-Bayo, *Historia de la vida y reinado de Fernando VII* (3 vols. Madrid, 1842), III, 21-23. *Cf.* Archives du ministère des affaires étrangères, correspondance politique, France, vol. 721.—W. S. R.

[5] An exact interpretation of these reforms is given by Carbia, *op. cit.*, XIV, 271.

Victoria. The conspirators marched with cries of "Long live religion! Death to the heretics!" Soon there arrived a crowd of priests wearing scapularies who exhorted the people to support the Catholic religion. But they were dispersed and taken prisoners; many of them were punished severely.

Rivadavia's reforms were also concerned with the moral and intellectual improvement of society. Within the bounds of the United Provinces there existed only one university, that of Córdoba. Its curriculum was eminently religious. Even during the colonial epoch Viceroy Vértiz y Salcedo had proposed to found a university in Buenos Aires. During his administration, Director Pueyrredón initiated measures to promote such a foundation. In consequence of the energetic measures of Minister Rivadavia these plans were later carried out during the administration of Rodríguez.

On August 12, 1821, the University of Buenos Aires was solemnly inaugurated. The general plan of the university was prepared by its first rector, Dr. Antonio Sáenz. The institution was organized in six departments: "preparatory studies, exact sciences, medicine, jurisprudence, sacred science, and elementary instruction" (for the primary schools existing in the capital and in the country were under its control). As Agustín Pestalardo wrote: "In this wise the university organization included all the grades of teaching, from the primary to the collegiate. Rivadavia thus carried out the plan which he had proposed: . . . the promotion of public education by a general system." [6] The university decided upon the methods and the texts that were to be used in the instruction of each subject. Its professors were to prepare the textbooks. This obligation was performed by not a few professors; we may mention the lessons in physical mathematics by Avelino Díaz, the course in philosophy by José Manuel Agüro, the course in civil law by Pedro Somellera, and the lessons in natural law and the law of nations by Dr. Antonio Sáenz. [7] To the new régime introduced into the primary

[6] A. Pestalardo, *Historia de la enseñanza de las ciencias jurídicas y sociales en la Universidad de Buenos Aires* (Buenos Aires, 1914), p. 35. See further, R. Levene, "El primer plan de estudios projectado para la Universidad de Buenos Aires y las escuelas de primeras letras," *Revista de la Universidad de Buenos Aires* (Buenos Aires, 1918), XXXVIII, 511-26.

[7] A survey of the condition of municipal schools in La Plata during the revolutionary epoch is found in Levene, "Un decreto del virrey Cisneros sobre

schools, which were now released from the jurisdiction of the
cabildo, Rector Sáenz gave his best efforts. From this viewpoint
the creation of the university involved a true educational reorganization.

In line with his idea of adopting a policy of centralization in all
its branches, Minister Rivadavia talked to the rector of the advantages which would result for the progress of learning if education
in all its grades "were to be inspected by the same persons and be
responsible to one single authority." In order to carry into practice so generic and abstract a proposition, Rector Sáenz, from
the very beginning, struggled against difficulties of every kind.
Going to the heart of the matter, he discussed the preparation of
an inventory of the existing educational material with the director
of primary instruction. A simple statement of this will serve to
disclose the condition of primary instruction better than any
eloquent discourse. There were found only a few books of reading,
writing, arithmetic, grammar, arithmetical tables, "an atlas with
various plates missing," and a large folio volume in French concerning the travels of a party in Spain, entitled *Viajes de la banda
por España* (*Journeys of the Band in Spain*). There was urgent
need of pencil cases, pointers, and catechisms dealing with the obligations of man and with Christian doctrine.

Still more serious were those difficulties of a financial character
which threatened to smother the nascent institution. The school
teachers protested against the reduction of salary to which they
had been subjected (from 600 pesos to 400) with an energy worthy
of the cause. Some mentioned in their petition that the cabildo had
subjected them "to a rigorous examination" in the expectation
that their salary would be 600 pesos. Others complained not merely
of the reduction in the emoluments, but also of the dismissal of their
assistants. They supported their views by pedagogical arguments.
They maintained that one master alone could not teach with success
one hundred pupils whom he was expected to instruct in reading,
writing, Castilian grammar, arithmetic, Christian doctrine, and
polite manners.

Rector Sáenz was endowed with singular strength. One by one
the difficulties were solved in the same year 1822. The rector had

---

instrucción primaria obligatoria," *Revista de Filosofía,* año IV, núm. IV, pp.
70-75.

enough energy left to lay before the minister the urgent necessity of assigning, in addition to the usual appropriation, 1,800 pesos for the founding of eight schools, not in the capital city which "was now regularly supplied with schools for boys," but in the country "which clamored for new establishments of that sort in those extensive districts where it had not yet been possible to found them." After the distracting events of 1820, the university gazed fixedly at the extensive and uncultivated plain enveloping Buenos Aires which was still colonial and within which threatening specters were moving.[8]

In the beginning of the eighteenth century, the Hermandad de la Santa Caridad (Brotherhood of Holy Charity), was founded in Buenos Aires to gather the poor from the streets. In time this institution became rich; and to it there was added a female hospital, an orphan academy, and other agencies. On June 1, 1822, Governor Rodríguez issued a decree signed by Minister Rivadavia directing the brotherhood to cease to administer various properties and to place its philanthropic institutions under the direct care of the government.

Rivadavia planned to invite the ladies of the society of Buenos Aires to engage in the noble activities of aid and charity. Because of her talents and exquisite culture, María Sánchez de Mendeville, wife of the consul of France, Washington de Mendeville, exercised great influence. In the salon of Mariquita Sánchez, as the people tenderly designated her, "a permanent club assembled. Stimulated by the notes of the harpsichord played by the mistress of the house, its members danced the minuet. Always animated by a patriotic spirit, they discussed current events. The club promoted intellectual life: poets reserved for it their latest verses; the master Esnaola brought to it his compositions, and the high clergy mingled with illustrious warriors." [9] Rivadavia entered this club only to dominate it, and by the aid of Madame de Mendeville on January 2, 1823, the *Sociedad de Beneficencia* was founded. Madame Mendeville could not be chosen its president because of the post occupied by her husband, but this important office was conferred upon an

---

[8] The importance of the founding of the University of Buenos Aires is pointed out by Ingenieros, *La evolución de las ideas argentinas*, I, 413-16.

[9] A. Meyer Arana, *La caridad en Buenos Aires* (2 vols. Buenos Aires, 1911), I, 149.

aristocratic woman, Mercedes de Lasala de Riglos. In the inaugural discourse of the society, Rivadavia formulated the objectives that the government wished to realize by its foundation: the perfection of morality, the cultivation of spirit in the fair sex, and the dedication of women to labor and social service.[10]

Ever since the close of the viceregal period, a trend toward the formation of a literary society in Buenos Aires had been apparent, but January 1, 1822, was the opportune moment for its inauguration. In order that it might be founded, Dr. Julián Segundo Agüero invited a meeting of Vicente López, Esteban de Luca, Manuel Moreno, Antonio Sáenz, Cosme Argerich, and other persons. Agüero explained to them that the project proposed to promote general learning and to advance science, literature, and art. This society—of which Dr. Agüero was made president—edited the periodicals *El Argos* and *La Abeja Argentina* which were distinguished by a spirit of impartiality and moderation in their comments regarding events at home and abroad.[11] In the meetings of this society important papers were read, such as those of Diego de Alcorta regarding the decline of the sciences, and of Francisco Pisco concerning religious toleration.

The idea of convoking a congress suited Minister Rivadavia. Hence, he appointed a commission composed of Dean Zavaleta, General Arenales, General Las Heras, and Dr. Cossio. Dean Zavaleta went to the provinces of Cuyo where the plan to convoke a congress was greeted with enthusiasm. In the execution of their mission, General Arenales and Dr. Cossio proceeded respectively to the north and to the coast, where the plan was also readily accepted. The provinces opposing it were Córdoba, Santa Fe, Santiago del Estero, La Rioja, and Catamarca. The chieftains Bustos and Quiroga did not readily accept the idea; for they said that congress did not wish to recognize provincial autonomy but rather to form a centralistic constitution. In spite of this disappointment, the government of Buenos Aires officially invited the provinces to send their deputies to congress. The instructions of Dean Zavaleta constitute a document of institutional importance. According to its provisions, the province of Buenos Aires fixed

---

[10] Correa Luna, *Historia de la sociedad de beneficencia* (Buenos Aires, 1923), declared that the act constituting this society was an inimitable document.

[11] Rodríguez, *Contribución histórica y documental*, I, 234 ff.

the following bases for the negotiations: (1) The reunion of all the provinces into one nation administered under a representative system. (2) The entrance of each province into a regulated peace which was to be supported both by the people and by their respective governments.[12]

On April 2, 1824, General Juan Gregorio de las Heras, one of the distinguished commanders who had participated in the campaign of Chile and Peru, was elected to succeed Martín Rodríguez. Las Heras gave the portfolio of minister of government to Rivadavia, but the latter declined to accept it, because he had decided to make a trip to Europe. Manuel J. García was then appointed minister of government, and General Francisco de la Cruz was made minister of war and the navy. The most important event of the administration of Las Heras was the meeting of the general constituent congress at Buenos Aires on December 16, 1824.

---

[12] *Documentos para la historia argentina*, XIII, 223-29, 256-60.

CHAPTER XL

THE CONGRESS OF 1824

To THE constituent congress which assembled in Buenos Aires in 1824, delegates were sent by four riparian provinces, namely, Entre Ríos, Santa Fe, Corrientes, and Misiones—which is now a national territory—by three provinces of Cuyo, namely, Mendoza, San Juan, and San Luis; by four provinces of the north, Jujuy, Salta, Catamarca, and Tucumán; by three of the interior provinces, namely, Córdoba, Santiago del Estero, and La Rioja; by the Banda Oriental; and by the province of Tarija, which was later separated from the territory of the United Provinces of La Plata. Invested with national sovereignty and with legislative and constituent faculties, congress opened its sessions on December 16, 1824.

On January 23, 1825, congress passed a "fundamental law" providing that the provinces should be governed by their own institutions until the national constitution was adopted. Another clause in this law provided thus: "Whatever is concerned with the objects of independence, integrity, security, defense, and national prosperity is within the special jurisdiction of congress."[1]

Political events of this epoch were closely linked to foreign relations, which were concerned with the war against Brazil—an event to be considered in the following chapter. After war was declared, the government of Brazil reënforced its army in the eastern province and ordered a blockade of the port of Buenos Aires, while the Argentine government concentrated its army on the banks of the Uruguay River and equipped a fleet which it placed under the command of Admiral Brown.

At this time, General Las Heras resigned his office, and proposed to congress that it should enact a law which would create a national executive authority. Congress favored his proposal, and on February 6, 1826, it approved a law which established the executive power of the United Provinces. Immediately afterward, it proceeded to select the president of the republic, and by a majority

---

[1] *Registro oficial de la República Argentina*, II, 71.—W. S. R.

of votes, with the exception of only three of its members, it elected
Bernardino Rivadavia.

Two days later, Rivadavia assumed office. In his inaugural
address he said: "In order to constitute the nation two principles
must be established: first, that the reciprocal subordination of individuals should be sustained; and, second, that all interests should
be reconciled and the management of affairs made active and harmonious. The president has entered upon his office with the conviction that one of his chief duties is to declare that the organization
of the nation will retrograde if it does not furnish to all the people
a head, a central authority which regulates everyone and from
which everyone may gain support. For this purpose, it is necessary
that everything concerning the capital city should be essentially
national." [2]

The law creating the executive national power had been framed
in view of the complicated and difficult situation facing the country
because of the war with Brazil. It was accordingly a means by
which to organize a prompt and effective defense and to attack the
enemy with advantage.

On the day after his inauguration, President Rivadavia sent to
congress a project which provided for the federalization of the
city of Buenos Aires and its suburbs by declaring that this territory should constitute the capital of the United Provinces. In
the province of Buenos Aires, this proposal met with much opposition, for it abolished that autonomous province. The minister
of government, Dr. Julián Segundo Agüero, defended the project
in congress; while Dr. Manuel Moreno and Colonel Dorrego attacked it. They based their arguments upon the fundamental law
of 1825 which affirmed the right of the provinces to regulate their
local affairs by their own institutions. Yet the project was approved
by congress.

Among the members of congress two tendencies became apparent:
the federal, and the unitarian or centralistic. A majority of the
members were unitarians and supported the policy being pursued
by President Rivadavia. There were among the ranks of this party
the following persons: Julián Segundo Agüero, Valentín Gómez,
and Manuel Antonio Castro. The federal group, which formed

[2] A sketch of parts of Rivadavia's career is found in A. Lamas, *Rivadavia;
su obra política y cultural* (Buenos Aires, 1915).

the nucleus of the opposition, had as its chief representatives Manuel Moreno and Manuel Dorrego. This party developed its policy
in the hall of congress and by means of the press. It counted on
the support of the people of Buenos Aires; for its leaders had
championed the autonomy of the province, and attacked the proposed law to federalize the city and the suburbs of Buenos Aires.
Thus, the federalist party opposed the centralistic tendency of
the administration of Rivadavia and the majority of congress. It
counted on the sympathy of all the provinces and their caudillos,
who beheld in Dorrego and Manuel Moreno the defenders of provincial autonomy.

Congress now devoted itself to the task of framing a constitution
for the Argentine nation. For this purpose, it invited the provinces
to suggest the bases and the character of the constitution which
it was about to form. Six provinces declared in favor of the federal
form of government: these were Entre Ríos, Santa Fe, Córdoba,
Santiago del Estero, San Juan, and Mendoza. Four provinces decided in favor of the unitarian régime: these were Tucumán, Salta,
Jujuy, and La Rioja. The provinces of Corrientes, Misiones, Catamarca, San Luis, Montevideo, and Tarija declared they would
accept the form of government which received the sanction of
congress.

The debate occupied several sessions of congress. The committee
intrusted with the task of formulating an opinion advised congress
that it favored the unitarian system. It made evident the advantages
of giving unity to the government of the nation. Some deputies
championed the autonomy of the provinces; they affirmed that the
federal régime was best suited to the country.[3] In the session of
July 19, 1826, a unitarian constitution was approved. Forty-two
members voted in favor of it. It was supposed that the new régime
would be accepted by the provinces according to the views previously expressed; for if only four provinces had decided in favor
of a centralistic régime, yet six had declared that they would adopt
the system of government sanctioned by congress, so that the new
régime counted upon the support of ten provinces.

Such was the theory. The facts proved to be different. Córdoba
was in rebellion against the congress of Buenos Aires, because it
had intervened in a dispute concerning the internal affairs of that

---

[3] Pelliza, *op. cit.*, II, 23.

province. Tucumán was engaged in a civil war against the provinces of Cuyo. In Buenos Aires, a provincial party had arisen which offered strong opposition to congress after it enacted the law of the federalization of Buenos Aires. Besides this condition of anarchy and civil war, it should be noted that six Argentine provinces had presented to congress in the form of an ultimatum a resolution that they would defend their respective autonomies.

The governor of Córdoba, General Bustos, was the first to reject the constitution and to rebel against the president. Other events occurred to provoke civil war. Colonel La Madrid, a partisan of the unitarian cause, had been sent to Tucumán for the sole purpose of collecting forces for the prosecution of the war against Brazil, but he promoted a revolution in that province which overthrew the local government. This event made the local chieftains believe that President Rivadavia wished to impose the unitarian régime by force. The chieftain Bustos wrote thus to the governor of Santa Fe: "That scoundrel La Madrid is acting like himself. In the Salado Valley a revolt was started against the arbitrary acts of the president and the advances of congress, but La Madrid aided the deposed governor. It is necessary, my friend, that you should not become negligent for the president is sending venial men to every quarter to start a revolt against us or to deprive us of the means of starting a revolution."

In the wake of Bustos, the chieftain Quiroga rejected the authority of the president and the unitarian constitution. The chieftain of Córdoba had written to him thus: "A communication has fallen into my hands . . . which states that it is necessary to destroy the chiefs Bustos, Quiroga . . .; I am on the lookout and am advising the other governors so that they may be on their guard." The constitution was thus abortive because the provinces and their chieftains violently rejected it.

The conflict regarding internal policies was entangled with the external conflict, namely the war with Brazil. Confronted by the opposition of the chieftains who were preparing for a conflict, Rivadavia accepted the mediation of England to put an end to the war. He sent Dr. Manuel J. García to Rio de Janeiro in order to sign a peace. But, acting beyond his instructions, Minister García made peace with Brazil by a treaty which stipulated that the Banda Oriental should be a dependent province of the Brazilian empire.

This convention provoked opposition on the part of the president
and congress who hastened to disavow the peace that had been negotiated. But the political situation became critical. Because of
his integrity of character, Bernardino Rivadavia did not hesitate
a single moment, and in July, 1827, he resigned his office of president of the republic. In his letter of resignation, which is a notable
document, he said: "Argentinians do not poison my life by doing
me the injustice of supposing that I am terrified by perils and discouraged by obstacles. I should have serenely encountered the greatest inconveniences if, by means of. this self-denial, I could have
promoted the security and happiness of my country. Consecrate
your efforts entirely to it. In front of its altar smother the voices
of local interest, of partisan differences, and, above all, of personal
affections and hatreds that are as much opposed to the welfare of the
states as to the improvement of public morals."

"Rivadavia descended from the presidency," said the historian
Saldías, "because of the passions and the demagogism of his era.
He fell amid a silence that he was foremost to preserve. He left
everything to posterity, which is free from the prejudices that dwarf
men and the injustices that belittle nations. His name symbolizes
an era, which left in the republic the brilliant vestiges of free government. No one has surpassed him there as a statesman and administrator, and, after the lapse of seventy years, what he accomplished as a constitutional reformer is still the desideratum
of the nations of South America." [4]

The resignation of Rivadavia having been accepted, Dr. Vicente
López was appointed provisional president. The new executive,
whose policy constituted a stage of transition between the downfall
of the unitarian party and the new régime which was imposed by
events, did no more than to dissolve the general constituent congress, to return to the province of Buenos Aires its suspended autonomy, and to convoke the representatives who were to designate
a governor.

---

[4] A. Saldías, *Historia de la Confederación Argentina* (5 vols. Buenos Aires,
1911), I, 235. See further, M. de Vedia y Mitre, "Rivadavia en el destierro,"
La Nación, Buenos Aires, May 20 and 21, 1920.

CHAPTER XLI

INTERNATIONAL POLICY

In the course of the preceding chapters, we have mentioned in detail or incidentally the diplomatic negotiations carried on by revolutionary governments after 1810. In particular, we noticed in its appropriate place the mission of Belgrano and Rivadavia in Europe, as well as that of García in Rio de Janeiro, for those missions were intimately connected with the political and military events of the moment.[1] We have reserved for treatment in this chapter the international policy that was followed with regard to England, the United States, and other powers until 1825, the year in which Argentina signed a treaty with England.

When considering the Revolution of 1810, we mentioned the diplomatic negotiations of Matías Irigoyen in England as an agent of the patriot government. The treaty of amity negotiated between Spain and England in 1809, which was renewed in 1814, prevented England from assuming a definite attitude in favor of the insurgent colonies of Spanish America. As an absurd and reprehensible measure of government, we recorded that, during the few days in which Dr. Alvear was in charge of the directorate (January, 1815), he had representations made to the head of the English cabinet to the effect that the provinces of the Río de la Plata would place themselves under its government and protection.

After the meeting of the congress of Vienna (1814-1815), the absolute sovereigns of Europe leagued together and constituted the Holy Alliance. The king of Spain asked the aid of that alliance in order to reconquer his colonial dominions in America. Certain governments of continental Europe were at times disposed to satisfy the wishes of Ferdinand VII, but during the reign of George IV, because of the attitude assumed by Secretary Canning, England opposed the execution of such plans.

In October, 1823, England appointed a consul to Buenos Aires,

---

[1] Important viewpoints are presented in the letter of Rivadavia to Pueyrredón from Paris, November 6, 1816, *La Revista de Buenos Aires,* XIV, 501-25. In regard to the mission of Belgrano to Brazil and England, see Belgrano, *op. cit.,* VII, 77-92.

and on February 2, 1825, a treaty of amity and commerce was signed between England and the provinces of the Río de la Plata, which should be mentioned as one of the organic antecedents of the present Argentine constitution, for it contained liberal provisions concerning such matters as commerce, navigation, and religion.[2]

This treaty was based upon the principles of reciprocity and equality. In respect to property, it prohibited to both contracting parties the system of odious and prejudicial privileges. By Article I it stipulated that there should be perpetual friendship between the governments and the citizens of Great Britain and the United Provinces of the Río de la Plata. Article II stated that the citizens of one party should enjoy the privilege of going freely with their vessels and cargoes to all those places, ports, and rivers in the dominions of the other party into which the citizens of other countries were admitted or might in future be admitted. Of equal importance was the privilege conceded by Article XII to the effect that subjects of Great Britain residing in the provinces of La Plata should not be molested because of their religion, that they should enjoy freedom of conscience, and should be able to hold religious services either within their own houses or in special churches or chapels. Likewise, they were granted the right to bury their dead in their own cemeteries. Such generosity in the concession of freedom of religious faith, provoked a proposal in the discussions in congress for modifications by delegates from Córdoba who maintained that the United Provinces should be left free to concede this privilege or to refuse it according to circumstances.

In 1816, Director Álvarez Thomas appointed Colonel Martín Thompson diplomatic agent to the government of the United States in order that he might solicit aid in support of the "just and sacred cause" of emancipation. As this first mission failed, Dr. Pueyrredón, in 1817, authorized Manuel H. de Aguirre to ask that the United States should acknowledge the independence of Argentina which had been avowed on July 9 of the previous year and to secure munitions with which to carry out the plan of invading Chile. In the beginning of 1822, James Monroe, president of the United States, informed congress that in view of the progress of the insurrection in the Spanish-American colonies it was proper

---

[2] C. A. Villanueva, *La Santa Alianza* ("La Monarquía en América," vol. III, 4 vols. Paris, 1911-14), pp. 107-73.

"to conclude that its fate is settled and that the provinces which have declared their independence, and are in the enjoyment of it, ought to be recognized." In accordance with this proposal, on March 28, 1822, the congress of the United States made effective the recognition of the independence of the new American states.[3]

But in the belief that the Holy Alliance continued to cherish the proposal to support the plans of Ferdinand VII to restore the Spanish colonies to him, President Monroe made more inclusive declarations in his message to congress on December 2, 1823—declarations of signal importance in international American law—which embodied a doctrine that bears the name of its author. In one of its most significant passages the Monroe doctrine announced: "We owe it, therefore, to candor and to the amicable relations existing between the United States and those powers to declare that we should consider any attempt on their part to extend their system to any portion of this hemisphere as dangerous to our peace and safety. With the existing colonies or dependencies of any European power we have not interfered and shall not interfere. But with the governments who have declared their independence and maintained it, and whose independence we have, on great consideration and on just principles, acknowledged, we could not view any interposition for the purpose of oppressing them, or controlling in any other manner their destiny, by any European power in any other light than as the manifestation of an unfriendly disposition toward the United States." [4]

The government of the United Provinces was engaged in improving the relations of amity and commerce with all independent nations. During a meeting in September, 1816, the congress of Tucumán decided that, when the declaration of independence had been sworn to, it should try to secure the recognition of La Plata by foreign nations, for which purpose diplomatic agents should be sent to Brazil, England, Russia, Sweden, and the United States.

[3] On May 4, 1822, President Monroe signed a bill that appropriated $100,000 to defray the expenses of diplomatic missions to independent nations of Spanish America. On January 27, 1823, the senate of the United States confirmed the appointment of Cæsar A. Rodney as minister plenipotentiary of the United States at Buenos Aires. See W. S. Robertson, "The Recognition of the Hispanic American Nations by the United States," *Hispanic American Historical Review* (Baltimore, 1918), I, 257, 261.—W. S. R.

[4] J. D. Richardson, *A Compilation of the Messages and Papers of the Presidents* (10 vols. Washington, 1896-99), II, 218.—W. S. R.

In 1819, a pact of union was signed by Argentina with Chile in order to carry out the expedition to liberate Peru. In 1826, these two nations agreed to maintain the independence of the new states against any attempt at foreign invasion. A treaty between Argentina and Colombia in 1823 was conceived in the same terms. These treaties support the solemn assertion that the entire policy of international diplomacy developed by the government of Buenos Aires until 1825 had as its prime object to assure the independence of the United Provinces from all foreign domination.[5]

---

[5] N. Piñero "La Política internacional," *La Nación, 1810—25 de Mayo—1910* (Buenos Aires, 1910), pp. 83-87.

CHAPTER XLII

THE WAR WITH BRAZIL

The war between the United Provinces of the Río de la Plata and Brazil was caused by the problem of the Banda Oriental. The antecedents of this dispute must be sought in the colonial period, in the conflict between Spain and Portugal concerning the boundary between their dominions in America—a topic that we do not propose to discuss here.[1] The diplomacy of Portugal was designed to extend the frontiers of Brazil as far as the left bank of Río de la Plata, and with this object the Portuguese had founded the colony of Sacramento, which was definitely regained by Spain through the work of Viceroy Cevallos.

In 1814, the Argentine army under General Alvear captured the fort of Montevideo which was held by the royalists. In 1816, under the pretext of restraining the incursions of the chieftain, José Artigas, Portugal ordered that the Banda Oriental should be occupied, but announced that it was not animated by any idea of annexation or conquest. Director Pueyrredón sent Colonel Vedia to demand the evacuation of the eastern province of General Lecor, the commander of the Portuguese army. Lecor refused. The Argentine government then prepared an army to free the Banda Oriental from the invader on condition that Artigas should respect the national authority. The eastern chieftain refused to do so; but as civil war began to rage in the provinces of the Río de la Plata, and as the cause of independence was intrusted to the hands of San Martín, the government of Buenos Aires decided not to involve the country in the hazard of a war, especially as it could not count upon the obedience of the chief of the Banda Oriental. Nevertheless, Artigas made a separate resistance to Portuguese domination, but in February, 1820, he was defeated in the battle of Tacuarembó. Freed from him, the Portuguese found the definitive possession of the eastern province so easy that in 1821 an assembly declared that "the eastern province of the Río de la Plata is united with and in-

---

[1] On the conflict between Spain and Portugal concerning the boundaries of their dominions in South America, see C. L. Fregeiro, *La batalla de Ituzaingó* (Buenos Aires, 1919).

corporated in the United Kingdom of Portugal, Brazil, and the
Algarve, under the name of the Cisplatean province." Shortly
afterward, Prince Pedro of Brazil declared Brazil's independence
of Portugal and the forces that occupied the eastern province were
divided into two factions: the Brazilian faction that followed General Lecor, who favored the annexation of the Uruguayan territory to the independent empire of Brazil; and the Portuguese faction commanded by Alvaro da Costa, who favored the relinquish-
ment of the Banda Oriental.

Meantime, Uruguayans from Buenos Aires and Montevideo, led
by General Juan Antonio de Lavalleja, strove to secure the evacuation of the Banda Oriental by the Portuguese. Thirty-three in
number, in April, 1825, they embarked, and in the course of
their Uruguayan campaign they recruited some 2,000 patriots.[2]
They fought the battles of Sarandí and Rincón de las Gallinas in
which they triumphed over the Portuguese forces. In August, 1825,
the Uruguayans organized a province and named Lavalleja governor. In a congress which met in the town of Florida, they declared
the act of annexation to Brazil to be null and void, and added
"that the general, decided, and constant vote of the eastern province was for union with the other Argentine provinces." The constituent congress assembled in Buenos Aires accepted the incorporation of the sister province and approved the certificate of the
deputy, Gomensoro, who entered congress as representative of that
province. The Argentine government notified Brazil of these events;
and, on December 1, 1825, the emperor responded by declaring
war on Argentina.

General Las Heras, the governor of Buenos Aires, at once formed
an army of observation of 8,000 men which was stationed on the
coast of Uruguay under the command of General Rodríguez. The
declaration of war had lighted the patriotism of the Argentinians;
the governors and chieftains of the provinces sent forces to Buenos
Aires, thus promoting the success of the campaign.

The war was waged at the same time upon both land and sea.
As Brazil had declared a blockade of the port of the Río de la

---

[2] M. Falcao Espalter, "Los treinta y tres orientales," *La Prensa*, Buenos
Aires, April 19, 1925; J. Beverina, "El congreso de 1825 y la cuestión oriental,"
La Nación, August 30, 1925.

Plata, the Argentine government undertook the formation of a squadron which it placed in charge of Admiral Brown. The Brazilian squadron had sailed up the estuary as far as the island of Martín García; Brown left in pursuit, and on February 9, 1827, the engagement of Juncal took place. This was won by the Argentine fleet which captured all the Brazilian vessels in this action. On June 11, another fight took place at Pozos with results favorable to the cause of La Plata.

The land campaign was as glorious as that waged on sea. As General Rodríguez resigned the command of the army of observation, President Rivadavia appointed the minister of war, General Alvear, as commander in chief of the army. This army, styled "republican," numbered 5,500 soldiers, who established their camp near Arroyo Grande, one of the affluents of the Río Negro. In this great crusade there accompanied the army such distinguished military leaders as Paz, Soler, Lavalle, Olavarría, and Brandzen. The last-mentioned leader died in one of the battles. Alvear organized the army in three divisions: the vanguard, composed of Uruguayan cavalry, was commanded by General Lavalleja; the second division was under the orders of Alvear and General Mansilla, the chief of the general staff; while the third division, composed of infantry, was led by General Soler.

The army of Brazil was composed of 10,000 soldiers, including 2,000 Germans.[3] The first engagements were favorable to the republican army. On February 20, 1827, the battle of Ituzaingó was fought, which resulted in a decisive triumph for the united Argentine and Uruguayan army. Alvear had penetrated into Brazilian territory where an enemy was less expected. The Marquis of Barbacena, who commanded the Brazilian army, stated at Rio de Janeiro that if he had lost the battle of February 20, it was not because of a lack of munitions (for there was so large a supply that when they fell into the hands of the enemy, the latter considered them a precious acquisition), but that the battle was lost because proper precautions had not been taken, and "because the army was sur-

---

[3] It is not clear that the Brazilian army had so many Germans enlisted. When General Lecor arrived in Brazil in 1816, he brought some 5,000 Portuguese soldiers with him. See *Livro do Centenario* (4 vols. Rio de Janeiro, 1900-10), II, 32.—W. S. R.

prised during its march." At the crisis of the battle, Colonel Brand-zen led his squadron to a charge in echelon, but the terrain was broken by a ravine where the brave chief lost his life.

The strategy of General Alvear consisted in compelling the enemy's soldiers to engage in partial combats in their own terri-tory. Nevertheless, it has been asserted that the success of this engagement was not so much due to the maneuvers of Alvear as to the decision of the chiefs of the army who operated on their own account; for the commander in chief had directed the principal movements of the cavalry, leaving the infantry and the artillery out of his maneuvers. The battle of Ituzaingó, as Argentine and Uruguayan writers designate it, or the battle of Paso del Rosario, as it is styled by the Brazilians, has been described and judged in very different ways. From a strategic viewpoint, Dr. López com-pared it with Chacabuco; Dr. Saldías likened it to Maipú; Bal-drich characterized it as a fine tactical triumph, while Paz, a dis-tinguished participant in that battle, assures us in his *Memorias Inéditas* that there was no strategic foresight on that occasion and that the final outcome at Ituzaingó was "due more to the momentary aspirations of individuals who sought to derive advantage from the mistakes of the enemy than to the tactical dispositions of General Alvear, who did not make any." Ituzaingó, he added, "could be called the battle of the disobediences: there all of us commanded, all of us fought, and all of us triumphed, directed by our own in-spirations." [4] This viewpoint of General Paz has been modified in the light of fresh investigations regarding our military history.[5]

In the second campaign of General Alvear, the Argentine army continued to cover itself with glory. It won new military triumphs, among which we may mention Camacuá and Yerbal.

While the Argentine arms were being crowned by success both by sea and land, internal politics made the situation of the national authorities precarious. When the centralistic constitution of 1826 had been promulgated, and when disturbances had been provoked in the interior provinces by the agent of congress, Colonel La

---

[4] C. I. Salas, "Bibliografía del coronel Federico de Brandzen," *Renacimiento,* Buenos Aires, December, 1909.

[5] See J. Beverina, "La batalla de Ituzaingó y el general Alvear," *La Nación,* Buenos Aires, September 16, 1923.

Madrid, the provinces, and the chieftains refused to give their support and obedience to President Rivadavia. He accordingly accepted the mediation of England, in order to negotiate peace with Brazil. For this purpose, as we have already noticed, he sent Minister García to Rio de Janeiro. In the letter of instructions given by the government to Commissioner García appeared the following: "Señor García is fully authorized to adjust and conclude any protocol or treaty whatsoever providing for the cessation of the war and the reëstablishment of peace between the republic and the empire of Brazil, on honorable terms and with reciprocal guarantees to both countries, having as its basis the restitution of the Banda Oriental, or the erection and recognition of said territory as a separate, free, and independent state."

Ignoring the instructions given him, Minister García arranged a peace humiliating to the national honor. The principal clause of the treaty was that providing for the renunciation of Uruguayan territory by the Argentine Republic as follows: "And in virtue of the fact that the emperor has solemnly promised to establish a régime in the eastern province as good or better than that which exists in other states of the empire, the Argentine plenipotentiary trusts that when his Majesty considers the real cause of the disquietude existing in that province as well as the customs, inclinations, and interests of its population which is foreign to Brazil, he will become convinced that there is no better solution than to give it a separate and independent existence, thus satisfying the demands of the Argentine government. . . . With regard to the armies of both contracting states, they should not maintain any more forces on sea and land than those which are necessary for the maintenance of order, and they should proceed to dismantle the island of Martín García. Further, they should solicit the guarantee of a friendly power in order to assure the free navigation of the Plata River." [6]

In truth, this act was a satire: Argentina had triumphed in its campaigns by land and sea, yet it terminated the war by relinquishing everything to the vanquished. In his council of ministers President Rivadavia repudiated this treaty of peace. He thus expressed to congress his opinion concerning that pact: "On May 24, 1827,

---

[6] Rodríguez, *La patria vieja*, pp. 40-41.

there was subscribed in Rio de Janeiro the humiliation, infamy, and dishonor of the Argentine republic." [7]

There are preserved in the historical museum of Argentina five imperial standards which were captured in the course of the war. It is possible that those flags are not precisely trophies of the battle of Ituzaingó, but of the preliminary campaign, taken from the imperial army encamped at Santa Ana. In any case, "they symbolize to the historic conscience of the peoples of La Plata, the most eloquent demonstration of the strength displayed by the Argentine people in the turbulent age of Rivadavia and Dorrego in favor of the embattled Banda Oriental, even at the risk of compromising the stability of the Argentine provinces which were not yet unified into a body that constituted a nation." [8]

---

[7] García's justification may be found in López, *Historia de la República Argentina*, X, 173-75.

[8] C. L. Fregeiro, "Bandas imperiales del Brasil existentes en el Museo Histórico Nacional," *Humanidades* (Buenos Aires, 1921), II, 94-167.

CHAPTER XLIII

THE ADMINISTRATION OF DORREGO

PROVISIONAL President López convoked the legislature of the province of Buenos Aires, which assembled on August 3, 1828. On the 12th of that month, it elected as governor Colonel Dorrego, who during the presidency of Rivadavia had been the champion of provincial autonomy. After taking the oath of office, Dorrego delivered an address in which he said: "Gentlemen, your votes have summoned me to an honorable but arduous task. Moreover, if there is anything flattering for me in this invitation, it is the fact that it involves the reorganization of our province. . . . Your disapproval will not only be sufficient to make me relinquish the post which you have intrusted to me, but since I am an ardent lover of public opinion, if I am not fortunate enough to win its support, I shall not increase my disgrace by employing force to combat it or by using intrigue and tenacity to lull it. I shall resign with pleasure an office that cannot allure one who esteems what is right when public opinion does not approve his acts. The epoch is terrible: my path is strewn with thorns. Hence, it will not be possible to smooth it, unless each citizen coöperates with all the knowledge and resources in his power." [1]

With these pledges, Colonel Dorrego began his administration. He was both a military and political figure. He had fought valiantly in the war for independence, and had developed his political personality during the directorate of Pueyrredón, at which time he had led the opposition. He was a federal democrat: he had defended federalism against the monarchical and unitarian propaganda of leaders of the directory. His articles opposing the administration which were published in the columns of the *Crónica Argentina* had alarmed the government of Pueyrredón. During a night of panic in 1817, the director summoned Colonel Dorrego before him and appealed to his patriotism to cease the campaign of conspiracy of which he accused him. Dorrego responded that he defended the democratic and federal cause against those persons who wished to monarchize the country. Pueyrredón became irri-

---

[1] M. A. Pelliza, *Dorrego en la historia de los partidos unitario y federal* (Buenos Aires, 1878), pp. 362-64.—W. S. R.

tated and said: "Colonel do not forget that you are speaking to your superior." Colonel Dorrego retorted thus: "I do not recollect on which battlefield I have met the general." A few days later, Dorrego was deported to North America.

Upon his return from exile, six years later, the governor of Buenos Aires, Martín Rodríguez, commissioned Colonel Dorrego to go in pursuit of Dr. Tagle, who had promoted a conspiracy, and to bring him in dead or alive. Tagle had been a minister of Pueyrredón and had asked for and approved the exile of Dorrego. The latter found the conspirator, who, being aware of the decisive orders of Governor Rodríguez, prepared for death. Nevertheless, Dorrego helped him to secure a horse, pointed out the road by which he could flee, and said: "Go, doctor, and may you be happy." Such was the man, obsessed by his ideals, but tolerant and cultured, who undertook to exercise the office of constitutional governor of the province of Buenos Aires.

"The epoch is terrible," Dorrego had said in his inaugural address; and he was right, for it was an age of internal anarchy and foreign war. Manuel Moreno was his minister of war, José María Rojas was minister of the treasury, and General Juan Ramón Balcarce minister of war and the navy. Among the new measures adopted should be mentioned the decree abolishing the forced issuance of paper money, and the law of the press promulgated on May 9, 1828, which contained individual guarantees for freedom of thought. The true glory of this administration consisted in the negotiation of an honorable peace with Brazil. After the resignation of Rivadavia the country decided to continue the war and, for this purpose, Colonel Dorrego provided the necessary forces. Brazil then undertook to offer, as the basis for the negotiation of a convention, the independence of the Banda Oriental. The treaty of peace was signed on September 5, 1828.

In recognition of this achievement, the legislature of the province of Buenos Aires decided to confer upon Dorrego the title of general. He replied to the representatives in a communication dated August 6, the principal part of which we shall quote because it is a beautiful page of moral sublimity: "He who signs this," said Colonel Dorrego, "has read with feeling the motion presented to your excellencies providing that you should grant him the title of general of the army of the province. This distinction with which the author of the motion has wished to honor the undersigned is appreciated by him at its true worth, but this obliges him to declare to your Excellencies that he believes himself sufficiently honored with the title of colonel which he possesses; that in his career he has maintained the principle of not accepting any rank which was not conferred upon him as a reward for a military engagement or for some remarkable success, and that, firm in this resolution, in 1816 and 1820 he declined to accept the office with which today it is your desire to distinguish him, even though it was the highest in the military service, because it was in reward for services which, though important to the province, were performed in the midst of an internal war."

After the constituent congress of Buenos Aires was dissolved by Provisional President López, there assembled in the city of Santa Fe a national convention which was to designate a provisional executive and to promulgate a constitution that should be republican, representative, and federal. The national convention of Santa Fe approved the treaty of peace with Brazil that had been negotiated by Colonel Dorrego.

After peace was made with Brazil, the Argentine army returned to Buenos Aires, but one of its divisions under the command of General Lavalle mutinied, because, upon the resignation of Alvear from the command of the army, President López had appointed Lavalleja in his place. On December 1, the troops revolted and decided on the deposition of Governor Dorrego. The latter, surprised at so strange an act, left the fort of Buenos Aires accompanied by his ministers and sallied into the country with the intention of joining Juan Manuel de Rosas, and smothering the military uprising. General Lavalle addressed a proclamation to the people, inviting them to meet in the church of San Roque in order to designate by direct vote the person who should replace Dorrego. In part, the people responded to the invitation of Lavalle, and in the portico of the church he was proclaimed governor.

Meantime, in conjunction with Juan Manuel de Rosas, Dorrego was able to collect 2,000 men. He marched toward the north where he expected to join the forces of Colonel Pacheco and those of Santa Fe. Lavalle immediately left the city in pursuit of Dorrego and defeated him at Navarro. Colonel Escribano, a subordinate of Dorrego, took the latter prisoner and sent him to the camp of

Lavalle, who without regard to the most elementary legal formalities, ordered that in the course of two hours the constitutional governor of the province of Buenos Aires should be shot. Unfortunately, the order was carried out, and on December 13, Dorrego was executed. Immediately afterward, General Lavalle addressed to his minister in Buenos Aires a note in which he said: "I inform the provisional government that Colonel Dorrego has just been shot by my order in the presence of the regiments which compose this division. History will judge whether or not Colonel Dorrego deserved to die, and whether his sacrifice to the tranquility of a people who had been thrown into mourning by him was animated by any other motive than the public welfare. I hope that the people of Buenos Aires may be convinced that the death of Colonel Dorrego is the greatest sacrifice that I could make for their sake."

"History will judge whether or not General Dorrego deserved to die," said General Lavalle; and history has pronounced its judgment to the effect that Dorrego's life was precious and necessary for his country, and that his death, decreed by a military commander who led a mutiny in the army, was an error.[2]

The execution of Dorrego signified for the country in the first place the death of a virtuous citizen, endowed with the qualities of a politician and a statesman: he had a place among the men who were necessary to the country in those blind moments. This execution had, moreover, important political consequences. From the shadow of Dorrego, who was a respecter of the law and a cultured man, there emerged the avenger, Juan Manuel de Rosas. Henceforth, there were no ideals to influence the course of the political struggle, but only private passions, petty ambitions, or the spirit of vengeance. To quote Pelliza: "The first of December, 1828, terminated the struggle of parties that possessed principles. The struggle now moved toward the unknown. For many years afterward there was no constitution; neither was there any order in public affairs. Personal factions succeeded the political propositions of the past, and the only prospect of the future was a huge

---

[2] P. Lacasa, *Vida militar y política del general argentino Don Juan Lavalle* (Buenos Aires, 1858). On the disquietude caused by the return of San Martín at this juncture, see M. de Vedia y Mitre, "La revolución de Diciembre y sus consecuencias," *Humanidades* (La Plata, 1923), VI, 205-63; and P. Abad, *El general San Martín en Montevideo, 1829* (Montevideo, 1923).

bonfire ignited by a war of extermination—a bonfire which threatened to consume the nation. When the revolution was neither supported by right, nor drew its strength from national opinion, the people opposed it, for it did not promote the general interests, it caused a harmful disturbance in all the relations of the State with foreign powers, it caused direct injury to public and private fortune, and it caused a moral misconception that diminished the importance of the country. Upon the day following the military uprising which caused the downfall of Dorrego, our credit sank to the lowest point; the national authority with which the governor had been invested was insulted by men who were armed and financed by the nation—men who had acted without any authority, and who could not have been invested with authority for such a step. The responsibility of the victor was immense both before the nation and before the bar of history." [8]

Upon the death of Dorrego, all the Argentine provinces with the exception of Salta and Tucumán, protested against the military uprising of Lavalle. The national convention which had gathered in Santa Fe pronounced the execution of Dorrego to be high treason, and asked from all the provinces the military forces necessary to make war upon Buenos Aires. It intrusted those forces to Estanislao López, the governor of Santa Fe. The caudillo, Quiroga of La Rioja, addressed a communication to General Lavalle in which he said: "The undersigned cannot tolerate the outrage that you have committed against the peoples in general; if upon this occasion he should view with serene countenance the fortunes of the republic in such destructive hands without taking upon himself the vengeance which he threatens to exact, he would become unworthy of the honorable title of son of the country." [4]

General Lavalle arranged with General Paz, commander of the second division of the army which had just arrived from Brazil, a plan of attack upon the chieftains Bustos, Quiroga, Ibarra, and López. One division of the forces of Lavalle, under command of the Prussian colonel, Frederick Rauch, was defeated at Vizcacheras.

[3] Pelliza, *Historia argentina desde su origen hasta la organización nacional,* II, 79-80. See further, A. Dellepiane, "El monumento de Dorrego, su significación artistica, histórica y filosófica," *Revista de la Universidad de Buenos Aires* (Buenos Aires, 1925), año XXII, 2a. serie, pp. 269-85.

[4] D. Peña, *Juan Facundo Quiroga* (Buenos Aires, 1906), p. 200.—W. S. R.

López and Rosas then attacked Lavalle, who in the end of April, 1829, was defeated at the bridge of Márquez. Lavalle being vanquished, he signed with Rosas the convention of Cañuelas which provided that hostilities should cease, and that as soon as possible an election should be held for the choice of representatives of the province. A little later, the Treaty of Barracas was arranged between Lavalle and Rosas. In accordance with this treaty, Juan José Viamonte was made governor of the province of Buenos Aires and Lavalle agreed to retire to Uruguay. Thus did General Lavalle fall, shrouded in silence and defeat.

CHAPTER XLIV

ROSAS

Juan Manuel de Rosas sprang from one of the most illustrious families that settled in La Plata during the colonial era. From the marriage of León Ortiz de Rosas and Agustina López de Osornio, there was born in Buenos Aires (94 Sarmiento Street) on March 30, 1793, a son who was named Juan Manuel. When still a child he was taken to the paternal ranch in the district of Salado, which was one of the leading estates in the province. At the age of nine he entered one of the best known schools of Buenos Aires which was under the management of Francisco Javier de Argerich. When the first English invasion occurred he was thirteen years old; he gathered some companions, invited them to serve under the orders of General Liniers, and on August 12, 1806, thus participated in the reconquest of Buenos Aires.

In 1808, his father intrusted Juan Manuel with the management of the family property. His mother doubted whether her son would manage the ranch honestly. Juan Manuel accordingly withdrew from the paternal roof, and associated himself with Juan Nepomuceno Terrero. Rosas later explained this incident in his life by declaring that "I did not wish to receive any capital from my parents. . . . I left home to work without any more capital than my credit and my industry. Encarnación Ezurra [his wife], had no property, nor did her parents. I wrote my father's will," said Rosas, "at his direction. In one of its clauses, it stated: 'My son Juan Manuel has declared to me that the inheritance which belongs to him after my death he concedes to his very beloved mother, Agustina López de Osornio.' When my mother died, my maternal inheritance passed to my brothers." [1] With Terrero, Rosas engaged in the business of salting fish and garnering the products of the country. In 1815, he established the first meat-salting establishment of the province of Buenos Aires in the district of Quilmes. So important was this business that the landed proprietors thought they saw in it the cause for the decrease in the number of cattle; and they in-

---

[1] Saldías, *Historia de la Confederación Argentina,* I, 14.

duced Director Puyerredón in 1817 to suspend the industry of salting meat. Later, in company with Terrero, Rosas bought land within and without the limits of Salado, and engaged in raising livestock. To quote from the work by Saldías on the history of the Argentine Confederation:

"Here Rosas began to lay the foundations of his influence and his fortune. . . . Furnishing an example of austerity of customs and love of labor, he lived, in more than one sense, a common life with his employees. He was the first one to attempt the hardest tasks, for he was not only reckoned as the most accomplished horseman but also as the gaucho who was most skilful in overcoming by force of habit and dexterity the difficulties which at this time daily confronted those persons who lived in the pampas confident of their own strength. His ranches were transformed into true centers of a population that was subjected to the rigorous discipline of labor which educates and ennobles. Both the gauchos and those who were not gauchos considered it an advantage to work in them. They trusted in modest comfort and in hope of the advancement that came to those who distinguished themselves by ability and constancy. A species of lord of the manor, exercising both civil and criminal jurisdiction, Rosas punished drunkenness, idleness, and theft, either expelling from his estates or delivering to the authorities persons who indulged in those vices which he abominated." [2]

During the recurring crisis of the governments in 1820, the militia of the south had played an important rôle. Rosas had left his estate to join them and to march with them against the Indians, or even to check irruptions from the province of Santa Fe. On June 8, 1820, he was appointed commander of the fifth rural regiment. When, on October 1, 1820, political factions made a revolutionary movement in order to depose Governor Rodríguez, Rosas at the head of the fifth regiment of "colorados"—rural militia that were so designated because of the color of their uniforms—supported the authority of the governor. In the words of Saldías: "Eye-witnesses, journalists of every political complexion, the most bitter enemies that Rosas later had and who wrote about these affairs— all agreed in stating that the people of Buenos Aires did not know which to admire the more, the heroism with which the colorados of

[2] *Ibid.*, p. 19.

A Woman Grinding Corn; a work done by Jean L. Pallière, from *El Hogar,*
Buenos Aires, July 7, 1916.

the fifth regiment fought and conquered, or the example of behaviour and discipline which they furnished after the combat. . . . At the end of the afternoon, Rosas commanded his men to march, and at the head of his colorados, he presented the detachment to the captain general of the province. General Rodríguez, visibly moved, paused a moment in front of Commandant Rosas, lifted his cap, extended to him a friendly invitation, placed Rosas at his left, and they entered the fortress together." [3] Rosas continued to strengthen his prestige in the campaign that took place after the war with Brazil ended. When, in 1828, Governor Dorrego left the city of Buenos Aires, deposed by the uprising of Lavalle, he went to join the militia of Rosas. After Dorrego was defeated and executed, Rosas opposed Lavalle, and in conjunction with the forces of López, vanquished that general at the bridge of Márquez. Later, Rosas signed the Treaty of Barracas which placed the provisional government of the province in the hands of Juan José Viamonte. The latter governed for three months; then he convoked the legislature, which designated Juan Manuel de Rosas as governor and captain general of the province of Buenos Aires.

Such were the personal antecedents of the man who occupied the political stage of the country during an historic period of twenty years that has been styled "The Tyranny of Rosas." Before passing judgment upon this ruler and chieftain one must study him in action and in the task of government. But we say now that any murder or other crime imputed to Rosas and which has been proved, deserves the condemnation of history. In the same manner that posterity has harshly judged the shooting of Colonel Dorrego, history has allowed its condemnation to fall upon Rosas, whenever the unjustifiable death of a single man has been proved. We shall notice in time what share of the responsibility pertains to him, and what part it is necessary to adjudicate and to apportion to our historic past—one of continuous revolutions, of violent governmental crises, of the transformation of political parties with principles into personal parties—and to the society of the epoch which was tormented and agitated by the phenomena of moral and political dissolution.

While Rosas was vanquishing Lavalle, General Paz led his army toward Córdoba where he routed Governor Bustos at San Roque.

---

[3] *Ibid.*, pp. 72-73.

The chieftain Quiroga, who enjoyed great prestige in La Rioja, joined Bustos, and thus they formed an army of 5,000 men. In a plain to the northeast of Córdoba, at a place called Tablada, a battle took place on June 23, 1829, between the forces of Paz and those of Quiroga. The latter was defeated. Quiroga then tried to make a conjunction with General Villafañe who was approaching with a reënforcement of 1,500 men but on February 25, 1830, Paz compelled him to give battle, and on the plain of Oncativo defeated him again. In this battle Father Aldao, second in command of the forces of Quiroga, was made a prisoner. General Paz stated: "Vanquished once more at Oncativo, Quiroga withdrew to his provinces with the remainder of his army. The governments of these provinces prepared to continue the war. In Cuyo, the Aldaos, brothers of the prisoner, took up arms again; in La Rioja, there remained the caudillos Villafañe, who retired with his division of more than 1,000 men, and Brizuela; in Catamarca, there was Eslabes Figueroa, and in San Juan and San Luis other minor chieftains." [4]

After these last triumphs, eight provinces of the interior designated General Paz as "supreme military chief." On the other side, on January 4, 1831, the riparian provinces signed the "federal pact" and were thus linked in an offensive and defensive alliance. Further, this treaty contained a general declaration of rights and guarantees in favor of all the inhabitants, and it was agreed to invite the other provinces of the republic, when they were at liberty, to reunite in a federal congress. According to the judgment of writers on constitutional law, the "federal pact" is more than a treaty of union: it is a constitution embodying fundamental principles.

This was a time of intense expectancy. Politically, General Paz represented unitarianism which was triumphant in the interior of the country. The riparian provinces, at the head of which was the governor of Buenos Aires, Juan Manuel de Rosas, and the governor of Santa Fe, Estanislao López, represented the triumph of the federal cause of the chieftains. From a military viewpoint, General Paz signified the man who was acquainted with the vicissitudes of war, a tactician and strategist, who selected the site of a battle in advance and calculated its results. On the other hand, though López and Rosas did not possess the military skill of their adversary, yet

---

[4] J. M. Paz, *op. cit.,* II, 204.

they had veteran troops. Which party would triumph? If success should crown the efforts of General Paz, a unitarian restoration would doubtless take place throughout the country; if, on the other hand, victory should remain with the party of Rosas and López, a federation would be definitively imposed. The moment was therefore decisive. Rosas appointed Juan A. Balcarce general of the army of Buenos Aires. López intervened personally, and from Mendoza Quiroga agreed again to struggle against General Paz. But while the stage was being anxiously prepared, an unforeseen accident happened to General Paz; on May 1, 1831, at a place called Tío, where he was surveying the terrain, he was thrown from his horse, and taken prisoner.[5]

Once Paz was captured, the unitarian cause was lost. La Madrid took charge of the remainder of the army, but Quiroga, seeking revenge for Tablada and Oncativo, defeated him in the fierce battle of the fortress of Tucumán. In this manner the cause of the unitarians in the provinces of La Plata was ended forever. The flood tide of unitarianism had been signalized by the presidency of Rivadavia. After his resignation, the triumph of the federal cause had been assured, once autonomy had been restored to the provinces at whose front fought Colonel Dorrego. As we have seen, the successes of Lavalle in Buenos Aires and of Paz in the interior were transitory. Federalism was assured throughout the country; as yet, not in the form of a triumphant political party, but incarnated in the personal predominance of the chieftains.

---

[5] A letter of López, May 12, 1831, which informed Rosas of the imprisonment of General Paz is found in Beverina, *El general José María Paz, sus campañas y su doctrina de guerra,* apéndice.

CHAPTER XLV

THE CHIEFTAINS

THE POLITICAL anarchy that broke out in 1820 and 1827 had its personification in the caudillos or chieftains. Behind them moved legions of people, impelled by respect for courage. Anarchy was a social condition, as we have said in another place; the chieftains were the visible expressions of this anarchy. If, after 1810, Argentine democracy broke out in a turbulent and revolutionary fashion, the elements produced by it bore traits of the original democracy. The Argentine social masses possessed an instinct for their own government and for popular sovereignty; they displayed it in numerous revolutionary movements that occurred during the colonial era and particularly in the Revolution of 1810. In the political realm, the democratic sentiment, turbulent and inorganic, had produced the crisis of the patriotic governments; and when these organizations, for reasons of stability and national order, tried to establish strong and absorbing governments or to transplant a monarchy, the popular masses moved against Buenos Aires by a single impulse. The battle of Cepeda had a double significance; as we said in another place, it represented the democratic opposition of popular instinct to the monarchical leanings of statesmen, and also involved the principle of federation *de facto* in opposition to the unitarian tendency of Buenos Aires. The chieftains, who were faithful exponents of the instincts of the masses, raised the banner of democracy and federation. The cause was great, but the means employed by the chieftains to secure its triumph were barbarous; "because the social nucleus which executed it was barbarous; because its methods were barbarous and the roads into which it flung the people were bloody." [1]

This important phenomenon of Argentine caudillismo has been explained by Domingo Sarmiento in his famous book *Facundo*, as the result of the struggle of the country districts against the cities, of barbarism against civilization. With more exactness, other

[1] Estrada, *La política liberal bajo la tiranía de Rosas*, pp. 30-31. Mitre's views in regard to the origin of Argentine caudillos is found in his *Historia de Belgrano*, III, 31. See further, Varela, *op. cit.*, III, 333.

writers take the view that the gauchos did not constitute
the conscious people but that neither were they a plague of
bandits. They formed the population of the country districts, dislodged and corraled by the governments of the cities. Once they
triumphed, the chieftains engaged in cajoling those people but
they did nothing to promote their welfare.[2] The historic period
which extends from 1820 to 1830 has been called the Argentine
middle ages to signify that it was an era of chaos and retrogression.

In European history the term "middle ages" is applied to the
period that extends from the fall of the Western Roman Empire
(fifth century) to the fall of the Eastern Roman Empire (fifteenth
century). The middle ages were characterized by one typical institution, feudalism, which involved the division of land and of political authority among numerous "feudal lords." There were feudal
lords more powerful than the king himself, who for a considerable
time played a rôle that was purely decorative. Many historians, in
fact, affirm that this epoch is the "night of history," but more
careful studies have demonstrated that, if the middle ages were not
a brilliant period, they were a fruitful period in the sense that our
modern civilization grew and evolved thereupon. In fact, during
the ancient period there existed the vast Roman Empire which
included almost the entire known world that had been subjected
to a single authority; during the middle ages, and as a result of
feudalism, the western part of this huge empire broke up into small
states that were subordinated to the authority of feudal lords, and
when these lords were eliminated, these states were subordinated
to the authority of a king. Thus there were born from the extensive
Roman Empire the modern nationalities of Europe. Accordingly,
the middle ages was not a barbarous epoch.

Some analogies exist between that period and the age of the
Argentine chieftains. The caudillos, like the feudal lords, were petty
kings in the territories under their control; some of them were more
powerful than directors or presidents. The chieftains López and
Ramírez vanquished Director Rondeau. Quiroga and Bustos disobeyed President Rivadavia. The epoch which was dominated by
the caudillos was one of chaos and anarchy; but just as the feudal
lords furnished the bases for the European nationalities, so the

---

[2] See further, Alvarez, *op cit.*, pp. 104-5.

Argentine caudillos assured the triumph of democracy and asserted the principle of federalism.

In addition, the chieftains were nationalists, that is, they promoted the organization of the nation, but upon the basis of provincial autonomy. All the movements of rebellion against Buenos Aires, and of rivalry among the provinces had, nevertheless, an instinct and a common tendency toward nationality. Two facts disclosed this tendency on the part of the caudillos: (1) The inter-provincial treaties which they framed. (2) The meeting of national congresses which they promoted by their initiative.

The first important inter-provincial treaty was that of Pilar, signed after the battle of Cepeda by the provinces of Buenos Aires, Santa Fe, and Entre Ríos. The first article of this convention provided that: "The contracting parties declare that the vote of the nation, and in particular that of the provinces under their control, with regard to the system of government that should be adopted, has been cast in favor of the federation which in fact they accept. As they are convinced that all the provinces of the nation aspire to the organization of a central government, they pledge each one of the contracting parties to invite the other provinces to coöperate by sending their respective deputies in order that they may agree to whatever may suit them and promote the general welfare." At the same time that this treaty manifests the national spirit of the caudillos, it affirms the principle of federalism.

On February 8, 1822, a treaty was signed by the governments of Buenos Aires, Santa Fe, Entre Ríos, and Corrientes which recognized the principle of Argentine nationality and pledged the contracting parties to convoke a national congress. By this treaty the differences that might arise among the provinces were "reserved to the sovereign, legitimate, general congress of all the provinces upon the occasion when the condition of American affairs should be marked by perfect tranquility and by the absolute cessation of political operations—a congress whose apt innovations would be obeyed as the emanations of national sovereignty."

In the same year, 1822, Martín Rodríguez, the governor of Buenos Aires, signed with the riparian provinces the so-called quadruple treaty by which they promised to aid each other and to promote the entry of the other states into the pact. Other treaties were later signed by the provinces, by the initiative or consent of their respective caudillos. All of these insisted upon the recognition of the autonomy of the states as integral parts of the nation. Another manifestation of the national instinct of the chieftains was their notion that national congresses should be assembled. This spirit of organization, by which they were animated, was certainly personal and egoistic. Each caudillo desired to organize the congress in his own way in order to decide its measures, but these plans were in the end proposals of organization.

The caudillo, Bustos, promoted the meeting of a general congress in the city of Córdoba. By the treaty of peace arranged between Buenos Aires and Santa Fe in the end of 1820, during the administrations of Rodríguez and of López, respectively, the province of Córdoba was the intermediary in the negotiation and its governor Bustos, caused the insertion of a stipulation in the treaty to the effect that the provinces of Santa Fe and Buenos Aires should be obliged to send deputies to the congress which, at the end of two months should assemble at Córdoba. In fact, on October 21, 1821, there gathered in that city the deputies of ten provinces; the civil war which was raging in the north prevented the provinces of Salta, Tucumán, Santiago del Estero, and Catamarca from sending representatives to congress. The deputies who assembled at Córdoba addressed to the governments that had not sent representatives a note which contained this passage: "Appointed as deputies to the next general congress, we have met at a convenient point animated by the purest intentions, profiting by the lessons of bitter experience, guarding, so far as possible, against ulterior misfortunes, and desiring to give to the country a new era of glory and peace." But all was in vain. The deputies who had gathered at Córdoba returned to their respective provinces feeling that the attempt of Bustos to convoke a general congress had failed.[3] Henceforth, the desires of the chieftain Bustos took another direction; for some years later he dissolved the junta of representatives and levied contributions at will.

---

[3] In accordance with Rivadavia's instructions, the deputies of the province of Buenos Aires maintained that it was impossible to constitute the national authority at once because of the following reasons: (1) there was no person in the country in whom to deposit this authority; (2) it would be impossible to grant a chief executive sufficient authority; (3) the empty national treasury could not be replenished from a poverty-stricken people, *Documentos para la historia argentina*, XIII, 114.

After 1818, the caudillo López of Santa Fe, championed the autonomy of that province.[4] In 1819, when the congress of Buenos Aires framed the unitarian constitution—an occasional cause for anarchy—López joined the chieftain Francisco Ramírez of Entre Ríos, and routed the soldiers of Director Rondeau at the battle of Cepeda. At this juncture, the Treaty of Pilar was signed, which recognized the autonomy of the contracting provinces; in the same year, 1820, López triumphed over General Miguel Estanislao Soler at the glen of Cruz; Dorrego routed him in the ravine of Pavón, but López avenged himself at Gamonal. In the personal struggle for supremacy between López and his rival, Ramírez, the caudillo of Entre Ríos, the latter was killed. Already eliminated from these struggles, the Uruguayan caudillo, Artigas, had taken refuge in Paraguay. When the congress which had assembled in Buenos Aires framed the unitarian constitution of 1826, the province of Santa Fe refused to obey the national government. But when the constituent congress had dissolved, the provincial deputies reassembled, and formed a national convention in the city of Santa Fe. Although the delegates of eleven provinces made their appearance, yet the convention did not open its sessions because of the obstacle interposed by the chieftain Bustos. In accordance with the terms of previous pacts, the members of the convention had authority to designate a general executive and to convoke a constituent congress for the purpose of framing a federal republican constitution.

Tucumán had its caudillo, a type that represented its people, Bernabé Aráoz. In 1814, Director Posadas appointed him governor-intendant of the new province of Tucumán, which by a decree of that period had been carved out of the province of Córdoba, and which had within its limits Santiago del Estero and Catamarca. In 1819, Aráoz promoted an uprising in order that he might once more gain control of the government, and on March 22, 1820, the province declared itself to be an "independent republic," with him as supreme president. In the same year, a congress assembled in the city of Tucumán with representatives from that province and from the province of Catamarca. The historian, López, justly criticizes this miniature congress and states: "It is composed of

[4] J. L. Busaniche, *Estanislao López y el federalismo del litoral* (Buenos Aires, 1927).

three persons: Dr. Arteaga, the curate, Pedro Miguel Aráoz, and José Antonio Olmos. The first is a miserable pickpocket, the second, a generous spirit but incapable of resisting the suggestions of his relative Bernabé, and the third is a flute that simply pipes the tune furnished by Arteaga." Nevertheless, this congress did not, as has been claimed, entertain a desire to separate from the rest of the nation. In 1824, Bernabé Aráoz was shot by order of the governor of Tucumán, Abraham González.

The caudillo Quiroga, "the tiger of the llanos," played a prominent rôle in the political history and the sanguinary wars of our republic. We have seen him in action, triumphing over La Madrid in the battles of El Corneta and Tala, and vanquished at La Tablada and Oncativo by the forces of General Paz. At the fortress of Tucumán, he struck another blow at La Madrid, who had taken charge of the army of General Paz when the latter was made prisoner. After an agitated and unfortunate career the chieftain, Quiroga, came to reside in Buenos Aires. To quote Saldías again: "In his conversations with the leading men, whose society he frequented, Quiroga ingenuously confessed his errors, and admitted that he had more than once regretted having rejected the constitution of 1826; that he had acted as he did because of suggestions from men residing in Buenos Aires. The most curious fact is that he sought to associate with the unitarians who were in Buenos Aires and that they reasoned with him concerning the necessity that he should promote the organization of the nation under a federal régime, because this was the undying wish of the people. One night, in the house of Simón Lavalle, he avowed that Rosas was in accord with him in that respect; that as soon as the provinces should be at peace both of them would take steps to convoke a congress at Santa Fe [he should have said in Buenos Aires]; and that he would stake his life that the constitution framed there would be federal. Availing themselves of his offers, various leaders and émigrés of the unitarian party obtained favors of him. By his interposition, Colonel Wenceslao Paunero was allowed to proceed from Bolivia to rejoin his family at Colonia; and he offered Rivadavia his guarantee and his services to the end that he might be allowed to remain in Buenos Aires." [5]

---

[5] Saldías, *Historia de la Confederación Argentina,* II, 223.

Was Rosas in accord with this desire of Colonel Quiroga?[6] In 1834, a sanguinary dispute arose between the governors of Tucumán and Salta. Rosas asked Quiroga to proceed to the northern provinces charged with a special mission to prevent civil war, but as the latter insisted that as soon as possible a congress should be assembled for the purpose of framing a constitution, Rosas addressed a letter to him in which he expounded the reasons that rendered the convocation of a congress inopportune. Let us quote some paragraphs of the letter: "No one can be more fully convinced than you and I of the necessity of organizing a general government and that this procedure is the only means of insuring existence and respectability to our republic. . . . Who in order to form an orderly and compact entity does not previously arrange in a regular and permanent form the parts that should compose it? Who organizes an army out of groups of men without commanders, without officials, without discipline, without subordination—men who do not for a moment cease to spy upon and struggle with each other, thus involving the others in their disorders? Who forms a living and robust being from limbs that are dead or that are torn asunder and diseased with the most corrupt gangrene, for the life and vigor of this new complex being can be no different from that which it receives from the very members that compose it? . . . Notice that a federal republic is the most chimerical and disastrous which can be imagined, whenever it is not composed of states well organized among themselves, for, as each state preserves its sovereignty and independence, the force of the general authority with respect to the internal affairs of the republic is almost negligible."[7]

Was this letter due to the inspiration of Rosas? Some writers affirm that it was not. Did Rosas express with sincerity the sentiments that it contains? Here the reply of most writers is again in the negative. They adduce other documents, in sharp contrast with this letter, in which Rosas seems to make a farce of the plan of federation. From this analysis it may be deduced that the caudillos, with the possible exception of Rosas, were not the disorganizers of the nation; and that the delay in framing a constitution

---

[6] Peña, *Juan Facundo Quiroga*, p. 335.
[7] *Ibid.*, pp. 391-92.—W. S. R.

for all the provinces was rather due to the condition of society and of the age.

We wish to repeat the words with which we began this chapter: our democracy was turbulent and inorganic, and the caudillos, its fruits and typical exponents, possessed such traits.

CHAPTER XLVI

ROSAS

On december 8, 1829, Rosas entered upon the duties of governor and captain general of the province of Buenos Aires. He appointed as his ministers Tomás Guido, Manuel J. García, and General Juan R. Balcarce. The legislature passed a law delegating to the governor extraordinary powers. That law ran thus: "There will be very special powers, in accordance with which he is authorized to regulate, in conformity with the exigencies of present circumstances, the interior administration of the provinces in all their branches, preserving intact their liberty and independence; to minister to their necessities in the most efficacious manner; to thwart the attacks that the anarchists design against them; and to insure order and public tranquility. . . . In order to promote these objects he is invested with those extraordinary powers which he may judge necessary until the meeting of the next legislature to which he shall give an account of the use which he has made of this special authorization." This delegation of extraordinary authority was made by the legislature in view of the civil war that agitated the country; for General Paz, victorious in the interior, was preparing for a struggle against the riparian provinces.

During the provisional government of Viamonte, orders were given for the transfer of the remains of Colonel Dorrego from the field of Navarro to Buenos Aires. It accordingly devolved upon Rosas to receive them on December 13; he arranged a funeral suitable for a deceased captain general. This was an imposing ceremony; there were present the leading representatives of the government, the army, and the clergy; the people en masse and the school children surrounded the hearse. Upon this occasion Rosas made a speech in which he said: "Dorrego, illustrious victim of civil dissensions, rest in peace! . . . Today the country, honor, and religion have been satisfied by paying the highest honors to the first magistrate of the republic, who was sentenced to die at a time when law was ignored. The deepest blot in the history of the Argentinians has been laved with the tears of a just, grateful, and sensitive people. Your tomb, surrounded at this moment by representatives of the province, of the magistracy, of venerable priests, of warriors of independence, and of your mourning compatriots forms the glorious monument which the government of Buenos Aires has dedicated to you in the face of the civilized world—a monument which will make known until the last generations that the people of Buenos Aires were not accomplices in your misfortune."

Public opinion, as well as the chief civil and military leaders, supported Rosas in the execution of his functions during the first period of his rule. In the war which he undertook against General Paz, the latter was taken prisoner, so that order was restored throughout the country. At the end of Rosas's first term of office, on three successive occasions the legislature insisted that he should continue in charge of the province. But as he refused to do so, it appointed as governor General Juan R. Balcarce who had served as minister of war during the previous administration.

The psychology of Rosas is not simple. Certain facts help to explain his contradictory manner of life. Thus, a few days after he assumed command of the province, Rosas was the object of a great demonstration on the part of the people, of the merchants, and of the legislature. In celebration of his elevation to the governorship, orders had been given to mint a medal on which there was inscribed under the bust of Rosas: "He cultivated his fields and defended the Fatherland." Rosas refused this homage, and replied in a note which, because of its suggestiveness, we shall cite in part: "This event, . . . though indeed it displays the liberality of the representatives, yet is a step perilous to the liberty of the people and perhaps a motive of just anxiety to those persons who do not understand the conscience of the undersigned; for this is not the first time in history when prodigality in the distribution of honors has stimulated public men until they reached the level of tyrants." [1]

No less singular than the foregoing episode is the fact that, after fulfilling the duties of his office for a year and a half, Rosas threatened to resign. This rumor began to spread and soon it became public. The protest against such a studied or sincere decision was general. Tomás Guido wrote a letter to convince Rosas that he owed something to his country which had higher claims than the superficial tranquility of private life. "Without doubt," added Guido in his epistle, "you would be much happier scattering a fist-

---

[1] *Historia de los premios militares* (3 vols. Buenos Aires, 1906), III, 164.

ful of wheat over the land than in exercising a discretional power
to distribute rewards and punishments among its citizens; but if
there are enchantments in rural occupations that the good man
knows how to appreciate, there is also something seductive that
satisfies the conscience in the administration of justice and in the
performance of great actions." In a succeeding passage of his letter Guido ventured to drop this warning hint: "If I should see you,"
he said to Rosas, "elevated to the supreme magistracy by the abuse
of force, by the strategems of a party or by the fascination of a
people deluded by pompous promises; if I should see you engaged
in perpetuating your authority, in defrauding the people of their
rights, in violating guarantees, in overthrowing or ignoring the
vital institutions of a free country at a time when I should lack the
courage to labor for your overthrow, never would I degrade myself
in the least to justify by words your continuance in office." [2]

The Indians in the southern part of the province of Buenos Aires
had ravaged the frontier of the country. Rosas conceived the daring
project of despatching an expedition into the wilderness. Governor
Balcarce placed the necessary forces at his disposal; Rosas also
asked aid from the government of Chile and from the caudillos
Quiroga and López. The expeditionary army was organized in
three divisions: the left under the command of Rosas, the center
under the orders of Ruiz Huidobro, and the right under Félix Aldao.
The Chilean government declined to participate because of the
internal condition of the country; while the caudillo, Quiroga,
declared that he was not conversant with Indian warfare. The
expedition, composed of two thousand men, reached Bahía Blanca
on April 20, 1833. The forces traversed the courses of the rivers
Neuquén, Limay, and Negro. After some engagements with the
Indians, the divisions of the center and the right withdrew. Left
alone, Rosas undertook to extend the theater of operations. The
division under his command conquered the territories that stretched
one hundred and sixty leagues to the west and northwest up to
the foothills of the Andes, and on the southwest it subjugated the

---

[2] This letter of Guido was first printed, with an illuminating commentary
by Correa Luna, in *La Prensa*, Buenos Aires, August 19, 1923. The important
interpretative work of E. Quesada, entitled *La época de Rosas* (Buenos Aires,
1923), which was first published in 1898, has recently been reprinted with an
introduction by N. Binayán.

tribal bands of the Tehuelches to within two hundred leagues of the river Valchetas. Says Saldías:

"The results of this heroic campaign lasting one year were, in the first place, to determine the limits of the province of Buenos Aires in accord with the governments of Santa Fe, Córdoba, San Luis, and Mendoza; to destroy all the clans of the important caciques Chocori, Pitrioloncoy, Mittao, Paynen, Cayupán, . . . who raided these provinces; to put out of action in killed or prisoners more than six thousand Indians; and to release more than two thousand captives whose names were recorded in the publication that was officially circulated for the information of their relatives who already considered them lost." [3]

General Balcarce became head of the government of the province at a juncture when public opinion sympathized strongly with Rosas. On the occasion of the election of deputies to the legislature, a schism took place between the group that followed Balcarce and the partisans of Rosas. The latter violently opposed the governor in every manner, particularly by means of the press. One of the periodicals that supported the federal party was called *El Restaurador de las Leyes (The Restorer of the Laws)*, a name which the legislature had bestowed upon Rosas. Governor Balcarce ordered the fiscal, Pedro José Agrelo, to bring charges against that periodical because of the aggravating articles published in its columns. The people bunglingly thought that the accusation was directed against Rosas, and on the day set for hearing the accusation of the fiscal, more than two thousand citizens invaded the Plaza de la Victoria. Soon they rushed off in the direction of Barracas, where they joined some ten thousand men from the country who laid siege to the city. This uprising was designated the revolution of the restorers. [4] The legislature dismissed Governor Balcarce and gave charge of the province to General Viamonte.

General Viamonte began his administration on November 4, 1833, and resigned on June 27, 1834. His ministers were Guido and García, but the political situation, which steadily grew worse, made it impossible for this government to last long. Rosas had returned from his campaign into the wilderness, and the legislature

[3] Saldías, *Historia de la Confederación Argentina,* II, 170-71.
[4] Levene, *Lecturas históricas argentinas,* II, 275-77.

had rewarded him by a grant of the island of Choele-Choel in the Río Negro in Patagonia, by a sword, and a gold medal.

On June 29, 1834, when the term of General Balcarce, which had been filled out by General Viamonte, came to an end, Rosas was named governor and captain general of the province, but he would not accept the post and in the letter sent by him to the legislature he said: "Honor, and that virtue without which no one can call himself a patriot, at present imperiously prevents me from occupying such an elevated post." The house of representatives insisted on the appointment; Rosas replied expressing thanks for the marked signs of appreciation which this act implied, but again declining to accept it. The house then addressed a note to him declaring that "whatever might be the merit of the reasons upon which the second refusal was based, naught could resist the irresistible force of public exigency, of the welfare of the country, and of the uniform desire of the province that imperiously proclaim your Excellency as the chieftain designed to determine its destiny." Rosas refused to accept the appointment for the third and for the fourth time. The fourth refusal was accepted by the legislature, which then appointed Tomás Manuel de Anchorena; but he also declined the appointment, as did also Nicolás Anchorena, Juan N. Terrero, and General Ángel Pacheco, who were successively named. On October 1, Manuel Vicente Maza, who was president of the legislature, took charge of the province.

During the provisional government of Maza, a civil war broke out between Latorre and Hereida, who were respectively governors of the provinces of Salta and Tucumán. Maza arranged with Rosas for the caudillo Quiroga, who was now residing in Buenos Aires, to be sent north on a mission of conciliation. For some time, Rosas had been solicited by the caudillo of La Rioja to promote the convocation of a national congress which would frame a constitution. Upon confiding to Quiroga the peace mission destined for the provinces of the north, Rosas promised that he would write Quiroga a letter which would explain the grounds and the motives that induced him to think that the time for the political organization of the country had not yet arrived. We quoted some excerpts from this letter in the preceding chapter. Quiroga left Buenos Aires on December 18, 1834; while on the journey he received the news that Governor Hereida of Tucumán had vanquished Governor Latorre of Salta, and that the latter had been assassinated.

On the return from his mission, while passing through the province of Córdoba, Quiroga was warned that the Reynafés, who dominated this province, were conspiring to murder him. In fact, on February 16, 1825, at a place called Barranca Yaco, Quiroga was assassinated by a band under the command of Captain Santos Pérez. This event caused much excitement in Buenos Aires. By whose order had Santos Pérez assassinated Quiroga? The majority of writers assert that this was done by order of Rosas, who cherished the desire to eliminate this rival caudillo. Other writers throw the responsibility for this murder upon Estanislao López, governor of Santa Fe, or upon the Reynafés who dominated the province of Córdoba, or upon Ibarra, who was the caudillo of Santiago del Estero. History has not been able to pronounce the final verdict with regard to this tragic episode.

CHAPTER XLVII

DICTATORSHIP

ON MARCH 7, 1835, as Dr. Maza had declared that it was impossible for him to govern the province, the legislature appointed Rosas governor, and transferred to him the sum total of public authority. By virtue of this delegation of power, the new official was to defend the federal cause and to hold office as long as he might consider advisable. Rosas accepted this appointment, but imposed the condition that the people should vote directly and declare whether they approved of the act by which the legislature had delegated all public authority.[1] The plebiscite took place on March 26, 27, and 28, when the people of the city of Buenos Aires, with the exception of a few votes, by a direct expression of their will, delegated to Rosas the entire public authority.

Rosas selected Felipe Arana as minister of government and foreign relations; José María Roxas y Patrón as minister of the treasury; and General Pinedo as minister of war and the navy. Among the measures adopted by the government, the following should be mentioned: the annulment of the laws concerning the confiscation of property which, "in order to satisfy hatreds and ignoble pretensions," had been in force up to this time. Nevertheless, this measure was not carried out; and Rosas had the properties of exiled unitarians confiscated. Another measure was the negotiation of a treaty with Great Britain by virtue of which the slave trade was abolished. Another was the foundation of the *casa de moneda* in 1836 to replace the former national bank. By five emissions that were authorized between the years 1837 and 1846 there were placed in circulation 107,831,666 pesos of paper money. In 1853, the *casa de moneda* was transformed into the bank

---

[1] The proclamation of Rosas upon receiving command is printed in Levene, *Lecturas históricas argentinas*, II, 278-79. There is a large mass of documents concerning early phases of Rosas' career in the Archivo general de la nación. See further, Saldías, *Historia de la Confederación Argentina*, II, 244; Estrada, *Lecciones de historia argentina*, II, 445; and Ingenieros, *La evolución de las ideas argentinas*, II, 87-88.

of the province.[2] Lastly, Rosas permitted the reëstablishment of the Society of Jesus, which had been expelled during the reign of Charles III. He directed that the former Jesuit church and academy should be restored to the order, and authorized it to develop university education.

During the tyranny, Argentine poets and writers had taken refuge abroad in order to carry on a campaign in favor of liberty. The intellectual lights of the country were thus snuffed out. Only a single man of letters, Pedro de Angelis, who had arrived during the epoch of Rivadavia, placed himself at the service of the dictator. In 1830, Angelis published an *Ensayo histórico sobre la vida de Rosas,* and gave to the world up to the date of the battle of Caseros, numerous writings, most of which tended to praise the policy of Rosas. But his most important work, *Documentos para la historia argentina,* is a very valuable contribution to the study of Argentine national history.

The policy of Rosas also affected the University of Buenos Aires. It caused removals of professors from their posts, as well as changes in the administrative and teaching régimes which gradually dissociated them. In 1838, it was required that the students should pay the cost of their education, on the pretext that the governmental budget could not bear the expense of the professors' salaries. In 1846, a commission was appointed to inspect the programs of study and the texts. Its duty was to examine them in order to see that they harmonized with Roman Catholic doctrine and with the existing political system.[3]

Public opinion, as well as the sentiment of the middle and lower classes of society, had designated Rosas as the arbiter of the destinies of the province of Buenos Aires and of the entire republic. The social atmosphere was prepared for a dictatorship.[4] Rosas had himself said in 1829: "This is not the first time in history when prodigality in the distribution of honors has stimulated public men until they reached the plane of tyrants."

Among the most abject spectacles in which the people of Buenos

---

[2] There are numerous legajos of documents in the Archivo general de la nación concerning economic and financial problems during the age of Rosas.

[3] See further, Ingenieros, *La evolución de las ideas argentinas,* II, 536.

[4] J. V. González, "Origen y fin de una dictadura," *La Nación,* Buenos Aires, February 3, 1921.

Aires participated were the parochial entertainments arranged in homage to the dictator. The portrait of Rosas was placed on a triumphal car that was drawn by magistrates and citizens who took the places of beasts of burden. The image of Rosas was transported through the city and thus feelings of respect and fear were diffused among the people. His portrait was even placed on church altars; and from their pulpits the priests preached the worship of Rosas.

This servile sentiment of the populace assumed all the forms that might flatter the personal vanity of the dictator and make his will omnipotent. In theatrical performances, the people preferred scenes representing actual politics: the plot was concerned with incidents and conflicts that took place between a federalist and a unitarian. The last-mentioned appeared on the stage true to the type that Sarmiento has described: "He marches straight ahead," states Sarmiento of the unitarian type, "with head aloft; he does not retreat though he sees a building fall; he talks with arrogance, and ends a phrase with disdainful gestures and decisive attitude." The show ended by exhibiting the unitarian as a guilty and perverse person upon whom punishment fell. The crowd then became delirious, and offered an ovation to "the holy federal cause." [5]

In 1833, during the administration of Balcarce, an institution designated the "Mazorca" was organized in order to spread the views of Rosas. There are authors who affirm that the Mazorca was composed of a brutal and a licentious rabble. Others maintain that this institution included decent and respectable persons. Pelliza's verdict is worthy of notice: "In both of these judgments there is truth, but in neither of them is the truth absolute but rather relative. Because of unsettled conditions the Mazorca had in its ranks good men and peaceful citizens and it is also beyond doubt that among its members in friendly brotherhood were the worst rascals and assassins who placed their whips and their daggers at the service of the dictator." [6] The institution of the Mazorca seems to have inspired the popular celebrations that were held in honor

---

[5] See further, A. Zinny, *Historia de los gobernadores de las provincias argentinas* (5 vols. Buenos Aires, 1920-21), I, 150.

[6] Pelliza, *Historia argentina desde su origen hasta la organización nacional*, II, 188.

of Rosas. In his interpretative study of Rosas, the eminent sociologist, Ernesto Quesada, expressed this view:

"The excesses, the abuses, the crimes, indeed all the barbarous
methods of terror and dominion that served Rosas, are absolutely unjustifiable and merit the most energetic condemnation:
no excuse should extenuate them; no pardon should be granted
them. Rosas knew it: he performed the barbarous acts or he tolerated them because he considered them necessary. Were they perhaps the product of a neurotic temperament, the invention of a
madman, an anachronism in customs, a strain on the epoch, an inexplicable phenomenon? Nothing of the sort. These reprehensible
measures can be easily and logically explained: they were inherent
in the customs of the epoch and in the doctrines of our thinkers.
They were resorted to by all factions: federalists and unitarians,
rosistas and émigrés, tyrants and subjects—all of them became
in turn, and as circumstances permitted, victims and executioners,
executioners and victims." [7]

This was not the first occasion in our history that a régime of
excessive rigor was invoked in order to insure the triumph of a
certain cause. Thus, in the year 1810, when the revolution began,
one of its armies imprisoned in Córdoba the chief leaders, directors, and authors of the first reaction against the patriots.
Convinced that it was necessary to furnish a warning, the governmental junta ordered their execution. The expedition proceeded northward, and after the triumph of Suipacha, the junta
commanded that the chiefs of the Spanish army, Córdoba, Paula
Sanz, and Nieto, should be executed. The conspiracy of the regiment of nobles, owing to the order issued by General Belgrano
that its soldiers should remove the galloons that adorned their
uniforms, was also repressed in the same manner; for rebellious
sergeants, corporals, and soldiers were condemned to death. In
1812, a conspiracy threatened the stability of the revolutionary
government; Martín Alzaga was found to be implicated in the
plan and the triumvirate ordered that he should be shot, in company with thirty-eight fellow conspirators. Their corpses were

---

[7] E. Quesada, *op. cit.,* p. 99. Estimates by an enemy of Rosas of the number of
persons put to death during this age may be found in J. Rivera Indarte, *Rosas
y sus opositores* (Buenos Aires, 1853), pp. 275-318.

exhibited for three days in the Plaza de la Victoria. Amid the crowd that gathered to behold the spectacle there was a youth who was no more than fifteen years of age:—he was named Juan Manuel de Rosas.[8]

These facts demonstrate that the terror—though indeed used only partially and to support the elevated cause of the revolution— had antecedents in our country: but Rosas undertook to establish it as a governmental régime and in order to serve a personal cause. The political anarchy of 1820, already studied above was the result of forces which agitated society in a certain manner. The strong hand of Pueyrredón could scarcely restrain momentarily the crisis that broke out violently after his resignation was precipitated. This powerful historic force—of turbulence, of anarchy, of revo- lutions—is what caused the downfall of Rivadavia, who repre- sented the theoretical type as well as the organizer par excel- lence. In advance of his age, forgetting that the preliminary task was to consolidate the country, Rivadavia was above all a doctrin- aire who legislated as though for a nation that was already con- stituted. After his fall, Colonel Dorrego became governor of the province of Buenos Aires, who, if he did not have the breadth of view and the ample talent of his predecessor, had the correct con- ception of the actual condition of his people and of his age. But Dorrego was shot: the execution of the constitutional governor of the province of Buenos Aires was the first violent provocation. The political parties possessing principles—the federalists and the unitarians—who had played a brilliant rôle in the constituent con- gress of 1826, brought on a crisis, and impelled by ambition and interest became transformed into personal parties. From this time forth the historic currents which since 1810, had agitated and moved society toward anarchy and the fiasco of all attempts at or- ganization, were let loose and now ran unbridled and violent. To quote Ernesto Quesada again:

"The previous political struggle had provoked passions that reached the last stage of irritation. The two traditional parties could no longer exist side by side; and the unitarian party, which was undoubtedly in a minority, had been dislodged. The revolution was permanent, and there resulted an abnormal condition, with martial law, suspension of the guarantees of citizens, and all the

---

[8] J. M. Ramos Mejía, *Rosas y su tiempo* (3 vols. Buenos Aires, 1907), I, 109 ff.

horrors that such a condition occasioned. The governors enjoyed what, in the terminology of the age, was styled the *suma del poder público*. . . . It was not possible to think of constituting the country on any different bases in those blind moments. The struggle of both parties was to the death, and it permitted no pause. It was life over a volcano. The reciprocal hatreds were unprecedented; a tranquil existence was impossible. Governments had no other recourse than terror. . . ." [9]

The successive and violent crises of the patriot governments showed the revolutionary condition of the country. A government rose to fall in a short time, overturned by an internal commotion. In this sense, Rosas checked the dissensions and, taking advantage of the prevailing moral dissolution, he maintained himself in power during a period of twenty years.

We said that Rosas is a social product: (1) because he was the result of anarchy and of the successive crises of the governments which since 1810, had not endured for the term set either by law or the constitution and which had fallen as the result of anarchical, revolutionary explosions; (2) because the terror established by Rosas as a régime had historic antecedents in our country, and had been employed by governments, although not with the character of an organized system; and (3) because the social psychology of the epoch determined the creation of this product which was founded in the sentiments of an uncultured people, as the majority was composed of negroes and the inhabitants of the suburbs of Buenos Aires—a majority that gave an explicit manifestation of the public will when the people by the plebiscite of 1835, conferred on Rosas "the sum total of public authority." [10]

---

[9] E. Quesada, *op. cit.*, p. 55.

[10] Appreciations of the historical significance of this era by Dr. Tejedor and B. Mitre may be found in "Una época: la tiranía y la resistencia," *Atlántida* (Buenos Aires, 1911), II, 321-23.

CHAPTER XLVIII

REACTIONS AGAINST ROSAS

SUCCESSIVE and continuous campaigns of liberation were organized aganist the government of Rosas. The reactions that resulted were as follows: The Asociación de Mayo (Association of May), the uprising of Berón de Astrada in Corrientes, the conspiracy of Maza, the revolution of the country south of Buenos Aires, the campaign of Lavalle, the coalition of the north, the campaign of General Paz. The last and triumphant reaction was the liberating campaign of Urquiza, who routed Rosas in the battle of Caseros.

The liberal revolution of 1830 in France against Charles X for the purpose of insuring a constitutional monarchy, had the virtue of affecting the political and philosophical ideas that prevailed in all countries. In Buenos Aires, a representative nucleus of young men headed by Esteban Echeverría, Juan María Gutiérrez, Juan Bautista Alberdi, Vicente Fidel López, and Miguel Cané induced a well-known bookseller named Marcos Sastre to fit out a hall in his store to accommodate frequent literary meetings. Thus was brought into existence the so-called literary salon, at whose initial meeting Alberdi, Gutiérrez, Sastre, and Vicente López y Planes spoke. Rosas later said to the last-mentioned member that he did not belong there. Some time afterward "the bookstore of Marcos Sastre had to be closed; he was warned by the police that its little meetings were not pleasing to the political authority and openly distasteful to the ecclesiastical authority. Foreign Jesuits intrigued effectively against the young Argentinians." [1]

This persecution convinced the founders of the literary salon of the convenience of organizing themselves into a society, similar to the societies of the Carbonari then in vogue in Europe. In 1837, Gutiérrez, Alberdi, and Echeverría formed the Association of May or rather the *Joven Argentina*, which was closely modeled upon analogous European institutions, especially the Young Italy

---

[1] J. Ingenieros, "La filosofía social de Echeverra y la leyenda de la 'Asiociación de Mayo'," *Revista de Filosofía* (Buenos Aires, 1918), año IV, núm. 2, pp. 225-97.

founded in 1830 by Mazzini. Esteban Echeverría was charged to formulate "the symbolic words" or the program condensed in "the social dogma of May," according to which, in order to make it possible to fulfil the second proposal of the emancipatory movement of 1810, namely, to organize society and to constitute a free government, encouragement had to be sought from the labor of those persons who had brought about the May Revolution. The members of the Association of May invited all Argentinians to join them, irrespective as to whether they were federalists or unitarians, and asked them to cast aside party hatreds.[2]

The governor of Corrientes, Colonel Berón de Astrada, was the first to issue a challenge to Rosas by publishing a manifesto in which he invited the governors of the provinces to deprive the dictator of the power to negotiate with foreign nations and of the delegated authority with which they had intrusted him. Berón de Astrada was able to gather an army of 5,000 men; he entered into collusion with the Argentine unitarians residing in Montevideo, and signed an agreement with the president of the Uruguayan Republic, General Rivera, in which the latter agreed to lend his support. General Echagüe, governor of Entre Ríos, and a partisan of Rosas, invaded the province of Corrientes, and at the battle of Pago Largo, on March 31, 1839, he completely routed the forces of Berón de Astrada. Numerous leaders and officers were put to the sword. This fate was also meted out to the leader of the uprising. The name of Berón de Astrada, who perished gloriously on the field of battle, will ever be found in the roll of the self-denying defenders of liberty.

Scarcely had the uprising in Corrientes been suppressed, when Rosas received news of a conspiracy formed by his enemies and by many important federalists. This plot was headed by Colonel Ramón Maza, son of the president of the house of representatives, and had its origin in the Association of May, whose principal members directed it. The plan was vast and the spirit of the conspiracy was also to compromise the country near the city of Buenos Aires. When Colonel Maza undertook to leave that city, he was conducted to prison; his father, who was implicated in the conspiracy, was assassinated in his office in the hall of the legislature; and upon the

---

[2] Ibid.

following day, Colonel Maza was shot; he was accused of having planned to assassinate Governor Rosas.[3]

On August 2, 1839, the liberating expedition which General Lavalle had prepared against Rosas in Montevideo in conjunction with the agents of France, who were involved in a diplomatic controversy with our government, began to march toward the island of Martín García. Thence it proceeded in the direction of Entre Ríos. In combination with this campaign, a revolution was prepared in the southern part of the province of Buenos Aires. But as Lavalle marched toward Entre Ríos and not to Buenos Aires, as he had promised, the revolution broke out on October 29, 1839, headed by Manuel Rico in Dolores, by Pedro Castelli in Chascomús, and by Ambrosio Crámer in Monsalvo. Rosas rapidly equipped an army which he placed under the command of his brother Prudencio, and on November 7 the battle of Chascomús was fought in which the revolutionists were vanquished. The heads of the revolutionary chieftains were exhibited for several days in the plaza of Chascomús.

In Montevideo, an "Argentine commission" was busy with a plan to depose Rosas. There happened at this time a rupture of relations between our country and France, an important event which we shall study attentively in the following chapter. In 1837 and 1838, the French consul presented a claim to the government of Rosas; but as that government did not yield to the demand of France, its agent arbitrarily announced a blockade of the port of Buenos Aires, and joined General Rivera and the Argentine commission, which was composed of unitarians. In conjunction, therefore, with the diplomatic agents of France, General Lavalle had organized a liberating expedition which seized Martín García, despite the valient defense made of this Argentine island by Commandant Jerónimo Costa. On September 2 the army of Lavalle composed of 550 men embarked in French vessels and landed near Gualeguay. Governor Echagüe gave battle on the plains of Yerúa but Lavalle defeated him. From Entre Ríos the victor marched to Corrientes, the heroic province that had previously revolted under Berón de Astrada. The governor of Santa Fe, Juan Pablo López, marched with an army of 2,500 men to attack Lavalle but the latter evaded a battle and with light divisions sought to defeat the army of

---

[3] New evidence concerning this incident in the struggles against Rosas is presented in Rodríguez, *Contribución histórica y documental*, II, 447-519.

López in detail. General Echagüe had invaded the republic of Uruguay, where President Rivera offered resistance, and at the battle of Cagancha, on December 19, 1839, Echagüe was defeated. Dissensions began to appear in the liberating army. Rivera beheld a rival in Lavalle and, for the purpose of discrediting him, he wrote to Governor Ferré that he should not repose all confidence in the leader of the campaign. In the beginning of 1840, General Lavalle marched toward Diamante; General Echagüe, a partisan of Rosas, sallied out to meet him, and at the rivulet called Don Cristóbal, a sanguinary battle took place which was favorable to Lavalle; but three months later at Sauce Grande, Echagüe avenged himself. Then Lavalle decided to invade the province of Buenos Aires; and landed at San Pedro. In the expectation that the country would rise in support of the expedition, Lavalle advanced to Merlo. The delay gave Rosas time to quiet the panic produced by news of the advance of Lavalle's army. The liberating army did not dare to venture up to the city, and its commander decided to retire toward the province of Santa Fe.[4]

One of the most heroic attempts made against Rosas was led by Marco de Avellaneda who organized "the coalition of the provinces of the north." On April 7, 1840, the government of Tucumán issued a decree which declared "that the existence in the first city of the republic of a government invested with the sum total of constitutional authority is a scandal in the eyes of South America and of the world, to which none of the other cities of the republic can consent without disgrace to its honor and its interest, since this postpones more and more the desired era in which the constitution of the Argentine people will be framed and sanctioned. . . . It has been resolved and decreed: Article I, Dictator Juan Manuel de Rosas is not recognized in the character of governor of Buenos Aires; Article II, the authority conferred upon him by these provinces to maintain relations of friendship and harmony with foreign nations is hereby withdrawn. . . ."

This coalition was formed by the provinces of Tucumán, Salta, La Rioja, Catamarca, and Jujuy; at the head of its army was General La Madrid, who got into touch with Lavalle in Santa Fe.

---

[4] Levene, *Lecturas históricas argentinas,* II, 282-90; Rodríguez, *Contribución histórica y documental,* III, 37 ff.; and J. Beverina, *Las campañas de los ejércitos libertadores* (Buenos Aires, 1923).

Rosas despatched General Oribe with an army of 10,000 men in pursuit of Lavalle; and on November 28 on the fields of Quebracho Herrado, of the province of Córdoba, a battle took place which was fatal for the army of liberation. Lavalle, who was morally and materially undone, then divided his army: La Madrid was in Tucumán; Colonel Vilela proceeded to Catamarca; Colonel Acha was to invade the province of Santiago del Estero; and General Lavalle should march into La Rioja. General Oribe also divided his army, and thus separate engagements took place. Colonel Vilela was routed by General Pacheco at San Calá, and Colonel Acha was defeated by Father Aldao at Machigasta. Acha was able to recover himself and to vanquish Father Aldao at Angaco; but Benavídez soon defeated him and he was shot.[5] General Pacheco routed La Madrid at Rodeo del Medio and the latter was compelled to flee to Chile. At Famaillá, General Oribe overtook the remainder of the army of Lavalle, on September 19, 1841, and routed it completely. Avellaneda was taken prisoner and executed. His head was displayed in the public square of Tucumán.

With a few followers Lavalle advanced to Salta, intending to leave Argentine soil. In Jujuy, he was entertained in the house of Dr. Bedoya; but a rosista party fired upon the house and a ball killed him. His soldiers carried his corpse to Potosí where it was buried in the cathedral.

While the last remainders of the army of Lavalle and of the coalition of the north were being destroyed, General Paz, who had escaped from prison after eight years of incarceration, gathered an army against Rosas in the province of Corrientes. This was joined by a battalion of soldiers organized there who, after the battle of Famaillá, had traversed the forests of the Chaco, and returned to their province. General Echagüe, governor of Entre Ríos, made war upon the province of Corrientes for the purpose of destroying the army of General Paz. The forces of both chieftains camped on the banks of the river Corrientes. General Paz knew the terrain on which he operated, and one night he decided to cross the river; on November 28, 1841, he took Echegüe's army by surprise and defeated it at the battle of Caa-Guazú. Because of

---

[5] E. Quesada, *La guerra civil de 1841 y la tragedia de Acha* (Córdoba, 1916), p. 311, maintains that the battle of Angaco was relatively the most bloody encounter in Argentina's civil wars.

the skill, the military art, and the strategy displayed, this battle should from the military viewpoint be included among the most important battles of its kind. It was a great misfortune, however, that this was a battle in a civil war, and not in a war for emancipation.

The triumph of Caa-Guazú set free the province of Corrientes and opened the road for General Paz as far as Entre Ríos. He planned to advance thence to Buenos Aires. Everyone believed in the success of this great campaign, because of the important victory gained, the discipline of the army, and the skill and valor of General Paz. But again discord arose among the leaders of the reaction. Rivera strove to have the command of the army taken away from the governor of Corrientes; becoming aware of this intrigue, Paz retired, and General Rivera became head of the forces. General Oribe then pursued them, and on December 6, 1842, General Rivera was completely routed at the battle of Arroyo Grande. General Oribe decided to attack Montevideo, but this campaign was delayed, and the fort was not besieged until February, 1843. Montevideo organized a resistance against the besieger and intrusted the command to General Paz. Discord again broke out between Rivera and Paz, but the difficulties were smoothed away; the latter took charge of fortifying the city, while General Rivera aroused opposition to Oribe in the country. On the other side, while General Oribe beleaguered Montevideo by land, Rosas ordered a blockade of the port. Montevideo made a patriotic defense. Within its walls "foreign legions" were formed, who aided General Paz to resist the siege. This situation lasted for a long time. General Urquiza, who was in the service of Rosas, finally proceeded to Uruguay and on March 27, 1845, defeated General Rivera in the battle of India Muerta.

The province of Corrientes organized a new campaign against Rosas. General Paz sallied out of Montevideo, and in conjunction with the governor of that province, Joaquín Madariaga, and by the aid of 4,000 Paraguayans, he prepared an army of liberation. Urquiza, having defeated Rivera at India Muerta, now decided to invade the province of Corrientes, where he defeated Juan Madariaga, brother of the governor, who commanded the vanguard of Paz's army. The "Treaty of Alcaraz" was signed by Paz and the governor of Corrientes, by virtue of which the provinces that

they represented bound themselves in an alliance and agreed recip-
rocally to recognize each other's autonomy as had been stipulated in the federal pact of 1831. Rosas disapproved of this treaty;
hence Urquiza, pretending to respect his orders, again invaded
the province of Corrientes, and defeated Madariaga at the ranch
of Vences in November, 1847.

CHAPTER XLIX

FOREIGN COMPLICATIONS

AFTER THE year 1824, when the discussion between Spain and England concerning the Falkland Islands was terminated, the government of Madrid continued to occupy those islands and to appoint their officials. When the revolution of 1810 occurred, the new government succeeded Spain in the exercise of all rights over the Falkland Islands. But in December, 1831, a North-American warship committed an outrage against their authorities, because of the watch which they maintained along their coasts to prevent whale fishing. The minister of foreign relations of Buenos Aires demanded from the chargé d'affaires of the United States satisfactory explanations for this insult; but that diplomatic agent did not give satisfaction and left Argentina. In this state of affairs the crew of an English corvette of war came to the islands in January, 1833, and landed there, in order "to operate in that territory as in a possession that belonged to Great Britain." The government of Buenos Aires immediately protested to his Britannic Majesty through the Argentine minister in London, who at that time was Dr. Manuel Moreno. The latter set forth in conclusive form the Argentine title to the possession of the islands by saying: "The United Provinces have proved by irrefutable documents that their title to the Falkland Islands, that is, to the isle of Soledad, or Puerto Luis, (separated from Puerto Egmont by a branch of the sea) is based upon a legitimate 'purchase' from France; 'priority of occupation, cultivation, and formal settlement'; in fine, 'well-known and tranquil possession for over half a century, until the moment when they were forcibly despoiled on January 5, 1833. This title is based especially upon the principle that occupation confers a real and exclusive dominion over the land in possession— a principle that is consecrated in the codes of nations as one of eternal justice which is the basis for the inviolability of all property, private and public. . . . A nation cannot better demonstrate its right to the place which it occupies upon the face of the globe than that it has first taken possession of it, has cultivated it, and has created the riches that are found within its district. . . ." [1] The Argentine title is therefore indisputable; but Great Britain remains in possession of the islands.

The French consul raised divers issues before the government of Rosas which provoked a diplomatic rupture with France. In May, 1837, Rosas started a war with Bolivia because the president of that nation, General Santa Cruz, allowed unitarian armies to be organized within its territory. The lithographer, César Hipolyte Bâcle, received an order from the government of Buenos Aires to prepare plans and itineraries for use in time of war. Bâcle declared that he was ill and obtained permission to withdraw into the interior of Argentina. However, Rosas was informed that he carried on a correspondence with the president of Bolivia and that he was proceeding toward that country. Upon Bâcle's return there were found in his possession plans and papers that he had prepared in order to turn over to the enemy. The government then obliged him to reside in the province of Santa Fe; and shortly afterward he died. The French viceconsul, Aimé Roger, presented a claim in favor of this subject of France, but he made it in so violent a manner that Rosas gave him his passports.

During the same year, Roger had presented another remonstrance which was due to the fact that Rosas obliged foreigners who had resided in the country for two years to serve in the national guard. This act of Rosas was based upon a law passed in 1821 and which had as its purpose to arm foreigners as well as citizens for the defense of the city or the frontier against Indian invasions.

In 1838, Admiral Leblanc, commander of the French squadron near La Plata, asked Rosas to give an explanation regarding the Bâcle affair and also in regard to the forced military service of French subjects. Felipe Arana, the minister of foreign affairs, showed Leblanc that only six Frenchmen had served in the Argentine army of whom five were volunteers and that the sixth had been enrolled because he was a robber; further, he argued that the French

---

[1] R. Greenhow, "Memoria sobre las Islas Malvinas," translated by J. T. Guido, *La Revista de Buenos Aires* (Buenos Aires, 1867), XII, 161 ff. See further, Manuel Moreno to Arana in J. M. Rosas, *Papeles de Rosas* (edited by A. Saldías, 2 vols. La Plata, 1904-7), I, 212; see also W. S. Robertson, *Hispanic-American Relations with the United States* (New York, 1923), pp. 170-75; P. Groussac, "Les Iles Malouines; nouvel exposé d'un vieux litige," *Anales de la Biblioteca* (Buenos Aires, 1910), VI, 401-579.—W. S. R.

claim would have been justifiable if the government had imposed this military obligation solely upon the French, while the law treated in identical manner all the foreign residents, whatever might be their nationality. Minister Arana thus rejected the pretensions of the French agent. In consequence, on March 28, 1838, the latter announced a blockade of the port of Buenos Aires and of the entire coast of the Argentine republic.

As the declaration of a blockade made difficult the unfolding of the policy of Rosas, he accepted the friendly mediation of the English minister Mandeville. In this situation, the conflict was complicated because of the political condition of Uruguay, where General Rivera was besieging the city of Montevideo. The French viceconsul had an interview with Rivera, in which they agreed that he should not accept the mediation of the English minister; thus France maintained its position. For this reason, Leblanc avowed that he had received fresh instructions from his government to maintain the blockade. Rivera and the French agents thus formed an alliance and, in conjunction with the "Argentine commission" they seized the island of Martín García. This event promoted the triumph of Rivera in Uruguay, where he was elected president.

The liberating campaign of Lavalle had been made in large part by resources furnished by Admiral Leblanc. Lavalle's legion had proceeded to the province of Entre Ríos in vessels belonging to the French squadron; and the expedition to the province of Buenos Aires had been carried out in the same manner. When Lavalle drew near the district of Morón, the support of the French agent decreased, and this fact influenced Lavalle not to attack the city of Buenos Aires.. At this very juncture, Baron Mackau arrived as plenipotentiary of France. In October, 1840, the English minister, Mandeville, proposed to Mackau that a fresh negotiation be undertaken with Rosas. Mackau accepted the proposal, and at once negotiations were begun between Minister Arana and the French plenipotentiary. By the treaty of peace, signed on October 29, 1840, the government of Rosas agreed to pay indemnities for the losses or injuries that French subjects had suffered, upon condition that the French minister should immediately raise the blockade and should deliver up the island of Martín García. Article III of the treaty stipulated that the government of Rosas should grant the unitarians who had taken up arms against the dictator permission to return to their country. Lastly, it provided that this government should agree to maintain neutrality in the politics of Uruguay.[2]

After General Lavalle had been defeated at Quebracho Herrado, Rosas sent General Mansilla as emissary in order to urge him to lay down his arms.[3] As the negotiations of Mackau prejudiced the liberating army, which had been equipped by the aid of French agents, Lavalle rejected the Mackau Treaty. The Parisian press commented as follows on the negotiations of the French plenipotentiary: "The treaty of October 29, 1840, has been faithfully executed by Rosas. We desired three things which we have obtained, and which only Rosas could assure to us: to settle the fate of our compatriots who live upon the left bank of La Plata River; to put an end to a purposeless war that brought us neither honor nor profit; and finally, to relieve France in the future of all connection with those parties that are excited about the French question."

A constant intention of Rosas was to intervene in Uruguayan politics: for Montevideo was the refuge of Argentine émigrés. The constitution of the Uruguayan state was promulgated on June 18, 1830, and in conformity with it Rivera was chosen to serve as president of the republic. When his constitutional term ended, he was succeeded by Oribe. But Rivera started a civil war with his successor; this is the starting point of the two traditional parties that have since agitated Uruguayan politics; the *Blanco* party, of Oribe; and the *Colorado* party, of Rivera. Oribe linked himself to the policy of Rosas; while Rivera, chief of the colorados, allied himself with the unitarians, who were enemies of the dictator. Thus, when Rivera joined with Argentine leaders to overthrow Oribe, Rosas undertook to support the authority of the Uruguayan president. Rivera was, nevertheless, a shifty leader; while he was allied with the unitarians, he secretly negotiated with Rosas. Besides, he began to arouse and to stimulate the first dissensions among the leaders of the reaction; for he was vexed at the successes won by Lavalle, and, alleging that those leaders did not wish to recog-

[2] The text of this treaty is found in Díaz, *Historia política y militar de las repúblicas del Plata* (12 vols. Montevideo, 1877-78), V, 103-7.

[3] The instructions to General Mansilla directing him to make known to Lavalle the treaty of peace between Argentina and France are found in Rosas, *op. cit.*, I, 189-91. The pronunciamiento of Urquiza, May 1, 1851, is found in *Archivo americano y espíritu de la prensa del mundo* (61 nos. Buenos Aires, 1843-51), nueva serie, núm. 25, pp. 195-97.—W. S. R.

nize him as supreme director of the war, he delayed the succor that he was to give the liberating army. This fact favored the development of the policy of Rosas.

General Oribe, who had triumphed at Arroyo Grande over the forces of General Rivera, decided to cross the river and to besiege Montevideo, the defense of which had been intrusted to General Paz. As we have stated, Rosas supported the pretensions of Oribe. When the siege was announced, England and France, who felt that their interests were being injured, protested to Rosas, invoking the provisions of the Mackau Treaty. Rosas replied that General Oribe was the constitutional president of Uruguay, who had been deposed by a revolution led by Rivera, and that the Argentine army was scarcely an auxiliary division. Besides, if Rosas did intervene in Uruguayan politics, it was only in reprisal for what Rivera—who had become president of Uruguay—had done by intervening in Argentine politics through aiding the unitarian army. Rosas ordered that Montevideo should be blockaded and placed his squadron under the command of Admiral Brown who soon took possession of the island of Ratas. The English admiral, John B. Purvis, refused to recognize the blockade, and sequestrated the Argentine squadron. Rosas presented a complaint because of this act of Admiral Purvis. The admiral was superseded, but two new agents, Ouseley for England, and Deffaudis for France, demanded that Rosas should raise the siege of Montevideo. Rosas refused to grant this request; and these agents accordingly asked for their passports and declared a blockade of Argentina's ports.

As Dictator López of Paraguay had allied himself with Corrientes in order to resist Rosas, the latter prohibited commercial intercourse with those regions by refusing to grant vessels permission to enter or to leave Argentine ports if they sailed to or returned from either Paraguay or Corrientes. As foreign ships wished to navigate the rivers, Rosas gave orders that the pass of Tonelero at Vuelta de Obligado should be fortified. At this place a bitter fight took place on November 18, 1845.

Being desirous of settling the questions that were pending, Count Walewski, envoy of France, and Lord Howden, envoy of England, began negotiations with Rosas but without success. At last, an end was made to the Uruguayan question, in August, 1850, by a negotiation of Minister Arana with the envoy of France, Le

Predour, by virtue of which the blockade maintained by French ships was terminated, and Rosas withdrew his soldiers from the siege of Montevideo.[4]

In September, 1843, the government of Chile sent an expedition to the Straits of Magellan, which disembarked at the port of Hambre, with the intention of starting a settlement there and in the territory of the straits. Shortly afterward, in 1847, the Argentine Government received news of this event, and after a study of such an important matter, it took the proper diplomatic step. "Since the most remote times," said the government of Buenos Aires at that date, "in which the Spanish monarchy took possession of this part of America and in which the provinces and intendancies of Chile as well as those of the Argentine Confederation were established, the orders for the surveillance and policing of the Strait of Magellan as well as for other objects related to it, and also the measures concerning the adjacent islands and Tierra del Fuego were always directed to the governors and viceroys of Buenos Aires, as the authorities to whom this part of the Spanish dominions was subject. Upon severing the bonds that united them to the motherland and upon constituting themselves sovereign and independent states, the republics of South America adopted as a basis for their territorial division the same demarcation that had existed among the viceroyalties which had respectively constituted them. In the belief that this principle, which has been accepted by Argentina, is incontrovertible, and being without the least doubt concerning the authority that the governors of the province of Buenos Aires have exercised in watching the Strait of Magellan, it is evident that the colony which the honorable government of Chile has directed to be founded in this strait, infringes upon the integrity of Argentine territory. . . ." [5]

The Chilean minister of foreign relations replied to this note of Minister Arana by declaring that he believed the right of Chile to be indisputable, "not only to the land upon which the colony

---

[4] Pelliza's opinion in regard to foreign intervention in La Plata is found in *Historia argentina desde su origen hasta la organización nacional*, II, 309-10. *Cf.* Saldías, *La evolución republicana durante la revolución argentina*, pp. 313-14. [See also J. F. Cady, *Foreign Intervention in the Río de la Plata*, Philadelphia, 1929, especially pp. 244-71.—W. S. R.]

[5] Pelliza, *Historia argentina desde su origen hasta la organizacion nacional*, II, 354-55.—W. S. R.

recently established at the Strait of Magellan is located, but to the entire strait, and to the lands adjacent, and to other lands that are thus designated."

The Argentine government intrusted the investigation of this question and the collection of the proof of its title to Pedro de Angelis. But the claim was postponed by the Argentine government, because it was engrossed in the grave conflict that was still going on with European powers.[6]

---

[6] J. J. Gschwind, *La política internacional argentina durante la dictadura época de Rosas* (Rosario, 1925), pp. 47-85.

CHAPTER L

NATIONAL POETRY

AMONG THE poets of 1810, Vicente López y Planes, the celebrated author of the national hymn, and Esteban de Luca, who sang the epic poem of the revolution, are prominent. Juan Cruz Varela (1794-1836), the commentator and panegyrist of the liberal reforms of Rivadavia, was a poet in whose productions, especially in the tragedies of *Dido* and *Argia*, the classic influence reached its culmination.[1]

After the revolutionary age, the romantic period in the history of Argentine letters began, during which the writers were masters of their own inspiration. The Argentine romantic school, an echo of the great literary movement that swept through Europe in the beginning of the nineteenth century, eulogized the originality of the poet, exalting his imagination and discarding every kind of model. Our picturesque and varied natural scenery and the special circumstances of the historic moment, furnished Argentine poets with inexhaustible fountains of inspiration; thus arose the beginnings of what can be called the cultivation of a purely national poetry. The government of Rosas had expelled from the country a classic Pleiad of writers in the forefront of whom figured Echeverría, Juan Cruz Varela, Florencio Varela, Rivera Indarte, Mármol, Sarmiento, López, and Mitre. They made the feelings of Argentinians vibrate with emotion; and prolific and exuberant fantasy overflowed in the poem, the novel, the theater, and history.

Echeverría is one of the richest and most complex personalities of our past. Sociologist, historian, politician, poet, he is in fine, an author with a great reputation. In 1825, he went to Europe, where he completed and strengthened his culture. In the words of a literary historian: "The romanticism which had affected the European literary world and which was to have so powerful an influence in Spanish America was then at its height. . . . It was Echeverría's fortune to be in Paris when the romanticists achieved their most resounding triumphs, with defenders like Sainte-Beuve, Janin, and Nodier. The influence of those authors aroused the spirit of Eche-

---

[1] Rojas, *op. cit.*, II, 593.

verría, and he passionately dedicated himself to literature. He read much: in a lamentable disorder which is reflected in various of his works, he passed from classic Spanish writers to the French romanticists, from the satanism of Byron to the theocratic marvels of Châteaubriand, and finally became passionately fond of Goethe and Schiller." [2]

Four years later, Echeverría returned to his native land. In 1831, he published the *Profecía del Plata* and, in 1832, the poem *Elvira*. In 1834, he wrote the *Consuelos*, and then his celebrated *La Cautiva* in which he painted with the hand of an artist the immensity of the pampas and the indomitable fiber of their inhabitants. This lofty spirit conceived many other poetic compositions. He fixed with precision the character of the national poetry with these words that are worthy of reproduction: if it is desired to conquer poetry, one must invest it "with a distinctive, original character, which reflecting the colors of physical nature that surround us, will be at the same time the living picture of our customs and the most elevated expression of our prevailing ideas as well as of the sentiments and passions that arise from the clash of our social interests in the sphere within which our intellectual culture moves." [1]

In 1843, José Rivera Indarte published a volume of poetry. He was not exactly an inspired author; he was rather a littérateur who, after having endured the sufferings of the dungeon and of exile, directed against the dictator his best-known works, *Tablas de sangre*, and *Rosas y sus opositores*. His most widely-known tract is one whose title proclaims its content: *Es acción santa matar á Rosas.*[4]

The origins of the romanticism of the representative poet, José Mármol, are characteristically Spanish. It was inspired by Zorilla and Espronceda, just as the romanticism of Echeverría was of French origin. No writer poured out more passion against Rosas in his works than Mármol. His literary product was certainly not the best, surcharged as it was with violent notes and strong tones of vengeance and desperation. Mármol shone with original inspiration in *Cantos del peregrino*, in which he described the nature of our

---

[2] E. García Velloso, "Historia de la literatura argentina," *La Nación, 1810— 25 de Mayo—1910* (Buenos Aires, 1910), p. 252.

[3] Rojas, *op. cit.*, III, 163. See further, R. A. Orgaz, *Páginas de crítica y de historia* (Buenos Aires, 1927).

[4] That is "To kill Rosas is a holy deed."—W. S. R.

country. As a playwright he wrote *El Poeta* and *El Cruzado*, and
as a novelist he excelled, by a just estimate, in his popular work,
Amalia. This novel depicts an epoch of anxiety and anguish; it
revives for moments in magistral form, episodes of the dictatorship
of Rosas, the persecutions suffered by free men and lofty spirits.
Amalia is thus an emotional novel, with decided historical value;
for it illustrates the customs and the passions of an epoch in our
past.

Poet, historian, and biographer, Juan María Gutiérrez is one of
those spirits that has exercised and still exercises most influence
upon Argentine culture. From the very beginning, he figured with
Echeverría and Alberdi; he laid the bases of the great party of
principles which by cruel sacrifices was destined to overturn the
dictatorship. The best-known poems of Gutiérrez are *Á mi bandera*,
Á la juventud argentina, and the *Canto á Mayo*. The last was
awarded a prize in the literary contest held in Montevideo on May
25, 1841. In 1870, he published a volume under the title *Poesías*.

Among his valuable productions of an historical character
should be mentioned *Bosquejo biográfico del general San Martín*
(*Biographical Sketch of General San Martín*); *Noticias históricas
sobre el origen y desarrollo de la enseñanza en Buenos Aires* (*Historical Notes on the Origin and Development of Teaching in Buenos
Aires*)—the most complete treatise that has been written on that
subject; *Bibliografía sobre la imprenta de Buenos Aires hasta
1810* (*Bibliography relating to the Press of Buenos Aires to 1810*);
and biographical studies concerning the poets of the revolution.
One may, perhaps, say of Gutiérrez that his output makes him
our most distinguished man of letters.

The fatherland is the perennial theme that inspires Olegario
V. Andrade, a vigorous and imaginative poet. His poetic compositions, "La libertad," "La América," "Al general Lavalle," "Á
Paysandú," "El nido de cóndores" ("The Condor's Nest"), "Á San
Martín," are patriotic songs, par excellence. In the poems "Promo-
teo" and "Atlántida," the fancy of this poet is freely displayed.
The second of these was his last work. It is a hymn to the progress
of the Latin race. All the productions of Andrade bear an unsurpassed stamp of poetic exaltation.

Gaucho poetry is the popular poetry of the inhabitants of La
Plata. By the end of the eighteenth century, the colonial chroni-

Rosas

Alberdi

Juan María Gutierrez

San Martín

Upper left, Dictator Rosas; portrait in the Museo Histórico Nacional, Buenos
Aires, attributed to Fernando García del Molino; from Pradère, *Juan
Manuel de Rosas; su iconografía.* Upper right, Juan Bautista Alberdi;
from Alberdi, *The Crime of War,* translated by C. J. MacConnell. Lower
left, Juan María Gutiérrez; from Chueco, *La República Argentina en su
primer centenario.* Lower right, General San Martín; medallion by Simón;
from Salas, *Bibliografía del general Don José de San Martín y de la emancipación sudamericana.*

clers spoke of the gaucherio or gaucho, who was described with his characteristic costume, arms, and customs. The inhabitant of the pampas or plains was passionately fond of liberty, singing, and dancing. The gaucho dialect was the official language corrupted by oral tradition. Without experience or education, the gaucho singer poured out his soul in the form of verse, without subjecting himself to rhetorical laws or principles, but vibrating with emotion and life.[5] Bunge said:

"The ethnic temperament of the gaucho and the milieu of his life operated jointly to produce the old *gauchesa* poetry. A descendant of Spaniards and Arabs, frequently of Andalusians, the gaucho had a genius eminently contemplative and poetic. In his veins there seethed the blood of ancestral warriors and artists, nomads, and singers. The small amount of Indian blood intermingled with his European and Asiatic ancestral strain merely added to his idiosyncrasy a certain savage passion for liberty." [6]

The Uruguayan, Bartolomé Hidalgo, is the author of dialogues between the foreman of an hacienda and Ramón Contreras which glorify the gaucho patriot. Hilario Ascasubi (1807-1875) composed "Santos Vega," "Aniceto el Gallo," and "Paulino Lucero," in the harmonious verses of which he sings of the gaucho, of civil war, and of the tyranny of Rosas. The poem "Fausto" of Estanislao del Campo (1834-1880) is remarkable because of the vivacity of its dialogue and because of the description which the gaucho Anastasio el Pollo makes to his partner, Laguna, of the performance of the opera, "Faust," which he has seen in Buenos Aires.

Yet, without doubt, the most vigorous example of gaucho poetry is the poem "Martín Fierro" of José Hernández (1834-1886). The gaucho, Martín Fierro, the hero of the work, is the personification of the gaucho persecuted by power who suffers every privation and injustice with a physical and moral energy that exalt the race. Not only is the poem "Martín Fierro" of great literary significance, but it is also particularly valuable as a record of observation and as an historical and sociological study of the gaucho, his customs, and his psychology.

[5] Writers who have made a special study of gaucho literature are Martiniano Leguizamón, Ricardo Rojas, and Leopoldo Lugones. The Uruguayan writer, Mario Falcao Espalter, is the author of a study entitled *El poeta oriental Bartolomé Hidalgo* (Montevideo, 1918).

[6] C. O. Bunge, *Nuestra América* (seventh edition, Barcelona, 1903), p. 152.

CHAPTER LI

THE PRONUNCIAMIENTO OF URQUIZA

THE DIFFERENCES between Urquiza and Rosas continued to increase after the years following 1832; they soon caused misunderstandings between Urquiza and Echagüe, the governor of Santa Fe and the docile instrument of the rosista policy. In 1847, the differences between these two men became serious. Urquiza framed a long list of charges against Echagüe and indirectly against Rosas. The latter soon realized that Urquiza was not his man. This dissidence became known, and assumed a political character after Rosas rejected the treaty of Alcaraz that had been signed by Urquiza and Madariaga.

To this conjunction of personal and political circumstances were added very serious considerations of an economic character. Ramón J. Cárcano has fittingly said: "Buenos Aires was the only market of foreign exchange for the provinces of Corrientes and Entre Ríos. The dictator wished to make them accept the irredeemable paper of his bank and in fact prohibited the exportation of any kind of metallic money. Not being able to withdraw the difference in their favor in specie the merchants from the interior who bought and sold in Buenos Aires were injured in the development of their resources. Because of political mistrust, he also prohibited the exportation of gunpowder, which was indispensable for making lime, the production of which, after cattle-raising, was the chief industry of Entre Ríos. The governor of that province protested repeatedly against these odious and injurious restrictions but Rosas always replied by a refusal or by silence." [1]

The period lasting more than nine years during which Uruguay maintained a struggle against the armies of Rosas has been designated the Great War. After the battle of Arroyo Grande (1842), Rosas ordered Oribe to beseige Montevideo. We have noticed the international complication that this event caused, and it is now our duty to refer to the rôles played by the chancellor of the government that was defending Montevideo, Manuel Herrera y Obes, by the diplomatic agent of that defense at Rio de Janeiro, Andrés

---

[1] R. J. Cárcano, *De Caseros al 11 de Septiembre* (Buenos Aires, 1919).

Lamas, and by General Guido, in his capacity as the representative of Rosas at the Brazilian capital.

While Herrera y Obes persistently influenced the mind of Urquiza against Rosas, Minister Lamas tried to induce the imperial government of Brazil to respect the pact of 1828 by which it had guaranteed the independence and integrity of the republic of Uruguay. To quote Cárcano again: "With the acknowledged authority and justly acquired prestige, Lamas explained to the emperor and the politicians of the empire his conception of the great international policy that should be realized in order to guarantee the peace and prosperity of the nations of South America: the maintenance of the territorial status quo; the independence and sovereignty of the constituted nationalities; the renunciation of any aspiration to reconstruct the viceroyalty of La Plata and of any ambition for the establishment of natural frontiers; the liberty of navigation and commerce; the opening of interior rivers to the flags of all nations, the neutralization of islands and canals, and the solution by arbitration of future as well as of pending questions. . . ." [2]

In 1848, the political situation in Brazil was changed by the accession to power of a liberal ministry determined to intervene in the questions of La Plata. In the name of Rosas, Minister Guido protested because of the repressive measures that had been used against his government. But the authorities of the empire did not grant the explanations that were requested. Nevertheless, subsequent events obliged General Guido to withdraw from the imperial court, and henceforth the Uruguayan-Brazilian alliance was a fact.

Perhaps Urquiza delayed for some time his pronunciamiento because he felt that it was necessary for him to join with Brazil in order to dethrone the tyrant. On January 5, 1851, there appeared in the journal designated *La Regeneración*, which was published in Concepción, Uruguay, an article entitled "El Año 1851" ("The Year 1851") which said: "This year 1851 will be designated in this part of America, 'The year of organization.' As the result of an admirable combination of science, patriotism, and firmness, there shall exist general peace with glory in the republic and between foreign nations and the republic. The great principle of the federal system, consecrated by victory, shall be strengthened in an assembly composed of delegates of the people."

[2] *Ibid.*

This article produced a great sensation in Buenos Aires. It was, indeed, true that Urquiza cherished the patriotic design of rebelling against Rosas. Friends of the latter tried to induce Urquiza to disavow the article, but the governor of Entre Ríos responded "that the province under his command—the press of which did not absolutely depend upon the government—which was organized and uniform in its opinions without any ungovernable or rebellious citizens, and was marching in its glory along the path pointed out by civilization, entertained with its chief the desire of beholding the republic definitely organized."

Five months after the publication of this article, on May 1, 1851, was issued the official pronunciamiento of Urquiza against Rosas. The province of Entre Ríos thereby accepted the resignation which Rosas had repeatedly made of the office of director of foreign relations and of affairs of peace and war that had been delegated to him by virtue of the treaty of January 4, 1831. On May 25, 1851, Urquiza addressed the following proclamation to the Argentinians: "People of the republic: twenty years ago, after a sanguinary struggle, accompanied by the horrors of anarchy, there appeared on the banks of the Paraná River, the consolatory hope of order and of national organization. A man came upon the political stage, who, simulating constitutional ideas and a love for the fraternity of the Argentine provinces, was hailed by the people and honored by their unlimited confidence. This man undoubtedly harbored sinister intentions in his soul, and no other thought dominated his mind than to elevate himself above the ruins of national dignity, to shatter into fragments upon the altar of his ambition the rich heritage of valor and glory bequeathed to us by our fathers. . . . Confederated peoples: the heroic province which has honored me with the management of its destinies has made resound in all its parts a united call for 'liberty, organization, and war against despotism.' . . . Our sister, the illustrious province of Corrientes, has already responded and linked her magnanimous resolution to that of Entre Ríos. The great Argentine-American alliance, the liberator of the republics of La Plata, has in its favor the power of arms, the elevated justice of its cause, and the benedictions of good people." [3]

---

[3] Pelliza, *Historia argentina desde su origen hasta la organización nacional*, II, 366-67.—W. S. R.

This splendid proclamation does honor to General Urquiza, for it makes known the noble aspirations by which he was animated. On May 29, a treaty of alliance was signed in Montevideo by the provinces of Entre Ríos and Corrientes, and by Brazil and Uruguay. In order to insure success to the liberating campaign, General Urquiza realized that it was necessary to march to Uruguay where General Oribe still kept up the siege of Montevideo. In the month of July, Urquiza crossed the Uruguay River with 5,000 soldiers from Entre Ríos and 1,500 from Corrientes; Oribe capitulated and thus the siege that had lasted for almost ten years was raised. Clemente L. Fregeiro thus describes the pacification of Uruguay:

"Urquiza, inspired by a sentiment that foreshadowed national Argentine egotism, and faithful on the other hand to his original thought, felt that the immediate military support of Brazil was necessary in order to insure the pacification of Uruguay. The treaty agreed to by the discordant Uruguayans, which was known as the pact of October 8, 1851, and which was framed through the fraternal mediation of the governor of Entre Ríos, put an end to the Great War. By the terms of this pact there did not exist either vanquished or victorious Uruguayans: all were to enjoy equal rights; it finally recognized—and this was only strict justice—that the citizens and the soldiers, who had fought against European intervention, had defended the integrity of national sovereignty. Urquiza did even more: in the name of liberty, he made the government of the defense of Montevideo realize its decrepitude, by an appeal from it to the vote of national sovereignty." [4]

Soon after raising the siege of Montevideo, Urquiza recrossed the Uruguay River and, on December 11, camped on the banks of the Paraná near Diamante. The allied army was composed of 28,189 men distributed thus: the forces of Entre Ríos, 10,670; the forces of Corrientes, 5,260; divisions composed of men from Buenos Aires, 4,249; Brazilians 4,040; Uruguayans, 1,907; soldiers concerned with the artillery, ordnance, and all others, two thousand. The crossing of the Paraná was begun on December 23,

---

[4] C. L. Fregeiro, "La defensa de Montevideo y el general Urquiza, según la correspondencia diplomática del canciller montevideano Manuel Herrera y Obes," *Revista de la Universidad de Buenos Aires* (Buenos Aires, 1917), XXXVII, 40-82.

1851. A historical military study of the campaigns of 1851-1852 states:

"The Paraná River, which is subdivided throughout almost its entire course into numerous branches, thus covering a considerable area in width, is reunited at Diamante into a single stream; the minimum width of the river at this point at low tide is 1,200 meters. On the other side of the river is the province of Santa Fe, but before reaching firm land, it is necessary to cross a large isle composed of low land and almost impassable by artillery. Further, while the Santa Fe bank is low and sometimes under water, the bank of Entre Ríos is high and steep. At Diamante it reaches a height of about forty meters above the level of the river. To cross from one province to another, the most opportune place had been selected, because of the small number of obstacles that it was necessary to overcome there in order to execute that grand operation." [5]

"The preliminary measures taken to prepare for the crossing were as follows: all the vessels that could be found—such as canoes, boats and launches—were gathered together at Diamante; three large rafts were built, each capable of carrying one hundred horses inside a stockade; the arrival was hastened of some vessels belonging to the first division of the Brazilian squadron, which were not only to be used to tow the barks but also to protect the passage of the army for which purpose a battery of artillery had already been placed on the banks of the river; and, lastly, at Diamante some work had been done to facilitate the approach of soldiers to the river and their embarkation." [6]

General Urquiza led the grand army up to the farms of Chivilcoy. General Pacheco, who commanded the vanguard of the rosista army, was at Mercedes, and upon learning of the proximity of the liberating army, he prepared to retire to the capital. General Pacheco left the cavalry in charge of Colonel Hilario Lagos, and on the morning of January 31, the vanguard of the army of Urquiza prepared for the battle. When the soldiers of Rosas were

---

[5] This was the same place at which, eleven years and eleven months earlier, General Lavalle had forded the Paraná River with a similar purpose in mind, namely, to overthrow a tyrant. See M. Ruíz Moreno, *La revolución contra la tiranía y la organización nacional* (4 vols. Rosario, 1905-8), I, 244.

[6] J. Beverina, *Caseros: estudio histórico militar de las campañas de 1851-52* (Varese, Italy, 1911), p. 186.

seen leaving the battlefield, the army of Urquiza was surprised.

On the morning of February 3, 1852—the day of the battle—General Urquiza distributed among his soldiers the following proclamation: "Soldiers; if the tyrant and his slaves hope, show the world that you are invincible, and, if at any moment victory does not smile upon any of you, seek your general upon the battlefield; for the field of battle is the point of reunion for the soldiers of the allied army, where we all have either to vanquish or to die." At nine o'clock in the morning Colonel Chilabert, who commanded the center of Rosas's army and had thirty cannon, began firing; the wings of that army were easily routed; but the center fought with intrepidity and for more than an hour the fight was concentrated against the artillery of Chilabert. A final effort of the allied soldiers broke the center of Rosas' army, and the battle of Monte Caseros covered the liberating army with glory. To quote Mitre:

"The battle of Caseros affords the singular psychological phenomenon of other battles of its kind: it was won before it was fought; from the generals to the last soldier of both armies, both victors and vanquished evidently anticipated the outcome, as did the whole world. In whatever manner it might have been fought, it would have been won by the allies, and under the existing conditions Rosas would have lost it a hundred times. . . . The truth is that in the battle of Caseros no one truly fought on the side of Rosas, with the exception of Colonel Chilabert. The dictator's battalions had neither opportunity nor courage to engage in formal combat, and some of those that did not mutiny either by killing their commander or by disbanding, upon arranging themselves in passive formation, placed their ramrods in the mouths of clean muskets, in order to show that they had not discharged their guns. This battle was more than a dispersion of the rosista army, it was a dissolution of that army because of inertia." [7]

After the defeat at Caseros, Rosas with a pencil wrote his resignation, which was conceived in the following terms: "Honorable representatives: the time has arrived to return to you the investiture of governor of the province and the sum total of power with which you deigned to honor me. I believe that I have fulfilled my

---

[7] See the letter of Bartolomé Mitre to Dr. Adolfo Saldías, October 15, 1887, written upon the occasion of the publication of the latter's *Historia de la Confederación Argentina*. This letter is printed in I, xx-xxi, of the edition (1911) of that work which is cited in this translation.

duty as have all the representatives, our fellow citizens, the true federalists, and my compatriots and companions in arms. If we have not accomplished more in the sacred support of our independence, our integrity and our honor, it is because we have not been able to do so. Allow me, honorable representatives, upon taking leave of you, to express again the deep pleasure with which I embrace you tenderly; and I beseech God to give glory to all of your Honors and to each one of you. In the country, and wounded in the right hand, excuse me for writing this note with a pencil and in scrawling letters. May God preserve the lives of your Honors— Juan Manuel de Rosas." [8] In company with his daughter, Rosas embarked immediately aboard the steamboat *Conflict* en route to England. He settled at Southampton, where he died on March 14, 1877.

Upon the defeat of Rosas, the task of national organization fell into the hands of General Urquiza. The Argentine provinces were vegetating in a state of profound prostration. Neither anarchy nor civil war existed among them; for they had all been subjected to the domination of Rosas. When General Urquiza addressed his proclamation to the people of the republic inviting them to withdraw from Rosas the management of war and foreign affairs, the provinces did not respond to the summons. General Gutiérrez, governor of Tucumán, declared against Urquiza, "the obscure oppressor of Entre Ríos"; while the province of San Luis expressed the desire that Rosas should continue to guide the destinies of the confederation. The provinces of San Juan, Salta, Córdoba, Catamarca, Santiago del Estero, La Rioja, and Santa Fe in turn declared their adhesion to the policy of Rosas. Although, indeed, peace and general tranquillity prevailed in the country, yet there were obstacles to the task of organization—obstacles which would doubtless be overcome, for that was the sentiment and general aspiration of the people.

Two great obstacles have to be surmounted in order to form a final judgment upon Rosas: (1) there are still lacking documents sufficient to serve as a solid basis for an impartial judgment; (2) the age of Rosas—more than twenty years of government—is extensive, and during that age there took place numerous events of internal and external policy which complicated it. In part, if

---

[8] Rosas, *op. cit.*, II, 246-48.

isolated events or aspects of the rule of Rosas are considered, one may venture an opinion. Thus, after 1835, Rosas governed by terror: this means of oppression will always be disapproved by history, and not a single life lost during this régime should be justified or excused.

An event that prejudiced, and in large part absorbed the policy of Rosas was the diplomatic and martial diplomacy that he carried on with France, England, Uruguay, Bolivia, Paraguay, and Brazil. In this particular, the policy of Rosas is pleasing to Argentine patriotism. The unseasonable and violent claims of France were restrained in time by the energetic hand of this government; the armed intervention of England and France, because of the siege of Montevideo, which involved various incidents, was haughtily met by Rosas who believed in the right to intervene in the politics of Uruguay, after the president of that republic had made alliances with the governors of Argentine provinces.[9]

The enemies of Rosas, the unitarians with Lavalle at their head, joined the French, and by the aid of that nation waged a war against Rosas. Were those Argentinians who united with foreigners to solve a problem of internal policy traitors to their country, or did they act rightly?[10] It has been said that the war which Rosas waged with Bolivia and with Uruguay, and that which he decided to carry on against Paraguay in 1850, had as an object to extend his authority to the limits of the former viceroyalty of La Plata. Nothing positive can be affirmed on this point; the ostensible reasons for this war with neighboring countries were the protection and aid that they furnished to the unitarian armies.

Something can also be affirmed with respect to the administrative and financial management of Rosas. In this respect, on February 16, 1852, the government of Buenos Aires decreed the confiscation of the ex-dictator's property. From beyond the sea, Rosas pro-

---

[9] General San Martín's judgment upon Rosas is found in a letter printed by R. Obligado in *La Nación*, Buenos Aires, July 9, 1894. The different conceptions of the dictator that have been entertained by Argentinians are summarized by Bunge, *Nuestra América*, pp. 165-66. [See further, W. S. Robertson, "Foreign Estimates of the Argentine Dictator, Juan Manuel de Rosas," *Hispanic American Historical Review* (Durham, 1930), IX, 125-37.—W. S. R.]

[10] This question is discussed by the following authors: E. Quesada, *op. cit.*, p. 268; R. J, Cárcano, "Rosas, esterilidad de su dictadura," *La Capital*, Rosario, November 15, 1917; and by Mitre in Saldías, *Historia de la Confederación Argentina*, I, xx-xxi.

tested and declared that "during the twenty years in which the press of the world served my enemies as an instrument through which to invent charges against me, no one thought of accusing me of pilfering the public exchequer, for no one either could or can present this charge without being confuted by authentic documents that prove the contrary." In his exile Rosas did not even have the food necessary for his table, yet he had been one of the richest landed proprietors of the country. To a friend in Buenos Aires he wrote: "I did not draw any salary; and I observed absolute scrupulousness in managing the property of the people . . . ; it is possible to ascribe anything to me; it is possible to accuse me of everything; I acknowledge and do not disavow the responsibility that belongs to me, but never shall it be possible to say of me that I abstracted a single real from the treasury for my personal use: one attempts to stigmatize me as a thief; I, who have been everything, who have done everything except to tolerate even the thought of indelicacy with respect to public funds." [11]

But Rosas did not succeed in ensuring peace. The sterility of this government of twenty years is also evident.

---

[11] Levene, *Lecturas históricas argentinas*, II, 299-300. See further, the opinion of Dr. José A. Terry as commented upon by D. Corvalán Mendilaharzu in an article entitled "Rosas: historia y fábula," published in *Nosotros* (Buenos Aires, 1914), XVI, 156-77. The manifesto of Rosas in which he mentions the money that he took with him on his journey to England is found in *Papeles de Rosas*, II, 255. Urquiza and some friends offered to send the ex-dictator some money with which to pay his living expenses. Upon acknowledging the receipt of one thousand pounds from Quiroga, Rosas described the economical life that he was leading on a small farm after the auction of the furniture of the house which he had occupied in the city. See M. P. Leguizamón, *Rasgos de la vida de Urquiza* (Buenos Aires, 1920), pp. 142-45. See further, the volume recently published by R. de Castro Esteves, *Inquisiciones acerca de Rosas y su época* (Buenos Aires, 1927).

CHAPTER LII

THE AGREEMENT OF SAN NICOLÁS

ONE OF THE first measures adopted by the victor of Caseros was to designate the gifted author of the national hymn, Dr. Vicente López y Planes, provisional governor of the province of Buenos Aires. Two months later the governors of Buenos Aires, Entre Ríos, Corrientes, and Santa Fe assembled at Palermo and decided to delegate to General Urquiza the management of foreign affairs. Among the men of Buenos Aires this selection was not received with sympathy, for General Urquiza had provoked jealousies— in honor of truth let it be said, unjustly—for, after the triumph at Caseros, he had entered the city wearing a poncho and a plush hat. On May 1, the legislature of Buenos Aires met and confirmed the appointment of Dr. Vicente López y Planes as governor.

Meanwhile, General Urquiza made his plans to accomplish the much-desired task of national organization. For this purpose he thought that since he was the official in charge of foreign affairs, the best solution of the matter was for him to invite governors of the provinces to a conference, in order that they might agree on the method of holding elections and the time and place for the meeting of congress. The agreement was drawn up at San Nicolás de los Arroyos on May 31, 1852, and was composed of nineteen articles. By Article I, the treaty of January 4, 1831, or federal pact, was renewed; by Article II, a federative congress was convoked; and by Article IV, it was stipulated that the election of deputies to congress should conform to the respective existing laws of the provincial legislatures and that each province should send two deputies. Article XIV, XV, and XVI provided that in case of domestic violence, the provisional minister of foreign affairs (General Urquiza) was empowered to take prudential measures to restore order. General Urquiza was invested with "the effective command of all the military forces of the provinces which shall henceforth be considered as integral parts of the national army." The minister of foreign affairs was authorized "to regulate the navigation of the rivers of the republic . . . and the general administration of the post offices." [1] The agreement of San Nicolás is the most immediate and fundamental organic precedent that explains the promulgation of the Argentine constitution of 1853.

The news that this agreement had been signed produced a bad impression in Buenos Aires. The journal *El Progreso* had published the complete text of the agreement. It was believed that the governors of the provinces had conferred excessive powers upon General Urquiza and political passion rose to such a pitch that a new delegation of the entire public authority was considered. The members of the legislature were disposed to offer a strong resistance to the governor. On June 14, Dr. López y Planes again assumed the command of the province, and sent to the legislature the text of the agreement with an explanatory message. An agitated debate then took place among its members which is known by the name of "Las jornadas de Junio" ("The Squabbles of June"); the result was the rejection of the agreement and this was followed by a civil war.

The agreement was attacked by Colonel Mitre, Dr. Ireneo Portela, Dr. Pedro Ortíz Vélez, Dr. Miguel Esteves Saguí, Dr. Marcelo Gamboa, and Dr. Dalmacio Vélez Sársfield. It was defended by the minister of public instruction, Dr. Vicente Fidel López, a son of the governor.

The first member who spoke was Deputy Mitre who said that he would omit the details of the agreement and that he understood that its prime idea was national organization. Then he asked: "But organization upon what basis? Upon the basis of an irresponsible dictatorship, which constitutes what might properly be styled a despotic power; and by saying this I naturally find myself within the sphere of real discussion and placed face to face with the great figure and the great principle that dominate this treaty like two colossi: the great figure of General Urquiza, invested with an authority which is without a precedent in our history. . . . I shall be told that General Urquiza will not abuse the immense authority thus deposited in his hands. I also believe this. But I refer to the act of authorization and not to the person; I examine the principle and omit the man. If he should abuse the act, he would become a tyrant, and he who has triumphed in the name

---

[1] *Registro oficial de la República Argentina*, III, 15.—W. S. R.

Upper left, Bernardino Rivadavia; from *El Hogar,* Buenos Aires, July 7, 1916. Upper right, Mariano Moreno; from Manuel Moreno, *Vida del Dr. Mariano Moreno.* Lower left, Domingo F. Sarmiento; from Chueco, *La República Argentina en su primer centenario.* Lower right, Bartolomé Mitre; from Chueco, *La República Argentina en su primer centenario.*

and in the interest of liberty cannot and should not be allowed to assume that rôle."

Dr. Vélez Sársfield spoke after Mitre. Minister Vicente Fidel López responded to Sársfield. "What I am about to add, gentlemen," said the minister, "is according to my manner of thinking, fundamental; because of that I shall persist in following the deputy who has just spoken: his speech is the only one that deserves a refutation; the others have been a heap of empty words, of commonplaces, that come adorned with one or another faded flower of rhetoric; and all this affects me as do those cadavers which it is customary to display decorated with tufts of ribbon and lace; a spectacle of death decked with the puerile vanities of life. The agreement of San Nicolás has begun to create a legal and circumscribed sphere of national affairs in order to give to power (the only center of fact that exists in the republic) a conventional origin distinct from that of victory, and a sanction of constituted wills distinct from that furnished by military force. To this existing *de facto* authority have been given various but well-defined faculties, which among us is a great step in advance. . . . There is much talk here about laws, and about laws that have been violated in order to create a dictatorship with illegal attributes, but the question that one should propound is, where is the law that defines the legal attributes of national power? As there is no such law, it must be that the origin is illegal, that is, it does not emanate from a law which does not exist, but from one which has to be created, so that it may fortify and sanction the power that has to labor in order that there may be such a law. . . . The deputy is poorly acquainted with constitutional rules who, because he finds the union of the military command and the management of the national treasury incompatible in the hands of the executive, has said that the agreement of San Nicolás has put the bayonets in one hand of the director and the pesos in the other, thus placing the nation at his feet. What well regulated power is there in nations that is not in this position? What is the executive in any nation, unless he is the commander of the armies and the administrator of the public finances?" [2]

The legislature rejected the agreement of San Nicolás; and the

---

[2] A. del Valle, *Derecho constitucional* (Buenos Aires, 1911), pp. 446-53, where a vivid description is given of the scene of the legislative debates.

governor and his ministers resigned on June 23. The legislature accepted the resignation of Governor López, and appointed its president, General Martín G. Pinto, as provisional governor. When this fact became known to General Urquiza, he accomplished a coup d'état by suspending the legislature, and again appointing Vicente López provisional governor of the province. López assumed the command, but relinquished it on July 23, and the provisional director of the confederation appointed General Galán in his place. General Urquiza left Buenos Aires on September 8 in order to open the session of the constituent congress at Santa Fe.

Four days later, the revolution of September 11 broke out, which was an uprising of the province of Buenos Aires against the government of Urquiza. The revolution was led by Dr. Valentín Alsina; its military chief was General Pirán. Governor Galán, who felt impotent to check the movement, left the city. General Pinto was then named governor; he designated as his ministers the two leaders of the revolution; Dr. Alsina as minister of government; and General Pirán as minister of war.[3]

The provisional government of Buenos Aires was now definitely constituted. Dr. Valentín Alsina was made governor. He soon designated Colonel Mitre as minister of government and foreign affairs; Juan Bautista Peña as minister of the treasury; and José María Flores as minister of war. The intentions of Governor Alsina were to weaken the power of Urquiza and to prevent the meeting of the congress of Santa Fe. Besides, he dispatched against Entre Ríos an expedition under generals Madariaga and Hornos, who were defeated.

Colonel Hilario Lagos, the commander of the Porteño campaign, harbored personal resentment against Governor Alsina, and prepared a plan to depose him from power. For this purpose he compelled the minister of war, General Flores, to leave the city of Buenos Aires, which remained in the power of the mutineers. The country around the city of Buenos Aires responded to the summons of Lagos; Dr. Alsina presented his resignation; and the president of the legislature, General Pinto, became the head of the government.

---

[3] The important part in the September revolution which was played by former partisans of Rosas is indicated by J. Victorica, *Urquiza y Mitre* (Buenos Aires, 1918), pp. 62-63.

The uprising of Lagos would have favored the plans of General Urquiza, but he preferred to reach a friendly adjustment. For this purpose, he appointed a commission that proceeded to Buenos Aires. Colonel Lagos urged General Urquiza to place himself at the head of the besieging army. Yielding to this plea Urquiza proceeded to San Nicolás de Arroyos. The committee of pacification had framed a convention with Buenos Aires, but one of its articles provided that that province reserved the right to accept or to reject any constitution which might be framed. Urquiza rejected this agreement by which the decisions of the constituent congress were to be submitted to the judgment of Buenos Aires. The siege of the city was kept up, and the director of the confederation intrusted a squadron to the command of Commodore Coe, which blockaded the port of Buenos Aires. The government of the city seduced the squadron which was thus placed under its orders; besides, the constituent congress, assembled at Santa Fe, upon framing the constitution, federalized the city of Buenos Aires. This news made a bad impression upon the soldiers of the army of Lagos who felt that the province of Buenos Aires would be despoiled if it agreed to the federalization of the city. In consequence, the siege of Buenos Aires was terminated; thus it came about that General Urquiza found himself without either a navy or an army.

While the Argentine Confederation was approving the national constitution, the province of Buenos Aires was being organized into a state, for which a constitution was framed that received sanction on April 12, 1854. This political charter was unitarian in character; its formulation had been intrusted to Tejedor and Vélez Sársfield. It created a legislature of two houses: one of senators (one member to be elected for every 12,000 inhabitants); and the other of deputies (one for each 6,000). It established freedom of religious worship. The slave trade was prohibited. In large part this constitution of 1854 embodied the principles and declarations of the constitution of 1826.[4]

In May, 1854, Pastor Obligado was designated as the first constitutional governor of the state of Buenos Aires. Mitre, Paz, Alsina, Vélez Sársfield, La Riestra, and other leaders were his principal collaborators. Obligado founded numerous schools for

---

[4] Varela's opinion of this constitution is found in his *Historia constitucional de la República Argentina*, III, 547-48.

primary education in the country around Buenos Aires; he appointed Canon Agüero director of the Colegio Seminario which later became the National Academy. He laid the bases of the towns of Fuerte Esperanza, San Martín, Santos Lugares, Las Flores, Lomas, Chivilcoy, and Bragado which were located on the sites of small forts. He undertook the construction of city water plants and installed the first gas plant.

Subsequently, and up to the date when Buenos Aires was reincorporated in the national union, the province made significant progress, especially in economic directions. In respect to the public land, the emphyteutic system that had prevailed since the age of Rivadavia was modified by permitting the sale of land at the rate of 16,000 pesos of silver per square league. Upon the basis of the casa de moneda the bank of the province was organized which gave a great stimulus to industry and commerce.

CHAPTER LIII

THE ADMINISTRATION OF URQUIZA

THE AGREEMENT of San Nicolás had fixed upon the city of Santa Fe as the place for the meeting of congress. It was installed there on November 20, 1852. Upon this occasion the representative of General Urquiza—for he was unable to attend the opening of congress—read an address in which he said:

"The sincerity of my intentions with respect to the people of Buenos Aires is demonstrated by my conduct. Upon assuming command on July 26, I deprived the governing authority of all those prerogatives which had caused so many misfortunes by their abuse. I issued a law of amnesty in favor of all citizens exiled from the country, without excluding anyone. I anathemized the right of confiscation, thus freeing from its cruel effects even the government itself, which had practiced this as a means of obtaining partisan vengeance. I also abolished the death penalty for political offenses. In the internal management of the province I have introduced many improvements: I took steps to guarantee property, to promote agriculture, to aid honest commerce, and I issued a law concerning municipalities which when put into force would elevate the capital to the rank of one of the most commodious and best administered cities of southern America. . . . I opened the navigation of rivers to all foreign flags, improved the ports, abolished internal customs houses, and recognized the independence of Paraguay as an established fact. . . . For I love the people of Buenos Aires; I mourn the absence of their representatives from this hall. But their absence does not signify a permanent withdrawal; it is a transitory accident. Geography, history, and various pacts link Buenos Aires to the rest of the nation. That province cannot live without its sisters; nor can its sisters live without it. In the Argentine flag there is room for more than fourteen stars; but not a single one should be eclipsed."

"From this moment," wrote Pelliza, "the constituent congress held in its hands the future of Argentine institutions. Outstanding among those persons engaged in that patriotic task was Dr. Facundo de Zuviría, a native of Salta, a student and a man of extensive knowledge. . . . Dr. Salvador María del Carril, a native of San Juan, was minister of the treasury under Rivadavia. . . . He returned to the public service, convinced of his former errors, and disposed to collaborate in the great work of making a constitution. José B. Gorostiaga, a native of Santiago del Estero, lacked traditions. . . . Dr. Juan María Gutiérrez, a porteño, represented the province of Entre Ríos. Mathematician and legist, he was perhaps not a statesman. He was too fond of literature and the poetic art to be a consummate politician. The country owes him much because of his literary laurels, and it was to be indebted to him for his intelligent efforts in framing the fundamental law. . . . Distinguished for his austere mien, was the Dominican, Juan Manuel Pérez, a native of Tucumán, who with Dr. Benjamín J. Lavaisse of Santiago, and Dr. Pedro Centeno of Catamarca, formed the ecclesiastical group in congress. . . . Juan Francisco Seguí, deputy for Santa Fe, a talented son of that province, had been invested with priestly vestments but his restless spirit and his indomitable flesh tore him away from monastic austerites." [1] Imagine then in this congress "old men full of experience like Pérez, Ferré, Zuviría, and Colodrero; young enthusiasts like Huergo, Seguí, and Llerena, and men in the full vigor of their intellectual energy like Gutiérrez, Gorostiaga, Zapata, Zavalia, Derqui, and many others who were devoted collaborators in the great work of constituting a nation, whatever might be the obstacles and difficulties encountered in the way."

The members of congress labored assiduously in order to frame the constitution. During the preparatory conferences, there was in the halls of congress a copy of *The Federalist*, a collection of essays on the constitution of the United States by James Madison, John Jay, and Alexander Hamilton, which could be used as a norm, because the Great Republic of the North had adopted a federal system, the spirit of which dominated the congress of 1853. This volume, which belonged to Rivera Indarte, disappeared at the very moment when the constitutional project was to be framed. At that juncture, there fortunately came into the hands of the deputies a new book, small in format, but notable because of the amplitude of its concepts, entitled *Bases y puntos de partida para la organización política de la República Argentina* (*Bases and*

---

[1] Pelliza, *Historia argentina desde su origen hasta la organización nacional*, II, 443-45.

Points of Departure for the Political Organization of the Argentine Republic), which was written by the publicist, Juan Bautista Alberdi. This book furnished the orientation and marked the path to be followed by the members of the constituent congress of 1853.[2]

"The constituent congress," said Alberdi in the *Bases*, "will not be convoked to form the Argentine Republic. It cannot reduce its territory, nor alter its geological formation, nor change the course of its great rivers, nor transform agricultural lands into mineral lands. . . . Accordingly, it is the facts, the conditions . . . which exist by virtue of the action of time and of the history of our country that will determine the constitution which the Argentine Republic will receive at the hands of its constituent legislators." [3]

According to this criterion, a constitution is not a body of doctrines or theories reflecting the learning of a legislator, but the true and faithful expression of the history of a people, of its customs, of its prevailing manner of life and feeling. Alberdi, therefore, asked whether the constitution about to be framed should be federal or unitarian. In order to reply conscientiously on this point, and to propose a positive formula for the solution of our political struggles, Alberdi studied Argentine unitarian and federalistic tendencies. The author of the *Bases* enumerated the following unitarian antecedents: (1) Unity of republican principles: the nation had always been democratic. (2) Unity of sacrifices in the war for independence: all the provinces had furnished their aid to insure independence. (3) The distinct pacts of union which had been negotiated among the provinces affirmed the principle of political unity. (4) The congresses, presidents, and directors, who were essentially national. (5) The unity of glories and of symbolic colors, the coat of arms, the very word Argentina, and so on. Among the federalist antecedents that Alberdi enumerated were the following: (1) The provincial rivalries. (2) The long periods of provincial isolation and independence. (3) The local peculiarities in soil and climate, and also in the character, habits, and language of the people. (4) The enormous and onerous distances that separated some provinces from others and the lack of good roads. (5) The

---

[2] On the personality of Alberdi, see R. Sáenz Hayes, *La polémica de Alberdi con Sarmiento y otras páginas* (Buenos Aires, 1926).

[3] J. B. Alberdi, *Las bases* ("Biblioteca Argentina," vol. III, Buenos Aires, 1915), pp. 102-3.

partial sovereignty acknowledged by the May Revolution as belonging to all the provinces.

Thus, reasoned Alberdi, the members of the constituent congress should take into consideration these historic antecedents, both federal and unitarian; they should also remember that the country had only made two essays at a constitution, both of which were unitarian: that formed in 1819 during the directorate of Pueyrredón, which was followed by the crisis of 1820; and that formed in 1826 during the presidency of Rivadavia, which was followed in 1827 by anarchy and resistance in the provinces.[4] Upon the basis of the plan sketched by the author of the *Bases*, and with some modifications, congress adopted the constitution which now rules us.[5]

On May 1, 1853, congress sanctioned the Argentine constitution, and General Urquiza, who was at San José de Flores, declared it to be the fundamental law of the nation on the symbolic date of May 25. The constitution was signed by the following members of congress: Facundo Zuviría, Pedro Centeno, Pedro Ferré, Pedro Días Colodrero, Luciano Torrent, Juan María Gutiérrez, José de la Quintana, Manuel Padilla, Agustín Delgado, Martín Zapata, Regis Martínez, Salvador M. del Carril, Juan del Campillo, Santiago Derqui, Ruperto Godoy, Delfín B. Huergo, Juan Llerena, Juan F. Seguí, Manuel Leiva, Benjamín J. Lavaisse, José B. Gorostiago, Fray José M. Pérez, Salustiano Zavalía, and José M. Zuviría.

The form of government provided by the constitution of 1853 —which, with the slight modifications proposed by the provincial convention of 1860, is our fundamental law—is representative, republican, and federal. Argentine federalism is not and cannot be of the strict character of North American federalism, where the states that formed the Union had an independent autonomous tradition. Argentine federalism is of a moderate type, in the sense that it recognizes the relative autonomy of the provinces, and organizes a central, consolidated authority. In this manner, the two

---

[4] José N. Matienzo took the view that Alberdi was an admirable example of the application of the scientific method to social affairs. See his *Juan Bautista Alberdi* (Buenos Aires, 1910), p. 10.

[5] On the sources of the Argentine constitution of 1853, see S. Baqué, *Influencia de Alberdi en la organización política del estado argentino* (Buenos Aires, 1915), pp. 167-68.

historic Argentine currents, the unitarian and the federal, have their expression in the political organization that rules us, but the predominant tendency is the federal.

From the viewpoint of the declarations and the rights that it proclaims, this constitution is one of the most liberal in the world. It invites all men, without distinction of nationality, to reside on Argentine soil, and assures them the enjoyment of civil rights. The members of the constituent congress of 1853 had an admirable vision of the future of the country: their political charter still endures; it both directs and stimulates the country's progress.

Though the constitution of the Argentine nation was adopted, there nevertheless remained pending a conflict with the province of Buenos Aires, which had announced that it would establish itself as an autonomous state. A document exists which makes clear the patriotism and exalted views that animated General Urquiza. This is a circular addressed to the governor of Entre Ríos in which Urquiza considered the situation produced in the country by the attitude of the province of Buenos Aires and promised to relinquish the post of provisional director of the Confederation, in order that the national constitution should be stripped of all personalness. "If it is neither just nor rational," said General Urquiza, "to admit that the province of Buenos Aires possesses an arbitrary veto by which it can prevent national organization, in the knowledge that this was not begun under its exclusive direction; if it is not judicious to recognize as a right the power to reconstruct a situation in which the republic has been placed for the space of forty-two years, under the influence of its governments, neither is it politic nor useful to leave that extensive province as a disturbing element, outside the Argentine association. . . . It would be both perilous and impolitic, if a question of such transcendancy should be converted into a personal question, as the government of Buenos Aires has desired. In this policy there is a despicable astuteness that tends to make issues of the highest general interest personal questions in order to weaken them. . . . It is to eliminate this pretext that I have decided to place in the hands of congress the resignation contained in my message. . . . Congress can eliminate my person. I ardently desire this; and I shall give thanks for it with special gratitude. But with the same power of mind, I shall urge the need of maintaining invulnerable and permanent the principle of the fusion of all parties, of the forgetfulness of all misconduct, and of tolerance for all past errors. Without this, there is neither salvation, fatherland, nor constitution. . . . We should not extinguish the parties, but act as though they did not exist: in fine, if we sincerely desire to put an end to our evils, let us not lose sight of this capital maxim of my policy: that wherever there is no union, there some day dissolution must take place." [6]

According to the provisions of the constitution, elections took place on November 20, 1853. General Justo José de Urquiza was proclaimed first constitutional president; and Dr. Salvador M. del Carril was proclaimed vice president. The president took oath and assumed office on March 5, 1854; he appointed Dr. José B. Gorostiaga, minister of the interior; Dr. Juan M. Gutiérrez, minister of foreign affairs; Dr. Santiago Derqui, minister of justice, religion, and public instruction; Dr. Mariano Fragueiro, minister of the treasury; and General Rudecindo Alvarado, minister of war.

Meantime, on October 22, 1853, an ordinary session of congress had met in the city of Paraná. "It is only necessary to look through the national register from 1854 to 1860 in order to appreciate the prolific labor of the ministers who aided Urquiza during the six years in which he exercised the first constitutional presidency of the republic." [7] With regard to foreign relations, we noticed that grave complications occurred during the rule of Rosas. Urquiza undertook the difficult task of restoring good relations. In fact, in 1853, the first international treaties were signed with England, France, and the United States, which established the principle of the free navigation of the Paraná and Uruguay rivers for the merchant vessels of all nations. These treaties were followed by others of amity and commerce with Chile, Brazil, Bolivia, and Paraguay in America, and with Belgium, Prussia, Naples, and Sardinia in Europe. Further, in 1856, Dr. Alberdi was commissioned to negotiate a treaty of recognition, peace, and friendship with Spain; by one of the clauses of this treaty it was provided that, to determine the nationality of Spaniards domiciled in the Argentine Confederation, the principles embodied in the Spanish constitution should be observed. Buenos Aires protested against this stip-

---

[6] *Documentos relativos á la organización constitucional de la República Argentina* (3 vols., Buenos Aires, 1911-14), I, 186-91.

[7] Victorica, *op. cit.*, pp. 91-92.

ulation, and the government did not ratify the treaty. Alberdi explained that his proposal was intended to encourage Spanish immigration to Argentina; for Spaniards would by preference have directed themselves to our country, as by that treaty their children were to possess the same status as born Spaniards. But the treaty was tactfully rejected.

In the matter of public instruction, a decree was issued which nationalized both the University of Córdoba and the Academy of Monserrat and which subsidized the provinces in order to promote public instruction. When he was governor of the province of Entre Ríos, General Urquiza had been the founder of the first national academy of the republic, the Academy of Uruguay.

A governmental problem of great importance, to which it was necessary to give special study, was the promotion of immigration and settlement. In 1851, when the campaign of liberation against Rosas was being prepared, Dr. August Brougnes came to La Plata with the intention of planting settlements and agricultural communities with families of foreigners. In 1853, the government of Urquiza approved the contract signed by the governor of Corrientes with Dr. Brougnes for the planting of agricultural settlements in that province. The first immigrants to arrive in the country in accordance with this contract reached Corrientes in January, 1855. In June, 1853, the province of Santa Fe contracted for 200 Swiss families who arrived in Argentina in 1856; this immigration resulted in the founding of the settlement of Esperanza, which during its early years suffered from drouths and locusts.

In the province of Entre Ríos, General Urquiza founded in July, 1857, the settlement of San José, granting to each family composed of five adults, four square miles of land, four work oxen, two milch cows, two horses, and one hundred Bolivian pesos with which to purchase such necessities as seeds, farm tools, and wood for the construction of a house. A certain author has aptly said that the settlement of Esperanza in the province of Santa Fe and that of San José in the province of Entre Ríos became the complement of the victory of Caseros.

With regard to railroads, in January, 1854, an order was given that a contract be arranged for the services of a North American engineer. In the following September, the decision was reached to study the project of a railroad from Rosario to Córdoba. According to an agreement with the government of Chile, in 1855, a decree was issued concerning the proposed transandine railroad.

A resolution providing for the publication of the work of Martin de Moussy concerning the Argentine Republic deserves mention. Since the preparation during the colonial era of the works of Félix de Azara that dealt with the land, its fauna and flora, no one had written about the country until Martin de Moussy described in his work the Argentine pampas and mountains, the adaptability of the soil for the development of cattle-raising and agriculture and for the exploitation of all its fecund natural riches. In order to carry on an active propaganda abroad an order was given for the translation from French of the work entitled *Extinction du paupérisme agricole, moyen de s'enrichir par la colonisation dans la République Argentine* (*Extinction of Agricultural Pauperism, the means of enriching oneself by colonization in the Argentine Republic*), written by Dr. Brougnes. To quote Pelliza: "Various foreign collaborators, both of the United States and of Europe, approached the new government and offered their services in all sorts of enterprises. . . . In 1855, an arrangement was made with Dr. Moussy for the publication of the work mentioned above. Arrangements were made with the engineer, Allan Campbell, for the survey of a railroad from Rosario to Córdoba, with Rusiñol and Fillol for the establishment of stage lines, and with the agent of the firm of Trouvé, Chauvel, and Dubois for the founding of a bank. José Buschenthal interested the government in the negotiation of a loan for the consolidation of its foreign debt. The chief item in this debt was four hundred thousand pesos fuertes which the government of Entre Ríos had borrowed from Brazil to pay the expenses of the crusade against the dictator of Buenos Aires." [8] A law was also enacted regarding federal justice for the entire territory of the nation, but which, because of the lack of funds and of lawyers, was not enforced until the administration of Mitre in 1862. Vicente G. Quesada states:

"Those persons who suppose that in the provisional capital of the Argentine Confederation there were no students of literature are mistaken. With a population relatively small, composed in

[8] Pelliza, *Historia argentina desde su origen hasta la organización nacional*, II, 502.

large part of employees and merchants, but the official seat of government, it attracted as guests for a longer or shorter time such celebrated foreign littérateurs as Martin de Moussy, Baron du Graty, Viel Castel, M. Bravard, Francisco Bilbao, Herr Burmeister, M. Lelong, and M. Brougnes—the last-mentioned persons being enthusiastic entrepreneurs of colonization. Among the senators and deputies were many persons who were fond of historical and literary studies, so that in the political centers literary culture lived modestly. . . ." [9]

In 1860, Minister Juan Pujol made an attempt to establish an "historic-geographic institute of the confederation." In 1861, Dr. Vicente G. Quesada founded the *Revista del Paraná*, the publication of which continued for eight months, being interrupted because of the civil war. It printed in its columns articles by the best-known writers of the epoch, as Juan Pujol, Benjamín Victorica, Francisco Bilbao, Vicente Quesada, Carlos Guido y Spano, Juan M. Gutiérrez, Juana Manuela Gorriti, and Juan B. Alberdi. Other important intellectual centers of the confederation were the University of Córdoba, the Academy of Monserrat, and the Academy of Uruguay, directed by Alberto Larroque.

[9] V. G. Quesada, "La vida intelectual en las provincias argentinas," *Atlántida* (Buenos Aires, 1911), I, 321-22.

CHAPTER LIV

THE CONFEDERATION AND BUENOS AIRES

THE ARGENTINE Confederation and the province of Buenos Aires had established separate organizations. In spite of this, in the end of 1854 and in the beginning of 1855, these governments signed treaties of peace and commerce according to which they agreed not to consent to any territorial dismemberment and to aid each other mutually in case of an external attack. Therefore, according to the spirit of these treaties, the separation of the province of Buenos Aires from the rest of the Argentine family was temporary. But subsequent events complicated this condition of separatism and the parties prepared for war.

There was formed in Buenos Aires a party that favored the principle of union with the Argentine Confederation. Its adversaries denominated it "Chupandino." This party had as its mouthpiece the journal *La Reforma Pacífica* which was edited by Nicolás Calvo and Juan José Soto. The friends of the government of Buenos Aires—and hence the adversaries of General Urquiza—organized a party that was designated "Pandillero" whose principal representatives were Mitre, Sarmiento, Mármol, and Juan C. Gómez. Thus, there existed two parties in the confederation: one which emphasized the tenseness of relations with Buenos Aires and asked Urquiza that he should subdue the dissident state by force; and the other which proposed formulas for a rapprochement in order to reach a peaceful solution.

The financial situation developing in the confederation was not happy. On the one side, Buenos Aires, with its busy custom-house, could meet with ease the expenses of its administration. On the other side, the expenses of the confederation in 1856 had been estimated at 3,000,000 Bolivian pesos, while the income did not amount to 2,000,000 pesos. It was necessary for the confederation to found a bank, which put into circulation 6,000,000 pesos of paper money. Part of this issue was intended for the service of the administration, and the rest for public works and loans for the purpose of stimulating commerce. The port of the confederation was Rosario; but its situation could not be compared with the advantageous position occupied by Buenos Aires. The congress of Paraná sought a means of remedying the financial condition. For this purpose, and in order to promote the growth of the port of Rosario, in the end of 1854, congress formed the project of "differential duties" which taxed the introduction into the ports of the republic of European goods proceeding from intermediate ports with the exception of those in southern Brazil, Uruguay, and Paraguay. In the hall of congress this project had as many advocates as opponents; finally, in 1856, it was put to a vote and approved by sixteen votes against twelve.

In the approval of this law the leaders of Buenos Aires beheld a hostile move. From the viewpoint of its financial results, the law of differential duties did not produce great advantages for the confederation, and unfortunately, it only had results in a political way, by increasing the resentment between the leading men of both states. This precarious condition of relations soon had a violent end. In the beginning of 1857, Dr. Valentín Alsina, who had harbored a personal resentment for General Urquiza, was elected governor of the state of Buenos Aires. Thus war became inevitable. In February, 1859, Governor Alsina issued a retaliatory decree in reply to the law of differential duties. By another decree, he dismissed from the military service Generals Pirán, Iriarte, and others, because they were not *personae gratae* to the government. In this state of affairs the congress of Paraná authorized General Urquiza to subdue the province of Buenos Aires, if necessary, by force. In its turn, the government of that province appointed the minister of war, General Mitre, commander of the army.

The commander of the porteño army stationed himself at San Nicolás de los Arroyos. On October 23, 1859, this army was near the stream called Medio in the province of Buenos Aires in the ravine of Cepeda, whither advanced a column of cavalry belonging to the army of General Urquiza. The army of Buenos Aires was totally routed, and Mitre was compelled to retire to San Nicolás, whence he set out for the capital. General Urquiza advanced to San José de Flores; he laid down as the condition for an adjustment the resignation of the governor of Buenos Aires. This was immediately presented and accepted by the legislature. Paraguay had offered its friendly mediation, and in this manner it was easy to frame a pact of union. Everything induced the hope that the adjustment was definitive.

The pact of San José de Flores, which was signed on November 11, provided for the incorporation of the province of Buenos Aires in the Argentine Confederation on one condition. This was that within a period of twenty days a convention should assemble in that province which would frame suitable amendments to the national constitution framed by the congress of Santa Fe, and that in turn these amendments would be submitted to the definitive ratification of a national convention.

In fulfilment of the pact of San José de Flores, on January 5, 1860, the provincial convention of Buenos Aires was installed. To this assembly there came the most representative men of Buenos Aires: Adolfo Alsina, Mármol, and Sarmiento; Elizalde and Mitre represented the autonomist element that had defended the integrity of the state; Vélez Sársfield and Ugarte represented the element that favored a national policy. The project of amendments to the constitution of Santa Fe was framed by a committee composed of Mitre, Vélez Sársfield, Mármol, Antonio Cruz, Obligado, and Sarmiento. Upon this occasion, Vélez Sársfield delivered a notable speech from which we extract a passage: "A people can be happy," said the orator, "even with a bad or a defective constitution: we have the example of England, a great and happy republic without any constitution whatever. It seems that nothing could be stable there, yet England is even governed by a constituent power. Something analogous took place in Buenos Aires. It is ruled by a constitution, the poorest with which I am acquainted, and still we are a free and happy people."

One of the chief reforms proposed related to the problem of a capital. The constitution of 1853 declared that the capital should be the city of Buenos Aires. The convention of Buenos Aires proposed that the capital of the republic should be at a place fixed by the national congress, with the consent of the legislature of the province in which the place to be federalized was located. Besides, as the custom house of the province of Buenos Aires was nationalized, by the pact of San José de Flores, this province was assured of its income for 1859, for five years.

On October 21, the modified constitution was solemnly sworn to in Buenos Aires. The *Te Deum* was chanted in all the churches of the republic to celebrate the union of the Argentine family. Upon this occasion, Governor Mitre said: "Only today, after a half century of anxieties and of struggles of tears and of blood, we are about to fulfil the testament of our fathers, executing their last wish in the act of constituting Argentine nationality under the sway of principles. Only today, after so many days of trial and conflict, with joy in our souls and with our hearts overflowing with hope, can we say, this is the constitution of the United Provinces of the Río de la Plata, whose independence was proclaimed in Tucumán on July 9, 1816, forty-four years ago. This is the constitution of the Argentine Republic whose decision was reached thirty-four years ago by the unitarian congress of 1825. This is also the constitution of the federal congress of Santa Fe complemented and perfected by the revolution of September by which Buenos Aires revindicated its rights, and as such, it is the definitive constitution, the true symbol of the perpetual union of the children of the great Argentine family."

On March 5, 1860, the constitutional presidency of General Urquiza terminated, and Dr. Santiago Derqui, who had been his minister, was elected president. President Derqui, who desired to consolidate the union of Buenos Aires with the confederation, intrusted the portfolio of the treasury to Norberto de la Riestra, who had been in charge of that department in Buenos Aires, and in the same spirit, he promoted Colonel Bartolomé Mitre to the rank of brigadier general.

At the proper time, when the provisional government of Buenos Aires had ended its term, a governor was elected. The choice fell upon General Bartolomé Mitre. Animated likewise by sentiments of order and national harmony, Governor Mitre sent a commissioner to Paraná, who signed with an agent of the confederation "the pact of June 6" which simply ratified what was stipulated in the pact of November 11 of the previous year, that is, that both governments considered the union of all the Argentine provinces as a definitive fact. In order to give external and patriotic forms to these pacts of union, Mitre invited President Derqui and General Urquiza to celebrate in Buenos Aires the glorious date of July 9. This resulted, in fact, in a very solemn celebration.

Two later events produced a fresh difference between Buenos Aires and the confederation: the revolutionary movement in the province of San Juan; and the rejection of the certificates of election of the deputies of Buenos Aires who had been elected according to the terms of the provincial constitution and not according to the national constitution.

At this juncture, Antonio Virasoro, who had been reëlected for a new term in spite of the subversive movement preparing in the province which was being patronized by some publicists of Buenos Aires, was governing the province of San Juan. In November, 1860, Mitre went to Entre Ríos, and conferred with President Derqui and General Urquiza concerning the events in San Juan. They decided to advise Virasoro to relinquish the office of governor, just a few moments before the news arrived that he had been assassinated by an armed mob, and that Antonio Aberastain had assumed the command of the province. In accord with Mitre, President Derqui decided that the national government should intervene. He selected as the agent of such intervention Juan Sáa, governor of San Luis, and, as his assistants, Colonels Paunero and Conesa, who believed in the policy of Mitre. The new governor of San Juan, Aberastain, opposed this intervention: Colonels Paunero and Conesa entered into accord with the agitators, and the battle of Pocito was fought in which Aberastain was taken prisoner and shot. President Derqui disapproved of the actions of the interventor who had ordered that Aberastain should be shot; and the government of Buenos Aires also made an energetic protest.

Thereupon, the national congress was convoked and the province of Buenos Aires elected its deputies according to local law. Congress refused to accept the credentials of the delegates; it maintained that the election should have been in accordance with the national constitution. The government of Buenos Aires was aggrieved by this refusal, and was indisposed to arrange new elections. It enacted a law that declared the pacts of November 11, 1859, and June 6, 1860, to be null and void.

Both the confederation and Buenos Aires now prepared for war. President Derqui proceeded to Córdoba, in order to organize the militia. Between Urquiza and Derqui a certain coolness had developed: Urquiza confined himself to organizing the militia of Entre Ríos and Corrientes. Nevertheless, before engaging in battle, the parties tried to reach an agreement, but these negotiations carried on through the good offices of the ministers of France, England, and Peru in Argentina did not succeed.

The national army remained under the command of General Urquiza, while the army of Buenos Aires was under General Mitre. On September 17, 1861, these armies clashed on the plains of Pavón in the province of Santa Fe; the losses of Mitre were greater than those of Urquiza; but the latter, who was discouraged and was not on the best of terms with Derqui, felt that he was defeated morally, and withdrew from the theater of war. Mitre advanced with his army to Rosario.

The battle of Pavón symbolizes the definitive union of all the Argentine provinces. President Derqui, who had no support, withdrew to Montevideo; the vice president of the republic, Pedernera, declared that the national government had renounced its authority. General Mitre was intrusted with the provisional government until the convocation of a congress.

CHAPTER LV

THE PRESIDENCY OF MITRE

AFTER THE battle of Pavón, as the national government of Paraná had renounced its authority, the government of General Mitre assumed control in the double character of provincial government and national government. Mitre was able to handle the difficult and complicated situation of the moment. He gave the portfolio of government to Dr. Eduardo Costa, who was his principal collaborator in the task of arranging the definitive organization of the nation. In the first place, it was necessary to reassemble the representatives of all the Argentine provinces and for this purpose he ordered that national elections should be held; and decided that the assembly should open on May 25.

General Urquiza held the office of governor of the province of Entre Ríos. The quarrel between the confederation and Buenos Aires during the years immediately preceding the battle of Pavón had been incarnated in Urquiza and Mitre respectively, and had a personal bias. In January, 1862, at a time when Mitre had decided to prepare for the meeting of the constituent congress, he wrote thus to General Urquiza: "In regard to what your Excellency said at the end of your note in reply to the suggestion which I made to you in my letter of the 14th concerning your retirement from public life, and in which you declared to me 'that your only ambition is to remain by a tranquil hearth and to behold from it the happiness of a free and united fatherland,' I still hope that your Excellency realizes the seriousness of the present situation and that, hearkening to the counsels of a sane patriotism, you will perform in favor of the tranquility and the organization of the Argentine Republic the greatest service that you can now undertake by voluntarily removing the only obstacle which can be offered to general confidence in the new situation—a sacrifice which should not be very difficult to your Excellency who has made other greater sacrifices in regard to the highest and gravest public interests. I do not believe that you will hesitate to make this sacrifice also which is only concerned with your person." [1]

[1] *Documentos relativos á la organización constitucional de la República Argentina*, I, 293.

General Urquiza responded to this proposition by declaring that "in whatever concerns the person of the governor of the province, neither his dignity nor the rectitude of his intentions, nor the importance of the measures employed to insure a general peace, give him the right to decide whether his remaining in power would be an obstacle to the public welfare, regardless of his own attitude toward the performance of an act which is really far from being a sacrifice. . . . The government of Entre Ríos must have the assurance that this suggestion is not a demand backed by armed force and humiliating to the privileges and interests of this province which has to maintain them at all cost, whatever may be the situation in which its confidence in the justice of the Argentine people whose name your Excellency invokes has placed it." [2]

Upon this occasion, the legislature of the province of Entre Ríos sent a note to General Urquiza in which it approved and lauded the policy that he had pursued during the time which had elapsed since the battle of Caseros. It further declared that the legislature of Entre Ríos would not allow him to give up office, because it considered the demand of Buenos Aires to be unjust.

When the national congress assembled, the first matter to be considered was to determine the site of the capital of the republic. Mitre took over the plan which Rivadavia had submitted to the consideration of the constituent congress of 1826, according to which, all the territory of the province of Buenos Aires should be federalized. Congress approved this project, but the legislature of that province rejected it, and framed a counter-project proposing that the federalization should be limited to the city of Buenos Aires. However, that legislature finally accepted the so-called "Law of Compromise," which provided that the national administration should be seated in the city of Buenos Aires for a period of five years.

In the first session of congress, Mitre read a notable message giving account of the manner in which he had used the power with which he had been invested. "At the instant," so ran the message, "when public authority is dissolved and when the material manifestation of Argentine unity is, so to speak, blotted out, one must consider that this eclipse is only temporary, and that this apparent dissolution is in reality a labor of regeneration from which the

[2] *Ibid.*, p. 297.

republic will soon emerge, strong, compact, and free. . . . With this end in view, it is also necessary to seize with a firm hand the visible symbol of nationality, which still subsists, and to raise it aloft in order to assure some persons of the loyalty of the design that fortified the arm of the people, and in order to remind others what was the thought that smoothed the path amid the turmoil of war and the fluctuations resulting from an undefined situation. The reorganization of the republic upon the basis of morality, of liberty, and of a reformed constitution has been the banner which in its turn reunited the desires of all, upon the day following the end of the struggle." [3]

Congress justly declared that General Mitre was *benemérito de la patria* (well-deserving of the fatherland). From this moment, the candidate for the presidency who was favored by public opinion because of his own prestige was Mitre. And thus the will of the people was consecrated in the assembly of electors that met on October 5: it elected him as constitutional president for the term of six years and made Marcos Paz vice president.

The problem of the location of the capital had precipitated in Buenos Aires the formation of two new political parties. The "nationalist" party, headed by General Mitre, favored the federalization of Buenos Aires; while the "autonomist" party advocated the principle of the integrity and autonomy of that province. Its leader was Alfonso Alsina. The autonomists were also dubbed "crudos" ("the raw ones"), while the nationalists were nicknamed "cocidos" ("the cooked ones").

The president of the republic formed a ministry that met entirely the political expectations of the moment, and augured progress in the government and the administration. The department of the interior was intrusted to Dr. Guillermo Rawson of San Juan, who had played a shining rôle in the congress of Paraná. In this ministry, Dr. Rawson displayed much activity both in political matters and in administrative affairs. He gave a vigorous stimulus to everything that related to means of communication, post offices and telegraphs, immigration, and settlement. The treasury was intrusted to Dr. Dalmacio Vélez Sársfield, our first jurisconsult, the author of the Argentine civil code. By his influence, Minis-

---

[3] H. Mabragaña, ed., *Los Mensajes* (6 vols. Buenos Aires, 1910), III, 167-68. —W. S. R.

ter Vélez Sársfield insured the enactment of the customs law of 1863, which granted privileges to the trade between Buenos Aires and Europe, and which resulted in an increase in the national revenues from 7,000,000 to 14,000,00 gold pesos.

Dr. Eduardo Costa was appointed minister of justice, religion, and public instruction. Upon him devolved the honor of organizing the supreme court of federal justice. With regard to public instruction he stimulated the development of secondary education; he founded national academies in the provinces of Catamarca, Salta, Tucumán, San Juan, Mendoza, and in the city of Buenos Aires. Foreign affairs were intrusted to Dr. Rufino de Elizalde, while the portfolio of war and the navy was given to General Gelly y Obes. In both of these departments the ministers were able to enlist the active and talented collaboration of President Mitre.[4]

In international politics, the task of General Mitre demanded energy in order to repress the uprising of the guerrillas as well as to suppress the revolutionary spirit in the provinces. In 1863, the guerrillas led by Ángel Vicente Peñaloza, nicknamed "El Chacho," subjugated the provinces of San Luis, La Rioja, Córdoba, Catamarca, Salta, Tucumán, and San Juan. The governor of Tucumán defeated him on the banks of the river Colorado. In the following year, El Chacho was again defeated by the national forces at Lomas Blancas in the province of La Rioja. Thence the guerrilla leader proceeded to Córdoba where General Paunero vanquished him. Then he went to San Luis where he suffered another check. In the province of La Rioja, he was assassinated by soldiers of the national army.

In addition to this commotion caused by Peñaloza's guerrillas, revolutionary movements took place in almost all of the provinces of the interior, but the president was able to overcome this menace to the organization of the country.

---

[4] On Bartolomé Mitre as an historian, see especially R. Levene, "Mitre historiador," *La Nación*, Buenos Aires, June 27, 1918.

CHAPTER LVI

THE PARAGUAYAN WAR

In 1814, there was created in Paraguay the unipersonal dictatorship of Dr. Francia which was to last for five years. Two years later, the term of the dictator was made one for life. Francia kept Paraguay in a most backward condition until 1840, when he died. In 1844, Carlos Antonio López was named president of the republic with the powers of dictator. López did not adopt any measure of a moral or economic character to lift Paraguay out of its colonial condition. In 1842, urged by the Paraguayan government to recognize its independence, Rosas affirmed that he could not do so, but avowed that he would never take up arms to disturb the peace of the Paraguayan people.

In 1844, López arranged a treaty of navigation and commerce with the province of Corrientes, which had revolted against Rosas. In the following year, the dictator of Buenos Aires prohibited trade with Paraguay and Corrientes, and did not allow entrance to nor departure from Buenos Aires to any vessels bound for or returning from these regions. But at the end of the same year the naval squadrons of France and England won the naval victory of Obligado.

In accord with Montevideo, López declared war on Rosas. A clause of the agreement of López with the government at Montevideo embodied the following proposal: "As it is important to all of us to encourage the separation of Corrientes and Entre Ríos from Argentina in order that these provinces may form an intermediate state, we must carefully ascertain the sentiment regarding this, for, once this is realized, it will be easy to promote an offensive and defensive league against Brazil by Paraguay, Bolivia, and the republic of Uruguay by means of treaties of alliance, which would serve to strengthen the allied states and to prevent future plots, as well as to promote the negotiation of boundary treaties."

In August, 1844, Brazil recognized the independence of Paraguay. As López had Paraguayan troops occupy the mission district in 1849, the legislature of Buenos Aires passed a resolution in March, 1850, which authorized Rosas to prepare the supplies and forces necessary "to bring about the reincorporation of the province of Paraguay into the Argentine Confederation."

López did not enter into the alliance with Brazil, the government of Montevideo, and General Urquiza (in representation of Entre Ríos and Corrientes) in 1851, in order to unseat the tyrant. He proclaimed the principle that a foreign power should not interfere in the political organization of another nation, thus forgetting that in 1845 he had united with the province of Corrientes for that very purpose. He later joined this alliance, because it did not contemplate any hostile step toward Paraguay and only aimed to reëstablish the governments of Montevideo and Buenos Aires. The Paraguayan author, Cecilio Báez, asks, "Does not it appear to you reader, that these pacts arranged for the purpose of overthrowing governments in Montevideo and Buenos Aires, foreshadowed the triple alliance of 1865, formed for the purpose of demolishing the tyranny of Solano López." [1] Upon the establishment of the government of the confederation at Paraná, on July 17, 1852, it acknowledged the independence of Paraguay.

On November 20, 1857, Brazil and the Argentine Confederation signed the convention which, reproducing a similar clause of the treaty of March 7, 1854, between the same parties, stipulated that the navigation of the rivers Uruguay, Paraná, and Paraguay should be free to all flags. In February following, President López signed a similar treaty with Brazil (in ratification of a convention of 1856). Thus the imperial government realized its objective, that is, the free navigation of the Paraguay River in order to form a connection by that waterway with the province of Matto Grosso.

In January, 1859, representatives of the government of Brazil, of the Argentine Confederation, and of Montevideo signed a treaty by which the contracting parties declared that the republic of Uruguay could not be incorporated or confederated with either Brazil or the Argentine Confederation and that Uruguay would not contract any alliance against the signatory powers.

That same year, Urquiza signed a secret treaty with President

[1] Báez, *op. cit.,* p. 87. [In 1843, General Oribe, who claimed to be the legal president of Uruguay, besieged Montevideo, which was defended by the opposing party led by Joaquín Suárez, who after March 1, 1843, served for a time as provisional president of the government in Montevideo. The period of 1842-1850 in Uruguayan history has been styled the "Guerra Grande."—W. S. R.]

López, which provided that the Paraguayan dictator would place at the disposal of the president of the Argentine Confederation the four wagons for the transportation of soldiers and munitions that were necessary in the operations against the province of Buenos Aires. This friendship of López for Urquiza was a return for the official and efficacious intervention of the latter in a serious conflict in which Paraguay was involved with the United States.[2] López was not able to coöperate in the war of the confederation with Buenos Aires, but in exchange his mediation became operative after the battle of Cepeda (October 23) and the convention of November provided that Buenos Aires should submit to the government of the confederation.

In September, 1862, President Carlos Antonio López died. At that time Paraguay was a poor, backward country; without learning, industry, or active foreign commerce. To quote Báez once more: "There was a fundamental error in the policy of President López, an error that proved fatal to Paraguay. That error consisted in not having elevated by liberty and enlightenment the moral standard of the people, whose destiny he confided to his son, Francisco Solano López with the Greek gift of the boundary question pending with Brazil and Argentina."[3] At the opening of the war Paraguay had 550,000 inhabitants. Solano López was able to organize an army of 80,000 men by enlisting old men as well as lads under fifteen years of age.

In 1864, General Flores—chief caudillo of the Uruguayan party of the colorados—invaded the republic of Uruguay in order to depose the president who belonged to the blanco party. Flores enjoyed a reputation for military ability. He had fought at Pavón by the side of Mitre, and was in favor with the court of Brazil because of his relations with Emperor Pedro II. Lamas, who represented the Uruguayan government stated to Elizalde, the Argen-

---

[2] The conflict between Paraguay and the United States was due partly to the activities of an adventurous citizen of the United States named Hopkins who organized the United States and Paraguay Navigation Company for the development of Paraguay. Differences arose between this company and the Paraguayan dictator; in consequence it demanded an indemnity. Although the United States sent a debt-collecting expedition to Asunción in 1859, yet the controversy was not adjusted until August, 1860. It would seem that the attitude of Urquiza to the dispute was not altogether altruistic. C. A. Washburn, *A History of Paraguay* (2 vols., New York, 1871), I, 355-87.—W. S. R.

[3] Báez, *op. cit.*, p. 120.

tine minister of foreign affairs, that a contingent was being prepared in our territory for the expedition of Flores, and that the revolutionists were being provided with arms. The Argentine government replied that it "had given assurances that it would fulfil the duties imposed by neutrality on a friendly government." Such events produced complications in the internal political divisions of our country; for, while the members of the party in power, in whose triumph Flores had participated, had sympathetic relations with that Uruguayan chief, the members of the federal party or party of the interior were carrying on a campaign of opposition to the government of General Mitre. Some Argentine steamers were seized by the Uruguayan authorities, events that provoked acts of reprisal on the part of the Argentinians. After lengthy negotiations, an agreement was temporarily reached.

In this situation, Uruguayan diplomats represented to the governments of Paraguay and Brazil that the expedition of Flores had been assembled and equipped in Argentine territory for the purpose of making an attack upon the independence of Uruguay and of reconstructing the former viceroyalty of La Plata. Above all, Paraguay insisted upon demanding explanations; this view was supported by certain European powers: France, England, Portugal, and Italy. Confronted by this unusual act of intervention which constituted an affront to the nation, the Argentine government gave no explanations.

At the same time, the imperial government demanded of Uruguay that it should put an end to the injuries suffered by Brazilians who lived in the Uruguayan plains and who were being despoiled of their property. The Uruguayan government did not give the satisfaction which was demanded; hence, Brazil concentrated soldiers along the frontier. Being requested to intervene in friendly fashion in this conflict, in order to make peace prevail among the Uruguayans, President Mitre sent Rufino de Elizalde, the minister of foreign relations, to Montevideo. However, the mission of the Argentine minister failed, and the Brazilian ambassador announced that the imperial army stationed on the Uruguayan frontier would opportunely receive orders to make reprisals in defense of Brazilian subjects. On August 30, 1864, the Paraguayan government protested because of this act of Brazil, declaring that it would consider "any occupation of Uruguayan territory by im-

perial soldiers . . . as an attack upon the equilibrium of the states
of La Plata, an equilibrium that was important to the republic
of Paraguay as a guarantee of security, peace, and prosperity." [4]
The government of Uruguay immediately took up arms for defense against attack. Marshal López of Paraguay seized the Brazilian steamship *Marquez de Olinda*, and ordered an invasion of
the province of Matto Grosso. The imperial army, in conjunction
with the Uruguayan army of Flores, triumphed in Uruguayan territory.

President Solano López now asked permission from the Argentine government to cross the territory of the province of Corrientes
with Paraguayan soldiers, in order to oppose the Brazilians. Mitre
denied the request. Without a previous declaration of war, the
Paraguayan naval squadron surprised two Argentine vessels, the
25 de Mayo and the *Gualeguay* which lay in the port of Corrientes.
This attack provoked intense indignation; and the Argentine government and people prepared immediately to repel the invasion.
As the minister of foreign relations of our country explained,
"Mitre did not wish to become involved in the war and did everything possible to prevent it. . . . Dazzled by the power which it
had at disposal, in the belief that there was no nation in the
Platean region that could resist it, the government of Paraguay
launched the enterprise. . . . It first wronged Brazil, then the
Argentine Republic, and, against the wishes of all, the dogs of
war were unloosed." [5]

On March 5, 1865, Solano López declared war against the Argentine republic. Two months later, the ministers plenipotentiary
of Argentina, Brazil, and Uruguay signed the treaty of the Triple

[4] T. T. Fernández, "Guerra del Paraguay, sus antecedentes," *Atlantida*
(Buenos Aires, 1911), II, 353.

[5] Dr. Elizalde in the chamber of deputies, June 3, 1868, quoted in B. Mitre,
Archivo del general Mitre (25 vols. Buenos Aires, 1911-13), II, 33-34. A scholarly
investigation of the causes of the Paraguayan War has recently been made by
Dr. P. H. Box in a monograph entitled, *The Origins of the Paraguayan War*
("University of Illinois Studies in the Social Sciences," vol. XV, Urbana, 1930),
where, in the main, the thesis is presented that the Paraguayan War had its roots
in the unsettled boundaries of the Platean countries and in their economic and
political instability, and further that it was precipitated by the bizarre and
reactionary foreign policy of Paraguay which threatened the nascent liberties
that had been made possible by the defeat of Rosas at Caseros.—W. S. R.

Alliance by virtue of which they formed an offensive alliance in order to make war against Paraguay. One article of this treaty expressly declared that the war was against the tyrant Solano López, and not against the people of Paraguay, and that the ranks of the attacking coalition would be open to the sons of that country who might desire to lend their support to depose the tyrant.

After the seizure of the Argentine vessels, the Paraguayan general, Robles, at the head of three thousand men captured the city of Corrientes.[6]

According to the treaty of the Triple Alliance, President Mitre became the commander in chief of the allied armies. Brazil placed its naval squadron at the service of the war, but proceeded so slowly that the vessels did not sail from Buenos Aires until April, 1866.

Three months after the declaration of war in 1865, President Mitre had delegated his civil authority to the vice president of the republic, Marcos Paz. The place of reunion for the allied armies was Concordia in the province of Entre Ríos. General Flores was the commander of the Uruguayan forces numbering 6,000 men, while General Osorio commanded the Brazilian soldiers. The Uruguayan army formed the vanguard, and marched toward Yatay where an engagement favorable to the Allies took place with Paraguayan forces under Duarte. In the month of August, General Mitre left Concordia, and marched toward Uruguayana, where the Paraguayan chief, Estigarribía had fortified himself. When terms of surrender were submitted to prevent a conflict, the Paraguayans capitulated.

The allied army soon advanced to the Paso de la Patria, where the Paraguayans had stationed a force of 30,000.[7] In May, 1866, the battle of Estero Bellaco took place, and a few days later, another sanguinary combat occurred, which, like the preceding one, caused great losses to both armies. On July 11 and 18, the battles of Yataití-Corá and Boquerón or Sauce took place. As the Paraguayan army continued to suffer great losses, President Solano López felt compelled to ask for a conference with General Mitre

---

[6] The Paraguayans made the great mistake of dividing their forces and invading Argentina by way of both the Paraná and the Uruguay. See Mitre, *Archivo del general Mitre*, II, 134-35.

[7] On the fording of the Paraná River, see J. I. Garmendia, *Campaña de Humaytá* (Buenos Aires, 1901), pp. 7-10, 24-25.

in order to arrange a peace;[8] the conference was unproductive, and precious time was lost; for during this pause the Paraguayans fortified themselves strongly at Curupaytí. At this place, there occurred one of the bloodiest battles of this war; the allied armies lost almost 9,000 men while the enemy lost only 50 men.

In the beginning of 1867, General Mitre came to Buenos Aires, while the Marquis of Caxias remained at the head of the allied army. About the middle of this year, Mitre returned to take charge of the army. He made a successful attack on Curupaytí and fought other engagements.[9]

Because of the death of the vice president, Mitre was compelled again to return to Buenos Aires during the first days of 1868. The Marquis of Caxias, who had again taken charge of the allied army, forced the pass of Humaytá, and reached Asunción.

During the entire course of the war the activities of the allied squadron were important. Aside from having aided in the concentration of the land forces at Concordia, and having transported the Brazilian forces to the scene of action, it furnished decisive coöperation in the attack and occupation of Corrientes, Uruguayana, Paso de la Patria, and Curupaytí.

There operated to lessen the importance of the coöperation of the allied squadron the fact that its management under Admiral Tamandaré was independent of the command of the army. Certain writers take the view that this lack of unified control was one of the chief conditions that retarded the termination of the war. Valotta said: "General Mitre, realizing the disadvantages in the independent command of the squadron, wrote a letter to the emperor of Brazil, demonstrating the necessity of placing the squadron under the control of the commander in chief of the allied armies. Hence, the government of Brazil had to reflect about the manner of satisfying this demand which was both necessary and reasonable.

"The appointment of the Marquis of Caxias as generalissimo of the land and naval forces of Brazil, was beyond doubt a step taken for the purpose of giving unity to the operations. Indirectly,

---

[8] On the conference of López and Mitre at Yataití-Corá, see J. S. Godoi, *Monografías históricas* (Buenos Aires, 1893), pp. 138-43.—W. S. R.

[9] In regard to the plan of campaign originally agreed upon by Mitre and Caxias, see Mitre, *Archivo del general Mitre,* III, 125-26.

it gave General Mitre the command of the squadron. But this was only a partial step and did not satisfy the supreme demands of the moment. There was no other solution except to place the Brazilian squadron at Mitre's disposal." [10]

President Solano López fled into the Paraguayan Chaco but made a stand at Cerro Corá at the head of 2,000 men. Unable to resist longer, López tried to flee again, but was overtaken and killed. The Paraguayan War was long and costly. The intervention of the Argentine Republic in this conflict was inevitable; the tyrant López had insulted its national sovereignty. The prevailing belief was that the war would last a short time; the fact that it was prolonged for several years was due in part to the heroic resistance made by the Paraguayan people and in part also to the misunderstandings that arose between the commanders of the Brazilian and the Argentine forces.[11]

---

[10] G. Valotta, *La cooperación de las fuerzas navales con las terrestres durante la guerra del Paraguay* (Buenos Aires, 1915), p. 21.

[11] On the prolongation of the war, see Mitre, *Archivo del general Mitre*, VI, 185-86. On the tactics of the Allies, see A. A. Maligne, "Historia militar de la Argentina," *La Nación, 1810—25 Mayo—1910* (Buenos Aires, 1910), p. 105.

CHAPTER LVII

THE ADMINISTRATION OF SARMIENTO

A YEAR and a half before the constitutional term of President Mitre had terminated, the question of his successor was warmly discussed, and various persons were named as candidates for the presidency. One of these candidates was Dr. Rufino de Elizalde; in opposition to him, Dr. Adolfo Alsina was placed in candidacy, and shortly afterward, Domingo Faustino Sarmiento. The two last-mentioned candidates came to an understanding by a coalition that adopted the slogan Sarmiento-Alsina for president and vice president of the republic. Finally, the victor of Caseros, General Urquiza, was also put forth as a candidate.

In order to explain the neutral position of the president of the republic in such a manner that no candidate might suppose that he was supported by the government, Mitre wrote to Dr. José M. Gutiérrez—one of the supporters of the candidacy of Elizalde— the historic letter which rightly has been designated "the political testament of Mitre." As he declares in that letter, Mitre's earnest desire had been "to prepare the country for the free election of a president under the best possible conditions for the great national party of principles." [1] With admirable foresight, considering the events of the epoch, Mitre defined in his letter the political position of the national executive, who because of the eminence of his post, could not allow the influence of the government to favor an official candidacy. He invited the people to a free and democratic election, and thus restored to them the enjoyment and full exercise of their true sovereignty, which consisted of government by the people and of the free expression of their will.

In May, 1868, Mitre sent a letter to Urquiza in which he made interesting political reflections concerning the country, and invited him to withdraw his candidacy. "An agreement between us to transmit the presidential power," wrote General Mitre, "in order to promote the success of any candidate whatever, even without the use of reprehensible means, would be an immoral act,

---

[1] Mitre, *Archivo del general Mitre,* I, 27. This document is also found in Levene, *Lecturas históricas argentinas,* II, 366–77.

Upper, Scene in a Bullfight; an engraving dated 1780; from Pillado, *Buenos Aires Colonial.* Lower, The Grandstand of the Jockey Club at the Race Track, Buenos Aires in 1916; photograph by the Translator.

an ignominy for our country and a shame for us, besides being an immense retrograde step in the road of constitutional order and of government of the people by the people. . . . A people have more need of morality, of liberty, and of justice than of tutors who wish to direct them by means of obscure intrigues." [2]

General Urquiza replied and among other remarks made the following statement: "If your Excellency's letter had reached me before the one I wrote to José M. Gutiérrez in regard to candidacies, I would have received the views expressed by you in time to consider them with serenity and to avoid committing myself by yielding to the desires and opinions of many of my fellow citizens who have demanded of me as a patriotic duty that I should not withhold my name from the people, whatever might be the result. . . . The merit of unrestricted popular suffrage depends neither upon your word nor upon mine: this depends solely upon the régime of the institutions among the people, who are not disturbed by the coercion of the general power in matters foreign to it. There is no candidacy that does not involve inconveniences that are more or less grave; the patriotism of all citizens should coöperate to remove them in order to promote the progress of the country after the election takes place. . . ." [3] The author of the letter then made some observations in regard to the policy of the first constitutional government of the confederation which had been headed by General Urquiza accompanied by a pleiad of men, such as Carril, Zuviría, Zapata, Gorostiaga, Gutiérrez, López, Pico, Alvarado, Pedernera, and Guido, who did not coöperate to form a government by a select circle but to form the impersonal government of the constitution which could shelter all parties under the banner of the fatherland.

When the electoral assembly met, it chose Domingo Faustino Sarmiento and Adolfo Alsina to be respectively president and vice president of the republic. They were inaugurated on October 12, 1868. The national ministry was organized as follows: Dalmacio Vélez Sársfield, minister of the interior; Dr. José B. Gorostiaga, minister of the treasury; Dr. Mariano Varela, minister of foreign affairs; Dr. Nicolás Avellaneda, minister of justice, religion, and public instruction, and Colonel Martín de Gainza, minister of war.

---

[2] See further, Mitre, *Archivo del general Mitre,* I, 95.

[3] Victorica, *op. cit.,* pp. 296-97.

On April 11, 1870, General Urquiza was assassinated on his ranch of San José de Flores. A few days later General López Jordán, who assumed responsibility for this act, took the office of governor of the province of Entre Ríos.[4] The national government ordered military intervention in that province to insure order and the maintenance of the constitution; as the governor was disposed to resist the national government, it ordered that all the forces of the interior provinces should be concentrated under the command of General José Miguel de Arredondo. General Conesa of the forces of intervention defeated López Jordán in an engagement; he, however, recovered himself and took possession of the city of Uruguay and then of Gualeguaychú. The most important battle of the revolution of López Jordán was that fought at the stream Santa Rosa, which forced him to flee to Corrientes, whose governor in turn fought and vanquished him. Three years later, López Jordán returned to invade the province of Entre Ríos, and after numerous partial engagements, he was defeated in the battle of Don Gonzalo.

The administration of Sarmiento stamped by the vigorous seal of his personality an historic moment in Argentine social and political evolution. His activities had given him sufficient distinction so that he might well occupy the chief magistracy of the nation; he was, at the same time, a man of thought and action. One does not know which to admire the more in him, the intelligent appreciation of the epoch, of its events, and of its men, or the efficiency and energy with which he carried out his ideas.

This administration was distinguished by the policy pursued with respect to caudillism or chieftainship and the development of public education which it passionately stimulated. Sarmiento was a statesman, who was able first to diagnose the ills that afflicted Argentine society, and then to propose a remedy. A sociologist and politician, he had written in his *Facundo* that caudillism was a plant indigenous to our soil, an historic force of our past; it was, therefore, necessary to resist it by descending to the founda-

---

[4] An undated extract from the *Standard* of Buenos Aires indicates that the murder of Urquiza was due to partisan spirit. This pathetic account states that when the assassins entered the courtyard of Urquiza's house "terrible shouts of 'Death to the traitor Urquiza' mingled with the cries of 'long live López Jordán,'" State Dept. MSS, Bureau of Indexes and Archives, Argentine Republic, vol. 18.—W. S. R.

tion of the social soul, and by removing the passions and instincts of the masses. He reasoned that the greatest enemy to the consolidation of democratic institutions and of liberty was ignorance, under the protection of which the caudillos had been conceived and raised. In order to make the war against the chieftains effective, he made the school the scene of combat. Henceforth, the schoolmaster was the soldier of this new crusade. For it, Sarmiento founded the first normal schools of the republic, from which came the masters who had charge of the civilizing mission of spreading a knowledge of the alphabet and of culture. It has been aptly said of him that he led a real cavalry charge against creole ignorance.

Sarmiento also favored the development of the railway system. He had one railroad built from Córdoba to Tucumán, and another from Concordia to Mercedes de Corrientes, as well as the line of Río Cuarto. Immigration was given a vigorous impulse. Numerous settlements were planted by foreigners throughout the republic. The financial condition of the country was also prosperous; for the public revenues increased by several million pesos per annum.

Early in 1871, yellow fever became a terrible scourge. "In five months," said one authority, "more than thirteen thousand people succumbed to it. The year was almost an idle one economically and administratively, as is shown by the register of the acts and proceedings of the government and by the budget of the army for the following year. The gravest internal disturbance of Sarmiento's administration, the revolution of 1874, coincided with an economic crisis which was the outcome of fifteen years with an unfavorable balance of trade. In administrative matters, as in the matter of his presidential candidacy, Sarmiento's presidency suffered from the harassing effects of obstacles. Nevertheless, he surmounted them all, and despite the burden of the past, he went upward and onward." [5]

The conduct of foreign relations was also put to severe tests. The cautious and persistent advance of Chile in the Patagonian region and near the Strait of Magellan compelled the Argentine government to consider this question that had been imprudently neglected since the time when Rosas presented claims. The attitude of Sarmiento, who when he was an émigré in Chile favored the

---

[5] L. Lugones, "Historia de Sarmiento," *El Monitor de la educación común* (Buenos Aires, 1911), XXXVI, núm. 459, pp. 257-58.

Chilean pretensions to the Strait of Magellan, is well known. The president rectified his errors with self-denying patriotism without hesitating to make the difficult confession that this implied.[6]

By the treaty of May 1, 1865, signed by the governments of Brazil, Uruguay, and Argentina in order to wage war against the tyrant Solano López, it was stipulated that the allies would respect the integrity of the territory of the republic of Paraguay, and bases were established according to which at the proper time definitive boundary treaties were to be negotiated. In 1869, after the Paraguayan War had terminated, the ministers of foreign affairs of the nations belonging to the triple alliance met at Buenos Aires in order to confer with respect to the treaty of peace and boundaries that it would be suitable to frame with Paraguay. At the end of this year, Mariano Varela, Sarmiento's minister of foreign affairs, said: "Victory does not confer upon the allied nations the right to fix among themselves as their boundaries the lines drawn by the tripartite treaty. . . . These boundaries should be discussed with the government that exists in Paraguay, and the adjustment will be made in the treaties drawn up after the contracting nations have exhibited the titles upon which each of them respectively bases its claims." In this manner the government of Sarmiento proclaimed "that victory does not confer rights."

Confronted by this doctrine, the imperial Brazilian government became disturbed and was on the point of breaking off relations with the Argentine republic. In 1872, General Mitre was intrusted with a diplomatic mission to Rio de Janiero which reëstablished amicable relations between Argentina and Brazil. The boundary treaties of those nations with Paraguay were signed in 1876 during the administration of Avellaneda and the secretaryship of Bernardo de Irigoyen.

In 1869, the first national census was taken under the direction of Diego G. de la Fuente. The census gave a population of 1,743,353, which was composed of 1,531,360 Argentinians and 211,993 foreigners. Forecasting future developments, the census of 1869 indi-

---

[6] *Ibid.*, p. 258. Estimates of Sarmiento may be found in C. O. Bunge, "Sarmiento, el escritor," *Nosotros* (Buenos Aires, 1918), XXIX, 332-35; and in J. M. Eizaguirre, "Sarmiento, maestro de energías," *Humanidades* (La Plata, 1923), V, 125-37. On Sarmiento's attitude toward the dispute concerning the Strait of Magellan while he was a resident in Chile, see J. G. Guerra, *Sarmiento, su vida i sus obras* (Santiago de Chile, 1901), p. 136.—W. S. R.

cated that in 1909 the Argentine Republic would have 6,591,100 inhabitants. According to the census of 1869, the revenues of the national government amounted to 12,496,000 pesos and the expenditures fell short of 9,620,000 pesos. The telegraph was extended to Rosario; Mariano Billinghurst inaugurated the first urban street-car line. Foreign commerce greatly increased; the leading places in that trade were held by England, France, the United States, and Spain.

CHAPTER LVIII

THE ADMINISTRATION OF AVELLANEDA

AT THE END of the term of Sarmiento, the following leaders were brought forth as candidates for the presidential nomination: Dr. Nicolás Avellaneda, who had been his minister of justice, religion, and public instruction; Adolfo Alsina; and General Mitre. In order to promote his own candidacy, Avellaneda had founded the national party. Alsina withdrew his name, and with the entire autonomist party of which he was leader, supported the candidacy of Avellaneda. From this fusion of the national party of Avellaneda and the autonomist party of Alsina there was formed the national autonomist party. Avellaneda was successful in the elections and took charge of the government on October 12, 1874.[1]

Before his inauguration, on September 24, 1874, a revolution led by Mitre broke out in protest against the official influence that was being brought to bear in the presidential elections. The motive that impelled a part of the people to revolt was thus explained by its leader: "Invited not only by those persons who have supported my candidacy, but also by those who have opposed me, to place myself at the head of a revolutionary movement, I replied in the negative, but stated at the same time that revolution was a right, a duty, and a necessity; that not to engage in it, with many comrades or with few, though it should be to do nothing more than to protest in manly fashion with arms in our hands would be a crying shame which would prove that we were incapable and unworthy of guarding and of meriting the liberties which had been lost."

On the day set for the pronunciamiento, which was to affect the entire republic, the governmental general, Ignacio Rivas, revolted with a garrison in the southern part of the province of Buenos Aires. General Arredondo, another revolutionist, went to San Luis, captured the government general, Ivanowski, had him executed, and then proceeded to Córdoba. General Arredondo triumphed over the government forces at Mendoza in the battle of Santa Rosa.

About the end of October, General Mitre disembarked in the southern part of the province of Buenos Aires and made a junction

---

[1] See further, P. Groussac, *Los que pasaban* (Buenos Aires, 1919), pp. 136-37.

with the forces of General Rivas. Mitre marched into the western part of the province, which he reached on May 25, and, when he approached the capital, Commandant José I. Arias at the head of government forces gave battle at La Verde and routed him completely. General Mitre surrendered his sword to Commandant Arias and signed a capitulation. In the interior, fate was also adverse to the revolutionary forces; General Arredondo was now vanquished on the battlefield of Santa Rosa by Colonel Roca. Thus the revolt was suppressed.

After the insurrection of 1874, with the exception of the uprising that occurred in Entre Ríos in 1876, which was speedily suppressed, no other insurrection disturbed national tranquility. Thus President Avellaneda was able to develop a progressive program during his administration. During the six years of his presidency, 268,500 immigrants entered the country. In 1879, the imports into Argentina amounted to 44,860,000 pesos, while the exports aggregated 47,765,000 pesos, leaving thus a balance of 3,000,000 pesos in our favor. One of the objects of this administration was to continue the educational policy initiated by President Sarmiento. Avellaneda founded numerous primary and secondary schools throughout the republic.

The administration of Avellaneda definitively settled the problem of the wilderness. In 1833, Rosas took possession of these lands as far as the Colorado River, but shortly afterward the indigenous tribes regained their positions and not only raided the frontier settlements but also made menacing incursions as far as the roads that linked cities of the littoral with the interior. This event made impossible the adoption of a plan for the settlement of the public lands by alloting them for occupation by nationals and foreigners.

General Julio A. Roca, Avellaneda's minister of war, conceived and executed the plan for the occupation of all Patagonia by the army of the nation. On May 24, 1879, on the banks of the Río Negro, General Roca celebrated this great achievement. This campaign also signalized the extermination of the savage Indian and consequently the elimination of that factor from the miscegenation of races which is taking place in our country. With the disappearance of this constant threat to civilization, the foreigner undertook to cultivate and settle Patagonia in conjunction with Argentinians. President Avellaneda sketched a comprehensive plan concerning the public domain and its allotment. To quote González again:

"Argentine and European capital was immediately employed over that immense area which is as varied and fertile as the richest on the globe; daring explorers and tradesmen have disclosed richest beds of metal ore and substances of incalculable industrial value, such as gold, coal, and petroleum; European capital seeks to open on its coast or in its interior new railroad or maritime routes; and a brilliant constellation of settlements begins to appear on the southern firmament of the fatherland which presages an indefinite expansion, the vigorous sprouting from the old trunk of an indefinite number of branches." [2]

Lastly, it should be noticed that this definitive conquest of the wilderness served as a basis for the law of 1884 concerning federal territories. Such territories or settlements may constitute vigorous entities, even from the political viewpoint, and, when they have fulfilled the conditions prescribed by law, they have the right to be transformed into provinces.

The administration of Mitre moulded the nation; that of Sarmiento continued Mitre's work and presaged that of Avellaneda. Avellaneda's administration "with its great achievements," said Groussac, "that is, national order irrevocably consolidated, the economic crisis averted, the wilderness subdued, and, finally, the capital definitely established in Buenos Aires—completes the work inaugurated by the victor of Pavón." [3] Avellaneda is the expected fusion of two forces created in our political history: the capital and the provinces. With Avellaneda there begins a political activity which embraces the entire extent of the national territory and which affects the life of every inhabitant.

"Avellaneda wrote only one book, namely, *Tierras Públicas* (*Public Lands*). However, the collection of his spoken and written words, which were dispersed in political speeches and letters, comprise twelve volumes. He did not bequeath to us either *Facundo* or the *Bases*, a history of the revolution, of independence, or of the republic; neither did he leave us our codes of law. But his words composed the eloquent glossary of those books, and even of scien-

---

[2] J. V. González, *El juicio del siglo ó cien años de historia argentina* (Buenos Aires, 1913), p. 237.

[3] P. Groussac, *Los que pasaban* (Buenos Aires, 1919), p. 212.

tific matters that were scarcely perceived during his era. And, as his word was the echo of his acts, we should seek his literary works in his deeds." [1]

Near the end of Avellaneda's term, two candidates were put forth for the presidency: Dr. Carlos Tejedor, who was supported by public opinion in the provinces of Buenos Aires and Corrientes; and General Julio A. Roca, minister of war of Avellaneda, who had just increased his prestige by a campaign against the Indians. The first-mentioned candidate had gained a solid reputation as a publicist and codifier of law (he was the author of the penal code) and his chances were better than those of Roca, who was favored by the administration. Roca resigned the ministry of war and was succeeded by Dr. Carlos Pellegrini.

Dr. Carlos Tejedor, governor of the province of Buenos Aires, had ordered the mobilization of the national guard and organized urban groups and associations in a military fashion. The national government enacted a law prohibiting provincial authorities from taking such steps on the eve of elections. Shortly afterward a decree was signed declaring that meetings of armed citizens would not be permitted. A clash between provincial sectionalism and national authority was inevitable. Tejedor took up arms against the national government, which in June, 1880, had to transfer its seat to Belgrano, and concentrate the national army at Chacarita. The most important engagements fought during this insurrection were Barracas, Puente Alsina, and Corrales. The contending parties soon entered into negotiations for peace, and, in order to promote these, Tejedor resigned his office as governor of the province of Buenos Aires. Upon doing so, he composed a notable manifesto in which he declared: "It is even necessary to save institutions by peace or by war, and to sacrifice for them individuals but not principles. . . . The constitutional authorities and the government itself remain unharmed. . . . There will be only one individual less, I, who have neither aspired to the office of president nor wish to hold it, and there will be one thing more assured to us—peace." [5]

The revolution of 1880 had dislodged the national authorities

[4] D. Peña, "Elogia de Avellaneda," *Nosotros* (Buenos Aires, 1917), XXVII, 41. See further, V. C. Gallo, *La presidencia Avellaneda* (Buenos Aires, 1918).

[5] On the revolution of 1880, see further, M. L. González, *Vida del teniente general Julio A. Roca* (Buenos Aires, 1914), pp. 144-52.

from the city of Buenos Aires by invoking the law of compromise, by virtue of which they only had the right to reside there for a period of five years. When this revolt was subdued, it was necessary to settle once for all the pending, historic question concerning the capital of the republic. This was a problem for which a definitive solution had not yet been found. The historic past, the geography of the country, as well as political and constitutional antecedents, designated the city of Buenos Aires as the capital of the republic. The constitutions of 1819, 1826, and 1853 had thus provided; but the convention of 1860 modified Article III of the existing constitution by providing that the capital of the republic should be located at a place to be determined by congress and by the concession on the part of the respective provincial legislature of the place which was to be federalized. Congress took a definitive step in this matter by passing a law on September 20, 1880, which, counting upon the consent of the legislature of the province of Buenos Aires, federalized the territory of the municipality of Buenos Aires.[6] "In this turn of events, which is styled that of the year eighty, the providential man was not Avellaneda but Tejedor, the insurgent governor of the province of Buenos Aires. He was designated as such by a paramount logic in order to hasten definitively the unity of Argentina."

The federalization of the city of Buenos Aires was the *point d'appui* necessary to secure political equilibrium and the consolidation of the national organization. Historic experience had demonstrated that it was only possible to govern the republic from the city of Buenos Aires, which had the prestige of its secular tradition and the extraordinary economic importance due to its port. Beyond doubt the law fixing the site of the national capital has been the most important event in the last fifty years of Argentine history, as it assured the preëminence of the president of the republic in the face of the political power which up to that time had been exercised by the governors of the province of Buenos Aires. The revolutions occurring after 1880 did not constitute a peril to national unity. New facts and new factors—the diffusion of culture, the development of primary, secondary, and university education, immigration, railroads, the influx of foreign capital—caused a fun-

---

[6] See further, D. Peña, "Apuntes para el estudio de la cuestión capital de la nación," *Atlántida* (Buenos Aires, 1912), V, 382.

damental transformation in the character of Argentine society.

I have said that the federalization of Buenos Aires in 1880 terminates a period of our history; for institutional equilibrium was attained by the lever of the capital of the republic. Besides, this date 1880 has an economic significance. Up to that time cattle-raising was the chief source of wealth and the exports were composed simply of wool and hides. Agriculture now began to develop in notable fashion and with this new factor manifest change in the mode of rural life took place. That inhabitant of the country known as the gaucho receded and vanished from the scene. In order to explain this event one should keep in mind the enormous increase in population caused by Spanish and Italian immigration and the extension of the railroad system which linked the provinces to each other and to the capital of the republic. Thus after 1880 both political and economic conditions helped to initiate a new period in Argentine history.

CHAPTER LIX

SOME LATER PRESIDENTS

On October 12, 1880, General Julio A. Roca assumed the duties of president and Francisco B. Madero became vice president. The new president appointed Dr. Antonio del Viso as minister of the interior; Dr. Bernardo de Irigoyen as minister of foreign relations; General Benjamín Victorica as minister of war and the navy; Dr. Juan José Romero as minister of the treasury; and Dr. Manuel Pizarro as minister of justice, religion, and public instruction.

During the term of General Roca there were no revolutionary uprisings, a circumstance that explains the development of various new enterprises. Among those that should be mentioned are the new military expeditions which were dispatched against the Indians, thus removing that peril and extending the area of land opened to cultivation and settlement. In the domain of public instruction, the law concerning teaching by laymen was sanctioned during this period. Bucich Escobar gives the following summary of social and economic developments:

"In the matter of foreign commerce dimensions were attained which had been previously unknown. Imports, which in 1880 aggregated 45,535,880 gold pesos, in 1886, reached 95,408,745 pesos. In 1880 exports reached 58,380,787 gold pesos and in 1886, 69,843,841 pesos. During the last year of General Roca's term, the total of foreign commerce amounted to 165,243,586 pesos gold; and if, indeed, the balance of trade did not favor the country in 1882, 1883, 1884, 1885, and 1886, this did not in any way affect the progress of industry. The unfavorable balance was simply due to an unusual and extraordinary increase in the imports which could not be counterbalanced by the exports, although these surpassed the totals that had hitherto been recorded. The revenues of the nation, which in 1880 amounted to 19,594,306 gold pesos, in 1886 reached 42,250,152 pesos. The expenses of public administration for those years aggregated respectively, 26,919,295 pesos and 54,458,335 pesos. The increasing deficit, which becomes apparent on comparing income and expenditure, is explained by the numerous public works that were undertaken during those years and by the loans that they required. When Roca came into office in 1880 the railroads had a total length of 2,313 kilometers. In 1886, when he left office, the Argentine railway lines had increased to 5,964 kilometers, that is, they had more than doubled. With respect to immigration, during the six years of President Roca's term there had been an extraordinary influx. In 1880, 41,561 immigrants entered the country; in 1886, this figure had increased to 93,116, having been 108,000 in 1885. During Roca's first administration 483,000 immigrants entered the country." [1]

Two years before the end of General Roca's term, an agitation began concerning the succession to the presidency. Various candidates aspired to succeed him. This political era had a special trait: the presidency absorbed and centralized all the power of the democracy, in such a manner that the fortunes of the candidates did not depend upon the electoral struggle of political parties but upon the wish of the president.

There were the following candidates: Dr. Bernardo de Irigoyen, who had served for four years as a minister of General Roca; General Victorica, who held the portfolio of war and the navy; Dr. Dardo Rocha, governor of the province of Buenos Aires and founder of the city of La Plata; Manuel Ocampo, ex-governor of Buenos Aires, who was supported by a coalition of parties; and, lastly, Dr. Miguel Juárez Celman, ex-governor of Córdoba, who was a relative of General Roca.

Despite the electoral activity of the party of opposition to the administration, the candidate who was supported by it won the election. Dr. Juárez Celman took office on October 12, 1886; Dr. Carlos Pellegrini became vice president. Dr. Celman appointed the following ministers: Dr. Eduardo Wilde, minister of the interior; Dr. Norberto Quirno Costa, minister of foreign relations; General Eduardo Racedo, minister of war and the navy; Dr. Wenceslao Pacheco, minister of the treasury; and Dr. Filemón Posse, minister of justice, religion, and public instruction.

This stage of our history can be described from both the political and the moral points of view. Politically the power of the president of the republic increased after the federalization

[1] J. Bucich Escobar, *Los presidentes argentinos* (Buenos Aires, 1918), pp. 111-12. [A kilometer is nearly five-eights of a mile.—W. S. R.]

of Buenos Aires to such an extent that the provincial governors, who up to this time had possessed great influence, needed the support of the president to prevent federal intervention in their respective provinces. From the moral standpoint great corruption had become general in the public administration. In the words of José N. Matienzo: "It is peculiar that, at the very time when political morality was declining, the government was promoting the juridical progress of the nation by promulgating the law of matrimony, the penal code, the commercial code, the mining code, and the code of procedure in criminal cases—laws which in large part are still in force and to which no one imputes intentions contrary to the public welfare. Private law and even penal law are compatible with despotism and with personal rule as both Roman law and Napoleonic law demonstrate. Laws were accordingly not lacking for the ordinary cases of social life. What was lacking was political liberty and civic dignity." [2] In this condition a great political and economic crisis took place.

The financial and political horizon of the country furnished a prospect that was not flattering. In financial affairs, various facts indicated the approach of a crisis. An excessive and false fever for riches stimulated speculation; the government suffered from the effects of an abuse of credit, and was compelled to make new issues of paper money. Dr. Aristóbulo del Valle remarked at that time, making an estimate of the rule of Dr. Juárez Celman, "that it was a politico-financial administration which was truly disastrous." In affairs of politics President Juárez Celman separated from the political chieftains of the party which had brought him to power. The opposition became more and more powerful, and had as its slogan not only antagonism to the president's rôle in politics but also to his economic and financial conduct.

Aristóbulo del Valle was the tribune of the revolution and Alem its civil leader. From the year following that in which Dr. Juárez Celman assumed the presidency, the opposition to the administration was built up. In the senate of the nation Aristóbulo del Valle made a clear and just criticism of the acts of the government. In 1887 he protested against the scheme of the executive with respect

---

[2] José N. Matienzo, *La revolución de 1890 en la historia constitucional argentina* (Buenos Aires, 1926).

to the leasing of sanitary establishments. In a certain passage he said: "Is it possible that the chief executive himself is inclined to say to the chamber: I have not the means and the necessary administrative authority or I lack both the means and the men needed to bring them to the proper condition unless they go out of the public dominion? I do not believe that there is a government or a ministry on the face of the globe capable of making such a declaration."

Del Valle repeated his criticisms with respect to the plans of the executive concerning free banks, and with regard to railroad companies which were guaranteed by the Argentine government a certain rate of interest on their invested capital, and lastly when he accused the government of making clandestine issues of paper money. "I do not justify any of the clandestine emissions bearing the seal of the nation which have been made by the national government. Neither do I justify the emissions put into circulation by the public treasury nor those which have been made in order to save the national bank or the bank of the province which are in danger of closing their doors. For rather than see the government of my country falsify the seal of the nation, I would prefer that both the bank of the province and the bank of the nation should fail. We are honeycombed by a moral disease—a great moral corruption that clings to our body like leprosy, that cannot be cured by any other means than by cauterization, that is, by rendering even-handed justice as is proper to do in the present case."

It was now the eve of a revolt and in conjunction with members of the civic union Aristóbulo del Valle was preparing the pronunciamiento. Leandro N. Alem was a politician of great austerity, a popular caudillo in the finest sense of that term, who has been consecrated by the masses inasmuch as he was the president of the civic union and the leader of the revolt. In a meeting organized by young men in the Jardín Florida a program of action was sanctioned for the new party, the young men's civic union. Condemning all official intervention in electoral proceedings, and demanding the purity of administrative morality throughout elections, the civic union made its slogan the freedom of suffrage. The new faction also aspired to guarantee to the provinces the full enjoyment of their autonomy and to assure to all the inhabitants of the republic the benefits of the municipal régime. Noteworthy were the speeches delivered in that meeting by del Valle and Alem.[3]

A new popular meeting on April 13, 1890, gave form and organization to the "civic union" party which symbolized the opposition to the president. The first person to speak at that meeting was General Mitre who described the significance of this step by saying: "This is neither a party assembly nor a coalition of parties. It is an association of sane wills in a group of living forces. . . . Divorced from the government, the people are expelled from public life— excluded from the sphere of action of the constitution." [4]

The ministry resigned en masse, and this crisis seemed to be met by the organization of a new cabinet. But it lasted only a month and a half, for the revolt of July, 1890, broke out. This uprising had as its military leader General Manuel J. Campos; the revolutionary junta was composed of Leandro N. Alem, Aristóbulo del Valle, Lucio V. López, Juan José Romero, Mariano Demaría, and Miguel Goyena.

Realizing the imminence of the movement, the government ordered the arrest of General Campos, but he won over to the revolutionary cause the officers who guarded him, and on July 26 various regiments rose in rebellion and succeeded in getting possession of the park of artillery. A furious battle took place between revolutionary and government forces that lasted two days. An armistice was soon signed, and the revolutionists were compelled to accept peace; for they had suffered losses, and were without munitions. From his seat in the senate Dr. Pizarro affirmed "that even though the revolt had been suppressed, the government was dead. At this juncture the resignation of the president and the vice president of the republic is necessary." On August 6, more than sixty deputies and senators sent a note to Dr. Juárez Celman asking him to resign.[5] The president at once sent his resignation to congress; and when it was accepted, Dr. Carlos Pellegrini became president.

Dr. Pellegrini selected the following ministers: interior, General Julio A. Roca; foreign affairs, Dr. Eduardo Costa; treasury, Dr.

[3] Mariano de Vedia y Mitre, *La revolución del 90* (Buenos Aires, 1929), chaps. iii-v.

[4] *Unión civica, su origen, organización y tendencias* (Buenos Aires, 1890), p. 81. —W. S. R.

[5] *Ibid.*, chap. xvi.

Vicente Fidel López; war and the navy, General Nicolás Levalle; justice and public instruction, José María Gutiérrez. The financial condition of the nation could scarcely have been worse. The national treasury had no resources. The national bank had no appreciable deposits. First, the government printed an issue of paper money, but the amount was inadequate to meet the needs, so that before a month had elapsed (September 5) a law was passed which authorized a fresh issue amounting to 60,000,000 pesos. The public had, however, lost all confidence in the national bank and the bank of the province of Buenos Aires. In March, 1891, these two banking institutions closed their doors.

On December 1, 1891, a new and important banking institution opened for business—the bank of the Argentine Nation. Said a writer: "The position of the new bank was so correct and fruitful that it brought the current of public opinion to the conclusion that the national bank belonged to the domain of an obscure and melancholy past—the contaminations of which it would be convenient to avoid—and that the bank of the Argentine Nation would guarantee to the future the restoration of the sane and vigorous credit of the country." [6]

Near the end of this presidential term, the civic union convoked a nominating convention which met in Rosario, in January, 1891, in order to select candidates for president and vice president of the republic. It chose Bartolomé Mitre and Bernardo de Irigoyen. The national party, which counted upon the support of the government and also upon the conditions existing in the fourteen provinces, presented as its candidate, General Roca. The civic union divided into two factions: one, which made an agreement with the national party providing for the elimination of Irigoyen's candidacy for the vice presidency; and the other, which was styled the radical or the anti-agreement faction, which eliminated the candidacy of Mitre and proclaimed the candidacy of Bernardo de Irigoyen and Juan M. Garro.

The policy of an agreement produced divisions within the parties, and General Mitre then withdrew his candidacy. Conventions of the national civic union and the national party met again, accepted the resignation of General Mitre, and nominated as candidates Luis

---

[6] *Investigaciones del seminario* (Buenos Aires, 1917), vol. I, chap. iv. See further, Hansen, *op. cit.*, pp. 443-44.

Sáenz Peña and José E. Uriburu, who were successful in the elections of April, 1892. A large group of young men, belonging to a faction that was styled modernist, had announced the candidacy of Dr. Roque Sáenz Peña; but he withdrew his name when the conventions of the national party and the civic union selected his father, Dr. Luis Sáenz Peña, as a candidate for the presidency.

The important work of President Pellegrini was financial. In this matter it is sufficient to recall the firm establishment of the bank of the Argentine Nation. From the political viewpoint, Pellegrini's action consisted in maintaining public order which was constantly threatened by the partisans of the civic union. To quote Groussac again: "Pellegrini efficaciously coöperated in the redeeming evolution which we behold fulfiled today. Ceaselessly did he condemn both by word and deed the monstrous doctrine that assimilates a military uprising with a civilian protest—a doctrine that has been the cause of secular misgovernment in Latin America. For more than twenty years he constantly scattered over the country the good seed of reason and patriotism, denouncing revolutionary propaganda—the negation of all progress—and pursuing as a crime of *lesa patria* the corruption which had been spread in the army in order to make it an abettor of civil discord." [7]

Having recognized this merit, it should be noticed that the error of Pellegrini was that he combatted the effects without removing the cause; for the determining factor of political convulsions was official pressure in the selection of the president and the corresponding lack of guarantee of freedom of suffrage. Indeed the very designation of his own successor was an equivocation, because Pellegrini had displayed that official influence in order to ensure the triumph of a distinguished citizen like Luis Sáenz Peña, although he was a septuagenarian.

The new government began its labors on October 12, 1892, with the following cabinet: interior, Dr. Manuel Quintana; treasury, Dr. Juan Romero; war and the navy, General Benjamin Victorica; foreign affairs, Dr. Tomás M. de Anchorena; justice and public instruction, Dr. Calixto de la Torre. During this administration, various commotions took place in the provinces that caused crises in the cabinet. Twenty-three ministerial crises occurred in nine months.

[7] Groussac, *Los que pasaban* (Buenos Aires, 1919), p. 253.

In a trying moment, Dr. Sáenz Peña sought the aid of Dr. Manuel Quintana, who accepted the portfolio of the interior and organized a new cabinet. A general convulsion had actually taken place throughout the republic incited by the radical or anti-agreement party which triumphed in Santa Fe, Buenos Aires, San Luis, and Tucumán, and which proclaimed Dr. Leandro N. Alem as provisional president of the republic. The president proclaimed a state of siege, which suspended constitutional guarantees, and the army of the nation, under the command of General Roca, succeeded in pacifying the country. Dr. Manuel Quintana then resigned; President Sáenz Peña tried to reorganize the cabinet but, realizing that his situation was untenable, he presented his resignation.

On January 23, 1895, the vice president, Dr. José Evaristo Uriburu, assumed the presidency of the republic. Upon him there devolved the task of dealing with the old and thorny question of the boundaries with Chile. Minister Dr. Amancio Alcorta handled the diplomatic negotiations skilfully, and a happy solution was reached during the second administration of General Roca.

In 1898, a national convention assembled for the purpose of making amendments to the constitution. With respect to representation in the house of deputies, which was set by the constitution in the ratio of one deputy for every 20,000 inhabitants, an amendment was adopted that fixed the ratio as one deputy for every 33,000 inhabitants. A change was also made in the number and organization of the ministry, for a law was passed that increased the number of the cabinet to eight.

The presidential candidate of the administration in the next campaign was General Roca, who was brought forth by the national autonomist party and supported by eminent public men like Dr. Carlos Pellegrini in order that the boundary controversy with Chile might be faced. Members of all parties united to oppose the administration candidate.

By the tragic end of Dr. Leandro N. Alem on July 1, 1896, the radical party had lost its leader. When reorganized under the leadership of Bernardo de Irigoyen, its national committee decided to coöperate with other parties in order to select candidates in opposition to General Roca. On this occasion the committee of the radical party of the province of Buenos Aires directed by

Hipólito Irigoyen, who was the successor of Alem in the direction of that party, protested against this decision. Faced by the possible decline of public sentiment, which he had a right to keep alive in the hope of better days, in his mind the ideal of an election that should be realized was one that would recognize the legality of the future triumph of his party. The manifesto of Hipólito Irigoyen further declared that the organic charter of the radical party precluded any understanding or transaction which might at that time or in the future preclude the full application of the principles which formed the program of the party.[8]

Despite the strong opposition made by all parties to his candidacy, General Julio A. Roca, on October 12, 1898, assumed the duties of president for the second time. Among his ministers who played important rôles were Dr. Joaquín V. González, who brought to the attention of congress a well considered code concerning labor and framed the 1902 unipersonal ballot law. General Pablo Riccheri, minister of war as well as the author of a project concerning compulsory military service which became law and has produced many improvements in our military institutions and in the education of the people; and Dr. Luis M. Drago, minister of foreign relations, who formulated the international doctrine that bears his name by announcing the principle that, since imprisonment for debt in private relations has been abolished by law, so also in recognition of the sovereignty of states, whether weak or strong, force should not be employed in the collection of public debts among nations. The establishment of the new ministries of agriculture and of public works instituted by the constitutional convention of 1898 promoted the development of agriculture and cattle-raising by the use of methods of rational exploitation, by the progress in means of transportation, and by the execution of great works of public utility.

The law concerning redemption that regulates our paper money was enacted November 3, 1899. It provided that the paper peso should be worth forty-four centavos in gold. This law aimed to regulate the value of paper currency by assuring its stability and its ratio to the gold peso.[9]

We have already explained the antecedents of the dispute over boundaries with Chile during the rule of Rosas. Chile claimed to

---

[8] José Bianco, *La doctrina radical*, pp. 68 ff.

[9] Hansen, *op cit.*, pp. 448-49.

Upper left, General Roca; from Chueco, *La República Argentina en su primer centenario*. Upper right, Hipólito Irigoyen; from Acosta, *El Dr. Hipólito Irigoyen, intimidades políticas*. Lower left, General Urquiza; from Du Graty, *La Confédération Argentine*. Lower right, Luis M. Drago; from Chueco, *La República Argentina en su primer centenario*.

have the sole right, not only to the possession of the Strait of Magellan, but also to the adjacent territory, a doctrine that would have enabled it to assert that it owned all of Patagonia. The dispute having been left unsettled, years later the relations between the two states were on the verge of a rupture. By the mediation of the United States a treaty was negotiated in 1881 by which both parties promised "to settle the controversy in a friendly and dignified" manner by agreeing that the cordillera of the Andes was the boundary from north to south as far as 52°, south latitude. In this manner the discussion regarding the indisputable Argentine title to Patagonia was terminated. As a compensation, on its part, Argentina recognized as the property of Chile one half of Tierra del Fuego, the adjacent islands, and the shores of the Strait of Magellan. In 1888, a supplementary convention was signed in order that the demarcation line might be surveyed. When the experts began their survey, new and serious difficulties arose which for the second time threatened an armed conflict. But, in 1893, a protocol was signed which settled questions concerning the demarcation line in Tierra del Fuego, the powers of the commissions, the problem concerning the point of departure of the demarcation line in the cordillera of the Andes, and the possibility that there should be Argentine territories on the shores of the Pacific. Above all, there had developed a divergence of opinion between the theory of the Chilean expert of *Divortium aquarum*, that is, of "investigating on the ground the line that divided the hydrographic frontiers which were tributary to the Atlantic and those which were tributary to the Pacific in order to fix the boundary marks therein;" and the theory of the Argentine expert who maintained that this was not the correct interpretation of the treaty of 1881 and argued that the frontier of the demarcation was the crest of the Andes from which the boundary line should not deviate. In fact, the protocol of 1893 determined that the rivers shall be crossed by the boundary line which connects the highest peaks of the Andes, and hence discarded the theory of a continental watershed.

In 1898, new conventions were signed, and, instead of being settled the dispute with Chile became more complicated, for Argentine public opinion associated it with the controversy of Peru—a nation that had pending the serious question of the fate of the provinces of Tacna and Arica, which it had lost as a result of the War of the Pacific. Norberto Piñero thus described how these differences were adjusted:

"By the negotiation and the pacts of May, 1902, by which we agreed with Chile upon the limitation of naval armaments, the equivalence of naval squadrons, and a treaty of general arbitration, we withdrew from the question of the Pacific which that country was discussing with Peru—an issue to which we were not a party. A few months after calm was restored, in November 1902, King Edward VII acted as arbiter in the Argentine-Chilean boundary dispute. Thus the traditional friendship of Argentina with Chile was renewed. Never since has it been affected in essence." [10]

The pacts of May, 1902, formed a landmark in Argentine history; for they eliminated the possibility of war with Chile, and made clear the neutral attitude of Argentina in the War of the Pacific. In the enjoyment of this peace Argentina was able in time to increase its riches, to improve its political institutions, and to labor for the advancement of its culture. From the economic and material standpoint the labor performed had an appreciable effect during the second administration of General Roca with regard to the construction of railroads, highways, harbors, bridges, and telegraphic lines, the amortization of both the domestic and the foreign debt, and the improvement of the credit of the country.[11]

When the second term of General Roca ended, various candidates for the presidency appeared. These were Dr. Carlos Pellegrini, whose candidacy was supported by the autonomist party; Dr. Marco Avellaneda, who was brought forth by a representative nucleus of citizens of the metropolis; Dr. Manuel Quintana, who counted upon the support of the government; and lastly, Dr. José E. Uriburu who was presented as its candidate by the republican party. The election returns gave the victory to Dr. Manuel Quintana for president of the republic, and to Dr. José Figueroa Alcorta for vice president.

Four months after the installation of the government of Dr. Quintana, on February 4, 1905, a revolt broke out. This uprising was caused by members of the radical party who since the presidency of Luis Sáenz Peña had remained away from the polls

---

[10] Piñero, "La política internacional," *La Nación, 1810—25 de mayo—1910*, p. 85.

[11] M. de Vedia y Mitre, *Roca* (Buenos Aires, 1928), chap. xviii.

and demanded as the condition of their participation the freedom
of suffrage.   In a manifesto addressed to the people of the republic
to explain the revolt, the consequences of the policy of "regimen"
and of "agreement" which had provoked the revolt of 1890 were
examined. This manifesto declared that in hours of uncertainty,
confronted by the peril of international complications, the republic
had tolerated these excesses in silence, in the hope of seeing fulfiled the promise which had been so often repeated of a spontaneous
reaction that would obviate the need of a fresh revolutionary commotion. "In the existing situation it is not possible to cherish this
hope without falling into an indiscreet error. Conditions in congress and in the provinces are the same. The republic cannot forget," it adds, "that the citizens who today direct its destinies are
the same who in 1893 enslaved the four provinces that have reassumed their autonomy, smothered their liberties—now about to
regain their sway—and imprisoned and exiled the most distinguished citizens of the country with a hateful extravagance of
arbitrariness and vexatiousness. The principles and the slogan of
the moment"—so ends the document—"are those of the park of
artillery preserved immaculate by the radical civic union, which
under the auspices of that slogan promises to the republic its
speedy reorganization with the free struggle of opinion fully guaranteed in order that those citizens whom national sovereignty desig-
nates may be invested with public office, whoever they may be.
The only persons who cannot hold public office under any circumstances are the directors of the movement; this is demanded by the
rectitude of their proposals and by the austerity of their doctrines."
The leader of the revolution was Hipólito Irigoyen. Although
the insurrection of 1905 gained successes in certain parts of the
republic, yet Dr. Quintana was able promptly to repress it.

During this presidency the University of La Plata was created
with a national character.   Its founder was Joaquín V. González,
the minister of public instruction. While the University of Córdoba carried out its mission after a classic model and the University of Buenos Aires in Napoleonic fashion filled a need by
giving to the country what it demanded in men expert in the
exercise of the liberal professions and publicists with political
capacity, the University of La Plata was born with a new spirit:
the ideal of higher culture for its own sake, which is to say, that

besides preparing men for professional careers, this university stimulates scientific investigation and diffuses general culture. There was initiated by this institution, said Dr. González, in his report to congress in 1905, "a new university current which, without affecting the course of the old currents, would in view of the future of the country consider the new tendencies in higher education, the new needs of Argentine culture, and the example of the best institutions of a similar type in Europe and America."

The opposition to President Quintana, which was organized by other parties than the radical group became stronger and stronger. In the election of deputies in 1906 it won a victory on the very day as that on which that magistrate died. During the same year the great statesman Carlos Pellegrini died, and also Bartolomé Mitre at the age of eighty-five years, who had lived to a glorious old age enjoying the respect and affection of his fellow citizens.

In 1904, the president had sent to congress the project of a national labor law of which Dr. Joaquín V. González was the author. Dr. Alfredo L. Palacios, the leading deputy of the socialist party, proposed that the section of the bill concerning rest on Sundays should be discussed and presented a project dealing with that matter. The proposal of Palacios was approved and the first workingman's law was enacted in 1905; this law prohibited labor on Sundays in such establishments as factories, mills, and commercial houses.

In 1907, also at the instance of Alfredo L. Palacios, a law regulating the labor of women and minors was enacted. This law fixed the minimum age at which laborers might be employed (minors at ten years), prohibited night labor by minors and women, and undertook to safeguard their health, education, and morality. During the subsequent years this social legislation, which was founded upon justice, was extended.

On March 12, 1906, Vice President Dr. José Figueroa Alcorta assumed the office of chief magistrate. He filled out Quintana's term. The new president had to overcome serious difficulties in order to secure peace. Among the ministers who were associated with Dr. Figueroa Alcorta were Dr. Rómulo S. Naón, minister of justice and public instruction, who founded the first rural normal schools for the purpose of decreasing illiteracy in the country;

and Dr. Ezequiel Ramos Mexía, minister of public works, who sketched a plan for railroads in Patagonia. The political episode which was most noised abroad was the prorogation of congress decreed by Figueroa Alcorta because it had refused to approve the budget for the nation.

To this administration fell the honor of directing the celebration of the first centenary of the May Revolution, an occasion when all the civilized nations sent distinguished delegations to celebrate the growth and increasing prosperity of the Argentine people. Because of this celebration, various international congresses of a scientific or political character were held in Buenos Aires. On account of the importance of the decisions reached, mention should be made among others, of the conference on railroads, the conference on jurisprudence and social sciences, and the Fourth International American Conference.

Two international questions came up for settlement during this administration. Acting as arbiter, and assisted by able jurisconsults, the Argentine president had pronounced an award which pointed to a solution of the boundary dispute between Peru and Bolivia. But the latter state rejected the award; and the citizens of La Paz engaged in manifestations that were hostile to the Argentine Republic. Hence, in July, 1909, Argentina severed diplomatic relations with Bolivia. A diplomatic negotiation also took place with the government of the republic of Uruguay. This was concerned with the jurisdiction over the waters of the Río de la Plata. This controversy was adjusted—although not definitively—in a friendly manner with the sister nation.

CHAPTER LX

RECENT PROGRESS

THE EXERCISE of the electoral franchise had been corrupted in
Argentina. It can be said that in general, after the anarchy of
1820, the electoral processes were those of violence or of imposition by fraud and force. Every election resolved itself into an
armed contest in order to gain possession of the polling place or
to sequestrate the ballot box and in another contest to undo the
victory of the adversary, now by wresting from him the legal
instruments of the electoral act, again by recourse to more violent
measures against the persons of the candidates themselves, by
thrusting them into prison or by kidnapping them. To be a great
citizen, a great patriot, a great tribune, signified in the language
of that period to be a bully and a hero capable of marching "with
fixed bayonets to the polls, of beginning with a secret volley upon
the group of inspectors, and of ending by the elimination of all
obstacles and the complete possession of polls, ballot boxes, and
registers." [1]

To this domineering caudillo there succeeded the henchman who
negotiated by purchase or by intimidation for the votes of the
lower classes to whose amorphous mass was added that of those
foreigners to whom certificates of citizenship had been given solely
for election purposes. Official pressure upon the host of office-
holders was the means by which the government assured its continuance. Bear in mind that this system favored the concentration
of personal influence or the domination of the chieftain of a party
or of a government, and though this should be considered a detestable system in politics, yet in the political history of Argentina
after the battle of Caseros great figures of patriots and statesmen occupied the presidency of the nation. But this election method
was denationalized and the mockery of the popular will was
offensive.

Men in public life and political parties, chiefly the civic union
and the radical party, demanded that the electoral system of the
state should be reformed, that freedom of suffrage should be

---

[1] J. V. González, *El juicio del siglo ó cien años de historia argentina*, p. 193.

guaranteed, and that administrations for themselves and for the judges and managers of electoral campaigns should not use force at the elections and should not favor the success of slates. The radical party refrained from voting at elections and more than once had recourse to revolt. In 1904 a new law was enacted for the districts of the capital city which assured the triumph of popular candidates, but it caused a conservative reaction and was abrogated. Such was the electoral situation of the country and such was political mendacity as a dominant instrument in the year when we had completed the centenary of the May Revolution. Argentine society had been democratic since its beginnings, still it had not yet found the system which would make the public will respected.

Just before the term of Figueroa Alcorta expired, two candidates for the presidency came forward: Dr. Guillermo Udaondo and Dr. Roque Sáenz Peña. The latter triumphed in the election. Roque Sáenz Peña was a romantic and idealistic figure, with a brilliant record in political life as a legislator and as a representative of Argentina in international congresses. He had enlisted as a volunteer on the side of Peru in the War of the Pacific. While leading a small band of soldiers at the Morro of Arica, Roque Sáenz Peña was wounded and made a prisoner by the Chileans. Well versed in his country's history, and having taken part in its political struggles, with personal experience and a direct knowledge of the operation of representative institutions in Europe, Roque Sáenz Peña was the statesman who added to these qualities that of his undefiled idealism. He was called to inspire the election law of 1912 which fundamentally changed the political physiognomy of the country.

The problem which President Roque Sáenz Peña studied and solved was that of electoral reform. The radical party had been struggling in favor of that reform, and presidents like Figueroa Alcorta had initiated it. But Roque Sáenz Peña had a comprehensive vision of this great reform which involved the definitive consolidation of Argentine democracy. It can be affirmed that the electoral law of 1912, which was proposed by Roque Sáenz Peña while the publicist Dr. Indalecio Gómez was secretary of the interior, signifies in the first place the elimination of the political oligarchy which had been influencing and determining the succession to the presidency and to the governments of the provinces. Further, the law of 1912 made such occurrences impossible by the system of secret voting which was introduced. In the second place this law signifies the entry of the people into politics as an integral entity in order to determine by free suffrage the destiny of the nation by the use of the incomplete ballot which accorded representation to the majority and to the most important minority.

Opponents of this reform represented to President Roque Sáenz Peña that the people were not competent to exercise by themselves this sovereignty and that it would easily degenerate into demagogic convulsions. Sáenz Peña responded in this fashion: "to fear the legality of secret voting is to show oneself intimidated by democracy, thus ascribing to the present generation a civic cowardice which is not present in the souls of the constituents or in the creative concept of a nationality, the fruit of courage and wisdom."

To quote Groussac once more:

"Those who believed that they saw in this initiative of the president, which he carried on with faith and tenacity until it was consummated, simply a political maneuver to prevent agitation, thus disarming a party inclined to violence, calumniate Sáenz Peña. Always well-tempered, even when his health was declining, his spirit was incapable of ensuring his personal tranquillity by deflecting the country from its straight and charted course. The design which he cherished and prosecuted with unaccustomed eagerness until it was realized, was aimed to promote not his own welfare but that of the public. Considering universal suffrage as the basis of representative government carried on by a party system, it was elementary logic to draw the intransigent radicalism from its unhealthy self-denial, opening to it with all loyalty the arena of legal contention in honorable and open polls." [2] As Amadeo appropriately declared, Roque Sáenz Peña was "the person who revived Argentine democracy." [3]

The new electoral law established secret and compulsory voting and the system of the incomplete ballot, that is to say, the triumph

---

[2] Groussac, *Los que pasaban* (Buenos Aires, 1919), p. 344. The discourse of Dr. Ramón J. Cárcano in favor of this reform is found in his *Otras cuestiones y juicios* (Buenos Aires, 1914), pp. 4 ff.

[3] O. R. Amadeo, "Roque Sáenz Peña," in *La Nación,* February 11, 1832.

of the candidates of the majority and of the most important minority. In the election of April, 1912, more than 100,000 citizens voted in the city of Buenos Aires; the radicals triumphed, while the socialists won the minority representation. The political situation and the earnest desires of the reformer are reflected in the notable document by which Roque Sáenz Peña explained to the people the new electoral law.

After sketching the domestic and foreign policy of Argentina, he reaffirms his faith in education, in order to base upon its progress the refutation of a specious argument—the lack of preparation by the people. According to Sáenz Peña, that argument ignored the great improvement that was going on by means of conscription and the schools. He has plenty of arguments in favor of the incomplete ballot, of secret voting which would put an end to venality, and of compulsory suffrage which would counteract the neglect to vote, but he avows that the law is scarcely a means of performing a task which only becomes a reality by the electoral conduct of the citizens themselves. Animated by his passion for the public welfare, he declares that he is in debt to his country and must use his "utmost efforts in order to bring its political probity to a level with its material greatness." The document ends thus: "I have made known to my country all my thoughts, my convictions, and my hopes. I wish that my countrymen would hearken to the words and to the counsel of its first magistrate. Let them vote!" [4]

After October, 1913, Dr. Sáenz Peña was on leave of absence because of his health. Vice President Dr. Victorino de la Plaza was president ad interim; and also definitely, for Sáenz Peña died in August, 1914. During the government of Dr. de la Plaza the general European conflagration took place, which later spread to America—an event of univeral economic and moral significance. Our country immediately suffered the economic consequences of this event. In the first place, there occurred a rapid decrease in the customs revenue which deprived the treasury of one of its chief sources of revenue, and compelled it to resort to the floating of short-term loans. The foreign debt of Argentina increased some 600,000,000 pesos. Two years later the World War was responsible for a change favorable to the public wealth.

---

[4] Roque Sáenz Peña, *Escritos y discursos* (2 vols. Buenos Aires, 1914), II, 109-19.

When the new election law was put into force, the radical party, whose members, as we have already said, had remained away from the polls, now took part in the elections and gained partial victories in the city of Buenos Aires and in some provinces. At the end of President de la Plaza's term the radical party announced as its candidates for president and vice president respectively, Hipólito Irigoyen and Pelagio B. Luna, who triumphed in the elections of April, 1916, supported by some 400,000 electors of the republic. When Irigoyen became president the country was enjoying great economic prosperity; for the World War had perceptibly stimulated Argentine production, increasing the exports and the general prosperity.

It became the duty of this administration to define the attitude of Argentina toward the World War. Following the policy inspired by President Irigoyen, the neutrality of Argentina was announced, thus inhibiting the country from all participation in the war—a policy in contrast with the attitude adopted by such American countries as Brazil and Uruguay which adhered to the cause of France.[5] A corollary to this policy was the later declaration presented to the League of Nations by the Argentine delegation to the effect that all sovereign nations were, by virtue of that fact, equal, and should therefore be invited to join the League.[6]

---

[5] In August, 1914, the Argentine government announced that it would pursue a policy of strict neutrality in the war which had broken out in Europe. After two Argentine merchant vessels had been torpedoed by German submarines, Germany yielded to Argentina's demand for an indemnity and guaranteed that no more Argentine vessels would be thus destroyed. After the United States published correspondence which showed that the German minister at Buenos Aires had secretly advised his government either to spare two Argentine vessels that were about to enter the submarine zone or else to sink them without leaving any trace, by large majorities both houses of the Argentine congress adopted resolutions to the effect that diplomatic relations with Germany should be severed. Nevertheless, although President Irigoyen gave the German minister his passport, he did not break off relations with Germany.—W. S. R.

[6] On July 12, 1919, Argentina's secretary of foreign affairs instructed the Argentine minister at Paris that President Irigoyen had decided to join the League of Nations. Subsequently the Argentine delegation to the First Assembly of the League proposed that the covenant of the league should be changed so that any sovereign state might be admitted to the Society of Nations and that all members of its Council should be elected by a majority vote of its Assembly instead of allowing the Great Powers the permanent tenure of five places. After the Assembly had decided against the consideration of any amendments to

Upper, A Glimpse of the Harbor of Buenos Aires. Lower, Members of the
Radical Party parading the Streets of Buenos Aires in 1916.
Both photographs by the Translator.

With respect to domestic politics President Irigoyen devoted special attention to social problems. He favored legislative reforms concerning conciliation and arbitration in conflicts between capital and labor, reforms concerning collective labor contracts to maintain the social entity of the employers and the social entity of the laborers on an equal plane; and, lastly, he planned the adoption of a code of labor laws. President Irigoyen decided to carry on a campaign against gambling; he put an end to horse racing and games of chance on week days. For the conservation of the oil resources he planned a legal reform by declaring that the petroleum deposits were the private property of the nation. By the use of official means, he reserved to the State the right to supervise all exploitation of this source of public riches and placed checks upon the disturbing action of great monopolies and the infiltration of foreign capital.

With respect to public instruction President Irigoyen created new primary schools. During his administration the University of the Littoral was founded and the reform of universities was accomplished. The University of the Littoral was created in 1919: its college of law and of industrial chemistry was established in Santa Fe; its college of medical science and of economic science in Rosario; its college of educational science in Paraná; and its college of agriculture and cattle-raising in Corrientes. The reform of universities signified the appearance of a new element in Argentine cultural life. Having been initiated in the University of Córdoba in 1918, this reform spread to the University of Buenos Aires in the following year and soon to that of La Plata. Among other nations it was later extended to Uruguay and Peru.[7] University reform signifies chiefly the following measures: (1) student cooperation in the administration of the universities; (2) a change in the methods of instruction, the appointment of professors by competitive contests, academic freedom, and liberty of attendance at classes. This reform undertakes to insure the autonomy of the universities.

---

the covenant, acting on insistent instructions from President Irigoyen, on December 4, 1920, the Argentine delegation withdrew from the Assembly. —W. S. R.

[7] The Peruvian author, José Carlos Mariátegui treats of this educational reform in his book entitled *Siete ensayos de interpretación de la realidad peruana* (Lima, 1928), pp. 89 ff.

Upon the termination of the first administration of Hipólito Irigoyen the political map of Argentina was as follows: in the greater part of the country the radical party was dominant and the minorities belonged to local or provincial parties. Besides, in the capital of the republic the socialist party had gained a great ascendancy among the masses, because of the constant activity of its leaders among whom were prominent Dr. Alfredo L. Palacios, author of the first workingman's laws, the publicist Dr. Juan B. Justo, and the parliamentarian Dr. Nicolás Repetto. The socialist party later suffered a division. There seceded from it a faction that organized the independent socialist party led by Dr. Antonio de Tomaso. Notice should be taken that the radical party possessed the fundamental traits of a national party, that it extended throughout the entire country, that it was a popular party which developed with the liberty of suffrage ensured by the Sáenz Peña law, and that it was genuinely Argentine, that is to say, a party which loved both the historic tradition and the men representative of nationality.

Among the figures in the political and social life of contemporary Argentina that of Juan B. Justo should be singled out. He was a man with clear ideas and a fine character. A thinker, his work as a publicist was in his books: *Teoría y práctica de la historia* (*The Theory and the Practice of History*) and *Política argentina y teoría científica de la historia* (*Argentine Politics and the Scientific Theory of History*). With energy he fought against these two evils of Argentine politics, falsehood and fraud. Juan B. Justo was a militant socialist, but by his labor he helped to consolidate the existing Argentine democracy. "He aspired to make of politics an intelligent and virtuous activity within the reach of all men." [8] He died in January, 1928.

In the presidential election of 1922 the political creed of the radical party symbolized by the names of Marcelo T. de Alvear and Elpidio González triumphed. The government of President Alvear was distinguished by a policy of strict construction of our constitution. He directed an administration signalized by a reign of order in the country and by respect for the rights of all men. During this presidency the prince who was the heir to the Italian

[8] Prologue by N. Repetto to *Discursos y escritos políticos* of J. P. Justo ("Grandes escritores argentinos," vol. XLV, Buenos Aires, 1933).

crown and later also the Prince of Wales visited Argentina.

The cabinet of Dr. Alvear favorably impressed the public mind not only because its portfolios were held by worthy personalities, but also because of the acts of its members. The minister of war, Colonel Agustín P. Justo, who had previously been director of the military college, was the author of important measures which promoted the metamorphosis of military institutions, such as the founding of an airplane factory at Córdoba, a new organization of the army, the establishment of military schools, and the acquisition of armaments. Dr. Tomás Le Bretón, the minister of agriculture, undertook to encourage plant breeding and the selection of seeds that would improve the yield of cereals; he increased the area devoted to the cultivation of cotton; he promoted the improvement of the methods used in the making of butter and cheese. One should also record that he organized railway tours for agricultural propaganda. The minister of the interior, Dr. José P. Tamborini, carried out the administration's policy with respect to provincial autonomy, and Dr. Antonio Sagarna, minister of public instruction, devoted special attention to university education and artistic culture.

After this administration began, a division took place in the radical party; for Dr. Alvear took an independent stand; he did not allow himself to be dominated by partisan influences. A group of citizens formed the anti-personalist radical group; but the prevailing sentiment continued to recognize ex-President Hipólito Irigoyen as the leader of the radical party.

In December, 1923, there died in Buenos Aires a very estimable man, Joaquín V. González. He did not attain this distinction simply because of the high public positions which he occupied (he was governor, senator, a member of a national cabinet, and the president of a university), but also because of the constructive work which he accomplished as an educator and publicist. He published fifty volumes concerning politics, law, pedagogy, literature, and history. His principal works were the following: *La tradición Nacional* (*The National Tradition*), *Mis Montañas* (*My Mountains*), *El juicio del siglo ó cien años de historia argentina* (*The Judgment of the Century or One Hundred Years of Argentine History*), *Patria y democracia* (*Fatherland and Democracy*), *Estudios de historia argentina* (*Studies in Argentine History*).

In the forefront of the great institutions which he founded is
the National University of La Plata. Joaquín V. González consecrated his energies to the elevation of the spiritual level of his
native land.

At the end of Alvear's administration the anti-personalist faction put forward Leopoldo Melo as candidate for the presidency
and Vicente Gallo for the vice presidency, while the radical party
proclaimed as its candidates Hipólito Irigoyen and Francisco
Beiró. The candidacy of Hipólito Irigoyen was popular throughout
the country. As Francisco Bieró had died, the convention of the
radical party selected Dr. Enrique Martínez as its vice presidential
candidate.

The first measures of Irigoyen during his second term, among
which are noteworthy the steps taken to conserve the natural resources of the country, were received with favor. He undertook
to remove the fetters which a combination of factors had imposed
upon the sources of production, so that in the year 1928 the stock
of gold in the bank of redemption totalled 500,000,000 pesos in
gold, the savings deposits in banks exceeded 1,600,000,000 pesos,
and the area under cultivation was increased by almost 1,000,000
hectares.

But after a few months passed, it became evident that the functions of the government were paralyzed so that administrative
transactions were interrupted. This lapse was attributed to the
advanced age of President Irigoyen.

The president continued in politics, however, as the chief of
the radical party. The opposition became vigorous in the halls
of congress, in political parties, in journals, and among the people.
Federal intervention in the provinces of San Juan and Mendoza
infringed upon constitutional rights and paved the way for an
election vitiated by fraud. In the elections of March, 1929, the
radical party was defeated in the capital of the republic. In Córdoba and in the province of Buenos Aires it secured a scant
majority. The congress which should have opened its sessions on
May 1 was not convoked; its meeting was postponed until September in which month, according to the constitution, the ordinary
sessions of congress terminate.

Financially, the situation was critical and the prevailing condition was disorder. The budget, which in 1916 amounted to 377,-

000,000 pesos, in 1930 came to 1,043,000,000 pesos, being thus almost tripled. In the year 1930 the deficit in the budget was 300,-000,000 pesos. In the administration of the government organic laws had been violated, as the minister of war himself acknowledged on the eve of the revolution by declaring in his letter of resignation that military institutions were managed on the margin of those laws, and that decrees had been signed which distributed generous gifts.

A revolution was about to break out but the government did nothing to correct its errors. The president trusted to his one-time popular prestige. On September 5, Irigoyen, who was ill, delegated his power to the vice president, Dr. Martínez. When the latter assumed the duties of president, he proclaimed a state of siege; the orders which he gave to prevent or to limit the revolutionary movement were not obeyed. On September 6, shortly before two years of this presidential term had elapsed, the political situation became critical. The president and the vice president resigned from office. Irigoyen was confined on a warship and soon imprisoned on the isle of Martín García where he remained until the *de facto* government came to an end.

I have stated that opposition to President Irigoyen existed in various classes of society. The insurrection of September 6 was eminently popular; it was executed with celerity by a part of the army led by Lieutenant General José F. Uriburu. The military chieftains requested the assistance of the leaders of the political parties and at daybreak of September 6 these leaders went to the barracks where they joined the soldiers in the pronunciamiento. In this participation by civilians, which was made evident before September 6 and ratified on the day of the revolution, there should be noticed in connection with the actions of leaders of both the right and the left parties the coöperation of university students. A French author named Benjamin Crémieux, who was visiting Buenos Aires, observing the progress and result of the revolution, recorded the following episode which enables one to comprehend the real character of the movement. On the balcony of a hotel in the Avenida de Mayo he watched the demonstrations of students and the charge of the *Escuadrón de Seguridad*. A lady who was a partisan of President Irigoyen remarked with disdain: "Look! They are all lads." She did not comprehend, declared

Crémieux, that one of the beauties of the insurrection was that it was to be a movement of youth. "Against the inertia and the governmental debility of irigoyenismo was pitted a desire for action."

A little later on the same day General Uriburu assumed charge of the government. On September 8, he and his ministers took the oath publicly to respect the constitution and the fundamental laws in force. They announced their desire to return as soon as possible to normalcy with absolute guarantees in order that the nation in free elections should choose its new and legitimate representatives.

The government *de facto* was directed by General Uriburu. He prorogued the congress and intervened in the provinces (with the exception of San Luis and Entre Ríos whose governments were not in the hands of the party that had been deposed from power). A prejudice against democracy inspired not a few acts of the new government, which eventually contemplated the possibility of a fundamental reform of the constitution and of the Sáenz Peña law concerning universal suffrage with secret and obligatory voting. The country was declared in a state of siege; the guarantees of political and individual rights were suspended. The censure of the press was established and certain daily newspapers of the capital city and of the interior were suppressed. Besides, numerous citizens were arrested.

The university problem acquired great importance. Acts of intervention took place in the universities of Buenos Aires, La Plata, and the Littoral by reforms in their statutes. These acts concerned with teaching began to be executed while Dr. Ernesto Padilla was minister of public instruction and continued under his successor, Dr. Guillermo Rothe. The fiscal policy of the minister of finance, Dr. Enrique Uriburu, undertook a partial reduction in the budget of the nation which in 1930, as I have stated, was over 1,000,000,-000 pesos, but the fiscal year 1931 came to an end with a deficit of approximately 200,000,000 pesos.

In the elections of April 5 in the province of Buenos Aires the radical party triumphed. The minister of the interior, Dr Matías Sánchez Sorondo resigned his post. Later these elections were annulled. On July 20 an uprising of troops took place in Corrientes but the provisional government suppressed the insurrection. It then issued a decree blaming the radical party for having incited the uprising and arranged that the electoral juntas should not certify lists of candidates for office in which there appeared the names of individuals who had served under the former régime. Ex-President Marcelo T. de Alvear, who was directing the reorganization of the radical party, was deported along with other members of that party.

In its "manifesto to the people" of September 6, the *de facto* government made known that it would not modify the constitution and the fundamental laws. Nevertheless, it intended to alter the electoral law concerning secret and compulsory voting, and, as I have said, it framed a plan for constitutional reforms. This attitude of the *de facto* government is explained by considering the revolutionary process in the course of which the leader of the movement had expressed ideas contrary to the constitutional system in force, but an important group of chiefs and officials of the army reminded him of the pledge that the constitution and the fundamental laws would not be modified which was a condition of their participation in the movement.[9]

When the conventions were convoked for the choice of candidates for the general elections of November 8, including those of the president and the vice president of the nation, the following selections were made: Lisandro de la Torre y Nicolás Repetto by the alliance of the socialists and the progressive democrats; General Agustín P. Justo and Dr. José Nicolás Matienzo by the anti-personalist radicals. To this party there later adhered the partisans who belonged to the national democratic party; but as their vice presidential candidate they substituted Dr. Julio A. Roca for Dr. Matienzo. Marcelo T. Alvear and Adolfo Güemes were nominated by the radical party. The *de facto* government issued a decree by which, invoking a right of the revolution to prevent the return to power of a consolidated group or one that had not repudiated the deposed régime, it declared that the radical candidates were ineligible. In consequence, the radicals made known that they would stay away from the polls.

In his speeches during the electoral campaign General Justo

---

[9] Juan P. Ramos, "La ideología de la revolución de Septiembre," in *Bandera Argentina,* September 6, 1933; Alfredo Colme, *La revolución en la América Latina* (Buenos Aires, 1932), pp. 65 ff.

Agustín P.
Justo
1932

proclaimed both the need of a prompt return to constitutional normalcy and of initiating a policy of peace and union among all Argentine citizens. At the elections of November 8, General Justo was elected president. Dr. Julio A. Roca was chosen vice president. When the government *de facto*, which had lasted a year and a half, came to an end on February 20, 1932, General Justo became president. His first act was to end the state of siege.

This was followed by important political and administrative steps: decisions tending to respect the autonomy of the provinces and to assure the dignity and morality of public functionaries; the execution of a rigid plan of economy which with other arrangements lessened the effects of the grave world economic crisis that also afflicted the country; in university affairs professors who had been ejected were restored to their chairs, and the autonomy of institutions of higher culture was maintained; further, measures of the government in respect to military affairs promoted a spirit of justice and discipline in military institutions; and with respect to foreign relations a pacifist policy was adopted which we shall consider in a subsequent passage. This organic and politic labor, which tends to promote a return to normalcy, has been received by widespread signs of public sympathy.

There participated in these measures with President Justo the following personages: Dr. Leopold Melo, minister of the interior; Dr. Carlos Saavedra Lamas, minister of foreign relations; Dr. Manuel M. de Iriondo, minister of justice and public instruction, Dr. Federico Pinedo, minister of the treasury; Dr. Antonio de Tomaso, minister of agriculture; General Manuel Rodríguez, minister of war; Captain José Casal, minister of the navy; and Dr. Manuel Alvarado, minister of public works.

Radicals oppose Justo, plan revolt, leaders imprisoned (1932)

The radical party made a public declaration that it considered Justo's government as a continuation of the government *de facto*, and its members engaged in revolutionary activities. In December, 1932, a plan for a rebellion headed by certain radicals was discovered, which incited congress to declare a state of siege. In some cases by order of the judge, and in other cases by order of the government the radical leaders Hipólito Irigoyen, Marcelo T. de Alvear, and others were arrested and cast into prison.

Before opening the regular sessions of Congress in 1933, President Justo raised the state of siege and set all political prisoners

POLITICAL MAP OF ARGENTINA

at liberty. His message read at the inaugural meeting of Congress made an excellent impression in the country; for he again mentioned his desire to reëstablish the sway of institutions and to assure the freedom of suffrage through elections that were reformed by law.

On July 3, 1933, Hipólito Irigoyen, who had twice held the presidency of the nation, died in Buenos Aires. No less than 100,000 persons followed his body in a civic procession directed by the radical party.

Because he had agreed to the negotiation of important treaties between Argentina and Brazil, the latter nation invited President Agustín P. Justo to visit Rio de Janeiro just as upon another occasion President Julio A. Roca had visited that capital. This journey of President Justo, which took place in October, 1933, resulted in many manifestations of sympathy by the people of the sister nation for the Argentine people. Among the treaties that were signed in Rio de Janeiro should be mentioned the anti-war pact by which Brazil and Argentina agreed not to recognize the validity of a title to territory acquired by a nation through the use of armed force. There should also be noticed the intellectual agreement concerning the exchange of professors and of publications between the two countries as well as the agreement concerning the revision of textbooks of history in order to excise from them all topics that might in any manner arouse the animadversion of the peoples of America. A policy of pacifism in America is one of the features that distinguishes the administration of Agustín P. Justo.

CHAPTER LXI

CONTEMPORARY CONDITIONS

IT IS not easy to depict the physiognomy of present Argentina. In the foreground there should be considered the rapid and constant changes which are taking place in its breast and the mobile character of a sparse population that occupies an extensive territory. Nevertheless, this nation has a personality of its own.

A general review of the Argentine Nation should include economic, political, and cultural traits. From the economic standpoint Argentina is one of the richest countries on the globe, a purveyor of raw materials, of resources that are present in the soil and subsoil; all of these are exploited rationally by an industrious population. In Argentina the riches are within reach of the laborer's arm; they have redeemed thousands of souls from misery and abjectness. We are now suffering from an economic crisis caused chiefly by the improper distribution of raw materials in the markets of the world.

From the political standpoint the federal régime is rapidly evolving toward centralization and even toward personalism in the government by virtue of the multiple faculties of the president of the republic; but the system of a free democracy and the purity of suffrage distinguish present-day Argentina as one of the countries in which the system of the popular will and representative institutions function in a superior fashion. Remember what has been said concerning corruption in electoral practices and the transcendental significance of the electoral law of 1912 which assured the beginning of a new political era. This democracy is not antagonistic to foreigners; it does not hate foreigners, but assimilates them rapidly. From the standpoint of civilization signs show that a distinctive culture has begun to develop which is open to the spiritual influence of the world, a culture which has elevated the country to a position of intellectual and recognized hegemony in America.

Argentina is a young country, as is known, and such antecedents explain her rapid progress and sudden transformations; but it is fitting to consider also that in spite of her youth, she is a nation that has an historic tradition which not only serves her as a basis to support all the changes without commotions but also as a fountain of liberal and nationalistic inspiration. This tradition springs mainly from the revolutionary stock of May, 1810, an eminently idealistic generation which insured the emancipation of the country, and from the generation of 1853 which made the institutional organization conform to the most liberal ideas with respect to the guarantee of individual rights and the assimilation of foreigners. It can also be affirmed that the generation of 1880 inspired by the postulates of Alberdi brought about the economic greatness of Argentina, and that for some years past a new generation has been struggling for her spiritual and moral greatness and for the first establishment of democracy.

Defects in the character of the Argentine people are responsible for such evils as administrative bureaucracy, which dissipates much energy that could be useful in productive labor; political mendacity which has vitiated our political system; a spoils system which has disposed of public offices; a misdirected fiscal régime which has long corrupted democracy; greed and a sensual desire for material things; and a blameworthy disinclination to solve grave problems such as public sanitation. The last-mentioned defect is responsible for an alarming percentage of infant mortality and for the prevalence of endemic diseases in sections of the country. In the midst of abundance, middlemen and speculators have made the cost of living high. A certain author has observed that the congenital disease of the Argentine people is hatred, or rather that in our society hatred checks energy and brings constructive efforts to naught.[1] Such vices and evils are being combatted with efficacy and no longer disfigure the physiognomy of this country, which with a brilliant military history, loves the arts of peace, is the seat of a prosperous and optimistic society, and nourishes generous ideals.

We quote the verdict of a contemporary English publicist who has studied the history of Argentina: "This country is destined by nature to be the seat of a great civilization, mainly European in character. That destiny has been in great part fulfiled and is in process of further fulfilment. It has in its favor the enthusiastic belief and pride in the country felt by every Argentine born and by thousands of Europeans who have made their homes in the

[1] González, *Patria y democracia* (Buenos Aires, 1920), p. 103.

country." [2] The consolidation of its component and distinctive elements has made a nation of Argentina, and the security of its political régime has assured the progress of a great contemporary democracy. After the era of constitutional organization three national censuses were taken, in 1869, 1895, and 1914. Statistics gathered at those dates speak eloquently concerning the economic and moral progress achieved by the country during a half century. Under the protection of the constitutional provisions that assured to foreigners the enjoyment of all the civil rights of citizens, immigration has added to the increase of the population in exceptional fashion. Let us notice the comparative figures of the three censuses:

Year				Argentinians	Foreigners	Total
1869	.	.	.	1,531,360	298,854	1,830,214
1895	.	.	.	2,950,384	1,005,427	3,954,811
1914	.	.	.	5,527,285	2,378,217	7,905,502

According to the calculations of the bureau of statistics, in 1920 the population of Argentina numbered 8,700,000. In 1928 the population exceeded 10,000,000.

The estimate of the national wealth, including real property, livestock, railways, tramways, plants, machines and rural utilities, divers industries, movable property, and other wealth, was as follows, in paper pesos:

1869	. . . .	2,375,000,000
1896	. . . .	6,712,000,000
1910	. . . .	14,540,000,000

In this fashion, since 1886 the patrimony of the nation has increased in a much greater ratio than the population—a phenomenon that has occurred in other civilized countries. The per capita wealth has doubled.[3]

---

[2] F. A. Kirkpatrick, *A History of the Argentine Republic* (Cambridge, 1931), p. 227.

[3] A. E. Bunge, *Riqueza y renta de la Argentina* (Buenos Aires, 1917). A law of November 3, 1899, provided that the government would redeem paper money (*billetes de curso legal*) with gold money at the rate of one paper peso for forty-four centavos gold (*moneda nacional oro sellado*). See E. Hansen, *La moneda argentina* (Buenos Aires, 1916), pp. 471-72. In a few years paper money and subsidiary currency (*moneda nacional*) became the circulating media in Argentine domestic transactions, while the gold peso (*peso de oro*) was often

According to the best calculations, the total value of Argentine products in 1919 aggregated 5,500,000,000 paper pesos distributed thus:

Agricultural products	1,399,745,469
Livestock products	1,456,163,780
Dairy products	58,597,536
Forest products	207,187,878
Mineral products	39,543,164
Sugar industry	138,000,000
Milling industry and meat packing industry	267,182,217
Coal, firewood, vegetables, fish, and other products	169,335,180
Manufactured products	1,675,252,181

The history of Argentine foreign commerce falls into five periods. The first period was an epoch of economic preparation in which pastoral industry was organized, agricultural industry was started, and the construction of railroads was accelerated. It extended from the middle of the last century to 1890. Beginning with 1864, a date for which there are statistics available, the balances of foreign commerce for the last twenty-seven years of this period were for the most part unfavorable. The second period was an era of economic activity that extended from 1891 to 1914. In twenty-two of the twenty-four years that are included in this era, the balances of foreign trade were favorable, with an annual average of 47,000,000 pesos gold. The third period extended from 1915 to 1920. It has been called the era of "economic independence." This era was marked by large favorable balances in foreign trade which made it possible to bring to the country bonds and stocks located in foreign lands, and to cancel debts held abroad. Fourth period: this began in 1921 and continued up to 1928. It was a period of unstable economic equilibrium.

Not being able to meet the large adverse balances in our trade, by the export of bonds, stocks, and other values the attempt was made to extinguish them by three possible means: the encourage-

used as a standard of value in international transactions. About 1914 a gold peso was normally worth about ninety-six cents in United States money, while a paper peso was worth about forty-two cents. In making quotations to foreign correspondents Argentine merchants often cited both of these values.—W. S. R.

ment of the introduction of captal for productive industries, the increase and appraisal of exports, and the reduction of imports.[4]

The active commercial intercourse that our country carries on with England, the United States, Italy, France, Brazil, Spain, Belgium, the Netherlands, Mexico, Germany, and other countries is shown exactly in the following figures:

| | *Value in gold pesos* | | *Totals in gold pesos* |
Years	Imports	Exports	
1913	421,352,542	483,504,547	904,857,089
1914	221,817,900	340,254,141	621,072,041
1915	226,892,733	558,280,693	785,173,376
1916	366,130,571	572,999,523	939,130,093
1917	380,321,178	550,170,049	930,491,227
1918	500,602,752	801,466,488	1,302,069,240
1919	655,772,294	1,030,965,258	1,686,737,552
1920	934,970,000	1,044,090,000	1,979,060,000
1921	635,000,000	672,000,000	1,307,000,000

In 1924, the actual value of Argentine commerce amounted to 1,840,104,575 pesos in gold, of which the imports came to 828,-709,993 pesos and the exports to 1,011,394,582 pesos. Upon analyzing the imports for 1924 an important change is discovered: namely, a decrease in the amount of imports of articles of consumption (which had been replaced by articles manufactured by national industry) and at the same time great increases in the importation of petroleum, iron manufactures, machinery, and articles for railroad and other industries.

Fifth period: About 1929 a new period began, one of universal crisis which extended to Argentina. As a consequence of the overproduction of riches there was a fall in prices and unemployment of labor. The crisis profoundly affects our country; for the time had come in which it could no longer dispose of its raw materials, because the consuming countries had rigidly restricted their purchases, and at the same time they had eliminated all foreign competition and checked importation by high customs duties. In addition to these circumstances there was a large deficit in the budgets of 1929, 1930, and 1931 because of the decrease in the amount of taxes, especially customs duties, and the increase of the foreign

---

[4] *Informe No. 1, serie C., no. 1, comercio exterior, Junio de 1923.*

debt. The following table gives the commercial interchange in 1930 and 1931 in paper pesos:

Year	Imports	Exports	Total
1930	1,679,960	1,395,690	3,075,650
1931	1,173,490	1,452,510	2,626,000

The total of imports and exports in 1931, which came to 2,626,000 in paper pesos, shows a decrease of fifteen per cent as compared with the total for 1930, and the latter was twenty-six per cent less than the interchange for 1929.

One of the events of highest economic importance in contemporary Argentina is the discovery of petroleum beds at Comodoro Rivadavia and Cacheuta. The oil of Comodoro Rivadavia, which is the most important, has been employed advantageously as a fuel to replace coal in boilers on both land and sea. As is known, petroleum in its natural state is a fuel superior to soft coal, for a kilogram of the latter only furnishes a maximum of eight thousand calories, while a kilogram of petroleum yields as much as eleven thousand calories.

One must recollect that in 1915 Argentina imported coal, petroleum, and their derivatives amounting to 48,000,000, gold pesos; once the extraction of the great riches that our soil possesses in its petroleum beds is accomplished, the products will be destined to fruitful applications in our country.

Not only has Argentina made economic progress. To confute those persons who lightly hold that our country is simply the great granary of the modern world, as Egypt was the granary of the old world, there exist incontestable proofs of our cultural and social progress. Buenos Aires, Córdoba, La Plata, Tucumán, Santa Fe, Rosario, and other cities constitute centers of modern culture because of their academies, schools, journals, universities, and investigational institutions.

Modern Argentina possesses representative men in art, science, history, and letters. In order to give an account of the special attention paid by the state to the development of public education in all its grades and specialities, let us notice the sums appropriated for that purpose in 1934: to the five universities of the republic (Buenos Aires, La Plata, Córdoba, Tucumán, and the Littoral) 20,700,000 pesos; to national academies, normal schools, and special establishments, 33,971,758 pesos; to primary education, 166,397,398 pesos, of which 101,397,398 went to national schools, and 65,000,000 to provincial schools. The total sum applied to university, secondary, special, and primary education in 1924 amounted to 221,069,156 pesos. In the territory of the republic there were 11,135 primary schools which were attended by a total of 1,545,238 pupils.

Before 1853, illiteracy was one of the gravest evils that afflicted Argentine society. After that date, the dominant concern of both provincial and national governments was to establish primary schools in order to reduce illiteracy. Though we are not yet ready to affirm that our country occupies a leading place among civilized peoples in the campaign against illiteracy, yet the progress made can be shown by figures. The number of illiterates more than seven years of age at each of the four census periods is shown by the following table:

	Illiterates over 7 years old			*Proportion per 100*		
	Male	Female	Total	Total	Male	Female
1869	548,579	562,440	1,111,019	78.4	81.7	74.8
1895	878,687	887,497	1,766,184	54.4	58.5	50.8
1914	1,117,881	1,096,035	2,213,916	35.1	38.1	32.6

Among the influential instruments of culture of contemporary Argentina should be mentioned its great dailies and reviews. These distinguished organs of public opinion not only furnish the most complete and telegraphic news in the world, but also the correspondence of the most reliable contemporary writers and columns of critical commentary concerning the domestic and international problems of the country. Such dailies and reviews have now attained the rank of tribunes of general culture and doctrine.

Argentina occupies a distinctive scientific position in America. It deserves credit for the organization of the Latin-American scientific congresses which were instituted by the Argentine Scientific Society presided over by Dr. Ángel Gallardo. As there was no basis for the exclusion of non-Latin peoples from these congresses, they were consequently transformed into Pan-American scientific congresses.

The Pan-American Scientific Congress that assembled in Lima in 1924 had as its collaborators distinguished scientists of America

Upper, Façade of the Colón Theatre, Buenos Aires. Lower, The Museum of Fine Arts in Buenos Aires. Both photographs by the Translator.

who either attended its sessions or transmitted their scientific studies. The Argentine delegation, presided over by an engineer named Eduardo Huergo, played a brilliant part and was distinguished by the original character of its contributions, especially in such subjects as pure and applied mathematics, medicine, and historical sciences.

The International Congress of Americanists is another institution with genuine scientific prestige. Its exclusive object is to promote ethnographic, anthropological, archaeological, linguistic, and historical studies of America, especially concerning the precolombian era. Argentina has always been represented in the meetings of this congress. In November, 1932, the twenty-fifth conference of Americanists met in the city of La Plata under the auspices of the university located there, thus commemorating the fiftieth anniversary of the founding of that city. Because of the valuable scientific papers presented on this occasion, the twenty-fifth congress of Americanists is one of the most important sessions of that congress which assembled up to 1934. The official Argentine delegation was composed of the following scholars: Luis María Torres, Félix F. Outes, Martín Duello Jurado, Emilio Ravignani, A. Metraux, Milcíades Vignati, Fernando Márquez Miranda, and the author of this history.

Among the symptoms of moral vitality, which have been noticeable in recent times, should be mentioned the capacity of the people for saving, the elevated and fruitful sentiment of nationality inspiring them, the political transformation brought about by the use of the secret and compulsory ballot, the improvement in military organization, and its influence upon democracy by the adoption of compulsory service.

In sum, Argentina has the optimistic impulse of a people that possess ample room and manifold means for the realization of the ends of justice and culture.

In 1923, the Fifth Pan-American Conference met in Santiago de Chile. In this conference, which represented all of America, questions were considered that tended to improve friendly relations among the people of the continent. The Argentine delegates, under the chairmanship of Dr. Manuel Augusto Montes de Oca, obtained excellent results with the pacific declarations formulated by their leader. He gave the impression that our country, dominated by the desire to develop its resources and culture, wishes to live at peace with all the nations of the world.

The Sixth Pan-American Conference met at Havana in 1928, in an expectant moment because of the policy of the United States which had taken military occupation of part of the territory of Nicaragua, under the pretext of insuring the lives of North American citizens and of guaranteeing the investments of their capital. This theme, which was complicated because of its possible international consequences, was not considered in the conference. However, the chairman of the Argentine delegation, Dr. Honorio Pueyrredón, spoke of the concept of the sovereignty of a nation, great or small, and of the principle of the non-intervention of one state in the internal affairs of other states. In that conference, the same delegate of Argentina proposed the plan for a declaration according to which the tariff policies of the nations of America should lead to the abolition of customs barriers in order to facilitate free commercial intercourse. But this project was not accepted and consequently the Argentine delegation left the conference.

In 1933 the Seventh Pan American Conference assembled at Montevideo. The international situation was very delicate, because a war had been raging for more than a year in the northern Chaco between Bolivia and Paraguay, and all efforts to prevent or to end the war had proved futile. In this conference the members insisted that negotiations for peace should be undertaken—negotiations that culminated in the arrangement of a truce. The Argentine delegation headed by Minister of Foreign Relations Carlos Saavedra Lamas, scored an important success by the adoption of the anti-war pact by all the American nations. Two months earlier upon the occasion of the visit of President Justo to Rio de Janeiro, that pact had been signed by representatives of Brazil and Argentina.

The seventh conference at Montevideo also deserves mention because of many other measures initiated there, such as the means of preventing the intervention of American states in the political life of other American states and the means of lowering economic barriers. There should also be mentioned the creation in Buenos Aires of an international institute on the teaching of American history for the purpose of eliminating from the texts used in primary and secondary schools any theme that might affect the dignity of the peoples of America.

After the adoption of the constitution of 1853 the Argentine Nation made notable political progress. With the exception of the critical years from 1852 to 1862, when there was a struggle between the Confederation and Buenos Aires, the nation developed along constitutional lines by consolidating the power of authority in order to combat the evils of anarchy and the civil struggles that had convulsed the country. Such consolidation of authority, carried to an extreme, implied the negation of the freedom of suffrage thus creating a revolutionary spirit among the masses which had its manifestations in 1874, 1880, 1890, 1893, and 1905. This entire process is a struggle between the anarchical and revolutionary spirit of the persons who did not exercise the franchise and the dominant centralism which influenced decisively the choice of the chief magistrates of the nation and the provinces. This phase of Argentine political life was brought to an end by the electoral law proposed by President Roque Sáenz Peña in 1912 which symbolized the consolidation of democracy by freedom of suffrage. The increase of the Argentine electorate may be seen by studying the following conspectus of presidential elections:

Year	Citizens registered	Citizens voting
1916	1,189,264	745,825
1922	1,586,366	876,354
1928	1,807,566	1,461,581
1931	2,117,980	1,555,629

From the standpoint of the evolution of the executive, legislative, and judicial departments of the government, the executive department has acquired predominance over the others. By virtue of the letter of the constitution and because of political customs, the power of the president of the republic has been and is enormous.

Lastly, with respect to the Argentine federal régime, a system of centralization is being evolved. This centralization operates in three distinct and concurrent ways: (1) By the economic attraction of the capital of the republic to which flows a great portion of the foreign supply of men, funds, and creative energy. (2) By the increasing power of the president of the nation. (3) By the cultural and spiritual attraction exercised by the city of Buenos Aires upon the entire life of the country by virtue of its atmosphere and prosperity, viewed as a manifestation of modern municipal life.[5]

Certain authors have formulated general principles for the interpretation of Argentine history. Sarmiento said that there was a curious coincidence in the regular alternation of our political changes by decades that were almost regular. In 1810, the Revolution; in 1820, the dissolution of government; in 1830, the triumph of provincial anarchy; in 1840, the terror; in 1851, the fall of Rosas; in 1860, the reconstruction, the republic constituted; in 1870, the translation of the constitution into action; in 1880, the federalization of Buenos Aires.

José Nicolás Matienzo has observed that the Argentine political body changes fundamentally at the end of three presidencies, or every eighteen years, during which period a political generation maintains its predominance and is then replaced by a new generation. After the battle of Pavón Bartolomé Mitre was elected president in 1862. He was succeeded in 1868 by Domingo Faustino Sarmiento, who had been a minister of the province of Buenos Aires while Mitre was governor of that province. President Sarmiento was succeeded in 1874 by Nicolás Avellaneda, who had been minister of public instruction. These three presidential periods ended in 1880, having lasted eighteen years. In that year the province of Buenos Aires lost its hegemony as a consequence of the cession of its capital for use as the definitive seat of the national authorities. Thenceforth the president of Argentina exercised a great electoral authority and checked the influenc of all the governors. This second cycle included the first presidency of Julio A. Roca to 1886; the presidencies of Juárez Celman and Pellegrini that lasted until 1892; and those of Luis Sáenz Peña and José Evaristo Uriburu which carried on the work of political centralization to 1898. Then came another cycle of three presidencies: that of Roca (for his second term); that of Quintana and Figueroa Alcorta; and that of Roque Sáenz Peña and de la Plaza, whose chief political act was an electoral reform initiated by Roca to give representation to minorities and terminated by Sáenz Peña

---

[5] J. V. González, "Sistema y forma de gobierno de la nación argentina," *Revista jurídica y de ciencias sociales* (Buenos Aires, 1924), año XLI, pp. 19-28,

by the adoption of secret voting and the incomplete ballot. The last period comprised the first presidency of Hipólito Irigoyen, that of Dr. Alvear, and the second presidency of Irigoyen which constitutes the cycle of political reform.[6] We have already explained that the second presidency of Irigoyen reached a crisis in the revolution of September 6, 1930.

Lastly, the publicist Rodolfo Rivarola has essayed an interpretation of Argentine history by designating the following thirty-year cycles. The first cycle, which begins in 1791 and ends in 1821, is concerned with the movement for independence. The second, extending from 1821 to 1851, is concerned with the aspiration for a constitution. The third is concerned with the consolidation of the republic and extends from 1851 to 1880. The fourth, stretching from 1880 to 1911, is concerned with the desire for a representative system. The fifth, which begins in 1911 and has not yet ended, is concerned with universal suffrage.[7]

It should be observed that the process of the evolution of a people is not subject to laws like those which regulate the physical world in which phenomena are repeated, while in history events succeed each other. The interpretations of Argentine history which have been noticed do not have a precise value, but they enable one to realize the extent of the horizon and emphasize the great collective preoccupations or dominant ideas of each Argentine generation.

---

[6] J. N. Matienzo, "Leyes históricas de la política argentina," *La Nación,* December 5, 1829.

[7] Narciso Binayan, *Ciclos en la historia argentina* (Buenos Aires, 1933).

BIBLIOGRAPHICAL NOTES

It is the purpose of the translator to furnish bibliographical notes that will be helpful not only to the specialist in Latin-American history but also to the general reader. An attempt has been made, therefore, to direct attention to books and articles in English. Some works on Latin America have been included. Abbreviated forms of titles have been used **throughout**.

BIBLIOGRAPHIES

Among the best bibliographical aids in English are the following: C. K. Jones, *Hispanic American Bibliographies,* Baltimore, 1922 (with supplements published in the *Hispanic American Historical Review*); R. H. Keniston, *List of Works for the Study of Hispanic-American History,* New York, 1920; E. M. Borchard, *Guide to the Law and Legal Literature of Argentina, Brazil, and Chile,* Washington, 1917; W. W. Pierson, Jr., *Hispanic-American History, A Syllabus,* Chapel Hill, 1926; S. E. Leavitt, *Argentine Literature, a Bibliography of Literary Criticism, Biography, and Literary Controversy,* Chapel Hill, 1924. Current publications are listed in the *American Historical Review* and the *Bulletin of the Pan American Union.* The *Hispanic American Historical Review,* 16 volumes to date, Baltimore, 1918-1922, Durham, 1926—, is most useful. A valuable survey of publications in 1935 is the *Handbook of Latin American Studies* prepared by several scholars and edited by L. Hanke, Cambridge, Mass., 1936.

A very useful guide is the *Catálogo de la biblioteca nacional,* 6 vols., Buenos Aires, 1893-1919. A helpful narrative is furnished by R. D. Carbia, *Historia de la historiografía argentina,* vol. I, Buenos Aires, 1925. The books belonging to the talented author and publicist, General Mitre, are listed in *"Museo Mitre," catálogo de la biblioteca,* Buenos Aires, 1907. Annotated lists of important current publications on Spain and Spanish America are printed in the *Revista hispánica moderna.*

GENERAL

A comprehensive survey of Latin-American history is found in W. S. Robertson, *History of the Latin-American Nations,* New York, 1932. On the Spanish background, see C. E. Chapman, *A History of Spain,* New York, 1918. The best account of Argentine history in English is that by F. A. Kirkpatrick, *A History of the Argentine Republic,* Cambridge, Eng., 1931. Among the older works should be mentioned W. Parish, *Buenos Ayres and the Provinces of the Río de la Plata,* London, 1852. J. F. Rippy furnishes an historical sketch of "Argentina" in A. C. Wilgus, ed., *Argentina, Brazil, and Chile Since Independence,* Washington, 1935.

Among important works in Spanish should be mentioned V. F. López, *Historia de la República Argentina,* 10 volumes, Buenos Aires, 1913. C. A. Villanueva, *Historia de la República Argentina,* 2 vols., Paris, 1914, utilizes material from the French archives. A convenient collection of sources is published in R. Levene, *Lecturas históricas argentinas,* 2 vols., Buenos Aires, 1913. A most valuable work is the scholarly series in progress entitled *Documentos para la historia argentina,* Buenos Aires, 1913—, which is being published by the College of Philosophy and Letters of the University of Buenos Aires. Among the older works should be mentioned P. de Angelis, ed., *Colección de obras y documentos relativos á la historia antigua y moderna de las provincias del Río de la Plata,* 5 vols., Buenos Aires, 1910. In addition to the studies edited by the College of Law and Social Sciences of the University of Buenos Aires, special mention should be made of the documents and monographs published in the *Boletín del instituto de investigaciones históricas* of the College of Philosophy and Letters of the same university, Buenos Aires, 1923—. A coöperative *Historia de la Nación Argentina* is now in progress under the direction of a committee of the *Junta de Historia y Numismática Americana* of Buenos Aires headed by R. Levene; vol. I bearing the subtitle, *Tiémpos prehistóricos y protohistóricos* was published at Buenos Aires in 1936.

THE AMERICAN ENVIRONMENT

The International Bureau of the American Republics published the *Argentine Republic, A Geographical Sketch,* Washington, 1903. See also G. E. Church, *South America: an Outline of Its Physical Geography,* London, 1901; C. R. Darwin, *Journal of Researches into the Natural History and Geology of the Countries visited during the Voyage of H. M. S. Beagle round the World,* London, 1891; T. Falkner, *A Description of Patagonia and the Adjoining Parts of South America,* Chicago, 1935; A. Hrdlicka, "Early Man in South America," *Bureau of Ethnology,* Bulletin 52, Washington, 1912; L. L. Domínguez, ed., *Voyage of Ulrich Schmidt to . . . La Plata and Paraguai;* Works issued by the Hakluyt Society, 2d Series, vol. LXXI, London,

1891; B. Willis, *Northern Patagonia, Character and Resources,* New York, 1914; P. A. Means, "The Native Background in Latin American History," in A. C. Wilgus, ed., *Colonial Hispanic America,* Washington, 1936; G. E. Church, *Aborigines of South America,* London, 1912; C. Wissler, *The American Indian,* New York, 1917.

Among useful treatises in other languages than English are the following: F. Latzina, *Diccionario geográfico argentino,* Buenos Aires, 1908; J. A. V. Martin de Moussy, *Description géographique et statistique de la Confédération Argentine,* 3 vols., Paris, 1860-1869; F. F. Outes and C. Bruch, *Los aborígenes de la República Argentina,* Buenos Aires, 1910. Scholarly studies of pre-Colombian America are found in the *Revista del museo de la Plata,* La Plata, 1890—. A serviceable atlas is by J. J. Biedma and C. Beyer, *Atlas histórico de la República Argentina,* Buenos Aires, 1909.

DISCOVERY AND CONQUEST

A useful work in English on the great discoverer is J. B. Thacher, *Christopher Columbus,* 3 vols., New York, 1903-1904. P. A. Means, *Fall of the Inca Empire and the Spanish Rule in Peru, 1530-1780,* New York, 1932, touches pre-Spanish Argentina. R. B. Merriman in *The Rise of the Spanish Empire in the Old World and in the New,* 4 vols., New York, 1918-1934, links Spanish activity in Europe and America in scholarly fashion. E. G. Bourne, *Spain in America,* New York, 1904, treats phases of early Spanish activity in America sympathetically. "The Office of Adelantado" is described by R. R. Hill in the *Political Science Quarterly,* XXVIII (1913), 646-68. R. B. C. Graham describes *The Conquest of the River Plate,* Garden City, 1924.

Among learned treatises in Spanish should be mentioned J. T. Medina, *El descubrimiento del Océano Pacífico,* Santiago de Chile, 1914; P. Groussac, *Mendoza y Garay,* Buenos Aires, 1916; P. Lozano, *Historia de la conquista del Paraguay, Río de la Plata y Tucumán,* 5 vols., Buenos Aires, 1873-1875; R. Levillier, *El descubrimiento del norte argentino,* Lima, 1925, and the same author's *Francisco de Aguirre y los origines del Tucumán,* Madrid, 1920. A useful documentary collection is A. M. Fabié y Escudero, *Documentos legislativos,* second series, vols. V, IX, and X, Madrid, 1890-1897.

SPANISH COLONIAL POLICY AND ADMINISTRATION

E. J. Hamilton has made an intensive study of *American Treasure and the Price Revolution in Spain,* Cambridge, Mass., 1934. *Trade and Navigation between Spain and the Indies* are described by C. H.

Haring, Cambridge, Mass., 1918. W. G. Roscher, *The Spanish Colonial System*, edited by E. G. Bourne, New York, 1904, is a useful, brief survey. L. E. Fisher's *The Intendant System in Spanish America*, Berkeley, 1929, touches upon La Plata. On Church and State, see T. C. Lea, *The Inquisition in the Spanish Dependencies*, New York, 1908; and J. L. Mecham, *Church and State in Latin America*, Chapel Hill, 1934.

Standard treatises in Spanish are as follows: R. Altamira y Crevea, *Historia de España*, 4 vols., Barcelona, 1900-1911; C. O. Bunge, *Historia del derecho argentino*, 2 vols., Buenos Aires, 1912-1913. E. Ruíz Guiñazu, *La magistratura indiana*, Buenos Aires, 1916; and V. G. Quesada, *Virreinato del Río de la Plata*, Buenos Aires, 1881. Important sources are found in the following: *Documentos para la historia del virreinato del Río de la Plata*, 3 vols., Buenos Aires, 1912-1913; *Recopilación de leyes de los reinos de las Indias*, 2 vols., Madrid, 1841; and *Real ordenanza para el establecimiento é instrucción de intendentes de ejército y provincia en el virreinato de Buenos Aires*, Madrid, 1782.

Colonial Culture

Here again there are few works in English that are devoted exclusively to La Plata. B. Moses, *The Spanish Dependencies in South America*, 2 vols., New York, 1914; and *South America on the Eve of Emancipation*, New York, 1908, are instructive and stimulating books. H. E. Bolton describes "The Mission as a Frontier Institution in the Spanish-American Colonies," in the *American Historical Review*, XXIII (1917-18), 42-61. La Plata is treated in R. G. Watson, *Spanish and Portuguese South America during the Colonial Period*, 2 vols., London, 1884. "Alteration of the Argentine Pampa in the Colonial Period" is described by O. Schmieder in the *University of California Publications in Geography*, vol. II, no. 10.

Works in Spanish that should be noted are the following: F. de Azara, *Descripción é historia del Paraguay y del Río de la Plata*, 2 vols., Madrid, 1849; A. Garland, *Estudio económico sobre los medios circulantes usados en el Perú*, Lima, 1908; M. Leguizamón, *El gaucho, su indumentaria, armas, música, cantos, y bailes nativos*, Buenos Aires, 1916; R. Levene, *Investigaciones acerca de la historia económica del Virreinato del Plata*, 2 vols., La Plata, 1927; and by the same author *Los orígenes de la democracia argentina*, Buenos Aires, 1911; V. G. Quesada, *La vida intelectual en la América Española durante los siglos XVI, XVII y XVIII*, Buenos Aires, 1910; R. Rojas, *La literatura argentina*, 4 vols., Buenos Aires, 1917-1923; and G. Funes, *Ensayo de la historia civil de Buenos Aires, Tucumán y Paraguay,* 2 vols., Buenos Aires, 1856. *Biblioteca argentina,* edited by R. Rojas, 18 vols., Buenos Aires, 1915-1916, is a useful series of Argentine classics.

THE STRUGGLE FOR INDEPENDENCE

A suggestive survey is B. Moses, *The Intellectual Background of the Revolution in South America,* New York, 1926. W. R. Manning edited an important collection entitled *Diplomatic Correspondence of the United States concerning the Independence of the Latin-American Nations,* 3 vols., New York, 1925. *Minutes of a Court Martial holden on board His Majesty's Ship Gladiator . . . of Capt. Sir Home Popham,* London, 1807; and *The Proceedings of a General Court Martial held at Chelsea Hospital . . . for the Trial of Lieut. Gen. Whitelocke,* 2 vols., London, 1808, are important sources on the English invasions of La Plata. I. Núñez, *An Account, Historical, Political, and Statistical, of the United Provinces of Río de la Plata,* London, 1825, is instructive. W. Pilling, *The Emancipation of South America,* London, 1893, furnishes a summary of the important work of Mitre on San Martín mentioned below. W. S. Robertson's *The Life of Miranda,* 2 vols., Chapel Hill, 1929; and *Rise of the Spanish-American Republics,* New York, 1918, deal with phases of the Argentine Revolution.

The following are useful works in Spanish: R. Levene, *Ensayo histórico sobre la revolución de Mayo y Mariano Moreno,* 2 vols., Buenos Aires, 1920; B. Mitre, *Historia de San Martín,* 3 vols., Buenos Aires, 1887-1888; and *Historia de Belgrano,* 4 vols., Buenos Aires, 1902. A recent work on San Martín is J. B. Otero, *Historia del Libertador,* 4 vols., Buenos Aires, 1932. Important documents are printed in the works of Belgrano, Bolívar, Pueyrredón, and San Martín. A periodical entitled *San Martín,* Buenos Aires, 1935—, is publishing materials concerning that hero.

THE CRITICAL PERIOD

Phases of the career of Rosas are considered in the following writings: J. F. Cady, *Foreign Intervention in the Rio de la Plata, 1838-1850,* Philadelphia, 1929; J. A. King, *Twenty-four Years in the Argentine Republic,* New York, 1846; L. B. Mackinnon, *Steam Warfare in the Paraná,* 2 vols., London, 1848; W. S. Robertson, "Foreign Estimates of the Argentine Dictator, Juan Manuel de Rosas," *Hispanic American Historical Review,* X (1930), 125-37. The reign of Rosas and also the framing of the present Argentine constitution are covered in W. R. Manning, ed., *Diplomatic Correspondence of the United States; Inter-American Affairs, 1831-1860,* vol. I, Washington, 1932.

A chapter on Argentina is found in A. Coester, *The Literary History of Spanish America,* New York, 1916.

The *Archivo americano y espíritu de la prensa del mundo,* 2 series, 61 numbers, Buenos Aires, 1843-1851, was the organ of Rosas. The best interpretation of Rosas is that of E. Quesada, *La época de Rosas,* reprinted in Buenos Aires in 1923. See also A. Saldías, *Historia de la Confederación Argentina,* 5 vols., Buenos Aires, 1911. On other personalities of this period consult A. Dellepiane, ed., *Dorrego y el federalismo argentino,* Buenos Aires, 1926; A. Lamas, *Rivadavia,* Buenos Aires, 1915; D. Peña, *Juan Facundo Quiroga,* Buenos Aires, 1906. Two treatises that cover this and the following period are I. Bucich Escobar, *Los presidentes argentinos, 1826-1918,* Buenos Aires, 1918; and E. Ravignani, *Historia constitucional de la República Argentina,* 3 vols., Buenos Aires, 1926-1927.

WELDING THE NATION

L. S. Rowe, *The Federal System of the Argentine Republic,* Washington, 1921, describes the formation and character of the present government of Argentina. A sketch by an Argentine statesman is that of E. S. Zeballos, *Rise and Growth of the Argentine Constitution,* Buenos Aires, 1907. That constitution is translated in J. I. Rodríguez, *American Constitutions,* vol. I, Washington, 1903. *The Argentine Civil Code* has been translated by F. L. Joannini, Boston, 1917. C. J. MacConnell has translated J. B. Alberdi's *The Crime of War,* London, 1913. T. J. Page, *La Plata, the Argentine Confederation, and Paraguay,* New York, 1859, records the impressions gained on an exploring expedition. An excellent monograph by P. H. Box discusses *The Origins of the Paraguayan War,* Urbana, 1930. G. C. E. Thompson describes *The War in Paraguay,* London, 1869. C. H. Haring, *South American Progress,* Cambridge, Mass., 1934, devotes a chapter to Argentina. Translations of Argentine poems are found in A. S. Blackwell, *Some Spanish American Poets,* New York, 1929.

The rôle of Alberdi is described by S. Baque, *Influencia de Alberdi en la organización política del estado argentino,* Buenos Aires, 1915; and by P. Groussac, "El desarrollo constitucional y las bases de Alberdi," *Anales de la Biblioteca,* I (1900), 194-287. M. Niño, *Mitre,* 2 vols., Buenos Aires, 1906; and R. Rivarola, *Mitre, una década de su vida política,* Buenos Aires, 1921, sketch Mitre's career. Other colossi of this period are treated by M. Leguizamón, *Rasgos de la vida de Urquiza,* Buenos Aires, 1920; and J. G. Guerra, *Sarmiento,* Santiago de Chile, 1901. Besides the voluminous *Obras* of Alberdi and Sarmiento, and the *Archivo del general Mitre* (25 vols., Buenos

Aires, 1911-1913), there should be mentioned the *Documentos relativos á la Organización constitutional de la República Argentina,* 3 vols. and index, Buenos Aires, 1911-1914.

NATIONAL PROGRESS

E. Tornquist and Others, *The Economic Development of the Argentine Republic in the last Fifty Years,* Buenos Aires, 1919; W. H. Koebel, *Modern Argentina,* London, 1907; W. A. Hirst, *Argentina,* London, 1910; N. O. Winter, *Argentina and Her People of Today,* Boston, 1910; A. B. Martínez and M. Lewandowski, *The Argentine in the Twentieth Century,* New York, 1915; L. B. Smith and others, *The Economic Position of Argentina during the War,* Washington, 1920; W. B. Parker, *Argentines of Today,* 2 vols., New York, 1920; L. Hutchinson, *Report on Trade Conditions in Argentina, Uruguay, and Paraguay,* Washington, 1906. *Argentina's Revolution and its Aftermath,* Foreign Policy Reports, vol. VI, no. 17, New York, 1931.

Among a host of books in Spanish may be mentioned the following: J. A. González Calderón, *Derecho constitucional argentino,* 3 vols., Buenos Aires, 1917-1923; J. N. Matienzo, *El gobierno representativo federal en la República Argentina,* Buenos Aires, 1910; M. C. Chueco, *La República Argentina en su primer centenario,* 2 vols., Buenos Aires, 1910; A. E. Bunge, *Los problemas económicos del presente,* Buenos Aires, 1920; J. A. Terry, *Finanzas,* Buenos Aires, 1918; E. Hansen, *La moneda argentina,* Buenos Aires, 1916; *Unión cívica,* Buenos Aires, 1890; W. R. Peralta, *Historia de la unión cívica radical,* Buenos Aires, 1917; R. Rivarola, "El Presidente Sáenz Peña y la moralidad política argentina," *Revista Argentina de ciencias políticas,* IX (1916), 5-56; M. L. González, *Vida del teniente general Julio A. Roca,* Buenos Aires, 1914; A. Acosta, *El Dr. Hipólito Irigoyen, Intimidades políticas,* Buenos Aires, 1918; and B. Villafane, *Irigoyen, el último dictador,* Buenos Aires, 1922. Additional sources will be found in the writings of Nicolás Avellaneda, Carlos Pellegrini, and Roque Sáenz Peña. The centenary numbers published by *La Nación* of Buenos Aires in 1910 and in 1916 contain a wealth of material on various phases of Argentine history.

INTERNATIONAL RELATIONS

A general survey of relations between the United States and Latin-American Nations is furnished by W. S. Robertson, *Hispanic-American Relations with the United States,* New York, 1923. In *Pan-Americanism; Its Beginnings,* New York, 1920, J. B. Lockey presents an account of early Latin Americanism. In two volumes concerning the Monroe Doctrine before and after 1826 respectively, D. Perkins touches upon Argentina. See also W. S. Robertson, "South America and the Monroe Doctrine," *Political Science Quarterly*, XXX (1915), 82-105. England's policy toward Spanish America in the age of Monroe is well described in H. Temperley's *The Foreign Policy of Canning*, London, 1925. The adjustment of an important boundary dispute is explained by M. W. Williams, "The Treaty of Tordesillas and the Argentine-Brazilian Boundary Settlement," *Hispanic American Historical Review*, V (1922), 3-23. A decade of Argentine foreign trade is studied in J. H. Williams, *Argentine Trade under inconvertible Paper Money*, Cambridge, Mass., 1920. A chapter on Argentina and the World War is found in P. A. Martin, *Latin America and the War*, Baltimore, 1925.

Two views of the Monroe Doctrine by Argentinians should be noticed, namely, D. L. Molinari, "Mito Canning y Doctrina Monroe," *Nosotros*, vol. XVII, pp. 86-94; and L. M. Drago, *La República Argentina ye el caso de Venezuela*, Buenos Aires, 1903. On the foreign policy of Rosas should be mentioned J. J. Gschwind, *La política internacional argentina durante la dictadura de Rosas*, Rosario, 1925. Argentine maritime interests are considered in S. R. Storni, *Intereses argentinas en el mar*, Buenos Aires, 1916. On Argentina's relations with the League of Nations, C. Díaz Cisneros has published *La liga de las naciones y la actitud argentina*, Buenos Aires, 1921. Important source material will be found in *Memorias* of Argentine secretaries of foreign relations to congress and in collections of treaties.

INDEX

Abascal, José de, Viceroy of Peru, character, 317; mentioned, 216, 294
Abbess, house of the, 186
Abeja Argentina, La, periodical, 368
Aberastain, Antonio, 462
Abreu, Diego de, 27, 45
Abreu, Gonzalo de, 37, 46
Abusos de la Mesta, Campomanes', 105
Academy of Loreto or of the King, 160
Academy of Máximo. *See* Academy of Loreto
Academy of Monserrat, 95, 160, 455, 457
Academy of San Carlos, faculty of, 93; mentioned, 158, 160, 171, 265; students at, 94. *See also* Academy of the Union of the South
Academy of the Union of the South, 328-29
Academy of Uruguay, 455, 457
Acadia, 104
Acevedo, Manuel A., 326
Acha, Col., 420
Achega, Domingo, 328
Aconcagua, Mount, 305; valley, 306
Acosta, José de, Jesuit author, 149, 157
Adams, John, President of the U. S., 193
Adelantado, described, 16-17
Advance of geographical knowledge, 1
Africa, 2, 73, 119, 278, 349
Agaces, Indians, 12
Agreement of San Nicolás, described, quoted, 443-44; opposition to, in Buenos Aires, 444-46; mentioned, 449
Agrelo, Pedro G., 267-68, 331
Agrelo, Pedro J., fiscal, 275, 281, 329, 407
Agriculture, 119, 121, 174-75, 487
Agüero, Canon, 448
Agüero, Fernández de, advocate of the consulado of Cadiz, plea for commercial monopoly, 112-13; quoted, 112; refuted, 114-15
Agüero, José M., 365
Agüero, Julián de Segundo, 364, 368, 371
Aguiar y Acuña, Rodrigo de, 144
Aguirre, Francisco de, plan for settlements, 36-37

Aguirre, Juan F., 168
Aguirre, Juan P., alcalde, 338, 339
Aguirre, Manuel H. de, 376
A la juventud argentina, Gutiérrez's, 432
Alberdi, Juan B., Argentine publicist, mentioned, 416, 432, 450, 454-55, 457, 517; quoted, 88, 451
Albernos, Felipe de, 65
Alberti, Manuel, Platean patriot, 217, 227, 228, 240
Albido, Ortuño de, 31
Albuera, battle of, 278
Alcabala, tax, 130, 346
Alcaldes, 56, 146
Alcazaba, Spanish adventurer, 17
Alcorta, Amancio, 495
Alcorta, Diego de, 368
Aldao, Father Félix, 420; and brothers, 394
Alem, Leandro N., radical leader, characterized, 491; mentioned, 492, 495
Alexander VI, Pope, bulls issued by, 4, 148
Alfaibar de Viana, Francisca, 188
Alfaro, Francisco de, 49, 57, 58
Alfonso XI, King of Spain, 126-27
Alicante, 107
Allende, Col. Santiago, mentioned, 243, 245
Almagro, Diego de, 17
Almojarifazgo, customs duty, 130
Alsina, Adolfo, 476, 477, 482
Alsina, Valentín, 446, 459, 460
Altolaguirre, Pedro, will of, quoted, 181
Alvarado, Commandant, 311
Alvarado, Manuel, 514
Alvarado, Pedro de, Spanish conqueror, 182
Alvarado, Rudecindo, cabinet minister, 454, 477
Álvarez, Juan, quoted, 349-50
Álvarez, Manuel, 189
Álvarez de Acevedo, Tomás, 83
Álvarez de Arenales, Col. Juan A., 215, 216
Álvarez de Arenales, Gen. Juan A., 317, 318, 368
Álvarez Jonte, Antonio, diplomatic mission, 257
Álvarez Jonte, Juan, 280
Álvarez Thomas, I., Director of La Plata, 292

Artigas, José G., Uruguayan patriot, brothers of, 253; early career, 253-54; denounced by Posadas, 290; forms federation, 334; mentioned, 282, 283, 291, 292, 294, 297, 330, 331, 332, 344; military career, quoted, 254

"À San Martín," Andrade's, 432

Ascasubi, Hilario, 433

Asia, 73, 74, 119

Asiento, mentioned, 109; of English, 104

Assembly (congress), of July 24, 1810, in Paraguay, 249

Assembly of 1813, at Buenos Aires, 270, 280-82; measures, 347; dissolved, 291; mentioned, 348

Assembly of 1821 (*Congreso Cisplatino*), quoted, 379-80

Assembly of Notables, at Bayonne, mentioned, 211

Association of May, 416, 417

Asunción, decline, 50; founding of, 22-23; mentioned, 30, 39, 41-42, 47; quarrels in, 26, 44-45

Atienza, Ramón de, 345

Atlantic Ocean, 36

"Atlántida," Andrade's, 432

Auchmuty, Sir Samuel, English general, captures Montevideo, penetrates Buenos Aires, 199, 200; mentioned, 198

Audiencia: mentioned, 80; of Buenos Aires, deportation, 243; founding and influence, 63, 103; mentioned, 67, 210, 212, 242; quoted, 211, 222; second founding and functions, 145-46; of Charcas (Chuquisaca), mentioned, 43, 46, 49, 150, 214, 215

Augustinians, 149

Avalos, José de, 67

Avellaneda, Dr. Marco, 298

Avellaneda, Marco de, 419, 420

Avellaneda, Nicolás, President of Argentina, mentioned, 480, 482, 526; administration of, 482-87

Avenida de Mayo, Buenos Aires, 511

Avenue Colón, 186

Avilés y del Fierro, Gabriel de, Viceroy of La Plata, 99, 170

Ayacucho, battle of, 235, 300

Ayohuma, battle of, 235, 284, 285, 301, 317

Ayolas, Juan de, 18, 20, 21, 25

Ayuntamiento. *See* Cabildo

Azara, Félix de, Spanish scholar, 33 n., 168, 179 n., 456; quoted, 180; on Indian policy, 350

Azcona Imberto, Antonio, Bishop of Buenos Aires, 152

Azcuénaga, Domingo de, 172, 173

Azcuénaga, Miguel, patriot leader, 227, 228, 240, 268

Azopardo, Juan B., 250

Azore Islands, 4

Aztecs, 16

Bâcle, César H., 424

Báez, Cecilio, Paraguayan author, quoted, 249, 469, 470

Bahia, 62

Bahía Blanca, 8

Bailén, battle of, 278

Baird, David, English general, 192, 198

Bajada del Paraná, town, 250

Balboa, Vasco Núñez de, 38

Balcarce, Antonio G., Platean general, mentioned, 240, 245, 247, 311, 327-28, 333, 338, 340

Balcarce, house of, Buenos Aires, 186

Balcarce, Juan A., 395

Balcarce, Juan R., Argentine publicist, 341, 386, 404, 405, 406, 407, 408

Balcarce, Marcos, 336-37

Balcarce, Ramón, 221

Balcarce Street, Buenos Aires, 186

Balderas, scribe, 26

Baldrich, J. A., cited, 382

Balvanera, church, 154

Banda Oriental del Uruguay, mentioned, 12, 50, 51, 84, 251, 252-53, 254, 297, 335, 344, 370, 373-74, 383, 384, 386. *See also* Cisplatean province

Banialbo, Lázaro de, 31

Bank of discount, 363

Bank of redemption, 510

Bank of the Argentine Nation, 493

Bank of the province of Buenos Aires, 448, 493

Baraona, Gaspar de, 66

Barbacena, Marquis of, Brazilian general, quoted, 381-82

Barcelona, 107

Barco, 36

Barracas, engagement, 485; place, 407

Barranca Yaco, 409

Barreiro, Miguel, 253

Barrenechea, military commander, 70, 71

Barreto, Doña Isabel, 182

Basavilbaso, Domingo, house of, 186

Basavilbaso, Manuel de, 171

Bases y puntos de partida para la organización política de la República Argentina, Alberdi's, described, 450-52; mentioned, 484; quoted, 451

Bauzá, Francisco, Uruguayan historian, quoted, 252

fluence, 526; resettled, 50. *See also* Porteños

Buenos Aires, province, conflict with Argentine Confederation, 239, 458, 462-63; convention of, 460-61; federalization of, 465; influence, 352-53; mentioned, 9, 13, 50, 83, 84, 136, 332, 334, 443, 448, 449, 495; relations with other provinces, 360-61; as a State, 447-60. *See also* Argentine Confederation

Buenos Aires, section of La Plata, 50

Buenos Aires, Viceroyalty of. *See* La Plata

Bulario Indico, León Pinelo's, 157

Bullfights, 184-85

Bulnes, Juan P., 328

Bunge, Carlos O., quoted, 433

Burma, 1

Burmeister, Hermann, 457

Buschenthal, José, 456

Bustos, Juan B., chieftain of Córdoba, mentioned, 333, 338, 343-44, 368, 373, 389, 393-94, 399

Byron, Lord, 431

Caa-Guazú, battle of, 420-21

Cabañas, Col., 250

Cabarrús, Count, 287

Cabedo, Fray Juan, Bishop of Darien, views on the Indians, 53

Cabello, Francisco, 99-100

Cabello y Mesa, Francisco A., 173

Cabeza de Vaca, Alvar Núñez, Spanish official, career, 24 n.; deposition, 25, 26; mentioned, 29, 32, 44-45, 74; return to Spain, 28; trip to Asunción, 24

Cabildo, ecclesiastical, mentioned, 162

Cabildo, of Asunción, mentioned, 69; quoted, 67, 251

Cabildo, of Buenos Aires, cited, 119, 124, 182, 256; mentioned, 42-43, 86, 157, 195, 205-6, 209-10, 212, 242, 339, 341; mocks cabildo abierto, 225-227; quoted, 43, 93, 112, 206, 227-28, 241; revolutionary center, 361; swept away, 361-62

Cabildo, of Chuquisaca, mentioned, 215

Cabildo, of Córdoba, quoted, 43, 88-89

Cabildo, of Lima, mentioned, 319

Cabildo, of Luján, quoted, 342

Cabildo, of Montevideo, quoted, 211-12

Cabildo, secular, functions, 44, mentioned, 39, 41; significance, 88 and n., 139

Cabildo abierto (open council), described, 71 and n.; mentioned, of 1806, 196, 205, 211-12; of May 22, 1810 (congress), 220; quoted, 223;

votes of, 224-26, 339-40. *See also* Junta of war

Cabot, Juan M., 305, 306

Cabot, Sebastian, explores South America, 6-7; mentioned, 38, 74

Cabral, Juan B., 284

Cabral, Pedro Alvares, Portuguese navigator, discovers Brazil, 73, 74; mentioned, 2

Cabrera, Alonso de, inspector, 22, 25

Cabrera, Francisco, 187

Cabrera, Jerónimo L. de, 37, 38

Caceres, Felipe de, accountant, mentioned, 25, 30, 32; shipped to Spain, 29, 45

Cacheuta, 521

Cadiz, 103, 107

Caesars, city of, 37

Cagancha, battle of, 419

Caingúas, Indians, described, 12, 13

Calchaquí Valley, 66

Calchaquian Indians, described, 11-12; mentioned, 13, 36; revolt, 65

Calderón de la Barca, Pedro, 171

Calderón Sanabria, María, 28

Calderón Sanabria, Doña Mencia, expedition to America, 28

Callao, bay, 318; port, 139

Calvo, Nicolás, 458

Camacuá, engagement, 382

Campana, Joaquín, 268

Campbell, Allan, engineer, 456

Campeche, 107

Campillo, Juan del, 452

Campo, Estanislao del, 433

Campo, Nicolás del, Marquis of Loreto, Viceroy of La Plata, 99, 118, 141

Campo, Sancho del, quoted, 19

Campomanes, Count, Spanish publicist, mentioned, 78; reasoning, 105, 164

Campones, Ángel, painter, 165

Campos, Gen. Manuel J., 492

Canada, 191

Canary Islands, 18

Cancha Rayada, battle of, 310

Candelaria, 21, 250

Cané, Miguel, 416

Cañete, 36

Cangayé, 66

Canning, George, English statesman, mentioned, 375

Canter, Juan, quoted, 270

Canterac, José, Spanish general, mentioned, 317

Canto á Mayo, Gutiérrez's, 432

Cantos del peregrino, Mármol's, 431-32

Cañuelas, convention of, 390

Chaves, Nuflo de, mentioned, 26, 27, 28, 30; founds a city, 29

Chiapas, 54

Chichas, district, 244

Chiclana, Feliciano A. de, Platean patriot, 197, 218, 221, 224-25, 244, 275, 331, 347

Chicos, stream, 31

Chilabert, Col., 439

Chile, disputes with Argentina, 428, 479-80, 495, 497; mentioned, 39, 82, 84, 119, 136, 234, 235, 297, 300, 454

Chilean expert, quoted on boundary, 497

Chilean minister, quoted, 428-29

Chilean Revolution, the, 301-3

Chilean squadron, 317-18

China, 1

Chiquitos: Indians, 137; province, 29, 137

Chiriguanos, Indians, 12

Chivilcoy, farms of, 438; town, 448

Chocori, Indian chief, 407

Choele-Choel: island, 408; river, see Río Negro

Chorotes, Indians, 12

Chorroarín, José L., Platean revolutionist, mentioned, 225; quoted, 274

Chorroarín, Luis J., teacher, 93, 162, 173

Chuquisaca, town, revolt in, 85, 206, 214, 215

Church and State, relations of, 148, 155, 209, 241; struggles between, 43-44, 152, 153. *See also* Clergy

Cisneros, Baltasar Hidalgo de, Viceroy of La Plata, deportation, 243; manifesto of, 218; mentioned, 226, 231, 242, 243; nickname of, 187-88; policy, 217; quoted, 111, 206-7, 219-20, 222; rule, 82, 111, 113, 207, 216, 240, 256, 258

Cisneros, Jiménez de, Spanish cardinal, 53

Cisplatean province of Brazil, 386

Citizen of Buenos Aires, a, quoted, 216

City, the, classes in, 179

Ciudad Real, battle of, 279

Civic Union, the, convention of, 493; mentioned, 491-92, 494, 502-3

Clergy, reform of, 364-65; regular, 149-50, 155; revolutionary views, 156 and n., 363; rôle and spirit, 155-56; secular, 149

Coalition of the northern provinces, 419-20

Cochabamba, city, 123; intendancy, 137; province, 214, 244

Cochin-China, 1

Cochrane, Lord, English sea-dog, 318

Coe, Commodore, 447

Colegio Seminario, 448

Colisberry, William, 314

Colodrero, Pedro D., 450, 452

Colombia, 300, 320, 322-23, 378

Colombres, José E., Bishop of Tucumán, 349

Colonia. *See* Sacramento

Colonial society, 177-90

Colonial soldiers, 74. *See also* "Blandengues," Patricios, etc.

Colonizing streams, conflict between, 38-39

Colorados del monte, militia, 343

Colorados, regiment, 392, 393

Columbus, Bartholomew, 17

Columbus, Christopher, agreement with Spanish crown, 3-4; colonial policy, discoveries, 5; mentioned, 73, 80-81; training, 2-3

Columbus, Diego, 181

Commerce, colonial regulations, 91-92, 101-3; trade with colonies of other states, 109-10; exports and imports, 101, 103, 119; fleets and galleons, 103-4, 106, 102-10; free trade proposed, 134, 174-75; illicit trade, 51, 102-4, 111, 230-31; inter-colonial trade, 108-9; national trade, 467, 481, 483, 488; trade during the revolution in Spanish America, 346-47, 349; trade with neutrals, 110-11, 133-34, 179 n.; reforms, 106-7; rôle of Lima merchants, 102. *See also* Asiento, Consulado, Contemporary conditions, etc.

Communism, among Indians, 61

Comodoro Rivadavia, 521

Comuneros: of Corrientes, uprising, 70-72; of Paraguay, described, 68; mentioned, 66; revolt of, 69-72

Concepción, Chile, 310

Concepción, Argentina, city, founding, 46; parish, in Buenos Aires, 158

Concepción, Uruguay, town, founding of, 93, 99; mentioned, 435

Conclusiones sobre toda la filosofía, Martínez de Aldunate's, 162

Concordia, 474

Condarco, Álvarez, 304, 305

Condillac, Étienne B., 329

Conesa, military officer, 462, 478

Conflict, steamboat, 440

Conflictos y armonías de razas, Sarmiento's, 87

Congress: miniature, in 1814, at Tucumán, 400-1; of Paysandú, in 1815, 294, 332; of Tucumán, 1816, members, 294-95, mentioned, 235, 237, 274, 281, 288, 327, 377, proceedings, 295-99; of 1818, 270; of 1819, 331

United Provinces of La Plata, congress of, 294-97, 316, 327; constitutions of, 316, 333, 336; declaration of independence, 298; establishes directory, 326-28; mentioned, 235, 312; policies, 329-39, 356, 358

United Provinces of South America. *See* United Provinces of La Plata

United States, mentioned, 236, 377, 481, 520, 524. *See also* United States and Paraguay Navigation Co.

United States and Paraguay Navigation Company, 470 n.

University of Brussels, 325

University of Buenos Aires, difficulties, 365-67; founding, 365; mentioned, 499, 507, 521; planned, 93, 162; Rosas' attitude toward, 411

"University of Burgos," 139

University of Chile, 161

University of Chuquisaca (San Francisco Javier), founding and services, 161, 163, 168-69, 234

University of Córdoba, described, 160-61; founding, 65, 94; mentioned, 160, 365, 455, 457, 499, 507, 521

University of La Plata, founding of, 499-500; mentioned, 507, 510, 521

University of Lima. *See* University of San Marcos

"University of Merchants." *See* consulado

University of Mexico, 157

University of Salamanca, quoted, 93

University of San Marcos, 157, 161, 319

University of the Littoral, founding of, 507, 521

University of Tucumán, 521

University reform, 507

Upper Peru, mentioned, 21, 58, 83, 84, 96, 214, 245, 246, 247-48, 251, 284, 294, 297, 309, 334, 348. *See also* Audiencia of Charcas, Bolivia

Uriburu, Enrique, 512

Uriburu, José E., President of Argentina, mentioned, 494; administration, 495-96, 526

Uriburu, Gen. José F., becomes dictator, 512; leads revolution, 511-12; views on constitution, 513

Urquiju, Cristóbal de, 106-7

Urquiza, Justo J., General and President of the Argentine Confederation, campaigns against Rosas, 437-39; delegation of authority to, 443; leads troops against Mitre, 459; mentioned, 422, 435, 444, 461, 462, 463, 470; murder of, 478 and n.; presidency, 454-57; pronunciamiento, 436-37; quoted, 436, 439, 465; reaction against, 440; reorganization of Argentina, 440-54

Uruguay, city, 478

Uruguay River, 8, 10, 454

Uruguay, State, mentioned, 425, 426, 469, 506, 507; negotiations with Argentina, 501. *See also* Banda Oriental

Uruguayan-Brazilian alliance, 1851, with province of Entre Ríos, 435

Uruguayana, town, 473, 474

Uspallata, pass, 304, 305-6

Uztariz, Jerónimo, 105

Vaca de Castro, Cristóbal, 35

Vaccination, introduced into La Plata, 190

Valchetas River, 407

Valdenegro, Col., 331

Valdés y de la Banda, Diego Rodríguez de, 48

Valdivia, Pedro de, conqueror of Chile, 37, 39

Valladolid, Spain, 28

Valle, Alejandro de, 154

Valotta, Guillermo, quoted, 474-75

Varela, Florencio, 430

Varela, Capt. José, 167

Varela, Luis V., Argentine historian, quoted, 255

Varela, Mariano, Argentine minister of foreign affairs, mentioned, 477; quoted, 480

Vedia, Col., 379

Vega, Lope de, Spanish dramatist, 171

Vega de Campeo, engagement, 306

Velazco, Bernardo de, governor of Paraguay, 249, 250

Velazco, Fray Pablo, 42

Vélez Sársfield, Dalmacio, Argentine jurist, 444, 445, 447, 460, 466-67, 477; quoted, 460

Vences, engagement, 422

Venezuela, mentioned, 286, 297

Venezuelan revolutionary movement, 300, 307-8, 320. *See also* Bolívar, Sucre, etc.

Venialvo, Lázaro de, 42

Venta y Media, engagement, at town of, 292

Vera, Alonso de (Dog Face), 34, 46

Vera Mujica, Col. Antonio, 74

Vera y Aragón, Torres de, adelantado of La Plata, founds Corrientes, 34; mentioned, 33-34, 42, 46; wife, 31-32

Verde, La, battle of, 483

Vergara, Juan de, 152

Vergara, Ortiz de, 29

"Veritas." *See* Bradford

Vernon, Edward, English admiral, quoted, 191

Vértiz, Juan José, governor of Buenos Aires, 153

56414

DEMCO